EDMUND
AN ANTHROPOL

Stanley J. Tambiah discusses the life ᴠ ....ᴜᴜ Leach (1910–89), one of Britain's foremost social and cultural anthropologists, and a man of extraordinary versatility, originality, and intellectual breadth. His substantial contributions to anthropology deal with topics including kinship and social organization, hill tribes and valley peoples, land tenure and peasant economy, aesthetics, British structural-functional methodology, the structuralism of Lévi-Strauss, biblical narratives and the myths of classical Greece. Leach was not wedded to any settled orthodoxy: what makes his work exciting is his experimentation with new ideas and his expansions of the horizons of the discipline. His distinctive view of the comparative method allows him to transcend the stale dichotomy between "them primitives" and "us moderns," finding instead a dialectic between "us" and "them" which opens up the possibility for illuminating common human propensities and capacities.

STANLEY J. TAMBIAH is the Esther and Sidney Rabb Professor of Anthropology at Harvard University. He received his Ph.D. from Cornell University in 1954. He joined the faculty at the University of Cambridge, where he taught for ten years, and was a Fellow of King's College. He went to the University of Chicago in 1973, and moved to Harvard University in 1976. He began fieldwork in Sri Lanka (1956–59), the island of his birth, and later worked in Thailand. He is the author of eight books.

EDMUND LEACH
AN ANTHROPOLOGICAL LIFE

STANLEY J. TAMBIAH

CAMBRIDGE
UNIVERSITY PRESS

PUBLISHED BY THE PRESS SYNDICATE OF THE UNIVERSITY OF CAMBRIDGE
The Pitt Building, Trumpington Street, Cambridge, United Kingdom

CAMBRIDGE UNIVERSITY PRESS
The Edinburgh Building, Cambridge CB2 2RU, UK
40 West 20th Street, New York, NY 10011-4211, USA
477 Williamstown Road, Port Melbourne, VIC 3207, Australia
Ruiz de Alarcón 13, 28014 Madrid, Spain
Dock House, The Waterfront, Cape Town 8001, South Africa

http://www.cambridge.org

First published 2002

Printed in the United Kingdom at the University Press, Cambridge

Typeface Baskerville Monotype 11/12.5 pt.   *System* LATEX 2ε [TB]

A catalogue record for this book is available from the British Library

Library of Congress Cataloguing in Publication data
Tambiah, Stanley Jeyaraja, 1929–
Edmund Leach: an anthropological life / Stanley J. Tambiah.
p.   cm.
Includes bibliographical references and index.
ISBN 0 521 80824 3
1. Leach, Edmund Ronald.   2. Ethnologists – Great Britain – Biography.   I. Title.
GN21.L36 T35   2001
301′.092 – dc21
[B]   2001035665

ISBN 0 521 80824 3 (hardback)

Contents

Illustrations

vii

Preface

What was the nature of my relationship to Edmund Leach, and what circumstances led me to compose an intellectual biography of him?

I first met Leach in 1956 at the University of Peradeniya in Ceylon (now Sri Lanka). He had come for a second brief visit to Pul Eliya village, where he had done his fieldwork in 1954, presumably to gain some additional information for the monograph he was writing. I had recently returned to Sri Lanka in 1955 to resume my academic post at the University, after completing my Ph.D. program at Cornell University (1952–54) in what was then a joint department of sociology, anthropology, and social psychology. The chairman of my doctoral committee was the sociologist Robin Williams Jr., who had introduced me to the writings of Max Weber, Durkheim, Talcott Parsons (and many other sociologists dead and living). I had some training in survey techniques and quantitative analysis, and on the anthropological side I had read many ethnographic texts on South and Southeast Asia.[1]

At that brief, but as it turned out fateful, meeting at Peradeniya, Leach asked me what research I was doing. I informed him about an economic survey which Dr. N.K. Sarkar (economist and statistician) and I had conducted in a district called Pata Dumbara in the Central Province, and I gave him a draft of an essay on the relation between kinship, residence, and land tenure which was based on qualitative anthropological case studies of selected households collected during pilot studies and the survey itself. Leach returned to Cambridge and wrote to me that he liked the essay, and he undertook the task of editing it, and himself presented it for publication in the *Journal of the Royal Anthropological Institute*.[2]

---

[1] Among my other instructors at Cornell I would especially mention Bryce Ryan (who had introduced me to sociology and anthropology, and to fieldwork, at the University of Ceylon during my undergraduate days, and was later on the Cornell faculty), Morris Opler, Lauriston Sharp, Peter Blau, and Ed Suchman.

[2] S.J. Tambiah, "The Structure of Kinship and Its Relationship to Land Possession and Residence in Pata Dumbara, Central Ceylon," *JRAI*, vol. 88, no. 1, 1958, pp. 21–44.

But this celebratory mood was deflated by another act of Leach's. The Pata Dumbara quantitative survey data were published by N.K. Sarkar and myself in 1957 under the title *The Disintegrating Village: Report of a Socio-Economic Survey*.[3] To my surprise, Leach published in 1958 a forceful critique of this survey in a Sri Lankan journal.[4] While complimenting both authors as being by instinct first-class anthropologists, he characterized the survey as an example of quantitative method, a statistical investigation predicated on taking individuals as units of population which misses out a wide range of sociological phenomena which are intrinsically inaccessible to statistical investigation of any kind, especially systems of relationship between persons. A social field does not consist of units of population but of persons in relation to one another.[5] He did however concede that the truths an anthropologist who works in a small geographical area (such as Pul Eliya) discovers are particular truths and that if scholars hoped to achieve conclusions which have general validity, the sociologist and the anthropologist ought to act as a team.[6]

I found Leach's comments and his explication of the anthropological perspective for the most part cogent and persuasive, and I wrote him a letter which must have conveyed my distress; back came his unexpected reply that I should write a rebuttal without pulling any punches, a piece of advice unlikely to be followed by a young academic.[7]

In any event, the critique reinforced and activated the decision I had arrived at that the anthropological method of field study was necessary to get deeply into the understanding of networks of kinship, caste, and patronage relationships, and while still employing questionnaires for eliciting certain kinds of information, I would engage in fieldwork as the anthropologist understood it. By 1958, in collaboration with Gananath Obeyesekere and a few students, I had begun an anthropological study of a somewhat remote village in the Laggala district (Central Province). On the basis of this fieldwork I had composed by 1959–60 a long essay

---

[3] N.K. Sarkar and S.J. Tambiah. *The Disintegrating Village: Report of a Socio-Economic Survey*. Ceylon University Press, 1957.

[4] E.R. Leach, "An Anthropologist's Reflections on a Social Survey," *The Ceylon Journal of Historical and Social Studies*, vol. 1, no. 1, 1958, pp. 9–20. This essay was reprinted in D.G. Jongmans and P.C.W. Gutkind (eds.), *Anthropologists in the Field*, Assen: Van Gorcum, 1967, pp. 75–88. In this reprint Leach inserted this footnote: "In 1958, when this was written Dr. Tambiah was in fact a lecturer in *Sociology* in the university of Ceylon, in 1966 he is a lecturer in *Social Anthropology* in the University of Cambridge and a close friend and colleague of the author" (p. 85).

[5] Ibid., p. 77.   [6] Ibid., p. 79.

[7] It was some years later, when I came to know Leach's writings better, that I realized that throughout his career he expressed a strong antipathy to statistical studies based on survey data.

on polyandry in this region, and had given it to the anthropologist Von Furer-Heimendorf, who after a lapse of some six years (1966) published it in an edited volume.[8]

In the meantime, in 1960, I had departed to Thailand to teach and to do research there as a UNESCO technical assistance expert attached to a research institute jointly founded by UNESCO and the government of Thailand.[9] My principal task was to lead a team engaged in anthropological research in three rural communities in central, northeast, and north Thailand.

In 1962, while in Thailand, I received a letter from Leach inquiring whether I would like to come to Cambridge University for one year on a Smuts Commonwealth Fellowship awarded by the University. When I expressed interest, three persons collaborated to have me elected. They were Leach of King's College; B.H. Farmer of St. John's College, a geographer who had written a major work on peasant colonization in Ceylon,[10] whom I had previously met there; and Sir Ivor Jennings, Master of Trinity Hall, who had previously been Vice-Chancellor of the University of Ceylon when I was an undergraduate there.[11]

At the same time Farmer got me elected as a Commonwealth Fellow of St. John's College,[12] which privilege was accompanied by a fine apartment in the Front Court, and dining rights at the High Table. I had a great time attending lectures and seminars in the Department, and seminars at the Centre for South Asian Studies situated on Laundress Lane and presided over by Farmer.

When my two fellowships concluded in 1964, Meyer Fortes, William Wyse Professor of Anthropology, offered me an assistant lectureship

---

[8] S.J. Tambiah, "Polyandry in Ceylon," in Christoph Von Furer-Haimendorf (ed.), *Caste and Kin in Nepal, India and Ceylon*, Asia Publishing House, 1966. Leach, who had earlier in 1955 published a short essay entitled "Polyandry, Inheritance and the Definition of Marriage with Particular Reference to Sinhalese customary law," *Man*, vol. 55, 1955, pp. 182–86, expressed to me his appreciation of my essay based on detailed ethnographic data.

[9] The Bangkok Institute of Child Research located at the Prasarnmitr Teachers College, now Sri Nakarinwirot University.

[10] B.H. Farmer, *Pioneer Peasant Colonisation in Ceylon: A Study in Asian Agrarian Problems*, London: Oxford University Press, 1957. I had myself engaged in a study of peasant colonization in the Gal Oya Development Project in 1956, and at the request of Farmer and Leach written a paper entitled "Agricultural Extension and Obstacles to Improved Agriculture in Gal Oya Peasant Colonisation Scheme" which was presented by Leach on my behalf at the Second International Conference of Economic, History, Aix-en-Provence, 1962.

[11] Jennings was at the time of my election also chair of the Smuts Fellowship Committee.

[12] It was at St. John's that I met Jack Goody, a Fellow of the College, and a distinguished anthropologist, whose friendship I have valued over the years.

in the Department of Archaeology and Anthropology.[13] Soon I was fortunate to become a founding Fellow of Clare Hall, a new postgraduate
institution established by Clare College. Leach was elected Provost of
King's College in 1966; three years later he sponsored my election as a
Fellow of King's, and I served there for a few years as Tutor for Graduate
Students and Director of Studies in Social Anthropology.[14] In 1973, after
spending ten years in Cambridge, I left for the United States to take up
a position as tenured full Professor at the University of Chicago. Three
years later I was invited by Harvard University, and I have now been
there for some twenty-five years.

During my stay in Cambridge I became closely associated with
Meyer Fortes, Edmund Leach, Jack Goody, Audrey Richards, and Ray
Abrahams, and I acquired there a detailed knowledge of theoretical and
ethnographic contributions to the study of kinship, politics, and social
organization. I became familiar with a range of studies subsumed under
the gross label British structural-functionalism, for example the work of
Malinowski, Radcliffe-Brown, Evans-Pritchard, Audrey Richards, Max
Gluckman, and Victor Turner. But my most important colleague, friend,
and mentor at Cambridge was Edmund Leach; his earlier writings on
Burma and Ceylon, his developing interests in structuralism, structural
linguistics, semiotics, and classification, and his adaptation of the contributions of Roman Jakobson and Claude Lévi-Strauss, positively stimulated me. My first monograph on Thailand[15] and many of my essays
in *Culture, Thought, and Social Action*[16] bear witness to Leach's influence,
though at the same time I was discovering on my own the possibilities of Austinian linguistic philosophy for a performative theory of
ritual.

I attended most of Leach's lectures, and when I began to teach in 1964
he lent me some of his lecture notes which aided me in preparing my
own lectures. I was welcomed by Celia and Edmund Leach at their house
in Storey's Way, and later at the Provost's Lodge at King's. Toward the
end of my stay in Cambridge, I began in 1971 a new phase of fieldwork
in Thailand, complemented by library study, on the relation between

---

[13] Professor Fortes and his wife Doris were unfailingly kind to me throughout my years at Cambridge.
[14] At that time Geoffrey Lloyd, the classicist, served as Senior Tutor.
[15] *Buddhism and the Spirit Cults in Northeast Thailand*, Cambridge: Cambridge University Press, 1970.
   The fieldwork on which this book is based was done in Thailand before I came to Cambridge
   in 1963.
[16] Cambridge, MA: Harvard University Press, 1985. This is a collection of essays, most of them
   previously published in journals, plus an introduction and a concluding essay.

Theravada Buddhism, kingship, and polity – both historically and in contemporary times.[17]

After I left England for the United States in 1973, I saw Edmund and Celia whenever I returned to Cambridge on brief visits while he was still Provost. In 1976 both Edmund and I were invited by Sidney Mintz for a term to help start the Anthropology Department at Johns Hopkins. We saw each other frequently. I hosted him at the University of Chicago when he came to receive an honorary degree. He visited Harvard on three occasions to give lectures.[18] And I visited Edmund and Celia at Barrington a few times after his retirement.

Let me now conclude by stating the circumstances leading to the writing of this biography. Soon after Edmund Leach died on January 6, 1989, various obituaries appeared in British newspapers, and in the Royal Anthropological Institute's publication *Man* and *Anthropology Today*. Sometime later, the British Academy invited me to write a *Memoir* about Leach, which I gather is treated as a definitive biographical sketch.

I considered this invitation as an honour. As I began to prepare notes for composing the *Memoir*, I realized that although I had read a great number of Leach's writings, as they appeared in print over the years, I had no coherent overview of his work as a corpus. I had not previously attempted to track systematically the trajectory of his major writings, noting their range, their continuities, transitions, and transformations, their innovative experimentations and their new directions. So I began to reread much of his work, and as my notes and commentaries became longer and longer I became aware that in fact I was writing a book-length biography. By 1997, I had composed a rough draft which I sent to Cambridge University Press; on the basis of two readers' reports there was a provisional acceptance for publication; and from this version I distilled the memoir for the British Academy.[19]

The composition of the biography did not stop there. After 1997, I began to read the Leach Papers deposited in the Modern Archive Centre at King's College. By the end of the summer of 2000, I had completed the

---

[17] On the basis of this work, I completed and published while at the University of Chicago *World Conqueror and World Renouncer: A Study of Buddhism and Polity in Thailand against a Historical Background*, Cambridge: Cambridge University Press, 1976. Edmund Leach wrote a magnanimous lead essay and review of this book in *The Times Literary Supplement*, 14 January 1977, entitled "The Dharma of Kingship."

[18] On one visit in 1979 Celia and Edmund were guests at my home in Cambridge, MA for a few days.

[19] See Stanley J. Tambiah, "Edmund Ronald Leach 1910–1989," *1997 Lectures and Memoirs. Proceedings of the British Academy*, 97, 1998, pp. 293–344.

draft of a substantial biography that included valuable new information contained in the Archive and also a discussion of some of Leach's writings that I had previously set aside.

I have in this Preface described some features of my long relationship with Leach. But the biographical text itself plainly gives evidence of my authorial role. My interactions with Leach, and my own understanding and interpretation of what he wrote and said are an integral part of the text. Leach speaks, writes, and narrates – but these representations are filtered, selected, arranged, and mediated by my own activity as narrator, commentator, and friend. Throughout much of the text, I am in dialogue with Leach, who cannot speak back now.

Acknowledgments

There are many persons and institutions who provided invaluable assistance in the preparation of the biography. As a former Fellow of King's College, Cambridge, I was able to live in the college as a guest during my several visits there. I appreciated very much the generous help given by the Staff of the Modern Archive Centre at King's, especially in regard to making available to me the Leach papers for the purpose of taking of notes from them, and for photocopying some of them.

Special thanks are due to Louisa Brown, Edmund Leach's daughter and executor of his papers, who with generous patience provided me with important information about the Leach family not contained in the Archive, and also scrupulously corrected factual mistakes I had committed. She gave me more information than I could include in this biography, and I hope that some day she will compose a social history of the extended Leach family. I must also include here a warm thank you to Lady Leach, simply Celia to her friends, for the information she has provided me, and for the warm hospitality she has shown me over many years.

Stephen Hugh-Jones, Leach's devoted disciple and close friend, has published his insightful, moving, and sympathetic sketches of Leach which are quoted by me in this biography. I have known him and Christine since their student days, and I thank them for their help. I had given a copy of my first draft of the biography to Stephen, and he and his colleague James Laidlaw in turn sent me some of the introductory notes to the two volumes of Leach's papers they were editing for publication by Yale University Press.[1] I also thank Geoffrey Benjamin

[1] The volumes have now been published. See Stephen Hugh-Jones and James Laidlaw (eds.), *The Essential Edmund Leach*, vol. I, *Anthropology and Society*; vol. II, *Culture and Human Nature*, New Haven and London: Yale University Press, 2000. They are indeed a great effort, and I hope that my independently composed biography will be viewed by readers as complementing and enriching their work.

for making available Leach's correspondence with him while he was in the field in Malaysia.

Susan Brown, who is planning to write a biography of Meyer Fortes, her teacher and friend, gave me an account of her interview with Leach which I have incorporated in my text. I have valued the friendship and hospitality of Susan, and her husband Mick Brown, a famous Cambridge physicist who had time to converse with an anthropologist and to explain to him some features of modern science.

I have many other Cambridge persons to thank. Among them are Geoffrey Lloyd, now Master of Darwin, and Patrick Bateson, Provost of King's, who allowed me to read some of the Minutes of the College Council.

Raymond Firth, whom Leach acknowledged as his mentor, gave me invaluable information, advice, and commentary on an earlier draft. I appreciated his prompt replies to queries. Rosemary Firth's published correspondence with Leach opened a window onto his undergraduate days. I thank Emiko Ohnuki-Tierney for providing sympathetic information and encouragement, and Mariza Peirano for a perceptive and morale-boosting commentary on the final draft. The generosity of Rubie Watson, Director of the Peabody Museum at Harvard made it possible to have copies of photographs made free of charge.

I regret that for reasons of editorial strictures about length I have not been able to include sketches of their pleasant and memorable encounters with Leach given me by some members of the anthropological profession, significantly younger than him, whom he had met in the United States, and whose generosity toward him was reciprocated. Triloki Pandey of the University of California at Santa Cruz invited Leach in 1983 to visit the University and give some lectures. Leach stayed in Pandey's home for ten days. Pandey's friends know him to be an entertaining raconteur and a generous host. When Pandey in turn visited England, Leach, then Provost, went in person to the station to meet him. Among other things, Leach took him on a tour of the college, the highlight of which was the viewing of the incomparable chapel and its treasures. A similar sketch was provided by Lina Fruzetti and Akos Ostor. When Leach once visited Harvard, Akos, a junior professor, and Lina, entertained him and took him on tours of New England; when they in turn went to Cambridge, he met them at the station, showed them the college and the chapel, and in addition drove them around on a local tour regaling them with the history and mythology of sites visited. A similar testimony has been provided me by H.L. Seneviratne of the University of Virginia at Charlottesville.

Leach had been much taken with Seneviratne's manuscript of *The Rituals of the Kandyan State*, and had enthusiastically sponsored its publication by Cambridge University Press. When Seneviratne and his wife visited Cambridge in 1975, Leach again took the time to give them a tour of the college and the chapel, including a viewing of a painting which he had rescued and brought to light. These memories relayed to me by younger scholars who had met him in the United States show a side of him unknown to many in the profession.

A portrait of Edmund Leach (credit: Louisa Brown)

CHAPTER I

Edmund Leach (1910–1989): achievements

Edmund Ronald Leach was born in Sidmouth, Devon, England, on November 7, 1910. He went to school at Marlborough College and later entered Clare College, Cambridge, as an exhibitioner and read mathematics and mechanical sciences, obtaining a first class BA degree in 1932.

After some years of civilian life in China he returned to England and studied social anthropology under Bronislaw Malinowski and Raymond Firth at the London School of Economics. He was an active member of Malinowski's famous seminar. An abortive field trip to Kurdistan in 1938, frustrated by the Munich crisis,[1] was followed by a prolonged trip to Burma in 1939 in the course of which the Second World War broke out. From fall 1939[2] to the summer of 1945 he served with distinction as an officer in the Burma Army. He saw much of northern Burma, and he gained an unrivaled knowledge of its hill tribes, particularly the Kachin, on whom he was an undisputed authority.

Leach gained his Ph.D. from the London School of Economics in 1947 where he also obtained his first teaching appointment. He carried out a survey in Sarawak and his report entitled *Social Science Research in Sarawak* (1950) set out the guidelines for subsequent investigations by a number of distinguished anthropologists (particularly Derek Freeman, William Geddes, and Stephen Morris).

Edmund Leach[3] relinquished a readership at the LSE in 1953 in order to return to Cambridge as lecturer (1953–58). In 1954 he published

---

[1] On the basis of this aborted field trip, Leach wrote *Social and Economic Organization of Rowanduz Kurds*, London School of Economics Monographs on Social Anthropologyn, no. 3, London, 1940.

[2] Although recruited in 1939, he was allowed to continue with his fieldwork and he did not begin active service until 1941. He volunteered to join the Second Burma Rifles and was involved in the British retreat from the Japanese. He later commanded the Kachin irregular forces behind the enemy lines.

[3] He disliked his middle name Ronald and he did not use it. But he always used the initials E.R.L.

Political Systems of Highland Burma which embodied some of the results of his work in Burma. A field trip to Ceylon in 1953 provided the information for a second work of distinction: *Pul Eliya, A Village in Ceylon* (1961). He was in due course promoted Reader at Cambridge, and in 1972 the university honored him by appointing him to a personal chair. His research and writing vigorously continued throughout his career, despite mounting administrative and other responsibilities.

Leach's escalating academic recognition was signposted by his winning twice the Curl Essay Prize (1951, 1957) and the Rivers Memorial Medal (1958). He delivered the Malinowski Memorial Lecture (1959), the Henry Myers Lecture (1966), the Mason Memorial Lecture (1970), the Cantor Lectures at the Royal Society of Arts (1973), the Munro Lectures at the University of Edinburgh (1977), and the Huxley Memorial Lecture (1980). He spent a year in the United States in 1961 as a Fellow of the Center for Advanced Study in the Behavioral Sciences, Stanford, and a term at the Johns Hopkins University in 1976 as John Hinkley Visiting Professor. He was the first and only anthropologist so far invited by the BBC to deliver the Reith Lectures (*A Runaway world?* 1967) which notably brought him to the attention of the general public.

In the United States, Edmund Leach delivered the Lewis Henry Morgan Lectures at The University of Rochester in 1975, the John Hinkley Lectures at the Johns Hopkins University in 1976, the Harvey Lecture Series, University of New Mexico (1983), and the Patten Foundation Lectures (1984–85) at Indiana University. I have most likely missed some other instances, but one might say that Leach accomplished a grand slam of distinguished lectures on both sides of the Atlantic Ocean.

Leach's wide-ranging substantial contributions to knowledge are attested by his impressive bibliography.[4] It is no exaggeration to say that in sheer versatility, originality, and range of writing he was and still is difficult to match among the anthropologists of the English-speaking world. His contributions have touched on kinship and social organization; hill tribes and valley peoples; land tenure and peasant economy; caste and class; myth and ritual; binary thought, classification, and liminality; information theory, semiotics, and symbolic communication; art and aesthetics; ethology and archeology; computer technology and model building; British structural-functional method and the

---

[4] See Royal Anthropological Institute of Great Britain and Ireland, *Edmund Leach: A Bibliography*, Occasional Paper, no. 42, 1990.

structuralism of Lévi-Strauss; biblical materials and the myths of classical Greece. ⌐

Altogether Leach was the author of some eight books, co-author of one, and editor of several essay collections. A hallmark of all his writings was a forceful, vigorous, direct and clear prose, effective in exposition as in debate. He was a tireless reviewer of books in anthropology and a variety of cognate disciplines, and a prolific essayist not only in professional journals but also in publications for the general reading public such as *The Listener, New Society, New Scientist, The Spectator, Encounter, The Times Literary Supplement, New York Review of Books, London Review of Books,* and *New Republic.* He in fact wrote for and spoke to a much wider public and audience than the vast majority of social anthropologists are prone to, and positively sought to have a dialogue with specialists in other disciplines. All this added to his fame in mature years both as a notable spokesman for the discipline and as a commentator on general contemporary issues.

Apart from a distinguished academic career as a social anthropologist, Edmund Leach rendered noteworthy services to education, knowledge and professional societies in general. In 1966, he succeeded Lord Annan as Provost of King's College, a college which counts among its twentieth-century luminaries Lord Maynard Keynes, E.M. Forster, Goldsworthy Lowes-Dickinson, Rupert Brooke, Arthur Waley, Arthur Cecil Pigou and Lord Kaldor. As Provost of King's until 1979, he also served as Fellow of Eton College. In addition to being head of a famous college, he served at the highest levels in the administration of the university itself. His fellow anthropologists honored him by electing him Chairman of the Association of Social Anthropologists (1966–70) and President of the Royal Anthropological Institute (1971–75). His gaining a wider academic recognition was signified by his election as President of the British Humanist Association (1970) and as a Fellow of the British Academy (1972). He was a member of the Social Sciences Research Council for a number of years beginning in 1968, and was elected Honorary Fellow of the London School of Economics (1974), Honorary Fellow of the School of Oriental and African Studies (1974), Honorary Fellow of Clare College (1986), and Foreign Honorary Member of the American Academy of Arts and Sciences (1968).

A high point of Leach's career was reached when he was knighted in 1975, and also elected a trustee of the British Museum (1975–80). In 1976 the University of Chicago conferred on him the honorary degree of Doctor of Humane Letters, and Brandeis University honored him in the same way.

This enumeration of achievements might unproblematically convey the idea that Leach by virtue of his own capacities, his social background, comfortable circumstances, public schooling and Cambridge education, and his considerable writings quite naturally ascended the ladder of achievement to become a much honored member of the British Establishment. However, the canonized Leach himself would not have settled for a hagiographic narrative, nor did he want himself to be considered as aspiring and conforming to the career of an honors list grandee. We have before us a complex person, subject to tensions and frustrations, blessed with a creative experimental and reflexive mind that was more concerned with restlessly probing than with consolidating knowledge. While he tested the presuppositions and limits of orthodoxy, he was deeply protective and conservationist about the institutions he valued.

Consider these examples where Leach "deconstructs" and subverts himself while in doing so he also makes a social commentary:

Adam Kuper wrote in *New Society* in January 1987, in one of the unusually informal, humorous and revealing interviews he had with him: "Professor Sir Edmund Leach – knight, former Provost of King's ... establishment figure incarnate now – says that when he has to revise his entry in *Who's Who* he always roars with laughter. 'Who is this comic clown? There I am, aged 76, with all this long list of honours. The whole hierarchy of the establishment – the good and the great – is a joke. But I use it. And why not? I still have (academic) political objectives.'" One should of course not miss the pride behind this comic stance.

Another window on to Leach's scheme of evaluations and what he thought was worth working for is provided by his reply (dated July 21, 1975) to my own letter to him congratulating him on his knighthood: "The Knighthood has elicited an enormous shower of mail from people all over the world, some of whom I haven't seen for forty years! On the other hand, my appointment as a Trustee of the British Museum, which is really much more distinguished but for which I have to do some work, though likewise announced in *The Times*, did not produce a single letter!" In his own distinctive way, he celebrated and turned to anthropological advantage his elevation by giving a witty and perceptive lecture on the ritual of investiture as knight. Again at the University of Chicago in the following year, as I walked beside him in the academic procession to the neo-Gothic Rockefeller Chapel where he would receive his honorary doctorate, Leach chuckled and directed my attention to the order of the procession: on the way to the chapel the president of the university with the candidates for the honor were last in position and to enter, and no doubt when the ceremony concluded, they would be at the head of the departing procession: a little lesson to me on processional order, entry, and exit, and the marking of status hierarchy.

CHAPTER 2

Childhood and youth

WEB OF KINSHIP

Especially toward the end of his life, Leach more easily, informatively, and "ethnographically" spoke for the public record of his early family life and regarded it as having both shaped his later life and posed problems for it. An interview with Adam Kuper in 1986 (in the writing of which Leach himself took an authorial role) begins with the statement that "An autobiographical interview must begin with family mythology rather than history," and includes the observation that "Even in childhood I thought of the world as consisting exclusively of kinsmen and family domestics, a good start for an anthropologist."[1] We shall make liberal use of this interview in which he sketched his family background as a descendant of closely intermarried Rochdale mill-owners.

It however emerges with pleasant surprise that the experience of his extended family life, and reflection upon its significance, was not a remembrance of things past in old age but had been a long introspective preoccupation, about which some fifty-five years previously he had dwelt at some length in his letters to Rosemary Firth, a long-time friend since teen age with whom he corresponded when he was an undergraduate at Cambridge.[2] On January 10, 1931, he had written to her "as partly an autobiographical essay" about his "family and social class background" (as well as his "undergraduate experiences in Cambridge"). For someone who described himself as "inward and self conscious," the Victorian art and hobby of letterwriting which he enjoyed was a way of clarifying matters for himself through dialogue, and Rosemary Firth surmises that the long letters written to her were written at a time "when – as he told

[1] Adam Kuper, "An Interview with Edmund Leach," *Current Anthropology*, vol. 27, no. 4, August–October 1986, p. 375.
[2] Rosemary Firth, "A Cambridge Undergraduate: Some Early Letters from Edmund Leach," *Cambridge Anthropology. Special Issue: Sir Edmund Leach*, vol. 13, no. 3, 1989–90, pp. 9–18.

me later – he was just beginning to formulate ideas of his own and break away from family influences."[3]

In the autobiographical letter of January 1931, in an irreverent vein, but nevertheless probing the past in order to situate himself, Leach had the following to say about his family and social class, which is worth reproducing as a fuller variant of his 1986 sketch (it is remarkable that both sketches reproduce virtually the same details, in proof of a long memory):

To know me you have simply got to know something of my family history . . . I had 6 great-grandparents[4] instead of the more usual number, and they were all "in cotton". That is to say, by a process of exploitation that would not be even dreamed of by the most ambitious of present-day industrialists, they proceeded to amass very considerable fortunes at the expense of the unfortunate population of Lancashire. However, what with factory acts and so forth and the reduction of working hours from 16–12, cotton ceased to boom or at any rate it didn't boom quite so loud, and when my father [born 1851] left school my grandfather had quite decided that the country was ruined (which was remarkably far-sighted of him). So my father instead of going into cotton went to NZ – perhaps rather an extreme alternative!

My father was one of 10 brothers (+3 sisters)[5] – (these Victorians were so prolific) and all educated at Marlborough.[6] After the first five had been in the cricket XI I fancy the rest got in automatically, but there it was, for nearly 20 years there was always a Leach in the Marlborough XI. Now if you understand cricket you know quite a lot about all these brothers. Cricket is a game that requires phenomenal patience, it develops that peculiarity the team spirit, and that entirely erroneous theory that an english [*sic*] public-school boy is a gentleman the world over.

However cotton was slumping when the third brother left school, and the rest of them were scattered all over the world – pioneers of the empire and the rest of it, but they took their cricket bats with them! Eventually one of them struck gold in the Argentine – it wasn't gold really, it was sugar. A really benighted spot 1,000 miles up country [from Buenos Aires] four days by pack horse from nearest railway station. However the team spirit prevailed – the brothers [actually six of them] assembled from the four quarters of the globe and began to work like galley slaves. It was all cricket of course, but it lasted nearly 15 years. At the end of that time they suddenly found themselves rich and growing richer, they

---

3 Ibid., p. 10.
4 Edmund Leach subsequently established that he had eight grandparents, and sometime in the 1980s had a chart compiled of his correct pedigree.
5 According to Louisa Brown, née Leach (pers. comm.), Edmund Leach's father was one of eleven brothers (one of whom, Sidney by name, died very young) and two sisters.
6 Aside from Sidney who died early, the two oldest sons may not have attended Marlborough according to Louisa's surmise.

merely had to sit down and take it easy; actually, they continued to work like blazes, but my arrival [1910] was an ill-omen for the sugar trade, the industry has been slipping ever since. The tragedy of a soap bubble. All very romantic of course, but it explains one or two things about myself; I and the whole of my generation of the Leach family suffer from "wander-lust". Not a single one of them has remained at home. We still want to play the pioneer although there be no more happy hunting grounds for the adventurers.

I have inherited another quality from the Leach side of the family, an odd way of being Rebel and High Tory at the same time. I can't quite explain what I mean by this, it's Lancashire ancestry I think; you'll understand it when you know me better. [It is worth noting here that Rochdale, the place of origin of the Leach family, was the home of the Cooperative Movement which it appears influenced the thinking of Edmund's father and possibly also himself. It is also relevant to mention that the Rochdale Pioneers, who were rebels, steadfastly loyal to one another, may have influenced the Leach family.]

And now for the other side of my family; my Mother's father was also "in cotton"; but you could hardly imagine two types more entirely different than my F. and M. My Father is all patience, a patience that on the one hand leads almost to obstinacy, and the other to an almost total absence of anger.

My Mother is all emotion, almost fantastically idealist in theory, and yet surprisingly practical. She is one of these people who do about 15 things at once and get them all finished. But I can't explain my mother; I don't properly understand her myself.

I have inherited from her a temper not too well controlled, an inquisitiveness that wants to understand something about everything; any elements of the aesthetic that may turn up here and there, and that cursed blessedness, imagination.[7]

There are many complex and multivalent themes and tensions suggested by the autobiographical sketches quoted above, and also further extended in other writings.[8]

The family home was Harridge, "located in (or near)" Rochdale, Lancashire. It was established by his grandfather Robert Leach, "wealthy flannel manufacturer, a product of the English industrial revolution."[9] Robert Leach and his wife, grandparents on the father's side, were married in 1844, and had thirteen children. This Robert Leach was the nephew of another Robert Leach, founder of the family fortune, who is alleged to have left a will dated 1816.[10]

---

[7] Firth, "A Cambridge Undergraduate," pp. 13–14.
[8] Such as Edmund Leach, "Masquerade: The Presentation of the Self in Holi-Day Life," *Cambridge Anthropology. Special Issue: Sir Edmund Leach*, vol. 13, no. 3, 1989–90, pp. 47–69.
[9] Ibid., p. 63.
[10] This at least was the date of his will; he apparently died intestate and his will was according to Leach probably forged. Ibid.

"It was characteristic of the class of such industrialists that within any local area, they were all closely intermarried and that they had enormous families. All four of my great grandfathers were mill owners who lived within four miles of one another. They were all related by marriage. One of them had 17 children. My mother's father's mother was one of 11 siblings." Louisa Brown, Edmund Leach's daughter, has informed me that her father's "family was and still is quite extraordinary in extended family connections. He [Edmund] had twenty eight first cousins, all of whom he knew, descended from some of the eleven brothers and two sisters, children of Robert and Mary Leach, his grandparents who died ten years before he was born."[11]

It is not far-fetched to surmise that Edmund's strong sense of a dense network of closely intermarried kin, whose local endogamy was made immediate, real, and earthy by their "class interest" in fusing and conserving their industrial fortunes, would inform his later professional interpretation of kinship morality and norms, groupings and alliances, as grounded in *ancestral* concerns and interests, in terms of property, debt obligations, and honor as "intangible wealth." This same sense also informed his view of "individuals" (placed within such a network of relations and norms) as manipulating and strategizing to perpetuate and expand these advantages – a view that would subsequently be in partial accord with Malinowski's self-interested individuals, and in greater accord with Raymond Firth's articulation of the notion of "social organization" (in contrast to "social structure") to signify the outcome of individuals pragmatically using and manipulating their positions within the parameters of their social existence. We shall in due course see how Leach would try to undermine attempts by certain anthropologists to essentialize kinship as a thing in itself and as having an autonomous self-referential basis.

We note how Leach subverts the picture of the local world of Victorian bourgeois stability by reference to the changing fortunes of the extended family, and the dispersal of his cricket-playing father and the majority of his brothers[12] in search of their fortunes in the far-flung empire, with six of them regrouping with the zest and loyalty of cricketers to make their fortune in sugar in Argentina, and when that bubble burst, their

---

[11] It is also in the same essay, "Masquerade," that commenting on a photograph of "the Chadwick brothers," Leach meticulously details the kinship ties (and gender values) surrounding the persons in the picture.

[12] Three brothers, John, Robert, and Harold, did not go abroad. Robert was a clergyman, and John worked all his life in his father's business, John Leach & Son.

return to England with their brood.[13] Leach credits his own wanderlust to this imperial and colonial entrepreneurial and civilizing past, and he revealingly attributed to this kind of "Lancashire ancestry" his "odd way of being Rebel and High Tory at the same time," the permissible dissenter within the ranks of Establishment, one of the keys to his life and work.

A brief sketch of William Edmund Leach (1851–1932), father of Edmund Leach, is relevant here. I owe this account to Louisa Brown who did not know him personally. Very little is known about WEL, known as Lens to his contemporaries and peers and as Uncle Billy by his numerous nephews and nieces. He was the fourth in age and also the fourth son among the thirteen children of Robert and Mary Leach. He has been described as being extremely intelligent and remarkably handsome from a very early age. He went to Marlborough and was a star sportsman, excelling in cricket.

After leaving school William took a boat to New Zealand. He traveled around Australasia, mainly in New Zealand, for a number of years, before leaving for Argentina in 1883 because his brother Roger had informed him of the excellent business prospects there. He became Chairman of the Leaches Argentine Estates, initially a very successful sugar business with lands the size of the English county of Surrey and a factory to refine the sugar cane (that still exists and operates) known as La Esperanza, not far from the town of Jujuy, in the northernmost state in Argentina, 1,000 miles from the capital Buenos Aires. William spent many years in Argentina and was always at the center of both business and social occasions.

His mother and father died within months of each other in 1900. Soon afterwards he married. It was not a love match: it has been suggested that Mildred, who had previously been very much in love with one of her cousins, was initially not at all happy about her engagement to a man very much older than herself and with whom she had very few interests in common. Being extremely dutiful, however, she took on her duties as a wife very seriously and became as interested and dedicated to the Leach family as to her husband.

It is not known why William Edmund Leach married so late, or, indeed, why he married when he did, presumably having nothing to compel

---

[13] In fact not all the Leaches returned to England. It seems that, although the majority of about 70 percent came back, the rest remained behind in Argentina, and their Spanish-speaking fully Argentinean descendants continue that affiliation. The Leaches Argentine Estates were nationalized by the Perón regime.

him to once his parents had died. It is possible he had been in love with another woman (or other women) earlier in his life but had felt unable to marry because of financial circumstances or social constraints – the Leach family of that era were very worried about contracting marriage with people from the "wrong" social class.

In any event, his marriage to Mildred was a satisfactory marriage of convenience and Mildred devoted her life to her elderly husband, living in the Argentine with him and subsequently returning to England where, during a period of convalescence for William Edmund in Devon, Edmund Ronald was born. Toward the end of his life, William Edmund bought Town Farm, near Ivinghoe in Bedfordshire, for his eldest son, Walter, who wanted to be a farmer. Walter, his wife, Meg, Mildred, William Edmund, and Edmund (and a number of relatives and domestics) lived at Town Farm from around 1930 onwards. William Edmund had stipulated that the farm was to be available for any family member who was in distress and temporarily homeless, and this condition was steadfastly honored.[14]

William Edmund Leach died at Town Farm on November 30, 1932. Mildred moved away from the farm after his death. She subsequently bought a house called Petersfield, in Kings Langley in Hertfordshire, and lived there for many years together with her daughter Mary and her family. She died in 1958.

In order to fit Edmund and Celia Leach and their daughter Louisa into this family narrative, I will anticipate future developments by mentioning that Celia and Louisa lived at Town Farm for about six months when during the war they were evacuated from Burma and while Celia was looking for a house to live in. In this she was greatly helped by Walter.

Celia bought in 1942 a large part-Elizabethan mansion called Gurneys in Holwell, Hertfordshire. When, after the war, Edmund joined them there, the proximity of his mother Mildred and sister Mary and her family at nearby Kings Langley meant there was a close contact amongst those kin during the 1940s and early 1950s. Gurneys, Petersfield, and Town Farm formed a fairly close triangle, each about fifteen miles apart. Gurneys was much adored by Celia and Louisa (who describes it as a "truly wondrous place, forever my home") and also by Alexander, the son born after Edmund's return. It was however not favored by Edmund,

---

[14] The farm exists today (2000) and is inhabited by Walter's oldest grandson and his family. Walter's oldest son and wife live in an adjoining bungalow.

mainly because he found the commute to London, where at that time he worked at the London School of Economics, tiring.[15]

The crooked timber of humanity (to use an expression popularized by Isaiah Berlin) from which Edmund too was fashioned manifested its singularity in Leach's life in this way: he alone, born last, when his father was 59, was, unlike his older Anglo-Argentine brother and sister and many cousins, solely brought up in Rochdale; he "grew up much as the youngest member of a large, elderly, predominantly female and Christian household."[16] (The elderly amongst whom he grew up included two great-aunts on his mother's side, famed as "the aunts.")

As regards Edmund's relationship with his father and mother, in talking of them he drew attention to the fact that his father was fifty-nine on the day he was born, and that his mother, although already related to his father before they married, was twenty-two years his junior and of quite different upbringing. He said he saw little of his father, but that does not imply he was alienated from him or quarreled with him. In fact as the birthdays of father and son coincided, Edmund has left an account of his going home from Cambridge in 1931 to celebrate his coming of age; he elides this event with the simultaneous celebration of his father's eightieth birthday, at which the latter's eldest brother, a clergyman of 82, delivered "a very fine speech . . . in eulogy of my father's cricket, followed by a touching reply." While "laughing" at these events Edmund did not "scorn" them, and he remarked, "when we laugh at 'the Victorians' we often ignore the cornerstone of their existence – loyalty. They were loyal to their family, loyal to their school, loyal to their friends, their traditions and their country . . . there is something very fine about that." Edmund's father died in November 1932, some months after Edmund had completed his Mechanical Sciences Tripos at Cambridge, and Edmund wrote that, although his father's death had been expected, "the end when it came . . . was a great shock to us. It is not easy to realise how much the structure of our lives depends on one cornerstone until it be removed. My father was a great gentleman. He had two ideals, loyalty and courage; they are not such bad ones these days."[17] Loyalty to friends and to

---

[15] He would drive his car to Hitchin, then take the train to King's Cross, London, and from there travel to Holborn by tube or bus. Louisa Brown also comments that "Gurneys, a part-Elizabethan mansion, did not accord with ERL's left-wing politics." Aside from numerous rooms, Gurneys had four gardens. Louisa also mentions other reasons for Edmund's dislike of Gurneys.

[16] Firth, "A Cambridge Undergraduate," p. 10.

[17] Ibid., p. 15. Louisa Brown describes her grandfather as "a patriarch," "an immensely handsome and *powerful* man . . . highly intelligent, and quite clearly from what has been written about him, a leader" (personal communication).

institutions he valued, personal courage and a sense of duty and responsibility (to whom, he could not fathom) must have rubbed off on Edmund from his father, although it was his "splendid deputy 'grandfather figure'" in the person of his mother's uncle, Sir Henry Howorth, who provided him with an alternative model to the cricket-playing pheasant-shooting enthusiasms of his male elders and numerous cousins.

There is another narrative of the birthday celebrations of his father and himself that Edmund wrote in his diary dated Saturday November 7, 1931:

Allwood called for me at 10 o'clock and I went home. Mother loving and yet sad – no wonder . . . Most wonderful luncheon party. Four over 80: Uncle Robert [father's brother], Aunts, Daddy. Four more over 69. Uncle Sam, Aunt Mary [father's sister], Aunt Edith, T'Emmie [father's sister]. Mother 60. Madge, Nellie Daniels, Walter [brother]. A most successful luncheon despite the fact that there was no parlour maid! Mrs. Allwood officiated. Uncle Robert delivered a long speech in praise of Daddy (and cricket) and Dad almost in tears failed to reply. Too too gloriously Forsyte. The Uncles and Aunts gave Daddy a rejuvenator!!! They eventually departed at about 5 p.m.

In the evening Walter, Mother and I and Edith and Mrs. Allwood went to the cinema at Luton. "Tell England" terribly harrowing but good. Anthony Asquith. Its fault like Journey's End is that it leaves you tied up in knots. The other film a comedy in the very worst taste. So ended my 21st very weary. Thank heavens we did not attempt a beano in town as well.

In this somewhat cryptic account, which gives us some inkling of the style of life of the English upper middle class in the 1930s, I have stated in brackets the relationships to Edmund of some relatives who could be identified. There is a strong possibility that the rest were his mother's relatives. The bilateral kin assembled testify to their importance in his youth, and that he carefully enumerates the ages of eight elders aged between sixty-nine and eighty, in contrast to his own twenty-one, might, to speculate, indicate his sensitivity to being a part of a circle of elderly people.[18] It is not clear exactly what sort of a contraption was the "rejuvenator" given his father to keep him going. Perhaps even more intriguing is his reference to his sad and loving mother, and his accompanying her together with his brother in the company of two elderly women (maternal relatives) to the cinema to round off the celebrations is suggestive of his ease and solidarity with elderly womenfolk.

[18] As Louisa Brown noted, one is reminded here of his Reith Lectures given in 1967 in which he suggested that anyone over forty should retire! We also know however that he did not "retire" until he was himself sixty-nine.

In comparison with his patient and detached father, it was his mother whom Edmund singled out as having a strong influence on his life. He explained in 1986:

Because she was so much younger than my father and because I was the youngest child (my sister was eight years older,[19] my brother four years older), my mother fastened her attention on me, particularly when I showed signs of being intellectually rather bright. She herself could have been a professional singer when she was young, but her marriage, which had clearly been "arranged," put an end to that. She was obviously frustrated by the complete absence of intellectual and artistic interests among her husband's relatives. She concentrated her energies on being the spider at the centre of the vast network of "relations"; "Aunt Mildred" made it her business to keep in touch with everyone, but I was her nearest and dearest. It made it very difficult to grow up. She slaughtered my girl friends one after another.[20]

Edmund appears to have always had a strong feeling for his family and kin, especially manifested in his willingness to help them if required. His father, according to Louisa, was "totally committed to the family until he died," and this "interest, perhaps obsessional," was continued by Edmund, and, as he himself averred, was carried into his anthropological studies.

But there was also ambivalence and tension in this web of kinship which included him.[21] Edmund seemed in his adult life to have distanced himself and even, as reported by Louisa, "disowned his huge family and refused to have anything to do with almost all family members unless there were matters of duty or business to attend to." The expression "family it is" conveys the strong positive and negative features of an involvement in extended kinship.

According to Louisa, the Leaches were class-conscious and were concerned about conducting their lives properly. As is evident from preceding accounts, Edmund Leach was, by comparison, different from them, and unorthodox in his political and social orientations (although as we shall see later he was conscious of certain class prejudices into which he was socialized). His older sister, Mary, was widowed early, had four children, and Edmund helped her with her affairs. His older brother, who was not

---

[19] To be exact, she was seven and three-quarter years older.
[20] Kuper, "An Interview," p. 375.
[21] Louisa Brown comments that "He was the youngest of his generation (of the 31 Leach cousins) and felt alienated from many of them as he was unable to speak Spanish, and had no knowledge of the Argentine or places referred to where his older brother, sister and cousins had lived when they were children" (pers. comm.). He was not good at sports, but no one in his immediate or extended family was as bright as he was. He was very alone until he went to Cambridge.

academically gifted, took to farming and inherited Town Farm. Both brothers liked one another and got on well.[22] "Most of the members of his generation, including his sister, brother and brother's wife (Meg) were staunch supporters of the Conservative Party. Many were shocked that he [Edmund] supported the Labour Party in the 1940s."[23]

Among all his relatives, it was his mother, Mildred, who was the most "significant other" for Edmund. The following features will further help to configure her persona. Mildred's mother was a Howorth, and as we shall see, it was a maternal great-uncle (mother's mother's brother) named Henry Howorth whom Edmund idolized as his role model. Mildred's father was a Brierley. The Howorths, Brierleys, and Leaches came from a long line of Lancashire mill-owners.

However it seems that, although they were all mill-owners, as the Howorths had made their money earlier than the Leaches, they were on that account deemed to be a cut above the latter in social prestige. This difference seems to have cast its reflection on the personae of Edmund's own parents. In relation to her justly admired and capable husband, Mildred, musically inclined, was considered more "refined" in her upbringing and even socially somewhat superior. We have already related Edmund's own sketch of his mother and her influence on him (the non-Spanish-speaking youngest adored child brought up solely in Rochdale). She was an ardent and pious Christian, and it seems that she would have liked Edmund to become a missionary. She would in any case, as an active Christian, have hoped he would perform good works and "ease the pain in the world."

Edmund was apparently not exaggerating about his mother "slaughtering" his girlfriends. Celia Leach confirms that Mildred was very possessive, that she in fact put a stop to any intentions Edmund may have harbored about marrying women to whom he had been emotionally attached. But Mildred had in fact approved of Celia, had kind words for her, never "interfered," and they had got on well. Edmund had not put his mother first after he had married Celia.[24]

---

[22] The story is told that when Walter was being tutored, Edmund, the smart child, sat under the table and whispered the right answers. Although they led very different lives, they were fond of each other and Edmund deeply respected his older brother.

[23] Louisa Brown (pers. comm.).

[24] Louisa Brown informs me that Mildred's children were "somewhat in awe of her" and that some of her ten grandchildren were frightened of her. She had arguments with Mary, who was widowed, about the upbringing of her four children, and she had also tried to interfere with Walter's marriage with Meg. She describes Mildred as "a sharply intelligent unhappy woman who did not stand for any nonsense." She was known as Madre (Spanish for mother, a title of respect) by her in-laws.

Among all the information on Edmund's familial relationships, I would like to highlight certain features, and even speculate in anticipatory manner on their relevance, not only for his own affectively charged interpersonal relations as he was growing up, but also for his later perception and conceptualization of kinship and social organization in his capacity as a professional anthropologist. The first feature is that, although he admired and had affection for his father, he felt distanced from him by virtue of an enormous age gap, and also by comparison with all his cricket-playing paternal uncles and cousins, who shared their Argentinian experiences and connections. One might sense in Edmund not only his rejection of his father as a role model and as a source of paternal authority, but also his separateness, even alienation, from his paternal kin, especially the males. Does this suggest that he might always have problems dealing with male authority figures, and furthermore, that he might be skeptical of uncritical conceptions of the unity and solidarity of (patrilineal) lineages?

Second, Edmund was emotionally, socially, intellectually, and aesthetically much attached to and influenced by his mother, despite certain tensions in that relationship, including his need to cut the umbilical cord by going to China. Her ardent Christianity must have, as he put it, rubbed off on him, and he must have been steeped in the Bible from an early age. Although in adulthood he rejected the Christian faith (and especially institutionalized Christianity) and joined the Humanists, the biblical narratives remained a part of his active memory, and would re-engage him as an interpreter in the last phase of his career.

It might be surmised that through his mother, his maternal kin, including the unusual Sir Henry Howorth, had as much interest for him as, and possibly more influence on him than, his paternal kin.[25] In anthropological terms, he had first-hand experience and appreciation of matrilateral kin, and of the significance of bilateral kinship ties. His intimate knowledge and experience of close intermarriage from generation to generation among certain families of Lancashire mill-owning backgrounds must especially have impressed on him the motivations and strategies behind endogamous marriage alliances, and also, later on in his professional life, must have enabled him to recognize as "familiar" the appeal and "facticity" of repeated marriages as resulting in affinity as an inherited relation on lines similar to patrilinearity as an inherited link.

---

[25] Of Sir Henry Howorth, Louisa remarks that he was born in 1842 and died in 1923 when Edmund Leach was aged twelve. Edmund may not have known Sir Henry well when he was alive, but in his reminiscences, he says he idolized him.

(I have in mind in these speculations some of the theoretical formulations of Lévi-Strauss and Louis Dumont on kinship and marriage which evoked a positive response in Edmund Leach as professional anthropologist.)

FROM PUBLIC SCHOOL TO COMING OF AGE IN CAMBRIDGE

Mothered with such singular affection, tolerance, and encouragement, the youngest Leach would in any case have found Marlborough a trial, but life was made more difficult by the fact that being the twenty-first in a line of Leaches sent to that school, of whom all had automatically played in the cricket XI, he was the odd man out. His housemaster, discovering he could hardly see the ball, lost all interest in him.[26] "Much later, when I had made my way into the Upper Sixth, I was ruthlessly coached so that I could bring honour to the school by winning a mathematics scholarship to Clare College, Cambridge. Without question, my years at Marlborough were the unhappiest days of my life, worse even than the six years of army service, 1939–45."[27] "Public school tradition," he had concluded, was "not only unutterably foolish, but often wholly vile."[28]

But Cambridge proved to be "a glorious experience." He won a mathematics exhibition to Clare College in 1929, where he was somewhat disappointed to find that he wasn't a real mathematician and changed to the Mechanical Sciences Tripos. While in the usual Oxbridge style claiming to have "spent a blissful two years of practical idleness," he must have studied conscientiously, knew he could get a First, and "damned well got it."

But one can sense that the blissful Cambridge years were also a time of searching and questioning about art, music, sex, literature, films and theatre, politics, and morals. He once told me that he could operate on two channels simultaneously – listen to music and read or write at the same time. He also had a great interest in painting. In fiction, he had disliked Aldous Huxley and Evelyn Waugh, but found in D.H. Lawrence's *Sons and Lovers* good cause for "a great deal of thinking," no doubt in relation to the perennially engrossing issue of sex and morals.

Thus the privileged undergraduates of Cambridge, largely selected from a limited range of private schools and sharing social class

---

[26] This is an exaggeration by Leach. Although he was shortsighted, Louisa Brown comments that "more to the point he suffered a lack of bodily coordination" (personal communication).
[27] Kuper, "An Interview," p. 375.   [28] Firth, "A Cambridge Undergraduate," p. 16.

conventions, were in the early 1930s not blithely unconcerned with questions regarding sexual norms, gender relations, and morals in general. They felt stirrings of class injustices and conflict, and the forebodings caused by the Nazi movement in Germany.

One of the main issues that no doubt had great personal relevance for young people who in one way or another had been exposed to Victorian conventions and religious orthodoxy was where they stood in relation to organized religion. Of his own religious legacy Leach not entirely jokingly remarked: "In practice I was brought up a hard-boiled Christian, and mud sticks if you throw enough."[29] Though he had a distaste for organized religion (and doctrines such as papal infallibility), he at the same time wrestled with the question of whether civilized society necessarily depends on morals and ethics, which have their basis in human judgments of value, and in the case of religion, rest on faith: "The importance of religion is not in the truth or untruth of what we believe, but in the way in which we react to that belief in the conduct of our lives." These undergraduate musings do not suggest a commitment to "atheism," a position attributed to him by certain persons (including, as rumor has it, some of the Fellows of Clare College, especially the chaplain of that time, who would later deny him a fellowship primarily on that account). And in the latter part of his writing career, the mytho-logic and moral and social valuations contained in biblical stories would deeply engage him for their revelations of general human thought processes and their application to existential dilemmas.

He was similarly debating the issue of the moral code in place, which, in Durkheimian fashion (though Leach had not read him yet), being the "mortar that upholds the brickwork of laws and constitutions together," society must uphold, but which was being questioned by the "new psychology," "the favoured infant of the moment," by which he was probably referring to the writings of Freud, Bertrand Russell (e.g. *Marriage and Morals*, 1929), and the edited volumes of F.C. Calverton and S.D. Schmalhausen (*Sex in Civilization*, 1929). It was via these readings that Leach first encountered Malinowski in print, the text in question being *Parenthood: The Basis of Social Structure* (1930).

With the poetic license and fizz allowed in personal correspondence he wrote, "In Cambridge as elsewhere, the male of the species, anyway talks sex, morning noon and night to the almost total exclusion of anything else." He wondered whether the absence of barriers between the sexes,

---

[29] Ibid., p. 10.

the experiment of coeducation in Edinburgh, while credible in theory, actually worked in practice. Can the relationship between the sexes be "*really* free?" Is there not deep consciousness of difference between them?

Generalizing about the Cambridge of his time, he wrote:

Official attitudes not withstanding, the sexes were not effectively segregated, but the goal of sexual liberation and the permissive society was a novelty and in high fashion. Commentaries on the work of Freud, Jung, Adler, and other renegade psychoanalysts were to be found on the bookshelf of every undergraduate who saw himself as a member of the intelligentsia. A clandestine study of Malinowski's writings could be a part of that pattern along with the liberationist propaganda of Bertrand Russell.[30]

We may thus say of Leach's undergraduate preoccupations that questions of the gap between ideals of perfection and practice, and between moral values inflected by social convention and deep psycho-biological impulses, were raised, although of course not settled (if settlement is ever possible). In later life Leach was genuinely committed to liberal and humanist positions on these matters, and he would grapple with the large issue of how necessary, how viable, how justifiable were challenges to institutions in place that, while being social legacies, require also dynamically to adapt to ever-changing circumstances. In his Reith Lectures, *A Runaway World?*, in 1967, he assumed the role of national critic and advocate of change in British society; as Provost of King's College (1966–79) and as President of the Royal Anthropological Institute in the early 1970s he would simultaneously be cautiously innovative and protectively conservationist of the institutions he cherished as British achievements toward which he also acted as benefactor.

GLOOMY FOREBODINGS AT CAMBRIDGE

The episode I am about to relate comes chronologically before Edmund's twenty-first birthday celebrations which were described above, but for narrative purposes has been postponed until now. An undated letter to his father written either in 1930, or more probably in 1931,[31] in his penultimate year at Cambridge, indicates that he felt he was unable to concentrate on his studies and that he was in considerable uncertainty about his future direction and his ability to live up to the expectations

---

[30] Edmund Leach, "Glimpses of the Unmentionable in the History of British Social Anthropology," *Annual Review* of *Anthropology*, vol. 13, 1984, p. 9.

[31] The Modern Archive, King's College Library, Cambridge.

of his parents. The letter in question was written on six foolscap pages in answer to a letter from his father which could not be found among Edmund's papers. Edmund's reply, written in longhand, has the appearance of a composition completed in one sitting and materializing as a spontaneous rush of words charged with much emotion. The letter was from an undergraduate of about twenty to a father almost sixty years older, and is diagnostic of the uncertainty he suffered from for a few years regarding his vocation in life. Since the letter is somewhat prolix it is reproduced as an appendix to this chapter, and I will state here its themes and its implications as I see them.

It comes as a surprise in the context of his previous intimations of an exhilarating life at Cambridge that at the time the letter was written he was in a depressed state. His torrent of words was a kind of confessional to his parents, in which he blamed himself for his inability to concentrate on his studies and his falling short of his parents' seeming overestimation of his talents. His listless state of mind may have been partly due to the difference between the regulated studies at Marlborough and the freer atmosphere at Cambridge where the student was to find his own bearings.

However, he situates and explains this *mea culpa* misery as related to the menacing state of the world which does not inspire him (and his generation) to purposeful commitment. Thus the letter is also a sermon to his father on why their worlds are so different. He pointedly tells his father that there is a generational gap between them. The dividing line is the First World War. In comparison with his father's pre-war generation (which he perceives as having been more stable),[32] he describes his own post-war generation as destabilized by various global developments. There is on the one side the "terrible tyranny" of American business which, replacing "the more sober commerce of the last century" (controlled by British imperium), has lost control of itself, being subject to destructive alternating business cycles of prosperity and depression. (Possibly Edmund is here reflecting the Marxist indictment of capitalism which was all the more compelling on the eve of the Great Depression.) Ranged against this is the Russian Soviet totalitarian regime, which is bound to destroy the American system. However, there was in any case little to choose between "the machine world of the Soviet and financial tyranny of Western big business." (There is no sense at this time of the Nazi danger which would be the third player that would plunge the

---

[32] Edmund's father was actually a young man in the 1870s, long before the First World War.

world into disaster, although in the following year, as we shall see, Edmund becomes aware of it when he visits Germany.) It is noteworthy that Edmund includes as integral to his apocalyptic drama, which he must have shared with many others of his Cambridge generation, an indictment of depersonalizing science and the threat of man's domination by the machine, and the consequent destruction of "culture." Edmund thus asks his father how he can expect him to think of his future, his career, in this unpleasant world that is his heritage.

However, there is also a pragmatic discussion of his career possibilities. Edmund rejects apprenticeship in Britain, and considers the openings in the Colonial Services. He thinks he is not good enough to compete for a post in India but that service in East Africa or Sudan might be a possibility despite the malaria.

But this half-hearted discussion is abandoned to tell his father that since "so much change must descend upon the world in the next ten years" it is not possible to predict what he will be doing at the end of that time. He was indeed right about this, not only because the world would be plunged into the Second World War (he could not have foreseen this disaster), but mainly because he would be an uncertain wanderer for a time, and subsequently become a victim of that war.

In due course Edmund seems to have emerged from his slump. He obviously worked hard in his final year and "damned well" got a First, and whatever his previous denunciation of commerce and science, he did after graduation sign on to go to China to practice commerce and engineering. But political developments at this time were menacing and he was sensitive to them, as were his peers.

THE GATHERING OF STORMCLOUDS

Leach's Cambridge years, 1929–32, were also the time of emerging rifts in the British class system. The General Strike of 1926 had already signaled a deep class divide. The Great Depression had epidemic global repercussions – very high unemployment, long lines of workers, their families living on the dole and queuing for everyday necessities. And menacing in this context was the rise of Hitler's party of National Socialism in Germany, its mobilization of a youth movement, the spread of Nazi sentiments, the build up of armaments, and the threat of aggrandizing war.

Leach had himself visited Germany in the summer of 1931 and from there he had written: "I have great fear of the future . . . I shudder to think what may happen in another 30 years, when the present youth of Germany holds the helm . . . For all the world the future seems to hold nothing but trouble."[33] The trouble came much sooner than he had thought.

In retrospect in 1986 Leach described the impact of these developments on Cambridge undergraduates and their mood as follows:

> the more intellectual among us were almost all of a radical, near communist, political persuasion. We were already coming to hate the social rigidities of the system in which we had been reared, the injustices of which were visible on every side. By comparison with the present generation of Cambridge undergraduates, we were very politicized. We had no use for compromise . . .
>
> The fact that in 1929–1932 Hitler was just coming into power added another dimension. We thought that we could recognize the encroachment of a "fascist mentality" in every aspect of British life, as evidenced, for example, by the reaction of the ruling class (to which we ourselves belonged) to the General Strike of 1926. Some became activist leaders of the political left. A few years later many of my contemporaries joined the International Brigade in the Spanish Civil War. At least one communist scion of the Cambridge intellectual aristocracy died in that vain defense of socialist democracy as we believed it to be. Recent revelations about the Russian recruitment of spies from among upper class Cambridge undergraduates in the 1930s is part of that same story. J.B.S. Haldane . . . who by then was avowed Marxist, was a kind of culture hero.[34]

It was in this environment that Leach's own socialist sympathies were crystallized. The havoc caused by the Depression, the long queues for the dole and for bread and clothing, had affected him deeply. It was this more than any other experience that, affluent as he was, decided for him that he would not settle for a life of conspicuous consumption, as evidenced over twenty years later when he returned to Cambridge as a don. Storey's Way was dubbed "Snobs' Alley," and the Leach House there (number 52) was a large mansion, with comfortable rooms and beautiful furniture, adorned with works of art, and, of course, stocked with thousands of books. As Louisa said of her parents: "In fact they lived as did other upper middle class, wealthy, privileged academics of their time. Money was not regarded as of importance – because there was plenty of it." At Storey's Way Edmund and Celia entertained a great deal, and they often had friends stay for long periods of time. Celia was a marvelous cook and the family ate extremely well. Edmund loved fine wines, and "every evening good wine was drunk . . . sometimes quite

---

[33] Firth, "A Cambridge Undergraduate," p. 12.   [34] Leach, "Glimpses," p. 9.

fabulous wines were drunk."[35] They made motoring trips to week-long gourmet retreats, and also went on motoring holidays in France. This way of life was combined with generosity and liberality to others in philanthropic acts. And of course, as one might expect, Edmund invested in a very impressive library. Politically he steadfastly supported the Labour Party, and when in later life he was a public figure, he sometimes went to bat for it as a counterweight to some other academic lending his name to a Conservative Party cause. Toward the end of his life, while living in retirement in Barrington, Leach changed his allegiance and supported the Liberal Democrats.

THE CHINESE INTERLUDE

Two extracts from his diary dated January 15 and 24 (probably 1933)[36] describe Edmund's recruitment and preliminary training by a well-known firm operating in the Far East. The January 15 entry reads:

The chief excitement since my last entry has been that I have obtained a job. Cambridge put me on to a firm called John Swire and Sons General Agents operating in China and Japan. In due course I interviewed . . . only this time I was fired off for my medical interview right away – Dr. L., 86 Brooke Street, too utterly Mayfair – rather a nice Scotsman.

Edmund got the job, and was "briefly told to 'come along at 10 a.m. 23rd of this month.' So that was that! I like my boss greatly – he adopts the attitude that the Chinaman has a very fine intelligence and must be treated accordingly. None of the hard faced jingo imperialism that was shown by my previous selection [board]. It remains to be seen how things go."

There is a revealing introspection in his feelings about and motives for wanting to go to China:

The great and obvious snag is that it is so far away. To me this is an asset, but M[other] is going to feel it terribly. Rightly speaking I suppose I am acting very selfishly in going abroad at all, but I feel very strongly that I could completely waste my life if I stayed at home. M[other] for all her good intentions treats me like a baby and accordingly I act like one. Responsibility is absolutely necessary to me . . .

---

35 Personal communication from Louisa Brown, who also remarks that she learnt from her father a love and knowledge of wine.
36 The Modern Archive, King's College Library, Cambridge. These extracts were probably copied by Louisa Brown and put on file. The diary itself is not available.

In the diary entry of January 24 he wrote: "For two days am I [sic] the city Magnate. I started work at John Swire's yesterday So far all is well. My work is very dull but plenty of it – working through ships manifests." There were three others in a similar position to himself. "All are Oxford and very pleasant Oxford at that. The office staff is almost exclusively Scotch, pleasant but hard working. The drudgery of commercial life will no doubt pall somewhat but I think it will be worth it." He again wrote at the end of this entry, "Office work is proving surprisingly wearying."

He had just moved to his lodgings at Cambridge House, and he described his associates as "very mixed and all ages: lawyers, artists, do nothings, business men. Nothing violently intelligent; nothing violently unpleasant. Alas, one of them possesses a wireless; he thinks it *so* good and it *is* so bad."

But there was something more engaging than the office routine (hours 9:30–1:30 and 2:30–5, with a quarter of an hour for tea): "I attend the School of Oriental Languages 3 times per week for Chinese. I think it will prove an easy language to *understand*, very difficult to read, and difficult to pronounce. The grammar is very simple." And perhaps even more significantly he had his first shaky glimmerings of comparative religion:

Today I had a lecture on Chinese religion – a notable feature is that "Ancestor Worship" does not really imply that the Ancestors are considered divine or even immortal. The whole idea is to inculcate the idea of filial piety in the young and it is the *example* that is valued . . . Taoism is now on the decline, having descended to mere superstition. But Buddhism is undergoing a revival on the philosophic side, once the Chinaman's interest in religion is aroused he tends to Buddhism in preference to Xtianity. The Temple worship of Buddha is however declining. Note here again there is no real suggestion of the "worshipping of images." Buddha is a saint in the R.C. [Roman Catholic] style.

Edmund's adventurous trip to China is described well by Stephen Hugh Jones:[37]

On graduation he went to China on a four year contract with the trading firm of John Swire and Sons (Butterfield and Swire), a move he put down to a combination of the family characteristic of wanderlust, his own love of travel

[37] Stephen Hugh-Jones, "Edmund Leach 1910–1989," a memoir prepared by the direction of the Council of King's College, Cambridge, 1989, pp. 10–11. There is a small correction to be made. Leach states that "he entered a four-and-a-half-year contract with John Swire and Sons which kept me in their London office for about nine months and then took me to China." Edmund Leach, "In Formative Travail with Leviathan," in R.M. Berndt (ed.), "Anthropological Research in British Colonies: Same Personal Accounts," special issue of *Anthropological Forum*, vol. 4, no. 2, 1997, p. 190.

and his need for a job. [We might also add the need to experience his separation from his parents, especially his mother.] He served in Hong Kong, Shanghai, Chungking, Tsingtao and Peking and there acquired skill in business, financial dealings and administration, activities he thoroughly enjoyed and which he used to such good effect in later years – later he once remarked, rather wistfully, that he wished he had been a "proper businessman".

Edmund was delighted by China; off duty from business, he spent his time exploring with fascination its alien cultural system, learning something of the language and collecting jade sculpture and ancient pottery. On holidays he travelled widely, travel which included climbing four of the five sacred mountains of the country . . .

At the end of his assignment he had planned to travel home to England via Russia by way of the Trans-Siberian railway. On arrival in Peking his plans were thwarted – the Stalinist purges had begun, Russia was in turmoil and the embassy would issue no visas.[38] Disappointment was tempered by the delights of Peking itself and Edmund soon fell in with the large polyglot community of expatriate Western artists and intellectuals living there. A chance encounter at an embassy party changed the direction of his life. There he met Kilton Stewart, a psychiatrist and former Mormon missionary with an interest in anthropology who invited him to join an expedition to the island of Botel Tobago off the coast of Formosa to visit the Yami.[39]

Half joking, half serious, Edmund described the Yami as "real primitives" and "the sort of people who 'real' anthropologists are expected to study" and they made an indelible impression upon him and remained a touchstone of his kind of anthropology. Using his engineering training, he made meticulous drawings of their boats and technology and these were the subjects of his first anthropological publications.

I might add to this account that the enchanting waiting-days in Peking were also a felicitous time for reading Confucius and indulging in the connoisseurship of collecting art. Leach acquired a small collection of Sung ceramics, and in the 1970s I heard him recounting with conspiratorial chuckles the deals made with antique dealers who would shoo him off when tourist-buyers appeared on the scene. (This collection he much later gifted to the Royal Anthropological Institute to be sold to enhance its finances.)

---

[38] This is how Edmund related the dreams-dashed episode: "The visit to Peking was to plan a voyage home by the Trans-Siberian Railway with a friend in the British Embassy. The theory was that we would get as far as Moscow by rail and then float down the Volga . . . At that point Stalin started bumping off his generals. The great Stalinist purges had begun. Our friend in the Russian Embassy said that all visas were cancelled but that perhaps if we hung around for three months things would clarify" (Kuper "An interview," pp. 375–76).

[39] Leach's account of this first encounter with Stewart is hilarious. "At a party in the British Embassy, a very drunk American named Kilton Stewart, a former Mormon missionary, announced that he was on the way to 'Bottle the Bugger. Would anybody like to come . . .' I said, 'Well, that sounds an interesting place. Where is it?'" (ibid.).

Appendix: A letter from a Cambridge undergraduate to his father

Clare College,
Cambridge
Monday [undated]

Dear Dad,

Very many thanks for your letter; it is in many ways rather a difficult one to answer but I will do my best.

Firstly I would assure you that my somewhat disgruntled attitude, which must appear to you as wholly inconsiderate and lacking in gratitude, is to that extent false; for I am in fact fully conscious of the obligations that I owe both to you directly, and more generally, to the world for the upbringing and education that I have received. It is only as to the method by which I am to make use of this education that I am groping in the dark.

Firstly of ability. It was altogether natural that you and Mother as my parents, should deduce from my somewhat spectacular scholastic achievements of early years an altogether false value of my ability. I have in fact never possessed that ability for I wholly lack, and have always lacked, power of concentration. So long as my education required merely a fragmentary interest in the outlines of a large variety of subjects I was nothing short of brilliant, indeed my inherent inquisitiveness has even now endowed me with a most formidable armament as a "Mr. Know-all." But all that is not ability, it is a form of rather worthless curiosity. Three years of concentrated Mathematics at Marlborough raised me to a standard in that subject that with really applied concentration on *my* part should have been achieved in one. It was really almost despite myself that I attained the somewhat mediocre honour of an "exhibition at Clare." But at Marlborough indeed, with all its intensive teaching, even lacking interest I was bound to learn something, but here [at Cambridge] with the compulsion removed my former nature asserts itself, and I find myself lacking altogether the *will* to work. Once again I am plunged into

26

a world in which my curiosity and inquisitiveness are exercised to their fullest, but in which my concentration is left to its weak self.

Thus then, and for the moment neglecting altogether the future, I am faced with a problem. Having failed in two successive exams [he is probably referring to two tests] and lacking all interest[1] in my work, how can I even at this eleventh hour redeem myself and achieve at any rate *something* as a culmination to my education.

It is easy enough to make fulsome promises of hard and devoted work during the next twelve months but quite another matter to carry that out. And I would rather you realized that fact than that I should falsely be the object of your trust. You say—Nothing matters—*so long as we know that you have tried your best*; but that *is* just exactly what I cannot promise you. My best, even though I myself say it, is very good, and for years now, I have never given anything like fully of it, nor as far as I can see am I capable of doing so. This matter of work then is wholly a matter for my own resolution, to succeed or to fail. That I must grieve you and Mother by thus revealing myself as spineless and futile, grieves me, but I had rather that you should accept me for what I am than as some magnificent genius about to burst into flower.

In the matter of career, I am against the same difficulty that I lack all genuine interest outside myself. There is nothing that I particularly *want* to do. Fortunately the choice is limited. As things are, for good or for bad, I must be an engineer. I refuse absolutely to undertake a job that requires three to four years apprenticeship "shop" work, and *that* in effect means I must go abroad; somehow in addition I must earn my living, but good jobs these days do not grow like thistles, and I shall have to take what fortune offers, which is not likely to be much. On the whole a cheerless aspect. There remains of course in some sense the possibilities of the Civil Services. The Indian Civil is at any rate I think beyond my standard, even if I were attracted by it which I am not. With the Colonial Services it is otherwise, the competition being less severe, and the choice, I understand, not wholly dependent upon examination. As a career administration in East Africa or the Sudan offers little prospect other than Malaria, but there are many counterbalancing attractions, and the work itself should be interesting.

So far, in this letter I have done little but confirm your worst fears as to my spineless lack of initiative, and indeed I can do little else. Mother

---

[1] I might add that the fact that I am studying Engineering, and not Physics or History or Economics has no bearing on the case. Whatever the subject be I lose interest in it as soon as I attempt to devote my whole attention to it.

is just enough when she stigmatises me as a shirker and a looker-on and declares emotionally that "I am afraid to get down into the reality of the world's pain to do my bit to heal it." You for your part fear that I am "unbalanced." In some ways the whole of my generation are. Ours is the *first* generation to have grown up wholly since the war, my education began with the peace. It being so it is inevitable that we should have a wholly different standard of values to all those who preceded us. The war marked the death bed of a great age, and gave birth to a new one altogether without standards or stability. Consider, only for a moment, civilisation as it is today. On the one hand we have the vast and terrible tyranny that is typified by American business, that is but the logical succession to the more sober commerce of the last century; so vast and unmanageable has this huge monster become that it has utterly lost control of itself, so that of its own mechanism it is *bound* to operate in alternate cycles of prosperity and depression bringing misery and destruction with every downward swoop of the pendulum. Against this you have arrayed the deadly efficient machine that is aimed at by the Russian Soviet; that this latter will succeed and destroy the former I hold to be inevitable. It is merely a matter of efficiency, it is as inevitable as that a modern battleship should defeat a gunship of the dreadnaught class. But the world will scarcely gain; in cruelty there is little to choose between the machine world of the Soviet and financial tyranny of Western big business.

Thirdly apart from these two lies the whole realm of science. The early achievements can little have realized what a Pandora's box they were unloosing when they delved into the mysteries of the elements. Today absolutely nothing short of universal annihilation can stop the progress of science. If man does not destroy himself in the process, a wholly mechanical world is *bound* to evolve during the course of the next two centuries; the machine is the symbol of the age.

This then is the first great difference that my generation has to face, the two chief factors that control the destiny of the age, Science and Commerce, are wholly outside the control of man. This has never been so before, and the fact alone must necessarily alter entirely one's out-look in life. It throws one upon a fearful kind of fatalism from which there is no escape. I think it is time to say that this post-war gen-eration which is the first to grow up in a world so utterly under the control of science, *hates* that science with all the fury that the peasants held for the necromancers of old, and yet we are the slaves of that sci-ence, and must not only obey it implicitly but must even further its development – inevitably; all must do this or perish in the struggle for existence.

And so there is gradually being taken out of life all that made it possible for man to be something higher than the beast. Culture is being killed by the speed at which we are forced to live, and we are compelled to struggle where our forbears were at ease to contemplate. Altogether it is not a particularly pleasant world to gain as a heritage.

Upon me it has, for me, this effect. I cannot seriously concern myself about my career. So much change must descend upon the world during the next ten years, that it is a safe prediction to declare that what I shall be doing at the end of that time will not be what I decide to do now. In a time such as this it is wholly impossible to live beyond the moment.

And that really sums up my whole argument and explanation. I cannot live outside the present, as the mood is so will I act, and I cannot mortgage the future by empty promises of optimistic forecasts. The times are out of joint indeed. Come good or bad it matters little.

Your most loving son,
Edmund

CHAPTER 3

Apprenticeship and the Second World War

Although he had read some of Malinowski's early writings as an undergraduate, Leach did not meet Malinowski until after his return from China in 1937. By that time Malinowski, famously established at the London School of Economics, had acquired a reputation not only as the most exciting author of anthropological works but also as a great teacher.

Since Leach, when he began his studies with him in 1937, must inevitably have been impressed by the mountain of achievements attributed to Malinowski, it is necessary before I continue with Leach's biography to give some details of how Malinowski, who was appointed Reader at the London School of Economics in 1923 and had by then published, among others, the famous text *Argonauts of the Western Pacific*, became so pivotal in establishing social anthropology as a professional discipline in Britain, and in attracting and influencing a large number of scholars from diverse places who attended his celebrated seminar.

Goody provides valuable information on how, with timely Rockefeller support,

a vigorous graduate programme was established . . . after the First World War under Bronislaw Malinowski at the London School of Economics. That was where most of the action took place during the thirties, not at the ancient universities. His intellectual status, his energy, his enthusiasm and his ability to raise funds resulted in a great expansion of field research. He was able to do this because of his connection with the London School of Economics and through them with the Laura Spelman Rockefeller Memorial[1] which provided the large bulk of funds.[2]

---

[1] In 1928 the Memorial became the Division of Social Sciences in the Rockefeller Foundation.
[2] Jack Goody, *The Expansive Moment: The Rise of Social Anthropology in Britain and Africa 1918–1970*, Cambridge: Cambridge University Press, 1995, p. 8.

In 1929 the Rockefeller Memorial permitted anthropologists to apply for grants or fellowships (Edith Clarke, Lucy Mair, and Audrey Richards were recipients), and in due course established the Fellowship Programme of the International African Institute in 1931[3], its inauguration being made possible by the key efforts of Dr. J.H. Oldham, who was a friend of Malinowski. Although he had not worked in Africa, Malinowski achieved a dominant position in the African Institute, and influenced the selection of Fellows. In due course some seventeen full-time Fellows were appointed. Destined to "form much of the core of the teaching of African studies for the next thirty and more years" they were "Fortes (South Africa), Hofstra (Holland), Kirchhoff (Germany), Nadel (Austria), together with the two Kriges (South Africa), Lucy Mair (Britain), Margery Perham (Britain), Margaret Read (Britain), Monica Wilson (Britain), Z.K. Matthews (a Tswana), another German, G.K. Wagner, another Austrian, the missionary, Father Schumacher (who worked in Ruanda), two Frenchwomen, T. Rivière, the niece of G.H. Rivière, and Germaine Tillion . . . and two linguists, Father Crazzolora (Italy), and J. Lukas (Germany)."[4] Grants were also made to, among others, Jomo Kenyatta of Kenya (later the leader of the independence struggle) and Fadipe of Yorubaland so that they could work at the London School of Economics, and "Indeed a number of the other Fellows were asked to come to London to work under Malinowski."[5] Thus it came about that Malinowski, whose own famous writings were based on innovative and unmatched fieldwork in Melanesia, came to be the teacher of a great array of scholars from many parts of the world, and mostly focused on Africa.

Malinowski started his famous seminar at the London School of Economics in 1924 soon after he took up his appointment as Reader. He was appointed Professor in 1927. The 1930s were the high point of the seminar which saw the coming and going of a number of scholars who became key figures in the field:

At first it consisted of Evans-Pritchard (who had studied history at Oxford), of Ashley Montague (whose main work was on the biological side), of Ursula Grant-Duff (the daughter of Lord Avebury, an important figure in the earlier history of British anthropology), of Raymond Firth (who had studied economics

---

[3] Goody, *The Expansive Moment*, p. 26, mentions that the initial selection included Gordon Brown, Meyer Fortes, Audrey Richards, Margery Perham and P. Kirchhoff; other early recipients were Lucy Mair and Edith Clarke.
[4] Ibid., p. 27.   [5] Ibid.

in New Zealand), and of Barbara Freire-Marreco (or Mrs. Aitken, who worked among the Tewa of Hano in the south-west of the USA). When Hortense Powdermaker, a trade-union organizer from America, arrived there in 1925 and eventually wrote a study of Hollywood as well as of the Copper Belt of Zambia, there were only three graduate students in anthropology: she herself, Evans-Pritchard and Firth, followed the next year by Isaac Schapera who had worked under Radcliffe-Brown at Cape Town. Evans-Pritchard, who did field-work among the Nuer and the Azande of the Sudan, was to fill the Chair at Oxford. Firth carried out research among the Maori (before going to London), in Malaya and above all on the Pacific island of Tikopia, prior to becoming the successor to Malinowski in London. Schapera worked extensively among the black population of Southern Africa and he too became a professor at the School. However, Powdermaker was soon joined by others who were to become well-known in British anthropology: Audrey Richards, a natural scientist from Cambridge who was to work among the Bemba of Zambia, Edith Clarke from Jamaica, and by Jack Driberg (a former colonial officer), Camilla Wedgwood, and Gordon and Elizabeth Brown of Canada, who carried out fieldwork in East Africa, Melanesia and East Africa respectively.[6]

Goody continues:

The list of students attending Malinowski's seminars at the School in the session 1932–33 consisted mostly of Africanists, all of whom produced valuable studies: H. Beemer (later Kuper), M. Fortes, M. Lecoeur, S.F. Nadel, S. Hofstra, M. Read, G. Wilson, M. Perham, L. Mair, A. Richards and potentially P. Kirchhoff, a total of twenty-four which included "Mr. and Mrs. Davis" (the distinguished Black American, Alison Davis), occasionally the sociologist, Talcott Parsons, and others. Not all the members of the seminar were aiming to work in Africa; his students, Fei and Hsu, followed at the School by Tien Jukung,[7] were important in extending social anthropology to China. But as the result of the benefactions of the Rockefeller Foundation much of the research of the School was directed to that continent, to the study of which the majority of the Fellows contributed important monographs. There can rarely have been a more effective use of funds in the history of research in the social sciences.[8]

Although Goody is primarily concerned in *The Expansive Moment* with documenting the developments and achievements of British anthropology in Africa, it is nevertheless true that the non-Africanists were a minority in the salon presided over by Malinowksi. However by the late thirties some significant scholars concerned with Australian "aborigines" and with Melanesia and Oceania had also studied with him. Leaving

[6] Ibid., p. 15.
[7] Goody is in error about T'ien Ju Kang, who followed much later and was actually a pupil of Raymond Firth.
[8] Goody, *The Expansive Moment*, p. 27.

aside one of his earliest and most prized associates and heir, Raymond Firth, others included Ian Hogbin and William Stanner from Australia, Reo Fortune from New Zealand, and the Chinese scholars, Fei Hsiao-t'ung, and Francis Hsu. M.N. Srinivas, from India, though based at Oxford, appears to have made visits to the LSE. Joining the seminar in 1937, Edmund Leach was one of the members of the last cohort before Malinowski left for the United States to end his career there at Yale University.

LEACH'S ENCOUNTER WITH MALINOWSKI

I consider him [Malinowski] the greatest and most original of all social anthropologists.[9]

Leach came to anthropology in 1936; he was then twenty-six years old. It might seem as if there was a discernible accumulation and direction of events that brought him to anthropology: aside from his retrospective comments about his childhood immersion in a world of kin and domestics, more proximately his travels and experiences in China and the final trip to the island of Botel Tobago would seem to point him toward anthropology. During his eight weeks in Tobago he had made as an "amateur anthropologist" some ethnographic notes, but more relevantly, as an engineer deeply interested in "design features," he drew accurate scale drawings of boats and houses.

Leach has himself said that no early decision or steady path led him to anthropology as his vocation. He had returned to London from China by sea bringing with him the notes, drawings, and photographs made in Tobago. Moreover, Chinese culture, art, and religion had certainly fascinated Edmund, and this appreciation "probably helped him to throw off some of his early Christian upbringing and to suggest the lines of a possible future career. For, despite his acknowledged efficiency, he disliked the business atmosphere and determined 'never again to bind himself to an office stool.'"[10]

When he returned to London, he began to consider an anthropological career and wrote to Rosemary, his childhood friend, "I feel that only then could the Hermit, the Wanderer and the pseudo-Philosopher

[9] Edmund Leach, *Custom, Law and Terrorist Violence*, Edinburgh: Edinburgh University Press, 1977, p. 6.
[10] Rosemary Firth, "Biographical Sketch of Sir Edmund Ronald Leach (1910–1989)," in C.S. Nicholas (ed.), *The Dictionary of National Biography*, Oxford: Oxford University Press, 1986–90, p. 258.

within me, find mutual satisfaction."[11] As he himself has narrated, he knew that Rosemary Upcott had married an anthropologist, Raymond Firth. "I asked Rosemary to introduce me to her husband, and that was the beginning of a lifelong discipleship. Characteristically, Raymond said, 'Well, this looks very interesting, though of course you have asked all the wrong questions!'"[12] Leach had discussions with Firth about making sense of his data, and then at the beginning of 1937, Firth introduced him to Malinowski who, according to Leach, "was at this time at the peak of his reputation, but his own great days of intellectual output were behind him."[13]

Leach formally joined Malinowski's seminar at the London School of Economics as a registered research student. He was then aged twenty-seven. Malinowski obviously made an enormous impression on him, and in retrospect Leach eulogized him as one of his two "supernatural beings" or "deities," the other being his mother's uncle, Sir Henry Howorth. In his own words, Leach was "converted" to anthropology in 1937.[14] The extraordinary career of Malinowski has been well recorded: notably his origins in Poland, his change of discipline from physics and mathematics to anthropology, his passage to England and training at the LSE, his fieldtrips to Melanesia, and his election to the first chair in anthropology at the LSE in 1927. Although an outsider, Malinowski had within a few years risen to preeminence in London, interacting with British anthropologists such as the Seligmans, Frazer, Haddon, Rivers, Marett, and the Finnish anthropologist Westermarck, and perhaps even more impressively, as time went on, he developed a large personal acquaintance with scholars in various other fields. "In Britain alone he co-operated with or was influenced by a range of men including Richard Gregory, Havelock Ellis, A.H. Gardiner, Julian Huxley, C.K. Ogden, Cyril Burt, C.S. Myers, J.C. Flugel, W. Powys Mathers, G.H.L.-F, P.H. Rivers, J.H. Oldham – all of whom were interested from different angles in the wider implication of his science."[15] Aside from the International African Institute already referred to, Malinowski also lectured for the British Social Hygiene Council and advised Mass Observation.

[11] Ibid.   [12] Kuper, "An Interview," p. 376.
[13] Stanley J. Tambiah, "Personal Accounts: Edmund Leach Situates Himself," *Cambridge Anthropology. Special Issue: Sir Edmund Leach*, vol. 13, no. 3, 1989–90, p. 37. Leach explained that Malinowski's *Coral Gardens* had been published in 1935, and Firth's *We, The Tikopia* in 1936, and Bateson's *Naven* in 1937.
[14] See Edmund Leach, *Social Anthropology*, Glasgow: Fontana Paperbacks, 1982, pp. 7–8.
[15] Raymond Firth, "Introduction: Malinowski as Scientist and as Man," in Raymond Firth (ed.), *Man and Culture: An Evaluation of the World of Bronislaw Malinowski*, London: Routledge & Kegan Paul, 1957, pp. 1–14.

In addition to being an articulate propagandist for his own "Functional School of Anthropology," Malinowski was an impresario adept at popularizing and demonstrating the relevance of anthropology to other professional groups and to the public at large. These feats certainly must have impressed the members of his seminar in the late thirties, and set a pattern for at least some of them to follow. Edmund Leach, by his own activities later, suggests such an emulative response.

In his colorful way Leach has conveyed the euphoria and specialness he associated with the seminar group, focused on the charismatic Malinowski and surrounded by a coterie of about a dozen or so anthropologists, most of whom were drawn from the British Commonwealth, the British Empire, and South Africa. They were a "pretty exotic group" who were certainly not upholders of the colonial regime, and there were also others, from Europe and China.[16]

On another occasion, remarking on the variety of persons extending beyond "the inward looking parochial community of British academia" who surrounded Malinowski, "a permanent Central European", and on how these British members were situated *vis-à-vis* others, Leach said that at one end was Evans-Pritchard, a very "English Englishman", while at the other end was Nadel, "a very typical Viennese Jewish intellectual." In between was Audrey Richards, "true English but handicapped by the prevailing prejudice against women academics." Others were Firth, a near English "colonial from New Zealand", and Fortes and Schapera, South Africans of Jewish origin.[17]

Leach himself described his felicitous relationship with and attitude to Malinowski in these terms:

If [Malinowski] liked you, he liked you, and you could do no wrong. Fortunately, he did like me. For the next 18 months (in retrospect it seems much more) I was in Malinowski's pocket. He was intensely charismatic. I did not know him at all well personally, but I attended his seminars . . . The seminar had an official allocated time from five to seven on the same day, but it usually started at two and went on indefinitely. By that time it was notorious, a sort of circus attended

[16] See Tambiah, "Personal Accounts." Leach mentioned the following as being at various times members of Malinowski's seminar: Raymond Firth, Evans-Pritchard, Fei Hsiao-t'ung, Francis Hsu, Kenyatta, S.F. Nadel, Audrey Richards, Lucy Mair, Phyllis Kaberry, Ian Hogbin, William Stanner, and I. Schapera. In this non-exhaustive listing one notes the absence of Radcliffe-Brown, whose career had a different trajectory, and who had recently arrived from Chicago to take up his Oxford chair. London and Oxford would develop into two rival foci, but Malinowski did interact with Radcliffe-Brown. It would seem that Leach's own contemporaries included Phyllis Kaberry, Ian Hogbin, William Stanner, Nadel, Kenyatta, Fei Hsiao-t'ung, and Francis Hsu. See Leach's account in "In Formative Travail" quoted below.
[17] Leach, "Glimpses of the Unmentionable," p. 16.

by all kinds of celebrities who were not necessarily connected with anthropology at all. But somehow we learned a lot.[18]

Leach made scattered references to it in his writings, but the following is the amplest account of Malinowski's "celebrated seminar, which had become something of a show piece," at the time he attended it:

The seminar was certainly a very lively institution. It met once a week at about 2 o'clock, continued till tea-time, broke off for three quarters of an hour while the participants, still talking, migrated across the road to take tea in Bush House and then returned for further argument until about 6. Most of the members of the seminar were devoted disciples of Malinowski and accepted the basic tenets of his brand of functionalism as a religious dogma.

Anthropology of this sort was not expounded in any other university institution anywhere in the country, and indeed was regarded with anathema by most of the small band of professionally qualified anthropologists then in existence. The LSE anthropologists thus had many of the characteristics of a sect.

In those days the physical appearance of the general region within a few hundred yards of Russell Square was very different from what it is now, and plenty of cheap lodging which students could afford was available. A substantial proportion of the members of Malinowski's seminar, at the time when I was a member of it, lived in and around Mecklenburg Square and Lambs Conduit Street and we all saw a great deal of one another. Hardly any of these people had been trained as anthropologists. This was true also of the staff. Malinowski had been a physicist, Firth an economist, Fortes a psychologist, and so on. Indeed, as compared with their modern equivalent, the research students were not only ignorant of the most elementary facts about general Anthropology, but they were also quite unfamiliar with even the most elementary texts in sociological theory. But what they lacked in formal academic training they to some extent made up by their greater maturity and life experience. Nearly all members of the seminar, staff and students alike, had had some sort of field experience in the environment of a relatively "primitive" culture. I do not recall that there was any particular political slant which dominated the ideology of the group as a whole. This was the period of the Spanish Civil War and some of us at least were peripherally mixed up with the anti-fascist movement for support of the legally-established government. But the anthropologists as such were not politicized.[19]

Several of the individual members of Malinowski's seminar in the 1937–38 period were "colonial" administrators home on study leave. Two such members of the Burma Frontier Service were a Mr. Ogden who had recently had a spell of administration among head-hunters in the Wa states on the borders of Burma and China, and a Mr. Stevenson who was engaged in writing a diploma thesis based on his work as an administrator in the Chin Hills of Burma

---

[18] Kuper, "An Interview," p. 376.   [19] Leach, "In Formative Travail," p. 55.

on the borders of Assam. This diploma thesis was subsequently published under the title H.N.C. Stevenson, *The Economics of the Central Chin Tribes*, and was for many years one of the standard texts of post-war undergraduate training in Social Anthropology. It should not be thought that either Stevenson or Ogden were proto-typical of the seminar as a whole. The group also included two Chinese intellectuals, Fei Hsiao Tung and Francis Hsu, as well as a variety of other people who have subsequently made reputations for themselves as professional anthropologists, notably W.E.H. Stanner and Phyllis Kaberry. But Noel Stevenson is important for my story because it was through him that I came to undertake fieldwork in the Kachin Hills on the borders of Burma and Yunnan.[20]

Malinowski's encounter with Freudian psychoanalysis is perceptively demonstrated and discussed by George Stocking.[21] It appears that Malinowski seriously engaged with Freudian theory in the early to mid-twenties, and had hoped that his revision of that theory on the basis of his first-hand study of the matrilineal Trobriand society would be considered a contribution to psychoanalysis. But the orthodox Freudians, especially Ernest Jones, the most loyal guardian of Freudian theory, rebuffed him, and disappointed, he concluded *Sex and Repression in Savage Society* (1927) thus: "it would be a great pity [if psychoanalysts] refused to collaborate, to accept what is offered in good faith from a field, where after all, they cannot be at home."[22] His involvement with psychoanalysis having virtually ceased by 1927, Malinowski later tried to integrate his broader view of individual human instincts and self-interest to the pragmatics of cooperative work in social life and to the elaboration of culture.

Malinowski's reflections on how the Oedipus complex might manifest itself in a matrilineal community were first elaborated in articles published in *Psyche* in 1923–24 and in *Nature* in 1923. He argues that among the matrilineal Trobrianders the tyrannical and ferocious father of Freud's *Totem and Taboo* (1918) was absent, and what prevails among them is a situation in which "the two elements decisive for psychoanalysis, the repressive authority and the severing taboo, are 'displaced', distributed in a manner different from that in the patriarchal family." Therefore the "repressed wish formation ought to receive a shape different from the Oedipus complex."[23] The interplay of biological impulse and social role was quite different in the two most radically different types of nuclear

---

[20] Ibid., p. 56.
[21] George W. Stocking, Jr. (ed.), *Malinowski, Rivers, Benedict, and Others: Essays on Culture and Personality*, History of Anthropology vol. IV, Madison: University of Wisconsin Press, 1986. See Stocking's essay "Malinowski's Encounter with Freud . . . " in this volume.
[22] Quoted in ibid., p. 41, from the original text (1927) at p. 238.
[23] Quoted in ibid., p. 35, from an article by Malinowski in *Nature*, published in 1923.

family complexes known, "the matrilineal family" of the Trobriands and "a patriarchal family of modern civilization."[24]

In an informal seminar setting in 1976 at The Johns Hopkins University in which he occupied center stage, Leach alluded to certain features which created the seminar's reputation as a kind of *avant-garde* group with liberalizing and relativizing attitudes to issues of sex.[25] Malinowski, he pointed out, was one of the early readers of Freud, and around 1928 he had launched into a debate with Ernest Jones about the universality of the Oedipus complex. In *Sex and Repression in Savage Society*, Malinowski's explication of Trobriand notions of conception which denied the "physical" contribution of the father, and of the roles of "father" and "mother's brother" in the family complex which in some respects reversed patrilineal patriarchal expectations, and thereby raised the issues of translation between cultures ("How could missionaries talk of God the Father to the Trobrianders?"), had seemingly relativized and contextualized the Freudian formulation generalized from the mores and practices of middle-class Europe. Malinowski had been fascinated by the sexual permissiveness of the Trobrianders, and his *The Sexual Life of the Savages in North-Western Melanesia* (1929), which probed and described Trobriand practices, had been sold in London's bookshops in Old Compton Street as pornography. This was the book that made Malinowski's name. "Malinowski was picked up by Bertrand Russell in his role as a public moralist in favour of sexual permissiveness." He was also picked up by Ogden and Richards, editors of *The Meaning of Meaning*,[26] the latter of whom "was also considered to have unorthodox or eccentric ideas on sex." Malinowski actually invited scandal, and when Leach joined his "circus-seminar" in 1937, it was associated in public opinion with the advocacy of heterosexual permissiveness.

Leach's humorous dwelling on this aspect of Malinowski's ethnographic writing which had implications for the Freudian universalistic predication of the Oedipus complex also more seriously relates, I hypothesize, on the one hand to Leach's own continuing interest since undergraduate days in Freud's postulation of certain "innate" propensities in the human psyche surrounding sex and food as they unfold in

---

[24] Quoted in ibid., p. 36, from an article entitled "Psycho-Analysis and Anthropology", *Psyche*, vol. 4, 1924, pp. 293–332.

[25] Regarding Leach's seminars at The Johns Hopkins in 1976, see Tambiah, "Personal Accounts."

[26] Malinowski wrote the piece entitled "The Problem of Meaning in Primitive Languages" which was included in C.K. Ogden and I.A. Richards (eds.), *The Meaning of Meaning*, London: K. Paul, Trench, Trubner and Co. for the International Library of Psychology, Philosophy and Scientific Method, 1923.

childhood, and on the other hand to Leach's recognition of Malinowski's "transformation" of the Freudian model to adapt to the Trobriand context. Leach's own creative use of some Freudian themes in his later structuralist transformational readings of myths and rites would seem to be, to some degree, not unrelated to his interest in Malinowski's polemic with Ernest Jones.[27] But it was not so much Freud's repressed unconscious that Leach was interested in as the unconscious "mytho-logic" and transformational relations between patterns embedded in myth, ritual, and art.

Leach described the immediate sequel to his engagement with Malinowski, which we note, while being fateful and influential, was also relatively brief,[28] thus:

> In the summer of 1938, inspired by a love affair with an archaeologist, I visited Iraq, planning to write a thesis on the Rowanduz Kurds. It came to nothing. After the Munich crisis and Chamberlain's gesticulations about "peace in our time" I was back in London with an aborted project. I spent the next academic year, 1938–39, working as Raymond Firth's research assistant, an extremely valuable experience from my point of view. Malinowski was on sabbatical leave at Yale (he never returned), but Meyer Fortes came back from West Africa at that time and taught me during the spring and summer semesters.[29]

It would seem that his beginnings as an anthropologist continued the shifts and frustrations that were not strangers to him. The field study of the Kurds was abandoned because "A broken relationship, a touch of dysentery, and the imminent threat of war all served to drive him home. He returned to London dispirited and uncertain of his future. He wrote: 'I've got an enormous amount of ability at almost anything, yet so far I've made absolutely no use of it . . . I seem to be a highly organized piece of mental apparatus for which nobody has any use.'"[30] But another opportunity came and he took it.

---

[27] I have in mind here Leach's essays such as "Magical Hair" (Curl Bequest Essay 1957), *Journal of the Royal Anthropological Institute of Great Britain and Ireland*, vol. 88, part 2, 1958, pp. 147–164; "Pulleyar and the Lord Buddha: An Aspect of Religious Syncrenism in Ceylon," *Psychoanalysis and the Psychoanalytic Review*, vol. 49, no. 2, 1962, pp. 81–102; "Virgin Birth," The Henry Myers Lecture, *Proceedings of the Royal Anthropological Institute*, 1966, pp. 39–49 and also correspondence in *Man* (n.s.), vol. 3, no. 1, p. 129, and vol. 3, no. 4, pp. 655–56; and "Michelangelo's Genesis: A Structuralist Interpretation of the Central Panels of the Sistine Chapel," *Semiotica*, vol. 56, nos. 1/2, 1985, pp. 1–30.

[28] Malinowski had made two previous visits to the United States in 1926 and 1933; he went back in 1938 on sabbatical leave, and remained in North America for three and a half years until his death in 1942 (Firth, *Man and Culture*, p. 4). One wonders what their subsequent relationship might have been, had Malinowski's life been longer.

[29] Kuper, "An Interview, p. 376.   [30] Firth, "Biographical Sketch," p. 258.

BURMESE DAYS (1 9 3 9 – 1 9 4 5)

Then, in the summer of 1939, the Firths left for Malaysia to conduct the research which produced, among other things, Raymond Firth's *Malay Fishermen* (1946), while I left for north-east Burma [in July of 1939] to undertake field research among the Kachin. The monograph that I had planned to write would not have had the quantitative detail which characterises Raymond Firth's book, but it was to be a socio-economic study of the same general kind. I hoped to display the organisation of the local community in terms of domestic production and the network of trading. Segmentary lineages and cross-cousin marriage didn't come into the story at all.[31]

There seems to have been an additional stimulus in Leach's choice of Upper Burma for his fieldwork:

In Malinowski's seminar he had met Noël (H.N.C.) Stevenson, a member of the Burma Frontier Service then home on study leave This link now came in useful. At Stevenson's suggestion, he set off for the village of Hpalang in the Kachin Hills of north-east Burma to carry out field research and to monitor the effects of Stevenson's social uplift project dubbed the "Kachin regeneration scheme."[32]

Leach arrived in Burma in August 1939, just before Hitler launched his awesome war. There was no going back to England this time round, and so Leach in due course signed up with the Burma Rifles and went into the field to Hpalang to conduct his research.

A brief chronology of events from 1939 until demobilization after the end of the Second World War will help us to follow the adventures and misadventures that Leach encountered during these years. The frustrations of this war plagued him in many ways, not least in the repeated loss of his field materials and manuscripts.

Nowadays, most US "graduate students" and British "postgraduate students" go into the field for their Ph.D. research equipped with some basic training in the language of their prospective subjects, as much

---

[31] Kuper, "An Interview," p. 376.

[32] Hugh-Jones, "Edmund Leach," (memoir), p. 14. At the time Leach first went to Burma in 1939, H.N.C. Stevenson had not yet published his book *The Economics of the Central Chin Tribes* (1943). I can myself confirm that those of us who attended Leach's lectures on economic anthropology in the sixties were told to read this book. Stevenson's discussion of the Tefa system ("debt" and "bond" slavery) provided Leach with material for making a striking contrast with the conceptions surrounding classical Greek chattel slavery, and his discussion of "feasts of merit" and the activities of the "feasters' club" with material for explicating the manner in which "tangible perishables" (such as food and livestock) were converted to "intangible imperishables" (titles, reputation, and relations of debt and power). Leach had anticipated Bourdieu's now famous concept of "symbolic capital" in *Outline of a Theory of Practice*.

reading as they can manage of the relevant literature, including in many cases anthropological writings, on the region they intend to work in, and frequently one or two prior reconnaissance visits, and in the case of Americans perhaps a stint with the Peace Corps. Leach went to Burma with little of this kind of special preparation. His main contact and advisor, H.N.C. Stevenson, had arranged for him to do his fieldwork in Hpalang, the Kachin Hills area, more precisely the Sinlum subdivision of northern Burma, where he had launched his Kachin Regeneration Scheme. But when Leach reached Rangoon, Stevenson was not there to receive him; he had gone to England to attend to urgent family matters.

Leach went north to Bhamo, from where on September 9, 1939, he composed a letter on his typewriter with multiple carbon copies, which he sent to his family members, his mother receiving one with a special addendum for her.[33] Since it was addressed to his close kin, it is written in an informal and jocular style, but it conveys his predicament of being at the mercy of a war for which he had little enthusiasm, and his being somewhat stranded, especially among Rangoon's government officials, who were quite clueless about his work intentions as well as distracted by the impact of the war on their future. An exception, however, and a pleasant surprise was his meeting with a district commissioner called Wilkie, whom he tracked down in the small town of Sinlum "dressed in grey flannels and a sports coat sitting in front of a roaring fire 6000 feet up in the air"; he found him to be a marvelous person entirely unperturbed by the war "and enthusiastic" about matters concerning the Kachins.[34]

Leach's letter reassures his family that Burma holds exciting possibilities for him, and it glows with his euphoric reaction to the glorious views of the mountains populated by "fantastic birds and beasts and enormous butterflies," and to the colorful variety of the heterogeneous local peoples jostling in the bazaar town of Bhamo, such as "three varieties of Kachin (Jinghpaws, Atsis, Hkauris)," Shans from the plains, Lisu, Chinese from Yunnan, "a few odd individual Burmese, Indians, and Karens." Furthermore, Bhamo was the site of active missionary activities by American Baptists and Roman Catholics.

Bhamo sat on the border between Burma proper and the area further north and east under the control of the Burma Frontier Service. From Leach's first impressions it appears to have been quite an exciting location for fieldwork. However, already committed to do a functional study

---

[33] A copy of this letter is deposited in the Leach archives at King's College.
[34] Being district commissioner at Bhamo, Wilkie operated in two spheres – for the subdivision of Bhamo, which came under the Burmese government, and for the subdivision of Sinlum which, administered by the Frontier Service, was responsible to the Governor.

of a village community, more pagan than Christian, he journeyed further east to the settlement of Sinlum to "learn some Kachin," and from there to Hpalang where he could say "goodbye to radios and newspapers, and temporarily at least forget the war." Hpalang in 1940 was a dispersed settlement of 130 households at an elevation ranging from 5,800 to 5,000 feet, sloping down toward the valley of the Namwan whose irrigated rice plots were worked by Shans. Hpalang itself was engaged in monsoon shifting cultivation (*taungya*), and Leach found that it did include a variety of subgroups speaking Jinghpaw, Gauri, Atsi, Maru, Lisu, and Chinese.

Leach conducted fieldwork in Hpalang for nine months in the years 1939–40 and, as we shall see shortly, he also contrived to get married during this time. Thereafter he was called to serve in the army. He was stationed in Maymyo from October to December 1940, and during this training period he had time to complete a draft of what he referred to as his "functionalist" monograph on Hpalang.

The Japanese invaded in 1941, and in 1942 in the midst of derailments caused by their advance, Leach lost all his papers – the draft monograph, notes, photographs, etc. In July 1942 while on sick leave in Calcutta he reconstructed the monograph on Hpalang from memory. But during his subsequent extensive travels in the Kachin Levies operation, he was fated to lose that document too. However, the memory of Hpalang was not lost forever – for he would reconstruct Hpalang again and present a distilled portrait of this "unstable Kachin *Gumsa* community" as chapter 4 in his post-war classic *Political Systems of Highland Burma*. Later on in his discussions of this book he would remark that Hpalang was "a microcosm of Kachin society." Now we are ready to retrace those Burmese days and to spice those years of hardship with some adventure and romance.

In one personal aspect 1940 was a most felicitous year. As Hugh-Jones recounts:

The same Kilton Stewart who had introduced Edmund to the Yami also introduced him to Celia Buckmaster. Edmund had planned to marry her when home on leave from Burma in the summer of 1940 but in the chaos of early war his leave was cancelled. Undeterred, Edmund sent her a telegram asking her to join him in the town of Maymo [Maymyo] and to marry him. The two mothers, Edmund's and Celia's, got wind of the plan and conspired together to prevent it. As a delaying tactic, Celia's mother sent a telegram in reply saying "are there any drains in Maymyo?" and signed "Buckmaster." Thinking the telegram had come from Celia, Edmund sent Celia the following reply, "Buy ticket and argue afterwards." Though initially completely mystified, she understood what was up and flew out to join him.

Celia Joyce, daughter of Henry Stephen Guy Buckmaster, barrister, flew out to Burma just before Italy entered the Second World War. The marriage took place at the Registry in Rangoon and Dr. Oscar Spate, the geographer, and his wife, Daphne, were the witnesses. The couple went off to the Kachin hills together. Leach was called for active service and officer training in the autumn of 1940.[35]

Being top of the class in the officer training course, Leach could have temporarily returned to civilian life until the planned expansion of the Burma army was achieved (the policy was that those who performed poorly in the passing-out examination would be made to return), but he shocked his commanding officer by volunteering to serve. He remarked:

As far as the Burma army was concerned, I was odd man out, but I was potentially useful because I spoke the Kachin language and the Kachins were, in effect, the Gurkhas of the Burma army. At first the army used me as a recruiting officer, which was weird as my political sympathies were not in that direction at all; but I was under orders.[36]

When the Japanese eventually arrived at the end of 1941, I got shunted into a crazy cloak-and-dagger outfit run by H.N.C. Stevenson, a Frontier Service officer who had had some training in anthropology under Malinowski. He persuaded the governor of Burma that if the British were driven out of Burma then we ought to leave behind a network of intelligence officers with local linguistic competence. I got sucked into this madhouse.[37]

In the meantime news of the fall of France reached the Leaches via a Roman Catholic priest, and thinking that all was lost, they quickly packed up; they first went to the district headquarters and from there to Maymyo. They spent some time in Maymyo and Louisa was born there on October 31, 1941. Concerned with their situation, Edmund and some other officers drove their families in a bus across to Schwebo, north of Mandalay. They were left there in a disused army barracks for three days and nights, without food and water. An Anglican priest prayed for them

---

35 Hugh-Jones, "Edmund Leach" (memoir), pp. 14–15.

36 I remember Celia telling me of some of her dealings with the Kachin women, to whom she would give sewing needles (they were expert at making colourful clothes) and who would say in their (broken) English, "husband gone far away," referring to Edmund's recruiting trips. The women sat around with her and they had a liking for a fermented rice drink. In the field Celia wrote and painted.

37 Kuper "An Interview," p. 376. As Hugh-Jones ("Edmund Leach," (memoir), p. 16) remarks, Leach's "reservations were right; recruitment to another people's conflict sowed the seeds of a guerilla war which continues to this day." The Kachins, together with other hill tribes, have for many decades waged a war against the Burmese government which they oppose for its alleged colonizing policies. Leach has asserted unambiguously, "I consider 'development anthropology' a kind of neo-colonialism" (Leach, *Social Anthropology*, p. 50).

and mercifully some local "Blackie-Whites" (mixed European-Burmese) brought them some food. On the third day a plane came. However, not all were evacuated, and the child helped to save Celia's life. As Edmund wrote, "when the crunch came in Spring 1942, nursing mothers [and pregnant women] who were wives of white officers were flown out, the rest walked to China and mostly died." Celia and infant were flown to Calcutta, and from there with army help they went to Simla. Celia made arrangements with a travel agent in Bombay and took a Dutch-owned boat, which called at Mombasa, then Cape Town, picked up some people from Tobruk, and eventually landed in northern Scotland. She and Louisa next went to Glasgow, and from there to London. Their final haven was Town Farm in Ivinghoe where Edmund's brother welcomed them. Edmund did not see Celia and Louisa for three and a half years.[38]

Edmund continues:

I was supposed to hang around Hpalang (the base of my earlier fieldwork) with a radio set. My assistant lost his stores and the radio, and we had to head for home. It is a long story. I reached Kunming (capital of Yunnan Province) after many adventures and seven weeks of walking. I was then flown to Calcutta, very ill from dysentery. I tried hard to get back to regular soldiering, but my official unit had been disbanded, and, after a period of sick leave, I was ordered to report to Colonel Stevenson at a remote airfield in Assam. This was August 1942.[39]

I went on my way fully prepared to have a showdown with Noël Stevenson. When I reached his mystery address and had got through all the 007 secrecy with which he was surrounded, I asked, "What's going on?" The answer came back: "Well, Colonel Stevenson fell out of an aeroplane yesterday and broke his neck." "Is he dead?" I asked. "No. If you hang around for a few days you may be able to see him." When medical permission came through, it was to the effect that Stevenson was terribly ill: "You must not upset him. You must agree with everything he says." So that was the end of my planned insurrection! Noël, of course, was enthusiastic: "Ah, Edmund, just the man I want to see. Marvellous. We'll get you into Fort Hertz [in the extreme north of Burma] tomorrow. We've cleared a strip, and we can get a Dakota in." My only thought was, "Oh, God! Here we go again!"

So I went back into Burma to create the Kachin Levies. The official army Establishment were delighted that Noël Stevenson was out of commission, and they dug up a retired Australian Burma Military Police officer who was to take formal charge of the Kachin Levies operation and keep me under control. Colonel Gamble and I got on like cat and dog. In the end he more or less had me

---

[38] This information was provided by Celia Leach.

[39] The arduous retreat into China took its toll and it is surmised that the bothersome skin cancer on his head late in life was probably caused by the exposure to the sun.

court-martialled. I was reduced in rank from acting major to substantive second lieutenant. In the outcome I was transferred to the Civil Affairs Service, where I had further extraordinary adventures. Among other things the Civil Affairs Service had responsibility for the civil administration of "liberated" Burma as the British army moved back in. In this role I ended up as a staff major, deputy to the chief civil affairs officer at 14th Army Headquarters, an Establishment figure if ever there was one. Anything more bizarre is hard to imagine![40]

The eminence he served under was General Slim and Leach had performed effectively in the civil administration of liberated Burma.

Leach would characterize his "extraordinary series of war experiences" as a "strange mixture of the absurd and the horrible." But there was one benefit that he derived from it: "I travelled very widely in the Kachin Hills and got to know a great variety of different sorts of 'Kachin.' This diversity provided the basis for my subsequent anthropological thinking."[41] In fact his wide-ranging recruiting trips and operations with the Kachin Levies had given him a panoramic and dynamic view of the connections between the varieties of hill tribes, and this knowledge would be the basis for a theoretical contribution of fundamental importance.

Leach gave this account of the places he visited during his military duties:

I visited the Northern Shan States, the Sima and Sadon Hills, the Htawgaw Area, Kamaing and the region north of Myitkyina in the course of recruiting duty. In 1942 I saw military service in the Northern Shan States and later made an undignified withdrawal from Burma on my feet. This took me through many Kachin byways little known to Europeans and enabled me to see something of the Chinese Shan states. By the end of August 1942 I had re-entered Burma from Assam and was engaged in raising a force of Kachin irregulars. My centre of operations this time was the Putao, Sumprabum, North Triangle area. In 1943 I visited the Nung country in the Nam Tamai on a political mission. In all, the only main sections of the Kachin Hills Area of which I have no direct experience at all are the Hukawng Valley and Jade Mines areas. There are comparatively few Europeans who have had similar opportunities for assessing the totality of Kachin culture.[42]

There is more to be reported and discussed regarding how the colonial context in which Leach did his fieldwork in Hpalang, his subsequent war

---

[40] Kuper, "An Interview," p. 377.   [41] Ibid.

[42] Edmund Leach, *Political Systems of Highland Burma: A Study of Kachin Social Structure*, London: G. Bell & Sons for the London School of Economics and Political Science, 1954. Reprinted with introductory note by the author 1964, pp. 311–12.

travels and experiences, and, after the war, his close study in London of the reports, records, and writings of colonial administrators on Upper Burma and northeast India, impacted on his composing *Political Systems of Highland Burma*. I have postponed considering this important authorial issue until chapter 16 because Leach discussed it in a retrospective assessment in response to questions raised in the late 1970s and in the 1980s about the colonial connection of British anthropology, and the alleged complicity of anthropologists in the imperial project. Chapter 5 is devoted to explicating the text of *Political Systems*.

CHAPTER 4

The anthropologist at work: teacher and theorist

THE CAREER START AT LSE

I got back to England in the summer of 1945, supposedly on short
leave, but after Hiroshima all return trips were cancelled. I was
demobilized in January 1946. After eight years I was still registered
for an LSE Ph.D. Raymond Firth was now professor and head of
the department. I was not at all sure that I wanted to have anything
more to do with anthropology, but between us we agreed that I
should reread all the literature of the Kachin (and of other Burma
frontier "tribes"), going back to the beginning of the 19th century,
and reassess it in the light of my "on the ground" experiences. I
completed the thesis in the spring of 1947. Radcliffe-Brown was my
external examiner. It is a messy affair. Bits of it reappear in *Political
Systems of Highland Burma* (1954), but that is a very different kind of
book.[1]

After completing the Ph.D., pursuant to a proposal made to the Colonial
Office by Firth, Leach went in 1947 to the newly acquired Crown Colony
of Sarawak to suggest what kinds of research should be done to collect
more information about the inhabitants. He carried out a survey in
Sarawak and his report entitled *Social Science Research in Sarawak* (1950)
which was gratifyingly accepted by the government set out guidelines
for subsequent investigations by a number of distinguished anthropologists: Derek Freeman who "worked with the Iban, Bill Geddes with the
Land Dayak, Stephen Morris with the Melanau, Ju-kang T'ien with the
Kuching Chinese, [and] Tom Harrison with the Coastal Malays."

On his return from Borneo, Leach joined the staff at the LSE as a lecturer, and one of his primary tasks was to be responsible for the teaching
of "primitive technology," then an integral part of undergraduate
anthropology:

But it soon appeared not only that his major interest was in social anthropology, but that with his usual devastating logic, he had concluded that what passed for primitive technology should properly be studied as examples of simple applied mechanics – or not at all. [This no doubt reflected his engineer's training.] So he turned to social anthropology completely, and also with his talent for administration, assumed responsibility for the general organization of undergraduate teaching in the department.[2]

It was in this phase of his early career at the LSE that he decided to resign his position in order to work full time for over a year on the book *Political Systems of Highland Burma*. It is interesting to note that while Leach's doctoral thesis was about "the hill tribes of Burma and Assam" and was oriented, following Firth's interests, in socio-economic interactions and agro-ecological adaptations and practices, this book, more closely focused on the Kachins (and their Shan neighbours), while using the same information plus a great amount of archival and historical sources, was of a different genre, "his own thing," and not entirely to the taste of his two immediate teachers, Firth and Fortes. (*Political Systems of Highland Burma*, widely regarded as a classic, will be discussed in chapter 5).

When the book was ready for publication, Leach rejoined the LSE in a new appointment as Reader. However, by this time Meyer Fortes had become head of the anthropology department at Cambridge, and Leach could not resist the resulting offer of a lectureship there even though it meant a demotion in rank.

In his 1984 piece "Glimpses of the Unmentionable," Leach with characteristic candor admitted that Oxbridge dons regarded themselves as "the elect," and he himself "in becoming a rude mechanical . . . did not cease to be a snob." The preeminence of Oxbridge was, he maintained, a cause for envy among British academics, who given the chance would readily move there. It also seems that there were other personal and familial reasons why a residential move to Cambridge was desirable. When Leach was teaching at the London School of Economics he and his family lived near Hitchin in Hertfordshire. In an informal interview with Dr. Susan Drucker-Brown[3] in April 1984 Leach explained, "I was

[2] "Obituaries. Professor Sir Edmund Leach. Critical Rethinker of Social Anthropology," *The Times*, Saturday 7 [month missing], 1989.
[3] Susan Drucker-Brown, who had done fieldwork among the Mamprusi in Ghana, was closely associated with Meyer Fortes who was her primary teacher. Because she was thinking of writing a biography of Meyer Fortes, she decided to interview Leach on the advice of Audrey Richards. In April 1984, she met Leach for a long relaxed and friendly conversation at King's College over lunch in Hall and coffee in the Combination Room. They touched on many matters but a main topic of conversation was his coming to King's and his perspective on his "difficult" personal

commuting to London. The children were in school. The boy made his way to the next village but I was taking my daughter to school in Letchworth and then going back to the station at Hitchin to take the train to London. Then I took the Tube to the LSE. I was spending three or four hours a day travelling and I was getting very exhausted. This was in the days of petrol rationing."

Since the Fortes–Leach relationship, as Leach represented it, appears significantly in this biography, it is relevant to understand the difficult situation in which Fortes found himself when he came to Cambridge from Oxford to take up the chair as William Wyse Professor of Anthropology. The anthropology section of the department was in decline. Evans-Pritchard, who had been Reader at Cambridge, left for Oxford when he was elected to the chair there. According to Leach's narration, Alfred Cort Haddon had done the department a disservice by giving the last three appointments in anthropology to G.I. Jones, Reo Fortune, and Ethel John Lindgren, by no means of stellar standing. When Fortes arrived he found that all the slots had been filled. But since Lindgren's appointment was provisional, he was able to maneuver to get rid of him, in order to appoint a more competent person. He succeeded in this unpleasant work – he had some allies – and this was how he came to invite Leach. He was keen to attract Leach, and seems to have promised him more than he could deliver.

It is common knowledge that Leach and Fortes had over the years a strained personal relationship (which was seemingly aggravated by intellectual disagreements). This may also have stemmed partly from the impact of an issue about the Cambridge of the fifties (and later), where the colleges elected a select few as Fellows who then derived prestige, social privileges, and some additional income from that association. This meant that a large number of university lecturers and assistant lecturers were effectively left out in the cold (professors were placed in one college or another, and the University Senate saw to it if colleges were slow to move).[4]

The following excerpts from Susan Drucker-Brown's interview convey Leach's view of the circumstances of his breach with Fortes:

I knew Cambridge. I had been an undergraduate at Clare. I knew that you could be a member of the Faculty and not a Fellow of a College and I knew

relationship with Fortes at Cambridge. I am grateful to Susan for making available to me a transcript of that interview from which I shall quote a few passages and remarks.

[4] This is different from the Oxford system where professorships are tied to particular colleges.

what that meant. So I insisted that I would come only if I had a Fellowship. And Meyer said I had. Of course, when I arrived, I discovered that I hadn't. He hadn't done anything.

He may have tried . . . But he had promised and there was no Fellowship and after that I did not trust him. That was the basis of the row . . .

He may have tried but then he stopped trying. And it took seven years to get a Fellowship at King's. When my name came up at Clare, where I had been an undergraduate, they elected Geoffrey Elton [the historian] who of course was very important . . .

Cambridge was a very lonely place if you didn't belong to a College. That is why all these [new] colleges were set up at the time . . . Darwin, Wolfson, Clare Hall . . . to accommodate these lost souls who were in the university but not in any college.

[Moreover] at that time I was rather hard up. My mother had not yet died. My father's will was with the lawyers. I was in debt. And there were some financial rewards from a college lectureship. If you had no fellowship you picked up supervisions here and there, thrown to you as to a dog.[5]

On this vexed matter of a college fellowship it is possible that this recounting of events some thirty years after they actually took place may not be an altogether accurate recollection with respect to Fortes's culpability. None other than Raymond Firth has informed me that "it is doubtful if Fortes actually *promised* a college fellowship." Apparently at that time Leach had consulted Firth who had counseled him that it would be unwise to accept a Cambridge lectureship "without a definite appointment to a college fellowship." Leach had recognized the force of this advice, but had felt that he could not "resist Cambridge" and proceeded to accept Fortes's offer. Firth observes: "my recollection is that Edmund knew when he went that no fellowship had been fixed up, though of course he expected it soon would be."[6]

As we shall see, the other biographical recollections that Leach authored in the late 1980s took a narrative form, the constructed purposive nature of this genre being fully transparent to him. In any case, the

---

5 Susan Drucker-Brown had at this point interjected: "What could Meyer have done? He told me that he tried to organize a strike so that no one would supervise for the colleges [if they did not elect anthropologists as Fellows]." Leach had replied: "It just wasn't practical. He couldn't do much. There was a period, when the new colleges were being formed, when Fellowships were available but now its gone back to what it was like before. You have to prove a teaching need. That is why most of the anthropologists are in King's." (Leach was here referring to the fact that during and after his tenure as Provost of King's, this college had generally elected a fair number of Cambridge anthropologists as Fellows.)

6 Personal communication, October 7, 1996. Firth also informed me that he has in his possession "a letter of Edmund's of 1953 more or less confirming" what he had told me, and that he was prepared to show it to me. Personal communication, November 24, 1996. I have not yet had the opportunity to meet Professor Firth and read that letter.

situation at Cambridge was frustrating to Leach as it certainly was for Fortes as well. And, as in any dispute, the parties to it can be expected to give different narrative versions, which with the passage of time are further changed by retrospective memory.

There is another clarification that needs to be entertained about Leach's relationship with Fortes. From his point of view his personal row with Fortes had nothing to do with his intellectual disagreements with him on theoretical issues, which will be dealt with in due course. And behind this disagreement, there was definitely respect for Fortes's intellectual achievements, and the appreciative memory of Fortes having been one of his teachers at the LSE and having enthusiastically invited him to come to Cambridge. Geoffrey Benjamin has conveyed to me some observations that support this formulation. It is noteworthy that in departmental seminars, if Leach was moved to launch a vigorous criticism of a visiting academic's paper, he was surprised if the visitor took this to be a personal *ad hominem* attack; "Also, having seen Edmund and Meyer together many times, I know that they were good friends and respected each other, despite agreeing to differ on so many issues. Even today, I meet anthropologists who mistakenly assume that the published disputes between them were based on personal animosity."[7] The other side of the coin was that he expected his ideas and interpretations to be challenged, and was willing to engage in polemical give and take. Some might think, not without cause, that Leach sometimes showed an "insensitivity" or "blind spot" regarding his exchanges with some colleagues and peers. But, as we shall see, his attitudes to and intellectual exchanges with most of his students were admirably tolerant and supportive, and he encouraged them to think for themselves to the point of disagreeing with his formulations. "In tutorial the last thing he wanted was agreement. He wanted *discussion* – until he was sure that what we said was indeed what *we* thought."[8]

There were possibly other reasons than those considered so far for the difficulty of having anthropologists elected as Fellows of Cambridge colleges that had to do with the ranking of this discipline in relation to others in the hierarchical valuations prevailing at Oxbridge, and also

---

[7] Geoffrey Benjamin, who was closely associated with Leach in the early to mid-sixties as an undergraduate and later as a graduate student – and whom I shall cite at some length shortly – has remarked in a recollection sent me that "Edmund never saw the issues in an *ad hominem* manner . . . At one Anthropology society meeting I saw him reduce____literally to tears with his thorough criticism of the talk she had delivered. But he drove her back to her hotel afterwards. Later, he declared to me that he didn't know why____had got so upset" (pers. comm.).

[8] Geoffrey Benjamin (pers. comm.).

the degree of influence in Cambridge University politics wielded by the founders of the Department of Anthropology and Archaeology such as Rivers and Haddon. Leach had something "startling" and frank to say about this in a piece written after his retirement which will be discussed more fully later.[9]

Be that as it may, Leach in due course became settled in Cambridge, and his reputation began to soar. He became Reader in 1957, and the department came to be seen as the arena for a titanic debate between Fortes and Leach which assumed mythological proportions especially in the common-room talk of outsiders. It was at Cambridge that Leach would develop his reputation as "critical rethinker of anthropology" and as one of the "most original minds in modern social anthropology."[10]

EARLY CAMBRIDGE YEARS: FORGING A PERSPECTIVE

To return to Leach's intellectual trajectory, his next fieldwork monograph, *Pul Eliya, Village in Ceylon* appeared in 1961.[11] This same year, Leach has said, was "a kind of watershed" in that he had brought out a book of essays, *Rethinking Anthropology*,[12] "which showed much more clearly than anything I had produced before just how far I had distanced myself from my teachers."[13] This was also the same time – the academic year 1960–61 – that Edmund and Celia Leach spent at the "Think Tank" at Palo Alto – when he had a fruitful encounter and dialog with Roman Jakobson and at the same time recovered a deeper consciousness of his own transformational bent via mathematics and engineering. The period at Palo Alto was a happy time. Leach's sense of intellectual excitement (which was also produced by his attending Gregory Bateson's seminars on dolphin communication and ecological adaptation) was matched by Celia's responding to the California light, weather, flora, and landscape with intensified painting and pleasurable outdoor living. She has spoken in glowing terms of this sojourn.

It is relevant to note that 1961 was also the year when Leach published two essays which signaled his fascination with Lévi-Strauss's work

---

9   Leach, "Glimpses."
10 These evaluations were made by Raymond Firth in a letter to the Department of Anthropology at the University of Chicago when Edmund Leach was proposed in 1976 as a candidate for an honorary degree, which was duly conferred on him.
11 Edmund Leach, *Pul Eliya, a Village in Ceylon: A Study of Land Tenure and Kinship*, Cambridge: Cambridge University Press, 1961.
12 Edmund Leach, *Rethinking Anthropology*, London School of Economics Monographs on Social Anthropology, no. 22, London: University of London Athlone Press, 1961.
13 Leach, "Glimpses," p. 19.

on mythology, namely "Golden Bough or Gilded Twig?"[14] and "Lévi-Strauss in the Garden of Eden: An Examination of Some Recent Developments in the Analysis of Myth."[15] This was the beginning of Leach's own increasing preoccupation with what he called "the interface between art and religious mythology," which for my narrative purposes will be left to what I call his "second phase."

The conjunction of all these influences, trends, different intellectual preoccupations, and productions in the same year seems both unusual and improbable, and for orderly commentary there must be some chronological sorting.

Leach undertook the field research in Ceylon (now Sri Lanka) on which *Pul Eliya* is based during the period June to December 1954, supplemented by a further brief visit in August 1956. He had from 1955 until 1957 begun to publish on his Ceylon materials,[16] and must have submitted his final monograph manuscript for publication before he went to Palo Alto in 1960, probably as early as 1957. *Pul Eliya* was theoretically primarily an argument mounted against the structural-functionalist approaches of Radcliffe-Brown and Meyer Fortes. It is a problematical and distinctive text and in my view deserves an extended scrutiny to highlight its significance (see chapter 7). Here let us note its dating in relation to other publications at this crucial period.

Rethinking Anthropology, although it came out in 1961, is actually a collection containing essays crafted over a period extending from 1953 to 1961. The first essay was "Cronus and Chronos," first published in 1953,[17] and the last was the capstone Malinowski Memorial Lecture (1959), which also provided the title for the collection. But the collection is given a unity by the fact that five of the six essays are concerned with issues relating to kinship and marriage. One central essay, "The Structural Implications of Matrilateral Cross-Cousin Marriage," will be discussed in chapter 5: it addresses the issue of representing Kachin marriage exchange and political hierarchy. I shall deal here with only two other essays pertaining

[14] In *Daedalus* (*Journal of the American Academy of Arts and Sciences*), vol. 90, no. 2, Spring 1961, pp. 371–87.

[15] In *Transactions of the New York Academy of Sciences*, series 2, vol. 23, no. 4, pp. 386–96.

[16] For example, "Land Tenure in a Sinhalese Village, North Central Province, Ceylon," Summary in *Man*, vol. 55, article 178, 1955, pp. 166–67; "Structural Continuity in a Sinhalese Village (Ceylon Northern Dry Zone)," *Proceedings of the Ninth Pacific Science Congress*, 1957. It was also during this phase that he wrote "Polyandry, Inheritance and the Definition of Marriage, with Particular Reference to Sinhalese Customary Law," *Man*, vol. 55, article 199, 1955, pp. 182–86, later reprinted in Leach, *Rethinking Anthropology*.

[17] "Cronus and Chronos," *Explorations* no. 1, 1953, pp. 15–23. Its companion, "Time and False Noses," appeared in *Explorations*, no. 5, 1955, pp. 30–35. They were combined under one heading in chapter 6 of *Rethinking Anthropology*.

to Leach 's call to his British colleagues to rethink anthropology, which included urging them to experimentally try out new ideas even if they didn't quite work out.[18]

An important essay contained in the collection is "Jinghphaw Kinship Terminology," completed in Calcutta in 1943, and first published in a 1945 volume of the *Journal of the Royal Anthropological Institute* which actually did not appear in print until 1948. This essay was innovative in that Leach attempted to uncover the "rules" that organized the "superficially extremely complex" terminology, and his approach foreshadowed an approach (which he would progressively refine) that seeks out the "structure of relations" in a mathematics-logical or algebraic sense. The rules constituted "the ideal patterns of Jinghphaw society," and he underscored the point that "any structural analysis of a kinship system is necessarily a discussion of ideal behaviour, not of normal behaviour."

It is noteworthy that this mode of analysis was attempted many years before Leach encountered the writings of Lévi-Strauss, who in 1953 recognized Leach's essay as having some affinity with his own structuralist approach. This is relevant to considering the thesis – which Leach himself wished to establish – that his own predilection toward a mathematical-transformational approach, stemming from his earlier training in engineering, preceded as much as it later converged with features of Lévi-Strauss's structuralism. It was in regard to this matter of intellectual affinities and influences that Leach would draw attention to his felicitous meeting with Roman Jakobson (and Morris Halle) in 1960–61 at the Center for Advanced Study in the Behavioral Sciences at Palo Alto. Leach was particularly taken with Jakobson's pattern of distinctive features in phonology – it rang bells of recognition that "he had been there before" – and with Jakobson's search for linguistic universals. Leach had been initiated into linguistic theory, and he had begun to see that his "deepest concerns were with what is now discussed under such grandiose labels as semiotics and cognitive science."[19]

---

[18] In doing so, I do not wish to detract from the seminal ideas concerning the definition of marriage and the relations between bridewealth and marriage stability among the Lakher and Kachin treated in the two remaining essays in the collection. I may also mention in this context another essay in a similar theoretical vein, published elsewhere – "Concerning Trobriand Clans and the Kinship Category 'Tabu'" (1958), relating kinship terminology to the dynamics of marriage, residence, and affinal payments, and attempting to solve a classical puzzle about Trobriand clans. It is also a contribution to the complex issue of interrelations between linguistic and social phenomena. This essay is published in Jack Goody (ed.) *The Development Cycle in Domestic Groups*, Cambridge Papers in Social Anthropology, Cambridge: Cambridge University Press for the Department of Archaeology and Anthropology, 1958.

[19] Leach, "Glimpses," p. 19.

"Rethinking Anthropology" is the centerpiece in the collection which bears the same title. It was delivered with fanfare and expectation on December 3, 1959 as the first Malinowski Memorial Lecture at the London School of Economics, and Leach did not fail to both stimulate and provoke his British audience. With characteristic ebullience he reminisced in later years that on this occasion not only he had denounced "butterfly collecting" but also "to the mystification of most of my audience, I referred to the significance of binary arithmetic and computer machine code as devices for modelling sociological process."[20] The lecture exhorted anthropologists to break out of the straitjacket of viewing "societies" and "cultures" as plural empirical wholes and as concrete bounded entities capable of being labeled as types. Rather than labor at sketching particulars in detail (this by the way was the target and context for understanding Leach's earlier notorious remark that he was "frequently bored by the facts" and "cultural peculiarities"[21]), anthropologists should search for *general* patterns – whether similar or transformational – that may turn up in *any* kind of society. The patterns he was offering were relations between terms symbolized as mutually connected and variable in a "topological" or "algebraic" sense. Relationships between pairs of opposites were a case in point. In the field of kinship, for example, this pattern could be explored in the relations between "incorporation" and "alliance," as variably contrasted in different "societies," such as Trobriand, Kachin, and Tallensi, in terms of "blood and appearance" or "controlled supernatural attack" versus unconscious "uncontrolled mystical influence."

I cannot exaggerate how much this analytic and interpretive perspective became a dominant theme which Leach would restate, refine, and elaborate in many of his subsequent writings. We shall encounter for example a further explication of the notion of "relational structures" in his BBC Reith Lectures, *A Runaway World?* (1968).

THE CAMBRIDGE DON AS TEACHER

In their obituaries and reminiscences, Leach's students at Cambridge have affectionately described his large and powerful presence in a

---

[20] Ibid.
[21] Leach, *Political Systems*, reprint of 1964, p. 227. "I read the works of Professors Firth and Fortes not from an interest in the facts but so as to learn about the principles behind the facts" (ibid.). In fact, his extensive reviewing activity and his comparative essays show "an unrivalled grasp of ethnographic detail" (Fuller and Parry, "Petulant Inconsistency?" p. 11).

strikingly similar way. Of his entrance into the lecture hall, one writes: "Often late and looking slightly flustered, a tall gangling bear-like figure of a man, hair flying and dressed in a pinstripe suit would lope into a crowded room . . . Behind his spectacles were small but mercurial eyes which quickly took everything in without staring and with fleeting eye contact. He noticed things without being obvious."[22]

He consciously did not present himself as a model of sartorial fashion or high table wit with elegant gestures, but he certainly possessed the skills of an actor and orator, who responding to audiences gave his well-organized, provocative, vibrant lectures, illustrated with slides and graphic figures drawn with chalk of multiple colors. In fact he took pride in displaying his practical skills and in being a competent mechanic, who was way ahead of other academics in using a personal photocopying machine (his students were eager recipients of the acid-smelling notes and queries he liberally distributed), and in the appreciation of the uses of a computer, which in time, becoming antiquated, challenged his electronic skills. (At home he meddled with the car, gardened with precision, and did the electrical repairs, and later after retirement installed the latest moving bookcases for economical storage and retrieval of his extensive library.) One feature that strongly reinforced the image of a cerebral-practical man was his pair of large capable hands with mobile muscular fingers, which more than anything lived up to the presentation of himself as an engineer turned anthropologist concerned more "with structural features of design than with aesthetics."[23]

As regards his relationship with and impact on students, they crowded to hear him, sensing that they were participants in the breaking of new ground. Equally encouraging of students thinking for themselves were Leach's conscientious and informal supervisions: students both undergraduate and postgraduate marveled, were gratified, and frequently overwhelmed by the numerous pages of written comments on their

---

[22] Hugh-Jones. "Edmund Leach" (memoir).
[23] Leach, "Glimpses," pp. 9–10. "I tend to think of social systems as machines for the ordering of social relations or as buildings that are likely to collapse if the stresses and strains of the roof structure are not properly in balance. When I was engaged in fieldwork I saw my problem as trying to understand 'just how the system works' or 'why it held together'" (p. 10).

  Louisa Brown, Leach's daughter, having read this paragraph which gives an admiring portrait by some students of her father's practical mechanical skills, remarked, from the perspective of a child growing up, that her father's attempts at electrical repairs at home were untidy (entangled wires on the floor), and often produced blow ups. She saw her father as having problems of physical coordination (which was why he couldn't play cricket).

essays and chapters which they received from such a busy man.[24] (As we saw earlier, Leach enjoyed letterwriting as a way of clarifying issues for himself and this penchant may have been transported to his missives to his students clarifying matters for them and himself.) When teaching, both in lectures and in supervisions, he would often present his ideas on a topic, and then declare, "Well that's how I see it; but you are free to think otherwise." And *ut fama est*, a young German student, Gerhardt, who was one of six undergraduates reading anthropology at King's in the fateful early seventies when student rebellion was in the air, had been distressed by some of Leach's "outrageous" remarks during a lecture at the department. Gerhardt had threatened to walk out (he may actually have walked out). Leach had reacted by holding an informal seminar for Gerhardt and other students every other Monday night in term time at the Provost's Lodge.

Other undergraduates were won over in earlier years without such high drama. Ray Abrahams, now lecturer in anthropology and fellow of Churchill College, was sent to Leach to be supervised, and in a memorable remembrance he writes of Leach in his early years:

When I began my course in Social Anthropology in 1955, I received a postcard from my Tutor informing me that he had arranged for Mr. Leach to supervise me. The news meant little to me. After two years in Classics, I had a purely instrumental attitude to supervision, and I expected to gain nothing more than academic guidance from it. Mr. Leach (he had a London doctorate) was therefore a shock. He did not dazzle me with intellectual fireworks in those pre-structuralist days, but he made an immensely powerful impression on me nevertheless. I am still not quite sure how he did it.

I was of course in some degree a ready candidate. I had read Classics because I happened to be good at it at school, and I had moved into a smaller, non-school subject which I read because it had seemed interesting. I also very quickly realised that the Department [of Archaeology and Anthropology] was a small friendly community to which students, undergraduate and graduate alike, genuinely belonged, and this helped to kindle and fuel my enthusiasm. But this was only a small part of it. All too many teachers are capable of dampening an enthusiastic student's intellectual excitement, but Edmund never had that awful power. Without apparent effort, he fired one's interest in whatever he touched upon, and by the end of my first term I was besotted. My friends began to threaten to boycott me if I did not stop talking about "that man, Leach", whom they had never even heard of, let alone met, before I started harassing them

---

[24] A testimony to Leach's role as a supervisor, recognizable as authentic by other students as well, is provided by Ray Abrahams, "Edmund Leach: Some Early Memories," *Cambridge Anthropology. Special Issue: Sir Edmund Leach*, vol. 13, no. 3, 1989–90, pp. 19–30.

with my reports about him. There was clearly a remarkable charisma to him with his tall, almost gangling, figure and his odd mixture of outspokenness and shyness.

I have mentioned his charisma as a teacher, but Edmund never simply charmed or excited. He worked at teaching very hard indeed, and he left me and others with an indelible image of the ideal lecturer and supervisor. His lectures, though often carefully written, came over with remarkable spontaneity, and were a rare mixture of clarity and excitement. He applied the same incisiveness of mind to technical problems of communication as he did to theoretical issues. His diagrams of Australian kinship systems, for instance, were masterpieces of blackboard work, using different coloured chalk to bring the unintelligible criss-crossings of the printed page into sudden clear focus. His seminars were even better. He generated a keen sense of purpose in the group, and he produced a set of detailed stencilled minutes every week for the participants. His comments on one's supervision essays were often detailed, and he read every word with care. In supervision itself he listened well, and unlike Omar Khayyam's "doctor and saint", he never left one feeling that one simply "came out of the same door as in I went."[25]

A student of Leach some years later, another undergraduate, Stephen Hugh-Jones, describes how he cast his spell:

As supervisees, we began by standing in awe of him but he treated us as his equals and consequently took our ideas seriously and as worthy of his time and effort. Every essay came back picked over, dismembered then en-riched and reconstructed through a type-written commentary which might double its length and our pigeon holes were regularly supplied with a series of Leach notes on various supervision topics, each produced on his up-to-the-minute photocopier. They were succinct and clear, on a paper smelling strongly of chemicals which made one's fingernails shriek and they made us feel we really mattered. His delight in ideas and theory went together with a fasci-nation for ethnographic details of which he possessed an unrivalled grasp. And he made us respect them too . . . He demanded high standards and in-dependent thinking, challenging our ideas especially when they agreed with his own.[26]

One of the legends of the Department of Archaeology and Anthropol-ogy was the impact made on it by two German students, Wilke Gerhardt and Arthur Merin. As may be expected there are various stories of this impact; one of them concerns their encounter with Edmund Leach.

---

[25] Abrahams, "Edmund Leach," pp. 19–20. In this piece Abrahams also provides a detailed tran-scription of the Part II Seminar Programme for Michaelmas Term 1956, conducted by Leach for his discussion group. It is evidence of the effort Leach put into the teaching of undergraduates, let alone into directing research students.

[26] Hugh-Jones, "Edmund Leach" (memoir), pp. 25–26.

Dr. Maria Couroucli, now teaching at the Université de Paris-X at Nanterre, France,[27] was a first-year student of archaeology and anthropology during 1971–72. I met Dr. Couroucli in 1998 when I was visiting Paris. She remembered my presence in Cambridge as a lecturer, and in conversing about Cambridge of the early 1970s, she told me about this incident between Gerhardt and Merin and Edmund Leach, about which I had heard intriguing and embellished stories. I requested her to write me her account of it from memory, and she kindly sent me this narrative of Leach's "special seminar for first year students," of which she was a regular member:[28]

I was in my first year of Arch and Anth in 1971–72. Among the first years were two German students, Gerhardt and Merin, who were a little older and more mature than the rest of us. They were leading a mildly rebellious movement towards the established order in the Faculty.

One day some of the first-year group found ourselves in the graduate seminar at King's.[29] Steve Hugh-Jones had come back from the field and was giving a seminar on ritual practices. He had brought with him a kind of incense used during an initiation rite which, he claimed, when burning, would produce a smell provoking sexual excitement in men. To prove this, he started burning some of the substance in an ashtray, at which point Meyer Fortes got rather uneasy about us being around and he made the point that first-year students should not participate in the graduate seminar. The first-years present contested this mildly, and then Leach came up with a proposition to organize a seminar for those of us interested in more work. So we met about four or five times in Leach's house. I don't remember the themes discussed in this "first-year seminar"; I think they had to do with the practice of fieldwork. Leach suggested readings, we worked on them and then discussed. We all liked the experience, it was new and exciting and we were flattered, I guess, that Leach would give us some of his time. I suppose the more politically-minded of us thought this was a kind of victory over the system, or a way to challenge established authority and hierarchy. Others wanted to know what "real" anthropology was all about before they decided to become anthropologists themselves. It was the time when the issue of colonialism and anthropology was very much in the air, and students were eager to discuss more general questions about the political and moral ramifications of doing anthropology. Rather than addressing directly those issues, Leach tried instead to explain why research was both meaningful and exciting, which is probably why the seminar was so successful.

---

[27] Dr. Couroucli is presently Chargée de recherche au CNRS, Laboratoire de sociologie comparative, Université de Paris-X, Nanterre, France.

[28] I have made very minor changes in the two opening sentences of her account.

[29] Dr. Couroucli is referring to the Anthropology Departmental Seminar held at King's every Friday, chaired by Professor Meyer Fortes, and attended by Faculty and postgraduate (graduate in American terminology) students. It was a notable institution. Many of the papers were presented by students who had returned from the field and were writing their doctoral theses.

Leach's relationship with and impact on his postgraduate students in part bears witness to the British virtue (much in evidence among established academics) of allowing them to develop and express their views, and of tolerating eccentricity within implicitly understood limits. Although he did not aspire to be the founder of a school, there were at least three cohorts of students who in their own right achieved high reputation and who regarded Leach as a (for some *the*) primary teacher and with admiration and affection. The first includes Frederik Barth, Ralph Bulmer, Anthony Forge, Jean La Fontaine, Martin Southwold, and Nur Yalman, and together the second and third Adam Kuper, Ray Abrahams, Geoffrey Benjamin, C.J. Fuller, Alfred Gell, Ralph Grillo, Stephen Gudeman, Stephen and Christine Hugh-Jones, Caroline Humphrey, Jonathan Parry, and Andrew and Marilyn Strathern.[30] "Leach may not have created a school, but he certainly had many fiercely partisan students whose personal experience convinced them that they were working with one of the most exciting and creative intellectuals of his generation."[31]

When I arrived in Cambridge in 1963 (to take up a Smuts Fellowship at the university and a Commonwealth Fellowship at St. John's College), Leach already had the reputation of being the *enfant terrible* of the profession. Stories circulated about how he could be severe with shoddy work, sometimes had a scorching effect on this or that graduate student, had now and then explosive rows with some colleagues, and could be impatient with boring or stodgy seminar speakers, who might be treated to a disconcerting clinking of keys in his pocket, or in extreme moments, his turning away and reading a newspaper. It was in this state of demanding mind and stirred emotion, evoked by some writings he regarded as adversarial or incompetent, that Leach wrote some of his most cutting and biting reviews, and forceful, even vitriolic, responses to those who ventured to take him on. British anthropologists who were more used to the thrust and parry of polemical review writing rather enjoyed and expected it of him, but many Americans, mostly subject to the etiquette of sugar-coated reference-writing, tended to approach Leach as an unyielding and aggressive defender of the faith, until he disarmed them with chuckling, even nonchalant, admissions of the vulnerability and impermanence of some of his past arguments. I have come across these two assertions which I imagine would have amused him, and even reflected

---

[30] This listing is not complete, and I apologize to those who regard him in this light and have been missed out, owing to my ignorance or oversight. I should belatedly add Jock Stirrat and Deborah Swallow.

[31] Fuller and Parry, "Petulant Inconsistency?" p. 14.

his own moods: "Do I contradict myself? Very well then I contradict myself; I am large, I contain multitudes" (Walt Whitman); "If you *can't* annoy *somebody*, there is little point in writing" (Kingsley Amis).

Coming to Cambridge in the early 1960s, I probably encountered Leach at the height of his intellectual powers and self-assurance, and his dedicated encouragement of younger aspiring anthropologists. I therefore concur (as will others) with Hugh-Jones when he says, "He was tough, but intensely loyal and supportive, especially to his graduate students to whom he acted as a veritable godfather, inspiring in them deep and lasting feelings of attachment and the awareness of the privilege of working with one of the most exacting and creative intellectuals of his time."[32] But behind it all, there was a realization that academic discourse and creative writing were necessarily dialectical and dialogical. More than once he wrote and said that in order to be creative one has to critique, even repudiate, one's immediate intellectual ancestors, stretch their thoughts and creatively transform them. (It is consistent with this view that he did not court or bank on loyal or unoriginal intellectual descendants.) Audrey Richards is said to have remarked that Leach could never get going unless he had some established orthodoxy to attack,[33] a proposition that Leach himself acknowledged as necessary.[34]

One reason perhaps why students – who were younger than he – found him compellingly magnetic was that he never gave the impression that he was preaching to them a doctrine which they were obliged or beholden to accept as a gesture of conformity. He did convey to them that he was on the attack, disputing orthodoxy, and testing the limits of current knowledge. That may have been his hold on his audience, who listened attentively, even entranced, and went away encouraged to think for themselves and to tackle the puzzles of the discipline on their own.

Leach reserved his greatest attention and affection for those doctoral students whose research particularly engaged him. As their supervisor and their friend he enthusiastically and conscientiously attended to their financial needs and communicated his assessments of their field research; he obviously enjoyed reviewing their field notes and texts on myths and rituals of the people being studied, and pondered their analyses and in

---

[32] Hugh-Jones, "Edmund Leach 1910–1989," *Cambridge Anthropology. Special Issue: Sir Edmund Leach.*, vol. 13, no. 3, 1989–90, pp. 5–6.

[33] See Adam Kuper, "In Uncle Henry's Footsteps," *The Guardian*, Tuesday, January 10, 1989.

[34] In terms of contemporary fashion words, Leach in his own way appreciated that discourse was dialogical in the Bakhtinian sense, that meanings were not settled and were stretchable in Derrida's sense of *différance*, and that creativity necessarily to some degree "distorted" the work of predecessors in intertextual writing.

turn offered his own analyses in an equal dialog. I will illustrate this with two cases, those of Nur Yalman and Geoffrey Benjamin.

The first case is quite distinctive in that it relates to a special time in his career when Leach, a postgraduate student, and Nur Yalman (now a professor of anthropology at Harvard University) conducted fieldwork at the same time in Ceylon.

Leach did his first five-month spell of fieldwork from July to November 1954 in the village of Pul Eliya, located in the dry zone of the North Central Province. Nur Yalman, who was a student of Meyer Fortes and Leach at Cambridge, was also in Ceylon in the same year doing his Ph.D. fieldwork primarily in a community in the Kandyan highlands (supplemented by short trips to the Eastern Province and elsewhere). Both of them had in consultation arranged this research to coincide.

More in the manner of equal fieldworkers than in the manner of teacher and student, Leach and Yalman engaged in an intense, frequent, and sometimes very lengthy correspondence with each other, exchanging and cross-checking information and offering provisional interpretations on wide-ranging topics. From this thick flow of correspondence one infers that both fieldworkers were in a state of euphoric immersion in their engagement with their subjects. Their correspondence continued after Leach returned to Cambridge, and apparently ended in late 1955 with Yalman's return to the university.

The Leach papers in the Modern Archive Centre at King's College contain a large number of the letters exchanged (though some are missing), and summaries of some of them appear in the appendix to this chapter. Here let me say that, aside from much exchange and discussion on matters of kinship, land tenure, and social organization, there was an excited engagement in a guessing game suffused with Freudian psychoanalytical resonances and structuralist oppositions concerning the symbolic significance of such entities as milk, milk rice, oilcakes, coconuts, lotus flowers, blood, and semen, and their male–female sexual connotations and implications, as they figured in rituals such as marriage, a girl's puberty rite, and in healing, exorcism (*bali*), and sorcery (*huniyam*) rituals and communal festivities, such as the famous ritual game (*ankeliya*) played by the village divided into two upper and lower sections (*udapila and yatapila*).

Below are summaries of a few selected exchanges, highlighting in particular Leach's letters.

1. Yalman from Teripehe to Leach, dated September 30, 1954: thanking Leach for writing to him "so copiously," Yalman sent fourteen typed

pages (half-foolscap size) which contained details of the field systems in Teripehe, which were different from those Leach had reported for Pul Eliya. Yalman also gave description of rituals such as: *gammadu* [*gammaduva* – a collective village riutal], *kemmura* [*kemvara?* – a collective rite for the deities], and *bali* [a rite for dispelling evil planetary influences].

2. Leach from Pul Eliya to Yalman, dated October 7, 1954: five foolscap pages, closely typed, in which Leach advises Yalman to concentrate both on rituals which express the ideal state of affairs and on disputes which reveal the real state of affairs.

3. Leach from Pul Eliya to Yalman, dated October 16, 1954: seven typed foolscap pages dealing, first, with kinship relations, marriage, property transmission, *aiya-malli* (older and younger brother) and *massina* (male cross cousin) relations, *vasagama* and *ge*, and, second, providing a very detailed ethnographic description of "girls' puberty rites" (*vadiyapamununa*). (It is a pity that Leach never published this piece, which is an example of his meticulous thick description and arrangement of information.)

4. Leach from Pul Eliya to Yalman, dated October 21, 1954 (presumably a reply to a long communication of nine closely-typed half-sheets sent by Yalman from Teripehe to Leach on October 17, 1954): this communication contained five foolscap pages of notes on ownership of cattle, and on *gedera* and *ge* names, and four foolscap pages labeled "comments on Nur's paper on 'connotations of food offerings.'" Yalman's paper was missing in the Leach papers, and Leach's comments, obviously triggered by Yalman's own reporting, contain much play on the ritual symbolism of male–female union and separation.

5. Yalman to Leach, dated November 15, 1955 (after Leach had returned to Cambridge). Leach had written in 1955 an undated letter to Yalman on the subject of polyandry.[35] In his reply, Yalman reported extensively on the features of kinship he had encountered on his trip to the east coast of Ceylon, and reported on the practices of some Tamil and Muslim communities which were reminiscent of practices among the Nayar of Kerala. For example, Yalman referred to males and females owning undivided common property, to men marrying and going away, but not far, and maintaining control over the properties of their sisters, to men going frequently to their sisters' houses

---

[35] Leach published his essay "Polyandry" in *Man* in 1955.

to eat, and to the mother's brother having first claim on his sister's children.

6. Leach from Cambridge to Yalman, dated October 18, 1955 (a few weeks before Yalman's letter to him reported above): Leach gives news of the Department of Anthropology and other departments: "Here term is under way again with an alarming growth of the undergraduate population. The postgraduates look promising." He comments in the letter: Michael Banks who worked among the Tamils of Jaffna (Northern Province) is "frankly terrible . . . but Frederik Barth with stuff from Surat [Pakistan] is obviously going to be A++, Jean La Fontaine is back from Kenya, and Bill Cunning from Canada. Grace Harris has taken her doctorate, but Al [Harris] is still the perpetual student." George Homans, who is playing Talcott Parsons's role,[36] in a very different style, is much in evidence. "Esther Newcomb, who I think is after your time (daughter of an American Social Psychologist) would seem to be planning to marry Jack Goody." Meyer is "very cheerful,"[37] Reo Fortune is much the same as before.

Back in Cambridge Leach and Fortes attended to some of Yalman's financial needs and to the continuation of his Bye Fellowship at Peterhouse, thereby enabling Yalman to continue with his fieldwork and to return to Cambridge to write his dissertation. Nur Yalman published his monograph *Under the Bo Tree* in 1967, six years after Leach's *Pul Eliya* (discussed in detail in chapter 7).

My second illustration concerns Geoffrey Benjamin, formerly Associate Professor at the University of Singapore, who did fieldwork under Leach's direction among the forest-dwelling Temiar of Malaysia in 1964–65. At my request he wrote me an account of his "memories of Edmund," and also sent me some of the correspondence between them. Benjamin writes:

When I first approached him, shortly before the Part II exams, about the possibility of continuing to do research in Anthropology, he was cautiously encouraging. It was assumed without question that he would be my supervisor. I had previously discussed with him my plans to join a long-vacation student "expedition" to Malaya to study the Temiars: such a trip had been advertised by a Malaysian

---

[36] Parsons had been invited for a year to Cambridge by Meyer Fortes (and others).

[37] The Leach Papers at King's College contain some friendly and cordial letters exchanged between Fortes and Leach when the latter was doing fieldwork in Pul Eliya. This cordiality apparently continues in 1955 when Leach returned to Cambridge. It is unclear when their relations began to deteriorate – probably soon afterwards.

Chinese student, and I had joined up. The expedition plan fell through, however, but not before I had read everything I could get hold of – which wasn't
very much – on the Malayan Aborigines.

It turned out that Edmund himself had once thought of working on the
Temiars. He knew of H.D. Noone's incomplete 1936 study, and he was a good
friend of Kilton Stewart, the American psychotherapist-cum-ethnographer who
had worked with Noone in the 1930s. Edmund and Stewart had met up in China,
and travelled together to Botel Tobago, on which Edmund wrote a couple of
early papers.

As my plans developed, and I managed to find funding – largely with
Edmund's help – Edmund got increasingly enthusiastic. His own experience
in Sarawak was valuable in this, but of course his visit there was too short to be
really satisfying. Supervising my work on the Temiars seemed like a proxy substitute. His advice on practical matters – from surveying, to remaining healthy,
to dealing with officialdom – was all right on the mark. This was especially so
as I had never been outside Europe before, and was far from being a boy scout
type. He was especially glad that I was doing "real" anthropology, at a time
when he felt that many researchers were turning away from basic exploratory
ethnography to more "applied" issues in relatively well known societies.

The degree of Edmund's involvement in my work is apparent from the letters
that flowed between us while I was in the field. The correspondence itself was
physically difficult to maintain, since I depended on a monthly helicopter visit
and occasional foot-porters to get the letters to and from the official mail system. In addition to his great help in administering to my financial and official
problems while I was living in very isolated circumstances, he took very serious
note of my findings as they progressed. He made valuable suggestions as to
how I should follow up on certain questions, and he indulged himself several
times in detailed analyses of some ethnographic snippets I had sent him. When
I came back to them later, these analyses usually turned out to have hit the
mark. It was clear that Edmund had a very good sense of the physical and social
circumstances in which I was living – which is why I think there was an element
of proxy fieldwork in his approach to my reports, made possible by his own skills
as a fieldworker and by his experience in Sarawak and Burma.

From a batch of correspondence between Leach and Benjamin then
engaged in fieldwork (1964–65), a few items will illustrate the nature of
this communication:

1. Postgraduate students in the field are always short of money and worried about their finances. In the case of Benjamin, Leach wrote him in
   late 1964 (probably December) that he was writing to the Ministry of
   Education about payment of his fare "by the direct route," to Christie,
   to inquire about how much money he had with the Horniman Trust,
   and assured Benjamin "that funds will be made available so that you

can stay in the field as long as you think desirable. I can organize a grant from the Esperanza Trust [this was created by Leach from his own funds and was administered by the Royal Anthropological Institute] if your other funds are inadequate." In a letter dated 10 May, 1965 Leach wrote: "I am now taking steps to get some money out of the Esperanza Trust. £200 from this source should reach your bank in K.L. [Kuala Lumpur] within the next month." In another letter he commiserated: "I am sorry to hear that the tape recorder has run into trouble. If you incur expense on this account, keep the bills and let us see what we can get back."

2. On the academic side, Leach's letters, while commenting on Benjamin's field notes, are peppered with references he might consult: examples are Rodney Needham's "original" essays on teknonomy and death names among the Penan; H.L. Shorto's *Linguistic Comparison in South East Asia and the Pacific* (Leach says he was writing to Shorto, and sending him a copy of Benjamin's "Linguistic Paper," with another going to John Lyons at Edinburgh); I.H.N Evans's *Negritoes of Malaya* (photocopies of some pages were enclosed); Skeat and Blagden, volume II (with the remark that these authors' notes about "the myths and beliefs of the 'Semang'" come from the writings in German by Hrolf Vaughan Stevens whose texts Benjamin may find worth checking in due course).

3. Benjamin sent ethnographic information on Temiar myths and rituals together with his own comments on them. Examples were "Stories of the Engku," "The Origin of Rats," "The Origin of Fish," "The Story of Karey," and so on. Leach was excited, "tremendously pleased . . ." with this "absolutely high quality stuff," and, as may be expected, he sent back to Benjamin his own analyses of them. At this time (late 1964–65) Leach was in many ways entranced by Lévi-Strauss's "recent monumental piece on South American myths called *Le cru et le cuit* (*The Raw and the Cooked*)," and remarked, "I must say that it does really look as if the Temiar had been invented by Lévi-Strauss!" He entitled one set of comments: "Some Lévi-Straussian comments on your myth series."

Leach's commentaries on information sent him by Benjamin are reproduced in an appendix to this chapter in order to convey some sense of the authentically pleased engagement with the research of one of his research students – and his irresistible urge to order, analyze, and comment on Benjamin's ethnographic texts.

There is one piece of advice Leach gave Benjamin which probably recalls his own practice. It may have served him well in an unanticipated way when during the Second World War he lost all his notes but had actually written such a synoptic account of Hpalang, an unstable (Kachin) community. This later aided his recall of ethnographic facts.

> When you finally leave the field and draw breath, the first thing you should drive yourself to do, although it may seem extremely tedious at the time, is to write up an absolutely straightforward ethnographic account of the Temiar addressed to an imaginary audience who really know nothing about them at all. The point is that at that stage of your work, as perhaps never again, you will have an overall but very detailed feel for what Temiar culture "really is". Once you get buried into details of a Ph.D. thesis the overall balance will get very heavily distorted. At this stage you do not even need to bother about what the precise subject matter of your Ph.D. thesis is going to be. You have enough stuff for about six different theses. But it is very important that the overall ethnographic framework is written up as soon as you leave the field so that you have something on which to base future decisions. (Leach to Benjamin, June 3, 1965)

Leach's correspondence with Benjamin was not unique. Others (such as Stephen Hugh-Jones and Christine Hugh-Jones) can provide similar testimony. At the same time it is crucial to recognize that Leach most definitely did not aspire to found a school with pliant disciples attached to him. He likewise baulked at others' efforts to monumentalize him. He fiercely rejected any effort by his former pupils (and other colleagues) to commemorate his career with *festschrifts*.[38] His position was that this genre of edited volumes containing disparate essays usually lacked coherence and never amounted to much as anthropology. In a curious way, such resistance also accorded with his own lack of enthusiasm for crafting a systematic totalizing theoretical system, recapitulating his previous works and cumulatively built up piece by piece. In fact he readily acknowledged in informal exchanges with those with whom he was comfortable that he was aware of his inconsistencies. He would maintain that creative thinking was possible only if you were prepared to take the risks. Inconsistency did not worry him because he thought it was consistent with a Hegelian dialectical mode of thought. His impulsion was to "experiment," "probe," "play" with new ideas, and push at the margins. He once remarked that with regard to his own works, he had

---

[38] Leach scotched many attempts by his pupils and colleagues to do him honor in this way. I myself was the recipient of a quick and firm missive the moment a rumor reached him that I and certain others were contemplating a *festschrift*.

a linear experience of time and a sense of moving on, and that he did not particularly care about what he had written years earlier. "But the reading public does the opposite. It tends to aggregate the author's works and treat them synchronically as a unity."[39]

THEORETICAL POSITIONING

There were two sets of contrasts, or "oppositions" in the structuralist sense, that Edmund Leach frequently employed in order to characterize the theoretical impulsions and tensions in his writings. One was that he was simultaneously a structuralist and a functionalist; the other was that he was attracted to mathematical equations of relations and transformations (as a schoolboy preparing to enter Cambridge he had concentrated on mathematics), but that having been trained as an engineer he had pragmatic concerns regarding how designs were drawn, implemented, adapted to context, and put to use. He once said that there was a tug of war within him between a pure mathematician *manqué* and an empiricist engineer *manqué*, who however recoils from counting: "I feel that sometimes I am on both sides of the fence."[40]

The statement that he was simultaneously a structuralist and functionalist needs an extended gloss and a large part of this biography is devoted to that purpose, with the following only a beginning. While rejecting the Radcliffe-Brownian (and Durkheimian) notion of "function" as contribution of a component to the maintenance and integration of a social "system" (itself viewed in organismic terms), and the Malinowskian notion of "function" primarily in terms of serving individual "biological" needs and, secondarily, societal needs, Leach in various writings seems to have adopted the notion of function as connection between components, such that functional relations constituted an interconnected totality ("the total interconnectedness of things"). The "interconnectedness" that Leach meant was, however, "relational systems" as "transformations" of one another.[41] This conception of functional relations thus rejects the Malinowskian notion of a cultural system as "a unique self-sufficient functioning whole" and the Radcliffe-Brownian notion of "whole societies," bounded and "distinguishable as species types and classifiable as such in a kind of Linnaean taxonomy." These were the perspectives he rejected first in his *Political Systems of Highland Burma* and

---

[39] See Tambiah, "Personal Accounts."   [40] See ibid., p. 34.
[41] See, for example, Leach's *A Runaway World?* The BBC Reith Lectures 1967, New York: Oxford University Press, 1968. This idea is elaborated in his later writings as we shall see.

even more explicitly and unforgettably as "butterfly collecting" in his famous Malinowski Memorial Lecture in December 1959, urging the view that anthropologists ought to be searching for generalizations for which cultural and social boundaries were quite irrelevant or impossible to impose. This view of function derived from mathematics and not from biology or psychology as was the case with the followers of Radcliffe-Brown and Malinowski. "Consequently, from my point of view there was no inconsistency between 'functionalism' and 'structuralism' (in its then novel continental sense)."[42]

Leach progressively clarified that his "structuralism" cum functionalism consisted in seeing "relational systems" as "transformations" of one another, that certain devices stemming from or assimilable to his mathematical and engineering training such as binary arithmetic, information theory, and computer coding, could be deployed for perceiving patterns in classificatory thought, myth and ritual, and in social processes. More ambitiously, he saw the possibility of establishing "cross-cultural transcriptions" as the objective of his notion of the comparative method. These ideas gave an underlying unity and continuity to the way he would tackle many of the issues he undertook to investigate.

At the same time he also successfully exploited aspects of the "functionalist" perspective he principally associated with Malinowski and Firth, which dynamically focused on how individual actors (including groups) used and manipulated ideal categories and rules and norms of social conduct in contexts of action to further their interests and goals. Leach deployed this pragmatic instrumental or strategizing perspective on many occasions – to illustrate how mythological genealogical variants (in "structuralist" terms variations on a theme) were manipulated by competing Kachin lineages to further their claims or more generally how myth variants were related to "function and social change," how double descent systems might make sense if considered as networks through which different activities were channeled, or how an imposing intricately carved but densely populated Hindu temple facade whose details could not be distinguished by the worshipper was meant to convey a sense of power and awe.[43] In this mood Leach would criticize on the one hand the formalism of some of the structural-functionalists who reified social systems as organizations of social

---

[42] Leach, "Glimpses," p. 19.
[43] See Edmund Leach, "The Gatekeepers of Heaven: Anthropological Aspects of Grandiose Architecture," *Journal of Anthropological Research*, vol. 39, no. 3, fall 1983, pp. 243–64. This essay is dealt with at length later.

principles, and on the other, the non-contextualized abstract codes of some structuralist exercises divorced from social uses or lacking empirical grounding.

While remembering that Leach had many irons in the fire at any one time, I would risk a broad two-fold temporal division of his writings into those written and published from about 1940 to 1961, and those written from around 1962 (and especially after 1965) into the late 1980s. During the first phase he was primarily concerned with refining, extending, and polemically criticizing certain formulations surrounding kinship, segmentary descent structures, and social organization of "tribal" societies made by the leading figures in British social anthropology, such as Radcliffe-Brown and Malinowski who were his elders, Meyer Fortes, Raymond Firth, and Evans-Pritchard, who were senior to him, and Max Gluckman, Audrey Richards, Jack Goody, and others who were his contemporaries. Of all these personages, Leach explicitly named on several occasions Malinowski and Firth as his teachers; less frequently, he also referred to Fortes as one of his teachers.[44]

One might say, to simplify and accent matters, that in his mind in the category of senior figures, Leach opposed Radcliffe-Brown, whose typing of structural-functional organic systems he rejected and whom he personally disliked, to Malinowski, his charismatic teacher whom he liked, and whose ethnographic writing he admired much more than his theoretical contributions. At the next level, he positioned himself in contrastive relations to his part-teachers slightly older than him, namely Fortes and Firth. Though a participant in Malinowski's seminar, Fortes had gravitated toward Radcliffe-Brown, whose theoretical perspective he whole-heartedly espoused, and Leach saw him as his sparring opponent and theoretical foil. Leach was benignly inclined toward Firth who was sponsor and friend and had initially taught him "most of what I know about anthropology."

While Leach repeatedly idolized his dead hero, Malinowski, it was also evident from his words and deeds that initially he had imbibed much from his other teacher, friend, and sponsor, Raymond Firth, who has outlived him. I would surmise that Firth's own dynamic treatment of the relation between normative rules and actor-oriented usages first of

---

[44] In "Glimpses," Leach states that "Raymond Firth and Meyer Fortes were my teachers and closest associates throughout my academic career." In *Custom, Law and Terrorist Violence*, Leach declares that he considered Malinowski "the greatest and most original of all social anthropologists."

all accorded with Leach's own intuitions about how people acted, and secondly, provided fire power against the officializing *doxa* of Radcliffe-Brown and his followers.

In his twilight years, in an informal mood in 1984, Leach ventured that Firth's work was a "disguised attack" on Oxford's "objectivist" (and formal jural) representations of social life. Firth "is saying that real life is not determined by formal structural arrangements and segmentary oppositions. Real life is a matter of ad hoc improvisations, of getting things fixed up by your friends regardless of what the rules may say."[45]

No doubt Firth would modify this conversational exaggeration, but it is clear that from the beginning, Firth, in his first major monograph, *We, the Tikopia*,[46] and later writings, would elaborate on what he meant by kinship as "the re-interpretation in social terms of the facts of procreation and regularised sex union," and move in the direction of illustrating, with rich ethnographic details, how kinship operated in the broader social life as a guide and not as a prescription for behavior.

In *We, the Tikopia*, Firth subtly subverts the reification of descent systems by demonstrating that to label a society as patrilineal or matrilineal is to say little, for it is more productive to break down such categories into more precise components referring to the transmission of rights from whom to whom and under what circumstances, and in this way assemble a number of connected formulations about the design of the society. He went beyond the architectonic delineation of patrilineal groups such as *paito* (ramage) and *kaianga* (clan), by focusing on the roles played by certain kinsmen such as the *tautina* (mother's brother), and by kinsmen on both sides of the house, with reference to an individual. Firth had a lively sense of the contextual and manipulated usages of kinship terms that went well beyond their internal analysis as a set.[47]

Subsequently, Firth in *Elements of Social Organization*[48] conceptualized this dynamic perspective in terms of the distinction and dialectic

---

[45] Leach "Glimpses," p. 14.

[46] Raymond Firth, *We, the Tikopia: A Sociological Study of Kinship in Primitive Polynesia*. New York: American Book Co., 1936.

[47] When I was writing my own essay "Kinship Fact and Fiction in Relation to the Kandyan Sinhalese," *Journal of the Royal Anthropological Institute*, vol. 95, part 2, 1965, pp. 131–73, Leach directed my attention to this essay by Raymond Firth: "Marriage and the Classificatory System of Relationship", *Journal of the Royal Anthropological Institute*, vol. 60, 1930, pp. 235–68.

[48] Raymond Firth, *Elements of Social Organization*, London: Watts, 1951, The Josiah Mason Lectures, 1947; also published New York: Philosophical Library, 1951.

between "social structure," the system of formal rules and arrangements, and "social organization" which is the outcome of individuals modifying, stretching, and contesting the structure in the course of attempting to maximize their yields in terms of a means–ends schema. There is no doubt that Firth's demonstration of the pragmatic uses and manipulations of the normative rules by individual actors accorded with aspects of Leach's own discussions of the relation between "ideal categories" and "actual behavior," which will be explicated shortly.

In time the intellectual interests of Firth and Leach diverged, but at no time were there any disputes between them. We, however, find Leach directing his missiles, and therefore a much greater portion of his writing, in the late 1950s and 1960s at the formulations of Radcliffe-Brown, and Fortes whose view of "kinship as a thing in itself" was frequently assailed. Fortes, as one of Leach's former teachers at the LSE, and as Leach's superior in the Cambridge department, was quietly unyielding toward Leach's intellectual contestation; whatever their differences, they both combined, together with Jack Goody, to run what was (arguably) considered the best and most exciting department in Britain.

There is another figure who more than anyone else has been venerated and mythologized as the personification of the sophisticated best of Oxford-style scholarship and raconteuring by Oxonian anthropologists themselves, and who should be brought on to this stage of major players. He is E. Evans-Pritchard. It is not easy to situate Leach in relation to him and his work.

That Evans-Pritchard was a widely read scholar, familiar with European writings, who wore his considerable learning lightly, was recognized. While Leach was not sympathetic to the ideal type segmentary model in which the Nuer kinship system was featured (it was too much in the descent system objectifying style of Radcliffe-Brown and Fortes), he recognized Evans-Pritchard's versatility in his other works, and relevantly for us, the fact that he took important account of the role of ideas. Leach recognized Evans-Pritchard's originality thus:

It was not until the mid 1950s, that under the influence of the later Wittgenstein and Oxford linguistic philosophy, British social anthropologists began to show a serious interest in ideas rather than in behaviour. The shift was initiated by Evans-Pritchard, though the presence of Louis Dumont in Oxford for several years was also relevant, as was my own heretical idealism which had a variety of sources. It was certainly tied in with my early grounding in mathematics, though mathematicians are not necessarily of an idealist inclination.[49]

Leach did not dispute with Evans-Pritchard, and they seem to have kept their distance. Though there was a similarity of class origins, there were matters that separated them. Their life-styles were different: Evans-Pritchard had converted to Catholicism and sought solace in the Church, while Leach was not enamored of participating in institutionalized Christianity. But even more importantly Evans-Pritchard, who had earlier been a member of Malinowski's seminar, in time became estranged from him and critical of his work, and joined up with Radcliffe-Brown at Oxford. Jack Goody in his *Expansive Moment* conveys the problematic dimensions of Evans-Pritchard's persona in his negative attitudes not only to those loyal to Malinowski, but also toward most of his peers as well. These attitudes were conveyed in his personal letters about which Goody writes, "It is not clear that in these personal letters we are necessarily dealing with the 'real' (or at least considered) views of Evans-Pritchard but rather with a particular way of expressing himself (or perhaps of creating a persona) in writing."[50]

Evans-Pritchard's letters to Fortes about Audrey Richards "reached an outrageous level,"[51] which in my view smacked of a certain brand of public school and officers' club macho banter. Goody reports Richards as remarking, "After all Evans-Pritchard can't speak about anyone else without sneering, friend or foe alike," and he comments "which from his letters to Fortes appears to be a reasonable assessment."[52]

An amusingly high point in Evans-Pritchard's flippant letterwriting to Fortes is reached in these sentences from Goody:

Evans-Pritchard's dislikes, especially in his latter years, were not confined to those close to Malinowski. He resigned from the British Academy when Leach was elected. Although he gave economy as the reason and had "nothing personal against Leach, even though he is very far from being a scholar", he was "tired of all the lobbying, jockeying, even cheating". His opinion was no more favourable to other anthropologists at Cambridge. Of my appointment as Fortes' successor (and I had been a pupil of them both), he wrote: "I was very sorry to see in the Daily Telegraph today the appointment of your successor in the Chair – a great mistake, in my opinion."[53]

---

[49] Leach, "Glimpses," p. 17.
[50] Goody, *The Expansive Moment*, p. 72.   [51] Ibid., p. 72.   [52] Ibid., p. 72.   [53] Ibid., p. 71.

It would seem that these attitudes of Evans-Pritchard should best be treated with some levity; in any case they did not alter the course of anthropology in Britain, least of all at Cambridge.

I have so far mentioned five anthropologists who figured with varying significance in Leach's professional concerns in the first phase. There is a sixth from across the Channel in France whose writings as the leading French theorist increasingly became more and more important for Leach to take into account and come to terms with, but with whom he did not have a close personal relationship. This person was Claude Lévi-Strauss. Leach's intellectual engagement and preoccupation with Lévi-Strauss's ideas in his own writings is a vital part of his biography. As we shall see later, admiration spiced with dissent was not in this case a prescription that could bind the two in a relation of enduring "alliance."

The rejection of psychoanalytic interpretations and the commitment to structuralism

Leach's penchant for experimenting with interesting ideas did also propel him to consider psychoanalytic concepts and interpretation in the late fifties, and his attempts to interpret some of the information on ritual and myth he had collected in Ceylon in 1954 (and 1956), and his dialog with Yalman on this matter, give a sense of his transition to structuralism.

I have already referred in chapter 2 to Leach's undergraduate dipping into Freudian texts, and later to the manner in which Freudian ideas were discussed and revised in Malinowski's seminar in the 1930s.[54] This backlog of ideas surfaced with new force and relevance in attempting to decode Sinhalese ritual.

The monograph *Pul Eliya*, though completed a few years before, was published in 1961. Since it is solely focused on land tenure and kinship, readers may be inclined to think that Leach's fieldwork in Ceylon did not extend to other matters. In fact he was much involved (as Yalman also was) in Sinhalese ritual and mythology and classificatory logic, and this important dimension of his writing is to be found in certain essays to be considered now.

---

[54] As Goody has remarked in *The Expansive Moment*, p. 121, "Few students in the 1930s could avoid having to make some kind of resolution of their interests in two major figures, Marx and Freud."

Let me begin with a portion of a letter Leach wrote to Nur Yalman from Pul Eliya, dated November 10, 1954. It was written just before he returned to England after his first spell of fieldwork. Leach gave this advice about symbolic analysis.

It seems to me that you are in the same position as an analyst with his patient's dreams. The analyst gains insights from hearing his patient's dream because of his wide general experience of symbolic representations, but that doesn't mean that the patient will necessarily accept the analyst's interpretations. The whole thing, especially verbal associations, adds up to a kind of detective novel, with a lot of false trails and just one or two really important clues . . .

It is important to make an assessment in your notebooks of just how far *your* evaluation of a symbolic situation was shared by the audience or by your informants. Obviously there are "levels of validity" in all this. Ernest Jones once wrote a charming essay discussing Italian Renaissance pictures of the Annunciation of the Virgin Mary where the "holy spirit" in the form of a dove floats down from heaven towards Mary's ear while an angel presents Mary with a *lily*. The artists who painted these pictures were painting to a convention; one doesn't know how far the convention was "conscious," i.e. symbolically the ear stands for vagina. Did the artist think that way? I don't think it matters. The psycho-analytical argument would be I think that the artistically sensitive person will in fact make these associations – at some level of consciousness – and his appreciation of the picture will be affected by this association.[55]

Leach's groundbreaking essay "Magical Hair" (1958)[56] can be considered some kind of turning point in which he rejects psychoanalytic plumbing of meaning in favor of a social structural logic. This was roughly the early phase in his theoretical and methodological trajectory when he begins to espouse the Lévi-Straussian procedure of searching not for the particular meanings of particular symbols but for patterned structural relations in ritual and myth of the relations between different parts and of the parts to the whole.

Thus another notable essay published four years later entitled "Pulleyar and the Lord Buddha: an aspect of religious syncretism in Ceylon"[57] demonstrates his own incorporation and translation of psychoanalytic insights into a structuralist perspective.

---

[55] The Modern Archive, King's College Library, Cambridge.
[56] Edmund Leach, "Magical Hair" (Curl Bequest Essay 1957), *Journal of the Royal Anthropological Institute*, vol. 88, part 2, 1958, pp. 147–64.
[57] Edmund Leach, "Pulleyar and the Lord Buddha: An Aspect of Religious Syncretism in Ceylon," *Psychoanalysis and the Psychoanalytic Review*, vol. 49, no. 2, 1962, pp. 81–102.

His commitment to this procedure was further signaled in a somewhat trenchant essay[58] criticizing his own former student and companion fieldworker, Nur Yalman, for providing an inadequate or incomplete interpretation of a Sinhalese girl's puberty ritual.[59] Although
Leach's essay was published in 1970 in a *festschrift* for Lévi-Strauss, it
seems that he had worked out his counter-interpretation some years
earlier.[60]

Leach judged Yalman's paper as preferable to an earlier paper by
Kathleen Gough[61] because, while Gough's discussion is limited to the
narrow context of the matrilineal Nayar, Yalman's canvas treats the ritual
on a wider canvas covering south India and Ceylon. But Leach says
that both Gough's and Yalman's papers can be criticized because both
write as if "particular items of ritual symbolism can be discovered by
direct intuition or by a rather elementary kind of question-and-answer
technique, and both authors select their ethnographic evidence to fit in
with preconceived interpretations."[62]

Yalman (with Gough), charges Leach, is still operating in respect of
ritual symbolism at the intuitive level of Frazer and Radcliffe-Brown.[63]
He prefers the Lévi-Straussian procedure which, instead of searching
for particular meanings of particular symbols, looks for the structural
relations between the parts and of the parts to the whole. Two major
criticisms are leveled at Yalman's paper. First, Yalman interprets some
symbolic elements which depend for their value on the etymological association of words. For example, what Yalman says about the word *dagoba*
(a "relic chamber"/Buddhist monument containing a relic) is etymologi-
cally correct, but its *historical* etymological association cannot be taken to

[58] Edmund Leach, "A Critique of Yalman's Interpretation of Sinhalese Girl's Puberty Ceremonial," in Jean Pouillion and Pierre Maranda (eds.), *Echanges et Communications; Mélanges
Offerts à Claude Lévi-Strauss à l'Occasion de son 60ème Anniversaire,* The Hague: Mouton, 1970, vol. II,
pp. 818–28.
[59] Nur Yalman, "On the Purity of Women in the Castes of Ceylon and Malabar," *Journal of the Royal
Anthropological Institute,* vol. 93, part 1, 1963, pp. 25–58.
[60] As noted earlier Leach and Yalman were exchanging field notes on the puberty ritual in late
1954, and Leach must have read Yalman's essay in draft form.
[61] Kathleen E. Gough, "Female Initiation Rites on the Malabar Coast," *Journal of the Royal Anthropological Institute,* vol. 85, 1955, pp. 45–80.
[62] Leach, "A Critique," p. 819.
[63] Radcliffe-Brown, confining himself to a simple culture (the Andaman Islands), argues a priori
that within any one cultural context the meaning of a symbol can be discovered by comparing
all the situations in which that symbol is used. The presumption is that the symbol has the same
meaning in all these contexts.

have relevance for the present-day actors just as the Greek work *Ichtheos* (fish), treated as a coded pun in the early Christian Church, has no relevance for a very large number of Christians who abstain from eating all flesh other than fish on all Fridays. (Yalman has glossed *dagoba* [dagaba], also known as *dhatu-garbhaya*, especially the word *dhatu*, as having these associated meanings in Ceylon: semen, seed, and sacred relics; and the word *garbhaya* as meaning womb.) Second, Leach grants that although Yalman is "possibly correct in claiming that in South India and Ceylon there is a one-to-one correlation between a stress on *female* puberty and pre-puberty rites which have the overall form of a marriage and the existence of high evaluation of close local group and endogamy, this matter of ethnographic interest cannot be treated in any *causal* sense."

Yalman's essay attempts to establish the thesis "that the puberty of girls rather than boys is ritualized in South India and Ceylon *because* the sexual purity of women is highly valued and *because* caste membership is traced through women rather than men," and that the rituals in question take "the form of symbolic marriage *because* it is desirable that all women capable of conception should be, in a ritual sense, married to members of their own caste."[64]

A causal proposition implies that a universal sociological law is intended. Yalman's propositions cannot be validated in a *causal* manner, and do not even appear probable once they are considered in relation to the following distributions in comparative cases: first, if the Sinhalese ritualize the puberty of girls but not of boys, Roman Catholic Christians ritualize the social maturity of both girls and boys. Orthodox Jews lay special ritual stress on the social incorporation of boys and perform for them the initiation rite of circumcision, but they, like the Sinhalese, trace group membership through females. Second, ritual forms borrowed from marriage ceremonial appear in the Sinhalese and Roman Catholic cases. Thus such parallel ethnographic facts cited contravert Yalman's *causal* theses.

Leach suggests that, while Yalman does informatively state that "the procedures of the ritual amount to a manipulation of the logic of binary opposition," and summarizes the transformational process by which the menstruating girl, at the beginning impure but as yet infertile, is at the end

[64] Leach, "A Critique," p. 827.

ritually transformed into a pure, fertile adult, yet he gives an inadequate account of the actual transformation process because he is interested in the "symbolism" of particular elements rather than in "structure"; he keeps reverting to "interpretations" of sex symbolism, marriage symbolism, and rebirth symbolism, and he is preoccupied with the "overtly" phallic symbolism of the paddy pestle, of bananas, and of the meaning of *redi mama*, washerman, as a symbolic father-in-law. By contrast, for Leach the paddy pestle is simply what it is: an instrument which separates husks from rice;[65] the washerman is simply a washerman.[66] And his structrualist procedure, he claims, systematically establishes that a large proportion of the distinguishable elements (rather than being considered as individual symbolic elements) "occur in opposed pairs – these opposed entities occur both at the level of material things and metaphysical ideas".[67] The oppositions are deployed in a change of status of the young girl in terms of the standard tripartite Van Gennep schema of separation – isolation (liminality) – aggregation. The ritual occasion serves to declare the girl's matured availability "as a purified fertile adult rather than to determine her fate in a symbolic marriage."[68]

---

[65] The pestle's paired term is mortar. In this ritual the pestle appearing by itself is an incomplete object, as is the infertile old woman with whom it is isolated in a room with the menstruating girl in the liminal phase of the rite.

[66] The Sinhalese terms used for the low-caste washerman and washerwoman are *redi mama*, literally "uncle cloth," and *redi nenda*, "aunt cloth." Yalman interprets these fictional (or pseudo-) kin terms as symbolically meaning "father-in-law"/"mother's brother" and "mother-in-law." Leach points out that parallel expressions not implying symbolic kinship are Uncle Tom and Aunt Jemima in the American South, and Nannie (grandmother) for nurse in Victorian England.

[67] Leach, "A Critique," pp. 822–23. Leach's list of oppositions or binaries explicitly or implicitly manipulated in the ritual:

(male)	is opposed to	female
semen	"	menstrual blood
milk rice	"	oilcakes
milk	"	blood
pollution (dirt)	"	purity (cleanliness)
yakshas (demons)	"	Buddha
fertility	"	infertility
"the room inside the dwelling house where the girl is secluded"	"	"the hut outside in the garden where the girl is washed"
old age	"	youth
dehusked rice (*hal*)	"	(paddy [*vi*] with husk)
paddy pestle	"	(paddy mortar)

[68] Leach, "A Critique," p. 826.

Appendix: Excerpts from Leach's correspondence with Benjamin regarding the Temiar[1]

Ethnography:Your stuff about healing rituals is very interesting and seems to me to tie up with some of the myth material handled in the rat myth. For example the fact that the man is half a rat and half a man makes him a kind of a witch. I think in the same way Shamans have their power because they are persons of ambiguous quality, half man and half beast, while mourners may likewise be thought of as in an ambiguous status and therefore sacred and therefore powerful. I am enclosing with this letter several pages of photocopy from I.H.N. Evans *Negritos of Malaya*, where he quotes material from Schebesta about shamans (Halak). You will note that if read carefully this material implies that quite ordinary people can perform the curing ceremonial. Notice too how the ideology reported by Evans links up with the kind of mythology you have been describing.

I find your myths very interesting, but my comments on them will be quite irrelevant by the time you get them. Nevertheless I am working on them. I feel that you should look very closely now on any ideas of "the soul" which your people may have. Is there some idea about transmigration of souls and repetitive rebirth?

I think you want to follow up your point about the healing procedure being "just a technical act". You will note that Evans also says p. 207 that "the evil is expelled from the patient's body by virtue of the breath"... but he also gives a very elaborate mythology as to why this particular breath should have a "virtue"... it seems to me that there must be more to it than you suggest. Evans has it that an orthodox shaman (*halak*) is a reincarnation of "Hanei the son of Karei" (p. 208); seemingly in this Evans version Rinden = your Engku (p. 208 4–5). I am willing to believe that your Temiar do not have an institution of trance mediumship but even so the "magic of curing" must have some kind of mythical justification. Crudely put: how is the curing breath supposed to work? To get at this you will need to get an "ideology of disease"... why do people fall sick? If the healing power of "shamans" is widely distributed this can be interpreted as saying "there are no shamans" or "we are all shamans". Evans mentions that shamans are reluctant to discuss their curing techniques

---

[1] I have made a couple of typographical corrections (SJT).

for reasons of taboo and it may be that you are similarly being cut off from important areas of thought because breach of taboo might endanger the healer's potency.

I think your pursuit of what you call "ethno-ethnology"... the categories by which Temiar themselves specify their difference from "the others" is a most important and quite first rate line of attack.

(Leach to Benjamin, late 1964, probably December)

1. Running through the whole set [of Temiar myths] is the theme that the "first men" were male not female. This poses the question of how do they reproduce without committing incest. The solutions offered are: first women are (a) ants (b) rats (c) fish (d) unspecified females. But in the case of (d) the puzzle is unresolved since it appears that these females are the "same as" their male spouses... Engku and Aluj *themselves* seem to become pregnant.

2. The first woman, a "non-human" creature of Nature, seems to be linked with a very ambivalent attitude towards (a) women in general (b) affines. The "rat" story especially seems to equate "rats" with witchcraft of a destructive kind. If so, there is a direct equivalent here with Kachin ideology where *yu* = affine (*mayu*) = rat = witchcraft. (The logic of this association is that rats work destructively in a mysterious way, destroying the food when it is safely in store or in the ground.)

3. Of these original non-human affines, the fish clearly fall into a normal "edible" category. Do Temiar really eat either ants or rats?

(Leach to Benjamin, late 1964, probably December)

As you point out these nice antitheses ultimately run into a contradiction. Good versus evil should also stand for evil versus good. But this is also very Lévi-Straussian. In his new book [*Le cru et le cuit*] the structure of myth is compared in a most involved way with the structure of music. You will appreciate this much better than I do, but I think I am right in saying that in any serious music the crux of the matter is the point at which the sensitive listener is led to a crisis, a kind of contradiction in which the next note is not what you expect but what you don't expect. This too is fundamental in myth. One line of logic must lead to a hypothesis that the wild outside is the other world full of dangerous powers where are located the spirits of the dead. This wild outside is in this sense a source of evil. But from another point of view the tame inside is where the living human beings actually reside and suffer misfortune and the other world where things are perfect and which is a source of benefits must also therefore be located in the wild outside. So I did not find it at all surprising that it is in this area that you find the inconsistencies in Temiar myth and ritual. I find it especially interesting that it seems to be almost explicit that everything will be alright if you keep your categories distinct. On the other hand not only do illnesses result from confusing categories, but also the power of the Hatar seems to depend upon his special abilities in bridging categories. The prototype deity who was the first Hatar is a human being who is also a non-human being, and he is an earth-bound creature who can visit the sky. But that's enough. You are doing a terrific job.

(Leach to Benjamin, May 10, 1965)

CHAPTER 5

"The Political Systems of Highland Burma"

Leach's first major work, *Political Systems of Highland Burma*, is widely regarded as a landmark in political anthropology. It is a classic, still widely read as a set text, and in the eyes of many arguably his best book. This masterpiece already contains many of the issues he grappled with throughout his career: his critique of many of the orthodoxies of "structural-functionalism" *à la* Radcliffe-Brown, his admiring engagement with Lévi-Straussian "structuralism" as deployed in *The Elementary Structures of Kinship*, and simultaneously his rejection of some of the substantive, methodological, and theoretical submissions in that book, and thirdly, his attempt to straddle and combine some features of "functionalist" empiricism and pragmatism with "structuralist" rationalism and deductive formalism (an exercise with philosophical ramifications that engaged Leach more consciously in later years).

Leach has remarked that his first book, among other things, is "organized as a kind of dialogue between the empiricism of Malinowski and the rationalism of Lévi-Strauss and these two contrasted strands of my thinking should be apparent to the reader in all my later writings."[1]

In another version of his relation to the two perspectives that would engage and stretch his mind, Leach said that "first indoctrinated by Malinowski and Firth" he was "at the outset a 'pure' empirical functionalist. Much after I was greatly influenced by the very unempirical structuralism of Lévi-Strauss. This came about because Lévi-Strauss's first magnum opus, *The Elementary Structures of Kinship*, the first edition of which was published in 1949, makes great use of the ethnography of the Kachin of North Burma, a people among whom I had lived during much of the period, 1939–45." Antithetically, he added that "a great deal of the ethnography on which Lévi-Strauss had relied was quite inaccurate, but

---

[1] Leach, *Social Anthropology*, p. 44.

Figure 5.1. Edmund Leach during fieldwork in the Kachin Hills of northern Burma (credit: Louisa Brown).

I also knew from first hand experience that a number of [Lévi-Strauss's] insights concerning this society were very penetrating."[2]

One of Leach's achievements in *Political Systems of Highland Burma* was to argue against the view that "the boundaries of society and the boundaries of culture can be treated as coincident" and thereby powerfully to dissolve the older ethnographic fixation on tribes as bounded entities and wholes, and to unveil for our viewing a landscape of highland Burma as an open system of many lineages linked in circles of wife-givers (*mayu*) and wife-takers (*dama*), communicating with one another diacritically through variations of dialect, dress, and other local differences, and capable of dynamically generating as well as contesting tendencies toward extra-local hierarchical political formations. It was a model of an open-ended system, constrained but not determined by certain "objective" conditions, and capable of an expanding multiplication as well as incorporation of new lineage segments. In this way he changed extant notions of tribes, ethnic identity, and repetitive equilibrium as timeless static ontological entities of anthropology. The book also proposed a stimulating view of the patterning of myth and ritual and their role in political action, and grappled in an exploratory way with the integrated use of historical materials in anthropological analysis.

In a separate essay, "The Structural Implications of Matrilateral Cross-Cousin Marriage,"[3] published in 1951, some three years before *Political Systems*, Leach had already produced the first English-language commentary on Lévi-Strauss's *The Elementary Structures of Kinship* especially as it bore on his Kachin materials. As Leach saw it, Lévi-Strauss's exposition of the Kachin (and other highland Burmese societies, such as the Chin and Haka Chin) was in terms of a formal scheme of generalized exchange deriving from the premises of descent and marriage rules. Lévi-Strauss theorized that the generalized exchange of the Kachin type based on asymmetrical matrilateral cross-cousin marriage would automatically transform egalitarian circles into ranked hierarchies (and ultimately break the exchange ring) because of the accumulation of women at one end accompanied by speculative inflation in bride prices.

According to Lévi-Strauss the matrilateral cross-cousin marriage pattern establishes a system of exchange of women that is directional, in that the wife-takers from one group must in turn be the wife-givers to a third, and so on. As a result there is a greater element of risk (compared

---

[2] Ibid., p. 44.
[3] Edmund Leach, "The Structural Implications of Matrilateral Cross-Cousin Marriage," *Journal of the Royal Anthropological Institute*, vol. 81, 1951, pp. 23–55.

with patrilateral cross-cousin marriage) in this form of marriage in that one group when giving up a woman must assume that the other group will eventually give them a woman at a later period. This introduces the possibility of speculation, for groups may be able to hoard women if they are in an advantageous position politically and economically.[4] With the practice of polygamy, hierarchical relations can develop through the accumulation of women, and the resulting accumulation of affines. Thus the social organization generated from this kind of marriage pattern develops feudal tendencies. The conditions of equal, stable reciprocity start to break down, as some groups gain in status and material goods. The system can regain stability either by regressing into a system of restricted exchange, or by developing into a complex structure of kinship, where elements such as chance and personal choice become principles of marriage (as in the modern West).[5]

In the above mentioned 1951 essay, Leach set out to demonstrate that the Kachin *gumsa* type social order was not inherently unstable and threatened with break up by virtue of *internal intra-kinship* processes generated by the marriage rules toward greater and greater inequality and imbalances as Lévi-Strauss maintained; what has to be considered in a fuller analysis is how arrangements by which women travel "down" and marriage goods move "up" in compensation are interlocked with territorial sovereignty, land tenure, and patron–client relations, so as to maintain in dynamic tension a stratified political system of the *gumsa* type. Leach provides an elegant analysis of how the prescriptive marriage exchange among the Kachin is integrally linked up with and sustained by the wider political and economic circumstances, and here we see his version of structuralism and functionalism displayed at its best. It should be noted however that Leach appears to be asserting that the *gumsa* system can be presented as stable and in equilibrium in terms of a "model," but that in fact it was an "unstable" form owing to various dynamic processes which are described in the book.

The Kachin *gumsa* ranked categories consist of, first, a chiefly class at the top (say three chiefs of a district domain marrying in a circle, being *mayu/dama* to one another, and forming a loose political federation, and second, an aristocratic class of village headmen who marry daughters of the chiefs above and also marry women of their own status, thereby forming a loose inter-village union. The headmen's rights over village land

[4] Claude Lévi-Strauss, *The Elementary Structures of Kinship*, trans. J. H. Bell et al., London: Eyre & Spottiswoode, 1969, p. 265.
[5] Ibid., p. 475.

are validated by their respective chiefs who are their territorial overlords. The last level is the commoner class, who form intra-village local circles. The senior members of the commoner local descent groups, together with the village headman who heads his own descent group, control the affairs of the village. This stratum takes wives from the aristocrats above them and also marries in *mayu–dama* exchange among themselves. Thus Leach demonstrated that "matrilateral cross-cousin marriage plays an integral part not only in maintaining this class structure but in defining 'feudal' relationships between chiefs, headmen and commoners."[6] In the totality of relations three dimensions were simultaneously correlated, affirmed, and fused – political (the feudal relations between chiefs, headmen, and commoners), territorial (differential land tenure rights in terms of "landlords" and "tenants"), and kinship (especially *mayu–dama* as father-in-law and son-in-law). Affinal alliances are also one of political subordination and economic dependence. *Vis-à-vis* Lévi-Strauss's "mechanistic" model deriving from kinship categories and marriage rules themselves taken as structuring the system, Leach was arguing that kinship structures *per se* should not be essentialized and reified as formal systems containing an exhaustive internal logic, but should be explicated in terms of how actors use and manipulate them within the larger political economy, which, while providing directives and incentives to action, is also in turn constituted and changed by the dynamic strategizing acts and normative ideological constructs of the actors.[7]

One issue in the exchange between the two proud and unyielding stalwarts concerned ethnographic facts: Lévi-Strauss had been mistaken in thinking that women moved upwards "hypergamously" thus creating the demographic and social inequities and bottlenecks at the top.[8] Leach,

---

[6] Leach, "Matrilateral Cross-Cousin Marriage," p. 84.

[7] This in my view is an instance and an occasion in which Leach's structural and functional perspectives meet and combine to illuminate and come close to Bourdieu's theoretical ambition stated years later in formal terms in *Outline of a Theory of Practice* to combine "rules" with "practices," to steer clear of "mechanistic sociology" and "spontaneous voluntarism," and to track the relation between objective structures, the cognitive and motivating dispositions they shape (habitus), the strategies of action to realize practical aims in social situations, and the final outcome as "practices" ("regulated improvisations"), which recursively have a feedback effect on objective structures. (Whether in fact Bourdieu has actually realized this ambition is a debatable matter that need not concern us here.) Unlike Bourdieu, who has attempted to produce a systematized theory of practice with an attendant set of concepts, Leach as I have remarked before was uninterested in such ambitious theorizing, and implicitly illustrated the relation between semantics and pragmatics, structuralism and functionalism, cultural rules and individuals' manipulating to maximize their power and status by means of empirically oriented analyses.

[8] On the basis of my understanding of the ethnography I would venture this opinion: the Kachin system of "hypogamy," women marrying down and bridewealth moving up, does not cause a

who possessed direct authoritative empirical knowledge, had established that the direction of exchange was such that women moved in one direction (from higher-status wife-givers to lower-status wife-takers) and bridewealth and other marriage goods went in the opposite direction (thereby materially advantaging the wife-givers). When Lévi-Strauss responded that he would now substitute the term *anisogamy* for movement of women in either direction, Leach replied that this move did not save his model which was *empirically* wrong in misunderstanding the direction of passage of women and goods. This perhaps was the origin of their testy dissent,[9] and a prelude to other differences that would be aired later. In the last section of this chapter, I shall review in greater detail, for the benefit of kinship specialists, the controversy between Leach and Lévi-Strauss regarding the interpretation of the Kachin marriage system.

To return to *Political Systems*, "my most influential book," Leach was to remark that at LSE and at Cambridge, "its 'idealist' standpoint provoked hostile comment in both localities ... The notion that the persisting element in social relationships is a patterned structure of verbal concepts (which are open to very diverse interpretations) rather than a patterned structure of empirically observable 'groups' knit together by mysterious 'ether' called 'kinship' was as repugnant to Fortes in 1980 as it had been in 1954."[10] This remark brings us to another critical theoretical and philosophical position first espoused in this book, and subsequently reiterated in many other writings, but apparently not fully comprehended by many of his readers, and in any case capable of generating disputes as to what Leach was actually saying and whether he was being altogether clear and consistent in his exposition.

Leach's assertion in *Political Systems* was that events and behavior on the ground are "only seen as structured when they are ordered by means

dearth of women at the top stratum because chiefs and aristocrats, who are demographically a minority, have the political influence and lineage prestige to have multiple wives (and concubines) (polygyny), and they therefore procreate enough women for taking wives of equal status among themselves and for giving daughters in marriage to those of headman and commoner status. Polygyny however was not a widespread institution, thus there is no reason for a demographic problem of shortage of women dislocating the system. Lévi-Strauss would not have been off the mark if the Kachin system of marriage was "hypergamous" (women marrying men of higher status with dowries going with them in the same direction) as, for instance, happens in many parts of north India. This kind of asymmetry does cause imbalances and encourages periodic counter-moves toward abolishing high dowries and encouraging endogamy.

9 See Leach, " 'Kachin' and 'Haka Chin'; A Rejoinder to Lévi-Strauss," *Man*, n.s., vol. 4, no. 2, 1969, pp. 277–85; also Leach, "Imaginary Kachins," *Man*, n.s., vol. 18, no. 1, 1983 pp. 191–99 for Leach's critique of an essay by Nugent on the Kachins.

10 Leach "Glimpses," p. 20.

of verbal categories."[11] The three categories of ideal political order that the Kachin themselves used in their political dialogs were *gumlao* and *gumsa*, which were respectively "democratic egalitarian" and "ranked-aristocratic" in their connotations and gave conceptual gloss and a mental ordering to their own activities; and the third, *shan*, which pertained to the monarchical/feudal conceptual ordering of the neighboring valley-centred people.

With regard to the Kachin verbal categories, Leach performed the further interpretive act of formalizing their contrasting relations as models in the following way. The prescriptive "matrilateral cross-cousin marriage" implies the ritual superiority of wife-giver (*mayu*) to wife-taker (*dama*). Under certain circumstances this ritual asymmetry may be converted to differences of rank, and may find expression as the *gumsa* model (which was spelled out earlier) in which asymmetrical marriage alliances can link up chiefly lineages to headmen's lineages and these in turn to commoner lineages supported by differences of land rights and residence, political authority, patron–client relations, and so on.

The *gumlao* category is envisaged as an ordering whereby the marriage alliances link up groups with local lineages of equal status. The rules of succession to local lineage office among the Kachin favor *ultimogeniture*, which thereby carries a structural contradiction, in that the eldest son, superior in age status to his youngest brother, is motivated to break away, migrate, and set up his own *gumlao* local group or community.

In Leach's language *gumlao* and *gumsa* categories are "transformations" of each other in the mathematical/structuralist sense. The *shan* model is predicated on entirely different principles – for example, the *shan* chief who is polygamous receives wives and concubines as "tributes" from his petty chiefs and political subordinates, and as wife-taker is superior to the givers, thus reversing the Kachin *mayu–dama* evaluation; and the building blocks of *shan* monarchical polity are not segmentary descent lineages. A fundamental misunderstanding is generated when a Kachin chief gives a wife to a *shan* prince: the former in his own terms as *mayu* is the ritual superior; the latter in accepting a tributary gift from a political subordinate is in his terms the superior overlord. Therefore the *shan* model is not a transformation of the *gumlao–gumsa* dyad; individual *gumsa* Kachin chiefs may try to "become" *shan* by adopting *shan* pretensions and

---

[11] Introductory note to the 1964 reprint of Leach, *Political Systems*, p. IX. Leach refers to Vilfredo Pareto's *Traité de Sociologie Générale*, edited by Pierre Boven, Lausanne and Paris: Paget & Cie., 1917–19, and to its English translation, *The Mind and Society*, edited by Arthur Livingston, New York: Dover Publications, 1963.

claims, but such developments are subverted by the Kachin themselves whose basic valuations and practices resisted this kind of political subjection. As Parry and Fuller put it: "Partly because a *gumsa* polity had a more precarious productive base, partly because a *gumsa* chief was liable to alienate his kinsmen by treating them like a Shan prince's subjects – which he could hardly afford to do since his wealth ... was in people rather than land – the nearer such polity got to the Shan model, the more likely it was overthrown by a 'democratic' rebellion."[12]

Now we are in a position to come to grips with Leach's famous thesis of "oscillating equilibrium," which asserted that over a period of 150 years, which is the historical time span he has dealt with, the Kachin communities may be seen as oscillating between the *gumlao–gumsa* poles. He was later to explain that this oscillating model was influenced and adapted from "Pareto's discussion of the alternating dominance of the 'lions' and the 'foxes' and his conception of a 'moving equilibrium.'"[13]

What did Leach try to convey and what polemical issues was he addressing in his model of "oscillating equilibrium?" This thesis generated discussion and criticisms, which Leach later addressed, and my exposition takes this into account. First of all he had in mind the alleged "static equilibrium" model of stereotype structural-functional theorists who described their societies as integrated wholes maintaining themselves over time in static or repetitive equilibrium. (Nor does his model, Leach asserted, have any affinity with Fortes's "developmental cycle" which is based on the empirical biological facts of life-cycle aging and how that affects the membership and structure through time of the domestic group.) His concern with historical process over a large span of time – to some extent communicated by Pareto's notion of moving equilibrium[14] – had led him to transform and formalize the indigenous Kachin categories into his own construction of an "as if" model, between whose poles could be situated particular Kachin communities in time and space. He repudiated those readings of his text that inferred that he

---

[12] Fuller and Parry, "Petulant inconsistency?" p. 12.

[13] Introductory note to the 1964 reprint of Leach, *Political Systems*, p. ix.

[14] Leach's reference to Pareto is brief, and some of his readers have been intrigued by his use of Pareto especially when he was little read by Anglo-American anthropologists. As far as I know Pareto was introduced to Anglo-American social scientists by Talcott Parsons in his *Structure of Social Action* published in 1937. I have inquired from Professor Raymond Firth whether Leach might have got to Pareto via Parsons, but this seems unlikely because Parsons was in London attending Malinowski's seminar around 1932–33, many years before Leach joined it in 1937 after his return from China. We may conclude that Leach had found Pareto on his own, and there is no evidence that he interacted or communicated with Parsons at the time of writing *Political Systems*.

was saying that Kachin communities mechanically and inevitably moved through an everlasting cyclical process, with the additional connotations of a historical determinism that such a view carried. There were two kinds of processes that he adduced to counter this reading. Over a span of time particular communities may stay put or move at different paces and in different directions, and there is no way in which all these circumstances could be aggregated or summed up as constituting one integral total moving equilibrium system, or a system moving unidirectionally.

Leach expanded on the complicated dynamics of individual Kachin communities in this way:

There are instances of present day *gumlao* type in which we find a tradition that "formerly, x generations ago, we had chiefs," and then there was a rebellion in which the chiefs got killed or driven out. On the other hand, if we look today at those localities which are, by tradition, the focal points of the *gumlao* system, we usually find communities of the *gumsa* type, or something extremely close to this type. I do not claim that this evidence is sufficient to prove that over a period there is always a constant oscillation between the polar extremes of *gumsa* and *gumlao*, but I think there is a very strong suggestion that this is sometimes and often the case . . .

The asymmetry of the *mayu–dama* relationship is, as it were, inconsistent with the dogma of status equality between lineages which dominates *gumlao* theory; consequently a *gumlao* community which adheres to *mayu–dama* rules rather easily slips into practices of a *gumsa* type . . .

My hypothesis is that a *mayu–dama* type marriage rule will never be found associated with *stable* types of *gumlao* organization. Where *mayu–dama* rules and *gumlao* organization are found in association, then the latter may be regarded as a transitional phase.[15]

Secondly, even if in chapters 7 and 8 of his book he had proposed that the outcome for any one part of the Kachin region was "a long-phase political oscillation," the facts at the end of the cycle are quite different from the facts at the beginning, and the "system on the ground" is not in equilibrium in the same way as the "system of ideas." Moreover, the flux is not a social automatism produced by the marriage rules and other "internal" constraints:

the ultimate "causes" of social change are, in my view, nearly always to be found in changes in the external political and economic environment; but the form which any change takes is largely determined by the existing internal structure of a given system. In this case, the *gumlao* order and the *gumsa* order are both unstable; in situations of external disturbance the tendency is for *gumlao* systems

---

[15] Leach, *Political Systems*, pp. 210–11.

to turn into *gumsa* and *gumsa* to turn into *gumlao* ... I do not claim to be able to predict what will happen to any particular community in any particular circumstance.[16]

Leach's "as if" model related to a "set of verbal categories" with which the Kachin themselves "interpret to themselves and others the empirical social phenomena which they observe around them." Leach clarified that there is a clear distinction (which he admitted might have been blurred at some points in the original text) between *gumsa–gumlao* as ideal type thought categories and their correspondence to the "empirical facts on the ground." The categories must not be equated with actual relations, a mistake persistently committed by Radcliffe-Brown and his followers. Moreover, "Kachin verbal usage allows the speaker to structure his categories in more than one way," and in the political dialog with their opponents, they may make "different assumptions about the relations between the categories."

Leach's explication of the gap between "ideal categories" and "actual behavior", "rule and practice" focused on how individual Kachin actors driven by self-interested power motives instrumentally manipulated the ambiguous meanings and contested the application of those categories to their on-the-ground situation. And when wearing this hat, Leach would argue that

to the individual himself [different social systems] present themselves as alternatives or inconsistencies in the scheme of values by which he orders his life. The overall process of structural change comes about through the manipulation of these alternatives as a means of social advancement. Every individual of a society, each in his own interest, endeavours to exploit the situation as he perceives it and in so doing the collectivity of individuals alters the structure of the society itself.[17]

Entitled "The Structural Categories of Kachin *Gumsa* Society," chapter 5 of *Political Systems* is crucial, for it is there that Leach begins to expound and develop his "dynamic theory" as Firth characterized it, that distinguishes his kind of anthropology from the structural anthropology of Radcliffe-Brown and Meyer Fortes who aspired to delineate "principles of organization" that constituted a "system" in equilibrium. Rather Leach was concerned to expound how the main "categories" and concepts of Kachin society were dynamically "used as symbols in arguments about status and obligation."

[16] Ibid., p. 212.   [17] Ibid., p. 8.

The array of "categories" reviewed is long and exhaustive, ranging from territorial divisions and groupings through property and rank to supernatural beliefs and political and religious offices, but one interesting point of exposition was that, compared with analytical terms in English (frequently employed by anthropologists), the Kachin applications and understandings of *their* terms especially in the social arena are wider, or less specific, and more ambiguous, and it is this fluidity of context-bound usage, integrally linked to the situation, application, and interests of the individual actor employing those "symbols", that provides the *nexus* and the disjunction or elasticity between "ideal rules" and norms and "actual practices." This it seems to me is the way Leach creatively incorporates and transforms the insights of Malinowski's loose talk about individuals acting to pursue their self-interest, and Firth's more complex treatment of the twin concepts of social structure and social organization.

Leach had already propounded the thesis that myths (and genealogical claims) might vary from individual to individual according to the status, group affiliation, and other circumstances of the teller; there is no "true" version of a myth, but many versions of a type that provide a common focus for contestation and dialog.

Let me cite from chapter 5 a few examples which grapple with the issue of "translation" of the other's usages into anthropological English, and the simultaneously implicated issue of the relation between ideal concept and action on the ground. First Leach states that

There is one particular characteristic which all concepts here discussed have in common which seems to be of fundamental importance. In every case the meaning of the Kachin concept, when translated into English, appears in some degree vague and ambiguous. In English, for example, it may seem unsatisfactory that a simple term which I translate as "village" should denote an aggregate of any number of houses from one upwards . . . a Kachin does not notice the ambiguity, it is simply that in the field of ideas with which we are dealing, Kachins habitually use broader verbal categories than we do.[18]

Leach then launches the criticism that in their recent work on Africa some anthropologists

have been tempted by vagueness of this kind to introduce new more specific categories of their own which have no equivalents in the native language. In my view this is methodologically a mistake. If one attempts to interpret a social

---

[18] Leach quickly remarks that as regards rice agriculture "the Kachin has a language of the utmost precision, whereas English has practically no vocabulary at all. But in matters social, it is English which is the more precise language" (*Political Systems*, p. 105).

structure by means of analytical categories which are more precise than those which people use themselves, one injects into the system a specious rigidity and symmetry which may be lacking in the real life situation.

In my view the ambiguity of the native categories is absolutely fundamental to the operation of the Kachin social system. It is easy enough to produce a neat paradigm of the Kachin kinship system and demonstrate its beautiful symmetries . . . *It is only because the meaning of his sundry structural categories is, for a Kachin, extremely elastic that he is able to interpret the actuality of his social life as conforming to the formal pattern of the traditional, mythologically defined, structural system.*[19] (emphasis added)

Thus the important Leachian point: "the ideal structure" of Kachin society is both elaborate and rigid, while the "real" or "actual" Kachin society is flexible in form.

Second:

People of the same lineage, whatever the scale, may be described as "brothers" (*kahpu-kanauni*), or as of the same "sort" (*amyu*), or of the same "branch" (*lakung*), or of the same "hearth" (*dap*). These words are used interchangeably and one cannot distinguish consistently the degree of segmentation as conveyed by the expressions such as "maximal lineage", "medial lineage", "minimal lineage" and the like. Nor is there any clear distinction between exogamous and non-exogamous levels of segmentation . . . Finally one cannot distinguish between actual and putative descent.[20]

Every Kachin chief is prepared to trace his descent back to the Creator, and in this operation to put forward genealogies of forty or more generations.

It is quite impossible to assert at what point such descent lines become purely fictional. My own point of view is that Kachin genealogies are maintained almost exclusively for structural reasons and have no value at all as evidence of historical fact. Commoners are only interested in genealogy as a means of establishing correct relations with their immediate neighbours in the same community; the genealogies of commoners are consequently usually short, four or five remembered generations at the most. Chiefs on the other hand are concerned to establish their legitimacy as members of a "youngest son" lineage and also to establish their seniority to other chiefs over a wide area.[21]

Third Leach illustrates similar flexibility in the application of "concepts of affinal relationships."[22] Thus formal rules of exogamy say that a man shall not marry a woman born of his own lineage; but classificatory "brothers" and "sisters" of *lawu-lahta* status (belonging to lineages of

---

[19] Ibid., p. 106.   [20] Ibid., pp. 126–27.   [21] Ibid., p. 127.   [22] Ibid., pp. 136–40.

distant or inadequate connection) frequently marry. Similarly, marriage between classificatory "father's sister's daughter" (*hkri*) and classificatory "mother's brother's son" (*tsa*), although in theory incestuous (*jaiwawng*), and considered intolerable if the partners come from the same local community, is possible if they belong to different local communities. Theory and practice of what is allowable in the way of extra-marital relations is even more vaguely defined.[23]

What do all these complex moves and clarifications amount to in the explication of Kachin political process "as shifts in the focus of political power" over a span of 100–150 years? In an important review, published in 1958, Ernest Gellner charged Leach with holding a position that was an "idealist error"[24] in so far as Leach emphasized verbalized thought categories as providing the phenomenological map for viewing and interpreting the world out there, but that the dynamic behavior of actors and the untidy "facts on the ground" did not bear a direct correspondence to the ideal categories which were manipulated for personal advancement in the power game. The persisting element in social relationships was a pattern structure of verbal concepts, open to diverse interpretations, rather than empirically observable and existing kin groups.

It may come as a surprise to many readers, including some of his disciples, that in fact while rejecting Gellner's attribution of "error," Leach did accept and did again and again explicate in the later decades of his career his "idealist" position, which he conjoined with his "humanist" and "empiricist" orientations. This idealist–humanist–empiricist position radically separated him from what he saw as Radcliffe-Brownian empiricism and quasi-rationalism which saw societies as "concrete" systems held together by principles of kinship and descent, and theoretically capable of being represented in "the method of science involving observation, classification and generalization," in short a natural science of society. According to Radcliffe-Brown, "The fundamental problems . . . [of a theoretical science must] depend on the systematic comparison of a number of societies of sufficiently diverse types."[25] Leach's objections are that aside from the myopia of structural functionalists regarding the

---

[23] Kachin concepts relating to debt (*hka*), "wealth objects" (*hpaga*), land tenure, rank, and class, including the connotation of *gumsa* status, etc., are also discussed by Leach as subject to similar inconsistencies and flexibilities between theory and practice. Ibid., pp. 141–95.

[24] Ernest Gellner, "Time and Theory in Social Anthropology," *Mind* (N.S.), vol. 67, no. 266, April 1958.

[25] See Edmund Leach, "Social Anthropology: A Natural Science of Society?" Radcliffe-Brown Lecture, 1976, published in the *Proceedings of the British Academy*, vol. 62, 1976, pp. 157–80. In this lecture Leach assembled in one place all the objections he had to the Radcliffe-Brown brand of structural functionalism.

issue of "the lack of fit between ideal categories and empirical discontinuities," their static classificatory types failed to see their societies "as continuously adaptive sub-systems within an unbounded matrix."[26] In other words, Leach came to underscore as part of his credo what he already had perceived in *Political Systems*, that "historical process" is an open-ended process that cannot be represented in causal determinative evolutionary terms.

Leach's ultimate philosophical-anthropological position which combined idealism, humanism, and empiricism is best spelled out in chapter 14 at a more appropriate point in relation to the contrastive positions of realism, rationalism, and weak empiricism[27] he attributed to some of Lévi-Strauss's writings, although he shared much with Lévi-Strauss as a "structuralist," with whose views his own converged in many ways.

Here let me close this discussion of *Political Systems* by raising an issue regarding the implications of Leach's "idealist view" of the Kachin actors' own ideal categories of *gumsa–gumlao* for the representation of "history." In his introductory note to the 1964 edition, and much later again in 1984 in "Glimpses," Leach gives a few hints as to how he might now develop better what he had struggled to see in 1954. The book had been "concerned with the theme that empirical political behaviour among the Kachin is a compromise response to the polarised political doctrines of *gumsa* and *gumlao*" and with how "these polar doctrines are actually presented to the actor through the medium of conflicting mythologies, any of which might conveniently serve as a charter for social action." Lévi-Strauss's writings on myth, which appeared subsequently, might further advance our understanding of Kachin tradition.

Much later, after the lapse of some thirty years, Leach would return to the issue of the nature of historical writing in terms of the actors' perceptions and formulation rather than in terms of the categories and schema of the (Western) observer, and at the same time combine with it the related but different, what may be termed "postmodern," concern regarding the impact of the ethnographer's presence on those studied and the degree of validity of the authorial claim to objective reporting.

---

[26] Ibid., p. 160.

[27] An example is Leach saying that despite some intriguing insights on the part of Lévi-Strauss, there was "a very wide discrepancy between the details of the [Kachin] ethnography and what Lévi-Strauss had supposed to be the case . . . I was shocked to discover that he himself was in no way put out by these discrepancies; he blandly assured his readers that my ethnography must be wrong! From then on I knew that when it came to the crunch I was just as much an empiricist as any of my British colleagues" ("Glimpses," p. 18).

In this context he drew attention to the writings of Marshall Sahlins and Valerio Valeri on Hawaii and his excitement about them. Though he does not clarify the thoughts stimulated by them, I infer two themes that lie embedded in the Kachin book capable of further elaboration. On the one hand, Leach mused that he had in a pioneering and groping way tried to see in Kachin thought and action how *they* formulated for themselves via myth, ritual, speech acts, etc., the way they saw their "historical" process unfolding. We now perceive more clearly how to read historical ethnography from the point of view of the observed rather than the observer. To this positive achievement, Leach linked another radical but less well thought out or argued submission. He seemed to come to the realization much more sharply than before "that in no circumstances has the 'European' observer – anthropologist, missionary, ship's captain, traveller – ever been able to give an objective account of the 'manners and customs of primitive society.' The very fact that the observer was there at all completely altered the nature of what was observed. The 'Death of Cook' business is an extreme example, but the case is general."[28]

The assertion that the "observer's presence completely altered the nature of what was observed," stated in this unqualified absolutist manner, would be questioned in many quarters, and can readily be shown to be at odds with Leach's idealist–empiricist position set out in *Political Systems*, and as we shall see, reinforced with a materialist bent in *Pul Eliya* (examined in chapter 7). Moreover, it is not quite the view espoused by Sahlins and Valeri who also have carried further the task of writing history in terms of the actors' categories.

However, toward the end of his career in the 1980s, Leach was, without repudiating his own past, voicing the controversial claim that "all ethnography is fiction," as for example in a paper given in 1987 at the Association of Social Anthropologists conference on "History and Ethnicity."[29]

We shall comment later on what Leach might have meant by this assertion and whether it was expressed in anticipation of, and sensitivity to, what would become unsettling "postmodern issues." Already early in his career he was reaching for answers to questions that few, if any, of his

---

[28] Marshall Sahlins, *Islands of History*, Chicago: University of Chicago Press, 1985. Leach also mentioned in the same context Valerio Valeri *Kingship and Sacrifice: Ritual and Society in Ancient Hawaii*, Chicago: University of Chicago Press, 1985.

[29] See Edmund Leach, "Tribal Ethnography: Past, Present, Future," published in *Cambridge Anthropology*, vol. 11, no. 2, 1987, pp. 1–14; reprinted under the same title in E. Tonkin, M. McDonald, and M. Chapman (eds.), *History and Ethnicity*, London: Routledge, 1989, pp. 34–47.

contemporaries mulled over. How the anthropologist is to read the colonial texts of administrators, missionaries, and travelers – in which Leach had immersed himself – and from then infer how their power-imbued presence and interventions impacted on events and outcomes, and how their own assumptions and preconceptions affected what they saw and recorded, judged and tried to change; how far one can visualize what the "indigenous" people observed themselves, said among themselves and to the "observers", and what the relation of the latter was to "empirical" happenings on the ground; these and many more issues already broached in *Political Systems* will engage us for many more years. Parry and Fuller have correctly opined that Leach's "attempt to grapple with the problems of history and a culturally specific 'historicity' was years ahead of its time."[30]

THE DISPUTE BETWEEN LEACH AND LÉVI-STRAUSS

Two buffaloes can't share the same wallow. (Kachin saying)

In this section I review the famous and perhaps fateful dispute between Leach and Lévi-Strauss concerning the characterization of the Kachin marriage and socio-political system.

For the benefit of the imaginary "ordinary reader" I have set out in the preceding section of this chapter the main features of Leach's characterization of Kachin society. The dispute between Leach and Lévi-Strauss involves arguments regarding the accuracy of ethnographic data cited and the interpretations based on them. There are many technical and specialized issues at stake, and only professional anthropologists (and not all of them) will be able to or want to follow them. But the exchange had and still has much relevance for the practice of anthropology, and fully deserves close attention. In Lévi-Strauss's first French edition of *The Elementary Structures of Kinship* (*Les structures élémentaires de la parenté* [1949]), the Kachins figured centrally in his theory of generalized exchange (Part II chapters 15–18). He had based his account on written sources but had no first-hand experience of Kachin life. Leach, who spent the years 1939–43 in the field in Upper Burma, and also knew the extant sources, began publishing essays on the Kachin in 1945 and 1951, followed by the book *Political Systems of Highland Burma* (1954). As will become clear soon, Leach, while entranced by some of Lévi-Strauss's insights and interpretations, nevertheless was in some places trenchantly critical of Lévi-Strauss

---

[30] "Petulant inconsistency?" Fuller and Parry, p. 13.

on both ethnographic and theoretical grounds. Lévi-Strauss had played an important role as a dialogical catalyst for Leach's own writing. He took account of Leach's criticisms in the French and English reissues of *Elementary Structures* in 1967 and 1969 respectively, was for the most part unyielding and defensive about the accuracy and plausibility of his original treatment of the Kachin, and moreover, implied that it was Leach who had come round to Lévi-Strauss's point of view in his 1954 book. This elicited a tense but forceful and effective reply from Leach in 1969.

The dispute was famous because it engaged the polemical skills of France's most eminent anthropologist and Britain's rising star and soon to be arguably its most prominent anthropologist. The dispute significantly affects my narrative biography of Leach.

The dispute about the Kachin, although intermittent and spasmodic, nevertheless stretched over some eighteen years (1951–1969) and strained the relationship between the two men. By and large, despite *some* overtures, they were distanced in personal terms. In the meantime, as on the very different topic of myth analysis, there were friendly exchanges between them in the years 1962–66, during which time Leach, influenced by Lévi-Strauss's structuralist analysis of myth, had himself begun to engage in his own style of myth analysis, especially of biblical materials. Thus many of his subsequent writings that extended into the 1970s portray the manner in which Lévi-Strauss was both a stimulant and a foil for Leach's own explorative and experimental writing, and for his creative melding of structuralist and functionalist perspectives.

The reader should keep in mind that the Kachin dispute was alive over a long period of time, and its continuation has to be interwoven with the developments and change of direction in Leach's own work in the 1960s and later. I shall now lay out the nature and course of the Kachin controversy in some detail.

Korn and Needham state:

There are three editions of Lévi-Strauss' work "on elementary structures of kinship": the first edition of 1949, the French reissue of 1967, and the English translation of 1969. The second French edition was quite extensively revised, and the translation [of 1969] contains some further variations. Readers who use the translation for any scholarly purpose will need to resort to the second French edition, not only to check the rendering of the argument but also to see whether even a minor discrepancy between the texts of the two versions will affect whatever point is at issue. The 1967 text, in its turn, will then demand comparison with the original version of 1949, in order that the extent and significance of the major revision may be gauged.[31]

These editorial remarks indeed bear importantly on the rights and wrongs of the controversy between Leach and Lévi-Strauss.

Leach's relevant writings on the Kachin are "Jinghpaw Kinship Terminology" (1945), "The Structural Implications of Matrilateral Cross-Cousin Marriage" (1951),[32] *Political Systems of Highland Burma* (1954), and " 'Kachin' and 'Haka Chin': A Rejoinder to Lévi-Strauss" (1969).

Before I recount and comment on the Leach–Lévi-Strauss dispute on the representation and interpretation of the Kachin system of marriage, it is important that I report the contents of a letter Lévi-Strauss wrote Leach in early 1950, recognizing the ethnographic significance of Leach's essay "Jinghpaw Kinship Terminology" and explaining that he was not able to take it into account in the first French edition of *Les structures élementaires de la parenté* (1949) because the book was already in press.[33]

The letter reads as follows:

> Laboratoire D'Ethnologie,
> Musée De L'Homme,
> January 28, 1950

Dear Professor Leach,

This is to thank you for your kind letter of January 26 together with the reprint of your paper on the Kachin system. I was already well acquainted with it having red [*sic*] it on its publication in the Journal of the Royal Anthropological Institute. Unfortunately at that time my book was already printed though not yet published and it was impossible to acknowledge even by a footnote the tremendous importance of your contribution. I am well aware that my two chapters on the Kachin need to be completely rewritten on the new basis provided by your material and you may rest assured that this will be done in case a second print or an english [*sic*] translation (there is some talk about it in the U.S.) gives me

---

[31] Francis Korn and Rodney Needham, *Lévi-Strauss on the Elementary Structures of Kinship : A Concordance to Pagination*, London: William Cloves & Sons, 1969. The three texts in question are: Claude Lévi-Strauss, *Les structures élémentaires de la parenté*, Paris: Presses Universités de France, 1949; *Les structures élémentaires de la parenté*, Paris and The Hague: Mouton, 1967; *The Elementary Structures of Kinship*, (Boston, MA: Beacon Press; London: Eyre & Spottiswoode, 1969; revised edition, translated from the French by J.H. Bell, J.R. von Sturmer, and R. Needham, and edited by Rodney Needham).

[32] Both republished in Leach, *Rethinking Anthropology*. My references to these essays are taken from this collection.

[33] Edmund Leach Archive 5/17, King's College Library, Cambridge.

the opportunity to do so. The extension of the system into the "remote" *mayu* and *dama* – to make use of a Gilyak expression – which you so aptly described is all the more important as it provides a link between a Gilyak and a [*sic*] Crow-Omaha types of kinship systems, a relationship which I have been suspecting for a very long time without having the operational means to demonstrate it. This is now available thanks to you.

Notwithstanding the technical points which you rightly correct (extension of the system, theoretical nature of the five clans cycle, etc.) it seems however that there is a basic agreement between us as regards the ultimate explanation of the system. It is true I have taken some liberties with the Haka Chin material. This I hope may be excused considering that I did not attempt to describe the ethnography of the Kachin but rather to define a specific pattern with the help, not only of Jinghpaw material but also of neighbouring types. As soon as I shall start on my next volume dealing this time with the "complex" structures I shall avail myself of your kind offer to elucidate the doubtful points. I shall also have many corrections to make in other chapters, especially the one on the Murgin about whom Prof. Elkin wrote me that he has fresh material and the chapters on India for which there are new contributions (Elwin on the Muria and others). Incidentally I was much interested to learn about Held's present whereabouts from your review of his last book in *Man* (we did not receive the book in Paris) and to hear that he still clings to his eight classes theory which I have discussed at length.

I am sending you by the same mail an old reprint on kinship which take [*sic*] up the problem in a slightly different way than in my book.

Thank you again for your kind attention please believe me,

Yours sincerely,
C. Lévi-Strauss

P.S. You will probably notice a very unfortunate slip on page 490 where in the description of the Lolo system "black" and "white" were inverted.

In the light of the controversy I shall now review, I leave it to the reader to judge whether Lévi-Strauss lived up to his promise that he would completely rewrite his two chapters on the Kachin on the basis of the new material provided by Leach, should a second printing of his French edition or an English translation of the text give him an opportunity to do so. There was indeed a reissue of the French edition in 1967 and an English translation in 1969, but these texts virtually ignore the 1945 essay, and are concerned with contesting Leach's 1951 essay on "The Structural Implications of Matrilateral Cross-Cousin Marriage" in which he launched his broadsides against Lévi-Strauss's flawed characterization of the Kachin system.

Leach's 1951 critique of Lévi-Strauss's sketch of the Kachin system of marriage

In his 1951 essay, Leach made some strongly worded criticisms of Lévi-Strauss's analysis of the Kachin system as discussed in the original 1949 French edition. Lévi-Strauss, using numerous earlier sources on the Kachin (e.g. Wehrli, Gilhodes, Hanson, Hertz, and a commentary by Granet) had attempted an extended analysis of the Kachin system as "a particularly favourable illustration" of "generalized exchange" which was a more "complex structure" than "restricted exchange."[34]

In that essay Leach begins his commentary on Lévi-Strauss's *Les structures élémentaires* with this "principle criticism of the book. . . that it attempts far too much" in the way of aiming at establishing, or at least indicating, "the general laws of development governing all Asiatic societies, ancient and modern, primitive and sophisticated. This enormous programme is only covered by adopting a decidedly cavalier attitude towards the facts of history and ethnography." Remarking that he was concerned in his essay "only with that part of Lévi-Strauss' argument which deals with Kachin type marriage," Leach launches his critique of Lévi-Strauss's "strictly logical deductions from the work of Hodson, Warner and Granet"[35] and his own reexamination of the original Kachin sources.

Leach states that Lévi-Strauss shows a tendency "to confuse descent lines with local lines." Lévi-Strauss, following his sources, describes Kachin society as made up of five exogamous patriclans which marry in a circle. Leach had already shown in his 1945 essay on "Jinghpaw Kinship Terminology" that this circular marriage system does not represent empirical fact but is simply a kind of verbal model which the Kachins themselves use to explain the general pattern of their system. The empirical situation however is as follows: the major clans are segmented into dispersed lineages, the exogamous unit is really the lineage at the lowest level of segmentation, and "in essentials, this smaller lineage is a local descent group associated with a particular domain (*mung*), though some members of it may reside elsewhere."[36]

---

[34] Lévi-Strauss, *Elementary Structures*, p. 233.

[35] Leach, "Matrilateral Cross-Cousin Marriage," p. 77. In his grand work, Lévi-Strauss stated that his theoretical objective is "to find the origin and regulatory function of kinship in all its forms," and furthermore to demonstrate "that all known and conceivable types of kinship and marriage can be integrated into one general classification, as methods of exchange, either restricted or generalized" (Lévi-Strauss, *Elementary Structures*, p. 233).

[36] Leach, "Matrilateral Cross-Cousin Marriage," p. 81.

Thus in practice the famous Kachin "wife-giving" – "wife-receiving" (*mayu–dama*) relationship is "the affair of local descent groups only. If there happen to be two groups in the same domain which, from the lineage point of view, are segments of the same clan, it is more than likely that they will intermarry and be in *mayu–dama* relationships."[37]

It is crucial to realize that Leach, the field researcher, foregrounds the importance of the pattern of interrelation between local descent groups in the political unit in a single contiguous area called the *mung*, the domain ruled by a chief. The area of the domain is usually segmented into village clusters (*mare*), and these again into villages (*kahtawng*): "the relationship between a village and its parent village cluster is in almost all respects, identical with that between a village cluster and its parent domain."[38] It is on this territorial, political, and local lineage group grid that Leach plotted the dynamic linkage between the levels of class stratification (chiefs, aristocrats, commoners), the formalized marriage links between them, and the land tenure organization (landlord–tenant relationship) in the *gumsa* type of social formation (which has been described earlier in this chapter).

While praising him, despite errors of ethnographic fact, for putting forward "several wholly original suggestions which are not only empirically valid, but are of the utmost importance for understanding the Kachin situation," Leach criticized Lévi-Strauss for seriously misunderstanding and confusing his sources on Kachin marriage. In particular he charged Lévi-Strauss with the "inexcusable carelessness" of assuming that W.R. Mead's statements in *Handbook of the Haka Chin Customs* (1917) about the Haka Chins were applicable to the Kachins. The blunder was that "not only are the Chins geographically remote from the Kachins, they do not so far as we know even practise Kachin type marriage."[39] Since there would be a heated exchange later about this accusation of confusion, it is relevant to note that in a footnote Leach further explained that "The Haka Chins are neighbours to the Lakher on one side who do practise Kachin type marriage, and to the Zahau Chins on the other, who do not. Concerning the Haka themselves there is no evidence."[40]

The crux of Lévi-Strauss's whole Kachin analysis in the 1949 text "turns upon two apparent paradoxes": the complex system of prestations in the preferential marriage exchanges, and poverty in terms of reference in contrast to richness in terms of address. Leach devastatingly replies

---

[37] Ibid., p. 81.　　[38] Ibid., p. 83.　　[39] Ibid., p. 78.　　[40] Ibid., p. 78, footnote 2.

that the system of prestations he cites is Chin and not Kachin, and that the second attribution "is simply an error of the literature," as can be seen from his own documentation in his 1945 essay on Jinghpaw terminology.

But there is more at stake stemming from Lévi-Strauss's deductions from the sources and Leach's characterization of the Kachin system based on his "fieldwork in the Kachin area at various times between 1939 and 1943", and his critical appraisal of the written sources. For Lévi-Strauss, the system of "generalized exchange" in his terminology, expressed by the exchange of women for goods in terms of asymmetrical cross-cousin marriage, was typified by the Kachin type of marriage. Following most of his predecessors in this field, Lévi-Strauss assumed that Kachin type marriage "necessarily implies a circular system of marriage clans of the general type A marries B, B marries C, C marries A." But Lévi-Strauss went further and on purely theoretical grounds reached the interesting conclusion that ideally Kachin type marriage operates in a circle, with wealth objects circulating in one direction and women in the other, and the status of the participating groups will remain equal. But this starting model can be subject to strain. In theory the system can be extended in either direction to include more groups, and the more of them there are the more impractical it will be to keep all transactions within the circle. "In practice, argues Lévi-Strauss, there will be competition for women; this will lead to an accumulation of women in one part of the circuit rather than in another, with a consequent development of brideprice differentials."[41]

Leach continues: Lévi-Strauss recognizes that despite their form of marriage Kachins are nevertheless reported as being a class-stratified society, and he infers "that despite the social difficulties that ensue, the acquisition of several women must be highly valued in Kachin society."[42] Now come two crucial observations by Leach which are at the heart of characterizing Kachin marriage. "The reader is clearly intended to infer that throughout the social structure *the wife receiving group will rank higher than the wife giving group, the nobles at the top being the accumulators of women*" (emphasis added).[43] Thus Lévi-Strauss imagined the intermarrying groups to be like "exogamous castes" which practice *hypergamy*, and "he goes on to argue that a similar rule may have been a factor in creating the Indian caste system as we know it."[44]

---

[41] Ibid., p. 80.   [42] Ibid., p. 80.   [43] Ibid., p. 80.   [44] Ibid., p. 80.

The following are Leach's statements of differences from Lévi-Strauss's characterization and his alternative account of "the genuine Kachin system" of the *gumsa* type.

The Kachin ideal, as Lévi-Strauss asserted, is that a series of *mayu–dama* lineages should marry in a circle; but he also perceived the system as becoming unstable as the number of units in a single network of relationships is increased: "Lévi-Strauss suggested that the instability will arise from competition to accumulate women from polygynous marriages; the empirical situation is that instability arises from a competition for bridewealth."[45]

Integral to Leach's account is the layout of a Kachin domain (*mung*). In a hypothetical domain consisting of a simple village cluster of four villages, each village has a hereditary headman, and one of these is also the chief of the whole domain:

The chief's "ownership" [of the domain] is recognized by the fact that all persons in the domain, who are not of his own lineage, must present him with a hind leg of any animal killed in sacrifice or in the hunt and by recognition that the same persons are under obligation to provide free labour for the chief on stated occasions, as at the clearing of the chief's field or the building of the chief's house. The village headman's ownership on the other hand is recognized in the fact that he disposes of the cultivation rights in the village lands among the householders of his village.[46]

Neither type of ownership can properly be said to include the right of alienation.

The political relationships between chief and village headman, and headman and villagers, may suggest some resemblances to those of English feudal tenure, but it is important to note that while there is "some clear difference of class status as between chief's local descent groups, village headman's local descent groups, and commoners' local descent groups ... *the class distinctions are defined namely in terms of the rights to non-utilitarian prestige symbols* [such as the right to make a particular kind of sacrifice or to put up a particular kind of housepost], *and the difference in the economic standards of aristocrats and commoners is normally very slight*" (emphasis added).[47] There are processes of lineage fission when lineages grow large – at all three class levels, the principle that the senior lineage is always the youngest son's line, directs the fission with those who are shed going "down hill." Thus the upper classes shed their

---

[45] Ibid., p. 80.   [46] Ibid., p. 83.   [47] Ibid., p. 83.

demographic surplus into the class below; in time the lineages which split away from aristocratic lineage tend to go down hill and become common lineages.

Leach drives home the critical differences between his characterization of the Kachin dynamics and that of Lévi-Strauss in these terms:

Matrilateral cross-cousin marriage plays an integral part not only in maintaining this class structure but in defining the "feudal" relationships between chiefs, headmen and commoners.

The two most general principles that govern the Kachin marriage system are that a man will do everything possible to avoid marrying into a class beneath him, and that a man will seek to make the maximum profit – either in terms of bride price or political advantage – out of the marriage of his daughters. Lévi-Strauss' view that polygyny is highly esteemed for its own sake is erroneous. The factors which influence chiefs (and sometimes village headmen) to acquire more than one wife are firstly the importance of having a male heir to carry on the local descent groups, and secondly the political advantage that comes from maintaining relations with several different *mayu* (wife-giving) groups at the same time.[48]

We have described earlier Leach's own schema for the manner in which marriage operates among the *gumsa* Kachins: the chiefly class in multiple domains marry in a "cousin circle path" among themselves, and pass on surplus women to the less aristocratic class of village headmen, who in turn do the same *vis-à-vis* the commoner class. This structure "is not, as Lévi-Strauss supposed, analogous to hypergamy in the Indian caste system, *but hypergamy reversed* [hypogamy]. Women may marry into their own class or the class below, but never into the class above" (emphasis added).

Leach proposed that his explication of how the *mayu–dama* (wife-giver–wife-taker) marriage tie was dynamically linked and fused with the political feudal and territorial landlord–tenant relations resolves what appeared to Lévi-Strauss as an outstanding paradox: if the Kachin system is ideally one of intermarrying egalitarian marriage classes, how come their brideprice payments are large and complex?[49]

Lévi-Strauss's explanation, says Leach, is that "these large brideprice payments are a kind of pathological symptom" representing the conflict between egalitarian generalized exchange and aristocratic

---

[48] Ibid., p. 84.
[49] Ibid., p. 85. "The class status implications of the Kachin marriage operate with much more marked effect among the aristocratic classes (who tend on the whole to marry near relatives) than among the commoner classes (who do not)": see n. 1, p. 87.

developments, and the tendency of marriage classes to convert themselves into privileged classes. Leach retorts: "Yet the system as I have
now described it is neither contradictory nor self-destructive." While it
is true that bridewealth moves from commoners toward aristocrats, and
from aristocrats toward chiefs, yet the main item in a brideprice is the
gift of cattle, and cattle among the Kachin are a consumable commodity.

On balance the chief does tend to accumulate wealth in the form of cattle. But
prestige does not come from the owning of cattle; it derives from the slaughter
of animals in religious feasts (*manau*). If a chief becomes rich as a consequence
of marriages or other legal transactions he merely holds *manau* at more frequent
intervals and on a larger scale, and his followers, who partake of the feast
benefit accordingly. Here is the element which is necessary to complete the
cycle of exchange transactions, the absence of which struck Lévi-Strauss as
paradoxical.[50]

Leach thus offered a cycle of accumulation and redistribution of cattle
through feasting (a thesis proposed earlier by H.N.L. Stevenson). "The
chief converts this perishable wealth [of cattle] into imperishable prestige
through the medium of spectacular feasting. The ultimate consumers of
the goods are in this way the original producers, namely the commoners
who attend the feast."[51]

While applauding Lévi-Strauss's important insight that the full recognition of the structural implications of marriage requires that marriage
be seen as one item in a whole series of transactions within kin groups,
Leach remarks that he yet fails to recognize that "the reciprocities of
kinship obligation are not merely symbols of alliance, *they are also economic
transactions, political transactions, charters to rights of domicile and land use.* No useful picture of 'how a kinship system works' can be provided unless these
several aspects or implications of kinship organisation are considered
simultaneously" (emphasis added).[52] In marriage exchange Lévi- Strauss
is fundamentally interested in the exchange of women and not at the same
time in the counter-prestation, and his inference of instability stems from
this. But at a more general level, Lévi-Strauss, following the theorizing of
certain others, considers kinship simply as a system in itself; if it is simply
considered without reference to its political, demographic, or economic
implications it is inevitably thought of as a logically closed system. (We
see Leach here enunciating his critique against what he called "pure
kinship" theories, a view that – to anticipate his subsequent writing – he

---

[50] Ibid., pp. 88–89.   [51] Ibid., p. 89.   [52] Ibid., p. 90.

would later in *Pul Eliya* elaborate in criticism of the structural-functional perspectives of Radcliffe-Brown, Evans-Pritchard, and Fortes.)

Lévi-Strauss's revisions and counter-attacks

In the French reissue of *Elementary Structures* (1967), and in the English translation of it (1969) which carried some additional changes, Lévi-Strauss stated his reply to Leach's critique of 1951, and also taking into account Leach's *Political Systems of Highland Burma* (1954), set out to vindicate his original sketch of the Kachin system. He countered that Leach's *Political Systems*, influenced by his own writings, told a different story from that given in his 1951 essay.

Recognizing that although Leach's full-length monograph, *Political Systems of Highland Burma* (1954), reports the results of fieldwork conducted in a manner more up to date and systematic than that of his predecessors, and that "his analysis of the Kachin kinship system is much more firm, complete and precise than his predecessors', and therefore infinitely preferable," Lévi-Strauss launched a lengthy and testy critique of Leach's 1951 essay. He writes in the 1969 English edition: "What I published in 1949 on the Kachin has been vigorously attacked, and on now re-reading the original text, it seems to me that it has much more often been distorted than really contradicted. It is true that, since his highly polemical article of 1951, Leach has been anxious to emphasize that he has drawn considerably closer to my point of view, but as he has republished this article in his book of 1961 [*Rethinking Anthropology*], I believe it necessary, without seeking a retrospective quarrel, to justify what I originally wrote."[53]

Levi-Strauss then proceeds to discuss the many criticisms made by Leach, none of which, in fact, seems to him to have any serious basis.[54] I shall selectively consider his major submissions.

Kachin and Ha Kachin

On the question of his assuming that Mead's statements about Haka Chins were applicable to the Kachins, Lévi-Strauss, while freely admitting to "having been perhaps over-eager in combining the two types," obdurately resisted giving any ground to Leach.

Leach himself had stated that the Kachin population speaks a number of different languages and dialects and that there are a number

---

[53] Lévi-Strauss, *Elementary Structures*, p. 233.   [54] Ibid., p. 235.

of different languages and dialects and wide differences of culture between one part of the area and another. In Leach's own words, "the
term Kachin designates a highly heterogeneous population consisting of
about 300,000 people scattered over an area of 50,000 square miles, a
rectangle roughly 250 miles long and 170 miles across . . . the southern
Kachin are closer to the Chin than they are to the northern Kachin."[55]

Furthermore, Leach himself has acknowledged that it is not language,
or dress, or culture that the Kachin conglomeration has in common;
"what justifies the collective name of Kachin is *the existence of a common
social structure* within all the groups so designated." The actual words of
Leach quoted are: "I assume that within a somewhat arbitrarily defined
area – namely the Kachin Hills area – a social system exists. The villages between the hills are included in this area so that Shan and Kachin
are at this level, part of a single social system."[56] On the basis of this,
Lévi-Strauss concludes that Leach is "surely unwarranted in criticizing
me for having likewise used a common social structure in bringing together the Kachin and the Chin groups, which certainly differ much less
from one another than the Kachin differ from the Shan."

Since we have two very skilled debaters at work here, I suggest that
we look out for creative and tendentious misreadings and exploitation of
ambiguities. Clearly those who are familiar with the text of *Political Systems*
know that Leach took pains to distinguish between the structural features
of the *gumsa* (and *gumlao*) formations and those of the *shan* (in terms of
the superiority of the *shan* overlords and aristocrats as wife-takers over
the wife-givers, which is the reverse of the *gumsa,* and the *shan* penchant
for polygamy and concubinage, and how the gumsa structure cannot be
transformed into the *shan* monarchical polity, though individuals may
shakily pass from one into the other). In the statement quoted above,
Leach is saying that in the *context* of contiguity and contact between hill
and valley peoples, they can be viewed as being part of a single social
system.

Lévi-Strauss readily admits that Leach had said that so far as we know
there is no evidence that Chins even practice Kachin type marriage,
but he then cites two statements by Leach which he interprets in his
favor. Leach had stated in a footnote some pages later that, "although
Lévi-Strauss confused Kachin practice with Chin, he might still think
that the scale of Kachin bride-price payments is paradoxically large."[57]

---

[55] Ibid., p. 236.   [56] Lévi-Strauss quotes from Leach, *Political Systems*, p. 60.
[57] Lévi-Strauss, *Elementary Structures*, p. 237, quoting from Leach, "Matrilateral Cross-Cousin
Marriage," p. 88, note 3.

Lévi-Strauss interprets this passing remark as showing Leach as having "a doubt in this article about the presumed heterogeneity between the Haka Chin and Kachin." But Leach is merely saying he had disagreed with Lévi-Strauss's thesis of a fundamental contradiction in the Kachin system which led to accumulation of wives at one end and the escalating inflation of brideprice payments and that Lévi-Strauss might still, in order to argue his case, try to use the Kachin data as confirmation of his argument predicated on Head's data about Haka marriage payments!

Lévi-Strauss then cites the following passage from Leach (1961) as showing "a remarkable change [that had] taken place in Leach's thinking as regards the close affinity of the Kachin and Haka Chin systems:

> The Lakher, an Assam tribe who are neighbours to the Haka Chin of Burma, whom they closely resemble in general culture. These last live some hundreds of miles to the south-west of the Kachin groups and are not in direct contact with them. Kachin and Haka Chin cultures are, however, so similar in their general aspects that at least one distinguished anthropologist has confused the two groups."[58]

Lévi-Strauss triumphantly says that

> Leach thus took six years to realize that there was some justification for the liberty I had taken in constituting a type of social structure by borrowing elements from peoples who were undeniably geographically distinct . . . he simply forgets to give me credit for having demonstrated this identity between the social structure of the Kachin and that of the Haka Chin. The very fact that I was able to deduce the structure of the Haka Chin marriage system solely from their system of economic prestations shows that, contrary to Leach's assertions, I never isolated the former from the latter. Indeed, it is not because I confused them that I thought them similar; it is because I had established that they were similar that I asserted that – as far as the marriage system was concerned – it was justifiable to merge them. Therefore, I have done no differently than Leach, when he recognizes that the category Kachin rests neither on language, nor on culture, nor on geographical proximity, *but solely on a common social structure.*[59] (emphasis added)

---

[58] Leach, *Rethinking Anthropology*, p. 116. The passage in question is taken from Leach's essay "Aspects of Bridewealth and Marriage Stability among the Kachin and Lakher." Among other things, Leach shows in this essay that while the Kachin and Lakher are similar in their high evaluation of class hypogamy (and devaluation of class hypergamy) and in their "feudal" political structure, there are important differences in regard to marriage stability and marriage payments. The Lakher counterintuitively combine easy divorce with expensive and complicated payments. The essay does not give evidence for saying that Haka Chin and Kachin have identical social structures.

[59] Lévi-Strauss, *Elementary Structures*, p. 237.

We shall later review Leach's forceful reply to this argument about the logic of merging the Haka Chin and Kachin.[60]

On the instability of the Kachin system

Next Lévi-Strauss takes up the issue of the paradoxes built into the Kachin system which consequently pushed it into disequilibrium. He remarks that Leach disputes that "the Kachin system tends to heighten the inequality between wife receivers and wife-givers"[61]and says that Leach has himself described the Kachin chief as, thanks to his cattle, in a position to give feasts, and thereby gain prestige which is capitalized, and that this process enables social climbing by the dual process of lavish feasting and converting the accruing prestige into recognized status by validating retrospectively the rank of the individual's lineage.[62]

Lévi-Strauss rejects the "absurd idea" he says Leach attributes to him, namely that women are exchanged for goods:

It is clear that, as in all other social systems, women are exchanged for women. The reason I claim the Kachin system to be basically unstable is completely different. It does not relate to the economic nature of an alleged counterpart to prestations of women, but to the distortion of matrimonial exchanges in a system of generalized exchange. In fact, the longer the cycle of exchanges tends to become, the more frequently it will happen, at all stages, that an exchange unit, not being immediately bound to furnish a counterpart to the group to which it is directly in debt, will seek to gain advantages either by accumulating women or by laying claims to women of an unduly high status.[63]

Lévi-Strauss in the most revised English edition of 1969 continues to sketch the thesis of how generalized exchange establishes a system of operations conducted "on credit."[64] The exchange is based on trust

---

[60] Pertinent to the debate is that it seems to me remarkable that the passage from Leach that Lévi-Strauss quotes is not read by him as intended to be a comment on his confusion. Leach is saying that one cannot automatically deduce that, because two groups have *similar cultures* in their general aspects (groups also known to be *not* in direct contact), they have similar *social structures* (the inverse of the argument that the conglomerate of Kachin groups, who are in contact, may have some *dissimilar cultural features* as regards dialect and dress, etc., but they can be shown in terms of empirical evidence to have a *similar social structure*). A famous dictum of Leach is that the boundaries of society and the boundaries of culture cannot be treated as coincident.

[61] Lévi-Strauss, *Elementary structures*, p. 237.

[62] It is doubtful to me whether this addresses and confirms the issue of the progressive disequilibrium in the system as stated by Lévi-Strauss when the class is described as accumulating women and hiking up the marriage payments as well.

[63] Lévi-Strauss, *Elementary Structures*, p. 38. It seems to me that this statement clearly shows that Levi-Strauss fails to see that among the Kachin it is the superior class or stratum in status that gives women to the inferior stratum (*hypogamy*) and the process he describes cannot happen.

[64] Ibid., p. 265.

and confidence that the cycle will close and that after a period of time a woman will eventually be received in compensation for the woman initially surrendered. In the final analysis, this also implies that the participating group is willing to "speculate," and unlike restricted exchange, generalized exchange combines with risk the possibility of gains at every turn. Now comes the famous argument:

Generalized exchange not only results from chance but invites it, for one can guard oneself doubly against the risk: qualitatively, by multiplying the cycles of exchange in which one participates and quantitatively, by accumulating securities, i.e., by seeking to corner as many women as possible from the wife-giving lineage. The widening of the circle of affines and polygamy are thus corollaries of generalized exchange (although not exclusive to it) . . . In other words, generalized exchange seems to be in particular harmony with a society with feudal tendencies . . .

The speculative character of the system, the widening of the cycles between certain enterprising lineages for their own advantage, and, finally, the inevitable preference for certain alliances, resulting in the accumulation of women at some stage of the cycle, are all factors of inequality, which may at any moment force a rupture. Thus one comes to the conclusion that generalized exchange leads almost unavoidably to anisogamy, i.e. to marriage between spouses of different status; that it must appear all the more clearly when the cycles of exchange are multiplied or widened; but that at the same time it is at variance with the system, and must therefore lead to its downfall.[65]

The fantastic development of presentations and exchanges, of debts, claims and obligations is, in a way, a kind of pathological symptom. But the disorder it reveals and for which it acts as a kind of compensation is inherent in the system; viz., the conflict between egalitarian conditions of generalized exchange and its aristocratic consequences.[66]

Leach had criticized Lévi-Strauss in the 1951 essay for not distinguishing between hypergamy and hypogamy, and mistakenly theorizing on the basis that in the Kachin marriage system the wife-givers (*mayu*) are inferior to the wife-takers (*dama*). Since this issue is critically integral to how the Kachin social system is imaged, let us see how Lévi-Strauss now attempts to reconceptualize this while holding on to his original thesis of how the generalized exchange of the Kachin type inevitably leads to the pathological instability mentioned above. Lévi-Strauss asserts that

[65] Ibid., p. 266. One notes that Lévi-Strauss importantly changes the language of his 1949 text, and introduces in the 1967 and 1969 editions a new word, *anisogamy*, to cover both arrangements – *hypergamy* and *hypogamy*. We shall see how he defines and develops *anisogamy* shortly.

[66] Ibid., p. 267.

"the reason for his not distinguishing is that, from a formal point of view, there was no need to distinguish between the two. To make this point clear, in the pages that follow I shall use the term anisogamy, from Botany, which simply means marriage between spouses of different status without any implication as to which of them is higher or lower."[67] He next indulges in a convoluted discussion (which not every reader may wish to puzzle over) of how hypogamy (representing the maternal aspect of anisogamy), in a regime of patrilineal descent, is the sign of a relatively unstable structure, and hypergamy of a stable structure. Hypogamy is therefore a sign of instability in a patrilineal society inclined toward feudalism "because it makes cognation a means to agnation, whereas hypergamy more logically assumes that, in an agnatic system, cognatic relatives are not pertinent."[68]

Is this an elaborate obfuscation or a brilliant clarification?

By making the following statement in *Political Systems* (1954), Leach is supposed to have drawn appreciably closer to Lévi-Strauss's point of view:

Matrilateral cross-cousin marriage is a correlate of a system of patrilineal lineages rigged into a class hierarchy. It does not necessarily follow that the bride-givers (*mayu*) should rank higher than the bride-receivers; but it does follow that if class difference is expressed by marriage, then *mayu* and *dama* must be exclusive and one of the two must rank above the other.[69]

Leach is merely saying that from a formal point of view, if a society is organized in terms of patrilineal lineages, and *if class difference is expressed by marriage* (note the direction of this connection *contra* Lévi-Strauss), then the asymmetrical ranking could go either way. In the Kachin system wife-givers are superior; in the north Indian caste system the wife-takers are superior; but once you further take into account that in the Kachin system it is the wife-takers (husband's side) who make the significant marriage prestations, and that in the Indian case the significant marriage prestations go with the bride to the takers, and then also take in the implications of the ongoing obligations of affines as being in the same direction as marriage prestations, you arrive at quite different socio-political formations. But the fateful question remains: in class terms, in which direction was the exchange of persons and goods in the Kachin system, and what distributional results did those transactions have? Did Lévi-Strauss get them right, or was he wrong? The question is all important, because

---

[67] Ibid., p. 240.   [68] Ibid., p. 241.   [69] Leach, *Political Systems*, p. 256.

Lévi-Strauss's theory of generalized exchange, predicated on circulating connubium and progressively developing instabilities on the basis of "speculations" on cornering women and hiking up marriage prestations, rests on certain ethnographic assumptions. The stakes for Leach are equally high because his theory of *gumsa* and *gumlao* as ideal categories constituting the two poles of a continuum with the possibility of oscillation between them rejects the Lévi-Straussian account on fundamental points, including the way dynamics are generated in Kachin society.

The relation between gumsa *and* gumlao
Lévi-Strauss charges Leach with saying one thing about the Kachin system in his 1951 article and then saying something quite different in his 1954 book that in fact corresponds to his own treatment of the instability of the Kachin system: Leach having asserted previously that the system "is neither contradictory nor self-destructive" gives a different interpretation subsequently that "in point of fact coincides with the one I had put forward five years earlier."[70]

In the 1951 article Leach had explicitly said that he was writing primarily about "the Kachin *gumsa* type of political organization," and that there was an alternative *gumlao* system the structure of which "is somewhat different."[71] Lévi-Strauss states that,

By contrast, in his 1954 book Leach emphasized the duality of the two types. He shows that depending on the region and sometimes even the village, Kachin society may be organized either on an egalitarian basis (*gumlao*) or a hierarchical and semi-feudal basis (*gumsa*). He also shows that the two types are structurally linked and that theoretically at least, it could be conceived that Kachin society oscillates between the two types.[72]

To seemingly devastating effect Lévi-Strauss quotes from Leach's *Political Systems* (1954):

Both systems are in a sense structurally defective. A *gumsa* political state tends to develop features which lead to rebellion, resulting, for a time, in a *gumlao* order. But a *gumlao* community . . . usually lacks the means to hold its component lineages together in a status of equality. It will then either disintegrate altogether through fission, or else status differences between the lineage groups will bring the system back into the *gumsa* pattern.[73]

---

[70] Lévi-Strauss, *Elementary Structures*, p. 239.   [71] Ibid., p. 239.
[72] Ibid., p. 239, Leach, commenting on *Political Systems*, pp. 287–88.
[73] Leach, *Political Systems*, p. 204, edited by Lévi-Strauss, *Elementary Structures*, p. 239.

In fact Leach acknowledges his debt to Lévi-Strauss in stating his thesis of oscillation:

The hypothesis that there might be such a relationship originates with Lévi-Strauss... [who] made the further suggestion that the existence of *mayu–dama* type marriage system while leading to a class stratified society, would for that very reason result in a breakdown of Kachin society. The material I have assembled here *partly* supports Lévi-Strauss' argument *though the instability in Kachin* gumsa *organization is not, I think, of quite the type that Lévi-Strauss supposed.*[74] (emphasis added)

Lévi-Strauss concludes: "Leach might well have added that this empirical confirmation of my interpretation completely invalidates what he himself advanced in 1951."[75] But the words emphasized in the extract above intimate that Leach may have a different account from that given by Lévi-Strauss of why and how the oscillation occurs in terms of the self-contradictions of *gumsa* and *gumlao*, and we have to await his vindication of this position. In the meantime, Lévi-Strauss, riding on the wave of an assumed conquest, asserts that the *mayu* and *dama* (wife-giver and wife-taker) categories recognized by the *gumlao* are not the result of the Kachin political system, but rather its cause; in other words, Lévi-Strauss maintains when it comes to the crunch that it is matrilateral marriage (a component of kinship *per se*) and its speculative possibilities that activates and engenders the political system (feudal structure).

Leach's closing rejoinder

Let us now review Leach's reply as regards the identity of structure between Kachin and Haka Chin.[76] Leach comments that in the revised French edition of *Elementary Structures* (1967), "the sections relating to the Murngin and the Kachin have been substantially modified... on the other hand many of the ethnographical errors have been retained."

Chin and Kachin

Leach asserts that Lévi-Strauss's blunder is "even less excusable now that Lévi-Strauss having admitted his error, goes to great lengths to argue that it is of no consequence."[77] The original Haka Chin derived from Head's *Handbook on the Haka Chin Customs* (1917), which Lévi-Strauss described and still describes as "an unrecognized treasury

---

[74] Leach, *Political Systems*, 1964 edn., pp. 287–88.   [75] Lévi-Strauss, *Elementary Structures*, p. 240.
[76] Leach, "'Kachin' and 'Haka Chin.'"   [77] Ibid., p. 278.

of contemporary ethnography." It is actually a "pamphlet of forty seven pages, originally priced at eight annas" authored by "a Frontier Service administrative officer with no professional competence as an ethnographer." Leach remarks that

> although there is independent evidence that the "general culture" of the Haka Chin and of their neighbours the Lakher is broadly similar to that of the Kachin, there are very few facts recorded in Head's handbook which might be applicable to the Kachin situation. Haka Chin territory and Kachin territory are everywhere separated by a gap of several hundred miles and although Jinghphaw and Haka are both Tibeto-Burman languages, the differences between them are very substantial.[78]

Leach remarks that the ethnography about many of the peoples in question in Upper Burma is uncertain and contradictory. (The interested reader should read the text for all the details.) For example, while Parry's evidence indicated that the Lakher aristocratic lineages had a Kachin type marriage rule, Loffler has rejected this thesis, and Needham has also expressed his skepticism. Leach dismisses Lehman's submission that the Haka Chin he studied in 1957–58 have a prescriptive Kachin type marriage system similar to that of the Lakher as a mistaken outcome of being "rather thoroughly indoctrinated with the views of Needham, Leach and Lévi-Strauss."[79] Lévi-Strauss's retrospective use of Lehman to justify his original confusion is astounding. Another difficulty stems from the fact that, while Head's details of Haka brideprice resemble in some ways those recorded by Parry for the Lakher and for the Lushai, and by Stevenson likewise for the Zahau, the Lushai and the Zahau are at the same time reported as *not* having a Kachin type marriage rule.

In the face of these difficulties, non-concordance, and disagreements, Leach launches this furious protest at Lévi-Strauss's unyielding defensive claims:

> Lévi-Strauss defends his original error by the argument that, since he was able to deduce correctly the structure of the Haka Chin matrimonial system from a study of their system of economic prestations (as reported by Head 1917) he was fully justified from the start in confusing the ethnography of the Haka Chin with that of the Kachin. But in fact he deduced nothing of the sort. He supposed erroneously that the Haka system of prestations, as described by Head, was part of the same ethnographical complex as the Kachin system of marriage,

---

[78] Ibid., p. 279.   [79] Ibid., p. 279.

as described by Gilhodes (1922); that is, he supposed that the Haka system of prestations fits ethnographically with a system of circulation connubium. The Kachin in question *do* have a system of prestations associated with marriage, but it is a different system and is in fact much *less* like the Haka system (as described by Head) than that of the Lakher, or the Lushai or the Zahau. If we were to take Lévi-Strauss' justificatory statement seriously, then any old evidence from any part of the Assam–Burma–Tibet–Yunan border area would serve equally well to justify any proposition Lévi-Strauss cares to propose, because he has laid it down as dogma that once upon a time, in an unspecified remote past, circulating connubium and échange généralisé prevailed throughout this area! In short, all the most notorious fallacies of the Frazerian comparative method are being smuggled back into circulation all over again.[80]

Both for methodological and ethnographic reasons, Leach has cause to call for caution in dealing with the peoples of the Upper Burma region – the Kachins (and their subgroups), the Lakher, the Lushai, the Chins (and their subgroups) – as a unity as if separate pieces of information about them could be considered to produce a common synthetic system labeled the Kachin type. Lévi-Strauss by virtue of his grand sweeping enterprise was tempted to give these people a social structure unity which not only Leach but other contemporary anthropologists with field experience have questioned.

Leach had pointed out in a 1957 essay on "Aspects of Bridewealth and Marriage Stability among the Kachin and Lakher"[81] that while the Kachin (Ordinary Jinghpaw) and Lakher were alike in their system of descent, and their valuation of hypogamy, there is a significant difference in the nature of the institution of marriage, especially as regards the degree of effective membership of women after marriage in their natal patrilineage, of tolerance of divorce, and the complexity and expensiveness of marriage payments. Leach thus remarks in his 1969 rejoinder that Lévi-Strauss has failed to draw attention to the fact that there is now "a reasoned interpretation" which links the development of prestation in marriage to the legal permissibility of divorce, and on this issue discriminates between Lakher, Haka and Gauri on the one hand, and Jinghpaw on the other.

Kachin hypogamy

The rejection by Leach of the model of circulating connubium as applicable to the Kachin (and their neighboring peoples) is also integrally

---

[80] Ibid., p. 281.
[81] Edmund Leach, "Aspects of Bridewealth and Marriage Stability among the Kachin and Lakher,"*Man*, vol. 57, 1957, pp. 50–55, reprinted in Leach, *Rethinking Anthropology*, pp. 114–23.

linked to the implications of Kachin hypogamy which Lévi-Strauss failed to understand; Leach explores the inadequacies in Lévi-Strauss's resorting to the "cover up" term of *anisogamy*.

According to Lévi-Strauss' original argument a system of échange généralisé is naturally in balance – that is to say, on average, any particular group gives out as many women as it takes in. However, instability is likely to be accumulated by "l'accumulation des femmes à telle ou telle étape du circuit" and this must lead to status inequality between wife-givers and wife-receivers. Lévi-Strauss argued further that the usual imbalance is for the wife-receivers to be the superior, so that the pattern tends to become hypergamous (325), (336), (587).

In the light of criticism by myself, Lehman and others, he has now come to recognise that, in the Burma–Assam area, the normal imbalance goes the other way – the status of wife-givers being higher than wife-receivers. The critical sentence at (336) has tactfully been omitted – but he now argues vigorously that the question whether the wife-givers or wife-receivers rate the higher is quite irrelevant. All the same, in order not to get caught out by the ethnography once again, he has coined a new term, "anisogamy" to embrace both "hypergamy" and "hypogamy" and, in general, he has inserted this new word into his text wherever hypergamy formerly occurred (cf. [306] and (325)). However he has forgotten about [544–5] (587–8), where the argument is still in terms of hypergamy and where we are still assured that the Kachin system exhibits l'échange généralisé on the point of breakdown. It exemplifies "the case, which is the most frequent where the rule requires marriage with a woman of an immediately inferior status. Where then will the women of the highest class find their husbands?" [544] (587)

Moreover Lévi-Strauss has still retained the whole of the fallacious argument (325–327) [307–308], which rested on his double error that Haka Chin data apply to Kachin and that among Kachin the *dama* are of higher status than their *mayu*.

The thesis of (325)[306], (588)[545] is that the equal status of the participant groups breaks down firstly because those with privilege tend to accumulate an excess of women and then because, once a hypergamous structure has been established, there is a surplus of women in the top rank. Lévi-Strauss claims that this state of affairs is well illustrated by the Kachin case because, on the one hand, they have rules which require an individual to marry a member of his own class[82] – which is consistent with l'échange généralisé while, on the other, the Kachin institution of polygamy (implying an accumulation of women in one class) is associated with "the fantastic development of prestations, and exchanges and 'debts', of credits and obligations, which is, in a sense, a pathological symptom" (326) [308].

[82] Leach further explains that the rules are wrongly stated by Lévi-Strauss's sources: "The correct formula is not that an individual must marry into his own social class but that a man must not marry a woman of lower social status than himself and a woman must not marry a man of higher social status than herself."

The only fantasy in all this is in Lévi-Strauss' mind.[83]

In fact, by 1969 when Leach wrote his last reply on "Kachin" and "Haka Chin" he had also, as never before with such certainty, come to reject the main tenets of Lévi-Strauss's theory of "generalized exchange," including the paradigm of "circulating connubium."

At the level of terminology, "the speakers of Jinghphaw do not ordinarily think of their *mayu/dama* system as one of 'circulating connubium', but imagine it rather as a rank order system senior/junior."[84]

I should emphasise that the expression "Kachin type marriage" is an expression which I coined to denote a system in which localized patrilineages are related more or less permanently as wife-givers and wife-receivers and in which there is a legal prohibition against marriage between a man of the wife-giver group and a woman of the wife-receiver group. The system does not entail an ideology of circulating connubium, though, in the Kachin case, one well known myth does represent the system as circular. There is no evidence that either the Lakher or the Haka Chin have any kind of ideology of circulating connubium. In Lévi-Strauss' concept of "échange généralisé", on the other hand, an ideology of circulating connubium seems to have a central position. Moreover, Lévi-Strauss fastens his attention on "preferred marriage with the real or classificatory mother's brother's daughter" and ignores the only rule which is significant in the practical situation, namely the prohibition on marriage with a real or classificatory father's sister's daughter (cf. Lehman 1963).[85]

Gumsa *and* gumlao*: stability–instability*

Leach made his final rejoinder in these terms to Lévi-Strauss's charge that after having affirmed in 1951 that Kachin society was in equilibrium, Leach recognized in 1954 that it alternated in constant oscillation between two contradictory forms. (I have already earlier in the chapter described at some length how Leach dealt with *gumsa* and *gumlao* as ideal polar categories, how they related to dynamic conduct and facts on the ground, and what he meant by "oscillating equilibrium" [a concept borrowed from Pareto] in terms of an "as if" model, and in relation to the historical motion of individual Kachin communities which cannot be stated or predicted in mechanistic or determinate terms. He had also

---

[83] Leach, " 'Kachin' and 'Haka Chin,' " pp. 280–81. The numbers in round brackets refer to pages in the first French edition of Lévi-Strauss, *Les Structures Élémentaires*, of 1949 and those in square brackets to pages in the second French edition of 1967.
[84] Ibid., p. 278.
[85] Ibid., p. 279. The reference is to F.K. Lehman, *The Structure of Chin Society: A Tribal People of Burma Adapted to a Non-Western Civilization*, Urbana: University of Illinois Press, 1963.

stated in the 1954 work that "external" circumstances played an important role in acting on the "internal" features of *gumlao* and *gumsa* type communities, and in engendering their motion.)

"The development of rank hypogamy in a system of prescriptive asymmetric marriage alliance does not necessarily threaten its basic structural arrangements as Lévi-Strauss (1949) has suggested" (Lehman 1963: 131): thus Lehman writing about the Haka Chin; he is repeating a proposition by Leach (1951) made with relation to the Kachin ... Lévi-Strauss has misrepresented me; having been reared as a mathematician I do not, unless I am being exceptionally careless, confuse the notions of equilibrium and stability. What I said in 1951 was that "Lévi-Strauss is led to attribute to the Kachin system an instability it does not in fact possess" and I stick by that. An unstable system is one which has a tendency to change into some other *system without any tendency to return to the original position*. A system in equilibrium may be one in which everything is stationary, but it is more likely to be one in which the parts are in oscillatory movement around a central position – the pendulum of the clock is not ordinarily stationary, but it is at all times in equilibrium. My account of the Kachin political system is of a system in long term equilibrium, though in my book (Leach 1954) I made it clear that the equilibrium in question was "as if" (Leach 1954: 285). In fact, Kachin society over the last 140 years has undergone radical changes, but these changes have been a response to external pressures, they have not been generated from within the system, as Lévi-Strauss' analysis would have suggested they ought to be. Besides which both *gumsa* and *gumlao* practise "Kachin type marriage" as I have defined that concept, and both will on occasion resort to forms of circulating connubium (*hkau wang hku*).

Moreover, Lévi-Strauss' scheme would imply that the norm of the Kachin system, being based on échange généralisé, should be of the egalitarian *gumlao* type, while the aristocratic *gumsa* pattern should be anomalous and should itself disintegrate only in the direction of class or caste hierarchy. But in practice the norm of the Kachin pattern is quite emphatically centred in the *gumsa* model which is capable of oscillating in two directions. It can move either in the direction of becoming "more Shan" (i.e. from *gumchying gumsa* through *gumrawng gumsa* to *gumsa* to *Shan* in Maran La Raw's (1967) terminology) or it can move from *gumchying gumsa* to *gumlao*; but the factors which "determine" what shall happen are economic and political, not structural. Alliances between affinally related lineages break down not because there is no woman available to act as the symbolic re-affirmation of the alliance but because, for one reason or other, the hierarchical status difference implied by the *mayu/dama* relationship has ceased to correspond to the economic and political facts. It is not the instability of the marriage system which breaks up the political network; it is the instability of economic and political status which breaks up the pattern of marriage relations.

In Lévi-Strauss' view, the circulation of women in a system of échange généralisé is a system in itself; the circulation of prestations in the other direction is another system in itself: the two should not be confused [276]. But certainly that is not how the Kachin themselves think about it. They are not, of course, specialists in the theory of structuralism but they know very well how their marriage system really works. They know that political power consists in the control of material assets and that women are pawns in the game of politics. Lévi-Strauss, as always, has everything back to front.[86]

To conclude: Leach's rejoinder of 1969 is crisp (and presumes knowledge of his earlier writings). He explicitly refers to the 1951 essay (which is problematic for Lévi-Strauss's own model in so far as Leach imaged the *gumsa* system as a class-structured feudal system/self-maintaining system, not automatically doomed to pathological instability), and situates it in relation to the 1954 schema of oscillating equilibrium. What Leach now says emphatically, and which he did not say so emphatically in 1954 (but implied in the 1951 essay), is that the norm of the Kachin pattern for the actors themselves is centered in the *gumsa* model, and although the social dynamics may consist in movement away from it in the direction of *gumlao* or of *shan*, it nevertheless revolves around the focal point of *gumsa*. This is in line with some of his statements in the 1954 book that the asymmetry of *mayu–dama* is incompatible with *gumlao* equilibrium, and their co-presence may be regarded as a transitional phase that moves toward *gumsa*. The categories of *gumsa* and *shan* implied a much stronger incompatibility, and a durable systemic transition or transformation from *gumsa* to *shan* was unlikely.

This final statement, which attempts to integrate the *gumsa* ranked "feudal" system sketched in the 1951 essay as the focal point of Kachin society around which dynamics occur, and the model of *gumsa–gumlao* as polar ideal categories on a continuum on which there is movement in both directions, is offered by Leach as his final answer to Lévi-Strauss that is in conformity with his own authoritative ethnographic knowledge of the Kachin.

Leach concluded his rejoinder in this manner:

It fills me with regret to have to write in this vein of an author whom I greatly respect, but the fact is that by tinkering with his 1949 text in the pretence of bringing it up to date he has made confusion worse confounded. What was formerly a classic (though somewhat dated) work, the defects of which could be tolerated because of its intellectual originality, has become a hybrid monster. It

---

[86] Leach, " 'Kachin' and 'Haka Chin' ", pp. 283–84. The references are to Lehman, *The Structure of Chin Society*, and to Maran La Raw, "Towards a Basis for Understanding the Minorities of Burma: The Kachin Example", in P. Kunstadter (ed.), *Southeast Asian Tribes, Minorities and Nations*, Princeton: Princeton University Press, 1967.

is a real tragedy that the English edition which has now appeared is based on this revised version rather than the original.[87]

This chapter does not exhaust all the theoretical and interpretive formulations contained in *Political Systems*. Many of the following chapters will take up themes not mentioned or developed here where they are relevant to the topics being discussed.

[87] Leach, " 'Kachin' and 'Haka Chin,' " p. 284.

CHAPTER 6

"The Frontiers of 'Burma'"

Some six years after the appearance of *Political Systems of Highland Burma*, Leach published a lengthy essay entitled "The Frontiers of 'Burma,'"[1] but my guess is that it was written, or at least its principal ideas were sketched, during the time that *Political Systems* was being fashioned.

This essay, which ranges over many topics, is important to consider for many reasons. It may be considered an extension of *Political Systems*, and amplifies submissions made in it, but even more significantly it introduces new issues not contained in the book.

I will therefore recount the main points Leach discusses and comment on them, especially because, for unexplained reasons, most specialists of Southeast Asia have not acknowledged or have ignored this piece, although it does in an original, prescient, and provocative manner discuss the spatial ordering and political dynamics of pre-colonial Shan polities and their relations with the "hill people." Leach argues that these features distinctively differ from the modern European notions of nation-states bounded by frontiers and exercising exclusive sovereignty over their subjects. These themes have been revived and even replicated in some modern texts dealing with the history of map- and boundary-making, census classification, and the reification of tribes and minorities as separate entities.

When considering the merits and demerits of this essay it is relevant to bear in mind that it is dealing with texts and sources available before 1960, and that the author signals that he is proposing some "sweeping generalizations."

Leach sketches in macropolitical terms the confluence and "external" differential impact of two major civilizations, Indian and Chinese, on the societies of Burma. At the same time he also consolidates and formalizes the "internal" dialectic within the frontiers of Burma between the two

[1] Edmund Leach, "The Frontiers of 'Burma'", *Comparative Studies in History and Society*, vol. 3, no. 1, 1960, pp. 49–68.

categories of "hill people" and "valley people," in which the different ecologies and socio-political systems of these categories occupy a major place. In this second perspective his own personal knowledge of the region is much in evidence.

The "Burma" in quotes in Leach's title implies "the whole of the extensive imprecisely defined frontier region lying between India and China and having modern political Burma at its core."[2]

THE CATEGORIES: "HILL PEOPLE AND VALLEY PEOPLE"

Leach's propositions are that

the historically significant contrasts in present-day "Burma" are differences of ecology and differences of social organization ... The two sets of differences nearly coincide; roughly speaking the Hill People are patrilineal and hierarchical, the Valley People have a non-unilineal kinship organization linked with charismatic despotism. This coexistence is not a *necessary* one; if we are to explain why it exists then we must seek an historical explanation. The explanation which I offer is that the Valley People took their social organization and their politics from India while the Hill People took their social organization along with their trade and kinship system from China. It is a possible explanation; I do not claim more than that. (p. 51)

Hill people and valley people have practiced diametrically opposed modes of subsistence associated generally (with some exceptions) with, respectively, mountain ridges and valleys forming well-watered alluvial basins favorable for rice farming. In the main hill people enjoy a meager standard of living sustained through shifting agriculture, though there are exceptions that will be considered later. The hill people are characterized by a great variety of both language and tribal organization. The indigenous religion of most groups is "animistic," usually involving some form of ancestor worship. "Over the past century the Christian missions have made many converts, but true 'Hill People' are never Buddhists" (p. 52).[3]

---

[2] Ibid., p. 50. Hereafter in this chapter I shall convey the page numbers of quotations from the essay in parentheses in the text itself, and not in numbered footnotes.

[3] Leach qualifies this generalization by saying that apart from individual conversions, there are certain exceptional circumstances in which groups of Hill People have become economically prosperous and sophisticated and have adopted the religion and manners of their valley neighbors. For example, the Palaung inhabitants of Tawngpeng in the Burma Shan states who are prosperous tea growers have become Buddhists and have organized their Tawngpeng State in exact imitation of the political model provided by their Shan neighbors (p. 53).

The term valley people is not the equivalent of "lowlander." While the major populations of the lowland plains of Burma, Thailand, and Assam are Valley People, "so also are the dominant elements in the population of the Shan States, South-West Yunnan and Laos, all of which are upland districts," but also have alluvial terrain occurring at high altitudes permitting profitable rice cultivation.[4]

The languages of the valley people are less diverse than is the case with hill people. The majority of the Valley People speak Khmer, Tai and Burmese dialects. These languages are not spoken as a mother-tongue by any Hill People but bilingualism is common (p. 52).

"The most distinctive cultural characteristic of the Valley People – apart from the practice of wet farming – is their adherence to Hinayana Buddhism" (p. 52). The valley people, mostly Burmese or Shan, consider that Buddhism and civilization are synonymous, and they express their contempt for their hill neighbors by using the epithet *kha* ("slave," "savage"). "Nevertheless, a *kha* who becomes a Buddhist is thereby civilised, he has 'become a Shan', and within a generation or two the barbarian origin of his descendants may be forgotten. This type of assimilation has been going on for centuries. What is recorded of Cambodia in the 13th century is strictly in accord with what we know of North Burma in the 19th century" (p. 53).[5]

THE IMPACT OF INDIA AND CHINA

"Besides the two internal continuities – the ecological categories Hill People and Valley People – there have been two external continuities, the persisting influence of India and China" (p. 53). Every Southeast Asian society which has "possessed even a modest degree of cultural sophistication has been quite emphatically subject to Indian or Chinese influence; usually to both" (p. 53). These influences are diverse, and Leach selects particular ones for emphasis. The influence of China has been mainly in the fields of trade and communication and it has affected the hill people rather than the valley people. In contrast, the influence of India has been felt particularly in the fields of politics and religion and has affected the

---

[4] Leach also states another exception regarding Valley People. Certain parts of Burma include dry zones in which rice farming is possible in valleys only with the help of artificial irrigation engineering. People who are condemned to live in parched outlands without this facility live at an altogether lower level.

[5] Leach's authority for Cambodia is P. Pelliot, *Mémoires sur les coutumes du Cambodge de Tcheou Ta-Kouan. Oeuvres posthumes de Paul Pelliot*, no. 3, Paris: Librairie d'Amerique et d'Orient, A. Maisonneuve, 1951.

valley people rather than the hill people. Never interested in Burma as a potential dominion, China had a persistent interest in overland routes to India and also in the natural resources of Burma's mountains and forests. Chinese records, dating back to the fourth century AD, describe detailed itineraries and also state that the tribes "living South-West of Yung Chang produced rhinoceros, elephant, tortoise-shell, jade, amber, cowries, gold, silver, salt, cinnamon and cotton, hill-paddy and pani-cled millet, a catalogue which apart from the cinnamon, is accurate and comprehensive to this day. So also in recent centuries when Northern Burma has been the main source of jade for all China, the jade mines were owned and worked by Hill People and Chinese interests remained basically commercial rather than political" (p. 54). We shall return to the economic interrelations between the Chinese and hill people later.

THE CHINESE AND INDIAN POLITICAL MODELS AND STRUCTURES

Already in early Han times, in the first millennium BC, the Chinese had developed

an idea of the Nation State comparable to the concept of *imperium* which the Romans developed a few centuries later. This ideology postulates a central government which is the ultimate political authority for the whole of a large territorial area delimited by frontiers. The administration of this empire is in the hands of office-holders, an Emperor with an administrative staff of bureau-crats. The authority of the central government is maintained by military force, exercised by garrison troops permanently dispersed throughout the country and at appropriate positions on the frontier. Administration is financed by taxation which is levied in a systematic "legitimate" manner and not according to the arbitrary whim of local warlords . . . While no doubt practice often deviated from this model, yet the basic structure of both the Chinese and Roman systems possessed an extraordinary degree of stability. (p. 55)

The Indian political model is very different. Leach depends on schol-arship available in the 1950s (such as Weber on bureaucracy, Coedès on Hinduized states of Southeast Asia, and Hall[6] to develop this model as focused on the ideal ruler, conceived not as an office-holder such as the emperor sustained by bureaucratic continuity, but as a charismatic leader, such as the famed Asoka. The early historical states of the Burma region

[6] D.G.E. Hall, *A History of South-East Asia*, London: Macmillan, and New York: St. Martin's Press, 1955.

which achieved renown were of an Indian style, and they had four common elements: royalty characterized by Hindu or Buddhist cults, literary expression by means of the Sanskrit language, a mythology taken from the Epics, the Puranas, and other Sanskrit texts containing a nucleus of royal tradition and the traditional genealogies of royal families of the Ganges region, and the observance of the Dharmashastras (the "sacred" laws), especially the Laws of Manu.[7] Leach says it is outside his field to explain how this Indian colonization came about but he emphasized the pervasiveness of this political influence.

He now proceeds to give the following sharp, mostly true, but somewhat exaggerated sketch of charismatic kingship and "the empirical characteristics of *les états hindouisés*":

Most of them have been small, most of them have been shortlived; the continuity of state depends upon the personality of the monarch; every monarch has a successor, but every succession is an issue of dispute; the state dies with the King, the successor must create a new state from his own personal endeavours.

There was continuity of a sort, for the states were in every case built up around a heartland of irrigated rice cultivation and, whatever the vicissitudes of politics, the rice-land stayed in one place. But the state had no fixed frontier, no permanent administrative staff.

Scott's comment on the Shans is applicable to all the Valley Peoples of Burma:

"Shan history more than that of any other race, seems to have depended on the character and personal energy of the Sawbwa (Prince). An ambitious ruler seems always to have attempted, and often to have effected, the subjugation of his neighbours. When there were two or more such there was perpetual war; when there was none there were a number of practically independent chieftains dwelling in their own valleys. Hence the astounding number of huge ruined cities which are found all over Indo-China." (p. 56)[8]

In this respect the historical kingdoms of Arakan, Pagan, Pegu, Thaton, Ava, Ayut'ia, Manipur, and Assam (as well as some hundreds of smaller principalities located within the same general area) all had much in common. Hinayana Buddhism was everywhere the state religion mixed, as in Ceylon, with many explicit elements of Saivite Brahmanism. Everywhere royal polygyny was an exaggerated feature of the royal prerogative. The King was

---

[7] Leach is here presumably referring to the Burmese and Thai texts labeled as Dhammasathan, Thammathat, etc. R. Lingat's writings, such as "Evolution of the Conception of Law in Burma and Siam", *Journal of the Siam Society*, 1950, vol. 38, are not referred to by Leach though available at the time Leach composed this essay. Lingat's major text of relevance published later is *Les sources du droit dans le système traditionnel de l'Inde*, Paris and The Hague: Mouton, 1967.

[8] The quote is from J. George Scott and J.P. Hardiman, *Gazetteer of Upper Burma and the Shan States, 1900–01*, Rangoon: Government Printing, 1900, vol. II, part 2, p. 333.

regarded as a Chakravartin – a "Universal Emperor" – or else as an incipient Buddha. (p. 57)

In China succession was governed by law, and each emperor had a single legitimate heir specified by rules of descent. Usurpation was relatively rare and occurred only with a change of dynasty or in times of political chaos. The *literati*, who in theory gained office through personal talent and achievement, were in practice a largely hereditary bureaucratic class, but they were not relatives of the emperor. In contrast,

in the "Indian" states of "Burma" any one of a King's numerous offspring might "legitimately" succeed him and palace murders were the norm. The first act of any successful claimant was to carry out a holocaust of his most immediate rivals – that is to say, his half-brothers and step-mothers. He then apportioned his realm in fiefs to his close relatives who survived because they were considered trustworthy. They were usually the King's own wives and sons. The nature of this fiefdom is well indicated by the Burmese term for a fief holder – *myosa* – "the eater of the township." (p. 59)

Besides these "licensed royal plunderers" there was a hierarchy of commoner officials with elaborate titles, whose positions were directly in the king's personal gift. Two recognized ways of obtaining administrative office were to make oneself the client of a royal prince or to donate a daughter to the royal harem.[9] The "complete absolutism of the monarch's authority and the arbitrariness of the resulting administration were tempered only by the fact that the King, though also head of the Buddhist church, had relatively limited power to manipulate clerical offices." Leach sees this parallel hierarchy of relatively permanent church officials as introducing a few elements of stability and mercy into an arbitrary governmental system.[10]

Leach concludes this section with the following account of the spatial and administrative structure of the typical "Burma" state:

The typical "Burma" state consisted of a small fully administered territorial nucleus having the capital at the centre. Round about, stretching indefinitely in all directions, was a region over which the king claimed suzerainty and from the inhabitants of which he extracted tribute by threat of military force. These

---

[9] Pelliot, *Mémoires*, p. 14, made this observation regarding thirteenth-century Cambodia.

[10] Leach at the time he composed this did not have the kind of detailed documentation of the Buddhist Sangha, itself not a unitary entity, and its relations to the state/political authority before and after British colonial domination that is found in E. Michael Mendelson, *Sangha and State in Burma: A Study of Monastic Sectarianism and Leadership*, edited by John P. Ferguson, Ithaca, NY: Cornell University Press, 1975.

marginal zones all had the status of conquered provinces, and their populations were normally hostile to the central government. Insurrections were endemic and the political alignments of local leaders possessed the maximum uncertainty. Practically every substantial township in "Burma" claims a history of having been at one time or another the capital of a "kingdom", the alleged frontiers of which are at once both grandiose and improbable.

It is consistent with this general pattern that those who are now remembered as great Kings were practitioners of banditry on a grand scale whose fame rests solely on their short-term success in carrying fire and slaughter into the territory of their more prosperous neighbours. The "Just Ruler", that archetypal figure upon whom the Confucian ethic lays much stress, had no place in the value system of "Burma" kingship. The kings of Ava, Arakan, Pegu and Ayut'ia were forever pillaging each other's capitals, but conquest by the sword was never followed up by any serious attempt to establish a permanent political hegemony. Military success was simply a manifestation of the monarch's personal power, it did not serve to establish authority and it did not alter political frontiers. (pp. 57–58)

Let me, as an anthropologist of South and Southeast Asia, and having some knowledge of Buddhist formulations, make an intervention here. Leach does not give any value and credence to Theravada Buddhist notions of *dharmaraja* (righteous ruler) or to ideal notions of *cakkavatti* (Pali) or *chakravartin* (Sanskrit) as the just universal monarch, or of King Maha-sammata as the first "elected ruler," who were frequently invoked by monarchs and their monk-chroniclers of Southeast Asia. The same Leach who paid much attention to the "ideal categories" of the Kachin, including *gumsa* and *gumlao*, rank, merit and so on, and matched them against the dynamics of actual practice, sees these Buddhist usages as inflated "rhetoric."

I have to some extent sketched the Buddhist ideal conceptions of kingship prevalent in mainland Southeast Asia in my *World Conqueror and World Renouncer* (1976), and in certain other essays I have tried to answer the question of how Buddhist actors (the monarchs and their chroniclers) saw themselves as connected to and fulfilling these ideals,[11] and how I

---

[11] See S.J. Tambiah, *World Conqueror and World Renouncer: A Study in Buddhism and Polity in Thailand against a Historical Background*, Cambridge and New York: Cambridge University Press, 1976, part 1. Three relevant essays are "Buddhist Conceptions of Universal King and their Manifestations in South and Southeast Asia," Kuala Lumpur, University of Malaya, 1987; "The Galactic Polity in Southeast Asia," in S.J. Tambiah (ed.), *Culture, Thought and Social Action: An Anthropological Prospective*, Cambridge, MA: Harvard University Press, 1985, pp. 252–86; and "King Mahāsammata: The First King in the Buddhist Story of Creation, and His Persisting Relevance," *Journal of the Anthropological Society of Oxford*, vol. 20, no. 2, 1989, pp. 101–22.

would match these ideological conceptions with enacted practices and historical processes. Leach, however, is quite correct in his portrayal of the volatile and unstable nature of monarchical politics in the Burmese and other Southeast Asian kingdoms, and I have tried to conceptualize the interplay of the two levels under the caption "Divine kingship and perennial rebellion."

POLITICAL INTERDEPENDENCE OF HILLS AND VALLEYS

Leach posed the relevant question: in what sense did these explosive, ephemeral, yet recurrent states really possess "frontiers at all?" (pp. 58–59). The expanding polity of a king would begin in one valley, incorporate the next, and then claim sovereignty over the hill country separating valleys. There were two recognized methods by which the Valley prince or king might assert his authority over a hill chieftain: he would organize a punitive expedition and levy tribute, or he could pay protection money to the hill tribesmen as a reward for their loyalty. Such nominal overlordship did not entail the merging of the valley people and the hill people in any cultural sense. The hill chieftains might borrow certain manners, customs, and dress from their elegant valley overlords, but in fact they claimed to be lords in their own right.

The two categories, whatever the overall political structure, remained distinct in language, religion, and ecological adaptation. But it would be a mistake to see them as permanently ranged in implacable hostility. "The two categories of population are symbiotic on one another; they interpenetrate territorially and politically as well as culturally," for in the course of centuries the "civilization" of the valley people "fanned out along the river valleys and infiltrated upwards into isolated pockets right in the heart of the hill country" (p. 60). Some of these small pockets of valley people may have originated as garrisons guarding a strategic route; others may have been founded by colonists escaping the burdens of war and tyranny.

Leach gives a fine illustration of the high degree of political interconnectedness between adjacent groups of valley people and hill people from that region of northern Burma of which he had good knowledge, both historical and ethnographic, namely "the far North-West of Burma ... dotted with tiny Shan settlements surrounded by vast areas of mountain country inhabited only by Kachins" (p. 60). Though widely scattered, these various Shan statelets claimed a cultural unity; the inhabitants were Hkamti Shans, and formerly fell within the domain

of the Prince of Mogaung. The Kachins of the surrounding hill country admit no kinship with the Shans nor do they admit that they were
ever the subjects of the Prince of Mogaung. They are not the servants
but the allies of Mogaung, and they point out that the jade and amber mines which were the main source of Mogaung prosperity lie in
Kachin territory. Despite the nominal lordship of the Mogaung prince,
he exercised no administrative authority over the Kachins and levied no
tribute.

The principality of Mogaung was extinguished by military force in
1765 but the ancient ideology persists. The wide scattering and spatial
distribution of the Shan statelets is a telling confirmation of Leach's
thesis. He lists nine such localities, at a distance of 22 to 160 miles and in
various directions (northwesterly, northeasterly, and southwesterly) from
Mogaung.

Each of these localities is a small rice plain inhabited by a Tai-speaking
Buddhist population ranging in numbers from a hundred to a few thousand. In addition the Mogaung prince claimed suzerainty over all the hill
country lying in between, an area of some 10,000 square miles. "In turn
the Prince himself offered ambivalent allegiance to both the Emperor
of China and the King of Ava, a circumstance which proved disastrous
when in the latter part of the eighteenth century, the King of Ava went
to war with China over the control of the jade trade" (p. 61).

But the actual political dynamics of Mogaung were different from the
ideological and rhetorical claims. Mogaung as a typical "Burma" state
of the seventeenth and eighteenth centuries was in a sense a fiction: the
prince's claims of territorial suzerainty were optimistic; in fact he could
only undertake effective military or political action with the aid and
consent of the hill "subjects" who were not subjects at all.

Leach claims that this sketch of Mogaung is not an atypical instance, and that the conditions which prevailed in the eighteenth century have not altered substantially in recent times. Nearly all Indian-
style states of Burmese history have been of this general type. Moreover,
pursuing his theme of continuity he asserts that "the authority exercised by the central government of the Independent Sovereign State of
Burma over its outlying regions in the year 1959 is of a very similar
kind" (p. 61).

There were certain kinds of interrelations and interactions between the
"nominally dominant Valley People" and "their barbarous Hill neighbours." In the Mogaung case Kachins fought in the Shan armies and
they traded in the Shan markets. Shans and Kachins did not intermarry

and the Kachins had no interactions with the Buddhist priesthood, yet assimilation could and did take place. The laborers in the Shan rice fields were mostly Kachins living in voluntary serfdom. There is historical evidence that such persons, by adapting the manners, dress, and language of their masters, tended to merge with them in the course of a few generations. But in making this cultural transfer they have cut themselves off completely from their former associates in the hills.

The "argument from ecology" (p. 62) in the comparison is that the Valley People because of their wet rice farming live "in locally dense aggregates of population and this is an important factor in their cultural cohesion; in contrast, most of the Hill People, being shifting cultivators, live in small scattered settlements . . . the Hill country takes up ten times as much space as the Valley country but there are ten times as many Valley People as there are Hill People" (p. 62). (There are some hill people who resort to fixed cultivation on irrigated terraces, but since they do not form a distinct category in any linguistic or cultural sense their existence does not affect the general argument.)

There is a difference in productivity:

Hill farming of *any* kind requires a very high labour effort in relation to yield and consequently it can seldom provide any economic surplus over and above the immediate subsistence needs of the local population. It is the existence of such a surplus in the Valley economy which permits the Valley People to maintain their more elegant style of life. The converse is likewise true; throughout the whole hill region wherever a particular group has become exceptionally prosperous its members show a tendency to adopt a Shan (Tai) or Burmese style of living and to become converted to Buddhism. It follows that the contrasts of culture and language which have led to the conventional classification of "tribes and people of Burma" have no intrinsic permanence. Any individual can start as a member of one category and end up in another (p. 62).[12]

Thus in fact many valley people are simply descendants of hill people who have settled in the valleys. "If then we want to consider the nature of Hill Society as an ideal type so as to contrast it with Valley Society as an ideal type then it is here in the remote hill areas that we can observe it" (pp. 62–63).

[12] This account of interactional dynamics, as we can now appreciate, is Leach's argument against the exercise of linguistic distribution and considering linguistic groups as separate and enduring culturally bounded tribes/societies.

"POLITICAL STRUCTURE OF HILL SOCIETY"

In this section, Leach sketches the two contrasted kinds of authority structure, prevalent in Hill society, which are distinguishable in political ideology but are "nearly always juxtaposed in immediate association." These are "an ideology of rule by aristocratic chiefs," who are not endowed with personal charisma but hold their office by hereditary right as a senior member, and an ideology of "democratic rule" by a council of elders, each elder acting as a representative of a particular lineage, and no one lineage is intrinsically superior to another. These two ideological models are extensively described in *Political Systems* (1954) and in the 1951 essay "The Structural Implications of Matrilateral Cross-Cousin Marriage" as the *gumsa* (aristocratic) and *gumlao* (democratic) models pertaining to the Kachin of North Burma. I need not therefore recount here his treatment of these two contrasting systems and their dynamic connection as aspects of a single cycle viewed at different phases of its growth, except to note that Leach asserts that the two types of ideology "co-exist side by side throughout the whole of the northern and western parts of the 'Burma' hill country" (p. 63).[13] These dichotomies however differ in their particulars and should not be conflated as forming a common pair identical with the Kachin *gumsa* and *gumlao*.

Leach raises a question which he had not posed in quite these terms before. "Hills and Valleys stand in radical opposition and there is evidently a certain level at which Hill Culture and Valley Culture are totally inconsistent with one another just as one might say of early medieval Europe that Christianity and Paganism were inconsistent . . . Hill society attains its highest elaboration in areas which are remote from the contaminating influence of Buddhist civilisation" (pp. 64–65), as instanced by the Wa headhunters of the eastern Shan states. The cultural elements common to both groups are remarkably few. "Yet the pattern of political relations which I have previously described might have led us to expect something different. After all, the Hill People and the Valley People are racially the same and languages are very easily changed, so what is it that keeps the two groups apart?" (p. 65).

Leach suggests an intriguing and quite original answer to this query in terms of the relations between China and the hill people. Although

---

[13] Thus the parallels of *gumsa* and *gumlao* for the Kachin are these categories which Leach takes from the ethnographies of various writers: *thendu* and *thenkoh* for the Konyak Naga, Sema, and Chakrima (Angami) for the southern Naga, Zahau and Zanniat for the central Chin, and New Kuki (Thado) and Old Kuki for the western Manipuri Hills.

the hill people of "Burma" have for centuries experienced the spasmodic political influence of Indian-style states, *their most direct economic
contacts have been with the Chinese*. Many north Burma localities which were
"unadministered territory" were regularly visited by Chinese traders, but
never by Burmese (p. 65). "Chinese society, like that of the Hill People, is
structured into a system of unilineal descent groups, and the 'animism' of
the Hill People is fundamentally a cult of dead ancestors which has many
Confucianist parallels. These similarities make it possible for the Chinese
and the 'Burma' Hill People to communicate with one another and to
establish permanent social relationships in a way which is impossible for
the Hill People and the Valley People" (p. 65). In fact Chinese villagers
settle in the hill country, then live much like ordinary hill folk, and will
even intermarry with their "barbarian" neighbors, but the valley people
will not do these things.

This difference is embedded in the marriage patterns. "In the Valley
culture the population of each local rice plain tends to be endogamous.
The Prince, who has many wives, may take women from his immediate
followers. He receives the latter women as a tribute. Thus, in terms of
kinship, Valley society as a whole forms a closed system; the Valley People
do not give their women away to strangers" (p. 65). They repudiate
marriage with the barbarians even when they are willing to accept their
economic services.

Let me make a corrective intervention at this point. Let us accept as
a schematic representation Leach's equation of a "local rice plain" with
the limits of a princely kingdom (statelet), that is internally stratified and
is endogamous (closed) (except for dynastic marriages between princely
families). Leach now advances a further proposition regarding (ordinary)
valley people's marriage practices: that among them "each marriage is
an individual affair between a particular man and a particular woman;
it does not establish an alliance between kin groups" (pp. 65–66). This
last proposition about women being treated "as separate individuals"
is incorrect and not necessary to make the larger valuable comparison between Hill and Valley People, and exposes Leach's lack of first-
hand ethnographic knowledge at this time of the non-aristocratic kinship
and marriage patterns of valley agrarian communities in Burma, which
though locally bounded had complex internal patterns and networks.
Anthropological monographs sketching lowland Burmese patterns of
cognatic (bilateral kinship) networks, property inheritance of males and
females, marriage gifts, preferences and alliances including cross-cousin
marriage, residential patterns, and bilateral kindred groups, land tenure

and agrarian practices appeared later in time, such as Manning Nash's *The Golden Road to Modernity* (1965)[14] and Melford Spiro's *Kinship and Marriage in Burma* (1977).[15] In the meantime, Leach himself would in the mid-1950s study and document in unmatched detail and with masterly analysis a variant of those bilateral kinship norms and practices prevailing in an agrarian community in the dry zone of Sri Lanka. This study of *Pul Eliya, A Village in Ceylon* will be the subject of my detailed scrutiny in chapter 7. Since most anthropologists consider *Political Systems* and *Pul Eliya* to be totally different texts in substance and themes, I would suggest here that in "Frontiers of 'Burma'" Leach stresses the interrelations between kinship, ecology, agrarian forms, and political institutions which are central themes probed in the latter monograph. These corrections made, let me now return to Leach's perceptive explication of marriage in the hill culture and its close connection with trade objects and Chinese traders.

In contrast to the valley situation, girls in the hill culture "are married against a bride-price and the objects involved in bride-price transactions are the same sort of objects as are met with in dealings with a Chinese trader"[16] (p. 66). "Thus the ties of affinal kinship ramify widely, following trade routes and jumping across language frontiers and political boundaries" (p. 66). Leach is not maintaining that a single kinship network ramifies over the whole of "Burma" hill country, but that "everywhere in the hills a very high valuation is placed on extended kinship relations and also upon the permanence and stability of such relations. Individuals are regarded as representatives of particular lineages and particular places," and "women who are given in marriage serve to establish a relationship between lineages – a relationship which is likely to be repeated in further marriages or further trade." Hill culture is not a direct imitation from the Chinese but it parallels the Chinese in a way as does the valley culture in relation to the Indian style. The really crucial distinction is that in the hill system traditional offices are vested in particular lineages, while the valley system is dominated by charismatic individual authority, temporary and self-glorifying, and even tyrannical.

Before I embark on a commentary in the next section, I should record the positive impact of Leach's *Political Systems* and some of his

[14] Manning Nash, *The Golden Road to Modernity: Village Life is Contemporary Burma*, New York: Wiley, 1965.

[15] Melford Spiro, *Kinship and Marriage in Burma: A Cultural and Psychodynamic Analysis*, Berkeley: University of California Press, 1977.

[16] See Leach's explication of *hpaga* as valuable objects in *Political Systems*.

essays, including "Frontiers of 'Burma'" and "Structural Implications of Matrilateral Cross-Cousin Marriage," on Lehman's important monograph *The Structure of Chin Society* (1963).[17]Lehman studied the Chins in the late 1950s. What in particular influenced his interpretation was, as he put it, Leach's characterization of the Kachin political system and the relationship between the *gumsa* (aristocratic) and *gumlao* (democratic) political varieties as "in large measure conditioned by the external relationships of Kachin society to Shan civilization, an argument that holds for the Chin, but in a different way."[18] Lehman begins his book by asserting his version of Leach's submissions in "Frontiers of 'Burma'":

The structure and organization of the society and culture of the hill Chin . . . reflect their adaptation to an environment in which the neighboring civilizations are as important as their own physical habitat. Chin society and culture, therefore, must be understood in terms of a dual adaptation: first, an adaptation to local resources by means of a particular technology, and second, a response to Burman civilization.[19]

Thomas Kirsch's essay on *Feasting and Oscillation*[20] is another example that takes its main materials from the writings of Leach on the Kachin, and of Stevenson and Lehman on the Chin; it focuses on the centrality of "feasts of merit" in these (and other) Hill Peoples that are closely linked and articulated with their marriage alliances, and with the striving for greater control and wealth by the aristocratic lineages, and with the acquisition of prestige goods through trade. Kirsch phrases his approach in terms of a cybernetic model: the upland peoples face uncertainties with respect to rainfall and land fertility, and are highly motivated to produce,

[17] F.K. Lehman *The Structure of Chin Society: A Tribal People of Burma Adapted to a Non-Western Civilization*, Illinois Studies in Anthropology No. 3, Urbana, University of Illinois Press, 1963. Lehman acknowledges an intellectual debt to Edmund Leach and Rodney Needham. He also cites in many places H.N.C. Stevenson, *The Economics of the Central Chin Tribes*, Bombay: Times of India Press, 1943, which was a source for Leach as well.

[18] Lehman, *The Structure of Chin Society*, p. 140. Lehman explains that while Leach and Stevenson imply that the Kachin democratic variety is associated with an attempt to repudiate the privileges of inherited social rank, he sees Chin politics as based on the difference between status rank conceptualized as a hereditary fixed attribute of certain groups only, and class rank conceptualized as a function of changing wealth and power of lineages (p. 141).

[19] Ibid. p. 1. Lehman's formulation was also influenced by Julian H. Steward's theory of "cultural ecology." At the time Lehman was writing his monograph, Steward was a member of the Department of Anthropology in the University of Illinois and Director of Studies of Cultural Regularities.

[20] A. Thomas Kirsch, *Feasting and Oscillation: A Working Paper on Religion and Society in Upland Southeast Asia*, Cornell University Southeast Asia Program Data Paper no. 92, Ithaca, NY: Cornell University Department of Asian Studies, 1973.

and they have "adapted themselves to a narrow niche which is defined by their own cultural conceptions and resources as a total world."[21]

In "Frontiers of 'Burma'" Leach mounts two submissions that invite further consideration. The first one, which is a major contribution, is his spatial and political characterization of the indigenous (Shan) polities and their dynamic interaction with the Hill People's socio-political formations, and his comparison of those patterns and dynamics with modern European imperial political constructs of the nation-state; the second argument in his two-pronged critique is directed against the limits and deficiencies of language distribution and diffusion studies (historical linguistics) for the understanding of the long-term political and social processes of Upper Burma. I shall take each of these two issues in turn.

European and indigenous conceptions of polity

Leach begins his essay with this comparative observation:

the modern European concepts of *frontier, state,* and *nation* are interdependent, but they are not necessarily applicable to all state-like political organizations everywhere. In default of adequate documentary materials most historians of South-East Asia have tended to assume that the states with which they have to deal were Nation-States occupied by "Peoples" separated from each other by precise political frontiers ... In modern political geography a frontier is a precisely defined line on the map (and on the ground) marking the exact division between two adjacent states. (p. 49)[22]

Most such frontiers are the outcome of arbitrary political decisions or military accidents, and very few correspond to any economically significant feature of the natural topography. But from wars fought to defend such frontiers emerged "a European myth which asserts, not only that every political state must, *ipso facto*, have a definite boundary, but also that the frontiers in question *ought* in some way correspond with difference of culture and language" (p. 49).

In the ideology of modern international politics all states are sovereign, and all states rightfully possess a defined piece of territory. The attitude to frontiers and the dogma of sovereignty coalesce in the principle that

---

[21] Ibid. p. 6.

[22] We may note that Leach equates the words "frontier" and boundary or "border", which certain other writers such as Ainslie Embree have distinguished. Of this, more later.

"territorial sovereignty is absolute and indivisible" (p. 49). The alleged universality of this dogma is a byproduct of European imperial expansion and negotiations in Asia and Africa during the nineteenth and early twentieth centuries. The boundary between northeast Burma and China is a case in point. A distinguished example is the MacMahon line of modern political geography.

By contrast, the indigenous political systems of the Burma region which

> existed prior to the phase of European political expansion were not separated from one another by frontiers in the modern sense and they were not sovereign Nation-States. The whole of "Burma" is a frontier region continuously subjected to influences from both India and China and so also the frontiers which separated the petty political units within "Burma" were not clearly defined lines but zones of mutual interest. The political entities in question had interpenetrating political systems, they were not separate countries inhabited by distinct populations. (p. 50)

Thongchai Winichakul's *Siam Mapped: A History of the Geo-Body of a Nation* (1994),[23] a text published thirty-four years after Leach's essay, has been rightly recognized as a contribution to the understanding of the indigenous premodern Thai conceptions of space, influenced by "cosmographic or religious notions" as well as "profane or worldly ones." It also demonstrates how these notions were relevant to conceiving of indigenous center-oriented politics as overlapping and lacking bounded frontiers, and how Siam in the nineteenth century, influenced and under pressure from Western (British and French) imperial and nation-state notions of exclusive sovereignty, firm territorial boundaries, and frontiers which were given concrete form through the use of mapping and surveying and other "scientific" cartographic techniques, made the shift, especially in the time of King Chulalongkorn (1868–1910) and his successors, to a conscious imaging of itself as a nation-state, defined by these Western criteria. Thongchai phrases this shift in terms of how a new conception of Siam as a "geo-body" emerged, and how, projected back into the past, it came to play a new role in the creation of a new conception of Thai history, and of Thai national identity, which came to dominate Thai historical consciousness throughout the twentieth century.

One immediately notices that Thongchai's formulation of the Thai premodern conceptions of the layout of polities takes its cues from

---

[23] Thongchai Winichakul, *Siam Mapped: A History of the Geo-Body of a Nation*, Honolulu: University of Hawaii Press, 1994.

Leach's explication of the indigenous political sytems of the Burma region (and also from formulations advanced by O.W. Wolters and myself).[24] Remarking that there have been "few studies on the history of a national territory" in Southeast Asia, Thongchai gives this all too brief accolade to Edmund Leach: "only in [his] works on Burma have the effects of the arbitrariness and recent origins of boundaries been seriously considered."[25]

The Leach formulations on the structuring and dynamics of indigenous Burmese valley and hill societies, and Thongchai's narrative of the transition in Siam from such flexible indigenous forms to a European-influenced notion of territorially bounded geo-body would benefit from situating these shifts in the larger context of global processes in the late nineteenth century, especially in Europe and South America, and by extension in the Western imperial control of colonies, especially India. Happenings in India were reproduced in British, French, and Dutch expansions in Southeast Asia, and Siam as we know responded in kind to protect its shrinking territory and sovereignty.

Ainslie Embree has a chapter entitled "Frontiers into Boundaries: The Evolution of the Modern State" in his perceptive book *Imagining India* (1989),[26] which introduces us elegantly to the larger picture. Embree distinguishes the difference between the notions of "frontier" and "boundary." A "frontier" is "an area, often a zone of transition, not only between ethnic groups but also between geographic regions."[27] All the great empires and kingdoms of the past in Europe, Asia, and elsewhere functioned with frontiers.[28] A "boundary" is linear and is demarcated on the ground, along with its corollary, a system of relationships with neighboring states based on formal treaties. Linear boundaries are integrally associated with the forging of the modern nation-state. The development from zonal frontiers to linear boundaries was witnessed in Europe itself

---

[24] See O.W. Wolters, *History, Culture, and Region in Southeast Asian Perspectives*, Singapore: Institute of Southeast Asian Studies, 1982, pp. 16–17; and Stanley J. Tambiah on "the galactic polity" in *World Conqueror and World Renouncer*, chapters 7 and 8 and Tambiah, "The Galactic Polity."

[25] Thongchai, *Siam Mapped*, p. 16. Leach's "Frontiers of 'Burma' " is concerned primarily with the pre-colonial relations between valley and hill Peoples and not with modern nation-state making as such.

[26] Ainslie I. Embree, *Imagining India: Essays on Indian History*, Delhi and New York: Oxford University Press, 1989.

[27] Ibid., p. 68.

[28] In Asia they included the Chinese Empire, the Mughal Empire in India, and a host of other local kingdoms. They typically had forts as defensive frontier outposts, but these were not boundary posts.

in the last twenty-five years of the nineteenth century, a time of intense international tensions and an astonishing number of territorial changes.

Apropos our own interest in developments in South and Southeast Asia, it was the British who first introduced the new political device of linear boundary into the political society of the Indian subcontinent. The well-known McMahon line which demarcated an international boundary between British India and China was later, in 1959, affirmed by independent India as a permanent feature integral to its nationhood, and as marking a northern frontier that had been in existence for nearly three thousand years.[29]

Embree aptly remarks that a simple technological fact, the possession or lack of possession of accurate instruments for making land surveys, was decisive. "The process of marking a line on the ground on the basis of some kind of written description and then transferring it to a map with precision is an achievement associated with advances in surveying techniques in the eighteenth century."[30]

The relevance of this technology and its harnessing to the project of British empire-making is amply documented in Matthew H. Edney's *Mapping an Empire: The Geographical Construction of British India, 1765–1843* (1997).[31] Edney documents the British surveys of India, carried out from the time of James Rennel's survey of Bengal (1765–71) to George Everest's retirement in 1843 as surveyor general of India. The surveys in which geography and cartography served as the vanguard of the British East India Company's territorial and intellectual grasping and conquest of India reached their climax in the Great Trigonometrical Survey (GTS) – which adopted the technique of "triangulation" – begun in the beginning of the nineteenth century. This enterprise had multiple significances. As Edney puts it:

The imperial significance of the Great Trigonometrical Survey depended in part on the survey's configuration of the British rule of South Asia as being scientific,

---

[29] Sir A. Henry McMahon, who in Embree's words "gave his name to the most disputed of modern Indian boundaries" (Embree, *Imagining India*, p. 68) made this distinction in his piece on "International Boundaries," in *Journal of the Royal Society of Arts*, vol. 84, 1935, p. 4: "A frontier often has a wider and more general meaning than a boundary, and a frontier sometimes refers to a wide tract of border country, or to hinterlands or buffer states, undefined by any external boundary line. Such, until recent times, were the North-West Frontier and the North-East Frontier of India; the one comprising the wide indefinite area of independent tribes on the Indian-Afghan border, the other a wide tract of a similarly indefinite nature on the Indian borders of Tibet and China." Quoted by Embree, *Imagining India*, p. 68.

[30] Embree, *Imagining India*, p. 74.

[31] Matthew H. Edney, *Mapping on Empire: The Geographical Construction of British India, 1765–1843*, Chicago: the University of Chicago Press, 1997.

rational, and liberal, in active opposition to Asian rule, which it stereotypes as being mystical, irrational and despotic. The meaning of British rule – that the Company-State was not just another Asiatic tyranny – was *incorporated* into the very acts of surveying and observing the South Asian landscape.

The Great Trigonometrical Survey and, indeed, the whole mapping enterprise were significant for the ideological image of geographical space that they created . . . the surveys held the promise of a perfect geographical panopticon. Through their agency, the British thought they might reduce India to a rigidly coherent, geometrically accurate, and uniformly precise imperial space within which a systematic archive of knowledge about the Indian landscapes and people might be constructed . . . and the spatial significance of the trigonometrical surveys was *inscribed* onto the maps the British produced.[32]

The surveys thus were a cartographic instrument providing the knowledge for the control of India and the extraction of its wealth. While the GTS and its maps served the purpose of legitimating and extending British rule in India, it must also be admitted that the Trigonometrical Survey, one of the great monuments of nineteenth-century imperial science, was in practice undermined by the Company's internal division between the three great presidencies of Bengal, Madras, and Bombay, its inability to systematically aggregate uneven knowledge, its patronage system, and the impediments of the working conditions of its surveyors in the field, ultimately reducing the survey to "cartographic anarchy." Was this outcome a metaphor for the long-run unwieldiness of British India itself and a warning to ambitious nation-states of today in South and Southeast Asia and elsewhere, that their totalizing projects are usually impossible to achieve and undermined by various kinds of resistance? The same warning should be heeded by the post-independence nation-states of South and Southeast Asia, including Thailand which, though not colonized, bears much family resemblance to them, to be more considerate of the sentiments and aspirations of their minorities and marginalized border peoples.

Critique of the search for language origins and diffusion

I shall now consider Leach's rejection of the conventional hypothesis that the Tibeto-Burman languages had their point of origin in Tibet, from where the subsequent dispersion took place into Burma and elsewhere. He prefers the view that the variety of Burmese languages was always present in Burma and the migration theory from a point of origin is

---

[32] Ibid., pp. 319–20.

neither necessary nor substantiated. In any case he holds that his own thesis of the dynamic interactions between the two persisting political, kinship, and ecological structures of the hill people and valley people is a better key to understanding historical dynamics.

Leach challenges the "myth of philological origins" which influences existing histories of Burma, and which assumes that the "frontiers of language correspond to frontiers of culture and political power" (p. 50). The population is considered to consist of a large number of separate "peoples": Mons, Arakanese, Karens, Burmese, Kachins, Shans, Lisu, and so on, each group being assumed to have a separate history.

Such peoples are never treated as indigenous to Burma; each group arrived separately by migration from some remote original homeland ... The myth of philological origins, with its illusion of multiple discontinuities, has distracted the historian's attention from those elements of the modern Burmese social scene which have been persistently present throughout the last 2000 years. In particular, the historians have tended to neglect the continuing interaction between processes of political action and the permanent structure of ecological relationship. (p. 50)

Leach provocatively invites "the historian of Burma to look upon the present as part of a continuing process of interaction between two kinds of political structure, two kinds of ecology, two distinct patterns of kinship organization, two sets of economic contrasts" (p. 67). His analytical and interpretive procedure consists in first setting up a categorical contrast between two ideological structures as a continuing phenomenon, and then postulating a continuing process of interaction between them in the three aforementioned dimensions, and to focus on how individual persons undergo a change of identity by making the passage from one structure to another.

He proposes this processual sociological schema, continuously at play throughout Burmese history, as an alternative to, and replacement of, the approach of linguists, who see the Burmese terrain in terms of the distribution of different linguistic groups, and who search for the philological origins of these languages in the distant past, and their diffusion and geographical distribution through time. Leach persuasively demonstrates in *Political Systems* and in "The Frontiers of 'Burma' " that groups speaking different dialects in fact are not frozen as distinct entities, that they are not monolingual, that they have social exchanges of many kinds including intermarriage, and that speakers of one language not only learn other languages, but may, through migration and residential change, change their language and assimilate into their host society.

Was Leach unduly and unnecessarily dismissive of "the myth of philological origins" (p. 50), and excessive in his assertion that "language distribution can make no contribution to the history of an area" (p. 70)? The linguist Isidore Dyen of Yale University, who was invited to respond to Leach's critique of historical linguistics as applied to Burma,[33] accepts the value of Leach's sociological contrasts between the hill people and valley people, and concedes that "language distributions do not play an immediately determining role in historical events. Language boundaries rather reflect political and social changes. It is just as possible for a people who speak the same language to fight each other as it is for those who speak different languages. It takes very little time for partial bilinguals to develop among speakers of different languages who have come into contact" (p. 72). Dyen further suggests that "a historian looking to deal with groups for which records are available might wish to define the groups in the first place by criteria other than language, for such criteria might yield a simpler set of groups for his purposes than a linguistically determined collection" (p. 73).

At the same time Dyen concludes that there is value in classifying the languages of Burma and mapping their distributions. He maintains that there are scientifically plausible methods for attempting to locate the homeland of a set of interrelated languages and their subsequent historical dispersion. Interestingly one of his suggestions is that, measured by the "principle of least moves," the homeland of the Burmese language set, granted certain conditions, might likely be found in "an area occupied by a more diversified chain of languages rather than occupied by a less diversified chain" (p. 70). The inference from the application of this hypothesis is that a less diversified area may imply a migration from the more diversified area.

Applying this principle of least moves, Dyen suggests that Leach may have an argument in his challenge to the conventional hypothesis that the Burmese language reached Burma by migration from Tibet as an explanation of the language distribution of the Tibeto-Burman languages. "If the Tibeto-Burman languages of Burma are more diverse than those of Tibet, it would appear possible to entertain the hypothesis that the Tibetan came from Burma" (p. 70). And if one accepted H. Maspero's

---

[33] See Isidore Dyen, "Comment", in Appendix to Leach, "Frontiers of 'Burma,'" pp. 70–73.

divisions of the map of the Tibeto-Burman language territory[34] into western China, the Assam area (including northwest Burma), the Indian area, the Nepalese area, and the coastal area in which "Burmese and the doubtful Karen are spoken," then "of these areas the Assam area would at first blush appear to be the one with the greatest diversity and if so would be a reasonable candidate for the homeland" (p. 72).

In contemplating Dyen's reply, it is relevant to bear in mind that he was a follower of the hypothesis advanced by Sapir and Greenberg that "the homeland of the ancestral speakers of any group of related languages is likely to be located in or near the region exhibiting the greatest genetic diversity", and that this hypothesis itself is controversial.[35] While Leach may have an argument concerning the locus of the Burmese languages as explainable without a theory of migration whose origin point was Tibet, he seems to be more vulnerable regarding his rejection of the theory of the migration of the Tai (or Thai-Kadai) language speakers from their origin point in southern China, and their subsequent spread into a vast area southwards. We may also note that the Shans of Burma, who are his example of valley people in the "Frontiers of 'Burma,'" are classified as speakers of a language of the Tai type (and not of a Tibeto-Burman type).

Leach criticizes the assumption that, with the destruction of Nan Chao as a political entity in 1253, following conquest by Kublai Khan, there was a mass migration of Tai-speaking peoples to the south-west. "In the centuries which followed, it is supposed that evidence for this migration was that monarchs with Tai sounding names are recorded as the rulers of petty principalities all over Burma." This in turn is linked with the more general thesis that since Tai is a language of Chinese type it must have "originated" somewhere in central China. Yet in fact there is no evidence at all of any migration of Tai-speaking peoples into "Burma" from the north-east, and recent trends in linguistic research seem to indicate that Tai speech has no close affinities with Chinese. Its closest links appear to be with languages further south such as Mon and Indonesian.[36]

---

[34] Dyen cites H. Maspero, "Les Langues Tibéto-Birmanes," in A. Meillet and M. Cohen (eds.), *Les langues du monde*, Paris: Centre National de la Recherche Scientifique, 1952, pp. 529–70.

[35] See G.P. Murdock, "Genetic Classification of Austronesian Languages: A Key to Oceanic Culture History," *Ethnology*, vol. 3, no. 2, 1964, p. 122, cited by C.F. Keyes in *The Golden Peninsula: Culture and Adaptation in Mainland Southeast Asia*, New York: Macmillan, 1977, p. 17. Dyen's linguistic analysis in this vein, which has been questioned, relates to the study of Austronesian languages whose original home he located in Melanesia. G.P. Murdock supported Dyen's formulation.

[36] Leach refers to these works as his authority: Paul K. Benedict, "Thai, Kadai and Indonesian: A New Alignment in Southeastern Asia," *American Anthropologist*, vol. 44, 1942, pp. 578–601; and L.F. Taylor, "General Structure of Languages Spoken in Burma," *Journal of the Burma Research*

Nan Chao itself, asserts Leach, as a political entity was "unquestion-ably" of the Indian rather than the Chinese type: "it had no bureaucratic stability and its fortunes fluctuated violently according to the individ-ual aggressiveness of successive rulers," and it is an excellent exam-ple of the confusion which arises when such polities are "thought of as nation states of modern type" (pp. 55–56). "Nanchao should not be thought of as a state with borders but as a capital city with a wide and variable sphere of influence . . . there was no Nanchao nation which would be dispersed by the elimination of Nanchao as a separate political entity" (p. 56).

How do these assertions made in 1960 stack up in relation to later schol-arship? It seems that the classification and origins of Tai languages still remain an inconclusive and confused affair. We should note initially that the term "Tai" is used to refer to any group speaking a Tai language and the distribution of these groups is quite widespread. (The label "Thai" refers to the majority citizens of the "nation-state" of Thailand.) The old theory that Tai languages belong to the Sino-Tibetan language fam-ily has definitely been rejected, though it is possible that there may have been ancient contacts between Tai and Sinitic languages. Benedict's the-sis, which Leach cites, that Tai (or Daic) languages are genetically related to Autronesian-Polynesian languages seems to be still alive, though in a modified form.[37]

However, a dominant view among historical linguists pursuing the method of genealogical classification of the Tai languages seems to arrive at results which override Leach's disbelief in migrations of Tai speakers, whose original location was in south China. For example a group of French scholars (1988) have completed an interesting "map of the Thai language ethnic groups."[38] The map includes "the largest possible num-ber of ethnic groups speaking Thai languages spread over the greater part of continental Southeast Asia and southern China."[39] The authors use "Thai" in place of the more general expression "Tai." In a vast zone constituting, to use an expression coined by G. Condominas, an

Society, vol. 39, 1956. P.K. Benedict's *Austro-Thai Language and Culture, with a Glossary of Roots*, New Haven: HRAF Press, 1975, was not available to Leach.

[37] See Keyes, *The Golden Peninsula*, pp. 59–60.

[38] See Annick Léy-Ward and Sophie and Pierre Clément, "Some Observations on the Map of the Ethnic Groups Speaking Thai Languages," *Journal of the Siam Society*, vol. 76, 1988, pp. 29–41. Their mapping is based on and continues the work of many predecessors, and they particularly rely on the work of various French centers, the Australian Academy of Humanities, American scholars, and Mahidol University in Bangkok.

[39] Ibid., p. 29.

ethnolinguistic mosaic, the Thai-Kadai speaking peoples [are] spread through a large part of the Indochinese peninsula, the regions to the West as far as the banks of Brahmaputra, and to the north and east in China's southern provinces, Yunnan, Guangxi, Guizhou and a large part of Hainan . . . Politically the Thai speaking peoples constitute the nations of Thailand and Laos, while in Vietnam and China they are the largest minorities . . . Within the Shan states, they are also the largest minority in Burma.[40]

The authors in question, professing that "the aim of comparative grammar is to reconstruct a common initial language by comparing related languages," while accepting the contributions of Benedict, classify the Thai-Kadai languages into three main groups: Kadai, Dam-Sui, and Thai-Yay (subdivided into numerous languages, and further subdivided into dialects). Of the three main groups Thai-Yay is the predominant one in two senses: in terms of the number of languages and persons speaking them, and in terms of the areal spread of speakers.[41] The speakers of the Thai-Yay languages, estimated as exceeding 65 million, are to be found in Guangxi in southern China, and in the southern and southeastern parts of Yunnan Province; in Vietnam; in Laos; in Thailand (by far the largest number); and in Burma (especially the Shan, Khun and Khamti minorities).

The main conclusions regarding the Thai-Kadai languages as a whole are as follows:

1. The favored zones of occupation for the Thai-Kadai speakers are river valleys.[42]
2. As regards the origin and migration of these peoples, if one accepts the hypothesis that the Thai-Yay peoples originally lived in Guangxi in southern China, then Guangxi would be one of the poles of their concentration and the Menam Valley the other pole (with the Khorat Plateau and the Malaysian Isthmus the end points of their arrival). The intermediate less populated zones indicate the routes of migration toward the Shan states of western and northeastern Burma, and along the river valleys of the Mekong and Menam rivers (and secondary rivers) in a north–south orientation. In the course of the

---

[40] Ibid., pp. 29–30.
[41] The authors say that the territory occupied by the Thai-Yay group "is vast, extending east to west from southern Guizhou province to the bend of the Brahmaputra in the Assam region and it covers a large part of the Indochina peninsula, reaching from Yunnan in the north (if one excludes the Khamti peoples still further north) to the Malaysian border in the south." Ibid., p. 36.
[42] One exception is the Kelao grouped in the central region of China's Guizhou province.

great migrations southwards the Thai language speakers encountered Austro-Asiatic populations speaking Mon-Khmer.

3. On the basis of alleged linguistic evidence and historical chronicles the authors describe the stages of migration of the "Thai conquerors" (including the Central Thai of Li Fang Kuei or Taỳ-Nūng) as follows: in the eighth century they were still located in their original homeland, while during the eleventh and twelfth centuries their migrations occurred so that by the thirteenth century they were occupying approximately the areas where they are found today.

4. There were probably some displacements of populations resulting from wars; examples may be some small localized communities of the Phuan at Lophburi in Thailand, and Lao Song belonging to the Black Tai and Phu Thai in Thailand.

There are other somewhat different ways of dealing with the distribution of Tai languages. In May 1999 an international conference entitled "The Tai Peoples before the Coming of Civilization" was held at Thammasat University, Bangkok.[43] Numerous papers were read documenting the vast spread of Tai-speaking peoples and their life forms pertaining to the past and present in China (Guizhou Province, Hainan Island, Yunnan), Thailand and Laos (the Upper Mekong River Basin), northern Burma (Shan states), Vietnam, Northeast India, and elsewhere. It is interesting that a paper presented by R. Sethakul dealing with the Tai "Chiang" in the Upper Mekong River Basin, based on the submissions of James Chamberlain, asserts that linguistic and archaeological evidence shows that "the area of greatest dialect diversity of the Tai languages [was] along the eastern Sino-Vietnamese border" and that this area can therefore "safely be considered the homeland of Proto-Tai," from where diffusion of these languages was from east to west across northeast Southeast Asia.[44] Sethakul portrays the Upper Mekong River Basin as a vast area of Tai homeland. Along the Mekong river,

---

[43] The conference, held on May 27–28, 1999, was organized by the Thai Khadi Research Institute, Thammasat University, Bangkok. The Institute's Director was Professor Sumitr Pitiphat. I was privileged to attend the conference, which was part of the celebration of His Majesty Bhumipol's seventy-second birthday.

[44] The paper in question by Ratanaporn Sethakul was entitled "The Tai 'Chiang' in the Upper-Mekong River Basin: Their Origins and Historical Significance." He refers to James R. Chamberlain, "A Critical Framework for the Study of Thao Houng or Cheuang," paper presented at the First International Conference on the Literary, Historical, and Cultural Aspects of the Thao Hung Thao Chueang, Bangkok, January 18–19, 1996.

Tai-speaking groups, namely Lu, Shan, Laos, Khon, and Yuan, settled down and formed their principalities with walled cities (*Chiang*).[45] Tai chronicles state that principalities were formed in the twelfth to thirteenth centuries on the Mekong River Basin – distributed in an area ranging from Sipsong Panna in the southwestern part of Yunnan in China down to Luang Phrabang in the upper part of Laos, a region at present located in four different countries: China, Burma, Thailand, and Laos.

I should point out that this profile uses, via Chamberlain and Dyen, the original Sapir and Greenberg hypothesis that the area of greatest linguistic diversity is likely to be the homeland of a language complex. And this perspective could be seen as indirectly supporting Leach's rejection of the search for a single ultimate philological origin point in favor of focusing on the ecological, social, and political structures and processes operating in a known interactional arena composed of hill peoples and valley peoples whose linguistic variations and contrasts are a significant feature of their long-lasting communicational processes.

In conclusion, I shall briefly allude to some developments that go beyond the scope of Leach's essay. In the nineteenth century as well as in more recent times there have been known migrations of varieties of hill people into Burma, Thailand, and Laos from further north. The politics of majoritarian nation-state making in Burma since it gained independence from British rule in 1948 and in Thailand since the early decades of the twentieth century, but especially since the Second World War, have produced two different outcomes regarding the Burmese and Thai peoples and their respective hill peoples that Leach outlined. In the Burmese case, for various reasons, the policies of the government have generated organized rebellions and resistance from among the hill peoples, many of whom have been Christianized since British times – the Karens who staged a major rebellion in 1948 and have continued their politics of separation are a conspicuous case in point – and the picture of both contrast and interactions between the two entities that Leach dissected has deepened into a cleavage of enmity and warfare. In the Thai case, policies of sedentarization, border police patrolling of migration, and dubious regulation of opium production, combined with certain policies of economic development, schooling, and the spread of the Thai language, and even missionary efforts by monks at introducing

---

[45] The *Chiang* mentioned are Chiang Rung, Chiang Khaeng, Chiang Saen, Chiang Rai, Chiang Khong, and Chiang Thong (Luang Phrabang).

Buddhism, the "civilizing" religion, have over time begun to blur the boundaries between what Leach considered two contrasting forms of ecological social organizations, and to increase the process of more individuals and families becoming integrated, if not fully assimilated, in a hierarchical, inferiorized manner.[46]

[46] For example, for a recent essay on forms of accommodation with lowland Thai, and selective patterns of assimilation of some of their ways, on the part of the Akha in north Thailand, leading to subtle processes of redefinition of their group identity, see Deborah Tooker's unpublished essay "Modular Modern: The Compartmentalization of Group Identity in Northern Thailand.

CHAPTER 7

"Pul Eliya": *the challenge to descent group theory*

INTRODUCTION: THE ISSUES POSED

Leach introduces the monograph on Pul Eliya as having two aspects, firstly, as an addition to the already substantial literature relating to Ceylonese land tenure, and secondly, "as an academic exercise designed to provide a critical text of certain features of the theory and method of British social anthropology, especially as it related to the general field of kinship theory."[1] Whatever professional anthropologists may say in regard to its theoretical implications for kinship theory, there is no doubt at all that the monograph is a masterly, detailed, and unmatched account of the land tenure system prevailing in a village in the "dry zone" North Central Province in the year 1954.

It is possible that those anthropologists who have studied people who practice shifting agriculture with hoe technology or pastoralism – although these systems have land tenure concepts and inheritance rules – have for the most part little sense of the almost obsessive concern among people of South Asia, who practice sedentary plough agriculture in fields of fixed size and position, with values oriented toward possession of land and its transmission, and all the well-being, status, and symbolic capital that go with it.

Scholars of Sri Lanka (including A.M. Hocart, who for a time served as head of the Government Archaeology Department) have also marveled at the meticulous coding and indexing of the Kandyan kingdom's feudal religio-political structure and the hierarchy of castes in terms of land tenure. Perhaps nothing so famously and dramatically illustrates the centrality of land tenure as the organizing grid as the fact that in the kingdom's annual *perahera*, a procession in which the centerpieces were the sacred tooth relic of the Buddha and the four guardian deities of

---

[1] E.R. Leach, *Pul Eliya, A Village in Ceylon: A Study in Land Tenure and Kinship*, Cambridge: Cambridge University Press, 1961, p. 1.

the island, and in which the chief officials and departments of the kingdom paraded, the leader of the pageant was the "Peramune Rala," Officer of the Front, "riding an elephant and carrying a symbolic book that represented the *lekam miti*, the state records of the lands of the kingdom." (The *lekam miti*, or clerical rolls, were alleged to be a complete register of the land in use in the whole kingdom, and thus embodied the country's land tenure system.)[2]

Academic anthropologists in general have virtually limited their interest to *Pul Eliya*'s relevance for kinship theory, but Sri Lankan scholars of all types – historians, geographers, anthropologists, agronomists – have unstintingly acclaimed and appreciated it as a remarkable contribution to a subject for which many of them have a passion. The ancient and medieval hydraulic civilizations centered on the historic capitals of Anuradhapura and Polonnaruva have been hailed and saluted as engineering feats in colonial reports, local chronicles, and the writings of famous European scholars, such as Arnold Toynbee and Joseph Needham. Such writings have been important for shoring up national pride.

Clearly from the point of view of historical knowledge it is the writings of colonial public servants such as R.W. Ievers, H.W. Codrington, and R.L. Brohier, and recent Sri Lankan scholars such as R. Pieris, Paranavitane, and R.A.L.H. Gunawardena that matter as worthwhile accounts. In relation to this corpus Leach's study is exceptional. As Leach himself claimed, all these works are more or less synthetic accounts that give a kind of ideal model of both the macro-systems of monarchial regimes and the micro tank-villages, which, though composing the bottom stratum of the irrigation hierarchy, were in fact the mainstay of the dry zone agricultural economy. Although there had been previous partial accounts, Leach's study was the first full-scale empirical study of the actual "workings" of a particular social system in all the details of its singular particularity. *Pul Eliya* is a case study that illuminates the previous academic treatises in unexpected ways, and it did in fact stimulate a number of other field studies in Sri Lanka in which the relation between social structure and land tenure was a critical axis both for the people studied and for the anthropologists.[3]

---

[2] See H.L. Seneviratne, *Rituals of the Kandyan State*, Cambridge: Cambridge University Press, 1978, pp. 108–14. Also see A.M. Hocart, *The Temple of the Tooth in Kandy*, Memoirs of the Archaeological Survey of Ceylon, vol. IV, London: Luzac and Co. for the Government of Ceylon, 1931; Ralph Pieris, *Sinhalese Social Organization: The Kandyan Period*, Colombo: Ceylon University Press Board, 1956.

[3] For example, Gananath Obeyesekere, *Land Tenure in Village Ceylon: A Sociological and Historical Study*, Cambridge: Cambridge University Press, 1967; Marguerite S. Robinson, *Political Structure in a Changing Sinhalese Village*, Cambridge and New York: Cambridge University Press, 1975;

Keeping in mind those many omnibus wide-ranging monographs common to the field of anthropology which aim to touch on almost every aspect of the social and cultural life of single communities, Leach modestly and accurately says that his formal subject matter "covers an extremely narrow field," namely "the local land tenure system" and its relation to kinship. This narrow field in fact becomes an inexhaustible vista filled with ethnographic particulars that in my view constitutes one of the richest and most analytically illuminating documentations of virtually all aspects of a "peasant economy," both synchronically as it operated in 1954, and diachronically from 1890 or so to 1954. Land tenure is a canopy that covers much in the areas of production, distribution, consumption, and exchange.

Some wags have joked that because Leach lost all his Kachin field notes during the Second World War, he compensated by publishing all the information he collected in Pul Eliya. Leach genially admitted that there is something to this charge, but that there was a serious purpose behind his detailed documentation.

The resort to and handling of archival and contemporary first-hand information is truly amazing: cadastral surveys first done in 1890, and surveys later repeated; tax records from 1860 to 1893; land title registrations, plot ownership, and transmissions from 1890 to 1954; administration reports; court cases and litigation – all these are backed by Leach's own complete mapping of the Old Field and the residential compounds (*gamgoda*), and all categories of other land owned and used, and a thorough compilation of genealogies and much else. Serious fieldworkers who have tried to collect and diagram such information must surely be impressed with table 4, which gives a compilation of all owners of the Old Field at three dates –1889, 1890, and 1954–, with chart i, which gives a genealogy of Pul Eliya residents according to their residential succession in compounds from around 1890 to 1954, and finally with his complete mapping according to scale of all field strips in the Old Field in 1954 (map E).

Stanley J. Tambiah, "The Structure of Kinship and Its Relationship to Land Possession and Residence in Pata Dumbara, Central Ceylon," *The Journal of the Royal Anthropological Institute*, vol. 88, part 1, 1958, pp. 21–44; Tambiah, "Kinship Fact and Fiction in Relation to the Kandyan Sinhalese," *The Journal of the Royal Anthropological Institute*, vol. 95, part 2, 1965, pp. 131–73; Tambiah, "Polyandry in Ceylon – with Special Reference to the Laggala Region," in Christoph von Fürer-Haimendorf (ed.), *Caste and Kin in Nepal, India, and Ceylon Anthropological Studies in Hindu – Buddhist Contact Zones*, Bombay and New York: Asia Publishing House, 1966, pp. 264–358. Nur Yalman's *Under the Bo Tree Studies in Caste, Kinship, and Marriage in the Interior of Ceylon*, Berkeley: University of California Press, 1967 is contemporaneous with Leach's work, but of course they were in contact as teacher and student at Cambridge.

All this exhaustive and meticulously checked information is marshaled to cover the following aspects of economic life: land ownership and its transmission through time; the maintenance of the irrigation system; cultivation operations and landlord–tenant–laborer arrangements; credit and debt relations; labor organization, labor exchange, and sharing of rewards in different phases of a single cultivation season culminating in harvesting, threshing, and share distribution; forms of cultivation in compound gardens; and the fascinating system of shifting cultivation (*chena*) on dry land, according to the "wheel pattern." All these details are there not only to provide an understanding of the multiple dimensions of the economic life of the Pul Eliya people but also as ammunition for waging a theoretical campaign, ambitious and risky. The facts are marshaled and presented, as Leach warned, to the point of "unreadability," because the validation of his theoretical assertions depended on the empirical method he had chosen to substantiate the assertions. Thus, *Pul Eliya* is for Leach an experiment in method which would generate the empirical data that were needed to confirm his assertions. This experiment in method he compared with the usual anthropological fieldwork of his time in this way. From Malinowski onward, the so-called field study and case history took the form of anthropologists propounding a general hypothesis and then presenting this cases and examples to illustrate the argument: "The technique of argument is still that of Frazer. Insight comes from the anthropologists' private intuition; the evidence is only put in by way of illustration."[4]

Leach would try to avoid this kind of "subjectivism" by presenting as far as possible a dense aggregation and accumulation of observations on all relevant issues pertaining to land tenure and kinship to all the adult inhabitants (household heads, compound heads, their spouses, and marrying/married adults through time) in the small universe of Pul Eliya composed of 146 residents (and their close kin in neighboring villages relevant to them).

Covering quantitatively and qualitatively everything of significance in a small universe in relation to a chosen topic cannot of course be done in a literal sense, but it is important for any serious reader of *Pul Eliya* to realize that Leach harnesses his uncompromising empiricism to a theoretical end, namely that the quantitative patterns formed by the data would in themselves constitute a "social order" or "social structure." This would be a different representation of "social structure" from that

---

[4] Leach, *Pul Eliya*, p. 12.

propounded and allegedly confirmed by resort to "mystical" concepts by the leading British exponents of "structural-functionalism."

What is Leach's quarrel with this school of thought that "emanated from Oxford?"

During the period 1934–54 "the most important developments in anthropological work were concerned with the enlargement of our understanding of the nature and significance of unilineal descent groups."[5] The chief contributors to this effort were Radcliffe-Brown, Evans-Pritchard, especially in his study of the Nuer (1940), and Fortes, notably in his summing up (1953).[6] By virtue of its success and also its biases, this body of descent group theory invites its antithesis.

Radcliffe-Brown "consistently exaggerated the importance of unilineal as opposed to bilateral (cognatic) systems of succession and inheritance." Though uncommon in Africa, the main site for theorizing about unilineal descent groups (UDGs), cognatic systems are widely distributed throughout the world and far exceed in frequency other types, yet Radcliffe-Brown gave them little notice. A question that arises then is how do his generalizations apply to societies in which unilineal descent is not a factor?

A main assertion of Radcliffe-Brown, further accented by Fortes (and ultimately deriving from their reading of Henry Maine's *Ancient Law*), was that "in societies with a lineage structure the continuity of the society as a whole rests in the continuity of the system of lineages, each of which is a 'corporation', the life-span of which is independent of the individual lives of its individual members."[7] Fortes, while very aware of the fact, which Max Weber had made clear, that "in theory membership of a corporate legal or political group need not stem from kinship" and that in "primitive society" there could be other bases or means of incorporation such as locality and ritual initiation, yet saw "descent *per se* as the most effective basis of incorporation. This was especially so because "descent is fundamentally *a jural concept*" as Radcliffe-Brown argued, and its significance was that it served

as the connecting link between the external, that is the political and legal aspect of what we have called unilineal descent groups, and the internal or domestic aspect. It is in the latter context that kinship carries maximum weight, first *as the*

---

[5] Ibid., p. 5.

[6] E.E. Evans-Pritchard, *The Nuer: A Description of the Modes of Livelihood and Political Institutions of a Nilotic People*, Oxford: Clarendon Press, 1940; M. Fortes, "The Structure of Unilineal Descent Groups", *American Anthropologist*, vol. 55, 1953, pp. 17–41.

[7] Leach, *Pul Eliya*, p. 6.

source of title to membership of the groups or to specific *jural status*, with all that this means over and toward persons and property, and second as the basis of the social relations among the persons who are identified with one another in the corporate group.[8](emphasis added)

Descent had the advantage of providing unequivocal discrimination of rights *in rem* and *in personam* in respect of succession, as descent groups easily regulated rights over the reproductive powers of women, but deeper down nothing "could so precisely fix one's place in society as one's parentage."[9] Readers of *Pul Eliya* who come across Leach's barrage against theorists who consider kinship *per se* as "a thing in itself" will find their clues to this expression in the view that kinship, especially descent, is the very generative basis of jural status, succession and inheritance rights, and placement and incorporation in descent groups, which by a further extrapolation from the internal domestic domain to the external domestic domain also provides the grid for political and legal relations. Above all theorists, Fortes is the purest expounder of this vision of kinship as an autonomous system. Be that as it may, Leach remarks that in a society like that found in Pul Eliya, where no unilineal descent principle prevails, "it is locality rather than descent which forms the basis of corporate grouping."[10] It is only after one has worked through the ethnography that this statement can be tested and understood.

There are other entailments to the UDG approach which Leach criticizes as constructing a *static* and *equilibrium* view of society insulated from dynamics and change. "If anthropologists come to look upon kinship as a parameter which can be studied in isolation they will always be led, by a series of logical steps, to think of human society as composed of equilibrium systems, structured according to ideal legal rules."[11] In Leach's mind, and in terms of what would be a central concern and demonstration in *Pul Eliya*, the intrinsic equilibrium kinship model is particularly guilty of considering economic factors and activities to be of "minor significance," and thus the study of social adaptation to changing circumstances is made impossible. Fortes, in particular, reflects this bias: "The tendency towards equilibrium is marked in every sector of Tale society and in the society as a whole; and it is clearly *the result of the dominance in the lineage principle in the social structure* . . . The almost complete

---

[8] Fortes, "The Structure of Unilineal Descent Groups," p. 30.
[9] Ibid., p. 30. In his later writings Fortes would develop parentage, filiation, and solidarity of siblings as the fundamental building blocks of kinship.
[10] Leach, *Pul Eliya*, p. 7.   [11] Ibid., pp. 7–8.

absence of economic differentiation . . . mean(s) that *the economic interests do not play the part of dynamic factors in the social structure.*"[12]

The insensitivity to economic activities and relations of production in general stemming from the emphasis on the lineage principle was also reflected by Radcliffe-Brown who constantly stressed the jural and "legal aspects of kinship relations as manifested in *the rights of inheritance in contrast to the economic aspects manifested in work cooperation*" (emphasis added).[13] This last criticism, simply mentioned in one line in the introduction, would in fact become a central issue of exposition in the text: while inheritance, transmission, and possession of property over time are of vital concern to the Sinhalese peasantry, so are the organization and cooperative relations of labor in the operations of cultivation and harvesting of rice, and the rewarding of them through distribution of the product. The jural ties of kinship and inheritance stemming from "descent" are quite different from labor cooperation directed by ties of affinity. Furthermore, the stress on patrilineal descent and organization leads to "explaining away" the importance attached to *matrilateral and affinal kinship connections.*[14] Leach's thesis seems to be that if economic activities are a primary concern and basic to social life, and if changes in economic circumstances do engender changes in the kinship system, the latter cannot be regarded as "intrinsic and autonomous," and the possibility is raised as to whether economic relations are in this sense "prior" to kinship relations. What Leach means by "prior" is not clearly articulated at this point, and Leach's critics have seen this as a red rag. An attempt will be made later to contextualize this usage.

There is one final issue to which Leach gives attention, and which questions Radcliffe-Brownian orthodoxy. Leach is on record also on many other occasions as being skeptical of typologies of kinship systems. (Typologizing is a form of butterfly collecting.) In his book, Leach is not bent on offering the Pul Eliya case as simply a "bilateral system", in contrast to a "unilineal system". The distinction between non-unilineal and unilineal systems is not useful either: Pul Eliya does not belong to either type, and moreover, for some aspects of life in that village there is

---

[12] M. Fortes, *The Dynamics of Clanship Among the Tallensi: Being the First Part of an Analysis of the Social Structure of a Trans-Vorta Tribe*, London and New York: Oxford University Press, 1945, p. x emphasis added by Leach.

[13] Leach, *Pul Eliya*, p. 6.

[14] Fortes is famous for his thesis of "complementary filiation": in patrilineal systems with polygynous marriages each mother serves to internally distinguish the male siblings born of the same father; also marriage is an individual matter, and siblings will have different networks of affines through marriage.

at work a notion of "descent," and in others a contrasting notion of affinity. Similarly, Leach is not keen on distinguishing between "jural" and "economic" relationships where they are interactive and copresent. He would much rather be seen as offering the subversive agenda of persuading the unilineal descent group theorists to see in the Pul Eliya exposition reasons for loosening the primacy they accord in their accounts of unilineal societies to the structuring role of kinship *per se*, and to permit other existential activities and contextual circumstances a creative and structuring role.

Kinship as we meet it in this book [*Pul Eliya*] is not "a thing in itself". The concepts of descent and affinity are expressions of property relations which endure through time. Marriage unifies; inheritance separates; property endures. A particular descent system simply reflects the total process of property succession as affected by the total pattern of inheritance and marriage. The classification of whole societies in terms of such a parameter can only be meaningful in an extremely crude sense.[15]

This is the polemical challenge posed in trenchant terms, and aimed directly at the kinship theory of Radcliffe-Brown and his followers.

There is a larger, more encompassing theoretical issue about the form and nature of social action that is integrally linked to the empiricist method that was earlier described, and to the manner in which the anthropologist sees the relation between "custom" and the "behavior of individuals." Some of the writings of Emile Durkheim serve as a point of departure for Leach in setting up his debate.

For both Radcliffe-Brown and Evans-Pritchard, Durkheim's *Division of Labour* and Maine's *Ancient Law* were primary sources.

Individuals were presumed to be born free into a society composed of corporate institutions, the relations within which and between which provide a paradigm of social existence. The structural shape of such a corporation is intrinsically self-perpetuating and is independent of the individual life-span of its particular members. Social structure is thought of as a network of relationships between "persons", or "roles". The stability of the system requires that the content of such relationships shall be permanent. In such a society every individual who fills a role finds himself under jural constraint to fulfil the obligations inherent in that role. More crudely, the customs of a society are seen as providing a body of moral norms worked out in behaviouristic form; the discrepancies between individual behaviour and customary behaviour are due simply to the inability of the average man to live up to the moral demands of his society. He

---

[15] Leach, *Pul Eliya*, p. 11.

is represented as knowing very well what ought to be the case, but as devising immensely complicated fictions which will absolve him from the inconvenience of virtue.[16]

In contrast to this perspective,

There is another line of thought, which also comes from Durkheim, which stems from the thesis that the social is that which is *quantitatively* normal. In *Division of Labour* norms are jural norms, rules of behaviour supported by sanctions; in *Suicide* the norm is a statistical average. Throughout the later writings both of Durkheim himself and of his followers this same ambiguity between normative and normal constantly occurs. In British anthropology it corresponds in some ways to the opposition between the Radcliffe-Brown and the Malinowski versions of functionalist doctrine.[17]

In Radcliffe-Brown's schema society has the power to impose its will upon the individual through the operation of the sanctioned rules which constitute the structure of enduring corporate groups. In Malinowski's system, the individual is not a "slave to custom"; custom makes "sense" in terms of the private self-interest of the average person in a particular cultural situation, and actually no clear distinction emerges between customary behavior and individual behavior. Although Malinowski's conception is like Durkheim's "suicide rate," Malinowski's evaded the crucial issue of "just how the social fact of normal behaviour can emerge from a sum of seemingly arbitrary individual choices."[18] However Malinowski's virtue was that he did not invoke "the currently fashionable structuralist concept of social solidarity" which Leach dubs as a "mysticism" invoked as an ultimate explanatory device and absolute virtue toward which all social activity is of necessity directed.

Leach proposes a third way of thinking about the distinction and relation between custom and individual behavior, ideal model and statistical order, normative and normal. In a way the answer he searches for is an extension and elaboration of a perspective first broached in *Political Systems of Highland Burma*, in which he tried to probe the correspondence between *ideal type thought categories* (such as *gumsa* and *gumlao*) and the "empirical facts on the ground." The thought categories he warned should not be equated with actual behavioral relations. But *Political Systems of Highland Burma*, though an advance, had, as Leach recognized, "idealist" connotations, even "idealist pitfalls." *Pul Eliya* seeks to go further by incorporating a "materialist" dimension, so to say, and the answers

---

[16] Ibid., pp. 296–97.   [17] Ibid., p. 297.   [18] Ibid., p. 298.

Leach proposes to the grand question can only be sensibly reviewed and judged after doing our homework of closely attending to the ethnography he presents.

I have taken one liberty with the text. Reversing Leach's order of presentation I shall present the chapters on land tenure first, and subsequently the chapter on the kinship system. I do so because unless one fully grasps first what Leach had to say about the Old Field, one cannot appreciate his submissions regarding the flexibility of the kinship system that is integrally linked to the greater rigidity of the topographical system once it was laid out in a particular ecology.

THE TOPOGRAPHY OF THE TANK-VILLAGE

Leach discusses the ideal model of the land tenure system allegedly prevailing in many villages of the dry zone summarized by the phrase "one tank–one village" in the work of a number of previous writers such as Ievers, Codrington, and Pieris.[19] I shall bypass this, and summarize the main points regarding the "ideal model" of the Pul Eliya system, and thereafter the "actual" or "effective" system at work.

There are two tanks in Pul Eliya, the larger one with which we are concerned, which is deemed to be on Crown land, and the smaller one which belongs to a Buddhist temple, is nearly derelict, and has an insignificant role to play in the village economy. "It is by virtue of the Crown ownership of the main tank that the customary corvée work known as *rajakariya*, which is used to maintain the tank in good condition, is given a legal enforcement."[20]

There are four relevant categories of land. First is the original "Old Field," which is directly fed by the water of the main tank and whose extent is as a rule of thumb calculated to be as large as the area covered by the tank. It is critical to note that since 1900 the shape of the Old Field had been frozen. The second category of land is freehold land (*sinakkara*), previously sold in blocks to villagers, which in fact was monopolized by the wealthy of the village who developed it, and irrigated it with water remaining after the Old Field was serviced. Third, there is *badu idam* (land leased by the Crown), disadvantageously sited and never properly irrigable, but any irrigation channel developed was also private property.

---

[19] R.W. Ievers, *Manual of the North-Central Province, Ceylon*, Colombo: Ceylon Government Press, 1899; H.W. Codrington, *Ancient Land Tenure and Revenue in Ceylon*, Colombo: Ceylon Government Press, 1938; Pieris, *Sinhalese Social Organization*.

[20] Leach, *Pul Eliya*, p. 43.

Finally there is *olegama* land in the jungle adjacent to ancient abandoned tanks which villagers could develop and claim as their own; this category was of little relevance to Pul Eliya residents. In sum, the whole cultivation area taken together, the Old Field, the freehold land, and the *badu idam*, amounted in 1954 to about 135 acres. The Old Field itself was only 40-odd acres in extent, and the house-site *gamgoda* covered a mere 6 acres, "but in the ideology of the villagers themselves, it is the holdings in this traditional *paraveni* land which really matter,"[21] and provide the precedent for later development.

The *gamgoda* is the land immediately next to the tank's main bund, lying between the bund and the Old Field, on which the residential compounds – containing dwelling houses and gardens (on which grew coconut trees, plantains, areca palms, and the like) – were located. The house-sites fell into two distinct classes. First there were those which had been in existence from "antiquity" and were accepted as *paraveni* land (entailed property from "ancient times") when the survey of the village was made in 1900. All these ancestral house-sites cum *paraveni* compounds were lumped together near the northern end of the main tank bund under the expression *maha gam mada* ("main village mudland"). It is noteworthy that the second class of house-sites was made up of three additional house-sites located outside the *paraveni* residential area on ground purchased or leased from the Crown, and all the occupants of these houses had "for one reason or other an 'outsider' status *vis a vis* the rest of the community."

In 1954 there were thirty-nine individuals resident in Pul Eliya who were recognized as having the status of domestic family head. These heads and their families were grouped into thirteen "compound groups" (with the exception of one house-site outside the main residential area which amalgamated with a particular compound group). The total number of residents of Pul Eliya in 1954 was some 146 persons.

A fundamental principle to grasp is that the primary economic requirement for a villager is not that he or she should be the owner of land, but that he or she should be a member of the village with rights to a share in the water of the tank:

Under the traditional system, holders of land in the Old Field owned rights in a certain length of irrigation ditch rather than rights in a particular area of ground. A plot owner owned rights in water; he could cultivate as much or as little land as he chose . . . Individuals who work land served by the same irrigation channel

---

[21] Ibid., p. 171.

have an inescapable obligation to co-operate. This fact is a most potent source of friendship alliances, but it is also a major source of hostility.[22]

This last part is illustrated by several examples in the monograph. A fundamental principle in this tenure system is that each *panguva* (share) within each *bāga* shall have equal rights to the total available water, and correspondingly each *panguva* carries equal obligations with regard to the maintenance of the tank bund, field fencing, etc.

Some basic facts to grasp about the land tenure arrangements of the Old Field are as follows. This reduced sketch does not report all the details, but gives all the essentials to appreciate Leach's main submissions.

1. In the first place the Old Field is divided into two sections, the Upper Field and the Lower Field. The Lower Field has roughly half the area of the Upper Field.
2. The next segmentation to grasp is that each of those two fields is divided into sections called *bāga* – let us call them A, B, C.
3. Now,

    if we count the sections of the Upper Field as Ihala (A), Meda (B) and Pahala (C), then the corresponding sections in the Lower Field are arranged C, A, B. Each *bāga* also comprises an "end piece" (*elapata*). Thus the *bāga* are as follows:

    A. Ihala *bāga*: Upper end of Upper Field plus upper section of Upper Field plus middle section of Lower Field.
    B. Meda *bāga*: Lower end of Lower Field plus middle section of Upper Field plus lower section of Lower Field.
    C. Pahala *bāga*: End piece made up of lower end of Upper Field plus upper end of Lower Field plus lower section of Upper Field plus upper section of Lower Field.

    The general effect is that shareholders who own land in the lowest and least advantageous portion of the Upper Field also own land in the highest and most advantageous portion of the Lower Field.[23]

4. Next we come to the unit called *panguva*, translated as share (plural: *pangu*). A *bāga* contains a fixed number of *pangu* just as the ordinary capital of an English commercial company consists of a fixed number of "shares." Originally when the Old Field was laid out there were six *pangu* in each *bāga*, and, although over time there have been changes in the width of each *panguva*, the *bāga* blocks as *wholes have remained almost*

---

[22] Ibid., pp. 64–65.   [23] Ibid., p. 157.

unchanged. We should further note that each *panguva* itself has been over time divided into smaller strips (*issaraval*), and their arrangement is also logical.

For every strip in the *pangu* portion of the Upper Field, there is a corresponding width in the Lower Field. This pairing is an essential feature of the system. It is not possible to own *pangu* land in the Upper Field without also owning a corresponding piece of land in the Lower Field. Land can be bought or sold or alienated in other ways, but if an owner wishes to dispose of one-third of his *pangu* land he cannnot simply dispose of that worst portion of it which is in the Lower Field. He will have to divide off one-third of his Upper Field strip and also one-third of his Lower Field strip. This fragmentation makes very good sense if it is remembered that what is being disposed of is not really land at all, but rights to a proportion of the total water supply. The "fragmentation" that results is not an economic vice but a moral virtue!

The final detail which completes the logical perfection of the Pul Eliya system of equalised shares is that the order of strips in the Upper and Lower Fields is reversed. What I mean by this can be seen from reference to map E where the details of the Meda *bāga* are given for both fields. If the strips in the Meda *bāga* in the upper field are numbered α, β, γ, δ, etc., starting from the top of the *bāga*, then in the Lower Field they would have to be numbered in the reverse order starting from the bottom of the *bāga*. This feature, though not peculiar to Pul Eliya, is not found in all the villages round about, though in other respects the Old Field Tenure in all communities is very similar.[24]

There are two further complexities to take into account. The first relates to the variability among individuals regarding the ownership of shares (*pangu*).

(a) "It is possible for one individual to own several shares or alternatively for one share to be owned by several distinct individuals. Moreover, within one village community one particular individual may own parts of a number of different shares in different *bāga*. In theory, the number of shares is fixed from the start and should never change. But the number of individual shareholders is varying all the time. It follows that there is no precise correspondence between the number of strips (*issaraval*) in the field and the division into shares."[25]

(b) "Strips can sometimes be shared by more than one owner. For example, two persons may own a strip, which in turn has a site in the Upper Field and another in the Lower Field. Division is effected by cutting each strip in half and reversing the holding in alternate years.

[24] Ibid., pp. 158–59.   [25] Ibid., p. 157.

Each owner works the northern half of each strip in every other year. All this sounds most improbable but, in fact, this part of the ideal scheme is adhered to closely."

Leach in fact presents for scrutiny a table of the ownership in 1954 of *pangu* strips in the Upper Field and Lower Field respectively, and he shows that (except for a few small discrepancies) "the generalization 'that every *pangu* plot in the Upper Field has a counterpart plot in the Lower Field owned by the same individual is very nearly true'. This table confirms unambiguously that down to 1954 it was still the general practice in Pul Eliya that no one could acquire a holding in the Upper Field without simultaneously acquiring a corresponding plot in the Lower Field."[26]

Summary: ideal and actual transmission of land

While as regards the distribution of holdings, practice in 1954, as we have seen, corresponded fairly closely with the ideal theory, the correspondence between theory and practice was much less close *when it came to the matter of transmission of ownership rights from generation to generation*. In fact, Leach provides a truly remarkable piece of detailed documentation of the history of *every plot* in the Old Field from 1890 to 1954. He discovers that, despite all the talk of heirloom property inherited from ancient times, of 107 plots no fewer than 45 had changed hands by sale at least once during that stretch of time. A number of them had been sold several times over.

Traditional custom stipulated that all land should be retained in the hands of members of the local *variga* (sub-caste). "In 1890 only one of the recorded plot-holders was an outsider in this sense . . . In 1954 it was likewise the case that only one of the recorded plot-holders was an outsider . . . From the *variga* point of view the 1954 situation was a great improvement on the 1890 position."[27] The nexus between the frequency of sales to outsiders and the eventual outcome of retaining property within the *variga* is that "most sales of land are between members of the local variga and traders, who are outside the *variga* system, but as a rule land which is sold away to an 'outsider' is, within a short while, bought back again by some other member of the local *variga*."[28] Another conclusion from the detailed analysis of plot transmission is that it is not so much the land of the poor but that of the relatively wealthy that tends to be sold: "with scarcely any exceptions it is the lands of

[26] Ibid., p. 159. [27] Ibid., p. 173. [28] Ibid., p. 174.

the gentlemen of title (Vel Vidane, Gamarala, Mohottala, Badderala, Vederala) which have passed through the hands of the traders."[29] It is men of prestige – whose status depends on the control of traditional *paraveni* land and who enjoy the titular appurtenances that go with it – who sell to traders, mostly to finance the expensive rites of passage, especially marriage festivities, which are expected of them and validate their good fortune.

I want to highlight the critical issues opened up by the foregoing discussions, especially because many readers have missed their significance for Leach's main arguments. The first issue concerns the ideal and actual topographical layout and spatial distribution of plots (in strips composing *panguva*) in the Old Field, and the conventions concerning the cultivation of them. On this front Leach convincingly demonstrates that the Pul Eliya folk pretty much adhere to the traditional *bāga–pota* system, and this structural continuity found in the arrangements of the field system, at least from 1890 to 1954, is mainly to be attributed to the fact that the field system itself is taken to be enduring and imperative to continue. (Moreover, even when villagers developed freehold land bought from the Crown, they produced a pattern plainly modeled on the traditional *bāga– pota* system.) The topographical model is undergirded by an *egalitarian* ethos in respect to water rights.

The second issue is that when it comes to plot ownership and transmission there is a fairly wide disjunction between the ideal model of faithful transmission from holder to heir from generation to generation, and the actual circulation of these plots through sales to outsiders, mostly traders, and back again to the residents. In the course of this, much change can happen in the fortunes of the people, and in the scale of economic differentiation within the village society. It is this kind of flexibility and dynamics within the field of social relations – which in Pul Eliya can be equated primarily with "kinship relations" – that Leach thus sets out to document in micro-detail, in order to explicate to what extent kinship concepts and norms (as an "ideal system") direct and provide the pathways of action, and to what extent calculated actions taken on the basis of other interests (e.g. acquiring land titles) are *post factum* translated into and justified in terms of the idiom of kinship. In assessing this interplay between "land tenure and kinship," Leach wants us to be mindful of the topographical and agrarian arrangements of the Old Field system, such as the fact that the permanent concern is rights over water and irrigation

---

[29] Ibid., p. 175.

ditches; that owners of adjacent plots must cooperate in the operation of irrigation; that the vicissitudes of land sales may make unrelated or distantly related persons one's neighbors who all must cooperate in cultivation; that such considerations may actually dictate subsequent affinal alliance through marriage; that, because the layout of the land is fixed, maintenance of long-term alliances is sought so as to fit the facts of land tenure; in short, that "the recognition of kinship is constantly adjusted to fit the ground."[30]

This kind of documentation of "actual" or "effective" kinship behavior motivated by land and agrarian concerns can hardly be characterized as primarily ensuing from Sinhalese kinship concepts and rules *per se* (e.g. incest rules, kinship terms, prohibitions regarding marriage as well as alleged preferences), though such notions act as constraints that ought not to be contravened. Leach may have overstated his case when he claimed that he had demonstrated "that the kinship behaviours which are quite clearly apparent in the Old Field situations are *not* determined by jural rules of a moral kind, they are simply a byproduct of the economic facts of the situation."[31] But he certainly, at least in relation to Pul Eliya, makes us suspect that there is a gaping hole to any theory that might suggest that Sinhalese "principles of kinship" determine or produce the bulk of actual behavior on the ground. When he examines actual behavior he would try to demonstrate other theses, such as that statements of ideal model and actual behavior are of a different level, and that the actions of individuals may constitute an empirical "statistical" order which may, on the one hand, be unknown to the actors themselves, and on the other hand, in an unexpected way affirm the enunciations of the ideal model *because of translations of conduct into the idiom of kinship*. Finally, there is also the different demonstration that changes in the *contexts* of action are correlated with *changes* in collaborative patterns, once again demonstrating the malleability of kinship. (This proposition is substantiated in the section on patterns of labor cooperation later in this chapter.)

It is in the light of this background that we should now turn to Leach's minute documentation of "the kinship system" of Pul Eliya.

THE KINSHIP SYSTEM AND LAND TENURE

The very first sentence in chapter 4 on "The Kinship System" states that Leach is concerned in Pul Eliya "with the interconnections between

---

[30] Ibid., p. 234.   [31] Ibid., p. 242.

landholding and kinship."[32] In conducting such an investigation, the manner in which land is inherited and transmitted is therefore of critical importance, and in Pul Eliya itself this is a highly complex as well as adjustable issue, because of circumstances such as the fact that "Each child at birth becomes a potential heir to each of its parents considered as an individual."[33] The fact that each man and woman, husband and wife, holds their property rights separately, and can and does transmit them to children of both sexes, engenders a special dynamics associated with bilateral inheritance coupled with male dominance: "Men are the rulers and managers, yet women as well as men are owners of land. Rights over property are commonly exercised by men, yet they are transmitted through women as frequently as through men."[34] We thus note an asymmetry constituted of bilateral property rights and a paternal marking as regards property management, but unilineal descent as a principle of group formation is absent from this arena.

Beyond this inital flexibility, Leach gives notice of another "flexibility" which is a major focus of his documentation. Inheritance takes place within an existing kinship system, but in the Pul Eliya context "the application of kinship 'rules' is highly flexible for they are being re-adapted to fit the relatively immutable physical facts of the agricultural terrain and the irrigation system." He has already demonstrated the manner in which the Old Field topography and the irrigation system are structural continuities, and he now sets himself the task of showing why and how the human actors necessarily and flexibly manipulate their kinship rules relating to the more "immutable" terrain and tank irrigation system.

Leach foregrounds two prominent category words, the *variga* ("subcaste") and *pavula* ("family" kindred), and attempts to show how these are related. The exposition involves the consideration of many other phenomena and processes that intervene, such as marriage, endogamy, descent, filiation and affinity, and compounds (residential groups), which most anthropologists usually locate within the discourse of "kinship." Leach does not deny that "the frame of reference" in terms of which property transmission takes place in Pul Eliya is "kinship,"[35] but his argumentation relates to two issues regarding its *self-sufficiency* and *primacy* as a framework of interpretation of social action.

The first question is that, if it can be demonstrated that there is a gap between "ideal" kinship rules and actual kinship behavior, what

---

[32] Ibid., p. 67.   [33] Ibid., p. 67.   [34] Ibid., p. 37.   [35] See, for example, ibid., p. 65.

does this signify, and what is the basis for the difference? The second issue relates to the fact that some anthropologists, including the masters of "structural-functionalism" such as Radcliffe Brown, Evans-Pritchard, and Fortes, make a specialism of kinship, and think of it as a domain on its own account, as "a thing in itself" which engenders, and from which flows, all conduct in tribal or segmentary societies. What does Leach mean by kinship as "a thing in itself?" He means two theoretical orientations. One is that the phenomena of kinship, e.g. filiation, solidarity (or unity) of the sibling group, descent and groupings based on descent *per se*, and other such components of "unilineal descent group" (UDG) theory, are imputed by these theorists to form an interrelated *internal system*, and that this system or grid generates kinship conduct and explains it. (It is this separate systemic internally generative model that Leach attacks, not that there can be, and there are, kinship phenomena *per se*, such as genealogical ties, incest prohibitions, filiation and so on.)[36]

Secondly, by kinship as a "thing in itself" Leach accuses the above-mentioned view or approach as *essentialist*, in that "certain component kinship 'principles' or 'elements' are taken to have an intrinsic, and seemingly therefore general, signification based in 'nature', and at the same time carrying moral (jural) imperatives of amity, solidarity or some such morality." How this "morality," which is obviously a collective socio-cultural phenomenon, is connected with an initial situation allegedly based in the "nature" of human individuals is only asserted or implied but never answered.

Leach's objection is that such presentations of kinship as a separate domain can be misleading:

Kin groups do not exist as things in themselves without regard to rights and interests which centre in them. Membership of such a group is not established by genealogy alone. Properly speaking, two individuals can only be said to be of the same kin group when they share some common interest – economic, legal,

---

[36] Leach has extended a similar criticism toward anthropologists such as the componential theorists (e.g. F.G. Lounsbury, I.R. Buchler, and others) who assume that kinship terminology maps only genealogical relationships, and that the terms form a bounded set, whose rules of linguistic form can be generated internally. Ignoring contextual usages, and social behavior, these investigators treat kinship terminology as "a closed set – the elements of an algebraic matrix which refers to genealogical connections. Once the words have been isolated in this way the investigator is tempted to believe that this set of terms is logically coherent." They also fail to consider that most kinship words have non-kinship meanings. (Edmund Leach, *Lévi-Strauss*, London: Fontana, 1970, pp. 97–98.)

political, religious as the case may be – and justify that sharing by reference to a kinship nexus.[37]

Obviously, Leach knows that he cannot explain the origins and phonological particulars of the Sinhalese language of kinship (such as older and younger brother [*ayiya* and *malli*], and cross-cousin and brother-in-law [*massinā*]) which is employed as a nexus for describing and evaluating, and justifying and legitimating social relations. But what is the implication for orthodox kinship theory if Leach demonstrates that persons within an arena such as common *variga* ("subcaste") membership, who come together or divide because of economic, political, and other interests, continually phrase and rephrase their relations in terms of the appropriate language or "idioms" of kinship, converting unrelatedness or distant kinship into close affinal kinship, or rupturing previous close relatedness into hostility and factionalism? What if the primary arena and the stakes won and lost, as in Pul Eliya, have to do with the control of lands and water, from which stem status and symbolic wealth as well, and the language of kinship and subcaste is a categorical system, which while setting certain constraints and directives deriving from "genealogical" formulations of filiation, siblingship, etc. in fact serves, even more significantly, for validating transactional outcomes that are the result of persons' strategic actions in social space outside the scope and control of the former?

In my view, these are the questions at the back of his mind which direct, as well as derive from, Leach's close study of the "kinship system" of Pul Eliya, as it dialectically related to the "land tenure system."

The Variga court

All villagers of Pul Eliya "consider themselves to be members of a single endogamous *variga* of the *Goyigama* caste. All the villagers are, therefore, kinsmen of one another."[38] The *variga* thus sounds as if it is a "subcaste", and as if its essential identity is as a kinship collectivitiy, but Leach argues that there is nothing in the kinship structure *per se* which keeps it in being. Its continuance is much more linked to its being a "territorial corporation." The corporateness of the *variga* derived from the *variga* court which was presided over by the *ratemahatmaya* (the local chieftain), who traditionally also appointed the *variga* court officials. The *variga* court

---

[37] Leach, *Pul Eliya*, p. 66. [38] Ibid., p. 67.

dealt with nearly all disputes of the same village community which were primarily concerned with issues of caste and sex, and accusations of incest and improper marriage with a person who was an outsider to the *variga* to which Pul Eliya village belonged. Wrong *variga* marriages were neither forgotten nor forgiven. But at the back of these disputes lay issues of land rights and local residence rights.

The Nuwarakalaviya *variga* was corporate in that

> its representative leaders (the members of the *variga* court) ultimately decide who is and who is not a member of the group but also because the *variga*, as an aggregate, has title in all the lands of all the villagers comprising the *variga*; furthermore *variga* membership is directly linked with this title in land. Since it is land rights and place of residence rather than descent which provide the ultimate basis for *variga* status, the translation of the term *variga* as "sub-caste" must be used with caution.[39]

In short, the continuation of the *variga* is based in its corporation aspect with regard to land titles and residence, not in its functioning as a collection of kin. The *variga* as an endogamous subcaste is an "abstraction" or "idealist conception"; its continuation is tied to its deliberations regarding membership in a village on the basis of land and residence rights. When the *variga* court loses its political-legal context, the *variga* ceases to be functional. This argument must await further ethnographic documentation in the following sections for its plausibility to be strengthened.

Variga endogamy and the distribution of marriage

The terms *diga* and *binna* denote virilocal and uxorilocal residence respectively, and "this is a distinction to which Sinhalese profess to attach great significance."[40] The two most commonly expressed assertions regarding marriage are: "First, every Pul Eliya male, without exception, expressed a strong verbal preference for *diga* marriage. Secondly, it was very commonly asserted that a man had a 'right' to marry his *avassa nana* (true cross-cousin), though at the same time it seemed to be regarded as a rather feeble sort of thing to do."[41]

As may be anticipated, Leach proceeds with close ethnographic reporting and with quantitative distributions combined with analytical virtuosity, to probe the issues of how such "ideal assertions" are

---

[39] Ibid., p. 79.   [40] Ibid., p. 81.   [41] Ibid., p. 84.

translated into action, and what kind of patterning can be perceived when actual actions are aggregated and interrelated in relation to marriage choices, residential patterns, property transmission, and social cooperation.

What we have in this part of the Pul Eliya text is the argument and demonstration that principles of kinship *per se*, such as incest taboos, parent–child links (filiation), siblingship, kinship terminology as a categorical or classifying system, and of "ideal statements" such as the right to marry a true cross-cousin, and of allowable forms of post-marital residence, and the general "rules" of bilateral inheritance rights of male and female children from parents, act as framing rules and conventions, and in varying degree as orientating signs and variably as "constraints" of behavior, but they do not significantly determine nor can they adequately explain actual behavioral choices and actual outcomes.

The actual marriage and residential patterns are the outcomes of the actors, placed in different circumstances, making strategic decisions to maximize their interests which in Pul Eliya is overwhelmingly determined by control and access to *paraveni* land and water rights. And in this context, locality factors including spatial distance between marrying persons and their assets are also vital.

As we have noted before, Leach at this moment of his theorizing tended first to see his interpretive and analytical stance as showing the gap between the "ideal" system and the "actual behavior," and to conceive of "actual behavior" as constituting a "statistical order." While the actual behavior of individual actors was capable of being seen as strategic choices made to serve interests, and these choices made sense only if related to the actors' situational circumstances, the ensuing "statistical" or quantitative patterns formed by the separate acts might not be perceived by the actors. But there is a final twist to Leach's exegesis, which I shall explicate later, regarding the relations between the "ideal" formulations which do not significantly determine actual conduct, and the distributions of actual acts, which in fact constitute statistical patterns, and in an interesting way throw light on some of the ideal formulations.

Let us begin with some marriage statistics. A table dealing with a hundred marriages extant at various dates between 1890 and 1954, of which one or both partners were born in Pul Eliya, shows that in thirty-one of the marriages the conjugal home was set up in some village other than Pul Eliya. A table of thirty-nine extant marriages of living residents of Pul Eliya (1954) shows that twenty-one instances were *diga* marriages with the wife coming from another village, and eight were

binna marriages with the husband from another village (the remaining
ten were cases where both partners were from within Pul Eliya):

Both tables agree that in just over 50 per cent of all marriages, a Pul Eliya
spouse has found his or her mate in one of the four daily contact villages –
Pul Eliya, Wiralmurippu, Diwulwewa and Bellankandawala: rather over 20 per
cent found their mates in one of the three regular contact villages, Yakawewa,
Kadawatgama, Walpola, all of which lie within three miles of Pul Eliya itself.
The remaining 30 per cent of all marriages were distributed over some eighteen
different villages.[42]

What is the significance of the *diga*/*binna* distinction in practice?
"These terms do not have a great deal of practical significance when
applied to marriages in which both spouses come from the same community, but where the spouses come from different villages the relative
statuses of husband and wife are greatly affected."[43]

Diga is by far the most frequent form of residence:

Binna marriage is only resorted to in certain special types of cases. *Binna* marriages are, by and large, those of overprivileged females or of underprivileged
males ... Since it is deemed humiliating for a young man to enter into this
kind of dependent relationship, a man contemplating such a marriage likes to
move as far as possible from his own natal village to escape the jeers of his near
relatives.[44]

Marriages in which a man marries his true mother's brother's daughter are *not* common, "but many of those that do occur are *binna* marriages.
These again are often cases where a man's prospects of inheritance from
his own father are poor; by returning to his mother's natal village and
asserting his right to marry a daughter of his mother's brother (*mama*)
a man may lay claim to his mother's hereditary property."[45] There is
less tendency for a man to marry his father's sister's daughter although
this girl also is an *avassa nana* and her father is also a *mama*. "The reason
is clear. A man who is entitled to 'claim' in another village an *avassa*

---

[42] Ibid., p. 81.   [43] Ibid., p. 81.

[44] Ibid., p. 85. The following figures from the analysis of a hundred marriages between 1890 and
1954 confirm this argument: five *binna* husbands who came from more than 10 miles distant were
all landless men. One wife was also his cross-cousin. Of the eleven *binna* husbands who traveled
6–10 miles to find a wife, three were landless, three had been exiled from their home villages
for caste offenses, and four married relatively wealthy heiresses; the eleventh man married his
cross-cousin. For marriages within a 3-mile radius the *binna*/*diga* distinction is less critical, since
a man can work land simultaneously both in his natal village and in that of his wife.

[45] Ibid., p. 85.

nana who is his father's sister's daughter will be the son of a *binna* married father and the odds are that this *avassa nana* is herself a girl of no property."[46]

Marriage with a true cross-cousin is linked up with the notion of the "solidarity of the *pavula*" . . . A *pavula* (kindred) which is short of resources, either of men or of property, conserves its assets. The men marry endogamously and neither men nor dowries are lost. Correspondingly when a formal marriage is staged with ceremony it is an alliance between different *pavula*. A prominent feature of the ritual in such cases is that the male cross-cousin of the bride symbolically surrenders his claims to the outsider, the bridegroom from the other *pavula*. These ceremonial marriages only occur when a *pavula* is prosperous and pursuing a policy of expansion.[47]

No special characteristic distinguishes the marriages in which both spouses came from Pul Eliya itself. That the total proportion of such marriages is high is not surprising. Given the inheritance system previously described, most young men have everything to gain by marrying a local girl if a suitable candidate is available. Moreover, family and public opinion generally always approves of close endogamous marriages as tending to conserve property-holding within the local community.[48]

The meticulous fieldworker will appreciate the statistics on the frequency and geographical spread of *diga* and *binna* marriages in chapter 4, p. 87. Not only do *diga* marriages outnumber *binna* marriages, their geographical spread is also much less. In the same sample of a hundred marriages 82 per cent were *diga* in which the wife had been born within three miles of her husband; while in only 54 per cent of *binna* marriages had the husband been born within three miles of his wife. These (and other figures) are consistent with the view that two different types of bias are at work:

On the one hand, poor men and men with a caste taint not only tend to marry *binna*, but also tend to seek wives far away from their natal homes. On the other hand "respectable people", men and women alike, especially those who are likely to inherit property, tend (a) to marry *diga*, (b) to marry a spouse from very close at hand, and (c) as a corollary, to marry some very close relative – that is, first, second or third cross-cousins. Here (b) and (c) are really two aspects of the same thing; a high incidence of closely localized marriage over several generations has the automatic consequence that all *variga* members within a narrow geographical range are closely related.[49]

---

[46] Ibid., pp. 85–86.   [47] Ibid., p. 86.   [48] Ibid., p. 87.   [49] Ibid., pp. 87–88.

Leach concludes this discussion with two challenging "deconstructive" (to use current jargon) unmaskings, which in his own way of phrasing consist of contrasting the Sinhalese villagers' own "idealist" verbal formulations[50] with the patterns that emerge from the "actual" behavior of the villagers as quantitatively recorded by the anthropologist/sociologist. They have to do with two themes: first cousin (i.e. true cross-cousin) marriages and *variga* endogamy. It is I think important to note, as I have stated at the beginning of this discussion on marriage, that it is implicit often, and sometimes explicit, that what Leach reports as instances of "actual" behavior are motivated strategic actions on the part of actors as "agents" (to use current jargon again) in pursuit of maximizing their self-interest. But while individual actors or a group of actors (such as a *pavula*, whether "family" or "faction") may take calculated strategic actions to pursue their interest, the overall pattern formed by their separate acts may form a "statistical order" of patterning of which largely they may not be aware. In this sense it is a "latent" rather than a "manifest" order.

In the first of Leach's deconstructions, he states that "Although the Sinhalese will assert that a man has a *right* to marry his true cross-cousin, this does not constitute a rule of preferred marriage."

The real *preference* is for *diga* residence and a wife from a near locality; cross-cousin marriage is coincidental . . . When a man wants to marry, the total number of unmarried girls who are near at hand, of the right age, and not classed as "classificatory sisters", is not large. Nearly all such girls are likely to be quite close relatives, some may be true cross-cousins. Except where the man's poverty is a factor in the situation the latter have no special attraction. Of the (39) extant Pul Eliya marriages only two were first-cousin marriages . . . Considering the circumstances this incidence is low and suggests that, on the whole, marriage with first cousins is avoided.[51]

Second, Leach in a similar move deconstructs "the principle of *variga* endogamy" which is really undergirded by, and is an entailment to, a more consciously salient "prior" empirical imperative. *Variga* endogamy becomes a conspicuous issue only when it is rarely breached.

---

[50] "Idealist" formulation in the sense in which he treated Kachin uses of the terms *gumsa* and *gumlao*, and how they problematically corresponded to processes on the ground.

[51] Ibid., p. 88. This discussion on the incidence of true cross-cousin marriage fully accords with my own findings in the mid-fifties in the Laggalla region of Pata Dumbara district. See Tambiah, "Kinship Fact and Fiction."

On the face of it, the rule is a caste rule: *variga* endogamy is enforced because sexual relations outside the *variga* are considered polluting in a ritual sense. This certainly is how the villagers themselves think of the situation, and they react to *variga* offenses with that special kind of horror which, in Western society, is reserved for incest and sacrilege. Yet, objectively considered, the rule of *variga* endogamy is simply a formal justification of the state of affairs which exists. The systems of land and property rights being what they are, it is in any case convenient for these North Central Province villagers to marry close relatives from villages near at hand. Only the exceptional, underprivileged individual is going to go far afield to find a wife. The rule of *variga* endogamy serves to canalize these special cases. The ordinary man of property has no incentive to look outside the local group for a wife; the *variga* rule is designed for the others. There is an interesting contrast here between the villagers' analysis of the situation and that of the sociologist. "The villager says: 'We marry with members of our own *variga*.' He takes the existence of the *variga* as given. The sociologist sees the situation in reverse. *Variga* membership is only definable in terms of marriage and of *variga* court decisions. The members of a man's own *variga* are the inhabitants of those villages from which members of his own natal village have obtained approved mates within recent times. A court decision could at any time alter the boundaries of *variga* . . . The fact of territorial endogamy is really prior to the existence of the *variga* considered as an endogamous sub-caste."[52]

The nature of marriage

The flexibility of "marriage" and "heterosexual matings" is a marked feature of Pul Eliya society. "It is in fact often difficult to discriminate in this society between marriage and promiscuous mating."[53] Divorce may be effected as easily as common-law marriage. The couple simply separate and the marriage is at an end. Individuals who have been "married" five or six times are not thought in any way exceptional, though many long-lasting stable marriages do occur. "Divorce becomes less frequent as individuals get older, but the existence of children seems scarcely to affect the situation."[54] It is noteworthy that while few registered their marriages, the birth of every child born was, however, being registered and the names of the parents were recorded *in order to ensure the inheritance rights of every child.*

[52] Ibid., pp. 88–89.   [53] Ibid., p. 89.   [54] Ibid., p. 89.

In addition to the casual form of common-law mating, there was another form of marriage, numerically in the minority but sociologically important. This is the

> elaborate marriage ceremonial which includes the use of formal matchmakers, expensive feasting for assembled kinsmen, and, in some cases, the formal bestowal of dowry on the bride by the bride's parents . . . Such marriages form part of the strategy of village politics, the main issues at stake being the transmission of property from one generation to another. Expensive formal marriages are confined to the relatively wealthy; they can be thought of as political alliances with the kinsmen on either side assembling *en masse* to witness the treaty of friendship. But the parties concerned are likely to be rivals and potential enemies rather than natural companions.[55]

While both these kinds of marriage recognize every child as an heir to both its recognized parents individually, "the formal type of marriage does more than that, it establishes a relation of affinity between two sets of kinsmen, and it is this alliance aspect of the union which receives ritual emphasis."[56] The ritually emphasized marriage symbolizes alliance between rival factional groups, and it is often a statement of achieved status.

Descent, filiation, affinity

The distinction between *pater* and *genitor* has been repeatedly deployed in the recent Africanist literature (a distinction implicit in Malinowski's Trobriand analysis). From this perspective the Sinhalese situation is different in that the role of "the *pater* is ordinarily indistinguishable from the role of *genitor*,"[57] in that, except in the case of adoption, the rights that a father and his son have *vis-à-vis* each other stem "exclusively from the acknowledged biological fact that the son is the result of his father's cohabitation with his mother."[58]

The Pul Eliya practices introduce another lack of fit: vital to the Fortesian explicaton of African lineage systems is the analytical importance of the distinction between *descent* and *filiation*, which Leach does not reject, "But it is one which lays all the stress upon the relationships between parents and children while pushing into the background the co-existent relationships between the parents themselves, both in their capacities as husband and wife and in their capacities as members of distinct kin

---

[55] Ibid., pp. 90–91.　　[56] Ibid., p. 91.　　[57] Ibid., p. 94.　　[58] Ibid., p. 94.

corporations."[59] The theoretical interest of the Sinhalese material is
that

a clear cultural distinction is made between marriage reported as an alliance
between kin groups and "marriage" as the sexual union of a man and woman
for the purpose of procreating children. Marriage in the first case establishes
a relationship of *affinity*; "marriage" in the second case establishes the *filiation*
of the children; relationships of *descent* are not involved at all since there are
no unilineal descent groups in which the individual automatically acquires a
membership by virtue of his birth.[60]

In this kind of phrasing, Leach is preparing the ground for arguing that
the two axes of Fortesian unilineal descent group theory, namely patrilineal descent and "complementary filiation" (marriage among the Tallensi
is an individual affair, and individuates siblings by different mothers by
the same polygynous father, and is not a focus of "structural" significance), are inapplicable to the Sinhalese case, where marriage and *affinity*
become the channels for the structural generation of *pavula* as the most
salient grouping.

Finally, one further implication of the "ambiguity" of marriage in Pul
Eliya, which recognizes that cohabitation, and not necessarily formal
marriage, establishes the inheritance rights of consequent children, is that
in fact the *variga* court does not act to regulate the sexual exclusiveness
of the *variga*, but its judgments ensure that all *variga* heirs are recognized
as *variga* members, and vice versa, that no-one who is not recognized as
a *variga* member could inherit any part of the *variga* land. "Thus, despite
the ambiguity of its boundaries, it does seem that the *variga* as a whole
can usefully be thought of as a landholding corporation of which the
variga court members are the representatives."[61]

Compound groups

The compound (*vatta* – "garden") is an area of ground within the main
village (*gamgoda*) surrounded by a fence. Although fence positions are
changed from time to time, the general layout of the village had changed
little over the seventy years prior to 1954. Each compound is associated
with a particular group of people, namely those who own the land in the
compound and have the right to build houses there. Leach referred to
the compound group as *gedera*.

[59] Ibid., p. 94.   [60] Ibid., p. 95.   [61] Ibid., p. 95.

In Pul Eliya there were thirty-nine households, and the thirty-nine domestic family heads were allocated to thirteen compound groups. The villagers' claims to ownership of such compound land are phrased in terms of kinship.[62] Ownership of house-sites in the compound is directly related to ownership of the *paraveni* plots in the Old Field.

Leach demonstrates that neither the compound group, nor its prototype the *gedera*, can be described as a descent group, because there is no simple descent principle in terms of which compound group membership can be exclusively defined. Moreover, descent is an idea that was adapted to circumstances. Membership is established by asserting a claim based on pedigree, but recruitment to compound groups is not automatic. Nor is this membership an irrevocable commitment. Finally, pedigree can be adapted to circumstances: provided that a person has full title to ancestral *paraveni* land, "it will very quickly come to be asserted that the title itself is 'ancestral', and correspondingly that he has rights to a compound site by pedigree links, even if it was in actual fact purchased."

Pavula

Pul Eliya villagers do not discuss their society as being a collection of compound groups, but as made up of aggregates of people called *pavula*. *Pavula* is an elastic concept in terms of scale, extending from a woman as wife, a woman and her children, to "kinsmen" in the widest sense.

Leach offers a distinction between "ideal" *pavula* and "effective" *pavula*. In the Sinhalese case "ideal" *pavula* comprises the direct biological descendants of one woman, and this demonstration is important where legal rights to property and succession are concerned (as for example when a man marries two women in succession and raises a separate family by each, or when the rights of step-siblings and half-siblings are in question). The *pavula* in this "ideal" sense is a concept of kinship *per se*, and it is not usually an effective solidary cooperative group.

By comparison the "effective" *pavula* is a group of kinsmen who cooperate together, and express their cooperation by saying "we are of one *pavula*." The discussion of the "effective" *pavula* opens the way for Leach to demonstrate how far Pul Eliya norms deviate from the alleged building blocks of descent group theory.

---

[62] Ibid., p. 98.

The relation between "ideal pavula*" and "effective* pavula*"*

Leach engages in a detailed "forensic" analysis of " '*pavula*' membership and marriage" on pages 111–23 of chapter 4. This discussion is particularly relevant for the understanding of the *pavula* as kindred and faction in its most elaborate form. Especially as a caution to all those careless readers who all too easily accused Leach of reducing social structure solely to a statistical "by-product of the sum of many individual human actions,"[63] I would draw attention to the manner in which Leach makes a distinction and interplay between "ideal *pavula*" (kindreds defined as descendants of a common ancestress, which for him rates as a kinship concept *per se*) and "effective *pavula*" (political factions clustered around a leader and in whose formation *affinal* relationships are vital). A careful reading should also make it clear that both senses of *pavula* are part of the village discourse, and that the author first distinguishes between them and then relates them in his exegesis as anthropologist.

In the sense of the modular pairs of relationships that are at the heart of Leach's exposition, we have to take as a point of reference the contrast in the relations between "brothers" and "brothers-in-law," and much else flows from this contrast:

"Brothers" are always in elder-brother/younger-brother relationship. It is a relationship of inequality and polite respect. In contrast, "brothers-in-law" (*massinã*) are in a standing of equality and may joke together.

The reason for this difference in expected behaviours is plain. Brothers are expected to be co-resident; brothers-in-law are not. Co-residence implies joint-heirship to a common estate; joint-heirship is a relationship of restrained rivalry. Although brothers in this society are often seen to be rivals, this does not derive from any intrinsic principle of kinship; the rivalry is manifest only in so far as they are competitors for managerial control of the same piece of parental property. It is only because brothers are expected to reside virilocally (*dīga*) that personal relations between them are expected to be difficult.

Brothers-in-law do not ordinarily have managerial interest in the same piece of land, and it is for this reason that they are able to co-operate on a basis of equality without strain. This is not simply a theoretical ideal, it is readily observable as a fact. A labour team of any sort is far more likely to contain individuals related as *massinã* than it is to contain full brothers . . .

Brothers-in-law will only be co-resident if one of them has married *binna* (uxorilocally). In that event there is a contradiction between the rivalry for managerial control and the expectation of close co-operation between equals.

---

[63] Even Bernard S. Cohn in his "Review of *Pul Eliya: A Village in Ceylon*," *Journal of the American Oriental Society*, vol. 82, no. 1, 1962, pp. 104–6, makes this careless reading.

It is precisely the kind of situation in which, according to Radcliffe-Brown's well-known theory, we should expect a stereotyped joking relationship to develop.

In fact, as we have seen already, a *binna*-married husband is often a man who has come from far away and is in very inferior dependent status *vis-à-vis* his affinal relatives. Such a case is not likely to produce a situation of rivalry and formal joking. The difficulties only arise when the *binna*-married husband is a man from close at hand, a man with property rights of his own, a man perhaps of the same "ideal" *pavula*, even a cross-cousin.[64]

At another point Leach takes up the contrast in a slightly different way:

A characteristic feature of this society is that the bond between a man and his wife's brother is an extremely close one. Brothers-in-law address one another as *massinā* – cross cousin – and are often in a pronounced joking relationship. The feeling that brothers-in-law have a *right* to claim one another's assistance in all circumstances is very strong indeed ... Equally characteristic is the fact that the relationship between full brothers is marked with strain. The use of the differential *ayiya* (elder brother), *malli* (younger brother) emphasizes the fact that the relation is never one of equality. Often it is so reserved as to approximate an avoidance relationship.[65]

Full brothers (and their sisters) are by virtue of filiation heirs to their father's and their mother's property. But their relationships are not necessarily unitary or solidary on account of that. Full brothers are necessarily of the same "ideal" *pavula*, but this does not imply that they are at all likely to co-operate together. In this society the "solidarity of the sibling group" upon which Radcliffe-Brown laid so much stress is rather a matter of formality and ritual than of everyday fact.

In life crisis ceremonials and other situations, which call for polite visiting, brothers will be seen to stand together. But full brothers are seldom close friends and they do not ordinarily co-operate in their economic activities.[66]

Moreover the effective *pavula* is more likely to embrace half-siblings than full siblings, since the former, if children are of different fathers, are not competitors to patrimonial inheritance. One of the nice comparative touches introduced by Leach, with a bow to Malinowski, is that in the Sinhalese case, while on the one hand the roles of *pater* and *genitor* are indistinguishable, on the other hand the instability of the marriage tie, and the possibility that a man may be simultaneously *genitor* and *pater* to children by a woman who has other children by another marriage to whom the above-mentioned man is now *pater* (but not *genitor*), produces a situation to which Malinowski's phrase "sociological paternity" can be

---

[64] Ibid., pp. 118–19.   [65] Ibid., pp. 106–7.   [66] Ibid., p. 107.

applied. Thus the Sinhalese part-sibling relationships are of theoretical interest because the kind of relationship between a Trobriand father and a Trobriand son, which Malinowski labeled "sociological paternity," is not confined to societies with unilineal descent systems. In Pul Eliya there are several variant social relationships which may link a man to the children who are growing up in his house.

The composition of an individual's effective *pavula*, the group of individuals with whom he is in a good and amicable relationship, may be summed up as follows:

it will usually include kinsmen from other villages besides my own; it will nearly always include my brothers-in-law and my cross-cousins, but it may or may not include my "brothers" – for example, full brothers, half-brothers, step-brothers and parallel cousins. My full siblings are always members of "my (ideal) *pavula*" – for formal purposes, but this need not be the case for informal situations.[67]

It is in marriages accompanied by elaborate ceremonial that the two sides, the parents of the bride and groom, tend to be seen by Pul Eliyans as representatives of opposed factions which become allied together by virtue of marriage. It is important to bear in mind that the parents of bride and groom here are not related as first cousins, and may or may not be more distantly related.

Leach once again resorts to the distinction between "ideal *pavula*" and "effective *pavula*" first to describe the villager's own view of these occurrences as alliance and then to unpack their representation in terms of the anthropologist's own mapping:

Such marriages are arranged by the parents of the individuals concerned and the marriage ceremony involves the assembly of large numbers of kin from both sides. The villagers themselves refer to such marriages as linking the two *pavula*, and the strategy behind the negotiations leading up to such an alliance is explicitly designed to strengthen the position of "our *pavula*". To emphasise the equality of status of the two contracting parties it is usual to arrange two marriages at the same time, so that there shall be an exchange of personnel, even though there may be an interval of several years between the two marriages.[68]

The villagers represent this coming together of the kin of the two sides as a "binding together" (*bandi*). But such a notion of alliance between groups, remarks Leach, is an "idealist concept." My own view is that he is employing here "idealist" in the sense he used it in *Political Systems of*

---

[67] Ibid., p. 111.   [68] Ibid., p. 112.

Highland Burma, that is as a category and ideational term like *gumsa* and *gumlao*, which organizes the actors' perceptions of a flow of events on the ground which are actually fluid and dynamic and even ambiguous.

In theory, the guests at a wedding are supposed to belong either to the *pavula* of the bridegroom or to the *pavula* of the bride, "but since nearly everyone is likely to be quite closely related to both sides any allegiance to one party rather than to the other will be on grounds of political interest rather than biological descent."[69]

I draw the attention of the reader when reading pages 111–16 of the text devoted to the *pavula* to bear in mind that Leach is using the term "ideal" *pavula* in order to refer to links of descent of widening ranges: in the narrowest sense of full brothers (by filiation to their common parents), in the more inclusive sense of descendants of a common ancestress, and in the widest sense of people of the *same variga* who could as occasion demands find common ancestors to link up with and thereby claim kinship. In this manner the "ideal" *pavula* functions like a Chinese box concept.

To this kind of usage of "ideal" *pavula* Leach contrasts the term "effective" *pavula* to highlight two points: first, that in its make-up "affinal ties are here as important, or even more important than links of common descent", and second, that the membership of this group is "much more selective" in that the coming together is first dictated by "political" interest, and the kinship links can be invoked to "explain" this binding. "One cannot infer from a study of genealogy alone just which of a man's kinsmen will be treated as belonging to his 'effective' *pavula*."[70] "A man's effective *pavula* comprises those kinsmen who *at any particular time* can be relied upon to act as allies; the time element is crucial."[71] But although very elastic in size and indefinite in its boundaries, it is nevertheless structured on definite principles of choice.[72]

In these complexly constructed passages cited above, Leach as theorist is grappling with the issue of how to unpack the term *pavula* which the villagers use in different senses (polyvalence) according to context, and also its use as a composite term signifying bounded collectivities of kin, when in fact boundaries cannot be drawn according to criteria of kinship.

As an anthropologist dialogically questioning a certain kind of kinship theory predicated on the primacy of descent, Leach proposes that there is a contrasting distinction to be made between the "ideal" *pavula* and

---

[69] Ibid., p. 112.   [70] Ibid., pp. 112–13.   [71] Ibid., p. 113.   [72] Ibid., p. 116.

the "effective" *pavula*. He is repeatedly grappling with ties of "descent," which figure in the *pavula* as an entity made up of descendants of an ancestress, exemplified by the links between full brothers, and are opposed to ties of "affinity," exemplified by the links between *massinã* as cross-cousins and brothers-in-law, which he assesses are more important for the villagers, and are more selectively called upon. Since the "effective" *pavula* is assembled for political action, the element of choice in the assembling of its members is greater as is their commitment to help.

Both the "ideal" *pavula* and the "effective" *pavula* principles of recruitment and membership are simultaneously in play in the *pavula* that assemble at the formal ceremonial marriages which form the subject of the foregoing analysis. This is how Leach interrelates the two conceptions, and then assesses their relative weights.

When one encounters a group which purports to be a *pavula*, it is likely to be a combination of two distinguishable structures. On the one hand the "ideal" *pavula* (Rivers's *kindred*) lays emphasis upon the "solidarity of siblings", more particularly of full siblings. On the other hand the "effective" *pavula* ("personal kindred"/"kin-based political faction") lays particular emphasis on the mutual obligations of *massinã*, that is of brothers-in-law and the children of brothers-in-law.

It is consistent with this contradiction between the ideal and actual that whereas true cross-cousins, like brothers-in-law, are commonly close friends, parallel cousins, even when they live next door in the same compound, may be almost ignored except on formal occasions.

In theory, both the *massina* and the *ayiya/malli* cousins should be members of "my *pavula*", but for most practical purposes it is only the former who count.[73]

In practice, the *pavula* groups which manifest themselves on the occasions of weddings and other life crisis ceremonials are something of a compromise between "ideal" *pavula* (that is, kindreds defined as descendants of a common ancestress) and "effective" *pavula* (that is, political factions clustered around a leader). In such formal *pavula* full brothers may sit side by side, and fathers and sons may be of the same party, but relationships of affinity are given recognition besides those of biological descent.[74]

The concluding sections of the discussion on the *pavula* present us with an anthropological theorist grappling, in a summing up, with the dialectic and tension between two structural trends, and the ambiguities and manipulations, lapses and reactivations, as well as the boundaries and constraints that characterize village social relations. These sections

---

[73] Ibid., p. 120.   [74] Ibid., p. 112.

pose issues that Meyer Fortes sidestepped in his critique of Pul Eliya in his *Kinship and the Social Order*.[75]

Leach makes it quite clear, as he did many times before, that the whole social system of Pul Eliya (and its neighboring same-status high-contact villages) "presupposes the existence of the overall *variga* organization by which everyone in the village is necessarily a kinsman of everyone else."[76] In his discussion of *pavula* Leach is concerned with the dynamics within the larger universe of *variga* as recognized by the villagers.

Having discussed, with the aid of empirical examples, how in the relation between compound groups and *pavula* factions "kinship is allowed to lapse if it does not correspond to land tenure and territorial interests,"[77] and how many persons in *pavula* factions could equally well on the basis of kinship belong to either side but choose one of them, he remarks that such ambiguity is characteristic of the overall situation where everyone in the village is of a common *variga*: "Let me repeat: although recruitment to [an ideal] *pavula* is based in kinship alone, a *pavula* is in essence a political faction. Every individual is free to align himself with any leader of any *pavula* faction. He then turns his allegiance into a kinship tie by 'activating' an appropriate series of kinship links."[78] "One cannot infer from a study of genealogy alone just which of a man's kinsmen will be treated as belonging to his 'effective' *pavula*. In the 'effective' *pavula* kinship *serves as an explanation rather than as a cause of political alliance*."[79]

The "effective" *pavula* is often a group of kinsmen allied together for some specific political purpose, and its effectiveness depends "*upon the initiative of its leading members*." Agency and strategy figure importantly in this explication of *pavula* acting as a political faction: "But while I must stress the elasticity of the *pavula* concept I do not want to give the impression of a system of total fluidity. Political interests are closely linked with property interests and though the relative economic status of individuals is changing all the time it is not completely fluid."[80]

The pragmatic application of the *pavula* concept, and the elements of free choice and constraint in the choice of allies, become more apparent only when the distribution and location of landholdings in the Old Field and the freehold plots, and the reciprocities this aspect of land tenure encourages and even necessitates, are taken into account. It is to

---

[75] Meyer Fortes, *Kinship and the Social Order: The Legacy of Lewis Henry Morgan*, Chicago: Aldine, 1969, pp. 221–28.
[76] Leach, *Pul Eliya*, p. 123.   [77] Ibid., p. 123.   [78] Ibid., p. 123.   [79] Ibid., p. 113.
[80] Ibid., p. 124.

this dimension of the constraints stemming from the topographical lay-out that Leach assigned a "priority" over the more flexible domain of kinship relations, and it is to make clear the logic of this differential play that I reversed the order of chapters in the book, and outlined the to-pographical design and the plot distribution system first. One obvious lapse or omission in the text, which Leach could easily have avoided so as to save himself from criticism, would have been to state clearly that the egalitarian topographical model of *bāga*, upper and lower fields, three *pangu* (shares) and strips, and the egalitarian conception of watershares and agrarian duties associated with ownership, was a *historical-cultural* model of ecological adaptation and agrarian practices devised by the peasants in question. But it is necessary for the critics to appreciate the argument that this historical-cultural model is *more constrained* by *given* eco-logical, topographical, and climatic factors to which the peasants have to respond than by any other factors that are relevant to the shaping of that model.

Kinship terminology

Leach said that it was with some reluctance that he dealt with the Sin-halese terminology of kinship. Any reader who could conceivably think that Leach denied the existence and recognition of kinship among the Pul Eliya folk should read, for example, at least pages 125–28 where he makes the following statements.

The terminology is classificatory, and discriminates by sex and gen-eration. Ego makes a distinction between father's relatives and mother's relatives. The formal marriage rule is that a man should marry a girl of his own generation who is a classificatory cross-cousin (*nana*). There are for-mally expected behaviors between pairs of persons such as, for example, grandfather/grandson, father/son, mother's brother/sister's son, older brother/younger brother, and cross-cousins including brothers-in-law. The extent to which "these formally expected behaviours play a signifi-cant part in day-to-day relationships" is treated in the ethnography.

Of the *variga* he says, "owing to the fact that within the *variga*, everyone is related to everyone else in a variety of different ways, Ego is generally faced with some degree of choice as to how a particular individual should be classed."[81]

[81] Ibid., p. 127.

The reluctance to dwell at length on the terminology alone, and rest the discussion with the "formally expected behaviors" toward terminologically distinguished persons, stems from the consideration that the most critical structural principles of social organization in Pul Eliya derive from dynamics whose logic rests elsewhere. Perhaps the most significant counterintuitive demonstration for the Sinhalese case, which unilineal theorists of patriliny are called to contemplate, lies in the relative "weakness" of the patrilineal principle and the relative "markedness" of the affinal principle in the construction of Pul Eliya social life.

Thus older brother and younger brother, *ayiya* and *malli*, as true siblings do have claims by filiation on the property of their parents (not, however, to the exclusion of their sisters), but their relationship is divisive and full of strain, and their behavior correspondingly formal. Outside this range the relation between and labeling of classificatory brothers is diffuse and lax. The relationship between *massinā* carries firmer claims and obligations of cooperation "over the whole range of economic and social activities, and the term has a narrower closure in village discourse because of its association with marriage."

Leach sums up the overall argument as follows: "Expressed in another way we may say that the 'patrilineal descent' terminology, in *its wider ramifications*, does little more than specify the recognition of kinship in the most general sense; the affinal terminology on the other hand delimits the boundaries of the 'effective' *pavula* and is, therefore a matter of crucial structural significance."

Property transmission

Variga, *gedera* and *pavula* are not, in any strict sense, property owning corporate groups, but they are, in varying degrees, groups which endure through time independently of the life-span of particular individuals. The groups endure because the estates endure, but the groups have no corporate existence which could survive a dispersal of their landed property. *In this respect they differ from "lineages" which, in theory at least, owe their continued existence to a charter of common descent rather than of common property.*[82] [emphasis added]

The membership of factional groupings within the village keeps changing all the time, but, since the issues over which factional disputes tend to arise are recurrent, there is a tendency for opposition between families (*pavula*) to assume

[82] Ibid., p. 129.

a more or less stereotyped pattern. The factional disputes of this generation are, by and large, between the heirs of those who indulged in similar factional disputes a generation ago.[83]

We can by now guess the way in which Leach would treat the process of property transmission: "Ideally the cardinal rule is that land should never be allowed to pass outside the *variga*. Sales and gifts of land should only be between members of the same *variga*. If these rules were always maintained *variga* heirs would necessarily be within the *variga*."[84] In Pul Eliya land may be transmitted in a variety of ways: "It may be bought and sold, it may be transferred by gift, it may be bestowed by endowment upon a child while the parent is still living, or it may pass at death by inheritance proper."[85]

A detailed study of the actual transactions shows in what ways property transmission deviates from the "ideal" norms stated above, and yet in the long run how through circuitous pathways the Pul Eliya citizens manage to retain control of the land. To illustrate: land sales to outside traders, Muslims and Tamils, occur because of emergencies; also money borrowed from the same agents against land given on mortgage as security sometimes results in foreclosure because of inability to redeem. But although land does in this manner pass into the hands of non-*variga* outsiders, because the latter are traders rather than cultivators, they are likely, at the first opportunity, to sell the land back to a local villager.

Again there are ways in which plots of Pul Eliya land inherited by absentee owners in Wiralmurippu village, and vice versa, because of the density of affinal linkages between the two villages, are transferred back again by mortgage or half-share arrangements, and in the course of time ownership is also brought back into the home village by the process of inheritance, exchange of plots, and marriage reciprocities. Thus a dense measure of reciprocal indebtedness binds together not only members of a single village but also members of other villages of the same *variga* living within a few miles of one another. Leach thus insightfully demonstrates that, while individual mortgage or tenancy contracts may by themselves seem excessively onerous, in the larger context of all such contractual relations between affinal kin the economic burdens of indebtedness tend to cancel out. "The marriages of the relatively wealthy tend to be confined within the local 'close contact' area because the wealth involved

---

[83] Ibid., p. 129.   [84] Ibid., p. 130.   [85] Ibid., p. 130.

constitutes the capital on which the elaborate inter-village debt structure is built up."[86]

It is documentation and discovery of this sort that leads Leach to put forward the notion of a "statistical order" as opposed to the "ideal order" on the one hand, and the "randomness" or contingency of individual occurrences on the other. It is important for the reader of the book to follow the point he is making about "statistical order," because it lays the basis for his beginning statements to chapter 5 which have been misread and misinterpreted by a majority of his anthropological colleagues.

The discovery of *patterned outcomes* of particular acts or occurrences, which cannot be seen as exemplary manifestations of ideal rules, enables Leach also to argue that the institution of bilateral inheritance in Pul Eliya (and other communities like it) does not automatically lead to the dreaded consequence of fragmentation of holdings (the effect of an increase of population is a different issue), because of recombinations and exchanges of various sorts between the residents of affinally related villages, and realistic awareness by farmers as to what amounts of land it is viable to cultivate. The inheritance "rules" are one thing, the actual total outcome of land transactions another. Moreover, individual inheritance prospects are at all times "wildly unpredictable," but "individual luck" is not averse to statistical order.

We now come to the notorious passages on page 146 at the beginning of chapter 5, which have already been quoted. These passages are declared by many to be polemical, wild, and unsustainable, especially by those who have not given the book a close reading.

In order to construe these passages as meaningful, we first have to understand the logic and ordering of the land tenure system in Pul Eliya whose ecological pattern is summarized by the expression "one tank – one village." The gist of where Leach has hitherto brought us in this section is as follows: he has demonstrated that kinship concepts – which have "ideal" formulations – are manipulable and flexible in application; that simultaneously the rules by which land is inherited and transmitted and cultivated – which have ideal formulations – are flexible and manipulable and adjustable. In these senses both the "kinship system" and the "land tenure system" are subject to processes of modification and stretching, and the ordering that is emergent at any point of time is more of a statistical order than of a logical order.

---

[86] Ibid., p. 141.

But against the dynamic flexibilities of the kinship system and the land tenure system stands something that is virtually inflexible and permanently ordered, to which both the above systems must necessarily relate, and to whose exigencies and constraints the people as kinsmen and property owners must continually adjust. This is the topographical system, and its limits are framed by the size of the irrigation tank and the shape of the Old Field, and the agrarian rules regarding water-sharing and laying out of plots. This topographical system – which is man-made and culturally constructed (Leach might have saved himself a lot of trouble by saying this) – is thus considered immutable, and is itself constrained by the humanly uncontrollable (in this system of peasant technology and agrarian capabilities) features of dry zone climate, especially variable rainfall and heat (evaporation rates). These ecological conditions have prevailed through the centuries. It is these relatively immutable features of climate, topographical layout, and associated technology and labor organization of rice production, that Leach perhaps ill-advisedly labeled "the constraints of economics,"[87] which were "prior" (in the sense of their greater constraining power on the actions of Pul Eliya people as "natural" and as "instituted" factors, and had necessarily to be coped with) to "the constraints of law and morality" (in the sense of jural kinship norms and ideals which are more capable of being manipulated and "rationalized" *ex post facto*).

PATTERNS OF LABOR COOPERATION IN TWO DIFFERENT CONTEXTS

Labor cooperation "follows a pattern which is antithetic to that of land ownership, and the rewarding of labour has the effect of counterbalancing the unequal distribution of primary title."[88] "The distribution of primary titles gives a misleading indication of the way in which the economic benefits of cultivation ultimately accrue to different members of the population."[89]

Leach discusses two different contexts of organization of labor. The first is in the Old Field where hereditary rights are at stake. Here the

---

[87] It is a pity that Leach did not carefully specify and gloss what he meant by "economics," which in this syntax, read "literally," might be taken to be a domain that is "non-moral." But this reading is a mistake as the ethnography and his own exegesis show. What Leach was reacting to was to Fortes' equating "jural" kinship with "morality," and virtually excluding economic features and considerations as "external" to the shaping of kinship relations and morality.

[88] Leach, *Pul Eliya*, p. 241. [89] Ibid., p. 241.

following kinship pattern prevails: "a man cooperates with his father-in-law and his brothers-in-law, but steers clear of his father and his full brothers."[90] Contrasted with this is a situation where hereditary right is not pertinent but labor cooperation is called for. There are two such situations, namely tank fishing and shifting cultivation (*hena*). Here kinship as such is "incidental" in that a man is likely to cooperate with kinsmen of all kinds – father, brother, father-in-law, brother-in-law – and with casual friends.

From the comparison of these two different contexts, Leach draws the conclusion that, since changes in economic context produce changes in appropriate behavior, the pattern of kinship collaboration in the Old Field is *not* quite clearly "determined by jural rules of a moral kind," but is "simply a by-product of the economic facts of the situation."[91]

Brothers avoided in one constrained context may assist one another in another unconstrained context. Fathers and married sons, ill at ease where the disposal of parental property is at stake, may find it easy to collaborate where that divisive issue is not in evidence.

Labor teams in harvesting and threshing rice

In summary, the labor teams (*kayiya*) formed for work in the rice fields are particularly important at the peak time of the agricultural cycle when harvesting and threshing of the stacks of rice stalks on the threshing floor (the work of men only) take place.

The labor teams doing this intensive work were, as is to be expected, recruited mainly on the basis of affinal kinship: "Adult full brothers are very seldom seen working in the same *kayiya* though half-brothers, step-brothers, and brothers by adoption sometimes did so."[92] "Fathers and sons are likely to work together in one team so long as the sons are unmarried, but once the son becomes an individual householder they are likely to appear in different labour teams . . . On the other hand an old man who has already divided his property can work in comfort with his sons on whom he has become dependent."[93] "Individuals who lived in the same compound in different houses very seldom worked in the same team."[94]

Leach meticulously documented the labor teams in Pul Eliya engaged in the preparation and location of threshing floors (*kamata*) and in the

---

[90] Ibid., p. 241.   [91] Ibid., p. 242.   [92] Ibid., p. 265.   [93] Ibid., p. 265.   [94] Ibid., p. 265.

task of threshing after the *Yala* harvest of 1954. There were in all twenty threshing floors, and in theory these floors could be sited anywhere according to the owner's convenience. The "in group," that is those who resided in the main village and had well-established hereditary status there, had all sited their *kamata*, thirteen in total, in the top part of the Old Field (the *Ihala elapata* adjacent to the main village residential area) and had sorted themselves out according to their compound group affiliation. The seven *kamata* of the "outside group" were distributed in a dispersed way near their field locations.

The group of people who built their paddy stacks in a common threshing floor and used it ordinarily constituted a single *kayiya* (work team): "They had worked together reciprocally to help each other in the task of stack-shifting, and it was roughly the same people who worked in teams of two or three in the work of threshing."[95]

In understanding the general principles of labor-group formation, Leach says that the primary ties for people who do this work together are those of *ukas* (mortgage) and *ande* (lease, tenancy, share cropping), and obligations of reciprocity; kinship alone does not determine who shall join in a common work team.

It is important from now on to follow Leach's reasoning and manner of solving this "puzzle."

On the one hand he emphasizes that, in the formation of labor teams, "the element of choice" is present, and in this context "there is no clear-cut jural obligation that a particular individual should contribute his labour to one group rather than another."[96] In fact the owner–tenant links, and considerations of own advantage and convenience, are prominent.

On the other hand, when the actual membership of *kayiya* teams was plotted, Leach discovered that the people who worked together were linked as bodies of kinsmen by *pavula* ties, of which the most significant ones were those between affinal kinsmen.

Leach employs this empirical finding to underscore the argument that the multiple choices of these individuals based on economic calculations and advantage, which by no means can be said to be determined by jural obligations of kinship, nevertheless produce a statistical order and distribution, a "social fact" in the Durkheimian sense: "it is something quite outside the immediate awareness of the participants, just as the

---

[95] Ibid., p. 274.   [96] Ibid., p. 281.

suicide rate is quite outside the conscious awareness of any individual suicide."[97]

The positioning of the individual stacks – which need not have conformed to any kinship rule or constraint – did in fact produce a "total pattern which emerges at the end [as] a significant arrangement which represented the social structure in a quite valid way and in a manner which was consistent with the behaviour of the same individuals in much more formal situations such as village and family festivals,"[98] in which *pavula* as collectivities of allies and as political factions were the principal action groups.

Shifting cultivation

Shifting cultivation (*hena*) is the most open of the agricultural contexts studied by Leach. In legal-administrative terms the government gives permits to villagers to clear small acreages of forest land to conduct dry land cultivation of food crops, dry grains, and cash crops. In practice villagers ignore and violate these rules, and there are periodic collisions between them and the government officials, with the local *tulana* headman, who is supposed to enforce the rules, caught in between.

In 1954 the Pul Eliya villagers were not issued any new permits, but many of them recultivated the previous year's clearings, and Leach documented the details of a revived *hena* garden, cultivated according to a "wheel pattern." Further details can be read in the book, but here let me highlight the nature of the obligations and labor contributions of each *hena* plot cultivator. Ordinarily the group of cultivators would clear the forest land together, and burn the felled trees and branches, before marking out their plots (of variable size according to agreement). Thereafter there is obligatory cooperation between the *hena* plot owners only in regard to two matters: each cultivator is obliged to build a fence on his perimeter so that it properly joins with the neighboring fences on either side; and a night-watching roster of the *hena* garden to keep predators (deer, elephants, wild boar, etc.) at bay is worked out similar to the understandings of *pangu* (share) holders in the *baga* system of the Old Field. There is no labor cooperation needed thereafter – each household or family (man, woman, and children) does the planting, watching over the crops during the daytime, and the harvesting. Thus the group operating a *hena* garden is a cooperative labor team for a few purposes only,

***

[97] Ibid., p. 281.   [98] Ibid., p. 283.

and there is no sharing of economic yields, rewards, and responsibilities. Furthermore, the territorial site, though nicely patterned, is quite impermanent and *ad hoc*.[99]

Although it appeared that the villagers were quite aware of their "traditional" (*purana*) methods of organizing *hena* cultivation,[100] and that "fair shares for all the compounds" was a specially prominent articulation, and although representatives from seven compounds were involved in the revived wheel *hena* of 1954, there was otherwise "no overall systematic pattern" such as that he observed "in the distribution of *paraveni* holdings in the Old Field or in the organization of *kayiya* teams at threshing time."[101]

Leach concludes with this comparative statement:

In the irrigated fields the scarcity of labour and the scarcity of water together force the individual to exploit to the utmost those rights over neighbours and kinsmen which are latent in the total structure; and in this situation the kinship system is seen to operate in a definite and consistent way in accordance with a set of rules. But in *hena* cultivation, as practised here, there are no economic scarcities which force men to co-operate so that the manifestiations of kinship association are random and without significance.[102]

THE DIALECTIC BETWEEN "STATISTICAL" AND "NORMATIVE" ORDERS

Leach has this to say in 1961 about his earlier volume on *Political Systems of Highland Burma* (1954). He intimates that this book adapts and transforms Durkheimian ideas concerning "collective representation," and Durkheim's unacceptable proposition that "things sacred" and "things profane" are quite separate categories. Leach translates Durkheim's sacred/profane mutually exclusive oppositional categories into the related categories of "ritual" and "day to day" behavior. Ritual provides a formalized "outline plan" in terms of which individuals orientate their day-to-day behavior.[103] Leach transforms Durkheim's proposition that "things sacred" and "things profane" are quite separate categories into aspects of behavior that are present (in different strengths) in all behaviors. "Rituals, through which the members of a society manifest to themselves the model schema of the social structure within which they

---

[99] See ibid., pp. 291–95.
[100] Leach refers to another *purana* layout described as *pangu hena* described by villagers as another plan with similar practices.
[101] Ibid., p. 295.   [102] Ibid., p. 295.   [103] Ibid., p. 299.

live, occur all the time, in ordinary every day affairs just as much as in situations which are explicitly ceremonial."[104]

Applied to *Political Systems of Highland Burma* this formulation says that the formal (and ritualized) verbal categories of *gumsa* and *gumlao* are ideal categories, and "the divergences of individual behaviour from any standard norm are not then the result of moral error or of unenlightened self-interest, but arise simply because different individuals, *quite legitimately fill in the details of the ideal schema in different ways*" (emphasis added).[105]

But in *Pul Eliya* Leach is not content to rest here. While in the earlier book, he states that he had "argued that the ideal order tends to be constant which is reinterpreted to fit the changing circumstances of economic and political fact," he also suggested that "the facts of empirical reality are, in every variation, constrained by the ideas which people hold about which is supposed to be the case."[106] This is what he called his former "idealist position."

In *Pul Eliya*, his first big break with *Political Systems* is to suggest that the "quantitative" ("statistical") manifestation of conduct "possesses a structural pattern which is *independent* of any ideal paradigm. This does not imply that ideal relations are irrelevant, but it does emphasize that the ideal order and the statistical order are not just one and the same thing."[107]

As his ethnographic presentations unfold, Leach increasingly moves toward the position that the social structure viewed as a statistical order of aggregated individual acts should have primacy over the normative order conceived as social structure, and one could even dispense with the Oxford structuralists' assumption that "the individual is constrained by *moral* forces." Such a conclusion fits the reality that in Pul Eliya it is the topographical and tenure system, not Pul Eliya society, that is the continuing entity: "Members have to adapt to the layout of the territory rather than to adapt the territory to the private whims of individual human beings."[108] This is the basis for his conclusion that in Pul Eliya it is "locality structure" rather than "kinship structure" that has dominance as a "structuring" influence: "local group endogamy is not the survival of archaic caste prejudice, it is the necessary corollary of the fixed layout of the cultivated fields and the equal property rights accorded to both men and women."[109] The Oxford structuralists polarize "things social" and "things material." But this antithesis is wrong: in Pul Eliya, "society"

---

[104] Ibid., p. 299.   [105] Ibid., p. 299.   [106] Leach, *Political Systems*, p. 9.   [107] Ibid., p. 9.
[108] Leach, *Pul Eliya*, p. 301.   [109] Ibid., p. 303.

and "kinship" are not separate "things" with separate existence; they are a way of ordering experience in relation to land and property, and it is inadequate to isolate kinship – whose phenomenological reality is not denied and whose study *is* valid – "as a distinct category explainable by jural rules without reference to context or economic self-interest."[110]

It is quite likely that some – or even many – readers would find it disturbing to ponder what seems like a repudiation of the "normative" order in favor of the "normal." In fact Leach does not deny the role of "normative" ideal order formulations or of kinship conceptions in social life. He wants to relocate their relevance and their priority.

In the rest of this chapter, I will sum up what I take to be Leach's original "thought-struggles" – if I may coin this term – to formulate the dialectic between "ideal" and "statistical" orders, a dialectic in which they are by no means the same, but are nevertheless related in unexpected ways of feedback.

SUMMATION

Leach it seems to me convincingly demonstrated in *Pul Eliya* that a particular kind of structural-functional framework which accords primacy to the notion of social structure or system as constituted of social principles of organization of a jural-moral kind which then direct and engender actual behavior, and that deviance from these moral norms is due to the inability of persons to live up to the moral demands of society, is hopelessly inadequate to interpret social life.

In opposition to this view Leach establishes that "ideal formulations" by actors and "ideal categories" that they formulate (one could also say that this expression includes their "jural rules") are an order of phenomena that should be kept separate from the actual behavior of individuals/actors, which form another order of a "statistical" kind. They should be treated as separate frames of reference, the first being "normative" the second "normal." They are not congruent: one does not wholly or directly derive from the other. Moreover, the "normal" order as characterizing "social structure" should have primacy over the normative. But what then is the relationship between them, and what kind of answer or answers does Leach proffer? It is on this issue that anthropologists and social theorists might differ, and also his critics may have misread him.

That the people of Pul Eliya had "ideal concepts" and normative formulations, which anthropologists have labeled as belonging to the

---

[110] Ibid., p. 306.

domain of "kinship," is readily admitted and documented by Leach. He agrees that kinship terminology classifies kin; that certain kinds of kin terms, specifying parent and child, siblings – especially older and younger brother – and cross-cousin and brother-in-law, may also be accompanied by formulaic norms of "ideal" conduct, such as the famous "right" of a man to claim a mother's brother's daughter; and that incest taboos may serve as constraints on most actors. However, all these and other kinship particulars do not determine or predict actual conduct, because there is much cultural and social space *outside their scope* which provides the context, circumstances, and interests which actors pursue to reach their goals.

It would be absurd to think that the perspective of individual actors making strategic choices to maximize their interests and goals makes these motivated acts somehow amoral or non-social because they have "personal" or "private" relevance. The rules that define a game are different from the strategies and moves the players can adopt in playing the game, and those again are different from the actual performance of the players, for players manipulate and play with different skills, and opportunities, and cope with unexpected contingencies and accidents. An entailment of the individual strategizing perspective is that, while an actor may know what he or she is trying to attain, and may know what the result is for him or her, all the actors in a situation are not for the most part aware of the aggregate distributional patterns and outcomes of all their acts. This pattern of outcomes is what Leach called the "statistical order" (and the "curves," "averages," and other measures that are used to calculate the "normal").[111]

Leach's grappling with the issue of the relation between "ideal" *pavula* and "effective" *pavula*, of how both these structures interrelate, but in which it is the axis of affinity and *massinã* alliance that supersedes in social life the role of formal male sibling ties, is another variant example of the same general issue. Moreover, the unpacking of the alleged solidarity of male siblings by filiation and as primary heirs to parental property, by revealing how their being competitors to that patrimony creates a social distance between them, further accentuated by distinctions of age, is an acute diagnosis of contradictory trends built into that building block of "kinship principles" central to Africanist descent group theory, namely "solidarity of the sibling group."

---

[111] The neoclassical model of the market under conditions of perfect competition is an extreme ideal formulation of this logic.

But there are other revelations which surprise us in another way. The ideal formulation that inherited *paraveni* field plots in the Old Field are so precious for validating status that they ought not to be sold, especially to "outsider" traders of the wrong *variga*, or even worse of alien "race" (Muslims and Tamils), was right royally contravened by many of the titled and wealthiest farmers of the village. But there were circumstances and manipulations and strategies (including the unwillingness of locals to cultivate the plots as tenants or laborers to these "outsiders") by which the plots returned to the ownership of the Pul Eliya *minissu* (people); and there were similar processes of conversion into citizenship of new owners or their children by means of right marriage with Pul Eliya women, and transforming that property into "heirlooms." These processes demonstrate the routes by which actual gaps between ideal model and actual events are over time closed and *retrospectively* made to look as if the ideal norms have not been violated and have always been observed. In the case of the cooperating labor teams (*kayiya*) involved in the tasks of harvesting and threshing, whose membership is not obligatory on the basis of kinship, but open to choice, Leach finds that the total pattern of the teams (the statistical order) shows that the teams were bodies of kinsmen linked by affinal ties and *pavula* links. The outcomes thus affirm the Pul Eliya social structure as revealed by other outcomes in other formal situations.

There are other examples of how a master ethnographer meticulously engaged with micro-details and assembled his data according to a combined "idealist *cum* empiricist" perspective (which self-ascribed expression I shall gloss later when I compare Leach with Lévi-Strauss). But the most important documentation concerns the *dialectical relation* between ideal formulations and actual behavior, and concerning this what Leach labored to convince his readers, but seems not to have got across to many of them, is this formulation: despite various events over time (especially from 1890 to 1954) among the people of Pul Eliya and their closest neighbors, who consider themselves of the same *variga* which has to do with changes in the ownership over plots and associated water rights (especially in the Old Field and old residential area), and despite drastic changes in the economic status of individual families and their heirs (changes in regard to economic differentiation), and despite changes that made available new categories of land by virtue of governmental policy and legislation, etc., the people of Pul Eliya managed to maintain virtually unchanged the topographical layout of the "tank-village" in terms of two fields and three *baga*, and the notion of "shares" subdivided into

strips and their associated agrarian duties of tank and irrigation maintenance. This topographical system (a cultural model that was influenced
by certain given "natural" economic ecological factors) was existentially
more salient and relatively rigid and frozen. But the social system of the
locals, exemplified by their "kinship system," though framed in terms of
cultural ideal principles, was in fact much more flexible in its workings,
and this "adaptability" was primarily a response to changes in the ownership of prime land and water rights produced by inheritance, marriage,
sales, gifts, etc.

But when the anthropologist tracks these flexible dynamic social relations (many of which are given shape in the form of the dialectic between
ideal kin and subcaste rules and actual behavior), Leach discovers that
these actual relations (aggregated as "statistical orders") are themselves
significantly related to the manner in which the actors are spatially situated as contemporaneous contiguous owners and neighbors, or as potential neighbors or combiners of plots through marriage. The agrarian
system as such that requires that owners of neighboring strips must co-
operate to maintain irrigation, must get along to work the system of
water sharing, and also the system of strip location – that tells people
which physical combination of contiguous plots is worth possessing or
acquiring – ultimately has a steering role to play in the social relations
of people, and the actual patterns that "debts of social obligation" and
ties of amity assume on the ground. It is in this sense that "locality rather
than descent forms the basis of corporate grouping" in Pul Eliya.[112]

But there is one more alignment between ideal plan and contemporary reality, the past and present, to be grasped. The topographical
model, which Pul Eliyans hold to be ancestral, is a tripartite scheme
whose foundation and founding schema were formulated by them as
follows: the village was made up of three *bāga*, each the holding of a
single man – a *gamarāla* (hereditary chief and cultivator or primary grant
holder); but in turn each *gamarāla* sub-let numerous portions of his *bāga* to
tenants.

> This is an ideal construction which ... differs widely from the present facts
> of the case. But ... when the villages were explaining their system to me they
> constantly used a certain form of phraseology. The village consists of three *bāga*;
> the villagers are members of three *pavula*; formerly the head of each *bāga* was
> a *gamarāla*; formerly each *Gamarāla* was head of one of the three *pavula*. This
> displays very clearly the principle though not the facts.[113]

---

[112] Leach, *Pul Eliya*, p. 9.   [113] Ibid., p. 125.

The three *bāga* system is intact and has been so at least since 1890. The *gamarāla* system is gone, though the strips of land associated with that office still carry prestige and claims to leadership. A notable fact is that "even in 1954, although the *gamarāla* had ceased to be of practical significance, the three individuals who, by birth, should have been *gamarāla*, were still treated as *pavula* leaders." But there were others also, backed by land, energetic social climbers making their bids. Political factions form and reform in Pul Eliya, and in this process, it is how the compound groups align and aggregate that matters most. But, as Leach has demonstrated, the continuity, expansion, shrinkage, fragmentation of compound groups has been closely linked with the varying fortunes of the owners of land in the Old Field. And the people of 1954 imagined their society to be a continuation of their past, of which the concrete native of the topographical tripartite Old Field and its relatively invariant logic was the unshakable evidence.

It seems to me that Leach might have made much more of the *foundational* myth of the people of Pul Eliya, that their village was founded in the time of Dutthagamini in the second century BC, that in the Kandyan feudal period the village was classed as a *nindagam* over which the ancestors of the present *Disava* (1954) exercised ultimate title as hereditary feudal lords. And the most important segment of their foundational myth is what was mentioned above: that the village has always consisted of three territorial sections, headed by three *gamarālas*, each a head of a *pavula* (kindred and faction). The residents of Pul Eliya in persisting with this myth are enduringly wedded to the topographic layout which is the ground of their being in time. "The repeated assertion that the community consisted of three families (*pavula*) and that, in the old days, there had been three *Gamarāla*, was simply a projection of the *bāga* arrangements of the Old Field. It did not correspond to the actual facts as any living inhabitant of Pul Eliya had ever known them."[114] But they were persisting ideal thought categories and rhetorical speech acts.

THE FORTESIAN REPLY: AVOIDANCE AND CERTAINTY

Leach, the studied polemical provoker and tester of boundaries, did not want *Pul Eliya* to be taken simply as a bilateral kinship type of society that is differently constituted from the unilineal descent systems so systematically summed up by Fortes. He was famously against typologies. In any

[114] Ibid., pp. 303–4.

case *Pul Eliya* did not belong to either type grossly labeled as unilineal or non-unilineal. Such monolithic typing was useless. He had hoped to carry the war into the camp of the three magisterial theorists of descent group theory. Although *Pul Eliya* was primarily offered "as an example of a particular society which lacks a unilineal descent system," his ambition as theorist was "to introduce a wider scepticism." He hoped that his method of explication and demonstration, and the analytical process he deployed, "applied to societies *with* unilineal descent, might produce disconcerting results."[115]

Evans-Pritchard and Fortes were alive and still active when *Pul Eliya* was published in 1961. Evans-Pritchard did not respond, at least in print. Fortes, in the course of his weighty *Kinship and the Social Order: The Legacy of Lewis Henry Morgan* (1969),[116] which may be taken to be a full-fledged laying out of his theory of kinship, devoted some eight pages of chapter 12 to reviewing some of the ethnography of *Pul Eliya*, and illustrating his dismissive statement: "The special relevance of this study lies in the fact that the field data, which are presented in scrupulous detail unequivocally contradict the polemical stance."[117] Such a summary rejection does not promise a serious reading of *Pul Eliya* or a willingness to engage in a dialog.

There are two aspects of Fortes's response which I propose to consider. One is that it is my sense that his attempted rebuttal of Leach, via Leach's own ethnography, exhibits signs of cursory or spotty reading and/or unwillingness to seriously address himself to the task of engaging with the twists and turns and complexities of Leach's arguments and methods. From Fortes's own point of view there are some genuine problems in accepting all that Leach asserts; but there are also distortions produced by the old trick of "literal quoting" of sentences, isolated from their larger context and preceding formulations.

The second aspect is that both in his reply to Leach, and of course more so in the extended text of his own book, Fortes trenchantly and fiercely and without misgivings states and elaborates the architectonic principles of kinship and descent he had always held, and which he now holds, by favorably incorporating into his own schema the considerable ethnography and ideas propounded by numerous anthropologists of our time. In terms of a comparison popularized by Isaiah Berlin, Fortes is "the hedgehog" in contrast to Leach "the fox." Fortes's enduring commitment to a paradigm was immune to the wily strategems of Leach to draw him

---

[115] Ibid., p. 302.   [116] Fortes, *Kinship and the Social Order.*   [117] Ibid., p. 221.

out. There is little doubt that it was Fortes in particular who was the target of Leach's assaults in *Pul Eliya*; the late fifties and early sixties were the time of their most difficult and tense personal and theoretical differences.

Before I review Fortes's reading of *Pul Eliya* ethnography and Leach's interpretations, I have to make a framing statement which seems to have escaped Fortes.

The following facts are never in question in Leach's monograph. All villagers of *Pul Eliya* "consider themselves to be members of a single endogamous *variga* of the Goyigama caste. All the villagers are, therefore, kinsmen of one another."[118] Indeed, there are only some 146 residents in all in this small universe, and Leach's own elaborate chart 1 on compound succession and compound residents plots the kinship links, genealogically and affinally, of the compound heads. So in a sense everything that happens in the village can be said to involve kin in one way or another, a framing assumption for Leach, the unshakable proof of the primacy of "kinship" for Fortes.

Leach is concerned with *internal* analysis of various sorts to demonstrate that the attribution of *intrinsic* values to kinship does not explain the substantive differences in conduct between different categories of kin (for example, male siblings versus brothers-in-law), and furthermore, does not explain why the same kin behave differently to one another in *different contexts*; these, and other such changing values, can to a great extent be made to make sense in *Pul Eliya* by relating these persons in action contexts to "economic" factors such as differential ownership of valued land, location of plots in the rice fields and associated water rights, different types of cultivation (rice growing versus shifting slash-and-burn agriculture), owner–tenant relations, labor cooperation in harvesting and threshing, residential choice and location after marriage, marriage strategies for combining land, etc. By and large the logic and value of such internal analyses of changing contexts seem not to have engaged Fortes.

Concurrently, Leach's probing and struggling with the problem of how to relate "ideal thought categories" and "actual behavior," which began with *Political Systems* and is taken further in *Pul Eliya* in his attempt to distinguish between "ideal order" and "statistical order," and how to relate the latter to the former, and how much sense there is to characterizing "social structure" in terms of the patterns of statistical distributions rather than in terms of normative principles, which automatically

[118] Leach, *Pul Eliya*, p. 67.

determine conformity and define deviances – all these issues again do not engage Fortes.

Fortes claims he does not understand what Leach means when he charges him (and Radcliffe-Brown and Evans-Pritchard) with treating "kinship as a thing in itself." As I have clarified earlier, Leach in many places stated what he had in mind. He was opposed to that perspective which viewed kinship concepts and principles as forming an "intrinsic" and "internal" system which explained conduct; another way of saying this was that the phenomena of kinship were explained by reference to other kinship phenomena, which fitted into an autonomous system. It is incorrect to think that Leach did not recognize that there were some phenomena that belonged to "kinship *per se*" (see my earlier discussion) but he repudiated the claim that they constituted an intrinsic system as specified above.

In his reply to Leach, Fortes states that Leach's position is "that what we designate as the relations and institutions of kinship, descent, and affinity are in reality merely artifacts, or expressions of more funda-mental, more lasting, and more solidly real data of social life;"[119] "the implication is clear: Property constitutes the enduring, the basic staff of social life; the 'concepts'... relating to the universe of kinship are 'ex-pressions' – that is, secondary to, derivates of, this permanent reality."[120] This is Fortes's summary of Leach's main submissions, and although it is certainly the case that there are some eminently quotable polemical flourishes in *Pul Eliya*, the above references do not convey the heart of Leach's labors.

Fortes even resorts to some slapstick comedy when he suggests Leach might be guilty of this sin: no-one has demonstrated that "the system of kinship terminology, customary in any society, or the structure of kin-ship and descent relations operative in it, or indeed even the occurrence of some particular norm of kinship can be deduced from a knowledge of the economy or any strictly economic process, practice, or institution ... The point is too banal to emphasize."[121]

How does Fortes defend himself against the "kinship as a thing" slo-gan? He says, "Certainly none of those cited by Leach in the course of his study ever presented *kin groups* as 'things in themselves' without regard to rights and interests which centre in them." But what Leach was pointing to in this context was that the common interests are of economic, legal, political, religious, etc. nature, and these are not intrinsic to kinship links

---

[119] Fortes, *Kinship and the Social Order*, p. 220.   [120] Ibid., p. 222.   [121] Ibid., p. 222.

per se. It is people's sharing of these interests that is justified by reference to the kinship nexus. How does one deal with the play of these "externals" on the "internal forms" of kin concepts?

Fortes concedes that on the one hand genealogy alone is not sufficient to establish membership in kin groups without regard to rights and interests, but "on the other hand, without genealogy, there can, in certain political-jural systems, be no title to membership."[122] "By the same token ... marriage presupposes at least an incest rule ... and may prescribe partners, as in *Pul Eliya*, by genealogically framed criteria.[123] Similarly, inheritance, if intestate, presumes laws that define next-of-kin-right by criteria of kinship and genealogical speculation."[124] As a conclusion to looking at the issue in these terms, Fortes declares in a seeming reversal of Leach's thesis "that relationship by kinship or marriage appears to be *the necessary and prior condition* for economic and property relations in this community as in others of the same kind we are concerned with"[125] (emphasis added).

The senses in which Leach and Fortes are using "prior" in their texts need to be clarified. I have previously suggested that Leach uses "priority" in the existential sense of the Pul Eliyans having less freedom to change the topographical system once they had set it up, while they could be more flexible in manipulating the kinship system in relation to that agrarian reality and its constraints. In the above quotations Fortes is accepting that economic and property relations are *separate* from kinship and marriage and secondary to them.

Fortes seems to see priority ontologically in some kind of "initial situation" in the human condition: the mother–child relation is pegged to some ultimate biological and psychological starting point; other modular relations of filiation and siblingship are fundamentally tied to "familial relations." Then by the overlaying on this by "social recognition," humans develop the jural and moral rules of amicable kinship conduct and structural extrapolations of descent and marriage. All these develop according to some kind of necessary general existential and moral logic of amity. Economic and property relations are an extrinsic and external system, which interacts with the domain of kinship and marriage; these forces seem to come later in Fortes's "developmental" assumptions.

---

[122] Ibid., p. 229.
[123] This is an error: there is no genealogically framed prescribed rule of marriage in *Pul Eliya*; there is an alleged "claim" on a true cross-cousin, but first cross-cousin marriages are few. See my earlier presentation of the distribution of marriages in Pul Eliya.
[124] Fortes, *Kinship and the Social Order*, p. 222.   [125] Ibid., p. 223.

Political relations somehow seem to extend seamlessly from notions of descent which links the familial-domestic domain with the political tribal domain. But "economics" is an alien domain of private gain and ulterior motives of "mercenary commerce," an unguarded revelation of Fortes's prejudice. Interesting as all this spun web of kinship is, it remains a special "revelation" and speculation, and a special carving up of the entirety of social and moral life.

We know that Fortes was never seriously interested in the economic dimensions of social life, and he did not think "economic differentiation" in Tale society was a factor to be reckoned with. He exhibits his anthropological perspective when he declares that the problem that lay at the heart of Lewis Henry Morgan's researches and speculations, and remains the central one for us today, "is the problem of how kinship and polity are interconnected in tribal society."[126] Tribal polity was projected externally from the domestic domain and filiation via the connecting links of descent. That Morgan attributed a centrality to the development of private property constructs in the evolution of the patriarchal monogamous family is virtually ignored by Fortes. In reply to Leach's charge of the Oxford school's lack of interest in "economics" Fortes submits that "what functionalist anthropologists have always stressed . . . [is] the *concomitant variation and mutual dependence in tribal societies of economic and kinship and descent institutions*" and he cites Evans-Pritchard, Firth, and Audrey Richards. Whether Evans-Pritchard's *The Nuer* qualifies is debatable;[127] from Leach's point of view it would be curious to cite Firth and Richards whose pedigree and interests are more appropriately linked with Malinowski who was their major inspiration, as he was Leach's own.

Be that as it may, this is the Fortesian formulation that is stated as a rebuttal of Leach's concerns: "Systems of production, consumption, and exchange certainly act as external constraints and as media for the deployment of kinship institutions, norms, and relationships. They have never been incontrovertibly shown to be the ultimate *raison d'être* of such institutions, norms and relationships regarded as an internal system."[128]

Thus Fortes does – as Leach said – take kinship phenomena to constitute an "internal system." We are left in the dark as to how economic institutions serve as "media" for deployment of kinship. What is the sense

---

[126] Ibid., p. 219.
[127] *Ibid.*, p. 2. Leach criticizes Evans-Pritchard's monograph for discussing the social structure (segmentary descent system) and the ecology (territorial system) as separate halves and not interrelating the two. (See Leach, *Pul Eliya*, p. 305.)
[128] Fortes, *Kinship and the Social Order*, p. 229.

of "media?" The "field" through which kinship phenomena move, untouched, uncontaminated, and without a dialectical or mutual relation between them?

While Fortes, known for his analytical skills, is signally unhelpful in sorting this complex issue, we have from him an uncompromising stand that the phenomena of kinship are self-referential and internally linked and constituted. He is of the view that "marriage, parenthood, filiation, siblingship and other relations of kinship occur in similar arrangements in societies very different from the Tallensi in their modes of production of food, shelter, and services, in their property relations."[129] It is beyond my brief here to give an account of why and how Fortes thinks these arrangements are so general, but the answer is attempted in *Kinship and the Social Order*.

I would like to close by examining an attempted rebuttal of Leach by Fortes through the latter's reinterpretation of Leach's deconstruction of *variga* in *Pul Eliya*. *Contra* Leach, Fortes insists on the priority and *inviolability* of the *Goyigama* caste endogamy as the outer boundary of inclusion and acceptance by birth or incorporation into the *variga*. Unfortunately, he carries the war into Leach's camp by examining only one case; a more thorough search in the book might have deterred him. But right or wrong, what is made clear is his view that kinship (and subcaste) principles encode a lawful morality in their own right, which is what Leach is skeptical about.

There are at least two decisive cases presented by Leach where persons of ambiguous or wrong *variga* status, or of a non-Goyigama status and completely outside the *variga* system, were given *variga* status.

The first case concerns K. Menikrala, who was not married, and his two brothers, K. Dingirihamy and K. Wannihamy, who were both married to women of the *variga*.[130] The father of Menikrala and his brothers had originally been of the "wrong *variga*," but his sons were "accepted as full Pul Eliya citizens for most purposes." But Menikrala was referred to as a "scoundrel" because he was a blackleg willing to work in 1954 for the only Old Field landlord who was not a member of the Pul Eliya *variga* and against whom the leaders of the village were attempting to apply the usual sanctions (of denying him village agricultural labor).

Menikrala had other shortcomings. He "was considered to be unmarried and he therefore had no brother-in-law within the *variga*. This made

[129] Ibid., p. 221.   [130] See Leach, *Pul Eliya*, p. 253 for the details.

Menikrala's *variga* status inferior to that of his two married brothers."
"This case illustrates how the effective boundaries to *variga* membership
are established through the recognition of affinal ties rather than through
the validations of a status established at birth."[131]

The second case involves the deliberations of the *variga* court in 1954
and should be read in full.[132] To summarize: V. Arlis Fernando was a
carpenter practicing at Minhettigam village. He originally came from
Colombo and about 18 months previously had set up house with a *Vanni-
Vadda* woman from Kalawel Potana. Doing good business, and having
a child, Arlis "wishes now to make his marriage regular so that his own
children can marry his wife's relatives when they grow up. Since he is a
stranger in these parts he has to claim entry into his wife's variga."

His wife's relatives collaborated. It was so arranged that Arlis would
pay the fine (a quarter of which would go to the *Disava*), and the cost
of the feasting and of gifts to the courts would also be borne by Arlis.
Arlis's wife's two *massinā* gave false evidence that they had visited the
home of Arlis in Colombo and that they had verified that his family
was of respectable *Goyigama* caste status. (Everybody knew he was of the
"inferior" *Karava* caste.) Arlis was admitted into his wife's *variga*, he gave
a lavish feast, and the fine was reduced. A formal wedding of Arlis and
his bride was duly staged.

There is a third case,[133] which Leach interprets in one way, and Fortes
in another. It concerns two men, and also the sons of the second man.

At the beginning of the century, there was a resident in Pul Eliya,
named Ranhamy, who came from another district (Kurunegala) 40 miles
away, which if one follows the ethnography one realizes also falls outside
the entire *variga* system prevailing in the district of Nuvarakalaviya to
which Pul Eliya belongs. Ranhamy lived in Pul Eliya because he was a
cousin (*massinā*) of the Buddhist priest (who, if one follows the ethnography, one knows is again an outsider) of the local temple with its own
tank and lands.

In due course Ranhamy set up house with the daughter of one of
the leading men of Pul Eliya holding the *gamarāla* title. Ranhamy was
summoned before the *variga* court (the woman was guilty of having sex
relations with a non-*variga* person), but with the priest as his kinsman
and the *gamarāla* as father-in-law the case was not in doubt. "After a

---

[131] Ibid., p. 253.   [132] Ibid., "Appendix 1: Description of a 'Variga-Sabha'", pp. 307–9.
[133] See ibid., pp. 72–73.

payment of fine, Ranhamy was recognized as member of the local *variga* and formally married to Walli Etani."[134]

The priest in question had a gardener who was also called Ranhamy. He and his wife came from a village close to Nawana. "When the gardener's sons grew up they sought wives from the Pul Eliya area. Eventually one of them induced a girl from Yakawewa to set up house with him. This time the judgment of the *variga* court was that the girl and her whole family be expelled from the *variga*."[135]

Leach does report that "In the first case Ranhamy, the priest's cousin, was of *Goyigama* caste with respectable connections; in the second Ranhamy, the gardener was of dubious caste origins and a man of no substance." He draws this conclusion: "The discrimination in the rulings is revealing. The principle involved is clear. Where the 'sinner' is a desirable relative, his offence is purged with a fine; where he is undesirable he and his accomplices are cut out of the *variga* altogether."[136]

Fortes disputes this interpretation. His comment is that in the first case the "desirable" relative was a member of the *same* caste (*Goyigama*), whereas in the second case, the man was not of *Goyigama* caste. "Thus this case was a definite offence against caste endogamy, while the first case could be interpreted as tolerance of a breach of subcaste endogamy which yet kept within the bounds of the wider and prior endogamy of the whole caste. It is not simply a case of ulterior or mercenary motives being the main criterion."[137]

When this third case of the two Ranhamys is read together with the other two cases that are in the book but which Fortes ignores, it becomes clear that Leach's arguments concerned with the nuances of intra-*variga* politics about who is to be admitted to membership and who is not cannot be subverted.

Fortes is asserting that in *variga* affairs "the rule of caste morality" is the paramount consideration, and as long as the local people observe and enforce *Goyigama* caste endogamy, which is unshakable, they may tolerate non-observance of the *variga* (he calls it "subcaste") rule. But the first two cases show, firstly, that two of the three brothers whose father was of a wrong *variga*, but with a history of residence in Pul Eliya, achieved full Pul Eliya *variga* status by making the right marriages with local women, affinity providing a bridge to the full entry; and, secondly,

[134] Ibid., p. 73.   [135] Ibid., p. 73.   [136] Ibid., p. 73.
[137] Fortes, *Kinship and the Social Order*, p. 223.

that a man whom everyone knew to be of *wrong caste* was accepted into
the *variga* because of his economic success and his taking up with a
Pul Eliya woman. This latter case provides a contrast to that of the
poor gardener whose dubious caste origins could not be translated into
variga acceptance through the right marriage because he was poor, and
his wife's family were expelled from the *variga*. While Fortes is correct
to emphasize that breaking the rule of "caste endogamy" would ordinarily be a horrendous thing to contemplate, yet he should, as Leach's
report of village talk shows, have taken the "ideal" rule of *variga* endogamy to be also a serious matter for them.[138] And in their everyday
horizons, the *Goyigama* caste villagers of the district, divided into different *variga* (and having service relations with a few inferior caste individuals from a few well-known villages), take these *variga* affiliations
to be "paramount" because the outer boundary of belonging to the
Goyigama caste is taken for granted, and is not a matter of usual *variga*
court deliberations.

Let us briefly recapitulate how Leach gave his exposition of *variga* in
"ideal" terms and actual conduct. All villagers of Pul Eliya "consider
themselves to be members of a single endogamous *variga* of the *Goyigama*
caste. All the villagers are, therefore, kinsmen of one another."[139] For
Fortes such a declaration has absolute validity, and is in line with his
axial position that, just as a unilineal descent group is a corporation with
rights and duties stemming from descent concepts *per se*, so are the caste
and *variga* (subcaste) endogamous corporations regulating membership
through descent/pedigree and marriage.

Fortes rules that Pul Eliya membership cannot be acquired by purchase, or by right of occupational specialization, of property ownership,
or even by residence only. "The indispensable credential is a recognized
kinship status within the village subcaste."[140] But Leach provides incon-
trovertible evidence that this kinship status could also be acquired by
other means than "birth"; it too is negotiable.

Leach's attempts to unpack *variga* as a corporation and "kin group" are
incomprehensible to Fortes. If it is ideally bounded by common kinship,
variga, argues Leach, is also a "territorial corporation"; the *variga* members as an aggregate have title in all the lands of all the villages comprising
the *variga*. And the corporateness of the *variga* is enacted and manifested
in the proceedings of the *variga* court whose members ultimately decide

---

[138] As Leach reported: "Wrong *variga* marriages were neither forgotten nor forgiven." *Pul Eliya*,
p. 80.
[139] Leach, *Pul Eliya*, p. 67.   [140] Fortes, *Kinship and the Social Order*, p. 228.

who is and who is not a member. And if you scrutinize the court cases and judgments, it is the possession of land rights and history of residence in the village more than a person's "descent" that provide "the ultimate basis of *variga* status." Moreover, wealth, land rights, and residence as the back-up can provide the entry through marriage to a local woman of *variga* status to becoming a proper Pul Eliya citizen of "our variga." It is quite clear why an "outsider" trader who has purchased land in Pul Eliya and is not a farmer does not and cannot become a full citizen. Leach makes the final point that the *variga*, despite its "idealist" clothing as a kinship corporation, does not and cannot depend on its kinship criteria to continue its existence, for when the *variga* court loses its political-legal activities regarding ruling on membership, the *variga* itself, an abstraction, will cease to be functional. Local group endogamy is not the survival of archaic caste prejudice but a necessary corollary of the layout of the cultivated fields and the equal property rights awarded to both men and women.

Fortes does cursorily refer to other aspects of Pul Eliya ethnography on the labor groups in harvesting and threshing and the siting of threshing floors. He shows here no appreciation of the logic of Leach's argument that the constraints on cooperation (who helps whom) vary with the economic context, and yet in the positioning of individual stacks a significant total pattern similar to the statistical orders (social structure) emerges in a situation of free individual choice. Fortes merely points to the outcome as confirming the "social structure" and cannot understand why Leach puts emphasis on free choice in this context.

When it comes to the context of shifting cultivation (*hena*) on forest land, in which there are minimal imperatives for cooperative labor and sharing of rewards and responsibilities, a context in which no patterning emerges on affinal, *pavula*, or other lines, Fortes counters that "there is no social system in the world in which kinship rules and regulates every human activity."[141]

The disappointment I experience with regard to Fortes's responses to Leach, as I previously mentioned, is that he failed to either grasp or take seriously the internal comparative analysis involving the varying of contexts. These contexts vary from Old Field ownership and irrigation rights and duties and obligations to synchronize cultivation, to *Sinakara* collaborative land development, to labor arrangements and collaboration in cultivation, harvesting, and threshing (which tasks are entirely different from questions of ownership and transmission of property rights),

---

[141] Ibid., p. 228.

to shifting of agriculture. These different contexts are correlated with varying constraints on social relations, and the dialectical impact these processes had on the patterns of kinship and non-kinship ties, especially in terms of the links of descent and siblingship, marriage and affinity, and the micro-politics of *pavula* factionalism, are considered. Perhaps a great deal about these men's contrasting world-views is conveyed by the titles of their two books considered here: Leach's *Pul Eliya* is "A Study in Land Tenure and Kinship" (suggestive of the concomitant variation and dialectical relations and overlap between two domains) and Fortes's tome is called "Kinship and the Social Order" (intimating that kinship is the centripetal core of the larger expanding universe of social relations which constitute the social order).

In concluding this commentary on *Pul Eliya*, I want to signal the undeniable fact that Leach adopted a polemical style of argumentation, the forcefulness of which would have been weakened by caveats and qualified hedging, which he probably intentionally avoided for that reason. One eminent anthropologist, Douglas Oliver, on the whole a sympathetic reviewer of *Pul Eliya*, remarked that Leach's "all or nothing stand" on certain issues may be an "instance of the author's highly effective device for stirring up his colleagues to rethink their assumptions and previous interpretations."[142] Be that as it may, I hope my exegesis has helped to illuminate the sense of Leach's thesis which outraged the orthodox: "I am offering to my anthropological colleagues the awkward doctrine that, in this society, the kinship system is not a 'thing in itself', but rather a way of thinking about rights and usages with respect to land. The land is fixed, the people change."[143] The ethnography was presented in detail, he said, in order to justify this claim, and that plea should be honored: all concerned readers should return to the book and read it closely before passing judgment.

Though Leach in many of his writings combatively contested settled orthodoxies, he would also in the company of his friends and sympathetic students genially admit that his carrying some of his formulations to their limit made him vulnerable to criticism. He deliberately took the risks entailed in such polemics. The following example of correspondence with a future anthropologist illustrates my point.

Marguerite S. Robinson, while a graduate student at Harvard, wrote Leach a letter dated August 12, 1961, asking him for advice about the

---

[142] Douglas Oliver, "Pul Eliya, a Village in Ceylon: a Study in Land Tenure and Kinship," *American Anthropologist*, vol. 62, 1962, pp. 621–22.

[143] Leach, *Pul Eliya*, p. 145.

choice of a field site in Sri Lanka. She also wrote her comments on *Pul Eliya* which had been published earlier the same year. In his reply to her, dated September 27, 1961, he wrote:

thank you very much indeed for your nice remarks about Pul Eliya – in private and off the record, as it were, I would probably agree with most of your critical comments on the rather extreme position I adopted about kinship – but I think there was a case for overstating the argument in order to be provocative . . . especially around here [Cambridge] where as you know "kinship" has got rather out of hand.[144]

Thereafter Marguerite had quite lengthy communication with Leach, who was absorbed in her fieldwork ethnography, as he had been with that of Benjamin and Yalman.[145]

---

[144] Leach Papers, Modern Archive Centre, King's College.

[145] Marguerite Robinson did her fieldwork in 1963 at Kotagepitiya, Maswela, Gampola (in the central highlands of Sri Lanka). Subsequently she came to Cambridge as a Visiting Scholar and worked with Leach. Her monograph based on her fieldwork is entitled *Political Structure in a Changing Sinhalese Village*, Cambridge and New York: Cambridge University Press, 1975. Her writings on Sri Lanka bear the imprint of Leach's theoretical influence.

CHAPTER 8

"Hydraulic Society in Ceylon": contesting Wittfogel's thesis and Sri Lankan mytho-history

In academic circles Karl Wittfogel's *magnum opus* on "hydraulic society" as the crystallization of "oriental despotism" characterized by "total concentration of power" in a monarch who ruled through the services of "an agro-managerial bureaucracy" was long awaited. It was finally published in 1957 under the title of *Oriental Despotism*,[1] but some of his principal ideas on hydraulic organization in China, in which society he had specialized, and on the totalitarian form of the Communist regime in the USSR, which he abhorred and abandoned, were already known through his writings.

Leach, as we know, had in the mid-1950s conducted his field studies in the dry zone of north-central Ceylon, which was historically famous as the site of some impressive hydraulic achievements. His book on the study of a single "tank-village", *Pul Eliya*, was published in 1961 after some delay. But already he had read with interest Wittfogel's book, and, on the basis of his own readings on Ceylon and his own fieldwork, he composed and published in *Past and Present* in 1959 an essay entitled "Hydraulic Society in Ceylon."[2] It was a timely and contestational response to Wittfogel's grand but controversial thesis, and it in turn was provocative and had an air of historical sweep about it.

Leach's essay falls into two parts. The first is a critical commentary on Karl Wittfogel's thesis in *Oriental Despotism* that "hydraulic society" is integrally connected to centralized political despotism and a developed bureaucracy, which together undertake the engineering of the hydraulic works, their maintenance, and their regulation. Wittfogel developed this thesis by reference to an early formulation by Marx[3] about Asiatic society, its lack of private property, and its domination by absolute despotism,

---

[1] Karl Wittfogel, *Oriental Despotism: A Comparative Study of Total Power*, New Haven: Yale University Press, 1957.
[2] E.R. Leach, "Hydraulic Society in Ceylon," *Past and Present*, no. 15, April 1959, pp. 2–26.
[3] I shall later discuss Marx's formulations on Asiatic society.

which is the author of hydraulic works. Leach does not critique Wittfogel's application of his thesis to China, Wittfogel's own area of expertise, as such. But his commentary is on two aspects of Wittfogel's theory as a *general* formulation applicable to all hydraulic societies, and as an *ideal type* which applies to areas of full aridity that are made productive by bringing water from afar to feed irrigation systems of large scale.

Leach counters that chronologically the earliest successful societies seem to have been those of southern Mesopotamia followed by Egypt and the Indus Valley. "In each case the natural environment which faced the original inhabitants may be summarised thus: an alluvial and fertile soil, an arid climate, a terrain of flat swamp land subject to periodic flooding. In such a context urban development calls for formidable and resourceful engineering, but the first essential requirement of the agriculturalist is *not* irrigation on a grand scale but simply a little modest conservation of local water sources."[4] "Most of the hydraulic civilisations of the past have grown up in arid but not fully arid regions. And irrigation in civilisations like Sumeria did not require a despotic monarch to build vast aqueducts and reservoirs; it simply called for elementary and quite localised drainage construction and perhaps the diversion of river flood water into the flat lands on either side of the main stream."[5]

This is only a preliminary observation. Leach reminds us that Marx posited his model of "Asiatic society" primarily in relation to India not China. Also he states that Wittfogel's ideal type virtually ignores all comparative references to the states of southern Asia, and that Burma (Pagan), Cambodia, and dry zone Ceylon (Sinhala) were all sophisticated states of relatively small scale, for which we possess a fairly detailed political history, and which were all "hydraulic societies" flourishing at much the same time. Moreover they were all in regular contact with China. Wittfogel does not mention any of them. Leach makes his case by reference to the dry zone of Ceylon, which region on the basis of archaeological, epigraphic, documentary, and ecological evidence has been thought as fitting perfectly the requirements of Wittfogel's thesis.[6]

The ancient Sinhala civilization is located in the northern dry zone of Ceylon (now known as the North Central Province). It is not an area of full aridity, and regular cultivation is impossible without irrigation especially

---

[4] Leach, "Hydraulic Society," p. 7.   [5] Ibid., p. 7.

[6] See the essay by the human geographer Rhoads Murphey on the basis of a review of the evidence: "The Ruin of Ancient Ceylon," *Journal of Asian Studies*, vol. 16, no. 2, 1957, pp. 181–200.

because the soil is infertile and has no capacity for holding water.[7] Leach's important submission, informed by his own field study, is that the base of the agrarian economy, the small-scale system, does not rely on bringing in water from elsewhere, but is based on the local storage of local rainwater for use throughout the year. There are other major irrigation works, numerous and immense in scale, *but they are everywhere supplementary to the small-scale localized system.* Leach sees a long-term continuity of the contours of this latter system.

There is good archaeological evidence that the general arrangement of the irrigation system at the present time is very much the same as it was in the eleventh century. The modern irrigation works have a bearing on Wittfogel's propositions:

> The population is distributed over the map in small villages most of them containing fewer than fifty elementary families. Each village depends for its livelihood on an area of irrigated rice land watered from an artificial reservoir. The reservoirs (tanks) were first created in ancient times by building an earthwork transversely across the line of a natural stream and damming up the water behind it . . . A few of these village tanks, notably those located in the vicinity of ancient Buddhist temples are equipped with scientifically designed spillways and sluices but the majority are rather crude affairs.[8]

The construction and maintenance of these village tanks call for the expertise rather of "a foreman plumber than that of a university graduate in engineering."[9]

It seems there is no evidence that the ancient central state authorities ever concerned themselves with the details of village tank management. "Villagers were under legal obligation to maintain their tank in functioning order but there is no evidence of any bureaucratic machinery that might help to bring this about."[10] Leach interprets the references in the chronicles of the kings to monarchs receiving praise for their munificence in repairing village tanks, or for donating the revenues of particular tanks to Buddhist monasteries, as suggesting that these were special events, and that there was no overall routine procedure for control of or regulating the local works on a national scale.

---

[7] See B.H. Farmer, *Pioneer Peasant Colonisation in Ceylon: A Study in Asian Agrarian Problems*, London and New York: Oxford University Press, 1957, chapter 2.

[8] Leach, "Hydraulic Society," p. 8.   [9] Ibid., p. 8.

[10] Ibid., p. 8. It was only from about 1860 that a centralized Irrigation Department of the British Colonial Government was invested with the powers to interfere in matters relating to the maintenance and use of village tanks.

Now it is against this base of localized village tanks, the seeming periphery, that one must view the place and role of certain major irrigation works associated with the water supply of the various ancient capitals of the kingdom, Anurādhapura and Polonnaruva. These reservoirs were works of engineering on a grand scale, with high and wide masonry-faced embankments and complex sluiceworks and spillways to match. For example, before silting reduced the area, the Kalāwewa tank may have been nearly 40 miles in circumference, and it leads out into a complex feeder system about 55 miles long.

Such evidence bears out the inference that ancient Sinhala was a hydraulic society. According to Wittfogel's paradigm one would expect such a society to be ruled by an absolute tyrant monarch whose power was focused around the organization of hydraulic engineering, and that it would be serviced by a bureaucratic cadre of professional managers and engineers.

The Ceylon chronicles seemingly support the past existence of a despotic hydraulic monarchy. They celebrate the memory of Parakrama Bahu I who reigned in Polonnaruva from 1164 to 1197 for his works of irrigation and his benefactions to religion and the people. "It is alleged that he constructed 1,470 new tanks, including three giant lakes; 300 further tanks were built for the priesthood and 1,395 large tanks restored, besides 960 smaller ones; he constructed 534 water courses and repaired 3,621."[11] "His reputed statue at Polonnaruva stands to this day on the embankment of the largest artificial lake of all – 'the Sea of Parakrama.'"[12] The chronicle record also credits Parakrama Bahu I with building 101 dagobas, 476 statues of the Buddha, 300 image rooms, etc.[13]

If we look at the fabulous ruins of Anurādhapura and Polonnaruva we might persuade ourselves that this could be true, fitting perfectly with the Wittfogel picture of a totalitarian "agro-managerial" monarch who had at his disposal both a managerial bureaucracy and, even more importantly, a huge unpaid labor force mobilized through coercive methods.

Leach's deconstructive subversion of these expectations is along the following lines.

First, Parakrama Bahu's career was given over entirely to military conquest, and his exploits and financial exactions and extravagance finally brought the dry zone hydraulic civilization of Sinhala, which had

[11] Leach cites here J.E. Tennent, *Ceylon*, 2 vols., London: Langman, Green, Langman & Roberts, 1860, especially vol. I, part 3, Chapter 11.
[12] Leach, "Hydraulic Society," p. 10.   [13] Tennent, Ceylon, vol. II, p. 623.

endured for about 1,500 years, to an end. After him, following a half-century of chaos, the kingdom shifted into the eastern part of the wet zone, with the capital moving frequently from 1246 onwards, crystalliz-ing in the Kotte kingdom near Colombo in the sixteenth century at the time of the arrival of the Portuguese invader.[14]

Second, it is a fallacy to think that the dry zone hydraulic society logically required the centralized control of large labor forces.

In actual fact "the Sinhalese irrigation system was not created in a day, nor even in a lifetime."[15] What looks like a complex achievement of bureaucratic planning when viewed ahistorically and synchronically changes its aspect when viewed diachronically as a long term discon-nected effort. The Kalāwewa canal system, which now has a giant tank at its head and leads into a 55 mile long watercourse, which in turn feeds into three large tanks that provide water for the ancient capital of Anurādhapura, took about 1,400 years to build. The original Tis-sawewa tank at the *bottom* end of the system was first constructed about 300 BC. The Kalāwewa tank at the top end of the system was first con-structed about 800 years later, and elaborations and modifications went on for at least another 600 years. Leach finds support in the view of B.H. Farmer,[16] a Cambridge geographer and expert on peasant colonization schemes in Ceylon, that there never was a period when the whole sys-tem was intact: parts of what looks like a vast network were abandoned and went into disuse, while other parts were built over time, once again puncturing a static synchronic view. And so with all the other "stupen-dous" works. While myth invariably attributes their construction to a single outstanding monarch, archaeology shows each has been slowly developed over a long period of time. This is true not only of the tanks but also of the giant dagoba shrines built of many millions of bricks. An enormous number of man-hours of labor did go into building the big ir-rigation tank embankments and the Buddhist shrines, but this effort does not imply any massive control over labor resources by the "bureaucratic rulers." The work could probably be accomplished by a gang of about 600 corvée laborers working a hundred days in any one year, and the

[14] It was only in 1590, after nearly a century of complex civil war, that the hill city of Kandy finally emerged as the capital of an independent kingdom. Robert Knox's *An Historical Relation of the Island of Ceylon in the East Indies*, Glasgow: James MacLehose & sons, 1911, original edition 1689, was based on his residence in the Kandyan kingdom between 1659 and 1679.

[15] Leach, "Hydraulic Society," p. 13.

[16] Farmer, *Pioneer Peasant Colonisation*. It is moreover the case that the same irrigation scheme is frequently attributed to several quite different monarchs.

job would have taken some fifty years in the case of a major dagoba built of 20 million bricks, or about twenty-five years in the case of an embankment of 20 million cubic yards. The reliance on corvée service in Ceylon did "not necessarily imply that the scale of recruitment was large or that its imposition was arbitrary."[17]

Leach diminishes Wittfogel's twinning of bureaucratic planners and managers serving the despotic ruler together with the control of large-scale forced labor by suggesting that it was some of the literate members of Buddhist monastic institutions and not professional engineers in the service of the crown who provided the high-level engineering skill displayed in the design and construction of the large works, and that, secondly, the obligation of corvée service in the form of *rajakāriya* (work for the king) was enacted through a form of service attached to land tenure, which shares some features of what in Europe was termed "feudalism."

Wittfogel contrasted his profile of a static and archaic "hydraulic based despotism" (which he likened to the totalitarian police state of Russia, which personally he abhorred) with European feudalism which had the merit that "it led to a limping and multicentered type of absolutism and, eventually, to multicentered and private-property based industrial society."[18]

Leach's suppositions about "irrigation based feudalism" associated with caste-based service duties linked to tenure of land relies on Robert Knox's seventeenth-century account of the Kandyan kingdom, supplemented by some textual inscriptional evidence dating back to the early period, and by evidence of some long-term continuities in tank-village organization in the dry zone that he studied in the mid-1950s. Ralph Pieris's detailed historical and sociological account of the Kandyan kingdom preceding Leach's essay by three years[19] profiled the spatial patterning of "provinces," the hierarchy of feudal offices and their jurisdictions, the devolution of office tenures into land allocated to the king (*gabadagam*), to nobles (*nindagam*), and to monasteries and temples (*viharagam*), and the caste-based services due from categories of commoners and serfs at the local level of villages, and so on. Though it suffers

---

[17] Leach, "Hydraulic Society," pp. 14, 188.   [18] Wittfogel, *Oriental Despotism*, p. 52.
[19] Ralph Pieris, *Sinhalese Social Organization: The Kandyan Period*, Colombo: Ceylon University Press Board, 1956. It is relevant to note that the Kandyan kingdom included the north-central "province" of Nuwarakalaviya, which was part of the hydraulic dry zone region. A larger part of the kingdom was in the "hill country" wet zone and not arid.

from being a static account, Pieris's documentation confirms Leach's main inferences about the Kandyan system as a caste-based feudal system.

Leach summarized the main features of the historic Kandyan kingdom (which ceased to exist as such when it was conquered by the British in 1815), and the continuing aspects of the dry zone hydraulic society in the 1950s, which he knew first-hand, as follows. It should be noted that he takes it to be a highly probable assumption that the pattern of caste feudalism Knox and others described can also be construed as ancient for Ceylon.

The Ceylon system was one of "service tenure," with services of various kinds due to the landlord, including military duties.[20] Peasant society in Ceylon was, and is even today, divided according to occupational castes. The farmer caste which was the highest in status was also the most numerous. Other castes had the occupational duties of washerman, drummer, blacksmith, potter, spirit medium, and so on. As to their main occupation, all these castes were peasant cultivators, cultivating irrigated rice lands according to identical techniques. The farmers rendered military service or tax in kind, but the lower castes rendered their caste-specific work. In the "feudal" period, land was so distributed among the professionally specialized castes that the tenants of any particular superior landlord formed an overlapping set of reciprocal work teams. Even though under British rule the feudal duties to lay overlords were mostly abolished, villagers "still feel themselves under an obligation to carry out their caste services for their neighbours."[21] (However, the feudal caste services to the Buddhist temples and associated deities were not abolished, though commutation of service through cash payments became possible.)

"In the dry zone region each *variga* [subcaste] included some ten to twenty small single caste villages and was corporately organized with its own caste court. The *variga* as a whole was the client of the local baron and the baron was an ex-officio president of the caste court of each *variga* within his domain whatever its caste."[22] Each individual held land privately within his own village, and he was also under obligation to

---

[20] In my view, Leach thinks of European feudalism as land tenure exclusively associated with military service. Marc Bloch's authoritative account (*Feudal Society*, Chicago: The University of Chicago Press, 1963) explains that the fiefs of noble-vassals were tied to military service, but at the base, the system was imaged in terms of the manorial system, where the services of the freemen and serfs to the lord's demesne were akin to the services of the tenants to their overlords in the Ceylon system, except that the latter were organized in terms of occupational castes.

[21] Leach, "Hydraulic Society," p. 20.   [22] Ibid., p. 20.

contribute the duties of his caste to his *variga* lord (the local baron), who in fact transferred these duties so that they became reciprocally exchanged between members of the specialized castes – blacksmiths, washermen, mediums, and so on. It is necessary to bear in mind that "the service duties which attached to the lands of each particular *variga* group were over and above the *rajakāriya* – king's work – which was the general obligation to corvée. This now applies especially to the maintenance of irrigation works but, formerly no doubt, included all the monarch's constructional ventures."[23]

Leach has this to say about Buddhist temple and monastic properties in "Hydraulic Society". "When kings are credited with the construction of a tank they almost always give the revenues to a religious institution (*vihara*)."[24]

The differentiation of service obligations in terms of caste duties is closely bound up with the requirements of temple service. Temples, in their modern form, cannot be maintained without the specialised services of washermen, musicians, potters, painters and the rest and there is no reason to imagine that this is in any sense a modern development. If we couple this with the fact that, from the earliest times, we have reports of villages being gifted to temples along with their *gamvara* – that is the dues of the tenants; that the tenants of such villages are in some cases specified as carpenters, artisans, masons, serfs, drummers, washermen, etc.; and that a tenth-century inscription shows that villages were then administered not singly but in clusters (*dasagam* – lit. ten villages); then we can at least say that it seems likely that a caste organisation of labour . . . as outlined above generally prevailed in ancient Sinhala.[25]

There is more to be said than Leach has done about monastic and temple properties that are integral to the sketch of ancient hydraulic Ceylon. This lack will be rectified when we turn to the contributions of a Sri Lankan historian, R.A.L.H. Gunawardana.[26] From now on I propose to consider certain propositions by Leach which open him to contestations by Gunawardana which I shall address at the end of this chapter.

One is Leach's somewhat unyielding view – which in part is connected to Knox's characterization of the Kandyan king as a tyrant, but more importantly, is a continuation of the thesis he had already proposed

[23] Ibid., p. 20.   [24] Ibid., p. 22.
[25] Ibid., p. 31. The reference is to H.W. Codrington, *Ancient Land Tenure and Revenue in Ceylon*, Colombo: Ceylon Government Press, 1938, chapters 3 and 4.
[26] R.A.L.H. Gunawardana, "Irrigation and Hydraulic Society in Medieval Ceylon," *Past and Present*, vol. 53, November 1971, pp. 3–27.

in his essay on "The Frontiers of 'Burma' "[27] – that the South Asian monarch was an individual "charismatic" and unstable ruler, unlike the Chinese emperor whose lineage ancestry and institutionalized position were buttressed by orderly rules of succession. An associated thesis is that the South Asian polity had no organized bureaucracy unlike that of its Chinese counterpart.

Thus here in the characterization of the dry zone polity, Leach foregrounds his visualization of the self-aggrandizing monarch as incapable of being associated with centrally organized hydraulic engineering and with a systematized hydraulic bureaucracy. "The engineering activities, when mentioned at all, are treated as the arbitrary acts of merit of individual monarchs, and mostly such work relates to dagoba shrines and pleasure gardens [and ornamental lakes to embellish the capitals] rather than agricultural irrigation. The political background is one of constant civil war and palace murders."[28] Part of this sketch of the volatile instability of the polity is Leach's perception of the monarch's donation of tanks and the revenues deriving from them to monastic institutions, thus relieving him of centralized control and efficient maintenance.

A corollary of this overall picture of an unstable and weak bureaucratic center is that the system of large tanks and water channels which over time developed around the capital cities of Anurādhapura and Polonnaruva – the dry zone's core "nuclear areas" from the point of view of the economic historian Gunawardana – is from Leach's angle of vision considered of secondary relevance to the overall dry zone regime. Apart from the argument mentioned before that the system was never all intact, Leach makes this unqualified evaluation:

in the Ceylon case, although the major irrigation works provided food for labourers as well as amenities for palaces, the hydraulic system was not of crucial economic significance for the society as a whole. When the central government was disrupted and the major works fell into disrepair, village life could carry on quite adequately; for each village still possessed its own small irrigation system which was maintained by the villagers themselves.[29]

Since the construction of the major irrigation works was haphazard, discontinuous, and spread over many centuries, we cannot "infer from an inspection of these works the existence of a large labour force under

[27] Leach, "The Frontiers of 'Burma' " (1960).   [28] Leach, "Hydraulic Society," p. 22.
[29] Ibid., p. 23.

central government control; nor can we make inferences about the size of the population which was fed by the irrigation system. Still less can we make inferences about the nature of political authority in the ancient state."[30] In terms of current jargon Leach saw the tank-village organization characterized by his own Pul Eliya as the dominant mode of production and the real infrastructure of the dry zone hydraulic society.

But if he felt that he had disproved via the Ceylon case the generality attributed by Wittfogel to his theory of "oriental despotism," Leach agreed with Wittfogel (and thereby also Marx) that the Ceylon case affirmed a social factor common to a great many hydraulic societies – namely that they are "from a structural point of view, peculiarly static."[31] For Wittfogel the stagnant conservation of hydraulic society lay in its "monopoly bureaucracy." For Leach, the answer to the question, at least as it applies to the Ceylon case, is "much simpler." He provided a similar ethnographically substantiated answer in *Pul Eliya* published two years later as a critique of Fortes's structural-functional notions of kinship as a domain in its own right divorced from its integral linkage to economy: "Under Ceylon dry zone conditions once a village and its irrigation tank have been constructed, it is there for ever and since the irrigation area must always remain the same size, the population of the village itself can only vary between narrow limits."[32]

Such a situation of enforced physical immobility lends itself to the development of social arrangements whereby the populations of neighboring villages stand in fixed socio-economic relations one with another. Durkheim's analysis of *The Division of Labor* inclines us to imagine that complex "organic" systems of labor specialization are intimately connected with the existence of a monetary exchange medium, the payment of cash wages, and the free mobility of labor. "But in the 'caste feudalisms' of India and Ceylon, specialized occupations are professed not by individuals but by whole groups (subcastes), and provided these subcaste groups are physically immobile, complex organic structures of specialized labor can be maintained from generation to generation without any intervention of a money medium. The economic contract is a permanent one between settled groups continually resident in particular localities."[33]

Just as in the essay "Frontiers of 'Burma'" Leach dared to speculate on larger and more risky issues and comparisons embracing China and India than he had taken on in the monograph *Political Systems of Highland*

[30] Ibid., p. 23.   [31] Ibid., pp. 23–24.   [32] Ibid., p. 24.   [33] Ibid., p. 24.

Burma, so in this essay on "Hydraulic Society in Ceylon" he allows himself to similarly spread into a larger space, embracing China and India, than he occupies in the more ethnographically and, in some ways, more narrowly focused, text of *Pul Eliya*. In doing so he also manages to link up propositions in the two essays.

I suggest that there are many cases of hydraulic society where the characteristic pattern is "Indian" rather than "Chinese," and in which, in Wittfogel's terminology, the authority is "Feudal" rather than "Oriental." I believe that this links up with the basic difference between the Chinese acceptance of legitimate authority as manifested in patrilineal kinship and bureaucratic government as against the Indian reverence for personal Charisma. The Indian type of hydraulic society, of which Sinhala is an example, is cellular not centralised in structure; localised groups of technical specialists form a work team centred in a leader. The major hydraulic works are not created rationally and systematically but haphazard as pieces of self advertisement by individual leaders. But once started, such constructions survive and can be enhanced by later adventurers of the same type.[34]

Before I take up Gunawardana's commentary on Leach and Wittfogel, I want to suggest a limited affinity between Leach's formulation of "caste feudalism" and the immobile caste specialized village communities of the dry zone, and *one* version of Marx's stereotypical description of Asiatic society which, mired in stasis, stood apart from the European evolutionary sequence of development from primitive communities through feudalism to capitalism.

I allude to Marx at this point because Leach, in an informal discussion of his writings in the Department of Anthropology at The Johns Hopkins University in the spring term of 1976, at which I was present, made a passing remark that at the time he was writing *Pul Eliya* he had been reading Marx. This casual remark was not taken up for discussion, and I did not follow it up with him either. Marx was not mentioned once in *Pul Eliya*, but some readers of his argument that locality rather than descent forms the basis of corporate grouping in Pul Eliya, that kinship was a way of thinking about rights and usages with respect to land which was fixed, that his account was a study "in land tenure and kinship", etc. did remark that there was a materialist, even Marxist, streak in the work.[35] It was while recounting in some detail Leach's "Hydraulic Society in

[34] Ibid., p. 24.
[35] Raymond Firth told me that, in an informal conversation about the book, Maurice Friedman, then teaching at the London School of Economics, quipped that the book was "Marxism and water".

Ceylon" in this biography that I was reminded of that 1976 remark, and it put me on the scent to track which of Marx's writings might have particularly interested him.[36]

It would be an unnecessary digression and distraction to discuss in *detail* the intellectual antecedents and sources of Marx's thoughts on "oriental despotism," "Asiatic mode of production," "Asiatic society," "Asiatic system" of land ownership – terms he used interchangeably – which are to be found in three places:

1. The first discussion, in chronological order, appeared in some articles he wrote in 1853 in the *New York Daily Tribune*; the issues discussed there were clarified by some correspondence he exchanged with Engels at that time.
2. The second discussion is contained in the *Grundrisse*, which was composed in 1857–58 in preparation for his *Critique of Political Economy* and *Capital*.
3. There is a third and final reference – actually a few brief passages – in *Capital* which was first published in 1867.[37]

I shall selectively highlight some of the ideas in these discussions that have a bearing on Leach's view of hydraulic society in Ceylon.

In the *Tribune* articles Marx formulated two ideas. One was that climate and territorial conditions in Asia necessitated artificial irrigation by canals and waterworks as the basis of oriental agriculture. Unlike in Europe where private enterprise and voluntary association sufficed to meet irrigation needs, in Asia the civilization was "too low," and the territorial extent was too vast – by this he meant the dispersal of village communities – such that intervention by the central government was required. Marx, in agreement with Engels and endorsing Bernier, added that the basis of all social phenomena in the East was the absence of

---

[36] I had, however, many years earlier, made a study of Marx's writings on oriental despotism for another purpose, and I went back to that study to select the citations that I report here.

[37] Marx's major theses about Asian societies are in part a synthesis of previous writings and traditions. The proposition that public irrigation works, necessitated by climatic aridity, were a basic determinant of centralized Asiatic despotic states that monopolized land, fused three themes that had hitherto been relatively distinct – discussion of hydraulic agriculture by Adam Smith, geographical destiny by Montesquieu, and state ownership of agrarian property by Bernier. The second proposition, that the base on which this despotism sat was composed of dispersed and stagnant self-sufficient communities, embodying a union of domestic crafts and cultivation, had been advanced earlier by Hegel. Marx incorporated new evidence and arguments gleaned from the writings of English historians and political economists at home and of colonial administrators in India, and constructed a general schema in which the hydraulic state poised "above" and the autarchic villages dispersed "below" were dialectically linked.

private property in land, and this condition is related to the provision of artificial irrigation by the oriental state.

This is the formulation that Wittfogel embraced for his account of China, and which Leach rejected for Ceylon.[38]

But Leach, I surmise, must have paid attention to these features of Marx's formulation, which of course he transformed and reworked in his own way. Marx coupled the hydraulic formula with a thesis about property rights in land and the constitution of village communities. He highlighted stagnation and immutability of oriental society, which he largely attributed to the stability that the Indian village communities maintained despite political vicissitudes. He contrasted with this unchanging base the political instability of Asian empires and governments, whose volatile fortunes and efforts accounted for the periodic deterioration or revival of agriculture. Nevertheless this political instability at the top scarcely altered the social condition of the society below, constituted as it was by "the domestic union of agricultural and manufacturing pursuits," the latter represented by the handloom and the spinning wheel. This social organization, dispersed on the one hand over the surface of the country, and agglomerated on the other hand in small centers by the domestic union of agricultural and craft activities, was the *village system*, which gave to each of these small unions their independent organization and distinct life.

Marx thereafter gave a description of the village as a "simple form of municipal government" with its establishment of officers and servants, the headman, the accountant, the superintendent of tanks and watercourses, the Brahmin, the school teacher, and the village servants.[39]

---

[38] It is relevant to mention here that his formulation was also repudiated by Irfan Habib (*The Agrarian System of Mughal India, 1556–1707*, Bombay and New York: AsiaPublishing House, 1963). He dismissed with ease the possibility that the vast majority of Indian states and polities rested on, or sponsored, hydraulic systems. Indian historical geography was proof against this. Nor did the multiple layering of rights to the produce of the land in Mughal times support Wittfogel's thesis that the agrarian bureaucracy allowed no accumulation of private property.

[39] This picture of the village community based on an exchange of service, egalitarian and without conflict, is very similar to that painted by Sir Henry Maine. Marx and Maine seem to have used the same sources authored by Indian administrators. According to my investigations, Maine's *Ancient Law* (1861), written before he went to India, and *Village Communities in the East and West* (1871), published after his return (as was *The Early History of Institutions* [1875]), were written after Marx had already expressed his ideas on Asian society in the three main sources I have cited. But *The Ethnological Notebooks of Karl Marx* (ed. Lawrence Krader, Assen: van Gorain, 1972) show that between 1880 and 1882 Marx took notes from Maine's *The Early History of Institutions* and from J.B. Phear's *The Aryan Village in India and Ceylon* (1880), which was heavily influenced by Maine. Maine, on the other hand, shows no evidence of reading Marx, or rather, seems not to have referred to Marx in any of his books. Leach was of course familiar with Maine's writings.

It is interesting that the *Grundrisse* ruminations were a kind of dialectical *antithesis* to this sketch of the state as a universal landlord, because in this context Marx was concentrating on the village communities as the true center of gravity of Indian society. They were "corporations" which possessed the land "in common," and this was a special conception of "property."

The evolution of private property in human history was from communal to private forms, and at the earliest stage of human life the community dominated the individual; indeed it was the community that generated the notion of property and invested the individual with property rights. In short the early "natural" conditions of production had a double character: an individual's existence as a part of a "community," and his or her "possession" of land rights as a derivation from communal landed property. These features in turn generated a "specific mode of labor" which was always family labor and often communal labor. In the *Asiatic form* (which he distinguished from the Graeco-Roman and Germanic forms), there was no individual private property as such: there was only individual *possession*; the community was properly speaking the real proprietor, hence there could be only a communal property in land.

From this base, Marx projected the Asiatic state as a kind of epiphenomenon. The "all-embracing unity" which stood above all the small communities appeared as "the higher or sole proprietor," while the real communities appeared as only "hereditary possessors." The despot thus realizes the community of all, and oriental despotism therefore leads to a legal absence of property.

But despite the rise of oriental despotism, Marx maintained that the real foundation of Asiatic society was tribal or common property, which "in most cases is created through a combination of manufacture and agriculture within the small community which thus becomes entirely self-sustaining and contains within itself all conditions of production and surplus production." A part of the surplus labor was rendered to the despot as a tribute, or "to the higher community, which ultimately appears as a person." The "communal conditions for the real appropriation of labor" make possible irrigation systems and communications, which "will then appear as the work of the higher unity – the despotic government which is poised above the lesser communities."

Whereas in the *Grundrisse* Marx derived the despotic state as a kind of epiphenomenon projected upon the reality of a base constituted of real production communities, in *Capital* he more or less returned to the *Tribune* formulations, and to the views expressed in his correspondence with Engels, as regards the constitution of the ancient Indian village communities.

Although he clung to an idealized picture of the village community and reported that in its simplest form the land was tilled in common and the produce was divided among its members and special functionaries, Marx did make some perceptive remarks on the peculiar features of social division of labor, and the form of the surplus that left the community, which are remarkably close to Leach's own portrait of Ceylon's dry zone caste feudalism.

Marx observed that although the village community disclosed a systematic division of labor, this division was unlike that found in Western industrial manufacture, since artisans and artificers found (under conditions of demographic stability, Marx should have specified) an unchanging market, and were represented in small numbers in their villages. Moreover an artisan conducted in his workshop "all the operations of his handicraft in the traditional way" independently and without a supervising authority over him.[40]

Another feature of the division of labor in the local economy was that the craft and service specialists might not totally relinquish agricultural work, and more importantly, might be regarded as specialists who are primarily *clients* (though not exclusively) to one or more agricultural communities, which provided them with subsistence in return for satisfying their patrons' needs. Their specialization could not guarantee them an income from their products and services in a system of market exchange but it could in a redistributive system articulated around the dominant landowners.

A final comment on Marx's discussion. His characterization of oriental society combines two contradictory themes, but he provided no key to their synthesis. If the oriental despot was so powerful as to lay monopolistic claim to all land and reduce all peasants to mere "possessors" (not "proprietors") of land, and to extract the surplus labor and product of the cultivators by force, then how come the despotic regime was so unstable, and suffered changes of regime and dissolutions, which revealed it to be flimsy superstructure? Coming at the same puzzle from the other side, if the Indian village communities were so stable and self-sufficient, perennially reproduced themselves, and existed in a dispersed

---

[40] This point that, because in the Indian context each craftsman's operations were technologically simple, and that each craftsman performed more or less all operations entailed in the making of an object, the system of division of labor is significantly different from the industrial one, is best appreciated in terms of Adam Smith's famous example of the pin factory in *The Wealth of Nations* (1776).

parochial state, without being affected by the vicissitudes of monarchical politics, then how indeed did they in the first place, out of their placid inaction and secure autonomy, project the "mystification" and the illusion of a "higher unity" objectified in despotism?

This contradiction that Marx never satisfactorily resolved would also engage, among others, the two authors on Ceylon being considered here, Leach and Gunawardana, to whose essay I turn now.

I conclude with Gunawardana's main submissions as they bear on Wittfogel and Leach. Gunawardana is the pre-eminent living historian of early and, especially, medieval Ceylon, with a command of the Pali language (and the Sinhala language) and in possession of an authoritative knowledge of the written chronicles and inscriptions, and of the archaeological reports on the dry zone irrigation works.[41]

Unlike Leach who considered the contents of the chronicles as propagandist and did not take them at their face value, and did not study the inscriptional evidence in detail, but had studied the archaeological reports closely, Gunawardana assembles the claims the chronicles and inscriptions make on the behalf of monarchs as the sponsors of the major hydraulic works in a literal manner, and maps those claims *vis-à-vis* the archaeological record.

Gunawardana's linear narrative begins with the earliest stages of development of hydraulic works in the northern dry zone from the first century BC to the second century AD, when the attempts were very much of the order of the one tank – one village pattern, that is to say "rather unsophisticated attempts at water conservation than projects for large scale water diversion."

Following the chronicle accounts, he states that in the early centuries of the Christian era, under the sponsorship of kings such as Vasabha (AD 65–109) and Mahasena (AD 276–303), successful efforts were being

---

[41] Thus his 1971 essay "Irrigation and Hydraulic Society in Early Medieval Ceylon" (as well as his later major work *Robe and Plough: Monasticism and Economic Interest in Medieval Ceylon*, Tucson: University of Arizona Press, 1979, which I shall not consider here) makes references to chronicles such as the *Mahāvamsa* (ed. W. Geiger, Luzac: London, 1956), *Cūlavamsa* (ed. W. Geiger, Colombo: Ceylon Government Information Department 1953), *Pujavaliya* (ed. A.V. Suravira, Colombo: n.p., 1961); to the inscriptions in *Epigraphia Zeylanica*, Colombo: Department of Government Printing, 1933, and in S. Paranavitana, *Inscriptions of Ceylon*, Colombo: Archaeological Survey of Ceylon, 1970; and to various twentieth-century archaeological reports such as R.L. Brohier, *Ancient Irrigation Works in Ceylon*, Colombo: Government Publications Bureau, 1934, C.W. Nicholas, "A Short Account of the History of Irrigation Works up to the 11th Century," *Journal of the Ceylon Branch of the Royal Society*, n.s., vol. 7, 1960; R.W. Ievers, *Notes on Tanks Lying Below the Kalawewa Yoda-Ela*, Sessional Paper 29 of 1886, Colombo: Government Press, 1887; H. Parker, *Report on the Proposed Deduru Oya Project*, Sessional Paper 3 of 1889, Colombo: Government Press 1889.

made to harness the waters of Ceylon's largest and ever-flowing river, the Mahavali, its main tributary, the Amban Ganga, and other branches, to serve the area around the capital city of Anurādhapura.[42]

"The irrigation engineers of Ceylon," writes Gunawardana, "had succeeded by the end of the fifth century in developing two major complexes of irrigation works – one based on the Mahavali and its tributaries and the other drawing on the waters of the Malvatu and the Kala."[43] These complexes presupposed the "application of labour resources on an unprecedented scale" and a "highly sophisticated knowledge of surveying, levelling, hydraulics and of heavy construction." The crowning achievement was the construction of the Kalavava reservoir which fed the tanks at Anurādhapura and its environs by means of the Jayaganga canal whose course was 54 miles long, irrigating on the way an area about 180 square miles.[44]

In the subsequent three centuries – the fifth to the eighth – there was, we are told, further development and elaboration of these two main complexes.[45] Of the two complexes, the water resources feeding the canals and reservoirs of the Mahavali complex were more abundant and much superior to those of the Kala–Malvatu complex. In Gunawardana's estimation the two major complexes facilitated the opening of a vast extent of land, made possible multiple harvests a year, and sustained "the two most important 'nuclear areas' [a term he borrows from Burton Stein, the historian of the agrarian systems and polities of South India] in the Sinhala civilization of the period ... The economic importance of this region was further enhanced by the development of commercial relations with China and South-East Asia in which the port of Gokanna on the eastern coast would have played a prominent part."[46]

A momentous shift in Sinhala society was the shift of the capital from Anurādhapura to Polonnaruva in the period between the seventh and tenth centuries. Gunawardana suggests that this shift not only was made for military and strategic reasons,[47] but was supported by the economic

---

[42] "Of the irrigation works that the chronicles assign to Mahasena, the Minneriya reservoir which drew the water from the Alahara canal, was the largest built up to that time." Gunawardana, "Irrigation," p. 6. The "irrigation works spread over a wide region," attributed to Mahasena, "represent a mighty initiative to harness the waters of the Dry Zone." Ibid., p. 7.

[43] Ibid., p. 9.

[44] The Kalavava complex is referred to by Leach (spelt Kalāwewa) but its significance is viewed by him in a different way.

[45] Aggabodhi II AD 608–18 is credited with building the Giritale and Kantale reservoirs.

[46] Ibid., p. 11.

[47] Gunawardana does not discuss these reasons, but presumably he has in mind the successful invasions of the Cholas into the Anurādhapura region in the ninth century.

significance of the southern complex in both agrarian and commercial terms.

Thus we reach the final stage in the linear account. The reign of Parakramabahu I (1153–86) was "the last major phase of irrigation in medieval Ceylon" whose major efforts included a substantial addition to the irrigation system based on the Mahavali–Amban rivers by opening the Kalinga canal through a further extension of the Pabbatanta canal built by Makasena and by the construction of the vast reservoir, the sea of Parakrama (Parakramasamudra) at Polonnaruva.

Both Leach and Gunawardana agree on the invalidity of Wittfogel's thesis that oriental despotism was characterized by a total concentration of power in a monarch who ruled the hydraulic society through an agro-managerial bureaucracy. But the major difference between them lies in their perception of medieval Sinhala irrigation-based dry zone civilization. Leach as we have seen saw the tank-village localized system as the central continuing basis of that society, and the Anurādhapura-Polonnaruva regions' reservoirs and canals bringing water to the capital cities as making a limited *agrarian* contribution. Gunawardana in a sense inverts the Leach profile – he sees the two major complexes of reservoirs and canals as the infrastructure for the two nuclear areas focused on Anurādhapura and Polonnaruva, and these were the climactic achievements of Sinhala hydraulic civilization supporting a large population. If the two nuclear areas were the core, he grants that the local water conservation tank-village system was the dominant "ecological pattern" in the large area lying outside the core. This ecological pattern, which was achieved in the early phase, was already being superseded in the early centuries of the Christian era by the new technology of large-scale water diversion, large tanks, and feeder canals. He concedes that outside the two main nuclear areas, "large irrigation works sponsored by rulers of Anurādhapura and Polonnaruva were, if at all, of limited importance for agricultural activity."[48] And he is in line with Leach, though they differ in the emphasis they attach to it, that the localized tank-village units survived, and re-established themselves after the collapse of the major irrigation works "in about the thirteenth century and persisted right up to modern times."[49] In fact, he states that inscriptions confirm that a vast multitude of small village reservoirs always existed in parallel and independent of the two major complexes.

[48] Ibid., p. 15.　　[49] Ibid., pp. 4–5.

Acknowledging the assessment made by Brohier, Farmer, Leach, and others of the Polonnaruva complex, Gunawardana agrees that "it is doubtful . . . that all the irrigation works" built up to the thirteenth century "were functioning in full capacity, parallelly and simultaneously. These remarks would apply in particular to some of the irrigation works of Parakramabahu I in the vicinity of Polonnaruva."[50] Moreover, he recognizes that successive kings noted for their achievements in the chronicles and inscriptions typically incorporated existing tanks into larger schemes via new feeder canals, enlarged the capacity of pre-existing tanks, or even made obsolete some of the existing ones.

However, Gunawardana is unyielding in his final assessment, worded in dynastic terms: "the initiative of the Sinhalese kings had, by the beginning of the twelfth century, brought into being a vast array of irrigation works spread over a substantial part of the Dry Zone." The gradual cumulative development of the irrigation system "can be systematically traced over a long period of time and reflects a high degree of sophistication in technology unparalleled elsewhere in the whole of south Asia."[51] And all this had enabled the participation and contribution of Ceylon to the Indian Ocean trade, and brought it into contact with China and Persia.[52]

It is in relation to this thesis of a vast array of hydraulic works that now Gunawardana runs into a problem. While dismissing Wittfogel's notion of a royal despotism exercising a monopoly of power, he also dismisses that author's postulations of a large managerial agro-bureaucracy which planned, controlled, and regulated the works on behalf of the despot.

If "state enterprise was responsible for the construction of major irrigation works,"[53] and if Gunawardana attributes to royal agency such initiative, he does not have the information to even approximately answer who and how many were the extraordinary "engineers" who devised the plans and the technology, except to suggest that such personnel is presupposed. Nor is his supposition that large mobilization of labor would have been necessary to devise the major reservoirs and canals substantiated with actual evidence.[54] He can do no more than refer to "lists of officials" occurring "in the inscriptions of the ninth and tenth centuries when the main complexes were functioning" as evidence cited by commentators to suggest "the presence of hydraulic bureaucracy."[55] He opines that it "seems probable that the state took a special interest

[50] Ibid., pp. 12–13.   [51] Ibid., p. 13.   [52] Ibid., p. 13.   [53] Ibid., p. 20.   [54] Ibid., p. 21.
[55] Ibid., p. 21.

in the maintenance of what were called 'the twelve great reservoirs' in good repair", and finds in the inscriptions two terms in the early Brahmi script, *ananika* and *adikaya*, which "have been interpreted as connoting an irrigation engineer and a functionary in charge of work relating to canals."[56]

Leach had dismissed the possibility of a hydraulic bureaucracy and engineering corps in the service of a state, and had suggested that monks may have provided the planning for the large schemes, which were implemented over many decades by gangs of corvée labor, supervised and regulated by low-level officials at the local community level. And Leach had offered the answer that it is the devolutionary system of caste-based feudalism rather than a centralized agro-managerial bureaucracy mobilizing and commanding massive forced labor that delivers the answer as to how the dry zone hydraulic society functioned. And he had significantly singled out as a key to understanding how the system worked, the monasteries and temples to which monarchs are said to have gifted the revenues deriving from reservoirs and canals, and which utilized the caste-specific service tenures to stage their religious and ritual activities and to cater to their economic sustenance.

What Leach had barely recognized and had little knowledge for developing is the subject of Gunawardana's major contribution to the study of the integral role of monastic institutions in the functioning of the medieval religio-political system as independent, endowed with their own economic resources. The following paragraphs by Gunawardana illustrate the extent and implications of monastic property:

The strongest type of non-governmental property was represented by monastic estates with their tendency for expansion unhampered by fragmentation. Wittfogel . . . failed to realize the importance of the monastery and the temple as landowning institutions. In Ceylon, grants of land and irrigation works to monasteries can be traced from as early as the second century BC. And from this time onwards numerous references to grants of land and irrigation works made over to monasteries by royal personages as well as private individuals occur in the inscriptions and the chronicles. Some of these grants were very extensive. For instance, in the sixth century, a king called Mahānāga granted "one thousand fields" to the Mahāvihāra monastery at Anurādhapura, and his successor, Aggabodhi I, endowed the Kurunda monastery with a coconut plantation "three *yojanas* in extent".[57] In the latter part of the period under consideration,

---

[56] Ibid., p. 21.
[57] There are many interpretations of the term *yojana*, ranging from two and a half to nine to eighteen miles.

inscriptions recording such grants specifically state that their validity would last "as long as the sun and the moon". Monastic wealth accumulated gradually but steadily through donation as well as by purchase. By about the ninth century, monasteries had come to own, apart from movable possessions, a vast extent of property in estates, irrigation works and even salterns, some of them situated at considerable distances from the owning institution. The possessions of the Mahāvihāra, for instance, were scattered over a wide area extending to more than fifty miles each to the west and the east, and forty miles to the northeast; in addition to this, it had interests in property situated in the Kurunāgala district, about sixty miles to the south.

These developments turned the monastery into a largely self-sufficient economic unit. Its land was cultivated by tenant farmers while various types of workers like potters, weavers, lime-burners, washermen and sub-castes like the *pañcakula* which specialized in particular types of labour served its needs in return for allocations of land. Certain categories of craftsmen like carpenters, stone workers, bricklayers, blacksmiths and lapidaries were organized under master craftsmen and superintendents. At the Abhayagiri monastery, for example, such craftsmen as well as their superintendents were each given a field, one and a half *karīsas*[58] in extent, and a piece of unirrigated high land. In return, they were expected to give their labour for two months and five days each year and complete apportioned assignments within this period. Slave labour was known, but its scope was limited. Unskilled labour came mainly from the *corvée* which kings transferred to monasteries through immunity grants. The economic power that the monastery came to wield becomes particularly clear when its relations with tenants and craftsmen are examined. It would enforce its property rights through mild yet coercive measures like withholding irrigation water when tenants failed to pay their dues. Further, the monastery could exercise a strict control over its employees; for in addition to the frequently stated threat of depriving them of their lands if they failed to abide by its stipulations, it evidently owned the implements with which the agriculturists tilled the land and the artisans practised their crafts. A commentary on monastic discipline classifies all metal implements of craftsmen like carpenters, leather workers, tinsmiths, blacksmiths and lapidaries and agricultural implements like hoes, spades, and axes as the "indivisible communal property" of the monastery . . . This commentary is written in Pali but claims to be based on original Sinhalese texts and to adhere strictly to the traditions of the Mahāvihāra . . . It could be earlier or, more probably, somewhat later than the fifth century. At a level of technology and social relations when metal tools were not easy to come by, the ownership of the means of production would have placed the monastery in a domineering position *vis à vis* the tenant and the craftsman.[59]

Gunawardana's account of strong monastic estates organized in terms of caste-based service tenure would support Leach's thesis that feudal

---

[58] A *karīsa* is about 8–10 acres.   [59] Ibid., pp. 18–20.

organization was consistent with a complex hydraulic society as exemplified by Sri Lanka's dry zone from the fifth to the thirteenth centuries.

But there is one issue on which Leach is contested. Leach had taken the view that the tank-village of the interior, permanently constrained by the extent of paddy land that could be irrigated by its tank, made that system more or less immobile, reproducing itself and its fixed socio-economic relations continuously over time. This argument that Leach spelled out in *Pul Eliya* could not hold, argues Gunawardana, for the "two nuclear areas" centered on Anurādhapura and Polonnaruva, whose complex irrigation systems, developed up to the thirteenth century, "would have progressively extended the area under cultivation and also contributed to its greater exploitation. The resultant increase in agricultural production . . . made a progressive increase in population possible, even within each village [in the 'nuclear areas'], without upsetting the balance between land and population."[60] But as Gunawardana cautions, knowledge of great depth and detail is required "before the process and factors of social change in hydraulic society can be clearly understood."[61]

In the meantime, Leach wields the trump card: the unstable kingdom of Anurādhapura characterized by charismatic self-aggrandizing kingship was in disarray in the ninth century, and its successor, Polonnaruva, was abandoned in the thirteenth, and the two nuclear areas that were their alleged cores were rapidly depopulated, with their infrastructure of big reservoirs and canals reduced to ruins. The tank-villages however survived and have functioned to this day.

The classical chronicle narratives and ancient inscriptional claims, translated from Pali and decoded from earlier scripts, and nineteenth-century archaeological investigations and partial restorations under British rule – all these becoming more and more accessible to the larger public in recent decades – have been transported to, and become part and parcel of current political discourse, romantic imaginings of the past, and competitive, even acrimonious, arguments between persons of different political persuasions and ethnic affiliations as to their veracity and applicability to the present.

Some of the current claims and advocacies of "Buddhist nationalism and Buddhist democracy" in Sri Lanka invoke two conceptions. There is, on the one hand, the resort to idealized conceptions of righteous Buddhist kingship and of the Buddhist universal rulers (*Cakkavatti*), who are credited with meritorious public welfare services to their people,

---

[60] Ibid., p. 17.   [61] Ibid., p. 27.

especially in the form of hydraulic works. More relevant, as I briefly discussed in 1992, is

an equally well-entrenched and widely shared second axis, on which the Buddhist society of the past is projected. It is a conception of a rural society, whose base is a community of egalitarian peasant owners and cultivators. The irrigation "tank" watered their green rice fields, and the Buddhist temple in their midst served as the religious, moral, and cultural center, and its inmates, the monks, acted as their "advisors." Despite well-known traditions of "feudal" hierarchy, overlords, and differential privileges in Sri Lanka, especially in the last precolonial Kandyan Kingdom, this conception of a village community of ancient times – in which the irrigation tank and its surrounding rice terraces, the village community of peasant owners, and the combined duality of *vihara* and *stupa* constituted focal points of "moral" existence – has a powerful stereotypical hold in modern Sri Lanka, even among the urban middle classes and the proletariat.

The greatest Sinhalese novelist of this century, Martin Wickramasinghe is credited with this formula of Sinhala cultural identity: *vava* (tank), *dagaba* (temple), *yaya* (paddy field).[62] So important is this imprint that both in novels and in television dramas, the impurities and immorality of current urban life are uncritically castigated, while out there in the newly created peasant settlements and colonies, in the sites of ancient glory such as Anuradhapura and Polonnaruwa, might be found the ideal harmonious life. The new colonization schemes hold the prospect of regaining the lost utopia. This devaluation, if not rejection of urban existence as a necessary contemporary fact of life, may impede the ideologues from formulating and envisioning a "plausible" satisfying and creative urban form of life for Sri Lankans.[63]

This theme is amply developed and critically examined by H.L. Seneviratne in his most recent, timely, and original book, *The Work of Kings: The New Buddhism in Sri Lanka* (1999).[64] He shows how the term "agro-economy" (to translate the Sinhala usage [*krsi arthikaya*]), in tandem with notions of culture and environment, has become part of the language of political protest in present times.[65] Seneviratne gives a genealogy of "the idyllic village community centering on the tank, the temple, and the field," which has become part of the present-day nationalist

---

[62] I hasten to add that Wickramasinghe's formulation must not be associated with the current propagandist and chauvinist use of this romanticism by intolerant, chauvinist extremists who call themselves guardians of "national thought" (*Jatika Cintanaya*).

[63] Stanley Tambiah, *Buddhism Betrayed? Religion, Politics, and Violence in Sri Lanka*, Chicago: The University of Chicago Press 1992, pp. 109–10.

[64] H.L. Seneviratne, *The Work of Kings: The New Buddhism in Sri Lanka*, Chicago: The University of Chicago Press, 1999.

[65] Seneviratne (ibid., chapter 5) describes how a notable Buddhist monk, Inamaluve Sumangala, led a protest movement against a government project to build a tourist hotel at the site of Kandalama reservoir, allegedly built in the early centuries AD.

and middle-class world view and political discourse. This genealogy is particularly interesting because Leach and Gunawardana, by virtue of their discussion of hydraulic society (and I, too, in respect of the notion of "Buddhist state"), have also become members of the rogues' gallery.

Now considered indigenous, this romantic idea of the village community is borrowed from western conceptions of the village community and the idealized life of the peasantry, whose own view of their life was one of drudgery mercifully punctuated by some communal ribaldry and religio-theatrical alleviations. The idea first entered the Sinhala-speaking middle classes through Dharmapala. The writings of Ananda Coomaraswamy contributed to the idea of a noble peasantry living in idyllic harmony in its natural and social environment. The major recent writer who idealized the village and coupled with it the stupa, the tank, and the paddy field to construct a distinctive Sinhala culture was Martin Wickramasinghe. Sinhala poets of the "Colombo Period" like Mimana Prematilaka, Sagara Palansuriya, and P.B. Alvis Perera directly borrowed from English romanticizers of the countryside, adding another dimension to the idea of the idyllic village.

The idea also received a boost from an unlikely source the anthropologists and Buddhist scholars, through two concepts. The first is the concept of the "Buddhist State" proposed by S.J. Tambiah, Heinz Bechert, and Trevor Ling, who understood the Buddhist state as a symbiotic relation between the king, Sangha, and the people; and second, Edmund Leach's use of the term "hydraulic society" to refer to the ancient Sri Lankan irrigation-based civilization. Leach's work, however, was hardly a romanticization because he "deconstructed" the formidable tank by pointing out that the large reservoirs were not the work of some one single hero-king but systems that evolved over time – a point that cut down to size some of the tank building hero kings. Leach's term "hydraulic society" gained wider currency in Sri Lanka through the work of the historian R.A.L.H. Gunawardhana. This term has now trickled down into the nationalist-romantic-idyllic vocabulary as *vari samskritiya* (hydraulic culture), restoring the idea of the romantic hero-centered tank that Leach so imaginatively demolished. Inamaluve's term *krsi arthikaya* belongs to the same family of romantic-propagandist terms as *vari samskritiya* in contemporary ideological jargon and is probably inspired by it. That is to say the idea behind the term *vari samskritiya* and even the term itself is of western origin, just like numerous other items of "national" culture.

The idea of the Buddhist State trickled down to the Jatika Cintanaya ideology through the work of Gunadasa Amarasekera.[66] One or another version of this idea is now nearly epidemic in the newspapers and other media. In this we see a fascinating migration of ideas from intellectuals to demagogues via an

[66] "Jatika Cintanaya, or 'national thought', is an isolationist movement that advocates indigenousness in lifestyle and thought. It is led by Gunadasa Amerasekera, a dentist and novelist, and Nalin de Silva, a mathematician." Ibid., p. 233.

intervening range of interpreters, and the resulting unintended, unconscious, and unwitting complicity of intellectuals in the manufacture of socio-politically potent ideas of which they would want no part. In another contortion, the stupa – ricefield – tank trinity has been used in recent times as a model for inventing other trinities, like the school, the police, and the monastery of President Premadasa.[67]

[67] Ibid., pp. 260–62.

CHAPTER 9

The engagement with structuralism

The year 1961 may be taken by us to be a landmark in Leach's intellectual journey for that year saw the publication of work he had *already* completed in the form of a monograph on *Pul Eliya* and a reprint of essays in *Rethinking Anthropology*. The same year also saw the first attempts by Leach at structuralist analysis of myths influenced by certain Lévi-Straussian precedents. In 1955 Lévi-Strauss had published the essay "The Structural Study of Myth"[1] containing his famous decoding of the Oedipus myth, and in 1958 he had published the even more important *tour de force* "La geste d'Asdiwal,"[2] which in due time, but not immediately, came to have a special recognition as an exemplar in British academic circles.

Leach responded to the stimulus of Lévi-Straussian structuralist myth analysis with two 1961 essays: "Golden Bough or Gilded Twig?"[3] and "Lévi-Strauss in the Garden of Eden: An Examination of Some Recent Developments in the Analysis of Myth."[4] And in the following year, he published the remarkable essay "Genesis as Myth,"[5] an advance copy of which he had sent Lévi-Strauss who responded with a friendly scintillating reply.

"Genesis as Myth", brief though it is, dealt with three stories from the first four chapters of Genesis – the story of the seven-day creation, the

---

[1] Claude Lévi-Strauss, "The Structural Study of Myth," *Journal of American Folklore*, vol. 68, no. 270, 1955, pp. 428–44. A modified version was printed in his *Anthropologie Structurale*, Paris: Plon, 1958. The English version, trans. Claire Jacobson and Brooke Grundfest Schoepf: *Structural Anthropology*, New York: Basic Books, 1963.
[2] Claude Lévi-Strauss, "La geste d'Asdiwal," *Annuaire de l'E.P.H.E. (Sciences Religieuses)*, 1958–59.
[3] Edmund Leach, "Golden Bough or Gilded Twig," *Daedalus (Journal of the American Academy of Arts and Sciences)*, vol. 90, no. 2, Spring 1961, pp. 371–87.
[4] Edmund Leach, "Lévi-Strauss in the Garden of Eden: An Examination of Some Recent Developments in the Analysis of Myth," *Transactions of the New York Academy of Sciences*, series 2, vol. 23, no. 4, 1961, pp. 386–96.
[5] E.R. Leach, "Genesis as Myth," *Discovery* vol. 23, no. 5, May 1962, pp. 30–35. Reprinted in Edmund Leach, *Genesis as Myth and Other Essays*, London: Cape, 1969.

story of the Garden of Eden, and the story of Cain and Abel. Leach generously states that "this approach to myth analysis derives originally from the techniques of structural linguistics associated with the name of Roman Jakobson, but is more immediately due to Claude Lévi-Strauss . . . "[6] (Leach also referred to certain Pueblo Indian myths which focus on the opposition between life and death.)

For my purposes, the significance of this essay is how Leach sets out his interpretive procedure which clearly shows his acceptance of the basic tenets as set out by Lévi-Strauss, supplemented by Leach's own adoptions from information theory. Let me quote some passages: "It is common to all mythological systems that all important stories recur in several different versions."[7] "Another noticeable characteristic of mythical stories is their markedly binary aspect; myth is constantly setting up opposing categories."[8] "Binary oppositions are intrinsic to the process of human thought. Any description of the world must discriminate categories in the form 'p is what not-p is not.' " (For example, one could not formulate the concept "alive" except as the converse of its partner "dead"; "so also human beings are male or not female and persons of the opposite sex are either available as sexual partners or not available. Universally these are the most fundamentally important oppositions in all human experience.")[9]

"Redundancy" in the sense of alternate versions of the myth confirms a believer's understanding of, and reinforces the essential meaning of, the message (the word of God). Redundancy "increases information – that is the uncertainty of the possible means of decoding the message."[10]

"Every myth system will portray a persistent sequence of binary discriminations as between human/superhuman, mortal/immortal, male/female, legitimate/illegitimate, good/bad . . . followed by a 'mediation' of the paired categories thus distinguished. 'Mediation' (in this sense) is always achieved by introducing a third category which is 'abnormal' or 'anomalous' in terms of ordinary 'rational' categories."[11]

Leach concludes:

The novelty of the analysis which I have presented does not lie in the facts but in the procedure. Instead of taking each myth as a thing in itself with a "meaning" peculiar to itself, it is assumed, from the start, that every myth is one of a complex and that any pattern which occurs in one myth will recur, in the same or other variations, in other parts of the complex. The structure that is common to

---

[6] Leach, "Genesis as Myth," p. 11.   [7] Ibid., p. 7.   [8] Ibid., p. 8.
[9] Ibid., pp. 9–10.   [10] Ibid., p. 9.   [11] Ibid., p. 11.

all variations becomes apparent when different versions are "superimposed" one upon the other . . . Furthermore, it seems evident that much the same patterns exist in the most diverse kinds of mythology. This seems to me to be a fact of great psychological, sociological and scientific significance. Here truly are observable phenomena which are the expression of unobservable realities.[12]

Leach's own efforts in the structuralist mode in the early sixties conveyed his enthusiasm for Lévi-Strauss's path-breaking procedures and interpretations that spoke to his own mathematical and semiotic leanings. In the years 1962–63 there were some cordial exchanges between them as evidenced by their correspondence.[13] For example, Lévi-Strauss wrote to Leach (dated May 22, 1962) thanking him for "the Caste volume which is fundamental and will prove of great use,"[14] and "for the delightful time you all gave me in London."[15] Lévi-Strauss wrote again on September 6, 1962, saying that owing to a mistake made in the publisher's office a copy of "my last book"[16] was not sent to Leach (and some other "important persons") and that the mistake was being rectified.[17] More significantly, Lévi-Strauss wrote (dated January 4, 1963) that he had been "informed by Louis Dumont that you will probably stop over in Paris in March and early April," and that "Both Dumont and I would like to seize this opportunity to give our students a chance to meet you, since you loom large in our teaching, but so far mostly as a mythical figure . . . Should your stay in Paris be long enough, we would very much like to have you take part in a seminar of [*sic*] each of us; should it be very short, we would be ready to consider merging our seminars and holding a joint meeting."

In the event Leach seemed to have been unable to accept the invitation to visit Paris (there is no record of his letter to Lévi-Strauss), and Lévi-Strauss wrote a commiserating letter dated January 29, 1963, saying that "to be perfectly frank and even cynical, deep down in my heart I fully sympathize with your reaction. To deliver a lecture or to take part in

---

[12] Ibid., p. 22.
[13] This correspondence is taken from the Edmund Leach Papers, The Modern Archive, King's College Library, Cambridge. Lévi-Strauss writes from this address: Laboratoire d'Anthropologie Sociale du Collège de France et de l'Ecole Pratique des Hautes Etudes.
[14] Lévi-Strauss is probably referring to E.R. Leach (ed.), *Aspects of Caste in South India, Ceylon and North-West Pakistan*, Cambridge Papers in Social Anthropology, no. 2, Cambridge: Cambridge University Press, 1960.
[15] Lévi-Strauss was probably referring to his visit to deliver the Henry Myers Lecture.
[16] The book in question was probably *La pensée sauvage*, Paris: Plon, 1962.
[17] A letter from Lévi-Strauss, dated September 12, 1962, says that he was pleased to hear that Leach had received the book and was not one of the forgotten ones.

seminars is one of the worst chores of our profession and every time I have a good excuse I manage to withdraw from the ordeal." Continuing his friendly overture, Lévi-Strauss did not give up. He wrote: "will you stop over in Paris at the end of March? . . . so that I can at least arrange a small informal meeting at my home with the Dumonts and a few other of your admirers."

A high point in their mutual admiration and good will was soon reached in 1963 with Leach's review in *Man* (1963)[18] of two related books by Lévi-Strauss which would become in due course famously engaging texts, especially in their subsequent English translations, for many anthropologists in Britain and the United States. The books were *Le totémism aujourd'hui* (1962),[19] followed by the spectacular *La pensée sauvage* (1962).[20]

Invited to review the two books in *Man*, Leach seized the occasion to celebrate the tardy but now unstoppable arrival of Lévi-Strauss in British academic circles. Whereas the *American Anthropologist* immediately rated *Les structures élémentaires de la parenté* as "undoubtedly the most important book in anthropology in this generation," *Man* took two years to admit rather grudgingly that it was "the most important contribution made by a French anthropologist since the war . . ." But times are changing. When in 1952 Lévi-Strauss delivered lectures in London, Oxford, and Cambridge on the "structural study of myths" his audiences were uniformly baffled and uncomprehending; "ten years later his Henry Myers Lecture . . . intrinsically far more difficult than the earlier myth lectures, was received with tumultuous enthusiasm . . . [21] Lévi-Strauss is not the only influence currently affecting British social anthropology but he is certainly a dominant one; every serious anthropologist must read and re-read these books." Leach stating that in such a brief review it would "only be both presumptuous and misleading" to criticize the books, however, indicated their major submissions, notably that Lévi-Strauss more than his predecessors, who may have had inklings, systematically argues that totemism is "a system of logical categories rather than a system for providing functional satisfaction." In *La pensée sauvage* again Lévi-Strauss goes further than his predecessors in seeing in the general phenomenon

---

[18] Leach's review appeared as "Review of Lévi-Strauss' *Le totémism aujourd'hui*, and *La pensée sauvage*," *Man*, vol. 63, art. 50, 1963, pp. 76–77.
[19] Claude Lévi-Strauss, *Le totémisme aujourd'hui*, Paris: Presses Universitaires de France, 1962.
[20] Claude Lévi-Strauss, *La pensée sauvage*, Paris: Plon, 1962.
[21] Leach's characterization of the reception was probably over-generous to judge by much incomprehension evidenced at the ASA seminar in 1964. Quotations are from the review, see note 18.

of how things are named and classified that "it is in the relationships which exist between the individual members of sets of names that the structure of logic and mathematics first begins to emerge."[22] Such fulsome praise from Leach was unusual and uncharacteristic, and he would later follow it with longer explications spiced with much praise but also qualified by criticisms.

On March 22, 1963, Lévi-Strauss wrote to Leach "to thank you for your over-generous review of my two books in the last issue of *Man*. You were certainly right not to try to give a detailed account and your free interpretation was all the more interesting for me that it does not duplicate, but is rather complementary to what I have tried to express." He agreed that the translation into English of *La pensée sauvage* would pose tremendous problems and recognized that Rodney Needham "did extremely well" with the translation of *Totemism*.

"By the way," continued Lévi-Strauss, "I was amused to notice that the word 'pansy' has become *taboo* in English to the extent that you felt obliged to use 'violet' instead (not the same flower, of course!). If I had known it at the time when P.S. was written, I would certainly have quoted Shakespeare's 'pansies for thoughts.'"

The fulsome praise lavished by Leach in the brief aforementioned review in *Man* was soon followed by a longer and more measured consideration of *La pensée sauvage* (and its preceding complementary volume *Le totémism*), published in 1964. This seems to be one of the first attempts to convey the nature of the importance of these texts to an Anglo-American audience.

I have heard it from a person to whom Leach allegedly confided that "Telstar et les aborigènes" was first offered to *L'Homme*. The editor(s) referred it to Lévi-Strauss, who rejected it, to the chagrin of Leach.[23] If this is true, then we can sense the tensions and differences that are likely to occur between them, because whatever the sensitivity of the French master to criticism, Leach was the type of inquiring and creative scholar who, however appreciative of a compatible thinker, would apply his critical faculties to texts that engaged him and could not be restrained from extending the boundaries of their relevance.

---

[22] Leach, "Review," 1963, pp. 46–47.
[23] Edmund Leach, "Telstar et les aborigènes ou 'La pensée sauvage,'" *Annales: Economies, Sociétées, Civilisations*, vol. 19, no. 6, November–December 1964, pp. 1100–15. The English version was published as "Telstar and the Aborigines," Dorothy Emmet and Alasdair MacIntyre (eds.), *Sociological Theory and Philosophical Analysis*, New York: Macmillan, 1970, pp. 183–203, subsequent references are to the English version.

The essay begins with what Leach considers the major innovative proposition in *La pensée sauvage*, which Leach says he has read "from beginning to end at least three times and on each occasion . . . obtained a very different impression of how it all fits together."[24] Lévi-Strauss's basic point of departure is that even more basic to logical thought than the operation of words is the operation of the concrete entities to which the words correspond, and he thereby is "concerned to break down the conventional distinction between verbal and non-verbal aspects of culture. . . both are equally a means of communication, a language." Recent studies in structural linguistics and the closely related applied studies of communication engineers have enormously advanced our understanding of the way in which verbal forms of language actually operate as a means of communication. Lévi-Strauss is suggesting that we apply strictly comparable forms of analysis to the " 'language' aspect of non-verbal culture."[25] He may draw many of his ethnographic examples from exotic peoples but he is concerned with "the elementary principles common to all thinking, Chinese and Western European included, and not simply with the thoughts of 'primitive peoples' . . . Even if time should show that some of the items of evidence have been misplaced, the fundamental method of Lévi-Strauss's analysis is an innovation from which there can be no retreat."[26]

For centuries past sophisticated societies have sustained their superiority by maintaining a store of information in the form of written documents which are a special category of material things subject to human manipulation. "It is a common assumption that this ability to communicate by means of the written word is a unique cultural phenomenon peculiar to civilized societies," but Lévi-Strauss denies this is so, and attempts to establish that " 'uncivilized' societies likewise have their categories of material things which serve as a store of knowledge and a means of communication." The categories into which the formative world is ordered have the same function as the words of a sentence. In the age of electronics it is no more fanciful to argue this proposition and also to understand "that written documents are only one specialized and very inefficient device for storing information."[27] The point that Leach himself grasps and would develop in his own way is how "the latest miracles of the communication engineer" operating within the restrictions of digital binary oppositions, this vital age of the electronic

---

[24] Ibid., p. 185.   [25] Ibid., p. 185.   [26] Ibid., p. 185.   [27] Ibid., p. 186.

present, meet the thought operations of the golden age of the primitive past. "This time," writes Lévi-Strauss, "is now restored to us, thanks to the discovery of a universe of information where the laws of savage thought reign once more." (Leach with his engineering background and interest in semiology seems to have been particularly thrilled with this unexpected bringing together of the communication technology of the electronic age [Telstar] and the transmission of messages through the properties of the objects of the physical world by the Aborigines, and the displacement of literacy and writing from the centrality attributed to it in the transmission of messages.[28]) Lévi-Strauss breaks up the conventional accepted classificatory categories of anthropological analysis by other such moves, such as discussing the structural parallels between Australian totemism and the Indian caste system previously thought to be as different as chalk and cheese.

Lévi-Strauss's shakeup of the conventional taxonomic systems stems from his resort to the procedures of structural linguistics: he looks for comparable 'distinctive features' in non-verbal patterns of culture which will sort out the facts by means of binary discriminations. And it becomes possible to engage in a matrix analysis that was not possible in the conventional taxonomic typing.

The merging of linguistics and social anthropology was more significant than merely bringing Mauss up to date. The recognition that what makes man superior to all other creatures is the faculty to operate and manipulate the symbols through which he communicates, and the core of Lévi-Strauss's problem is the basis for the uniquely human capacity to perform such mental exercises of logical transformation.

Lévi-Strauss's theoretical move, which is an elaboration of Mauss's theory of the gift, is the argument that mathematical relations, linguistic relations, kinship relations, and transactional relations of all types are really "all of the same kind", and aspects of the same "thing," the Culture of Society.[29]

From this point of explication, Leach changes tack and embarks on an evaluation and critique of the Lévi-Straussian framework. Aside from the standard criticism that Lévi-Strauss may engage in selective and

---

[28] To anticipate a future onslaught: in 1979 Leach would give a provocative opening address entitled "Literacy Be Damned" on the theme of the increasing obsolescence of literacy in the age of electronic media. Edmund Leach, "Literacy Be Damned," opening address, National Communications Conference, June 13–15, 1979.

[29] Leach, "Telstar and the Aborigines," pp. 190–91.

even misleading use of the ethnographic evidence – cases in point are the mistakes committed in the representation of the Kachins of North Burma, or of the Penan death names as described by Rodney Needham, and the lack of fit between English and French naming customs of birds, dogs, and racehorses – there is a searching evaluation by Leach regarding Lévi-Strauss's treatment of totemism in terms of a binary logic.

1. Lévi-Strauss is certainly convincing that totems are in fact the "stuff of thinking," an aspect previously neglected by theorists. But in his fondness for binary operations, he distinguishes between "bonnes à manger" and things which are "bonnes à penser." But why cannot totems be both at once? He also evades the central problems for ethnographers: "why are totemic species held to be sacred?"

2. Binary analysis is a powerful tool of analysis no doubt, but one of its important disadvantages is that it cannot handle gradations of value of more or less, which can be more effectively handled by analog computers, which answer questions in terms of *more* or *less*, than by digital computers which can only answer *yes* or *no*.

3. Although Lévi-Strauss does take note of "good prohibitions" associated with totemism and of "culinary operations and utensils" in caste systems, he consistently plays down the importance of food customs as cultural indicators. If in totemism the central issue is the relationship of man to animals, then the dietary rules and preferences and prohibitions of a society that codes a whole range of dietetic possibilities (distinguishing between food and non-food, from that which is good and bad, pleasant and unpleasant, and so on) cannot be contained within the crude binary distinction that Lévi-Strauss employs. (Similarly, Goody has pointed out that a satisfactory analysis of the rules of incest calls for a consideration of the whole system of permissible, prohibited, and undesirable sex relations[30].)

4. It is a great step forward when Lévi-Strauss recognized that the "'totemic style' of logic can be discerned not only in systems composed of exogamous unilineal descent groups but also in the converse type of segmentary structure represented by an endogamous caste system. But this leaves out of account those social structures which are not 'segmentary' in any straightforward sense and which, on that account, do not readily lend themselves to binary analysis. Where, for example, do we meet with a totemic style of logic in the collective

---

[30] John R. Goody, "A Comparative Approach to Incest and Adultery," *British Journal of Sociology*, vol. 7, no. 4, 1956, pp. 286–305.

representations of societies which have a bilateral (cognatic) pattern of kinship organization?"

Although some of his writings were known to individual anthropologists, and although he had been invited to give lectures in Britain, it might be said that Lévi-Strauss made his official entry into British anthropological circles when the Association of Social Anthropologists (ASA) held a seminar in June 1964 in Cambridge to examine his writings on myth analysis and totemism. This seminar actually originated in the spring of 1963 when members of the ASA meeting in Oxford decided to devote a future session to this genre of his writings, and consequently invited certain persons, notably Mary Douglas, K.O.L. Burridge, Michael Mendelson, Peter Worsley, and Robin Fox, to prepare papers. Subsequently, Edmund Leach was invited to serve as the seminar convener in Cambridge, and seeing his role as "strictly catalytic," he circulated to participants copies of an English translation of "La geste d'Asdiwal" prepared by Nicholas Mann, who was at that time a Research Fellow in Romance Languages at Clare College (but who had actually done the translation some three years earlier as an undergraduate).

There was a certain amount of anxious comedy in the correspondence between Leach and Lévi-Strauss in which a third party, Rodney Needham, also took part. In a letter dated June 14, 1965, Leach wrote to enquire whether Lévi-Strauss would be willing to allow him to publish an English version of "La geste d'Asdiwal" in the collection of essays on totemism and myth delivered at the ASA seminar in 1964. Leach gingerly explained that he had "got landed" with the task of editing the volume, a task he found "a bit embarrassing," and he was somewhat relieved by receiving for inclusion Nur Yalman's review commentary of *Le cru et le cuit*. The point of his plea to Lévi-Strauss was that in its present form his task was "very much a case of Hamlet without the Prince of Denmark," and that it would make "a lot more sense if he could publish Asdiwal in English as part of the text." A very presentable English translation was already available and had been done by Nicholas Mann whose credentials he set out in some detail. Because publication of the ASA volume should not be unduly delayed, Leach urged Lévi-Strauss "to let me know more or less by return what is your reaction to this suggestion."

There was no reply from Lévi-Strauss, and Leach apprehensively wrote to Rodney Needham on July 5, 1965: "Are your relations with the great man sufficiently cordial to find out just what happened? I fear I am in the dog house for writing that thing in *Annales*, which was not sufficiently genuflectory."[31]

Needham's reply dated July 24, 1965 was reassuring: "I wrote very cagily and circumspectly to Lévi-Strauss, and today have this answer. 'Leach's letter was never received. It probably got wayled (sic) somewhere. Will you kindly convey my greetings to him and tell him how sorry I feel that I did not care to answer. Of course, he has my complete agreement to translate "Asdiwal" and to include it in the contemplated monograph.'"

A digression on Rodney Needham is I think useful. Needham together with Leach had been in the forefront of introducing and making known Lévi-Strauss's contribution to anthropologists in Britain and elsewhere. He had translated *Totemism*, was involved for a while in the project to translate *Les structures élémentaires*, and at this time in the early and mid-1960s he was on good terms with Lévi-Strauss (though later intellectual disagreements ruptured that relationship). In the years 1964–66 there is evidence of cordial correspondence between Needham and Leach. Leach had at times sought Needham's expertise in French for translating some difficult passages in Lévi-Strauss's writing; they exchanged their published essays (Leach had requested extra copies of Needham's papers on the Penan and on the Temiar). Especially Leach's "Animal Categories and Verbal Abuse," which Needham admired, evoked some witty puns and ethnographic information of a sexual nature.[32]

---

[31] Leach is here referring to "Telstar et les aborigènes" 1964, which was dealt with earlier.

[32] "Anthropological Aspects of Language: Animal Categories and Verbal Abuse," in Enic H. Lenneberg (ed.), *New Directions in the Study of Language*, Cambridge, MA: MIT Press. A choice communication from Needham dated October 24, 1964 has this passage: "This is what I wanted to inject into your subconscious for further rumination... *Night of the Iguana* is a pretty bad film, and clearly departs from Tennessee Williams, but at one point Ava Gardner (the character she portrays) says to an acidulous spinster who is persecuting Richard Burton Esq. that the trouble with her is that her 'quail' wants a man. So quail = cunt, bird = genitals (female), c.f. 'plump as young partridge.' There really is something there." In a sequel letter dated December 8, 1964 Needham thanks Leach for the "Animal Categories" reprint, and clues Leach to this "oddity, apparently found in American G. I. English that 'tail' = cunt; a piece of tail = accessible women."

It would appear that it was Needham who first alerted Leach to Lévi-Strauss's hostile reactions regarding the Kachin social system. Needham (July 1, 1965) "I [do] not remember whether I have ever told you that I have here a set of corrections and revisions to *Les Structures* which are being incorporated into the English edition. There is a fair amount about you, written in an edgy and sometimes sarcastic tone. Perhaps you would like to look at them when you come to examine Riviere." Leach served as external examiner for Peter Riviere's DPhil. and for James Fox's BLitt. theses.

In the volume edited by Leach that appeared four years later entitled *The Structural Study of Myth and Totemism*,[33] this translation of the Asdiwal essay appeared as the head piece followed by the contributions of the above-mentioned invited authors, *plus* a new piece containing Nur Yalman's observations on Lévi-Strauss's first major volume on Amerindian myths, *Le cru et le cuit*, which was published in Paris in the autumn of 1964, and had therefore not been available at the time of the Cambridge discussions.[34] The seminar discussions in Cambridge cannot be said to have been especially informative and productive. First of all, it did not seem as if either the main contributors or the other participants had an informed grasp of what Lévi-Strauss was actually saying.[35] The extant French texts posed varying degrees of difficulty to British readers. Secondly, there was a resistance to the newly arrived "new-fangled" structuralist perspective and interpretive procedures among many who thought themselves to be "empiricists" in the structural-functional fieldwork and theoretical traditions. In his introduction to the ASA volume Leach states without mincing words: "If this book provides illumination it will be because of the light it throws upon the assumptions and attitudes of particular British social anthropologists rather than because of any consistent analysis of the work of continental Europe's most distinguished living anthropologist."[36]

Declaring that he was "personally more closely addicted to Lévi-Strauss's methods than are most of my colleagues as represented in this book," both during the Cambridge discussions and in his ringing final remarks at their conclusion, later rewritten and extended in the Introduction to the edited volume, Leach, while accepting that other techniques for the analysis of myth and totemism are possible, clarified with vigor for his British colleagues Lévi-Strauss's main submissions. For example, Mary Douglas had been prominently critical of Lévi-Strauss's alleged "reductionist" and impoverished readings of myths, which moreover were demonstrations of his own ingenuity. Leach cautioned that

---

[33] Edmund Leach (ed.), *The Structural Study of Myth and Totemism*, London: Tavistock Publications, 1967.

[34] Claude Lévi-Strauss, *Le crut et le cuit*, Paris: Plon, 1964.

[35] By the time of the Cambridge seminar, these writings of Lévi-Strauss of relevance to the discussions, besides the Asdiwal essay, had been published: "La structure et la forme: réflexions sur un ouvrage de Vladimir Propp," *Cahiers de l'Institut de Science Economique Appliquée* seres M, no. 7, March 1960, pp. 3–36; *Le totémism aujourd'hui*, 1962 (English translation, *Totemism*, London: Merlin Press, 1964); *La pensée sauvage*, 1962. V. Propp's own Russian essay appeared in English translation in 1958 as "Morphology of the Folk Tale," *International Journal of American Linguistics*, part 3, vol. 24, no. 4, 1958.

[36] Edmund Leach, "Introduction," in *The Structural Study of Myth and Totemism*, p. vii.

Douglas might have grasped Lévi-Strauss's meaning more easily if she had read *Le cru et le cuit* where it is argued in very explicit terms that the mode by which myths convey meaning (or rather, experience) is similar to the mode by which music conveys experience. It was a mistake to suggest that Lévi-Strauss is suggesting "all myths are the same" – rather he is arguing that "at a certain level of abstraction the dialectical redundant structure of all myths constitutes a set of variations on a constant theme."[37] After the publication of *Le cru et le cuit* it is "possible to quibble only about details," "for Lévi-Strauss has shown that there *is* such a thing as 'a language of myth,'" and that structural methods for decoding unknown scripts have analogical applications for decoding myths. While myths were grounded in particular cultural contexts, there are certain myths which Lévi-Strauss finds especially interesting from a cross-cultural point of view. "Examples of universal myth problems are: Is death final? Is an incest rule necessary? How did humanity begin? Such problems are not only universal, they are quite fundamental, and I was astonished to find that some contributors to the seminar discussion actually referred to these themes as 'quite trivial'!"[38]

Since Lévi-Strauss's essay in English translation, "The Story of Asdiwal", would in due course become an important reference point, and for enthusiasts an exemplary demonstration of structuralist method, it is apposite to refer to some of its main submissions and strengths. Lévi-Strauss stated that the study of a native myth from the Pacific coast of Canada had two aims:

First, to isolate and compare the *various levels* on which the myth evolves: geographic, economic, sociological, and cosmological – each one of these levels, together with the symbolism proper to it, being seen as a transformation of an underlying logical structure common to all of them. And, second, to compare the *different versions* of the myth and to look for the discrepancies between them or between some of them; for since they all come from the same people (but are recorded in different parts of their territory), these variations cannot be explained in terms of dissimilar beliefs, languages, or institutions.[39]

This marvelous essay to this day evokes excitement, and has many interesting and unexpected revelations, but let me limit myself to its main virtue, which has been recognized by many, and which had special significance for Leach. Lévi-Strauss reads the myth with careful attention

---

[37] Ibid., p. xviii.   [38] Ibid., pp. viii, ix, xvii, xviii.
[39] *The Structural Study of Myth and Totemism*, p. 1.

to the thought categories and concepts of Tsimshian Indians: he systematically and dialectically tests the assertions and narrative patterns of the
myth (and its variations) to the extensive ethnography concerning the
Tsimshian Indians, compiled by Boas and others, which gives details of
their geographic and territorial circumstances, their economic activities,
the seasonal cycles and the movements of both people and fish, the requirements of hunting, fishing, and food collection, the people's social
organization (consisting of non-localized exogamous matrilineal clans,
divided into lineages, descent lines and households), their marriage patterns and post-marital residence patterns, their ritualized gift exchanges,
and finally, their cosmology.

Methodologically and interpretively perhaps the most stringent
demonstration ever presented by Lévi-Strauss, the Asdiwal essay examines the implications of a corpus of myths drawn from the same socio-
cultural context, and then examines the dialectical relations between the
myth patterns and the patterns of the socio-economic-cultural context
as lived reality. It exposes some unexpected outcomes of that dialectic
which goes well beyond a simple Malinowskian charter theory of myth,
while satisfying all the empirical expectations of the British "functionalist" approach. Thus in the Asdiwal essay Lévi-Strauss sets out what
we may call "the structuralist-functionalist" method and perspective of
a rigorous context-related analysis, which Leach himself accepted and
attempted systematically to follow in his later analysis of biblical narratives and early Christian doctrine and art. This controlled method,
which he espoused, was the opposite of the Frazerian "bits-and-pieces
from everywhere" form of the comparative method which he never tired
of denouncing. Ironically, one of Leach's later disappointments was with
Lévi-Strauss's progressive deviation in Frazer's grand manner from these
tenets in the later volumes of *Mythologiques*.

The Asdiwal essay had these revelations to make in the relation of the
myth to the ethnographic context. The myth's references to the physical
and political geography of Tsimshian country, to the places and towns
there, were accurate and thus showed a correspondence between the
two domains. Secondly, the myth accurately reflected "the economic
life of the natives which . . . governs the great sensational migrations between the Skeena and Nass Valleys, and during the course of which
Asdiwal's adventures take place." And now comes the unexpected: the
myth deals "with the social and family organization, for we witness several marriages, divorces, widowhoods, and other events," but most of
the crucial sociological representations had little to do with the actual

practices of the Tsimshian people, and frequently were inversions and imagined "negative" instances of these practices. The logic of this deviation engages Lévi-Strauss's speculative attention. Lastly, he deals with "the cosmology, for, unlike the others, two of Asdiwal's visits, one to heaven, and the other below the earth, are of a mythological and not of an experiential order."[40] Thus, with respect to the four levels distinguished in the myth analysis – the geographic, the techno-economic, the sociological, and cosmological – "the first two are exact transcriptions of reality; the fourth has nothing to do with it, and in the third, real and imaginary institutions are interwoven."[41]

It is this third level of representation, where the myth markedly deviates from sociological reality, especially in regard to post-marital residential patterns, that invites this kind of answer from Lévi-Strauss: the configuration of matrilineages, virilocal residence, children growing up first in the patrilocal home, then finishing their education at the maternal uncle's home, and after marrying returning to live with their parents, bringing their wives with them, and finally a minority of them settling in their uncle's village only when they were called upon to succeed him – these "comings and goings were one of the outward signs of the tensions between lineages connected by marriage," especially among the nobility whose mythology formed a real court literature.

Mythical speculations about types of residence which are exclusively patrilocal or matrilocal do not therefore have anything to do with the reality of the structure of Tsimshian society, but rather with its inherent possibilities and its latent potentialities. Such speculations, in the last analysis, do not seek to depict what is real, but to justify the shortcomings of reality, since the extreme positions are only *imagined* in order to show that they are untenable. This step, which is fitting for mythological thought, implies an admission (but in the veiled language of the myth) that the social facts when thus examined are marred by an insurmountable contradiction. A contradiction which, like the hero of the myth, Tsimshian society cannot understand but prefers to forget.[42]

This selectively summarized statement of the Asdiwal essay[43] has raised two important issues which remain continuing perplexities, and

---

[40] Ibid., p. 7.   [41] Ibid., p. 13.   [42] Ibid., p. 30.
[43] Towards the end of the essay, Lévi-Strauss also takes up the issue of what happens when myths travel from the center of their origin to other places. To quote: "Thus we arrived at a fundamental property of mythical thought, other examples of which might well be sought elsewhere. When a mythical schema is transmitted from one population to another, and there exist differences of language, social organization or way of life which make the myth difficult to communicate, it begins to become impoverished and confused. But one can find a limiting condition in which

therefore a perennial concern, for anthropologists: first, the relation between the structure of a corpus of myths and the socio-cultural context in which it is engendered and recited; second, while the understanding of the myth and its variants requires situating them in this context, what might be the dialectical correspondence and dialog between the message and meaning structure of the myths and the existential realities and practices of the people whose cultural possession and capital they are. These issues some might see as part of the more general issue of the relation between ideology and practice, others as part of the Marxist bifurcation and interrelation between infrastructure and superstructure, but this much is certain: there is no simple one-to-one correspondence between myth and social practices, if indeed the separation of these levels is justifiable. (A third perplexity which Lévi-Strauss does not raise here is the problematic relation between myth and ritual, a relation that becomes even more complex when there is recitation and enactment of portions of myths in certain ritual activities. These issues are of continuing interest in the discipline, inviting quite an array of variant answers.)

In terms of the tenets proclaimed and issues probed in the Asdiwal essay, Leach would quickly realize that his initial efforts at analyzing biblical materials fell short in regard to the grounding of the structuralist analysis of myth narratives in the social context and practices of the people who produced them, and that a deepened analysis and understanding of myths would be achieved if their dialectical relation to the norms and structural contradictions of their social life were probed. This, after all, was in accord with his own theoretical and methodological commitments as manifested in his study of the relation between ideal categories and on the ground practices in both *Political Systems of Highland Burma* and *Pul Eliya*.

Leach published in the *American Anthropologist* in 1965 a long, searching, and admiring review of Lévi-Strauss's *Mythologiques, vol. I: Le cru et le cuit*.[44] This famous text, later translated into English as *The Raw and the Cooked*, has become the most popular example worldwide of binary discrimination.

---

instead of being finally obliterated by losing all its outlines, the myth is inverted and regains part of its precision." He suggests that the Nass version of the Skeena version of the Asdiwal story is such an instance where "the double mechanism of the *weakening of the oppositions* [is] accompanied by a *reversal* of correlations," the formal coherence of which is contained in the parent Skeena version. See Ibid., pp. 41–42.

44 Edmund Leach, "Review of Claude Lévi-Strauss's *Mythologiques: Le cru et le cuit*," *American Anthropologist* vol. 67, no. 3, 1965, pp. 776–80.

Having been a little embarrassed by Lévi-Strauss's suggestion that Leach had not overcome the taboo implication of the word "pansy" in English in decoding the cover of *La pensée sauvage*, and sensing that he might be dealing with a polymath trickster figure playing with allusions, puns, and ambiguities, Leach wondered whether on the cover of *Le cru et le cuit*, the placing of the knife on the left and the fork on the right was an intended back-to-front mirror image. As it turned out, Lévi-Strauss had not noticed this printer's error until Leach picked it up. As Leach would find out, the task of serving as an explicator, interpreter, and translator of a master writing in a different language has its perils and frustrations.

Leach's attempt to translate and summarize for the English reader the contents of this French text signals his own problems with understanding some of Lévi-Strauss's concepts while at the same time he declares himself to be "one of the addicts" of the master, who however sometimes makes eloquent declarations in French which sound quite preposterous when translated into English: for example, "Thus we are not attempting to show how men think in myths, but rather how myths think for themselves in men."[45]

Whatever his qualms regarding certain particulars of the Lévi-Straussian decoding of South American myths, Leach, reminding readers of how the earlier skepticism of the method of the decoding of Cretan Linear B along the lines of structural analysis in the end concluded in certainty, makes this handsome affirmation: "Anyone who works his way through the astonishing book now before us and still claims that he doesn't believe a word of it has a resolution of disbelief which I must respect but cannot endorse. I myself am sceptical about details but I am now fully persuaded that the general methodology is legitimate."[46]

It is not necessary here to reproduce in full Leach's laying out for the English reader "some of the basic and persistent propositions which underlie all Lévi-Strauss' arguments [which] are gradually becoming apparent."[47] But it is highly relevant to set down those propositions and comments set out by Leach that Lévi-Strauss later rejects in a letter to Leach (see later) as a correct rendering of his views, as well as those critical questionings by Leach which Lévi-Strauss in turn will counter.

---

[45] Ibid., p. 776.
[46] Ibid., p. 778. Again Leach concludes his review (p. 780) with this praise: "But even if I myself am fascinated rather than wholly persuaded I must report in all seriousness that this book represents an intellectual feat which has seldom been equalled in anthropological literature. An English translation is urgently required."
[47] Ibid., p. 777.

The first proposition is that "The environment in which man exists is like a junk shop. Raw nature is a chaos which can be sorted out any way you choose by the manipulation of language, and to that must be added all kinds of worn-out residues of history ... Relationships *within* culture are highly organized, highly structured, but this is due to man's intellectual activity. Order is a human notion."

Next we come to an issue which revolves around Lévi-Strauss's use of the word *esprit* and Leach's understanding of it, which for Lévi-Strauss is a misunderstanding. This issue will continue to be a divider between them and is worthy of being introduced here. Leach cites the following passage in the text and offers his English translation of it as follows:

Les mythes signifient l'esprit, qui les élabore au moyen du monde dont il fait lui-même partie. Ainsi peuvent être simultanément engendrés, les mythes eux-mêmes par l'esprit qui les cause, et par les mythes, un image du monde déjà inscrite dans l'architecture de l'esprit (Lévi-Strauss 1964: 346).

Myths signify the spirit which elaborates them by means of the world of which it makes itself a part. Thus there can be generated simultaneously both the myths themselves (evoked) by the spirit which they cause and an image of the world already inscribed in the architecture of the spirit (evoked) by the myths.[48]

Leach remarks that he finds it disconcerting that Lévi-Strauss is scarcely interested in the meaning of myths (which have meaning for those who recite them), and that "the reality of myth [for him] seems to be almost metaphysical," nearly echoing "Durkheim's equation between God and society."[49]

Translating Lévi-Strauss's *esprit* as "spirit," Leach observes:

Spirit (*esprit*) is presumably Hegel's *objecktive Geist*, a concept which doubtless seems quite straightforward to continental minds but is quite incomprehensible to mine. In plain English such metaphysical discourse hardly makes sense, but Lévi-Strauss' general meaning seems plain enough. The world in which the members of a primitive society exist is not a world of objectively describable empirical things but a "collective representation" created by the culture out of the phenomenological facts in the world "out there." The whole body of myth carried out by a cultural group incorporates this collective representation which makes up the world as it is experienced much in the same way that the categories of a language "create" the particulars of which we are consciously aware. Any

---

[48] Ibid., p. 779.   [49] Ibid., p. 779.

particular myth only conveys meaning when considered in relation to the whole corpus of myth of which it is a part.[50]

From here Leach makes a transition to another perhaps more comprehensible critique which signifies his own functionalist methodological requirement that must accompany the structuralist exposition. Lévi-Strauss's book begins with a Bororo myth, and he elucidates it by reference to 19 other Bororo myths and 167 non-Bororo myths which span many different tribes and sources. He then ingeniously postulates transformational rules which will convert a Bororo myth into a Sherente myth, or a Mundurucu myth, but he does not tell us much about how the basic myth fits into Bororo culture. "For my taste, this emphasis is the wrong way round. Structural interpretation should be complementary to functional analysis and not *vice versa*."[51]

Lévi-Strauss wrote a letter to Leach dated August 17, 1965,[52] stating that he had read "with utmost delight your witty review of *Le Cru et le Cuit*" and that at the same time he felt "somewhat ashamed that you should spend so much of your valuable time trying to explain my book to the American reader."[53] (The word "ashamed" is a curious usage in this context and one wonders whether it carries the intimation that this role might land Leach in trouble.)

Lévi-Strauss addresses Leach's third criticism first,

about the lack of functional analysis – a criticism I was told, that Sartre had also made in private conversation with common friends. But don't worry: this will be covered in vol. IV where I shall explain *why* the Bororo, Gé and Tupi versions of the same myths are inverted along specific lines. If I did not do it in the first volume the reason is that by the time that vol. IV will be started, the unpublished Bororo myths collected by the Salesians and the Gé myths collected by Maybury-Lewis and Turner might be available, and also because I believe that anatomy should come before physiology, or else one would discuss the functioning of a body without knowing its structure, a procedure which can lead only to nonsense.[54]

Lévi-Strauss published the sequel to *Le cru et le cuit* entitled *Du miel aux cendres* in 1966.[55] From Leach's point of view this volume did not fulfill what was promised, and he would, as we shall see, hammer away at

---

[50] Ibid., p. 779.   [51] Ibid., p. 780

[52] Lévi-Strauss to Leach, August 17, 1965, Edmund Leach Papers, The Modern Archive, King's College Library, Cambridge.

[53] Ibid.   [54] Ibid.

[55] Claude Lévi-Strauss, *Mythologiques, Vol. II Du miel aux cendres*, Paris: Plon, 1966. The English translation entitled *From Honey to Ashes* was by John and Doreen Weightman, New York: Harper & Raw, 1973.

this lack and in turn attempt to demonstrate his own rendering of the complementarity of functional and structural analysis.[56]

Next, in his letter, Lévi-Strauss replies in combined fashion in one paragraph to Leach's first and second criticisms. He counters that the way Leach translates a sentence of his

does not make sense to me any more than it does to you. "Esprit" should not be translated by "spirit" but rather by "mind," and when I say "mind" I mean brain, so there is nothing Hegelian there. The misunderstanding starts with your point 1 for I don't believe that "raw nature is a chaos." Raw nature is orderly, or else there would be no physical science. The chaos is in the way in which we apprehend it at the level of sensory perception . . . the structure and functioning of the brain is, on a smaller scale, a reproduction of the structure and functioning of the physical world, and that in turn, myth and language alike reproduce the order of the brain and – by way of consequences – the order of the physical world of which there is a model in the brain. The whole system would thus look like a club sandwich: three layers of homologous orders: physical world, brain language and myth, separated by two layers of chaos: sensory perception and social discourse. Then, you see, I am much closer to the XVIIIth century materialism than to Hegel, since the objectivity of the mind results from the fact that the human brain exhibits the same properties in all individuals, and that its laws of functioning are the same as the laws of nature of which the brain is a part which makes knowledge altogether possible.[57]

[56] See Terence Turner, "Le dénicheur d'oiseaux en contexte," *Anthropologie et Société* 1980, vol. 4, Numéro 3, pp. 85–116. Turner also mentioned that Johannes Wilbert had published an exhaustive series of publications on *Folk Literature of Amazonian Peoples*. This valuable store-house has two volumes of Gé myths. In late August 1989 I contacted Terence Turner, an anthropologist who has done sustained fieldwork among the Kayapo and has been, among other issues, much concerned with the interpretation of their myths. I asked him whether Lévi-Strauss had fulfilled his stated objective of providing in volume II a "functional" analysis of the myths he mentioned both individually and in relation to their transformations. Turner was quite explicit that while Lévi-Strauss in certain places made scattered and shallow references to social structural specifics, he did not attempt "a principled and systematic discussion of how the myths he discussed related to their local, social, economic and material realities." Turner told me that he has had conversations with Lévi-Strauss in Paris on Kayapo myth texts in which he had expressed this judgment, and had himself published a paper that expressed his take on this relational nexus.

I also contacted David Maybury-Lewis, my Harvard colleague, in early September 1998, and he responded thus to Lévi-Strauss's stated intent to analyze in volume II the Gé myths collected by Maybury-Lewis. Although he had collected Gé (especially Sherente) myths he had never published them, but there were plenty of other published sources available to Lévi-Strauss. More importantly, he also stated decisively that although there are some references to the socio-cultural contexts of myths in *Du miel aux cendres*, Lévi-Strauss didn't go any deeper in this relational analysis than he had in *Le cru et le cuit*, and that there was no systematic or sustained relational analysis in it of the kind Leach had asked for. David Maybury-Lewis's own detailed critical "Review of *Mythologiques: Du miel aux cendres*" is to be found in *American Anthropologist*, vol. 71, 1969, pp. 114–20.

[57] Lévi-Strauss to Leach, August 17, 1965. Edmund Leach Papers, The Modern Archive, King's College Library, Cambridge.

Leach replied to Lévi-Strauss in a letter dated August 21, 1965[58] and on the matter of *esprit* and the human brain he had the following to say. He was aware that, in *L'anthropologie structurale*, *l'esprit* "had both an earlier and later existence as 'the human mind' " but that ever since reading Ryle's *The Concept of the Mind*[59] he had "tried to avoid the term simply because of the extremely wide range of different meanings which ordinary English speakers can manage to attach to it!" By translating "your *esprit* as spirit . . . I wasn't really claiming to translate it at all" and he stated that he was "still out of my depth here." (He might also have added, I suggest, that a popular pocket French–English dictionary glosses *esprit* as "spirit; soul; ghost; mind; intellect; wit; feeling.")

The crux of his own problem, Leach wrote, was how to understand Lévi-Strauss's conception in *Le pensée sauvage* (p. 173) of a mediator between "praxis" and "pratiques." Leach had thought that *esprit* performed this role.

But Lévi-Strauss's equating *esprit* with the mind and its structuring evoked in Leach these thoughts. If the human brain is a machine analogous in some way to a computer then it may be the nature of that machine that it sorts out any information which is fed into it in a "structured" way: "Different human brains can do many different things with the same raw material but whatever they do it will always be structured." If raw nature is orderly, if the "raw material is itself ordered in its very nature *this* ordering is irrelevant to the selector apparatus of the brain which will treat everything it receives as it comes." If following one line of analysis it may be possible on the basis of a broad-based comparison of ethnographic materials to say something general about how all human minds (brains) work, does this finding exhaust all that *esprit* means? Is it contrary to Lévi-Strauss's usage to speak of the *esprit* of a particular culture "in the way that we English might speak of 'the English mind . . . ?' "

If Lévi-Strauss does not use words in this way then clearly Leach admits his own reference to Hegel's *Geist* is quite off-center: "On the other hand it seems to me that some such concept is needed anyway. If *esprit* is what 'causes' myths, we surely need to get further than this to say that even if the Athenians in 1000 BC manipulated their experiences in much the same way as primitive Brazilians in 1962 AD nevertheless the Athenian

[58] Leach to Lévi-Strauss, 21 August 1965. Edmund Leach Papers, The Modern Archive, King's College Library, Cambridge.
[59] Gilbert Ryle, *The Concept of Mind*, London and New York: Hutchinson's University Library, 1949.

'mind' was different from the Bororo 'mind.' " But this difference is located, "not presumably in the *mechanism* of the brain but in the way it has been programmed (through the process of socialization)."

Leach says that in the disputed passage in *Le cru* (as quoted earlier in his 1965 review in the *American Anthropologist*) he thought it was to this difference of social programming rather than to the uniformity of the brain organization that *esprit* might refer. Leach supposed the *esprit* to be a mediator between the brain as natural object and the myth as cultural product, and it is in this sense he thought Lévi-Strauss had placed *esprit* as mediator between praxis and practice.

Throughout this exchange I have been reporting, Leach had adopted a conciliatory and on the whole admiring approach toward someone he recognized as having composed in *Le cru et le cuit* a truly great work of anthropology, and whose methods of decoding inspired his own efforts. But the points he raises, including his alleged mistranslation of *esprit*, would continue to problematize his appreciation and evaluation of Lévi-Strauss's contribution to the interpretation of myths. One critical concern was Lévi-Strauss's increasing tendency in the *Mythologiques* corpus not to address the functionalist and social-contextualist dimensions of specific myths but to embark on a grand comparative exercise spanning space and time in a neo-Frazerian fashion. Another was the role of cultural and social inputs in the programming (or, in contemporary terms, in the construction of the software) of the mind and its production of myths. Leach had trouble attributing everything to the hardwiring of the brain.

I myself as biographer would like to raise some queries and make some comments regarding Lévi-Strauss's framework as stated in his analogy of the three-layered club sandwich. His faith in nature out here in itself as orderly and lawful, which in turn is reflected in the objective findings of physical science, will be considered dated by many famous contemporary expounders of the philosophy and history of science such as Karl Popper (falsifiability but not verification), W. Quine (the indeterminacy of translation), Thomas Kuhn (revolutionary changes of paradigm and the impossibility of a pure sense-data language), Imre Lakatos (succession of research programs), Hilary Putnam (inseparability of the formal method of science from human judgments about the content of science), and the most anti-positivist and relativistic of them, Paul Feyerabend (experimental evidence modeled and manufactured according to theory).

The three orders viewed as homologous present certain difficulties. Even if we grant that the laws of functioning of the human brain are the same as the laws of nature, is the inclusion at the third level of both language and myth as manifesting laws of nature and being on the same level sustainable?

The viewing of language as naturally structured in the brain is in accord with Roman Jakobson's theory of distinctive features at the phonological level, but not applicable to many other aspects of his explication of utterances and other language productions. Natural structuring is in accord with a Chomskyan universalistic view of grammatical and syntactical features of language. But language analysis encompasses horizons and ranges of communication significance outside the limits of the Chomskyan paradigm, such as the extra-semantic, pragmatic, and performative features and implications of speech acts and utterances (as demonstrated in modern socio-linguistics and Austian ordinary language philosophy), or in another mode, the dialogical nature of linguistic communication, the constitutive features of speech genres, and interactions and dynamics of heteroglossia in a linguistic universe, as spelled out by Bakhtin and his followers. One can add to this list another related framework, namely the dynamic relation between discourse and practice as proposed by Bourdieu.

If language, only in some basic respects ordered in nature, has these other ramifications, it is extraordinary that Lévi-Strauss places myth at the same level as his conception of language, and speaks of it as if it were grounded in nature owing little or nothing to the interpersonal and intersubjective communicative features of language and contexts of language use.

As I have remarked in chapter 5, Leach's idealist/normative leanings (while accepting the propensity of the human brain to structure information in certain ways) were partial to the constructed and relativist nature of context-bound collective representations and normative evaluations. Therefore the view that human perceptions and cognitions, on the one side, and interpersonal social discourse, on the other, are to be treated as levels of chaos or noise sandwiched between the physical world and homologously structured brain, language, and myth, must shock both phenomenologists and discourse-practice theorists, among whom we might include the author of *Political Systems of Highland Burma* and *Pul Eliya*. We thus appreciate why Leach would insist on fitting myths into their cultural and social contexts, and on stipulating that structural interpretation should be complementary to functional analyses, and why he maintained that myth as a universal category on a par with language for which the brain is wired is an improbable albeit unprovable claim.

We have seen that it was the concept of *l'esprit* in French that generated the greatest misunderstanding between Leach and Lévi-Strauss. Leach's phenomenological subjectivization of *esprit* and aligning it with culturally distinctive collective representation were in line with a starting point he was fond of stating again and again. Leach's own theory of classification was premised on the thesis that "Raw nature [out there] is a chaos [in continuous process] which can be sorted out any way you choose by the manipulation of language." Human beings impose order on this chaos in terms of their variable perceptions. Order is a human notion by which "relationships *within* culture" are organized and structured.

This may be a sustainable position, but this is *not* the Lévi-Straussian view. (We should remember that *Le pensée sauvage* was dedicated as a riposte to his phenomenologist friend Merleau Ponty.) Lévi-Strauss unyieldingly maintained that raw nature is orderly, or else there would be no physical science.

There were further letters exchanged between Leach and Lévi-Strauss, and I have seen some of them which extended well into 1966. There was a "cordially yours" letter of congratulation dated April 22, 1966 regarding Leach's election as Provost of King's College ("I understand that it is terribly important"). Leach replied (May 2, 1966), apologizing that on account of an operation he had not been able to be present in Chicago "to celebrate your award of the highest world honour in anthropology." He remarked that "the office of Provost of King's is part of the mythology of the local Establishment. It is a great honour for British anthropology that I should have been elected."

There was one other letter by Leach of greater consequence, in response to a letter from Lévi-Strauss which is missing in the archives, that explains his use of Old Testament texts. I guess the text being discussed was Leach's essay "The Legitimacy of Solomon" (1966),[60] and I shall refer to this letter in chapter 11.

However, tensions were building up between them from another quarter and came to a head by 1969. It has to do with the dispute I have already recounted in chapter 5 concerning the ethnography and interpretation of Kachin marriage and social system, a dispute that intermittently smoldered over eighteen years (1951–69). To recapitulate significant dates: Leach had composed in 1945 his essay on "Jinghpaw Kinship Terminology", the relevance of which Lévi-Strauss acknowledged and promised

---

[60] Edmund Leach, "The Legitimacy of Solomon: Some Structural Aspects of Old Testament History," *European Journal of Sociology*, vol. 7, no. 1, 1966, pp. 58–101.

to take into account. In the meantime, Lévi-Strauss's *Elementary Structures of Kinship* was published in 1949 (the original French text). But in the reissue of that text in French in 1967, and in its first English translation in 1969, Lévi-Strauss had contested and commented on Leach's submission in the 1951 essay "The Structural Implications of Matrilateral Cross-Cousin Marriage" and in *Political Systems of Highland Burma* (1954). An embittered Leach then replied in "'Kachin' and 'Haka Chin'. A Rejoinder to Lévi-Strauss" in *Man* in 1969, surely signaling a rupture.

To this festering build up we have to factor in Leach's important writings on Lévi-Strauss's path-breaking procedures and interpretations of "primitive thought" and of mythology. He had declared his unambiguous commitment to "the structural method." But he had also voiced his criticisms of Lévi-Strauss's writings, the importance of which lie in their "innovations and beginnings, not in [their] conclusions."[61]

As his structuralist writings developed and proceeded further, the possibility of a continuing collaborative dialog with Lévi-Strauss receded, and Leach never again affirmed the Lévi-Straussian achievements so fully as he had done before. He increasingly voiced certain qualms about Lévi-Strauss's universalist reductionist assertions regarding the innate propensities of the human mind, his looseness with empirical evidence, and his drifting away from relating the derivation of myth themes and their patterns to their contextual grounding. But this is in the future.

---

[61] Leach, "Telstar and the Aborigines," p. 202.

CHAPTER 10

The comparativist stance: us and them and the translation of cultures

Leach was trenchantly committed to the view that modern anthropology is as much about "us" as it is about "them." He was also vociferous that "there is no class of 'primitive societies' which can be contrasted with 'modern societies' as 'static' is to 'dynamic.' "[1] This is one of the issues on which he registered his dissent from Lévi-Strauss's distinction between the premodern "cold societies," resistant to change, and the modern "hot societies," continuously volatile and changing.

Human beings are generative beings and they have always been in tension with their environment. Other peoples, whether of the past or in the present, are like us in certain features, a principal common feature being similarities in linguistic structure. "Neanderthal man, despite his strange appearance, was a human being like ourselves, a rational creature operating with language in the two crucial domains of metonymy and metaphor." To an audience of archaeologists, Leach enunciated his "universalist" position thus: "Human beings on the Australian continent some 40,000 years ago were rational men like ourselves, for their ancestors had needed to design sea-borne rafts and to exercise forethought."[2]

Leach was committed to the idea that the heart of anthropology is doing fieldwork in alien situations. Ethnography can describe *what* is happening in the location of fieldwork, but it cannot answer *why* a society is this way rather than another way in terms of a causal explanation. All such *why* narratives are endless regressions. Ethnography, however, can say something about *how* events and activities fit together: the old-style functionalism attempted to do this, but its error was that it presented a static equilibrium, not a dynamic account. Social systems are in fact open and not bounded, and never in equilibrium, and the model of an "organism" which social anthropologists at one time took over from

---

[1] Edmund Leach, "Masquerade: The Presentation of the Self in Holi-Day Life," *Cambridge Anthropology*, vol. 13, no. 3, 1989–90, pp. 47–69.
[2] Edmund Leach, "A View from the Bridge," *BAR Supplementary Series*, no. 19, 1977, p. 167.

Durkheim and Radcliffe-Brown mistakenly led them to believe that societies could be and should be imagined as closed systems in equilibrium.

The *how* exercise is akin to deciphering a text in an unknown language. There is an underlying assumption that the text embodies a human constructed order. The approach that an unfamiliar culture encountered in the field is like an alien "text" rests on the assumption that those human beings are like us, and that with effort we can intuit, associate, and analogize, and understand their utterances. Viewing the other as an irrational or noble savage is the result of our Western prejudice.

If the people an anthropologist studies in the field are people like us in the senses mentioned above, then their culture can be viewed as a transformation of ours and ours of theirs. We thus arrive at a point where we have to introduce a conception favored by Leach in the second phase of his theorizing, namely "transformational transcription." In the context of viewing culture as a "text," he associates transformational relations in the ways linguists such as Jakobson and Chomsky used the term. (As we shall soon see, Leach ultimately associated transformation with "mathematical" manipulations, and in his later writings resorted to that label to encompass quite a number of his structuralist demonstrations.) The assumption of similarities between societies in terms of deeper structural relations and permutations in thought patterns is a key proposition that Leach found to be very attractive and intellectually congenial, and it is this affinity that more than anything else attracted him to Lévi-Strauss's formulations on structuralism.

Thus Leach's firm repudiation of evolutionism in its crude nineteenth-century form, and of the quest for "the ultimate primitive who is *quite different* from civilized man," was linked to his commitment to a comparative method which looked for "cross-cultural schema" and transcriptions that spanned both the alleged "primitive societies" and the modern "civilized societies." "My own prejudices go all the other way. The data of ethnography are interesting to me because they so often seem directly relevant to my own allegedly civilized experiences. It is not only the differences between Europeans and Trobrianders which interests me, it is their similarities." He attempted to demonstrate the fruit of this comparativist view when he juxtaposed high Christian theology with "primitive" materials allegedly documenting ignorance of the facts of physiological paternity in his famous essay on "Virgin Birth."[3] Each schema compared entailed

---

[3] Edmund Leach, "Virgin Birth", The Henry Myers Lecture, published in *Proceedings of the Royal Anthropological Institute of Britain and Ireland*, 1966, pp. 39–49. Reprinted in Edmund Leach,

fitting together pieces of ethnographic evidence that came *from a single context* to form a pattern; this contextual stipulation separates the structuralist comparative method from the snippets-of-evidence prodigality of Frazer.

Leach's comparative stance contained a vital reservation when it came to interventions in societies other than one's own. During one of the Johns Hopkins seminars (1976), Leach quietly but firmly said: "In my own society I am a radical; where other societies are concerned I find myself in a double bind. I find it difficult to make judgements about other societies. Freedom and tolerance for me is the recognition and acceptance of differences between cultural systems, not within my own cultural system."[4]

Is there more to anthropology than the quest of understanding other cultures? Referring to the "proselytization" and intervention in other Third World societies and "primitive" societies by missionaries, experts, even Marxists, Leach took a position of personal distance from activism and intervention. He did not approve of "development anthropology" in a Third World country. His participation in activism in his own society was a different matter. He held "'development anthropology' to be a kind of neo-colonialism,"[5] and steered clear of its preoccupations.

The sequence in which the "Virgin Birth" controversy unfolded is as follows. In an essay written in 1961,[6] Leach had referred to the beliefs and attitudes of the Tully River Blacks concerning conception that Roth had reported in 1903. The famous passage by Roth that would later figure in the debate between Leach and Spiro was as follows:

Although sexual connection as a cause of conception is not recognized among the Tully River Blacks so far as they are themselves concerned, it is admitted as true for all animals: – indeed this idea confirms them in their belief of superiority over the brute creation. A woman begets children because (a) she has been sitting over the fire on which she has roasted a particular species of black bream, which must have been given to her by the prospective father, (b) she has purposely gone a-hunting and caught a certain kind of bullfrog, (c) some man may have told her to be in an interesting condition, or (d) she may dream of having a child put inside her.

Genesis as Myth and Other Essays, London: Jonathan Cape, 1969, pp. 85–112. Page references to quotations from this essay apply to the latter publication. The above quotation appears on p. 97.

[4] In thinking about tolerance of cultural differences, Leach was of course not saying that anything goes, such as mass murder, militant racism, genocide, and other crimes against humanity.

[5] Leach, *Social Anthropology*, p. 50. [6] Leach, "Golden Bough."

By whichever of the above methods the child is conceived, whenever it eventually appears, the recognized husband accepts it as his own without demur.[7]

In the above-mentioned essay, Leach had denounced Frazer who ten years later had completely rephrased Roth's report of the beliefs "so as to ridicule the childish ignorance of the natives concerned," and added that it was not a legitimate inference from Roth's statement "to assert that these Australian aborigines were ignorant of the connection between copulation and pregnancy."[8]

In 1966, Melford Spiro wrote that he had found Leach's interpretation implausible, and since Leach had not supported it either with data or with theory, he would hold instead that "the aborigines are indeed ignorant of physiological paternity, and the four statements quoted in Roth are in fact proffered explanation for conception."[9] In riposte to Spiro's challenge, Leach delivered "Virgin Birth" as the Henry Myers Lecture in 1966. Two years later Spiro replied in kind in a long essay.

This locking of horns triggered comments in *Man* (1968) by a number of anthropologists informed by their field knowledge of parts of the wider region. They were Phyllis Kaberry, H.A. Powell, A.M.W. Dixon, K.O.L. Burridge, and David M. Schneider.[10] There was a response from Leach to Spiro and Schneider, and thereafter both protagonists agreed to terminate their debate and to let readers compare their two main papers point by point, checking back to the original evidence.

I consider this debate to be significant enough to merit a review of the principal arguments made by Leach and Spiro, and also the evidence given and commentaries made by the above-mentioned correspondents. The controversy bears on issues of comparative method and translation of cultures, especially how to understand and interpret the statements of "informants" made in a language other than English, and to translate the inferred meanings of those statements into the English language (or some other literary language of the anthropologist). It also raises the issue of the relevance of the anthropologist's presuppositions and orientations that direct his or her questions addressed to informants, and how such "directed" interviews bear on the information elicited,

---

[7] Walter E. Roth, *Superstition, Magic and Medicine*, North Queensland Ethnographic Bulletin, no 5, Brisbane: G.A. Vaughan, 1903.

[8] Leach, "Virgin Birth," p. 87.

[9] M.E. Spiro. "Religion: Problems of Definition and Explanation," in Michael Banton (ed.), *Anthropological Approaches to the Study of Religion*, Association of Social Anthropologists, Monograph 3, London: Tavistock Publications, 1966, p. 112.

[10] This correspondence in *Man*, N. S., vol. 3, nos. 2, 3, 1968, is reported and discussed in due course.

and whether they meaningfully relate to the central concerns of the informants regarding the phenomena being talked about and observed.

What I propose to do now is first present and discuss Leach's 1966 essay on "Virgin Birth," then follow it with the 1968 counter-formulation by Spiro, and conclude with the contributions of the correspondents, and a coda on the implications of the controversy.

LEACH ON "VIRGIN BIRTH"

Leach's essay "Virgin Birth" is forcefully written, and was powerfully delivered (as I can attest as a member of the audience). It shows him in his best formidable form as a debater with whom it is deadly dangerous to cross swords.

The opening paragraph sets out the three themes which logically follow one upon another:

In the first place I review the classic anthropological controversy about whether certain primitive peoples, notably the Australian aborigines and the Trobrianders, were or were not "ignorant of the facts of physiological paternity" when first encountered by early ethnographers. I conclude, as others have concluded, that they were not. Secondly, I take note of the fact that the anthropologist's belief in the ignorance of his primitive contemporaries shows an astonishing resilience in the face of adverse evidence and I consider why anthropologists should be pre-disposed to think in this way. Thirdly, I suggest that if we can once lay aside this prejudice about ignorance and primitiveness we are left with some important problems for investigation. Doctrines about the possibility of conception taking place without male insemination do not stem from innocence and ignorance: on the contrary they are consistent with theological argument of the greatest subtlety. If we put the so-called primitive beliefs alongside the sophisticated ones and treat the whole lot with equal philosophical respect we shall see that they constitute a set of variations around a common structural theme, the metaphysical topography of the relationship between gods and men.[11]

After brushing aside Professor Clifford Geertz,[12] Leach engages with his main adversary in this context, "another American, Professor Melford

---

[11] Leach, "Virgin Birth," pp. 85–86.
[12] Geertz's appearance in this essay is only related obliquely to the theme of this essay, the alleged "primitive ignorance of paternity." Geertz in his well-known essay on "Religion as a Cultural System," in Michael Banton (ed.), *Anthropological Approaches to the Study of Religion*, Association for Social Anthropology, Monograph 3, London: Tavistock Publications, 1966, pp. 1–46, had labeled Leach's approach to religious matters in *Political Systems of Highland Burma* as an expression of "vulgar positivism." Leach proudly defends his espousal of the method of positivism, and defines what he understands by it. This elucidation is relevant for understanding Leach and will be taken up in this essay shortly.

Spiro," who, by common consent in Britain (including the press which had picked up on the wider-than-anthropological implications of the issue under consideration), had in this exchange been punctured by Leach's rapier thrusts.

As mentioned above Spiro had criticized Leach's interpretation in "Golden Bough" of Roth s report on the beliefs and attitudes of the Tully River Blacks concerning sex. Denying that Roth's statement implied ignorance of the connection between copulation and pregnancy, he stated that "The modern interpretation of the rituals described would be that, in this society, the relationship between the woman's child and the clansmen of the woman's husband stems from public recognition of the bonds of marriage, rather than from the facts of cohabitation, which is a very normal state of affairs."[13]

Professor Spiro, reports Leach, had declared himself to be personally persuaded that Roth's statements must mean that the aborigines in question were ignorant of physiological paternity, and had asked "by what evidence or from what inference can it be concluded that . . . the statements mean what Leach claims they mean?"[14] And Leach accordingly replies: "What is really at issue is the technique of anthropological comparison which depends in turn upon the kind or 'meaning' which we are prepared to attribute to ethnographical evidence."[15] The merit of his essays, he declares, "lies in its method."[16]

Leach sets out his method of inference and comparison which he later in the essay identified as "structuralist" *à la* Lévi-Strauss, and contrasts it with the neo-Tylorean perspective, which Frazer further distorted and which Spiro himself now espouses. This is for me the major issue in this essay and worth considering in some detail because it has many entailments.

Earlier, in reply to Geertz's allegation of "vulgar positivism," Leach had said that he was happy to follow that kind of positivism defined as follows. "Positivism is the view that serious scientific inquiry should not search for ultimate causes deriving from some outside source but must confine itself to the study of relations existing between facts which are directly accessible to observation." "Insight comes simply from seeing how the facts fit together." The structural method which Leach advocates "entails fitting the pieces together to form a pattern. *The pieces in each*

---

[13] Leach quotes from "Virgin Birth", p. 87.   [14] Leach, "Virgin Birth," p. 87.
[15] Ibid., p. 88.   [16] Ibid., p. 86.

pattern must come from a single context and we cannot accept the technique of Frazer's comparative method where snippets of evidence are drawn from here, there and everywhere" (emphasis added). Of course we do not have to describe all the evidence from every context: "Our aim is still comparative; we want to distinguish the variety of forms in which a single ethnographic pattern can manifest itself and then examine the nature of these variations."[17]

What then is Spiro's method? "He believes that explanation consists of postulating causes and ultimate origins for the facts under observation."[18] And his neo-Tylorean naivete consists in not simply taking an ethnographer's report that "members of X tribe believe that . . ." as an orthodoxy, a dogma; Spiro and all neo-Tyloreans desperately want to believe that "dogma and ritual must correspond to the inner psychological attitudes of the actors concerned."[19]

That Spiro's procedure is mistaken is illustrated by this acute and witty example:

We need only consider the customs of our own society . . . For example, a high proportion of English girls go through the *rite de passage* of a Church of England marriage service. In the course of this the husband gives the girl a ring, her veil is removed, her flowers are thrown away, a priest lectures her on the importance of child bearing, and she has rice poured over her head – a set of performances roughly analogous to those reported by Roth of the Tully River Blacks. But all this tells me absolutely nothing about the inner psychological state of the lady in question; I cannot infer from the ritual either what she feels or what she knows. She may be an outright atheist. Alternatively she may believe that a church marriage is essential for the well-being of her future children. Certainly her ignorance of the precise details of the physiology of sex is likely to be quite as profound as that of any Australian aborigine. On the other hand, the English marriage ritual does tell the outside observer a great deal about the formal social relations which are being established between the various parties concerned, and this is true of the Australian case also.[20]

Leach follows this with a footnote which is worth citing in full because it dramatically highlights the difference from, and the futility of Spiro's pursuit as he sees it:

Spiro maintains that the fact that a set of ritual data are structured in a manner which is directly parallel to a set of social relations is of no relevance unless we have direct evidence that the actors are consciously or unconsciously aware of

[17] Ibid., p. 86.   [18] Ibid., p. 88.   [19] Ibid., p. 88.   [20] Ibid., pp. 88–89.

the significance of this symbolism. Instead of looking for patterns in the way that people behave Spiro would adopt the naive procedure of asking the actor why he believes as he does – "and unlike some anthropologists, I believe him." If Spiro tries this out in the case of English marriage procedures he will get some astonishing results. These rituals are, as it happens, structured in an extremely clear and well-defined way, but not one bride in a thousand has an inkling of the total pattern.[21]

I do not intend in this exposition to report the details of Leach's coverage and assessment of the plentiful commentary surrounding Roth's original ethnographic report (much of which Leach alleges Spiro seems not to have consulted), or his arguments for asserting by reference to the earlier texts of Hartland and Roth, Malinowski's reports on Trobrianders, and the subsequent modern ethnographies by Meggitt on the Walbiri (1962) and Powell on the Trobrianders (1951), that "the aborigines were not 'ignorant about the facts of paternity' in any simple sense, but that the balance of evidence has *always* been that way."[22]

I do, however, think it is important to review why Leach thinks "a long line of distinguished anthropologists, which includes Frazer and Malinowski as well as Professor Spiro, have taken the opposite view," and why Spiro, manifesting a typical attitude, is "positively *eager* to believe that the aborigines were ignorant" while at the same time displaying "an extreme reluctance to believe that the products of aboriginal thought can be structured in a logical way."[23] Leach's explanation either anticipates or aligns itself with the early formulations of the "colonialist" critique,[24] and is in advance of some of the later neo-Marxist and "postmodern" commentary.

Leach asserts there is a long tradition of attributing ignorance to a native, which amounts to saying he is childish and superstitious, and incapable of logical rationality. When Spiro writes that "Religion persists because it has causes – it is caused by the expectation of satisfying desires,"[25] he takes the view that religious beliefs and rites including magic are obviously irrational but persist because they perform certain psychological and social functions; "he is simply rephrasing the old Frazerian argument that hope springs eternal in a context of total illusion."[26] It is interesting that Frazer and the neo-Tyloreans apply these

[21] Ibid., p. 120.   [22] Ibid., p. 91.   [23] Ibid., pp. 91–92.
[24] I have in mind here such texts as those written by Hymes and Talal Asad which I discuss below, in chapter 16.
[25] Spiro, "Religion," p. 177.   [26] Leach, "Virgin Birth," p. 92.

canons only to *primitive* contexts, but themselves participate in rituals without attributing to themselves a commitment to superstitious beliefs. A case in point is Frazer's presence during the nightly recital of grace in Trinity College Hall. Grace in a college hall functions as a "sign" (and not a "cause") saying that the meal is about to begin or end. If the university ordinances say that young men obtain degrees because they sit examinations, this does not mean that Cambridge undergraduates do not know that prior knowledge is required to pass exams. Therefore why not accept that "the relationship between ritual and copulation in aboriginal theories about the causes of pregnancy appears to be of a strictly analogous kind?"[27]

Leach's subsequent elucidations in the rest of the essay are predicated on two important propositions which are the hallmark of the anthropology he practiced:

1. Western scholars should apply the same standards of rationality and credibility that they attribute to the thought of their own society to the thought of the "natives" and "primitives"; double standards are indefensible.
2. You won't get anywhere by applying canons of rationality to principles of faith; while the religious person may claim the validity of "religious truths," anthropologists, as social analysts and not theologians, can only view "non-rational theological propositions . . . as data not as explanations."[28]

Thus, if certain groups such as the Trobrianders have persuaded their ethnographers that they were ignorant of the facts of life, then it is because that ignorance was for these people a *kind of dogma*. This same judgement applies and must apply to the assertions of miraculous birth of divine or semi-divine heroes that are characteristic of the mythologies of "higher civilizations." Take the myth of the virgin birth in the Christian context: it does *not* imply ignorance of the facts of physiological paternity; it serves to reinforce the dogma that the virgin's child is the son of God. Furthermore, the Christian doctrine of the physical-spiritual paternity of God the Father does not preclude a belief in the sociological paternity of St. Joseph, and in Jesus' pedigree in the direct line of patrilineal descent from David *through Joseph*.

What the Frazer–Hartland generation of anthropologists were guilty of is the adoption of two mutually inconsistent attitudes to these stories.

---

[27] Ibid., p. 93.   [28] Ibid., p. 93.

Where they come from present-day "primitive" people they are obviously survivals from their earlier primitive stage of ignorance. But the theology of the "higher religions" manifesting similar patterns was not amenable to anthropological investigation at all: the five volumes of Hartland devoted to the discussions of virgin birth contain scarcely a single reference to Christianity, and the corresponding volumes of *The Golden Bough* by Frazer "make no attempt to fit the details of Christian theology into a cross-cultural schema which includes 'primitive' materials."[29]

Leach thinks that the quest for the ultimate primitive who is *quite different* from civilized man, which appeals strongly to certain anthropologists, is a legacy deriving from the evolutionary theories in their crude nineteenth-century form. A case in point is the conjectural reconstruction of McLennan and Morgan, who began their fantasy with the promiscuous mating of early humans, which dictated the recognition of kinship through females. From there the next stage was predicated to be systems of matrilineal descent, and that the ignorance of physiological paternity must have prevailed in their original contexts of formation.[30] The ethnographers of Australian aborigines in their quest for the ultimate primitive imagined they had discovered a fossilized living specimen of primeval man who still manifested the primeval ignorance of physiological paternity.

In the course of his exposition, Leach suggests a correlation that is a masterly deconstruction of the projection of imperialist and colonialist presuppositions on to the colonized and inferiorized peoples subject to different strands of Christian dogma.

The Christian myth is comparable with a social system that is essentially patriarchal, in which it is taken for granted that the rulers are so vastly superior to the ruled that class difference almost ossifies into caste, a society in which they will graciously take slave concubines and elevate their sons to the ranks of the elite. Such societies have in fact repeatedly emerged in Christendom, notably in Byzantium and eighteenth-century Brazil, both countries where the cult of the Virgin was exceptionally well-developed ... it does seem to be a striking feature of Catholic colonialism (which distinguishes it sharply from the Protestant variety) that the rulers, with their bias towards Mariolatry have tended to pull their half-caste sons into the ranks of the elite. In contrast, the Protestant colonists who generally speaking tend to reject the myth of the Virgin Birth have always pushed their bastards into the ranks below, insisting that

[29] Ibid., p. 95.   [30] Ibid., p. 97.

the status of ruler-god is exclusive to the pure-blooded. God and Jesus fit well enough into the English Public School ethos; the Virgin-Mother has no place at all.[31]

This seeming diversion in fact recursively relates to the alleged ignorance of paternity among certain primitives.

The British nineteenth-century evolutionary anthropologists were mostly Presbyterian Scots soaked in a study of the classics and sharing, as far as one can judge, most of the paternalistic imperialistic values characteristic of the English ruling class of the period. Their theories reveal a fantasy world of masterly men who copulated indiscriminately with their slave wives who then bore children who recognized their mothers but not their fathers.[32] This fantasy had some indirect resemblance to American chattel slavery, but bears no resemblance whatever to the recorded behaviour of any known primitive society or any known species of animal. It was justified by *a priori* reasoning . . . The result was a theory appropriate to Protestant imperialists.

McLennan's arguments were accepted by his friend Robertson-Smith who passed them on to Frazer who passed them on to a host of admiring ethnographic correspondents. The whole argument was recapitulated in quite explicit form by Hartland and swallowed hook, line and sinker by Malinowski . . . back in 1913.[33]

We have to finally address the question as to what kind of theoretical construction Leach would offer in place of the long line of Victorian to Spiro-type (mis)understanding of primitive ignorance of paternity and the Christian dogma of virgin birth. Leach offers the results of what he elsewhere calls his method of "cross-cultural transcription" via structuralist "transformational" analysis. To recall the procedure: one seeks to fit the pieces together to form a pattern; the pieces in each pattern must come from a single context; patterns so derived from separate but parallel contexts can then be compared to see the nature of their variations. as possible transformations of one another.

Let us concentrate on one comparison in the essay. We have earlier seen the pattern of signs Leach put together with regard to the Christian dogma of virgin birth: the virgin's child is the son of God; the physical-spiritual paternity of God the father coexists with the sociological paternity of Joseph. The split between *pater* and *genitor*, and also between descent and filiation, enters the dogma that the child is divine

---

[31] Ibid., pp. 99–100.
[32] See John F. McLennan, *Primitive Marriage*, London: Quaritch 1865, chapter 8.
[33] Leach, "Virgin Birth," p. 101.

rather than human. But there is more: "In the theology of Christianity it is not sufficient that Jesus as mediator should be subsequently both human and divine, Mary must *also* function as a mediator and must therefore have anomalous characteristics when considered as a human being. What could be more anomalous than a human being who is sinless and a mother who is a virgin?"[34]

Leach compares this with the ethnography concerning South Indian "temple prostitution," misreported by Frazer, and aspires to show the merits of the structuralist procedure "by rescuing Frazer's suppressed evidence from oblivion."[35] His terse comparison is worth reproducing in full:

The locale is south Kanara. As in neighbouring Kerala most of the ordinary castes are matrilineal. The Brahmans are patrilineal and consider this fact to be an index of their social superiority. The original account comes from Francis Buchanan writing in 1801. He tells us that respectable married Brahman women when widowed or neglected by their husbands might become wives of the deity. The marriage rite consisted simply of eating some of the rice which had been offered to the deity. If the woman then chose to live in the temple she had the status of a sort of priestess and was fed and clothed at the temple's expense. She was free to have sexual relations with any Brahman but ordinarily became the concubine of a person of high standing such as a government official. Her children belonged to a respectable section (Stanika) of a special caste called Moylar. Women of non-Brahman caste could take up a similar profession but had to live outside the temple; their children also were Moylar but of an inferior grade. Within the general caste of Moylar there were a number of distinct endogamous sub-groups. Succession among all Moylar was from father to son, but each resulting patrilineage followed the caste custom of its matrilineal founding ancestress. The ordinary Brahmans, while professing to despise the Moylar, in fact behaved towards them as if they had high ritual status.

In this case the mother is a widow, the legal wife of a god. She is made pregnant by the action of a human being. The son is the founder of a patrilineal descent line originating in his mother but having status qualities derived from the mother's divine husband. Although the mother and the physiological father may both be Brahmans, the son is not legally related to either of them since he is of separate caste. This last detail creates complications and the theory that the Moylar son should rate higher than the Brahman father is disputed.

Taken together these facts add up to a pattern of some complexity. But notice how the Christian data form a very similar pattern with all the elements reversed.

[34] Ibid., p. 98.   [35] Ibid., pp. 104–6.

In the Christian case the mother is a Virgin not a widow. She is the legal wife of a human being, not of a god. The Son is the last not the first member of his patrilineal line. Although the mother and the legal father are both human beings the son is substantially related to neither of them since he is a god. This last detail creates complications and the theory that the mother is a lower order of being than the Son is disputed.[36]

Leach also refers to Australian and Trobriand[37] cases where some of the same variables occur in different combinations, and intimates the possibility of the same variables occurring in new combinations in Attis/Adonis mythology.

He himself would identify the beliefs or assertions considered in this essay as a species of religious dogma, which relates not so much to the ordinary matter-of-fact world of everyday events as to metaphysics. So much is clear when Christians say they "believe" in the doctrine of virgin birth, and their doctrines are compatible with positions of extreme philosophical sophistication. He hints at some human propensities to set up cosmological schemes in terms that we can more or less anticipate, given his previous favored tack. The "religious truths" are formulated in terms of the relation between the physical and the metaphysical, the "here and now" and the "other", and the relations between them, imaged in various ways – in terms of descent, ancestors versus descendants, or in terms of power and class status, gods versus imperfect man. But since disjunction and separation between the two worlds is cosmologically incomplete and unsustainable, there must also be links of connection, continuity, and mediation, such as dogma of virgin birth. Leach is careful to indicate that he can merely point to similarities in the theology of primitive as well as sophisticated societies, but he is not offering any *causal* explanation for their generation.

Further consideration of other essays relating to biblical and other Christian materials that will be discussed in later chapters will give us more indications of how Leach sees the structuring of dogma and mythical narratives as "religious truths," which have to be distinguished from alleged "historical truths" ("what really happened") and from alleged experimentally verified universal "scientific truths."

---

[36] Leach's source for Buchanan is John Pinkerton, *A General Collection of the Best and Most Interesting Voyages and Travels in All Parts of the World*, 17 vols., London: Longman, Hurst, Rees & Orme, 1808–14, vol. 8, p. 749.

[37] Leach, "Virgin Birth," pp. 104–6.

SPIRO'S COUNTER-FORMULATIONS

Spiro replied in 1968 to Leach's critique in a long but ponderous essay entitled "Virgin Birth, Parthogenesis, and Physiological Paternity: An Essay in Cultural Interpretation."[38] I shall select what I consider to be the main points made in an attempted rebuttal of Leach.

"Contrary to Leach's claim, Sharp and Malinowski, Kaberry and Austin, and most of the others who contend that the natives are ignorant of physiological paternity, do not claim it to be an *inference* based on the Australian cultural belief which they recorded; they claim, rather, that – the cultural belief aside – it is an *empirical finding*."[39] On the basis of their fieldwork inquiries "they concluded that the personal beliefs of the social actors corresponded to the cultural beliefs which they had been taught." For Spiro the reported belief is an "ethnographical fact," not an "ethnographical inference." However, in a footnote, realizing his vulnerability, Spiro admits, "All 'facts', to be sure, are inferences. 'Facts' obtained through anthropological interviews rest on a number of inferences concerning the reliability of our interviewing instruments, the motivation and veracity of our informants and so on. But to the extent that this is so, the factual basis for Australian conception belief is no less suspect than most other anthropological 'facts.' "[40]

To Leach's attribution of racist ideology to his opponents who ascribe "intellectual inferiority" to the native Australians, Spiro counters that while Leach argues that "ignorance is the opposite of rationality," on the contrary, ignorance is the opposite of knowledge (not rationality), and "the premiss ignorant = irrational is not only semantically false, but is culturally and historically absurd." (For example, on Leach's premise, Europeans were irrational until the nineteenth century because they were ignorant of human evolution.) Spiro enumerates four criteria for judging whether a belief is rational or irrational – whether it is validly deduced from some axiom, whether it violates inductive logic, whether it violates the law of contradiction, and whether it contravenes reliable knowledge or is empirically absurd. Spiro totally supports Ashley Montagu's (1937)[41] conclusion that of all the possible reasons which have been offered "for the limitations in Australian knowledge between coitus and conception, none includes faulty logic."[42] Spiro adds: "To be sure, this conception theory is false; but to hold a false belief is not in itself

---

[38] Melford E. Spiro, "Virgin Birth, Parthogenesis, and Physiological Paternity: An Essay in Cultural Interpretation," *Man*, (n.s.), vol. 3, no. 2, pp. 242–61.
[39] Ibid., p. 243.   [40] Ibid., p. 243.   [41] Ibid., p. 245.   [42] Ibid., p. 245.

irrational unless it violates the four [logical] criteria mentioned above."[43] Spiro concludes: "It is not true that those anthropologists [such as Roth, Malinowski, Kaberry, Spiro] who believe that the aborigines are ignorant of physiological paternity either view their ignorance as childish, or view them as intellectually inferior."[44]

It suits my purposes better to rearrange the order of Spiro's presentation by considering first his treatment of the Christian case and later that of the Australian/Melanesian evidence.

The argument from the Christian evidence

Leach had cited the virgin birth doctrine among Christians, and more generally the attribution of magical birth to heroes and gods in the religions and myths of "higher," especially Christian, civilization, as doctrines not taken to imply ignorance of physiological paternity in Christendom, and asked why then should ignorance of physiological paternity be inferred from reports of magical conception among Australians?

Spiro charges Leach with an obvious fallacy in his analogy for "he is comparing *ordinary* births among the Australians with the births of gods and heroes – *extraordinary* births – among Europeans." In the case of virgin birth among Christians, their dogma holds that the birth of Jesus "was a miracle," thereby making the reverse claim that "denies that the norm of procreative conception applies in his case." Furthermore, Spiro charges that the Christian dogma asserts that Jesus had no *human* genitor, while the Australian belief is not about virgin birth but about non-procreative births (the entry of an already formed spirit child into the vagina). The Christian double paradox is that a virgin conceives procreatively. There is much other circling by Spiro around the theme of the inappropriateness of Leach's analogy, but his own exegesis leads to a surprising conclusion. The Christian dogma of virgin birth is "abnormal," "extraordinary," "not rational but irrational," "absurd," and "to believe in the absurd requires a leap of faith."[45] Thus Spiro, who argues (as we shall see in the next section) that the Australian conception beliefs were "false" but not irrational (since they reason logically), now concludes that Christians believe "irrationally" and make claims beyond their normal reasoning. (This judgment, of course, cannot be the formulation of Christians.)

---

[43] Ibid., p. 245.   [44] Ibid., p. 245.   [45] Spiro, "Virgin Birth," pp. 250–51.

The Tully River conception beliefs, as interpreted by Leach, were stating that "the relationship between the woman's child and the clansmen of the woman's husband stems from the public recognition of the bonds of marriage . . . The virgin birth dogma, besides asserting that God is Jesus' father, also, as two of the synoptic Gospels (Matthew and Luke) say, provides Jesus with a pedigree which places him in the direct line of patrilineal descent from David through Joseph."[46] Spiro makes out as if Leach is interpreting the virgin birth *only* in the latter sense. Aside from this distortion, Spiro offers the alternative reading which he says is in line with the majority of the Church Fathers, that the function of the Davidic genealogy is not to assert that Joseph is the sociological father but to legitimize the Christian claim that Jesus is not only savior (=God), he is also Christ (=Messiah), thereby meeting the requirement in Judaism that the Messiah is a patrilineal descendant of David. Spiro as commentator suggests that Christian theologians have never solved the "dilemma and difficulty" posed by the assertion that Jesus is savior god and is also Christ (Messiah). I do not wish to enter this theological fray, except to say that orthodox Catholicism has firmly held that Jesus was simultaneously both divine and human and reacted against sectarian interpretations that advocated exclusively one side of this question. Leach's own preferred theorizing on the notion of mediator, applied in this instance to the Christian conception of Jesus' virgin birth, would see the necessity for the requirement that Jesus be considered divine and also seem to have a socially recognized father who was a patrilineal descendant of David. Anthropologically, if Joseph did not procreate Jesus, then the Judaic "descent" qualification is transformed to make sense in terms of the concept of sociological paternity and the public recognition of Mary's marriage to Joseph. Otherwise, we have to leave it, as Spiro leaves it, as a non-soluble theological puzzle. It may be said that Leach's solution is that Jesus is a divine (unnatural) child (god) born of an unsullied but married mother, which outcome legitimates his (legal) status.[47]

The argument from the Australian and Melanesian evidence

Spiro's citation and discussion of the Australian evidence – many sources are cited – is condensed and not entirely lucid. Leach had stated that

[46] Leach , "Virgin Birth," p. 42.
[47] He states this in reply to David M. Schneider in "Virgin Birth Correspondence," *Man*, (n.s.), vol. 3, no. 1, 1968, p. 129.

there is a "classically established reason" for supposing that the Tully River Blacks were ignorant: "They freely admitted to Roth that the cause of pregnancy in animals other than man was copulation." Spiro counters that if Leach is here asserting that we can best know about people's beliefs about themselves from their beliefs about animals, then on the basis of assertions by Malinowski and Austin for the Trobrianders, and Spencer and Gillin for the Arunta, he would have to concede that these are indeed ignorant of physiological paternity because they deny any procreative basis for animal pregnancy. Moreover, Roth said that if the Tully River Blacks made a distinction between themselves and animals, it signified "their belief of superiority over the brute creation."[48] I must here point out that there is a point at which Malinowski observes that Trobrianders are aware that their domesticated female pigs produce piglets because of copulation with wild boars who roam in the bush. Lauriston Sharp, affirms Spiro, states repeatedly that the Yir-Yoront are literally ignorant of physiological paternity. Spiro denies that most of the "recent ethnographers" who Leach claimed supported him, do not do that. They support Spiro whose citation (1937) of authorities is in places partial.[49] While Warner supports Leach, the evidence of others such as Stanner and Meggitt is confused or it is not possible to separate from their statements the beliefs of former generations from contemporary data. Roheim (1932), the psychoanalyst, asserted that following initiation Australians (men) repress their awareness of physiological paternity and render it unconscious.[50] (So the question remains: if Australians on a conscious level are "ignorant" through repression, does the evidence support Leach about "dogma" or Spiro about "ignorance"?)

The reporting of Malinowski was, as is well known, that the Trobrianderss did not assert physiological paternity; but then, he also reported that the father, as the husband of the mother, actually tended the child warmly and thereby even "shaped" his physical features to look like him. And

---

[48] Spiro, "Virgin Birth," p. 246. Roth in fact said something significant which Spiro misses, stating that "although sexual connection as a cause of conception is not recognized among the Tully River Blacks so far as they themselves are concerned, it is admitted as true for animals." Roth, *Superstition*, p. 22.

[49] Spiro, "Virgin Birth," p. 247.

[50] W.L. Warner, *A Black Civilisation*, New York: Nauper, 1937; W.E.H. Stanner, "The Daly River Tribes: The Theory of Sex," *Oceania*, vol. 4, 1933, pp. 26–8; M.J. Meggitt, *Desert People*, Sydney: Angus and Robertson, 1962; G. Roheim, "Psychoanalysis & Primitive Cultural Types," *International Journal of Psycho-analysis*, vol. 13, 1932, pp. 1–224.

to complicate matters, Malinowski (as Spiro recognizes) did in his 1932 "special foreword"[51] caution his readers to view Trobriand conception beliefs within the total context of Trobriand culture – a piece of advice that is in line with Leach's interpretive strategy. "Nowhere in this foreword, however, does he *retract* anything he had previously written about their beliefs," points out Spiro, and seals it with a 1937 statement by Malinowski which fully affirmed the verdict of Ashley Montagu that "in Australia practically universally... [that] pregnancy is regarded as causally unconnected with intercourse will... remain the ultimate conclusion of science."[52] But there is other commentary on Malinowski's position that problematizes his reporting, as we shall see, when we review Powell who worked among the Trobrianders, and who reports Malinowski as expressly stating "in the Special Foreword to the third edition of *Sexual Life* (pp. xxi–xxii), 'that previous publications notwithstanding he had not intended to commit himself one way or another in the matter of Kiriwinian clinical knowledge.' "[53] Was Malinowski then reporting only their official dogma?

Explicating the Trobriand view takes an interesting turn when we try to consider what Reo Fortune had to say, and the contrary inferences Leach and Spiro draw from it. What is one to make of Fortune's observation that when he accompanied a party of Dobuans to the Trobriands and tried to arrange a debate, the Dobuans became angry with him and turned their heads to the wall? Fortune attributed the Dobuan behavior to the fact that the two parties had quarrelled about their respective theories in the past and had no desire to revive the dispute.[54] Spiro charges that Leach was wrong to infer that the debate was about the Trobrianders' "doctrine" concerning conception theory. But it seems to me relevant to recognize that the Trobrianders were aware of the Dobuans' theory of the procreative role of the father, a theory that was an alternative to their own. From Leach's point of view, the dogma of masculine irrelevancy to conception that the Trobrianders held is partly to be understood in the context of the overall structural relationship "between the population of Kiriwina and that of Dobu."[55]

---

[51] B. Malinowski, *The Sexual Life of the Savages in Northwestern Melanesia*, 3rd edition, with special foreword, London: Ron Hedges, 1932.

[52] M.F. Ashley Montagu, *Coming into Being among the Australian Aborigines*, London: Routledge, 1937.

[53] H.A. Powell, "Virgin Birth Correspondence," *Man*, n.s., vol. 3, no. 4, 1968, p. 651.

[54] Reo F. Fortune, *Sorcerers of Dobu: The Social Anthropology of the Dobu Islanders of the Western Pacific*, rev. edn, London: Routledge & Kegan Paul, 1963, p. 329.

[55] Leach, "Virgin Birth Correspondence," *Man* (n.s.), vol. 3, no. 4, 1968, pp. 655–56.

The last portion of Spiro's essay is devoted to laying out "two different but equally valid interpretations" for Australian conception beliefs that are "ignorant of physiological paternity." He labels both as "functional" interpretations in contrast to Leach's "structural interpretation."

A first interpretation, deriving from Malinowski, is that the basis for the ignorance is "cultural." Since they do not know the causal relationship between sexual intercourse and conception, the Australians enunciated in default of a procreative explanation a non-procreative theory, "the function of [which] message is cognitive-explanatory, and the motivational basis for the natives' belief is the intellectual curiosity concerning otherwise inexplicable phenomena ... which is of central concern."[56] The sociological basis for paternity ("patrilateral filiation") *contra* Leach "is neither the message nor the function of the spirit-child theory";[57] it is "the unintended (though recognized) function" of the natives' ignorance.

Although from Spiro's point of view this interpretation poses no conceptual difficulties, it raises the serious ethnographical problem that "since most peoples seem not to be ignorant of physiological paternity," it is difficult to understand why the Australians did not discover the causal link.

Faced with this puzzle Spiro formulates his second functional interpretation, which, deriving from Ernest Jones,[58] argues that "the basis for the natives' ignorance is not cultural but psychological; i.e., it is based not on the absence of biological knowledge, but on its rejection."[59] To cut a long story short, Spiro, following the standard Freudian theory of a universal typical Oedipal conflict, suggests that the natives' procreative ignorance is motivated by a wish to deny physiological paternity engendered by the resentment over the father's punitive authority and/or by jealous rivalry with him for the love of the mother. This raises a conflict that is painful and charged with fear and guilt. There are different ways of coping with this conflict; Westerners ordinarily repress this hatred, but in the Australian case, the spirit-child theory, whatever the basis for its origin might have been, now serves as one of its functions "to

---

[56] Spiro, "Virgin Birth," p. 255.

[57] Leach rejects Spiro's attribution of "patrifiliation" to his theory (it is Fortes's term, not his), and says that "the Trobriand dogma, as repeatedly affirmed by Malinowski, is that the mother's husband is an affine and not a pater or a genitor in the sense that these terms are used." Leach, "Virgin Birth Correspondence," *Man*, no. 4, p. 656. Spiro "Virgin Birth," p. 255.

[58] Ernest Jones, "Mother-Right and the Sexual Ignorance of Savages," *International Journal of Psycho-Analysis*, vol. 6, 1924, pp. 109–30.

[59] Spiro, "Virgin Birth," p. 257.

resolve the natives' Oedipal conflict by providing them with the cognitive (cultural) basis for denial." Moreover, it serves a wish-fulfilling fantasy that the boy taking his father's place is his own genitor. The function of this theory is "ego-integrative" because it resolves an emotional conflict by comparison with the first interpretation in which the theory's function is cognitive for it satisfies an intellectual need.

In order to be fair to Spiro, I have taken time to summarize his two interpretations, but as one could have anticipated, Leach summarily dismissed them on the ground that there can be no simple causal explanation, *functional or motivational*, as to why the theory or dogma originated, and why it is maintained and perpetuated. (Spiro himself admitted that so far as he knows the evidence is lacking for testing the truth of his interpretations.) Leach also held that "the anthropologist has absolutely no information about what is inwardly felt by any professed believer,"[60] and rejected any attempt to characterize the "state of mind" behind the profession of faith. Spiro, in turn, held that Leach had similarly no evidence for testing the truth of his structural interpretation, but we have to recognize that Leach never pursued the causal explanation of the Australian dogma; he claimed he merely showed with close attention to contexts the structural and positional relations between the components of complexes and between the patterning of complexes. But he did postulate or infer "functional relations" between dogmas and their social and political contexts of action. This, of course, was not Spiro's approach to the "functional" interpretation of cultural and social phenomena.

Both Spiro's functional interpretations are speculative about origins and causes and merit the label of "just so" stories. It is also curious that in his psychoanalytic narrative he ignores Malinowski's famous attempt to demonstrate that the Freudian theory of Oedipal conflict was not applicable in its canonical form to the Trobriand matrilineal situation where the mother's brother rather than the father exercised the major part of "punitive authority," and a boy, who had mostly benign relations with his father, had to move before reaching adulthood to the residential location of his mother's brother. The whole drama of simultaneously loving and hating the father, and the painful emotional guilt generated and so on, seems so alien to the ethnographic reporting of actual family life witnessed and recorded by Malinowski and his successors who worked in the Trobriands. Ernest Jones, as we have remarked before, repudiated

---

[60] "Virgin Birth Correspondence," p. 655.

Malinowski's theorizing and put an end to Malinowski's flirtation with psychoanalytic theory.

THE CORRESPONDENCE ON THE SUBMISSIONS OF LEACH AND SPIRO

It is relevant that we recognize Phyllis Kaberry's voice in this controversy. She is the only anthropologist taking part in the virgin birth correspondence who wrote reaffirming that her fieldwork in Australia in 1934 and 1935–36 provided evidence that at least some of the Australian tribes were ignorant of physiological paternity, and whose findings supported Spiro's account of their beliefs. Her account of her findings is particularly interesting to ponder because of the cosmological significance of the spirit-child's connection with ancestors, and the nuances of the contribution to the child's procreation and formation provided by its "father" and "mother's husband" (even though his semen does not "cause" its conception).

Following are some excerpts from Kaberry's account of Australian beliefs.

The spirit-children were placed in pools by the Rainbow Serpent in the Time Long Past before there were any human beings ... Conception occurs when one of these enter a woman. Its presence in the food given her by her husband makes her vomit, and later he dreams of it or else of some animal which he associates with it. It enters the woman by the foot and she becomes pregnant. The food which made her ill becomes the conception totem of her child.[61]

According to Kaberry this implies that "the husband of the woman is the social father of the child and as a rule its spiritual genitor." Even if another man gives the woman the conception totem, he "will not dream of the spirit-child or have access to the woman sexually, or exercise any rights over the child, he will take the 'country' and the totems of the mother's husband."

Kaberry sticks to her point that the aborigines whom she studied, "despite over 30 years' contact with the whites, still had no idea of the true relation between sexual intercourse and conception." Yet she adds, the aborigines held that only after puberty did a woman conceive,

---

[61] Phyllis Kaberry, "Virgin Birth," *Man* (n.s.), vol. 3, no. 2, 1968, pp. 310–13.

and then "only when a man, generally her husband, prepared the way for the entry of the spirit-child." " 'Him make 'em road belonga picanniny' " but his semen remained in the vagina and had nothing to do with the child. Many women said, "the semen entered the uterus, and that the embryo floated in it 'like a water lily' as one expressed it." One argument provided against the Western theory of the semen's role in procreation is that a woman may sleep frequently with a man and yet not conceive (an infallible observation which other peoples in the region also made).

Kaberry remarks that, "The attitude towards half-castes should prove a crucial instance, but here again the system proved water-tight. It was asserted that the white man was the father since the woman was living with him at the time and he must have found the spirit-child." And the resemblance of the child to the white father in colouring and features, was that "too much [the woman] bin sleep alonga him" – that is that the constant proximity of the man externally moulded the child within the womb.

So what do we make of this Australian discourse? The ultimate creator of the spirit-children is the Rainbow Serpent who in the Time Long Lost placed them in the various pools; the spirit-children became human beings through the circumstances described before, and the pools and surrounding locality where the parents found them while they camped become their "own small country." The father's role, though not procreative, was regarded as facilitating the child's birth and its growth. "He bestows on [the child] its rights to his country and his dream totem."[62] Kaberry persists in describing the child's relationship with the father as "a derivative" one: he is "the husband of the child's mother," his "social father."

What puzzles me about Kaberry's exegesis is the resistance to combining all the features of Australian beliefs she reports into a complex whole, such that granting the foundational role of the Rainbow Serpent as the producer of the spirit-children is supplemented by the facilitating role of the father, through whose actions (e.g. the food he gives the woman, which she vomits, and which becomes the conception totem of the child) the child takes human form, and who is necessary in investing it with territorial rights and identity and its "dream totem." (Spiro's discussion does not address these significant features.) So, to echo Leach: why harp

---

[62] Ibid., p. 312.

on the theme of the "ignorance of physiological paternity" among the Australians when their cosmological and social conceptions of the continuity of Australian hordes over time by virtue of the combined "spiritual" actions of a foundational ancestral agent and the social relations between husband and wife, parents and children, give the physical features and social identity of successive generations which reproduce that continuity of society?

Leach restates in his reply to Kaberry his original comment on her evidence: "Kaberry's informants are saying that conception is not predictable in advance but is recognized by certain physiological signs after the event. They say that sex relations are a necessary preliminary to this condition and they say, as do most Europeans, that the fetal embryo has a soul."[63] He continues:

That really is what all this discussion is about. Trobrianders, Australian aborigines, and Englishmen all draw a subtle distinction between physical conception and metaphysical incarnation. It is a distinction which lies at the root of all theology and of most philosophy and, despite Dr. Kaberry's continued faith in her salad days' ethnography, such matters cannot be grappled either by the crudities of pidgin English or the highly selected citation of evidence. The issue is not "the true relation between sexual intercourse and conception," which is just as mysterious to me as it is to any Australian aborigine, but rather the nature of the truth that is being discussed.

We should now listen to the testimony of H.A. Powell who worked among the Trobrianders in the early 1950s.[64] In his contribution to the virgin birth controversy,[65] Powell attempts to clarify by resorting to two levels or frames of reference to the Trobriand statements. One is "the context of contractual interrelation of corporate groups" effected through marriage; alternatively, the context of the structural analysis of Trobriand affinal relationships. The other is the context and "content of their interpersonal relationships."

Powell says that, whatever the Trobrianders' "indigenous clinical knowledge of the facts of reproduction," "the formal dogma of kinship" as expressed in the first structural framework "denies the father

---

[63] "Virgin Birth," pp. 47–48.
[64] H.A. Powell wrote his Ph.D. thesis for the University of London in 1956 entitled "An Analysis of Present Day Social Structure in the Trobriand Islands."
[65] H.A. Powell, "Virgin Birth Correspondence," *Man* (n.s.), vol. 3, no. 4, 1968, pp. 651–56. These quotes are from p. 651.

any status as genitor." For this purpose and this context "the attribution of actual ignorance to the Kiriwinians is irrelevant."

At the same time Powell states that "I was in fact given an account of the reproductive process which is in accordance with beliefs held in many parts of the world (and which diverges from the 'scientifically ac-curate' accounts propagated by mission and other teachers to be *possibly* indigenous),"[66] though he also cautiously concedes that he cannot be certain that it did not derive from European influence. It is in a sequel to this statement in his thesis that the passage quoted by Leach occurs.[67] Powell thus intimates that the context of this second set of expressions is that of "interpersonal relations."

Powell suggests that both versions "are coexistent indigenous beliefs which … by European standards [are] mutually contradictory," and seeks a resolution by relating them "to what Malinowski might have termed different contexts of situation."[68]

Powell does underscore his dissent concerning a statement by L. Austen (1934), and we need to keep Austen in mind because both Leach and Spiro cite him as favoring their views. Austen emphasized the Kiriwinian "belief in the effect of sexual intercourse as a means of check-ing the menstrual flow, which is a necessary condition for conception."[69] This element in Austen's report, says Powell, "accords with an indigenous belief of the kind I recorded; it would seem to indicate that some connec-tion was recognized between sexual intercourse and conception."[70] But Austen then goes on to emphasize the strenuous denials by his informants that the male semen is the quickening agent, in effect denials that the male contributes physically to the forming of his wife's offspring. Powell suggests that these denials are consistent with the "matrilineal dogma" of the formal discourse, but that Austen's official status might have not made him privy to "the women's and children's talk" (of interpersonal re-lations) which does not have to affirm the formal dogma of "ignorance". We may also note here that Leach in reply to Spiro charges Spiro with tendentiously quoting Austen, and ignoring this statement by Austen: "*Until the menstrual flow has ceased, a female cannot conceive; and the monthly flow of menstrual blood is checked by sexual intercourse* [Tambiah's emphasis]. This is an acknowledgment made by all and is an idea found throughout

---

[66] Powell, "Virgin Birth Correspondence," p. 651.
[67] "Virgin Birth," pp. 47–48, note 5.   [68] Ibid., p. 651.
[69] Leo W. Austen, "Procreation among the Trobriand Islanders," *Oceania*, vol. 5, 1934, pp. 102–13. Austen had served as the local Assistant Resident Magistrate in Kiriwina.
[70] Powell, "Virgin Birth Correspondence," p. 651.

Kiriwina. It is not a modern introduction and is handed down from generation to generation."[71]

In his final summing up Powell acknowledges

the potential relevance of the Trobrianders' beliefs about and attitudes towards reproduction to the content of their interpersonal relations ... If from this viewpoint I were pressed on the extent and significance of the Trobrianders' procreative knowledge, I should reply that in matters of personal relationships they believe as though they were aware of physical paternity of some kind, but that in matters of corporate group definition and interrelation, to which the particularly Trobriand institutions of kinship and marriage pertain, they behave as though they were unaware of it. This does not of course preclude the possibility of a "carry-over" or "feed-back" from the one frame of reference to the other. Trobrianders, like other reasonably intelligent people, manipulate their cultural equipment skilfully in the pursuit of their personal preferences.

Thus the formal dogma could well be invoked to justify castration of boars, notwithstanding possible awareness of the advantages of using them for breeding, to justify the immediate preference for castrated porkers; but the recognition of physical paternity, indigenous or introduced, could be, and appears at times to have been invoked to justify a move towards patrilineal inheritance on the European model.

As Austen (1934:113) indicated, ideas vary from sex to sex and individual to individual as well as from situation to situation. There may be, or may have been, some Kiriwinans with extreme views corresponding more or less to the opposed positions of the present protagonists in the revived controversy. I suspect, however, that most could and would, if occasion arose, shift from one set of ideas to the other, or combine them, as occasion indicated; but this would involve the exercise of pragmatic, rather than academic, logic. If so, a combination of the opposed academic hypotheses might explain the total data recorded better than either one of them.

In the last analysis the crux of the academic argument is indeed what constitutes "ignorance" or "knowledge" of the "true facts". That at least some Kiriwinans recognized a connexion, however vague, between copulation and conception is indicated by the notions of "opening the way" and "stopping the menses"; is it not the case that some peoples who are not held to be procreatively "ignorant" are hardly better informed?[72]

Our next witness who participated in the virgin birth correspondence and who has impressive credentials is R.M.W. Dixon.[73] He conducted ten months of intensive linguistic fieldwork among the Tully River Blacks

---

[71] Austen, "Procreation," p. 103.   [72] Powell, "Virgin Birth Correspondence," p. 652.
[73] R.M.W. Dixon, "Virgin Birth Correspondence," *Man* (n.s.), vol. 3, no. 4, 1968, pp. 652–54.

(in 1963–64, with an additional short visit in 1967), the people about whom Roth reported in 1903. Dixon mastered these people's language, Dyirbal, an accomplishment that certainly Roth did not possess, or for that matter, many other reporters who communicate in pidgin.

Dixon recalls Roth's observation that there was the common belief in north Australia that animals and birds were once humans. Dixon, affirming this belief as stated in myths, indicates that it is difficult to reconcile this belief in animals as altered human beings with Roth's statement that "although sexual connection as a cause of conception is not recognized among the Tully River Blacks so far as they themselves are concerned, it is admitted as true for all animals: – indeed this idea confirms them in their belief of superiority over the brute creation."[74]

Dixon then follows a strategy of explication which parallels Powell's regarding the existence of two levels of discourse:

> The fact that animals are believed to be derived from humans might be taken to imply that any belief concerning animals should also apply to humans. It seems that this is the case. In the case of humans there are two levels of belief concerning human conception: these can be referred to as the "basic level of belief" and the "mystic level of belief". The basic level acknowledges the role of copulation in human conception, exactly as in animal conception. The mystic level is that described by Roth (1903:22) and discussed in detail by Spiro. The mystic level of belief may well be the only level normally explicitly acknowledged, the basic level being more implicit. The basic level of belief is for instance implicit in the semantic structure of the language. Thus there is a verb *bulmbinyu* "to be the male progenitor of", that has clear reference to the particular act of copulation that induced a conception.[75]

Dixon proceeds to illustrate how the distinction between mystic and basic levels of belief applies to other discourses as well. One example relates to toothache and rheumatism which at the mystic level are believed to be caused by a small grub and a species of bull ant respectively, but at the basic level are "acknowledged to be types of pain entirely different from those caused by grubs and ants biting. The interested reader may want to study the linguistic data relating to how in discovering that Dyirbal the 'everyday language' differs from a special 'mother-in-law language' used in the presence of certain taboo languages, Dixon finds

---

[74] Roth, *Superstition*, p. 22.   [75] Dixon, "Virgin Birth Correspondence," p. 653.

confirmation of the difference between the mystical and basic levels of belief concerning the cause of toothache."

Dixon concludes his submission in a manner that confirms Leach's formulation:

It can be seen that the mystic level of belief is indeed rather like, in Leach's words (1967:45) "a species of religious dogma; the truth which it expresses does not relate to the ordinary matter-of-fact world of everyday things but to metaphysics". The basic level of belief in each case corresponds to the commonsense knowledge that is common to all human beings. Explicit discussion is normally in terms of mystic belief, but basic belief is implicit in the reasoning, language and actions of the aborigines.[76]

Our next correspondent on the subject of virgin birth is David Schneider who worked among the Yap around 1947 and thereafter and can be relied upon to give some interesting ethnography in his distinctive discursive style.[77] To severely reduce a colorful narrative of Schneider's own dialogs with Yap informants which uncovered new levels of his understanding: the Yap, although exposed to German and Japanese efforts to edify them, held in 1947 that "conception was the reward arranged by happy ancestral ghosts, who intervened with a particular spirit to bestow pregnancy on a deserving woman." Coitus had no bearing on conception as evidenced by the fact that there were well-known cases of promiscuous women who were childless, and the contrary case of a woman with yaws with whom no one would think of sleeping, but who was rewarded by her own ancestral ghosts with two children.

However, the Yap told him that "if you want a sow pregnant you must get her to a boar which has not [been] castrated." It was explained to a much puzzled anthropologist by his Yap informants, who were puzzled by his puzzlement, that "people are not pigs," and there were many differences between them, the fundamental one being that people have ancestral ghosts and pigs do not.

This normative difference between animality and humanity is in itself, of course, significant (as in the other cases we have cited). But Schneider's understanding was seemingly sorely undermined when he discovered, after he left the field, that one of his dogmatic informants had said publicly

---

[76] R.M.W. Dixon, "Virgin Birth Correspondence."

[77] David M. Schneider, "Virgin Birth Correspondence," *Man* (n.s.), vol. 3, no. 1, 1968, pp. 126–29.

that the first child his wife bore had been the result of her incestuous relationship with her brother, and the accuser had been promptly killed by the brother. Schneider surmises that the accuser's phrasing may have become available from the talk of Germans, Japanese, and Americans, and that his "interest in coitus did not include its possible consequences in conception but focused on other consequences."[78]

This last line merits further comment. Schneider throughout his narrative reiterates that his Yap informants (they all seem to be male) showed "indifference" to the question of the relation between coitus and pregnancy, and he makes a comparative statement as to why this question, so important to a Western framework of understandings of the biology and sociology of kinship, does not seem of central significance to the Yap:

For me and for other western Europeans coitus plays the decisive role in conception, and the biological link between father and child (as between mother and child) is held to be, in itself, the basis for the social relationship between them. Hence it is a fundamental condition that we see coitus directly linked to conception, which is directly linked to the set of social bonds which we call the parent–child relationship . . .
  The father–child bond on Yap is explicitly framed in terms of reciprocal care while the mother–child bond is explicitly framed in terms of biological identity. What makes a woman a mother on Yap is that she bore the child. What makes a man a father on Yap is that he provides for his child who later provides for him. Whether the father is biologically linked to his child is quite as irrelevant as is his height, his weight or his accent.[79]

Let me at the conclusion to this section interject a "parallelism" between Australian and Christian conceptions that brings into relief a structural logic. There are grounds for concluding on the basis of testimony provided by certain authors that Australians, Trobrianders, and the Yap New Guinea peoples were aware that in the case of animals male coitus was necessary for causing pregnancy. Their proposition is that in the animal world, procreation requires copulation between male and female animals. This is the "ordinary" state of affairs. By *comparison*, in the human world as opposed to the animal, procreation is by an extraordinary process (the nature of which is complex involving both cosmological and social features). Christians, on the other hand, are by comparison opposing the combined human and animal kingdom, the domain of the "ordinary" processes of human procreation through male and female

---

[78] Ibid., pp. 128–29.   [79] Ibid., p. 128.

copulation, to the kingdom of God who enacts an "extraordinary" feat of "virgin birth." This *relational parallelism* should be borne in mind in making a comparison between Australian and Christian cosmological conceptions.

There are also grounds for inferring, on the exegesis provided by Dixon for the Tully River people and Powell for Kiriwinians, that the natives engaged in at least two situationally different dialogs – the formal "structural" or "mystical," and the "interpersonal" or "basic" – and that the second was not ignorant of physiological paternity. This second observation does not negate the first observation, because there the talk of human conception relates to the context of formal dogma that has structural/institutional implications.

CODA

We have reviewed two rival comparative approaches and interpretations of Australian and Christian conceptions concerning conception and pregnancy. The different formulations, aside from their semantic content and patterning, also have a rhetorical side to them, and in academic circles, as elsewhere, frameworks of knowledge claims are supported or opposed by allies, witnesses, and their "evidence and proofs" on both sides. The anthropological profession is itself not a unified community of practitioners, and the networks of persons and these persons' institutional associations and resources at hand have a significant role to play in which theories and frameworks, and which networks (and "schools" if that term is appropriate), dominate or segment the intellectual scene.

There is no way one can decide whether Leach or Spiro decisively won the debate, but it was my impression at the time the controversy was concluded that many academies in Britain, including the press there which had picked up on the newsworthy features of the exchange, deemed that Spiro had been bested by Leach's rapier thrusts. Although both had appealed to their respective authorities and witnesses, dead and living, if we only counted the correspondents in *Man*, it appears that Spiro had only one supporting him (Kaberry) while the remaining four (Powell, Dixon, Schneider, and Burridge) in varying degrees suggested that beyond the formal dogmatic discourse there was another level of discourse in which the relation between copulation and pregnancy was acknowledged.

An issue that we may consider as emerging from Leach's advocacy is whether the anthropologist (predominantly a Westerner or a person influenced by the Western categories and frameworks) might be engaging in an "asymmetric" comparison (to borrow a term from Latour[80]) which engenders judgments of "ignorance," falsehood, and irrationality that may be simply "a consequence of looking from inside a network [of knowledge] to its outside." Latour criticizes a "sociology of knowledge, that tries to account for non-scientific beliefs, if all questions of irrationality [and falsehood] are merely *artefacts* produced by the place from which they are raised."[81]

In the case of alleged ignorance of physiological paternity among the Tully River Blacks (and certain others), Leach followed certain strategies for understanding their allegedly strange beliefs. One was telling another story built around a similar structure but one that applied to his own Western civilization. Leach offered an analogy to the case of "the Australian aborigines" in the form of virgin birth taken from Christianity. This kind of exercise may well reveal parallel structures of reasoning both within and between cultures and societies.

Another strategy, which Malinowski himself recommended, was to see the unfamiliar reasoning in the contexts of its invocation and application. The more the anthropologist expands the contextual range of a mode of reasoning – to include marriage relations, land and territorial claims, ancestor beliefs and cults, distinctions and overlaps between animals and humans, humans and deities, and so on – the more comprehensible unfamiliar reasoning becomes.

Let me pose a hypothetical case. Suppose a people say that animals reproduce through copulation, but humans don't because they are extraordinary, they are not animals, it is their ancestor spirits who plant spirit-children inside women's wombs, and their living husbands only prepare the way for their birth. But let me follow this line of thought: present-day living human males are alleged not to be responsible for procreating children through copulation with women; but when these men (and women) die they become ancestors, and the longer they exist as ancestors the more potent their capacity to implant spirit-children in women. If we continue along this line of thought, we begin to see a cosmology in which the agency of current live male husbands themselves is *embedded* in an intergenerational process, and the contemporary living

---

[80] Bruno Latour, *Science in Action: How to follow Scientists and Engineers through Society*, Cambridge, MA: Harvard University Press, 1987. Latour says he borrows this term from Bloor.
[81] Ibid., p. 185. Apropos this comment, Mariza Peirano underscores the point that Leach throughout his life practiced "symmetric anthropology" (pers. comm.).

members are seen as part of a long-term persistence and reproduction of groups over time, in which ancestors as well as their successors are the critical links in the chain. When the anthropologist finds that his Tully River Black, or Kiriwinian, or Yap informant is "indifferent to" or does not see the significance of the questions and "facts" of "physiological paternity," he or she may not be aware that what is an imperative preoccupation of a Western investigator, given his or her embedment in a particular conception of kinship, in which physiological paternity is a crucial notion, may be insignificant to a people immersed in another kind of preoccupation focused on the structural continuity and relationships of descent and affinity between groups over time. Another pertinent line of inquiry that falls within the ambit of "structural" inquiry is that groups within a differentiated society, and groups or peoples in contiguous or neighborly relations, may voice contrasting dogmas as markers of difference within a wider arch of recognized discourse.

Anthropologists should be open to the possibility that their comparative question and focus of inquiry may be misplaced and asymmetric, *or* not attuned enough to situations of what Bakhtin called "heteroglossia." This, it seems to me, is the kind of important issue regarding the translation of cultures raised by the virgin birth controversy.

The Spiro thesis accepts that in all known human societies, except the *unique* "Australian aborigines" (and some other like-minded peoples), the relation between copulation and pregnancy was recognized. The thesis of unique "ignorance" of these people however changes when their cosmological conceptions are situated and contextualized in ampler frameworks of discursive understanding as those proposed above, and Australians are thereby seen as being members of a common humanity.

CHAPTER 11

The structural analysis of biblical narratives

Leach found in the Bible a treasure house of narratives, which he construed to be of a mythical nature, and which he found eminently suitable for his kind of structuralist analysis. Fully realizing that he was taking a risk in dealing with Old Testament and New Testament texts which had been subject to a long tradition of commentary by Jewish and Christian scholars, he made a serious effort not only to familiarize himself in detail with the Bible translated into English, but also to study commentarial works of scholars dealing with issues pertinent to his own analysis and interpretation. He was also sensibly aware that his approach to the Bible as a unitary mythological text amenable to his kind of structuralist analysis was at variance with that of biblical scholars who sought to distinguish different textual genres and to identify in the texts what portions were "historical" and what portions were not. He took care to say that he was by no means rejecting these scholarly pursuits or trying to prove them right or wrong. He was doing his own thing, and consequently set out his method of procedure and making inferences and establishing patterns. He was offering a new way of reading the Bible.

It is difficult to find out what the reaction of a range of biblical scholars is to Leach's novel way of reading the Bible. Obviously some of them have read the essays I am going to recount in chapters 11 and 12. But historians and commentators of the Bible, steeped in their own long traditions of framing issues and trying to solve them, while seeing something illuminating in Leach's essays and incorporating piecemeal portions relevant to their writings, are unlikely to embrace his presentations as requiring a necessary, paradigmatic change in their pursuits.[1]

---

[1] Leach himself mentioned the distinguished Judaic scholar J. Neusner, ("The Talmud as Anthropology," Annual Samuel Friedland Lecture, The Jewish Theological Seminary of America, 1979) as commenting favorably on his writings. Jacob Neusner at the time of delivering this lecture was Professor of Religious Studies, The Ungerleider Distinguished Scholar of Judaic Studies, Brown University. And I shall report later in this chapter another supportive view by Professor Abraham Malamat of the Hebrew University of Jerusalem.

On the other hand, most contemporary professional cultural and social anthropologists – there are some notable exceptions, such as Mary
Douglas – have not tried to seriously engage with biblical materials for
the purposes of their own professional writing. They may casually read
Leach's essays, and enjoy his stimulating and thought-provoking submissions, but are unlikely, because of their unfamiliarity with the biblical
"ethnography," to recognize the essays as being vital to, and as illuminating, their own anthropological concerns. Whether after a close reading
of the essays they agree or disagree, or partially agree or disagree, with
Leach is a different matter, but I hope that some of them at least will
closely read them and recognize his continuing relevance.

It may be said that in the latter part of his career Leach was more an
essayist than a writer of books (except for a couple written as introductory texts for pedagogical purposes).[2] His prowess as a forceful stylist and
in posing puzzles to solve was already demonstrated in *Rethinking Anthropology* (1961). In the writings that are discussed in this and later chapters
we see him as an essayist whose compositional strategies and mode of
exposition had been progressively elaborated and sharpened *pari passu*
with his confident capacity to treat grand issues of perennial interest to
the humanities and the social sciences.

"The Legitimacy of Solomon"[3] (subtitled as "Some Structural Aspects
of Old Testament History") was first published in 1966 and is, in my
view, the best essay in the structuralist mode composed by Leach. It is
longer than the usual précis, and he packs into it an enormous amount
of biblical material.

Leach right at the beginning asserts that he is employing an explicitly
Lévi-Straussian procedure, and that he feels "reasonably safe with Lévi-
Strauss' concept of *structure*," but out of his depth "when it comes to
his subtler notion of *esprit*" which appears in many sundry guises in his
writings.[4] Leach takes care to underscore that his essay is "a limited
exercise in certain of Lévi-Strauss' methods."

It is necessary to give notice of one problem about Leach's attempt to
use Lévi-Straussian procedure on biblical materials. Lévi-Strauss himself had been wary of dealing with biblical materials because, as Leach
admits, his narrow definition of myth "makes it appear that the myths of

---

[2] Examples are *Social Anthropology*, Glasgow: Fontana, 1982 and *Culture and Communication*,
Cambridge and New York: Cambridge University Press, 1976.
[3] "The Legitimacy of Solomon" appeared in *European Journal of Sociology*, vol. 7, no. 1, 1966,
pp. 58–101. It was reprinted under the same title in Edmund Leach, *Genesis as Myth and Other Essays*,
London: Jonathan Cape, 1969, pp. 25–83. All references here are to this second publication.
[4] Leach, "The Legitimacy of Solomon." p. 25.

the contemporary Amerindians are cultural products of an entirely different kind from the mytho-historical traditions of the Jewish people in the first century BC. My own view is that this distinction is quite artificial and that the structural analysis of myth should be equally applicable to both the time of men and the time of gods." Apparently Leach makes this declaration also in reference to Paul Ricoeur's challenge that Lévi-Strauss's structuralist method, while applicable to "totemic myths" of primitive peoples with notably thin historical records, may be inappropriate for the study of the Bible which constitutes a sacred history whose chronological axis is fundamental. For the theologian, the significance of the message of the Bible (the *kerygma*) is inseparable from the recognition that the events occur in a particular historical sequence.

Leach reports that Lévi-Strauss has taken a cautious and prudent line in responding to Ricoeur's challenge: "He advances the rather curious proposition that the Old Testament mythology has been 'deformed' by the intellectual operations of Biblical editors and he seems to imply that . . . a structural analysis of such materials must prove to be largely a waste of time."[5] By "deformed," Lévi-Strauss presumably means that "the intellectual operations of Biblical compilers have operated in conflict with the randomized non-intellectual workings of the structure of ancient Jewish culture, thus making the latter indecipherable."[6] Leach brushes aside whatever qualms Lévi-Strauss might have had, and sets out to demonstrate the applicability and meaningfulness of the structuralist procedure.

Lévi-Strauss's skepticism is perhaps not as formidable an obstacle as that which historians of the Bible and theologians of Christianity and Judaism might present on the basis of their specialist knowledge of interpolations and the "historical" intentionalities of those whose compositions constituted the Bible. Leach makes a spirited defense of his approach. He firmly stated his assumptions in another essay, which holds in the present context as well: "I take it for granted that none of the stories recorded in the Bible, either in the Old Testament or in the New, are at all likely to be true as history. In its present form the Bible is a much edited compendium of a great variety of ancient documents derived from many sources, but the end product is a body of mythology, a sacred tale, not a history book."[7] Leach is aware that

---

[5] *Genesis as Myth*, p. 114, footnote 18.   [6] "The Legitimacy of Solomon," pp. 29–30.

[7] Edmund Leach, "Why Did Moses Have a Sister?" in Edmund Leach and D. Alan Aycock, *Structuralist Interpretations of Biblical Myth*, Cambridge: Cambridge University Press, 1983, p. 35. This piece was first delivered as The Royal Anthropological Institute Huxley Lecture for 1980.

all scholarly opinion recognizes that the present recension of the books of the Old Testament is an assemblage of very varied writings which was finally edited and made fully canonical only around 100 BC. Likewise all agree that the purportedly "early" works in the collection contain numerous interpolations which have been inserted from time to time by later editors in the interests of consistency or with a view to providing traditional support for a disputed point of political or religious doctrine.[8]

Since the time of the assemblage, however, the stories of the Old Testament have retained the same structures despite the changing fashions of theology, and Leach argues that he is not concerned with true or false in historiographical terms, or good or bad theology in Jewish or Christian terms, but with "patterns or structures in the record as we now have it, and this record has been substantially unchanged over a very long period. To assess these structures we do not need to know how particular stories came to assume their present form nor the dates at which they were written."[9] Thus he takes the structuralist stand that he is doing comparison not in terms of content but in terms of structures, and that materials and stories that may share little content may well share "similarities" and "differences" of structure of a more abstract kind. These structural identities and differences include inversions, transformations, and contradictions.

So in sum, Leach bases his analysis

on a presumption that the whole of the text as we now have it *regardless of the varying historical origins of its component parts* may properly be treated as a unity. This contradicts very sharply with the method of orthodox scholarship. In the latter the occurrence of palpable duplication, inconsistency, etc., is treated as evidence of a corrupt text. The task of the scholar is then to sift the true from the false, to distinguish one ancient version from another ancient version and so on. For orthodox scholarship, the present text is not a unity but an amalgamation of documents which are still capable of being distinguished. I do not for a moment wish to challenge this proposition but I greatly wonder whether the effort can be worthwhile.[10]

In a lecture entitled "Against Genres"[11] given sixteen years later in 1982 at a seminar conference organized by the British Comparative Literature Association, Leach again blatantly declared his disagreement with "the ordinary theological exegesis" which assumes that the texts of the

---

[8] Leach, "The Legitimacy of Solomon", p. 34.   [9] Ibid., p. 33.   [10] Ibid., p. 80.
[11] Edmund Leach, "Against Genres: Are Parables Lights Set in Candlesticks or Put Under a Bushel?" in Leach and Aycock, *Structuralist Interpretations of Biblical Myth*, pp. 89–112.

gospels could be divided into genres such as "parables," "proverbs," "historical" episodes, and other narrative forms, and defended his thesis that "the same thematic patterning is repeated with variations in different gospels" and that "we shall only understand the texts as a whole if we recognize that some sections are structural transformations of other sections" and that these "transformations cut right across the conventional genre distinctions . . ."[12] This was a frontal assault on the theme of the seminar, "Parable and Narrative Form in the Bible and Literature," and consciously mounted as a challenge to scholars of comparative literature as "The Legitimacy of Solomon" was addressed against the historical preoccupations of biblical scholars.

There is another argument in defense of his method of dealing with biblical narratives that Leach made which also is aimed at the "historical" approach to them. Emphasizing "the very important distinction between structural contradiction (large-scale incompatibility of implication) and content contradiction (inconsistencies in the small-scale details of textual assertion)," Leach said that contradictions of the latter kind abound, mostly as a by-product of editorial glosses originally introduced with the purpose of eliminating still more glaring contradictions.

It is precisely the all-pervasiveness and random incidence of such inconsistency which makes the "historical" texts appropriate material for structural analysis, *for, under these randomized conditions, the underlying structure of the story ceases to be simply a chronicle of events, it becomes a drama* . . . it is the randomness of inconsistency which justifies the application of structural analysis . . . the editorial amendments of various hands have become woven into an involuted network which can convey a message which was not necessarily consciously intended by any particular editor [emphasis added].[13]

Moreover, any attempt to synthesize into a unitary whole a set of stories which purport to provide historical justification for rival political positions must end up as a text full of paradoxical contradictions. "The final result is a 'history' of randomized incidents with the structure of 'myth'. What the myth then 'says' is not what the editors consciously intended to say but rather something which lies deeply embedded in Jewish traditional culture as a whole."[14]

Let us now return to the Solomon essay (1966) and examine the structural patterns and existential dilemmas Leach extracted from the Old Testament materials he examined minutely in it. Leach makes a

---

[12] Ibid., pp. 92–93. [13] Leach, "The Legitimacy of Solomon", p. 45. [14] Ibid., p. 53.

fundamental point of method and interpretation in this essay, which he would try to implement and demonstrate in this as well as subsequent treatments of the Bible and early Christianity: "we may compare one myth with another and note the varying positions and mutual relations of the various elements concerned *but we cannot go further without referring back to the total ethnographic context to which the myth refers*" (emphasis added).[15] Lévi-Strauss had adhered to this structuralist and functionalist precept in the Asdiwal essay, but had progressively deviated from it in his later works where myth increasingly became a domain insulated from its connections with ritual action and social organizational context. This for Leach would become one of the major defects of the later Lévi-Straussian myth analyses. Leach, as we shall see, expounds the "total ethnographic context" in certain biblical materials in terms of postulating the normative categories relating to tribal segmentation, then mapping these segments on to territory as spatial allocations, and playing these against the references to alleged actual marriages and sex relations and to political maneuvers, and other practical realities on the ground. The myths reflect in their own terms the tensions, contradictions, manipulations, and fudging that this complex dynamic generates. The relations between these levels are not direct and one-to-one, but are dialectical interplays that are context-sensitive and open-ended, and exhibit themes and issues deeply embedded in Jewish culture.

Leach states that his

purpose is to demonstrate that the Biblical story of the succession of Solomon to the throne of Israel is a myth which "mediates" a major contradiction. The Old Testament as a whole asserts that the Jewish political title to the land of Palestine is a direct gift from God to the descendants of Israel (Jacob). This provides the fundamental basis for Jewish endogamy – the Jews should be a people of pure blood and pure religion, living in isolation in their Promised Land. But interwoven with this theological dogma there is a less idealized form of tradition which represents the population of ancient Palestine as a mixture of many peoples over whom the Jews have asserted political dominance by right of conquest. The Jews and their "foreign" neighbours intermarry freely. The synthesis achieved by the story of Solomon is such that by a kind of dramatic trick the reader is persuaded that the second of these descriptions, which is morally bad, exemplifies the first description, which is morally good. My demonstration is a long and devious one, and the reader must be patient if I offer a number of minor distractions on the way.[16]

[15] Ibid., p. 30.   [16] Ibid., p. 38.

Leach sequentially deals with groups of interconnected biblical stories, highlighting their structural identities. He begins with the biblical accounts of the sacrifice of Jephthah's daughter (Judges 11. 30–40) and the non-sacrifice of Abraham's son (Genesis 22. 1–18). He shows that the two stories are in structure mirror images of each other: "the second can be produced from the first by the simplest possible transformation rule: 'substitute for each element its binary opposite,'" and the "mythical outcome of the first story 'the father has no descendants' is the exact opposite to the mythical outcome 'the father has countless descendants.'"[17]

A second set is provided by the stories of Dinah (Genesis 34), Abimelech (Judges 9), Jephthah (Judges 11. 1–11), and Samson (Judges 13–14):

Here the common theme is a "contradiction"[18] which is the historical torment of all religious sects which acquire political ambitions but which have been of particular significance in Jewish history from the earliest times right down to the present day. On the one hand, the practice of sectarian endogamy is essential to maintain the purity of faith, on the other hand, exogamous marriages may be politically expedient if peaceful relations are to be maintained with hostile neighbours.[19]

The detailed structural arrangement of the sequences in the stories need not be repeated here, but the main points Leach makes are that "in a formal sense [in 'ideal terms'] the Biblical texts affirm the righteousness of endogamy and the sinfulness of exogamy, but that the structural 'message' keeps harking back to the contradiction stated earlier."

Leach directs the reader's attention to the way in which in these stories "the moral issue of the legitimacy of sex relations is intertwined with the political issue of 'How foreign is a foreigner?'"[20] It is in the probing of this issue – dramatized as the practical difficulty of deciding who is or who is not a foreign wife – that Leach excels in revealing the dialectical nexus between the "normative Judaism" propounded in the Books of Nehemiah and Ezra in the form of a "bigoted sectarianism which demands above all else that Jews shall separate themselves off sharply from all foreigners and that there shall be no intermarriage between Jew and Gentile," and the fact of such intermarriage which includes the famous cases of the half-Moabite origin of David, and the testimony provided

---

[17] Ibid., p. 35.
[18] Leach pays tribute to Lévi-Strauss's exposition of how interconnected myths pose irresolvable paradoxes of logic or fact and how the "variations on a theme" that recur in mythological systems serve to blur the edges of such contradictions and thus serve to remove them from immediate consciousness.
[19] Leach, "The Legitimacy of Solomon", p. 39.   [20] Ibid., p. 40.

by I Kings II. I–8 that Solomon the wise, the great king, the builder of the temple, "loved many strange women, together with the daughter of Pharaoh, women of the Moabites, Ammonites, Edomites, Zidonians and Hittites."[21]

The question of how foreign is a foreigner is a puzzle that emerges when the ideal type segmentary model of the tribal groups contained in the Old Testament is mapped on to an ideal type territorial allocation of these tribes in the idiom of distance from the core centers in the Kingdom of Judah in the south and the Kingdom of Israel in the north. Readers should consult the informative Skeleton Genealogy (figure 1) and Schematic Map of Old Testament Palestine (figure 2) compiled by Leach for "Legitimacy of Soloman." The traditional genealogy which represents the relation between the various tribal groups as one of binary segmentation serves to discriminate very precisely the exact "degree of foreignness" which separates one group from another, seen from the tribe (lineage) of Judah as the point of reference and ending with the Moabites and Ammonites, Canaanites, other Gentiles, and Kenites at the outermost periphery. Similarly, the territorial map of the Kingdom of Judah is primarily allocated to Judah (with some intrusive elements), and that of the Kingdom of Israel to the descendants of Joseph.

Benjamin receives a narrow strip dividing the two main blocks while the other Israelite tribes are distributed in a ring around the north and east. The heart of the matter is thus treated as a segmentary opposition between the descendants of Leah (i.e. Judah) and the descendants of Rachel (i.e. Ephraim, Manasseh, Benjamin) but with Benjamin both territorially and genealogically in a some-what equivocal position "in the middle."[22]

But the actual whole ethnographic context shows that the "squaring of this ideal pattern with the practical realities must at all times have been very difficult."[23]

The tribal composition of the Palestinian population was not tidily distributed. Even in the capital city itself the "Jebusites [Canaanites] dwell with the children of Judah at Jerusalem unto this day" (Joshua xv 63). Hebron, the reputed site of Abraham's tomb where David rules for seven years, is specified as the hereditary territory of Caleb the Kenazite (Edomite) with the gloss that it had formerly belonged to the children of Heth (Canaanites) (Joshua xv 14; Genesis xxxvi 9–11; Genesis xxiii 17–20). Even the formal rule book (Deuteronomy xxiii) equivocates about just how foreign is a foreigner. Edomites (and more

---

[21] Cited in ibid., p. 46.   [22] Ibid., p. 47.   [23] Ibid., p. 47.

surprisingly Egyptians) are not to be abhorred. "The children that are begotten of them shall enter into the congregation of the Lord in their third generation." Ammonites and Moabites on the other hand are absolutely tainted that "even to their tenth generation shall they not enter into the congregation of the Lord forever." Thus, even for the Patriarchs the distinction Israelite/Foreigner was not a clear cut matter of black and white but a tapering off through various shades of grey. The reason for this must be sought in later circumstance. The Jewish sectarians of the late historical Jerusalem were surrounded not only by foreigners, who were unqualified heathen, but also by semi-foreigners, such as the Samaritans who claimed to be Israelites just like themselves. How strictly should the rules of endogamy apply in such cases? . . .

The same kind of ambiguity is to be found woven into seemingly quite straight-forward historical traditions. "History" tells us of two Israelite kingdoms, one in the south (the Kingdom of Judah), one in the north (the Kingdom of Israel).[24]

The "history" that tells us of the two Israelite kingdoms poses contradictions. The kings of Israel are usually treated as more evil than those of the south. There is a recurrent tendency to treat the northerners as heathen. But at the same time the royal houses of Judah and Israel (Samaria) became allied by marriage and maintained the alliance over several generations. Leach lists many other such episodes that create ambiguities, oppositions as well as collaborations, between the north and the south.

In a nutshell, the irresolvable problems engendered in Jewish biblical history can also be seen as being an agreement with the following elementary formulas of general significance. This is the voice of Leach the comparativist. A taboo against incest coupled with a rule of exogamy provides a basis for forming marriage alliances between antagonistic groups within a single political community. Furthermore, it is the nature of real political communities that they consist of self-discriminated groups which are at any point in time either mutually antagonistic or in alliance.

A rule of endogamy provides a basis for expressing the unitary solidarity of a religious community, the chosen people of god. In real life the religious communities and the political communities seldom coincide. There is a total incompatibility between a rule of endogamy and the recognition that society consists of politically antagonistic groups allied by marriage.

The final editors of the biblical texts, members of an established Jewish church, whose members thought of themselves as the direct successors to the House and Kingdom of Judah, saw the Gentiles as the polar opposite

[24] Ibid., pp. 47, 49.

of the Jewish church. Again in polar opposition to David and Rehoboam stood the foreigners as exemplified by the Philistines.

But just as in the real world there were intermediate categories such as Samaritans who were neither Jew nor Gentile, so also traditional "history" provided intermediate categories, "the descendants of Rachel", "the House of Joseph", "the tribe of Benjamin", "the kingdom of Jeroboam", "the Calebites", "the Edomites". It is in the ambiguities of the relations between the men of Judah and these other historical-legendary-mythical peoples that we see the "resolution" of the endogamy/exogamy incompatibility described above.[25]

The last section of the essay addresses the question: "What was the legal basis of Solomon's kingship over the whole land of Israel?" In the Old Testament, conquest does not provide a legitimate basis for lordship over land (although Israelites both won land through conquest and lost it by defeat). The only fully legitimate mode of acquiring title to land is by inheritance (Exodus 32.13).

Land is ordinarily in the possession of men and is ordinarily inherited by the nearest male patrilineal kin, but in the absence of sons, a man's daughters will inherit before his brothers. It follows that, in ancient Judaea, title to land must have been held by women. The rule of endogamy, which was probably more fiercely applied to women than men . . . thus had the effect of preventing land from passing out to strangers through the marriage of property-endowed women. On the other hand, by declining to marry strange women, Jewish males were prevented from gaining title to the land of strangers.[26]

If these were the legal norms, then what do we learn about the legitimacy of Solomon's title from a consideration of his genealogy? Examining the New Testament, Leach finds that "Matthew's list of fourteen generations from Abraham to Solomon is consistent with the Old Testament record but is peculiar in that, in addition to the fourteen men, *it names four of their wives, each of whom is a prominent Old Testament personality*" (emphasis added). The four women are Tamar, Rachab, Ruth, and Bathsheba, and hypothesizing that the four women in question must have had something in common that makes them specially significant as ancestresses of Solomon, Leach subjects their stories to structuralist analysis and elicits many patterned relations such as parallels, inversions, and the mixing of, as well as the mediation between, these antithetical categories: Israelite/Foreigner, Endogamy/Exogamy, Tent Dweller/City Dweller, Virtue/Sin.

[25] Ibid., pp. 54–55.   [26] Ibid., p. 57.

He sums the implications of the stories of the four ancestresses, and a fifth woman, Abigail (associated with King David), as in the main harping on a single theme

which centres around the question of whether it is possible for a "pure blooded" Israelite to beget legitimate children from a woman who is not an Israelite, or conversely, whether it is possible for an Israelite woman to bear an Israelite child after cohabitation with a man who is not a pure Israelite. In a narrow sense, the answer to both the questions is "No", but legal fictions such as that embodied in the levirate rule or the principle that "the child of a harlot has no father" permit the issue to become obscured.

If then we ask "why should these equivocal ladies be mixed up with the genealogy of King Solomon?", the answer must surely be that, in terms of later Palestinian politics as distinct from Jewish sectarian religion, a doctrine of narrowly defined endogamous exclusiveness makes no sense. Moreover, taken all together, these stories make it possible to argue that not only is Solomon "directly descended" from Esau the Edomite and even from Heth the Canaanite, so that he is the legitimate heir to all forms of land title however derived![27]

The concluding sections of the Solomon essay take up a new issue in Leach's deployment of the structuralist method. Hitherto he had examined the biblical narratives in terms of the perspective that the variations-on-a-theme approach would be unaffected by the order in which they were cited. Now he asks the question of whether the chronological sequence of events as recorded in biblical history is itself of structural significance.

Leach's procedure was to take the biblical text from I Samuel 4 to II Kings 2 at its face value as a continuous history running from the death of Eli through the reigns of Saul and David to the succession of Solomon. He focuses on the genealogical and geographical details so lavishly provided by the text, and meticulously summarizes the stories focusing on the changing role positions of the principal *dramatis personae*, and the antitheses around which their actions revolve: Israelite vs. Foreigner; House of Judah vs. Houses of Joseph and/or Benjamin; Wives who are the daughters of Israelites vs. Wives who are the daughters of foreigners; Fathers vs. Sons; Full-siblings vs. Half-siblings; Legitimate king vs. Usurper king; Priest (Levite) vs. Non-priest.

The reader is advised to scrutinize the amount of detail systematically arranged and finally condensed into a dramatic play of three acts in which the basic patterns are foregrounded. Why should Leach go to this length, even, as he admits, to the point of unreadability? Because

[27] Ibid., p. 64.

he was demonstrating the structuralist method whose chief methodological canon was that the plausibility of the positions inferred must be demonstrated on the basis of exhaustively taking note of all the relevant evidence from every context.[28] (In Leach's eyes this is what separates his method from that of Frazer's simultaneous piecemeal citations from widely different contexts.)

Leach sums up his results in this way.

The "play" develops two themes in parallel. The first is that of *sex relations*. The sections of the story which I have called "prologues" ring the changes on sexual excess and sexual inadequacy. The second is a problem of *political relations*. In each "scene" an anti-king (usurper) struggles for supremacy against a legitimate king. In each case anti-king and king are supported by champions. In the course of the story the opposition between rival lineages (Judah v. Benjamin) is successively replaced by a rivalry between father and son and then by a rivalry between half-brother and half-brother, a convergence which is paralleled on the sexual side by "adultery with a rival's wife", "adultery with a father's concubine" and "incest with a half-sister." David, the original anti-King moves across the board to the position of King, and the champions Amasa and Joab make corresponding moves in matching repetition.

The varying statuses of the women tie in both themes with the issue of endogamy/exogamy//Israelite/Foreigner ... Each of the anti-Kings is tainted with Foreignness ... But they are never classified as outright foreigners as are the Philistines, Amalekites, etc.

In "Act III" the sexual and political themes are brought directly together in that the final bone of contention is *both* the Kingship *and* the sexual possession of Abishag ... When the rightful King (in the person of Solomon) is finally established his first acts are to wipe out (a) the surviving usurper (Adonijah), (b) the surviving champion of the House of David (Joab), (c) the surviving champion of the House of Saul (Shimei), thus bringing the story to a suitable "clear stage" conclusion.[29]

Leach's essay "The Legitimacy of Solomon" evoked favorable and worthwhile comments from two well-known biblical scholars and experts in Judaic studies. Professor Neusner's essay "The Talmud as Anthropology" has two main submissions. One is his criticism of two established approaches to the Talmudic literature. The old approach of comparative philology, which reached its heights in the nineteenth century, in the final analysis "has not vastly improved our understanding of the method and meaning of the Talmud."[30] The second approach using "historical

---

[28] One is reminded of Leach's similar insistence in his previous pre-structuralist text, *Pul Eliya*, on the methodological necessity of exhaustively citing the data on which the empirical patterns were based. Thus his "structuralist" and "empiricist" methods were congruent in this sense.

[29] Ibid., pp. 78–79.   [30] Neusner, "The Talmud as Anthropology," p. 3.

methods for the study of the Talmud, has on the whole, produced results of modest interest for people whose principal question has to do with the discovery of what the Talmud is and means."[31]

The historian's method and focus in the study of the Talmud is misconceived, because the Talmud is "not a history book" describing "concrete, one time, discrete and distinctive events of history." "The Talmud and related literature were not created to record things that happened. They are legal texts, saying how people should do things . . . or they are exegetical texts, explaining the true meaning of the revelation at Sinai; or occasionally, they are biographical texts, telling stories about how holy men did things."[32] The real purposes of the Talmudic literature are: "to lay out paradigms of holiness"; to explore "the meaning of being human in the image of God and of building a kingdom of priests and a holy people"; to probe and address questions of order and meaning in the conduct of every day life, as well as to reflect on "the understanding of the meaning of Israel and the world . . . The Talmud is about what is holy."[33] Neusner indicts theologians and historians as having mistakenly "asked the Talmud to speak in a language essentially alien to its organizing and generative categories of thought."[34]

For the understanding and interpretation of these central foci of the Talmud, Professor Neusner turns to anthropology for assistance in formulating "fructifying questions" and in gaining "fresh perspectives on the Talmudic corpus."[35] In particular he names two anthropologists, Edmund Leach and Mary Douglas, from whom Talmudists could learn how to read the stories of the Talmud and other ancient Jewish and Israelite texts, and "to become sensitive to their important traits and turnings, both those of language and those of substance."[36] He cites as "a stunning example, the perspective of the great structuralist anthropologist . . . upon the [biblical] story of the succession of Solomon to the throne of Israel,"[37] which, according to Leach, mediates a major contradiction in Jewish political life between the fundamental value of endogamy based on their title to the land of Palestine as a gift from God, and the intermarriage of Jews with "foreign" neighbors, whom they dominate by right of conquest.

---

[31] Ibid., p. 5.   [32] Ibid., p. 8.   [33] Ibid., p. 8.   [34] Ibid., p. 25.   [35] Ibid., p. 17.

[36] Ibid., p. 18. A third anthropologist he mentions is Clifford Geertz, especially his essay on "Religion as a Cultural System", which originally appeared in Banton (ed.), *Anthropological Approaches to the Study of Religion* and is reprinted in Geertz, *The Interpretation of Cultures*, New York: Basic Books, 1973.

[37] Neusner, "The Talmud as Anthropology," p. 18.

Neusner next cites some of the writings of Mary Douglas which have "made a considerable impact upon . . . the students of Hebrew Scriptures and the earlier strata of rabbinical literature, especially her book *Purity and Danger*,[38] which interprets the ordering and meaning of the laws of Leviticus." The following formulation of Douglas, which resonates with similar formulations by Leach, appears to have opened up new understandings for the above-mentioned students: "If food is treated as a code, the messages it encodes will be found in the pattern of social relations being expressed. The message is about different degrees of hierarchy, inclusion and exclusion, boundaries and transactions across the boundaries."[39]

Leach's essay "The Legitimacy of Solomon" also evoked authoritative comments from another well-known biblical scholar, Abraham Malamat, at the Hebrew University of Jerusalem.[40] He refers to the essay as "stimulating and substantial" and states that Leach's innovation seems to be the application of structural analysis in a diachronic fashion instead of the usual synchronic approach, and that this method "opens new vistas" in the study of the Bible, even if the structuralists "do not conceive of biblical history as 'real history'." He remarks that he is impressed by the distinction Leach makes "between the relatively antiquated 'form (or content) comparison' (often misused in Bible research) and 'structural comparison,'" which "together with the principle of contrast may serve as a new stimulant to Bible research."[41] Thus, an eminent biblical scholar endorses Leach's structuralist method as profitably and meaningfully applicable to the Bible, even if he denies that the Bible is "real history." Malamat gives his stamp of approval as follows: "All in all it seems to me that Bible research and structural anthropology may result in a fruitful mutual experience, revealing new insight into the former and rendering plenty of recorded material to the latter."[42]

---

[38] Mary Douglas, *Purity and Danger: An Analysis of Concepts of Pollution and Taboo*, London: Routledge & Kegan Paul, 1966.

[39] Mary Douglas, *Implicit Meanings: Essays in Anthropology*, London and Boston: Routledge & Kegan Paul, 1975, p. 249.

[40] Abraham Malamat "Comments on E. Leach: The Legitimacy of Solomon – Some Structural Aspects of Old Testament History," *Archives Européennes de Sociologie*, vol. 8, 1967, pp. 165–67. There is also a letter from Professor S. Talmon to Leach dated September 4, 1966 (The Modern Archive, King's College, Cambridge), saying that he "just read with great interest" Leach's paper on "The Legitimacy of Solomon." He requests an offprint "since it pertains to matters which are very much in my line."

[41] Malamat, "Comments on E. Leach," p. 165.

[42] Ibid., p. 165. An example is the analysis of biblical genealogies significant for the "orthodox historian" and structural analyst alike though the message to each is different.

Another comment by Malamat strengthens Leach's use of the Bible for structuralist analysis *contra* Lévi-Strauss's assertion that it is not amenable to such application because the contents of the Bible had over time been changed and altered by generations of literate commentators. Admitting that there were "editorial activities," Malamat asserts that "it must be stressed that the late Bible editors as a rule did not tamper too much with their sources, often transmitting them in 'fossilized' form. Thus as regards *Genesis*, E.A. Speiser, in particular, has shown that many of the narratives have been conveyed, untouched for generations, and included by the editors basically without change, the original meaning of the tales eluding them."[43]

Malamat's main questioning of Leach's interpretation relates to certain misconceptions that may derive from the reliance on "English forms of biblical names." Some of the examples he gives are these:

1. Jeroboam and Rehoboam cannot be inverse forms in the original Hebrew. Yet he remarks that "they remain a parallel set, perhaps brought about by their being contemporary throne names, both of similar connotation (Jeroboam meaning 'may the people increase'; Rehoboam 'the people are widespread')".[44]
2. Zeru'ah (mother of Jeroboam) and Zeruiah (sister of David) cannot be conflated as their spellings in Hebrew are distinctly different.
3. Linguistic comparisons between Rahab and Rechabites are not plausible as the Hebrew spellings are distinctly different.

It is not clear to me to what extent Malamat's disclosure of the philological differences in the spelling of these names in the original Hebrew vitiates Leach's structuralist assumption that takes these names to be variants or having parallel connotations, and therefore relevant for an analysis in terms of structural identities and differences.

Finally, Malamat gives information which richly supplements Leach's stimulating discussion of the dialectic between the injunction of normative Judaism that there shall be no intermarriage between Jew and Gentile, and the fact of intermarriages as illustrated by the half-Moabite origin of David, and by King Solomon's consorting with "strange women." This discussion is part of his larger elucidation of the relation between "sex relations" and "political relations," and the various shades of grey generated in the space within the Israelite/Foreigner binary distinction.

---

[43] Ibid., p. 165. Malamut cites Speiser's commentary on Genesis.   [44] Ibid., p. 166.

Malamat submits that "the policy of the Davidic dynasty in its early days was to conclude marriage with foreign princesses so as to ensure blue blooded successors to the throne."[45]

"Bath-Sheba, formerly the wife of Uriah the Hittite, a scion of the Jebusite aristocracy, was most probably herself a foreigner, descended from the local aristocracy of Jerusalem. Her marriage to David may be in keeping with the practice followed by conquerors of taking unto themselves the women of the vanquished rulers. Thus Solomon was of foreign aristocratic extraction through his mother's lineage, a fact which seems to have rendered him priority of accession over his brothers, despite the fact that he was not the firstborn. David, during his last years, married Solomon to Naamah, an Ammonite princess, from whose union Rehoboam, the heir to the throne, was born. Thus Rehoboam was of even less pure blood than his father. From amongst all the wives of Rehoboam it was Maacah . . . who became the "first lady" and mother of Abijah the royal heir (again not following the principle of primogeniture). The Jewish blood of the latter was by this time considerably diluted, and he may have been "acceptable" even to Germany of the thirties.[46]

There are two other essays by Leach based on biblical materials: "Why Did Moses Have a Sister?" and "Against Genres: Are Parables Lights Set in Candlesticks or Put under a Bushel?"[47] I shall concentrate here only on the first essay because it is centrally concerned with an array of biblical materials, and because the second essay is only concerned in part with them.

Beginning with the assertion in the Moses essay that, while the Bible is not true as history, "for the many millions of individuals who consider the Bible to be a sacred tale it is certainly true as myth," Leach says that "the nature of mythical truth is something about which anthropologists have something pertinent to say."[48]

There are a number of puzzles which interconnect and which Leach attempts to solve. One of them is as follows. The Roman settlement of Dura-Europos in Syria was destroyed by military action in the year AD 256. This abandoned site was excavated from 1927 onwards, and in 1932 a large part of the murals on the walls of the Jewish synagogue were rescued. They are now in Damascus. "One of these murals illustrates the Exodus story of Moses in the Bulrushes. Unexpectedly the picture includes the representation of a naked goddess. This picture dates from the 3rd century AD and is thus contemporary with the Gnostic heresies

---

[45] Ibid., p. 167.   [46] Ibid., pp. 166–67.
[47] Both essays were published in Leach and Aycock, *Structuralist Interpretations of Biblical Myth*, 1983.
[48] Leach, "Why Did Moses Have a Sister?" p. 33.

of the Christians."[49] Who is this goddess, and why is she featured? And what is her relation to the daughter of Pharaoh who finds the infant Moses?[50]

Leach introduces the idea that although the text of the Bible, as we now have it, clearly assumes that the deity is male, in Catholic practice the Virgin Mary, Queen of Heaven, the human mother of Jesus Christ immaculately conceived, has been turned into a goddess in all but name; and Protestants in turn, in emphasizing the mediating role of the Second Person of the Trinity, have made Him appear markedly effeminate.

He also refers to the point that during the first three centuries of the Christian era, the ambiguity of the sex of the deity was much more explicit, and that Elaine Pagel's study of the Nag Hammadi Gnostic gospels suggests that Gnostic Christianity espoused a deity in which female features are integral. Leach suggests that the strain of Gnostic Christianity may have had a counterpart in Judaism, and that some of the New Testament texts have some paradoxical features which would have been of fundamental importance for the advocates of Gnosticism. Leach notes as part of the larger context that the third century AD was a period at which the international Romanized cult of Isis was at its peak.

The Bible says that Moses had a sister Miriam (Mary) who, on a casual reading of the text, "seems to be a quite unimportant, almost redundant figure. So why is she there at all?"[51] Leach asserts that if the New Testament stories represent a more or less conscious transformation of the Old Testament stories, as some texts expressly state, then from a structuralist point of view the New Testament can illuminate the Old Testament just as the Old Testament illuminates the New. "All of which explains why part of my answer to the question, 'Why did Moses have a sister?' is derived from the complementary question: 'Why did Jesus not have a sister?' I am suggesting that we gain insight into the mythological significance of the shadowy women who surround Moses by looking carefully at the significance of the equally shadowy women who surrounded Jesus."[52]

Before launching into this close analysis of biblical narratives, Leach makes a preliminary statement about the predominant forms in which the relationship between God and man, "the central concern of the

[49] Ibid., pp. 34–35.
[50] The Dura synagogue mural is reproduced in the text of the essay, and it shows many women at the scene of the rescue of the infant Moses (midwives, women bearing gifts), but the issue that intrigues Leach is the presence of a goddess holding the infant and the conflation of that figure with the daughter-princess of Pharaoh who first discovered the child.
[51] Ibid., p. 36.   [52] Ibid., p. 35.

Bible," is articulated in the Bible.[53] The first is the Master–Servant image in which the human servant meets with God his master, directly face to face, or in a vision, or by inspiration. "The servant is a prophet. In principle, the ideology is egalitarian, all servants are of the same standing; anyone might become a prophet. In practice, the Grace of God falls only upon the chosen few, the Elect."[54] The principle of equality is at odds with the principle of hierarchy. Moses is superior to Aaron because he speaks with God openly "mouth to mouth".

"The capacity to prophesy, to act as the mouthpiece of God is strictly personal; it is not hereditary . . . "[55] But here, too, there is tension because of the possibility at the margins of the transmissibility of the prophetic role: "The dying Moses hands on his powers to Joshua who has previously been described as his 'servant, one of the young men'."[56]

Be that as it may, the act of prophecy nearly always takes place in the wilderness or on a river bank away from human habitation; in a cosmic sense such places stand at the boundary between This World and The Other.

Kingship is the second major image in the relations between God and man. The importance of this image is the way it contrasts with, and links with, that of the prophet. As a form of political organization, Kingship ensures continuity. Individual kings may die or be deposed or abdicate, but the office of Kingship is immortal, it is omnipotent. The idea that living kings are delegates of the deity, and worthy of being worshiped as god incarnate is expressed in the Bible.

"The prototype characteristics of the king are precisely the opposite to those of the Prophet. The Prophet lives an ascetic, solitary life in the wilderness and mountainous places, the king lives an erotic life, surrounded by women and courtiers in a palace in the city." Correspondingly, "God ceases to be a burning bush in the 'backside of the desert' and becomes a super king with his residence in the Holy of Holies in the Temple, at the centre of the Holy City, at the centre of the Holy Land."[57]

But the interesting feature, which becomes important in the later submissions of this essay, is that "yet in the limiting case, the Prophet himself, the scourge of princes, merges with the ruler who is deity incarnate.

---

[53] Leach treats three themes: the Master–Servant image, and the profile of the Prophet; the image of Kingship and its contrastive relation to the role of the Prophet; and lastly the Husband–Wife image, and some of the erotic aspects of this as represented in the contrast between Mary, the virgin mother of Jesus, and Mary Magdalene, the sinner who was close to Jesus. I shall only outline the first two conceptions here, and discuss the two Marys later.

[54] Ibid., p. 36.   [55] Ibid., p. 36.   [56] Ibid., p. 37.   [57] Ibid., p. 37.

Moses, like Jesus Christ, is a god-king as well as a man . . . Although the roles of Prophet and King are radically opposed, any particular character in the story may, and very frequently does, occupy both roles at different stages of his or her career."[58] A famous case is Moses himself: the first half of Exodus 2 links Moses with Kingship; he becomes the adopted son of Pharaoh's daughter. But the second half of the chapter, together with chapter 3, takes him into the wilderness where he becomes son-in-law to the Priest of Midian and communes directly with God. (The same pattern is discernible in the New Testament narratives in Matthew).[59]

"In general, the Kingship image represents God as an all-powerful but somewhat remote ruler who can only be approached through intermediaries such as living priests and deceased saints. In contrast to the Master–Servant image which fits with a pentecostal ideology and an egalitarian, congregationalist type of church organization, the Kingship pattern is systematically hierarchical."[60] (Leach develops this contrast between the hierarchical and egalitarian religious cosmologies in new directions in the essay "Melchisedech and the Emperor" which we shall consider in chapter 12.)

Leach suggests that the Old Testament's construction of an image of divine kingship is based to some extent at least in Egyptian precedents. "In the Pentateuch, the model that was actually used was that of the Egyptian Pharaoh . . . The fact that certain of the Patriarchs, in particular Abraham, Joseph and Moses are, by different devices, identified with Pharaoh, thus carries the implication that they are not just representatives of God but, in some degree, God incarnate in their own persons."[61]

Let us now review the main analytical and interpretive submissions of the essay. The Moses essay is a complex juxtaposition of Old Testament and New Testament stories to show the recurrence of an arrangement of male and female positions that closely parallels the Egyptian legends concerning the Pharaoh whose principal wife was at the same time his sister or half-sister. This practice (in so far as it really took place) was based on a structural pattern that anthropologists have labeled as *positional succession based on sibling incest*: "In myth, the God Osiris is married to his sister the Goddess Isis and is 'killed' by his brother Seth; the god Horus is the son of Osiris but posthumously conceived. The living Pharaoh of Egypt was treated as an incarnation of Horus. In mytho-logic the Queen mother and the Queen sister-wife were both representations of Isis."[62] Thus, in terms of positional succession Osiris (the dead Pharaoh) and his sister-wife Isis are succeeded by Horus the living Pharaoh and his sister-wife Isis, and this structural pattern is repeated over time, as dead and successor pharaohs and their chief sister-wife partners are represented as succeeding to these archetypal positions.

The next argument that Leach makes is that "both at the level of manifest plot and the level of manifest pattern, the Jewish and Christian versions are *transformations* of the Egyptian version," as exemplified by the stories about the patriarchs as they appear in Genesis and Exodus and the stereotyped late form of the saga of Osiris.[63]

The equations and substitutions made by Leach are detailed and I can only convey here some of the conclusions.

Abraham is assimilated to the pharaonic model and hence to the Osiris–Horus schema of positional succession. Abraham's principal wife Sarah was his half-sister. "The name Sarah means 'princess'; it has recently been suggested that it may have phonetic and historical links with Hera . . . In Genesis 12 Sarah becomes a minor wife of Pharaoh; the plain implication of the story is that Pharaoh and Abraham are virtually interchangeable."[64] Sarah is possibly a mythological transformation of Isis.

Joseph. The Joseph story repeats the Abraham pattern in the sense that just as Abraham went south into Egypt to avoid famine in the Land of Canaan, so does Joseph, grandson of Abraham, arrive in Egypt with the status of a slave as a consequence of his having boasted to his brothers that he would become king and rule over them.

In Egypt Joseph becomes the slave of Potiphar, "an officer of Pharaoh" (Potiphar = officer of Pharaoh = Pharaoh = [Osiris]). Joseph successfully rejects the seductions of Potiphar's wife (Potiphar's wife = Pharaoh's wife . . . = [Isis]). Later Joseph becomes the Pharaoh's viceroy and Pharaoh gives him as wife Asenath, the daughter of Potiphera, priest of On. (Note: Potiphar and Potiphera are alternate spellings and it is the Pharaoh who gives the girl in marriage.) (Asenath = Potiphar's daughter = Pharaoh's daughter = [Isis].) Thus finally Joseph = Pharaoh's (adopted) son = Horus – in the sense that Pharaoh establishes Joseph as his co-ruler in the same fashion that the senior Pharaoh ranked as Osiris makes the junior Horus, his son and heir, his co-ruler (as was the practice in Ancient Egypt).

Moses. We now come to the all-important Moses. Leach attempts to demonstrate that the story in Exodus represents a more complicated transformation of the Osiris–Isis–Horus pattern.

[63] Ibid., p. 39.   [64] Ibid., pp. 39–40.

Since Moses is the adopted son of Pharaoh's daughter, it should follow that Moses' father is the equivalent of Pharaoh's daughter's husband. By certain inferences, Leach arrives at this equation: Pharaoh's daughter is equal to Isis. The biblical text says that Moses' mother Jochabed was father's sister to his father Amram, implying an incestuous marriage according to the formal rules. In due course, Leach establishes that Jochabed = Pharaoh's daughter; that Moses in turn becomes the structural equivalent of Amram. If we follow through the various details, it finally transpires that all the female characters are representations of Isis while all the male characters are alternating representations of Osiris–Horus. Jochabed's daughter is Miriam, and she too will equate with Isis.

"Joseph and Moses are complementary characters. Both are directly linked with Pharaoh; both have a dual role as secular ruler and inspired prophet; the latter role of prophet is linked with the liminal 'wilderness' situation."[65] Leach here is referring to the journeys made by them in *opposite* directions. Joseph moves from Palestine, the land of suffering, and in the wilderness (betwixt and between) he has visions and makes prophecies, becomes a Midianite slave and reaches Egypt, the land of plenty, where he becomes deputy of the Pharaoh and son-in-law of the deputy Pharaoh. Moses moves in the other direction, with the signs reversed. He leaves Egypt, the land of suffering for Jews, and having become son-in-law of the Midianite priest he moves to the wilderness and there communes directly with God, and leads the Jews to the promised land of Palestine which he does not himself actually reach (but his succession passes to Joshua, a young follower, who does).

In the story of Moses in the bulrushes, the characters "Pharaoh's daughter," "the child sister," "the child's mother," are all unnamed but the sister is seemingly redundant (Exodus 2. 3–10). In fact the mother and sister play slightly different roles: the mother hides the child; the sister observes the discovery. It is a story of death and rebirth with a change of witnesses in between.

Leach now advances a somewhat "mind-blowing" parallelism between the Egyptian Osiris myth, the Old Testament story of the finding of Moses, and the New Testament story of the birth of Jesus.

In the Egyptian original it is Osiris who dies at the hand of Seth. The loving sister-wife Isis then reassembles the dismembered parts of Osiris' body and becomes pregnant by her dead husband-brother. From this pregnancy of a

---

[65] Ibid., pp. 44–45.

"Virgin" mother is born Horus. The infant is hidden in the reeds of the Nile delta to evade the vengeance of Seth. Horus is Osiris reborn.

But if the "infant Moses in the bulrushes" equates with the "infant Horus in the reeds", then the Pharaoh who orders the midwives to kill the male children of the Hebrews is Seth, the usurper King, brother murderer and perpetual enemy of Osiris–Horus.[66]

The whole pattern reappears in the New Testament story of the birth of Jesus. King Herod who orders the massacre of the innocents is a close copy of the Pharaoh of Exodus 1. The finding of the "babe lying in a manger" by "three kings"[67] equates with the baby lying in "an ark of bulrushes" discovered by a princess. The kings arrive as emissaries of Herod, the princess as emissary of Pharaoh (both Herod and Pharaoh are equivalent to Seth). "So Jesus, like Moses, is a Horus figure and we are led to start thinking about possible connections between Mary (Miriam), the virgin mother of Jesus, and Miriam, the virgin sister of Moses, and the archetypal figure of Isis who manages to be mother, sister, wife and daughter all at once . . . In myth there can be no finality."[68]

From now on, I shall select from parts of the remainder of Leach's essay, and focus on a theme that runs though it – the many Miriams of the Old Testament and the many Marys of the New Testament, and the links between them.

Miriam is Moses' sister, but there is nothing special or explicit said about her and *that is the puzzle*. Leach refers to four references to Miriam in the Bible. In the story of Moses in the bulrushes she is unnamed as Pharaoh's daughter and also unnamed and mixed up with Jochabed. In Exodus 15 she is named and described as the prophetess, the sister of Aaron. In Numbers 12 she is stricken with leprosy by God for complaining about Moses' irregular marriage to an Ethiopian. Miriam repents, is cured, and undergoes a purification ritual. In Numbers 20, after a statement of rules that are to be imposed on those who have had contact with a dead body, Miriam's death is reported. "Whatever else she may be, this Old Testament Miriam (Mary) is very much a tabooed person and in this respect at least she is an appropriate forerunner of her various New Testament successors."[69]

---

[66] Ibid., p. 43.

[67] Leach also suggests that the non-biblical tradition that turned the witnesses of Christ's nativity into three kings ties up with a convention in classical sources whereby the witnesses to a miraculous birth should be three gift-bearing Graces (ibid., p. 34, footnote 1). In the Dura-Europos panel there are three female figures bearing treasures, much like the three Graces.

[68] Ibid., p. 44.   [69] Ibid., pp. 46–47.

The Gospels refer to a number of different Marys, and several of them are mixed up. We are not straying into heresy, says Leach, if we make up a composite figure out of Mary, the sister of Martha and Lazarus, who anoints Jesus' feet with precious ointments in the house of Simon the Leper, and the Mary who performs a similar act in the house of Simon the Pharisee. "From a very early date this latter Mary has been identified with Mary Magdalene so that, throughout the Christian era, Mary Magdalene has been seen as the prototype of a repentant prostitute."[70] This composite Mary, if you follow the cross references, is, like Miriam, a repentant sinner associated with leprosy and also, like Isis, associated with death and resurrection. Mary (Magdalene) is said in the Bible to be "loved" by Jesus together with Martha and Lazarus; in the Gnostic texts a bond of erotic love links Jesus with Mary Magdalene.

Leach admits that

these traditionally established identifications cannot be justified from a strict reading of the canonical text though they fit perfectly with structuralist arguments. Thus whereas Mary, the sister of Martha, is witness to the resurrection of her brother Lazarus, Mary Magdalene is the principal witness of the resurrection of Jesus. In the mythic structure they are one and the same. On the other hand Mary, the Virgin, the mother of Jesus, has just the opposite characteristics. She is sinless and sexless instead of sinful and sexual; she is the vehicle of birth rather than the witness of resurrection, that is of rebirth.[71]

In the Moses story it is the mother who places the infant in the ark of bulrushes; she is witness to the death. It is the sister who observes the discovery of the infant by the Princess; she is witness to the rebirth. In the Christian story of the Crucifixion the mother of Jesus appears only once; she is witness to the death. It is Mary Magdalene who is consistently the witness to the rebirth. [72]

---

[70] Ibid., p. 46.   [71] Ibid., p. 46.

[72] Ibid., pp. 54–55. In order to understand the context for this "death and rebirth theme," Leach takes us through these developments. The religious ideology of the Old Testament was developed in a geographical context in which the sacrifice of the first born was very widespread especially in the time of King Moloch/Queen Ishtar (biblical Ashtoreth). Jewish reformers, turning from these abominations, endeavored to replace the institution of child sacrifice by alternative practices. Leach says here he agrees with Frazer "that the underlying rationale of child sacrifice is that a birth which 'opens the womb' is a mystical contaminating event which puts in danger not only the mother but all the senior members of her household, including the future of the mother's unborn children." In the Genesis stories the first-born son is not killed but he is deprived of his birthright. In all these stories there is a recurrent theme of replacement of a contaminated child by the sacred heir. "The Biblical Israelites, as described in the Pentateuch, retained the custom of sacrifice of the first born with respect to their domestic cattle, but 'redeemed' their first born children by means of an alternative animal sacrifice, and by treating circumcision as a kind of symbolic sacrifice of male children."

Leach takes us through a labyrinth of biblical details which he reads in terms of structuralist analogies and parallels, but the gist of his allusive juxtapositions and reductions is that Miriam, Moses' sister of the bulrushes, and Mary Magdalene show structural equivalence. Mary, the mother of Christ, witnesses his death; she is as Queen of Heaven the equivalent of Isis. Mary Magdalene, the sister of Lazarus (an alternative of Jesus), has the fused positions of the "sister-wife" of Jesus, who is the reborn Horus (Osiris risen from the dead). Mary Magdalene is a successor Isis to Mary, Jesus' mother. Miriam of the bulrushes is thus also the sister who witnesses the rebirth of Moses, who is the equivalent to Horus the god-king of Exodus 7.1. Therefore in this aspect Miriam can also be seen as his "goddess-queen."

Leach concludes by remarking that

the editing of the Bible texts into the canonical form . . . was a long term process which began, in the case of the Old Testament, around the third century BC, but continued for many centuries. The attempts on the part of both Jewish and Christian editors to eliminate all traces of "earlier" heretical beliefs was only partly effective. Miriam in the Old Testament and Mary Magdalene in the New Testament reflect strains of religious thinking in which the idea that deity might be partly female was readily acceptable. In antiquity, as in modern India, the timeless permanent aspects of deity were perceived as male, the ongoing time-bound, creative/destructive aspects of deity as female.[73]

Although orthodox Judaism and orthodox Christianity both endeavored to eliminate the female element, the canonical texts of the Bible retain large numbers of female characters who are mothers, sisters, lovers, and daughters to the male protagonists who are more obviously semidivine heroes of a standard type. These females seem to have inevitably taken on the attributes of goddess in other religious systems.

Of all the Jewish patriarchs the one who comes closest to having the attributes of God incarnate is Moses. Like Jesus of Christianity he is both King and Prophet. Certain paradoxes arise from this ambiguity. Divine kings need to come from

---

The relevance of all this for the main theme of this essay is that "the story of Moses in the bulrushes and the story of the Nativity of the child Jesus are both linked with stories of the massacre of children by royal command. They are not stories about sinful birth but about sinless birth; the purity of the infants concerned is established by the mass sacrifice of other children. The purified infants are replacements. The child that is discovered by the Princess and the child discovered by the Magi at Bethlehem are both children returned from the dead" (ibid., pp. 52–55).

[73] Ibid., p. 56.

a lineage of kings and their lineage must endure for ever. The books of Exodus and Matthew start off with a genealogy, from Jacob to Moses in the first case, and from Abraham, through David and Solomon to "Joseph the husband of Mary from whom was born Jesus, who is called Christ" in the second. But ascetic Prophets of the Wilderness can only be heirs of the spirit, never heirs of the flesh. So Joshua follows Moses and Jesus follows John by a person to person transmission of Grace which is wholly independent of the contamination of sexuality and birth from the womb.

The extreme ambiguity of the female characters with whom these two "sons of God" are associated derives from this contradiction; mytho-logic requires that the divine king-prophet shall be both married and unmarried, fertile and infertile, born of a woman but not begotten of man.[74]

The last paragraphs of the essay are an intriguing "revelation" that seeks its final evidence in art, in a manner similar to the way the essay's first puzzle was posed by reference to the Dura mural of infant Moses among the bulrushes. Leach presents two pictures which effectively make his point. The first is a picture by Gaddi which shows Christ crowning his mother as Queen of Heaven. "Apart from the fact that Christ is wearing his crown and the Madonna is not, the two figures are represented as virtually identical; they might be twins."

A similar convention is found in many examples of Renaissance and medieval art. Michelangelo's Pietà in Saint Peter's in Rome shows a young Madonna holding the dead body of her full-grown son.

The fact that the Madonna is young was Michelangelo's choice. So also was the fact that, as you probably do not know, he chose to give Christ and his mother identical features.

Moses has a sister because mytho-logic requires that his mother should be no older than himself.[75]

Let me conclude with some comments on the Moses essay followed by some observations on Leach's absorbed labors with biblical material.

"The Legitimacy of Solomon" was first published in 1966 and is readily recognized by many readers as Leach's most successful essay in the structuralist-functionalist mode. It is readily accessible because the problems dealt with are delimited, and the contradictions and their attempted mediations, and the difficulties of squaring ideal patterns with practical realities, are systematically explored in a long essay.

By comparison, "Why Did Moses Have a Sister?" delivered as the Huxley Lecture in 1980, actually deals with a multiplicity of themes

---

[74] Ibid., p. 56.   [75] Ibid., p. 56.

Figure II.I. Michelangelo's Pietà, Basilica of St Peter, Vatican (credit: Alinari/Art Resource, New York).

which Leach is artfully juxtaposing and trying to weave together. The Egyptian and the biblical materials from the Old and New Testaments traversed are varied and vast in scope, and the structuralist analyses are densely packed into a limited number of pages. Some readers may therefore find it difficult reading. But there are rewards for those who follow the master detective at work.

It seems as if the essay races through many entrancing issues at a breathtaking pace, and furthermore, as if Leach has let himself go and is having fun as he does so. Some readers may be entranced (as I have been) by the imaginative and intriguing linkages and structuralist equivalences and reductions he makes, while others preferring a linear and more literal narrative reading of the Bible may balk at Leach's excavation of structural parallels underlying the surface features of the text.

At times, the presenting and linking of themes may look Frazerian, but we must pay attention to Leach's methodological criteria and procedures. He stresses that his main historical context of analysis, his "ethnographic present," is around the third century AD, a period when "the international Romanised cult of Isis was at its peak," and he takes care to set out in detail the ways in which he derives the structural equivalences in Egyptian myth, and in the Old and New Testament narratives. He signals that he is not engaging in a historical analysis but is mining repeated structural patterns in the text. It is only after conducting these specified operations that at the end he ventures to suggest how the biblical materials may reflect certain existential themes and paradoxes of general, even universal, significance.

When one reflects upon all his essays on biblical narratives one notes with interest his assertions that they embody and convey religious truths or "metaphysical truths" and not other kinds of truth, "historical" or "scientific." Religious truths are presented in terms of a "mytho-logic." Leach seems to have concluded in the latter part of his career that if most religions are concerned with the mediation between omnipotent deity in heaven and human beings on earth, or between the supernatural realm and this world, then all the interesting action – the puzzles, the paradoxes and their attempted solutions, the transformational operations that result in a change of state – lie primarily at the level of this mediation. A virtually omnipresent human preoccupation is the transformational nexus between life–death–rebirth or resurrection, including the passage of the dead to ancestorhood and their regeneration in successor generations. The religious truths that in fact surface in the biblical materials revolve around liminal states and interstitial spaces, and with special beings who are simultaneously kings and prophets, saints and sinners, mediators and tricksters. The Bible affirms the role of the wilderness and the value of the reclusive life for having special experiences and acquiring special energies. It is from that space and regime that the prophet emerges to preach the message and perform heroic acts, even miracles. The religious truths also seem to focus on the dialectics of sexuality and procreation, incest taboos and marriage rules, and their observance and transgression, and on the tensions between endogamy and exogamy – all of which have implications for the maintenance of ancestry and group boundaries and personal identity. It also seems that religious narratives suggest in the face of official rules that the creative powers of foundational patriarchal leaders are linked to their breaking those rules (as seen from the un-orthodox marriages of Moses and Joseph). Lastly, Leach's establishing the immense importance and necessity of female figures in the biblical narratives, despite the male orientation of the edited canonical version, must be of interest and congenial to feminist writers on early and later Christianity, as well as on comparative religions.

CHAPTER 12

Anthropology of art and architecture

Leach had always on the side been interested in the objects and artifacts of the so-called "premodern"/"primitive" societies which had simultaneously aesthetic and religious/ritual and practical significances, and which in any case must be understood in the contexts of their use. The practice of removing objects from their contexts of production and use, and placing them in museums for viewing as exhibits, was an issue on which he had acerbic things to say. He was an advocate of informed ways of assembling museum objects that gave the alien viewer a sense of their multivalent attributes and the contexts in which they were originally deployed.[1] He was particularly interested in Melanesian objects, especially those from the Sepik River region, and from the Trobriands,[2] and in Hindu and Buddhist iconography.[3] He very much cherished his election as a Trustee of the British Museum.

It was however when he was engaged in his structuralist analysis of biblical narratives and Christian art and movements that Leach, who had a discriminating visual faculty and a phenomenal visual memory, began

[1] See Edmund Leach, "Aesthetics", in E.E. Evans-Pritchard, Raymond Firth, Edmund Leach et al., *The Institutions of Primitive Society: A Series of Broadcast Talks* Oxford: Blackwell, 1954, pp. 25–38. Reprinted as "Art in Cultural Context", in *Cultural and Social Anthropology: Selected Readings*, Peter B. Hammond (ed.), New York: Macmillan, 1964, pp. 344–50.

[2] The fine collection of Sepik artifacts collected by Gregory Bateson was deposited in the Haddon Museum at Cambridge University, and was much appreciated. Anthony Forge, a pupil of Leach, later studied Sepik artifacts and became an authority on them. Leach was very interested in the artistic, aesthetic, and textual researches of Giancarlo Scoditti, who did fieldwork in Kitava in the Trobriands. He was particularly taken with a wood carving of Monikiniki (snake figure) in Scoditti's collection. Malinowski had recognized Monikiniki as being in some sense the mythical founder of Kula, but had not recorded the relevant mythology. Leach had urged Scoditti to present the mythology he had recorded together with the iconographic decoding of the carving illustrated with photographs. I am grateful to Giancarlo for providing me with some correspondence written by Leach on this matter.

[3] In quite an early essay Leach included in his exposition the significance of iconographic features in Hindu–Buddhist sculpture: see Edmund Leach, "Pulleyar and the Lord Buddha: An Aspect of Religious Syncretism in Ceylon," *Psychoanalysis and the Psychoanalytic Review*, vol. 49, no. 2, Summer 1962, pp. 81–102.

to systematically examine and reveal the relationships between doctrinal cosmologies, their institutional realizations, and their visual and tactile representations in art and architecture. As previously underscored, Leach was irresistibly drawn to experimenting with and testing new ideas on anthropological materials, and to making interdisciplinary connections.

We have seen in chapter 11 his creative and effective use of a Dura mural of about the third century AD, and a painting by Gaddi and a sculpture by Michelangelo in the essay on Moses ("Why Did Moses Have a Sister?"). That piece was first delivered as the Huxley Lecture in 1980. But he had already delivered in 1972 as Presidential Address to the Royal Anthropological Institute the piece entitled "Melchisedech and the Emperor" which made very effective use of panels from S. Vitale at Ravenna and other murals and mosaics. He had personally made a trip to Ravenna and Rome (and other cities) to study the art he discusses.

In this chapter I shall recount three essays by Leach which portray his structuralist interpretations and anthropological perspectives on art and architecture, namely "Melchisedech and the Emperor: Icons of Subversion and Orthodoxy,"[4] "Michelangelo's Genesis: A Structuralist Interpretation of the Sistine Chapel Ceiling,"[5] and "The Gatekeepers of Heaven: Anthropological Aspects of Grandiose Architecture."[6]

"MELCHISADECH AND THE EMPEROR"

The essay "Melchisedech and the Emperor: Icons of Subversion and Orthodoxy" begins with a schema of a general cosmological system, exemplified in Christianity, in which "impotent Man on Earth is polarized against omnipotent God in Heaven." "Religion is concerned with mediation between the two spheres such that a channel is provided through which divine potency from Heaven is brought to bear upon the affairs of impotent Man on Earth."[7]

Leach says that ethnography reveals a variety of possible mediating systems of the above general type, but he singles out two particular patterns as especially frequent. The first he calls a "hierarchical model"

---

4 Edmund Leach, "Melchisedech and the Emperor: Icons of Subversion and Orthodoxy", Presidential Address of the Royal Anthropological Institute 1973, published in Leach and Aycock, *Structuralist Interpretations of Biblical Myth*, pp. 67–88.

5 First published as Edmund Leach: "Michelangelo's Genesis: Structural Comments on the Paintings of the Sistine Chapel Ceiling", *The Times Literary Supplement*, March 18, 1978. Revised version published in *Semiotica*, vol. 85, nos. 1/2, December 1985, pp. 1–30.

6 Edmund Leach, "The Gatekeepers of Heaven: Anthropological Aspects of Grandiose Architecture," *Journal of Anthropological Research*, vol. 39, no. 3, Fall 1983, pp. 243–64.

7 Leach, "Melchisedech," p. 67.

Figure 12.1. Melchisedech presents bread and wine to Abraham (credit: Alinari/Art Resource, New York).

and "an icon of orthodoxy"; the second he calls a "non-hierarchical model" and "an icon of subversion."

In the hierarchical model of orthodoxy, mediation is attempted through sacrifice. "The mediator is a human being, the priest of the sacrifice, who acts on behalf of a lay congregation. The sacrificial rite is viewed as an 'offering' to the Deity, and the priest, who stands in a superior position *vis-à-vis* his congregation, is in a supplicant status *vis-à-vis* the Deity."[8]

In the opposite non-hierarchical model of subversion, it is God who takes the initiative by offering grace to the faithful. "The individual devotee is directly inspired. The charisma is a direct gift from God which is in no way dependent upon the ritual efficacy of a mediating human priest . . . In empirical circumstances it is closely associated with millenarian belief and heretical radicalism."[9]

So far Leach's characterization of the two models of mediation between humans on earth and deity in heaven holds no surprises. But he next moves on to an issue on which he hopes to make a contribution. While a general theory of millenarian cults has been discussed in the recent writings of historians and social anthropologists, and though they have observed that in every case the basic chiliastic doctrine replicates ideas similar to those current among Judeo-Christians of the first century AD (as for example stated in the biblical book of Revelation), Leach knows of "no study which has attempted to apply modern millenarian theory to the known facts of early Christianity."[10] He gives notice that he would propose "a piece of second-hand sociological evidence" concerning the Arian heresy, and its repudiation by the fathers of Nicaea, about which there is little or no first-hand evidence.

Leach complains that although "the experts give full prominence to the way in which political intrigue influenced the outcome of individual Church Synods and Councils in early Christianity they have shown little interest in the social background of belief as such . . . Much preoccupation is given to the endless scholastic debates about the nature of the Trinity and the limits of Christ's humanity, but there is little attention to the question: 'in what sense was early Christian doctrine intermeshed with *its social context?*' " (emphasis added).

In pursuing this question, it is suggestive that if first-century Christianity consisted of a collectivity of overlapping millenarian cults, then from a comparative point of view, the history of the Puritan sects in seventeenth-century England becomes directly relevant. The reference here is to the study of the religion of the Levellers, the Diggers, the Seekers, the Ranters, the Fifth Monarchy Men, the Quakers, the Muggletonians, and so on by left-wing English historians led by

---

[8] Ibid., p. 67.   [9] Ibid., p. 67.   [10] Ibid., p. 68.

Christopher Hill.[11] From this study by Hill, and other studies of millenarianism, such as Norman Cohn's landmark portrayals of medieval Europe,[12] and keeping in mind Max Weber's conception of charisma and its routinization, Leach extracts certain features as possibly characteristic of millenarian movements as a general class. Of those he enumerates, the most salient for the theme of his essay can be seen to be the following.

Anxious concern for the end of time and the approach of the Last Judgment tends to reach a maximum in periods of exceptional political uncertainty. A necessary precondition for the formation of a *new* millenarian movement is that the secular context from which it emerges should *already* contain, in embryo, a self-identifiable community which perceives itself as alienated from the interests of the paramount political power. "Millenarianism is a creed for those who *feel* themselves to be deprived; it arises as a movement of protest against rulers who claim to exercise authority by divine will rather than as representatives of the general will."[13] While the missionary-apostles of the movement must always be persons of education and sophistication, those who join a *new* cult always feel themselves to be *politically* underprivileged.

Of particular relevance is the trajectory of these movements. In the initial phase the political theory of millenarian sects is always markedly egalitarian, with either communist or anarchist leanings, and their preachings inevitably come to be regarded as a threat to the legitimate forms of law and order.

The persecution and martyrdom which is a standard part of the syndrome is an automatic consequence of this situation . . . However, as time goes on, individual members of the persecuted anarchist minority begin to acquire social and political respectability . . . millenarian doctrines fade into the background. In the long run the heirs to the preachers of heresy are likely to end up as the mouthpieces of an established orthodoxy upon which the political regime leans for support.[14]

This overall process is in line with what Max Weber described as "the routinization of charisma," and the evolution of English Quakerism since 1651 provides a copy-book example of it.

---

[11] Christopher Hill, *The World Turned Upside Down: Radical Ideas During the English Revolution*, London: Temple Smith, 1972.
[12] Norman Cohn, *The Pursuit of the Millennium*, London: Secker & Warburg, 1957; Cohn, "Medieval Millenarism: Its Bearing on the Comparative Study of Millenarian Movements" in S.L. Thrupp (ed.), *Millennial Dreams in Action*, The Hague: Mouton, 1962.
[13] Leach, "Melchisedech," pp. 72–73.
[14] Ibid., p. 72.

Leach's next move is to find comparable evidence for the early Christian case, and he assesses this evidence to be "patchy but significant."[15] For example, the *Didache*, the relevant portions of which belong to the latter part of the first century, presupposes a situation in which the church had no central organization, no temples, no altars. The local sectarian communities were visited by "God inspired" prophets, but they also employed their own "bishop" who was an ordained minister. There was no large-scale hierarchy of church officials, though as early as the end of the first century the Bishop of Rome was claiming that he was uniquely qualified to decide issues of doctrine because of his direct apostolic succession from Peter and Paul.

One common heritage of the rival Christian sects was the belief that they were the new Israelites, the new Chosen People. The Jewish scriptures were interpreted as forefigurations of the Christian revelation. Christ is a second Adam; Moses leading the Israelites across the Red Sea was separating the Elect from the Damned. It is notable that in the *Didache* the sacrament of the Eucharist is viewed primarily as a common sacred meal through which the communicants assimilate to themselves the physical body of Christ as mediator. The doctrine of universal redemption is missing, and the Elect are presupposed. Jesus himself is a secondary being described as the servant (child) of God. All this suggests a similarity to the anti-hierarchical model.

In subsequent centuries there was a dialectical development corresponding to the success or failure of particular prelates in Rome or Constantinople or Alexandria or Antioch to assert paramountcy over ecclesiastical sees of varying scale. Wherever ecclesiastical hierarchy became elaborated millenarian doctrine fell into disfavour; vice versa, wherever a local schismatic church reasserted its independence millenarian belief once again became prominent.[16]

But by the fifth century Christianity had become the official state religion, so implicitly revolutionary doctrines were quite out of place. St. Augustine, who in his youth had inclined toward millenarian belief, now declared the millennium was simply a symbol standing for an entire Christian era. He died in AD 430, and spent the last years of his life teaming up with the political authorities in their suppression of the separatist, millenarian, and heretical Donatist movement.

At this point, moving closer to the heart of his own creative and original contribution, Leach introduces the Arian heresy and movement, so

---

[15] Ibid., p. 72.   [16] Ibid., p. 73.

as to delineate the cosmology associated with it in order to contrast it with the successor cosmology of the later established orthodox church, and thereafter to demonstrate the plausibility of his characterization by seeking visual iconographic evidence for it in church art.

Throughout the early centuries of doctrinal oscillation and evolution, the beliefs propounded by those who awaited an imminent millennium here on earth were invariably "Arian in style."[17] The particular doctrinal controversy known as the Arian heresy originated in AD 318 in Alexandria in a local quarrel between the bishop and his presbyter and was allegedly settled once and for all by the Council of Nicaea seven years later. But the issues that engendered the quarrel persisted for centuries before the Nicene ruling was accepted by the whole Christian Church. It would seem that representative early Christian Fathers of the second and third centuries expressed themselves in Arian style, and that the early Christian sects were both millenarian and Arian in disposition, the two features being closely linked. "The denunciation of Arianism in AD 325 was part and parcel of the decay of millenarian doctrine which followed logically from the political emancipation of the Church at large."[18]

The doctrinal and cosmological differences between the early Christian sects of an Arian disposition and the later orthodox churches revolved around the nature of deity and the humanity of Christ. A rough labeling is that the former was "monophysite" while the latter was "dyophysite." Leach describes their differences as follows:

Are the three persons of the Trinity eternal, coexistent, beings which are one with the First Cause, or is Deity a hierarchy of differentiated entities, parts of which are subordinate to the whole? Post-Nicene doctrine takes the former view. The Trinity is consubstantial, co-eternal. Likewise, in orthodox doctrine, the incarnate Jesus Christ was *both* "fully a human being with a human soul" *and* eternally, from the beginning "fully one with the First Cause of the Creation." Christ was one Person in two Natures. This doctrine has the direct implication that the Incarnation was a unique, once-for-all, non-rational, historical event which can never be repeated.

But the earlier Christians, as well as later schismatic opinion, diverged from this view in two directions. At one end it was held that Christ was always God and his human form only an appearance; at the other, the human Christ and the divine Logos, though housed in one fleshly body, were separate rather than fused. In either case, God as such has only one nature.

Monophysite doctrines of this latter kind have two important consequences. First they imply that there was a time when the incarnate Christ was not, and

---

[17] Ibid., p. 74.   [18] Ibid., p. 74.

hence that He is in some sense, a specially created being, secondary to the First Cause. But secondly they imply that any inspired human prophet who feels himself to be possessed by the Holy Spirit is really no different in kind, from Christ himself. Hence the incarnation ceases to be a unique historical event in the past; it becomes a perpetually repeatable event belonging in the present.[19]

The particular heresy for which Arius was condemned in AD 325 was the doctrine that the Christ-Logos was a created being, which carried the implication that *the Trinity is a hierarchy of separate persons of different degrees of efficacy*.

Now we come to Leach's innovative and unexpected correlational hypothesis concerning the early Christian dialectic and trajectory: "Visible hierarchy among deities goes with egalitarian politics among men; isolated monotheism goes with hierarchical politics among men."[20]

The second pattern consistent with Catholic orthodoxy (and anti-Arian in stance) has these features. At the top the doctrine of God-the-Trinity, consubstantial and coeternal. (The channels of mediation are the Cross and the Apostle.) Down below on earth is a religio-political hierarchy. In this system the legitimacy of any individual office-holder's actions derives from the delegated authority of some other office-holder higher up the system. At the top of the pyramid the legitimacy of the actions of the emperor-pope can derive from one source only, the direct authority of God himself. The common man can have no direct access to this ultimate power. His only approach is through the hierarchy of established *human* officers. "It follows that all theories about the commencement of 'new-time', or the immanent appearance of divine beings in human form, are politically subversive."[21] In Catholic doctrine, God and Jesus are one person in two natures, the completely divine, and the completely human. There is no hierarchy of greater and lower deities. This cosmology approximates the structure of sixth-century dyophysite orthodoxy in the reign of Justinian.[22]

In the pro-Arian type model of subversion, the present state of affairs is evil, and new time will come with the triumph of the revolution. The highest being is God the Father, "Christ-Logos" serves as mediator, and among humans there is a division between the Elect, the saints, who are

---

[19] Ibid., p. 75.   [20] Ibid., p. 83.   [21] Ibid., p. 76.

[22] Leach's diagram (figure 2, p. 77) gives the human hierarchy as follows. The emperor on top, with a dual structure of authority – one being bishop, presbyter, deacon, and the other governor, local official, police – meeting below at the level of the common man.

closer to redemption than the common man, and finally, the damned, including the "anti-christ" present rulers at the bottom.

In the Christian version of this doctrine God the Son – the Christ logos – becomes a subordinate function of the Father but closer and more approachable. This is consistent with, even required, in a context where rebellion is considered illegitimate by the existing secular hierarchy, and the radical sectarian's need for a directly approachable god by each individual whether he be priest or not.

In effect, God the Son and God the Holy Spirit become demi-gods; but equally, "the spiritual leaders of men are themselves almost demi-Gods since they are directly inspired by the Holy Spirit."[23] This model images the Arian millenarian heresy of the kind generally fashionable prior to AD 325.

Leach's final move is to propose a "testable hypothesis" that takes him into the territory of early Christian art. In structuralist theory, the geometry of cosmological ideas is their most fundamental characteristic. Therefore if his diagram of the cosmological schema is a "correct" structural representation of the difference between orthodoxy and Arianism then it should show up in the iconographic conventions of early Christianity.

But there is a hitch. Early Christian art was limited in quality, and very little of it now survives. "However it may plausibly be argued that where a datable early fifth-century mosaic contains an apparently 'established' convention, or repeats some theme of which there is an isolated instance in an earlier tomb painting from the catacombs, it is likely that the fifth-century picture derives from an original belonging to the fourth century or earlier."[24] This ingenious search leads Leach to a personage called Melchisedech, "a figure of considerable importance and the focus of much apocryphal mythology in the non-canonical literature of both sectarian Judaism and early Christianity."[25]

Since the pictorial evidence cannot be reproduced here in full, and Leach's interpretation of it is careful and therefore complex, I shall merely summarize the conclusions (leaving it to the expert scholars to peruse and assess the original text).

Only three major pictorial representations of Melchisedech as he figures in a passage in Genesis 14 have survived since antiquity. This passage says that "Melchisedech king of Salem brought forth bread and wine: and he was the priest of the most high God. And he blessed him, and said 'Blessed be Abram of the most high God... which hath delivered

---

[23] Ibid., p. 76.　　[24] Ibid., p. 78.　　[25] Ibid., p. 78.

thine enemies into thy hands' ..." The early Christian fathers treated this incident as a prefiguration of the Eucharist, in accordance with the principle of the recapitulation of time.

The first picture comes from Santa Maria Maggiore, Rome (see fig 12.1). In it Melchisedech as priest presents bread and wine to Abraham as communicant. They have equal standing. The Christ-Logos floats overhead in human form pointing at Melchisedech. There is no altar or other ritual paraphernalia. Leach suggests that the floating Christ-Logos refers back to the kind of argument presented by Justin Martyr in the second century that the Creator of all things who always remains above the heavens and is never seen by man is to be distinguished from another God, under the creator of all things, who appeared to Abraham, Moses, and Joshua. This picture thus is in line with the millenarian context of the early literature, in which Melchisedech figures, and in which the Arian view of a mediating deity (Christ) separated from God the creator was operative.

Plates 2 and 3 are taken from San Vitale, Ravenna, and San Apollinare in Classe, Ravenna. In these two pictorial examples, "God is off-stage and points at the scene with a three fingered hand projecting through the sky. Melchisedech is explicitly the priest at the Eucharist, engaged in a ritual involving an altar."[26] Both churches are of the same date; they were dedicated in 548 and 549 respectively. This is the time of Justinian, when the Arian view of the mediating deity is already thoroughly heretical, and the orthodox view would have been that of St. Augustine. In so far as Christ is Word, he is co-equal with God. The decorations of the two churches commemorated the reassertion of full Byzantine authority over Italy. Thus not only do the pictures embody explicit anti-Arian propaganda, but the original decorations of San Vitale include the Emperor Justinian and Empress Theodora and their hierarchized courts (Plates 4 and 5 in the text). The emperor and empress are distinguished by halos; they are living saints, near deities.

Leach provides other pictorial evidence from San Vitale, Ravenna, which contains representations of sacrifice, for example, Abraham's sacrifice of Isaac, Abel's offering of a lamb, and adds additional proof of this assertion that all the Ravenna mosaics are "icons of orthodoxy" in his language. There is much other close reading of the iconographic details of the Ravenna mosaics in the essay which correlates with the rival cosmological schemes of orthodoxy and subversion that Leach

[26] Ibid., p. 79.

had postulated from the textual readings in the first part of the essay.
Melchisedech, King of Salem, is in the Arian millenarian reading the
King of New Jerusalem, a "revolutionary" in new time; by the time of
Justinian orthodoxy, he is King of Peace as well as King of Justice and
Righteousness, and serves as a support for conservative attitudes, and
an appropriate symbol for a Christian Roman Emperor, between whom
as human mediator and human commoners there is a steep hierarchy,
and above whom there is no hierarchy of superhuman mediators for the
Trinity is consubstantial.

In conclusion, then, Leach has striven to substantiate a number of hypotheses in this experimental and innovative essay: that the "model" that
emerged as the outcome of structuralist and sociological analysis correlates with that which emerged from a study of iconography; that the
two contrasting theologies, one that is appropriate for rebellion against
established authority and the other that supports an established hierarchical authority, are not just polar attitudes but dialectical attitudes; that
the pictorial illustrations of Melchisedech showed a shift of iconographic
convention corresponding to his thesis, and that "the iconographic conventions themselves have a visual structure which is already implicit in the
power of any verbal agreement."[27] Correspondences of this sort "could
well have implications for our understanding of contemporary events as
well as those of ancient history."[28]

"MICHELANGELO'S GENESIS"

The next essay under the rubric of art and architecture that I shall
consider is "Michelangelo's Genesis: A Structuralist Interpretation of
the Central Panels of the Sistine Chapel Ceiling." It had a long run
on the lecture circuit: it had its origin as an illustrated lecture given at
the Courtauld Institute, London, on February 9, 1977, and a version
of it without illustrations (a mishap due to a printers' strike) was published in *The Times Literary Supplement* on March 18 of that year. Much
revised versions of the lecture were subsequently given to a variety of
anthropological/history of art audiences in widely dispersed localities
including Vancouver, Cambridge, London, and Sydney. The final version printed in *Semiotica* in 1985 was based on a lecture given to an Indiana
University audience in Bloomington in October 1984 as one of the
Patten Foundation lectures. Professor Sebeok generously made it possible

---

[27] Ibid., p. 84.   [28] Ibid., p. 84.

for eighteen plates of the panels of the Sistine Chapel to be reproduced in the essay, and thus we have at hand a richly illustrated essay in which the visual medium is subjected to a structuralist analysis.

Leach's topic is the patterning of the iconography in the principal pictures on the ceiling of the chapel. He is humbly aware that there is a vast bibliography of writings relating to Michelangelo and many treatises by art historians devoted to describing, commenting on, and interpreting the panels. But he is proposing that his structuralist mode of analysis has something to offer that has been missed by most of the art historians.[29]

We have already by now viewed so many of Leach's "structuralist" analyses that we may think that we do not need to have yet another statement of his analytical procedures. But since there are always some new twists and unexpected illuminations in his wide-ranging essays, it is wise to follow the route he maps so as not to miss some new insights sprouting among the familiar dogmas.

Obviously Michelangelo had to some extent intentionally evolved a design of the artistic project he was about to execute; and he was to some extent constrained by the materials he had to work with, by the existing structure of the chapel, by the wishes and requirements of his patrons, the principal one being the Pope, by the biblical treatment of his artistic theme, by prior and current art styles, etc. So what is it that Leach thinks his theory and method of structuralism can reveal that is special to it?

His answer is as follows:

Roughly speaking structuralist method (as I practise it) consists of making a meticulous and comparative examination of *sets* of human artifacts – the projected products of human thought – with a view to discovering their shared design content, their common structure. It is assumed that part of that structure is there because of the *intentional* operations of the designer who has to tackle, at a conscious level, the various technical and client oriented problems I have mentioned already. But other parts of the structure appear to be there by accident in the sense that they serve no immediate practical function. They are there because they have given the designer some kind of aesthetic pleasure without his knowing why. It is especially, though not exclusively, patterns of this latter kind which interest the theorists of structuralism.[30]

---

[29] Leach mentions that a paper by the art historian S. Sinding-Larsen ("A Re-reading of the Sistine Ceiling," *Acta ad Archaeologiam et Artum Historiam Pertinentia*, vol. 4, 1969, pp. 143–57) has conclusions "that dovetail in very well with those of my own account which relies on a quite different technique of analysis." He encountered this paper a good while after he had produced his first version, and therefore finds the coincidence of views reassuring.

[30] Leach, "Michelangelo's Genesis," *Semiotica*, 1985, p. 3.

On the other hand, among the various possibilities, one factor which quite certainly influenced the final outcome was Michelangelo's own sixteenth century, Florentine, apprehension of the Christian significance of the chapters of Genesis, through which he interpreted whatever instructions were given to him by his theological advisers.

Here Michelangelo was working within a long established artistic convention which is manifested in a whole series of quite explicit cross-references from the Old Testament to the New through the ordering of the designs. However, when he moulded that convention to fit in with the particular requirements of the total logic of his complicated overall design, it seems very likely that he did not fully understand, at a conscious level, just what he was doing. He did what he did partly because that was how the jigsaw puzzle worked out, but also because that was somehow how it had to be. My purpose is to show you, at least in part, just why it had to be like that.[31]

It is this kind of part-conscious, part-unconscious, subliminal logic that the structuralist is looking for because *he* believes that the structure of such a logic will help us to understand something of significance about the nature of aesthetics and of the operation of human minds in general.[32]

Freud and his successors have made us familiar with the idea of "unconscious thought" as a product of repression. The therapeutic value of psychoanalysis was supposed to consist of the release of this repression and thus to make the unconscious conscious.

Structuralists think of the "unconscious" in a much more mathematical way ... Conscious thought consists of *establishing relations between concepts in the mind* by metonymy ... or by metaphor ... But the further combination and recombination of such "concepts in the mind" through the process we describe as *imagination* is not a fully conscious operation. It is the outcome of some deeper level mental process, a kind of meta-thinking which does not, of itself, generate conscious thoughts but makes creative originality possible in that it consists of *the establishment of relations between relations* ... For structuralists, the unconscious is a kind of nonrational logic; what Lévi-Strauss has called "mytho-logic". The operations of this mytho-logic are apparent in the way that the products of human thinking are projected onto the material world and if we look hard enough in the right way, we can recognize what they are.[33]

Leach focuses in this essay on the nine main panels and the four corner panels of the Sistine Chapel ceiling (see figures 12.2 and 12.3), and lets us see how he carries out his structuralist program. Since I cannot reproduce here the eighteen plates to which Leach refers in detail I can

---

[31] Ibid., p. 4.   [32] Ibid., p. 4.   [33] Ibid., p. 5.

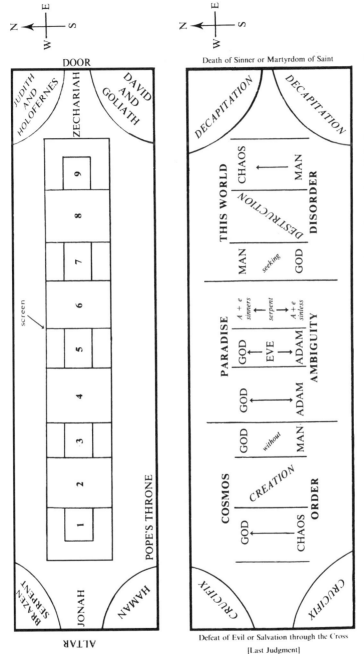

Figure 12.2. Leach's own diagram of the structural arrangement of the nine main panels and the four corner panels in the Sistine Chapel ceiling.

945 - ROMA - Soffitto della Cappella Sistina - Michelangelo - Vaticano

Anderson

Figure 12.3. Michelangelo, ceiling of Sistine Chapel, Vatican (full view) (credit: Alinari/Art Resource, New York).

only summarize the main points and leave it to the interested reader to go to the original essay.

First a few words about the chapel itself as it was in 1508:

The proportions are those of Solomon's Temple in the Book of Kings. The length is twice the height and three times the width. The orientation is West East with the altar at the West end. In 1508 as the visitor entered at the East end he saw to his right (on the North side) a row of large rectangular pictures relating to the life of Christ while on the opposite (South) wall there was a row of similar pictures relating to the life of Moses. The scenes served to emphasize the legal authority of the Pope as successor to both Moses and Christ in the capacities of law giver, priest, teacher, and ruler. Most of the pictures are still as they were then but Michelangelo's fresco of the Last Judgment, which now fills the West wall behind the altar, was not painted until 1535–1541.

And now the panels:

Notice at once that the nine center panels are arranged in alternation small-large-small-large (Plate 4 and Figure 1). This was dictated in part by the physical form of the roof. But, besides having to adjust his overall composition to the peculiarities of the shape of the vaulting Michelangelo also took account of the various uses of the floor space below.

As it is today the screen which separates the ante-chapel from the chapel proper comes under Panel 7 (Plate 11) "Noah's Sacrifice" but the screen was originally closer to the altar and stood directly beneath the border between Panel 5 (Plate 9) "The Creation of Eve" and Panel 6 (Plate 10) "The Fall".

This detail is important because it meant that the distinction between the Chapel proper (at the Altar end), which was reserved for the Pope and the Cardinals, and the Ante-Chapel, which was sometimes open to aristocratic laity, is marked in the ceiling as the distinction between Sacred and Profane.

All the main panels to the West of the screen (as it then was) show God in his role as Creator; all the main panels to the East of the screen towards the door, show sinful man without God. Directly over and to the East of the screen is the crisis of the Fall, the boundary between this World of Suffering and the Other World of Paradise. It is relevant, as we shall see in a moment, that in medieval churches the screen separating the nave from the choir was commonly fronted by a crucifix and known as the "rood-screen" on that account.

Figure 1 (cf. Plate 4) summarizes the general structure of the iconography. Panels 1, 2, and 3 show God in the Cosmos without Man. Panels 4, 5, and 6 show the Garden of Eden Story in which God and Man are together in Paradise. Panels 7, 8, and 9 relate to the story of Noah where sinful Man is in this World separated from God. Thus the middle triad mediates the two extremes. This mediation pattern is repeated in various symmetries.

Panel 8 "The Flood" (Plate 12) (which was the first to be painted) represents the *destruction* of the World and is symmetrically opposite to Panel 2 "The Creation of the World" (Plate 6). Midway between we have Panel 5 (Plate 9) where "The Creation of Eve" – symbolizing The Church – mediates directly between God and a seemingly dead Adam, whose deadness is emphasized by the manifestly dead tree against which he "sleeps". And let me remind you again that this figure of Eve stands at the exact center of the entire ceiling. As we shall see, there are several other such triads.[34]

Let me here interject the point that Leach is throughout his explication probing the logic of the arrangement of the panels as triads; and invoking his favorite Euler diagram, he focuses in particular on the intersecting boundary between two opposed categories as the mediating and creative and ambiguous betwixt and between component. Thus the middle panel in the triadic arrangement of panels, and again the middle part *within* a panel, are focused on as special zones of the sacred, the sites of ritual action, and the locus of intermediaries who combine opposite values, or who are generative in producing the paired polarities.

What kind of readings of triadic structures in the panels does Leach offer? Here are some examples:

Panel 1: The division of light from darkness is also made to serve as the emergence of God himself from the void; order out of chaos. As already indicated the position of this panel at the apex immediately above the altar is crucial.

At one level, the sequence of images is:

Panel 1 – the emergence of order out of chaos
Panel 2 – the creation of the world
Panel 3 – God by himself surveying his creation

But at another level these three panels form a triad representing the three Persons of the Trinity. At the center (Panel 2) is God the Creator of all things. At the altar end (Panel 1) is God the Son, the *light of the world*, the *Logos* of St. John's Gospel Chapter 1. Panel 3 – "the Spirit of God moving upon the waters" – is then The Holy Ghost.[35]

Compare the diagram in figure 1 with Michelangelo's Panel 1 – God dividing light from darkness, order from chaos' (Plate 5). Notice how the light and the dark half of the picture are separated by the half-formed emergent figure of God himself. God *is* the boundary, the entity that is both itself and not itself. Incidentally the light is on the side towards the high altar. With all that in mind let us go back to my diagram of the general layout (Figure 1).[36]

---

[34] Ibid., pp. 9–10.   [35] Ibid., p. 16.   [36] Ibid., p. 17.

Leach explicates the manner in which different episodes and persons in the Genesis account are elided or fused; for example, in Panel 7 Noah's sacrifice is presented in seemingly wrong sequence as occurring before the Flood (Panel 8); but Panel 6 depicting the expulsion from the Garden of Eden is logically followed by the sacrifice of Abel by Cain. Thus Panel 7 depicts both sacrifices in the middle panel.

Similarly, Leach clarifies the ambiguity in Panel 9 depicting the story of the drunken Noah and the sin of Ham. But Michelangelo's model for Noah is that of delving Adam by Jacopo della Quercia;

So it looks as if the Noah story and the Adam story are here purposely elided. And after all, why not? Adam and Noah were both "First Men". But there is a difference: Adam suffered disaster because of his sins; Noah survived because of his virtues.

Likewise in Panel 8 "The Flood" (Plate 12) there is ambiguity about the discrimination between the Sacred and the Damned. If we follow the Bible story then it must be presumed that all the figures in view are about to meet their end since Noah and his family are already safely housed in the strange windowless Ark in the background (from which the white dove of the Holy Spirit emerges from the roof). But matters are not so simple. The symbolism here was well established. The Ark is the Church; the Flood is a prefiguration of the sacrament of Baptism which washes away our sins. In that case the figures in the foreground are, as they appear to be, "saved" rather than "damned".[37]

Leach brings to our attention that the panels simultaneously cross-reference Old Testament episodes with New Testament ones, that there is both a prefiguration of events to come from the Old to the New as well as an inversion in the meaning from negative fall of man to positive redemption of man through Christ.

It is only quite recently that the critics have noticed that for an ordinary lay observer the sequence is back to front, Creation in reverse. Entering by the door at the East end we start with Man alone in his corruption and are led back step by step to assimilation with God. The unstated text for the whole composition is the passage from St. Paul: "As in Adam all die; so also in Christ shall all men be made alive."

This Old Testament/New Testament inversion is reiterated all the way through. The key points for our understanding of this fact have already been mentioned. First, Eve, whose creation has pride of place at the Center, is also the Virgin Mary, the second Eve, the "Church of my Salvation", just as Adam is also the second Adam, Christ the Redeemer. But furthermore, where one might

[37] Ibid., p. 18.

expect a Crucifix above and in front of the rood screen, we in fact encounter a cruciform Tree of Life around which is coiled the Serpent of the Garden of Eden.[38]

In the section devoted to "the triads within the triads" Leach treats us to the ambiguities, prefigurations, inversions, and elisions in each of the three crucial central panels relating to the paradise world of the Garden of Eden where God and Man come face to face:

In Panel 4 (Plate 8) in which Adam is separated from God but an uncreated Eve and a pre-incarnate Christ nestle in the womb of time, that [ambiguity?] is provided by the left arm of God the Father. The future Sin and the future Redemption of Mankind are both already preordained.

In Panel 5 (Plate 9) Eve (the Virgin, the Church) mediates between the living God and the "dead" Adam. But in Panel 6 (Plate 10) the middle position of mediation/ambiguity is taken up by the unambiguously female Serpent who has a face very like that of Eve in the previous panel but facing in the opposite direction while on the left the as yet sinless but about to be corrupted Eve, nestling in Adam's groin, has become outstandingly seductive though she still retains the face of the perky uncreated Eve of Panel 4 (Plate 8). The forbidden fruit take the form of figs (not apples) while the idle hand of the as yet sinless Eve points to her womb.[39]

On the right of the picture the sinners cower from the wrath of God as they are driven from Paradise. They have both lost their pristine beauty and are aged and haggard. But notice how, even in this arid world of despair, hope is renewed; a sprig of greenery which really belongs to the border of the adjacent panel has been allowed to overflow into the desert sky.

But the key ambiguity comes, as it should, at the center in the form of the Serpent/Tempter coiled around the Tree of Life and in that of the Tree itself. There are really two serpents; one faces the still innocent Eve and *grasps* her by the hand; the other is the arm of God, the Biblical Cherubim who drives out the sinners from the Paradise Garden armed with a flaming sword which turned every way, to keep the way of the tree of "life".

But the two serpents combined to provide yet another key symbol. There was a medieval tradition that the crucifix on which Christ died to redeem our sins was cut from the Tree of Life that grew in the Garden of Eden. Here, in the picture, the Serpent, the Cherubim and the Tree are combined in a cruciform image which stands, let us remember, above and just in front of the rood screen. This device of the double headed serpent forming a cross is repeated in the corner panel to the right of the altar.[40]

---

[38] Ibid., pp. 20–21.

[39] Leach cites here Les Steinberg, "The Line of Fate of Michelangelo's Painting," *Critical Inquiry*, vol. 6, no. 3, 1980, pp. 441, 443.

[40] Leach, "Michelangelo's Genesis", pp. 21–22.

... the theme of the double serpent turned crucifix recurs in the corner panel to the right of the altar (Plate 15). The text for this picture comes from Exodus. The Israelites wandering in the Wilderness complain to God who punishes them for their lack of faith by sending a plague of serpents. Moses appeals to God. God instructs Moses to set up a brazen serpent with the promise that those who gaze upon this seemingly idolatrous figure will be cured. Michelangelo depicts this scene using a long established convention. Moses does not appear. The saved and damned are separated, the saved being on the altar side, to the left of the picture as shown in Plate 15. As before, the serpent is two headed though here it is an explicit symbol of salvation instead of an explicit symbol of damnation. In this case the crucifix-serpent is lit by the glory of God shining from the divine light of Panel 1 (Plate 5) immediately above.

The association between the story of *The Brazen Serpent* and the Crucifixion has direct biblical sanction. It comes in St. John's Gospel: "And as Moses lifted up the serpent in the wilderness even so must the Son of Man be lifted up: that whosoever believeth in him should not perish but have eternal life." That much the orthodox critics have noticed, but they have not paid any attention to the consequential feedback for our understanding of the corresponding imagery in Panel 6 which, as we have seen, puts the Crucifix in the Garden of Eden (Plate 10). The implication is surely plain. As we proceed from the altar towards the door the Serpent in the Tree of Life stands for damnation through Adam; as we reverse our steps and move from the door to the altar the same image is symbolic of Christ on the Cross of Death and stands for salvation through Christ.[41]

Leach deals with a number of other inversions,[42] but the summary implication of all of them is that "at a grand scale level, the Old Testament message concerning the Creation and the Fall, that appears in the panels when read in sequence from altar to door, should be inverted and read as a New Testament message of Redemption through the Crucifixion and the Eucharist when the same panels are read from door to altar."[43]

The New Testament meaning, he claims, is ordinarily the direct converse of the manifest Old Testament meaning, and this argument rests on the "mytho-logic" uncovered by his structuralist reading. Modern orthodox scholarship tends to be scornful of ambiguity, "yet many practicing artists would themselves maintain all artistic statement is ambiguous."[44]

---

[41] Ibid., p. 25.

[42] Having examined certain panels in detail he sums up: "The switching from Old Testament to New Testament entails a dramatic reversal of roles. The villainous Haman turns into Christ; the villainous Holofernes into John the Baptist. But in the latter scene the saintly Judith becomes the villainous Herodias." Ibid., p. 27.

[43] Ibid., p. 27.   [44] Ibid., p. 28.

And as a parting shot he says that so far he has "exercised great restraint" but that

A more thoroughgoing polysemic, structuralist interpretation would take it for granted that all the identifiable female figures in the total composition should be seen as aspects or transformations of the same mythical persona. And indeed, if we adopt that view then even within the limited subset of pictures which we have considered, the Virgin Queen of Heaven appears in *all* her traditional roles.

Starting from the door end she is: (i) the victor over Satan (Judith); (ii) the suffering mother (The Flood); (iii) the wife of the Lord (Sacrifice Panel); (iv) the sister (The Fall); (v) the daughter of God (Creation of Eve); (vi) the mediating Queen of Heaven (Haman and the Last Judgment).[45]

In conclusion, I would venture the view that "Michelangelo's Genesis" is one of the best essays that Leach attempted on the anthropology of art. He once again boldly ventures into a field that is considered the province of art historians, and while acknowledging their scholarship and contributions, he proffers his own "structuralist" analysis of an artistic production as capable of bringing to light certain features unconsidered or unseen by most of them. The essay demonstrates well the systematic nature of the structuralist method he espoused and developed, and the imaginative revelation of the powerful, creative, and transformative role of ambiguous in-between middle terms in triadic arrangements.

"THE GATEKEEPERS OF HEAVEN"

I shall consider one final essay by Leach in which he again focused his anthropological searchlight on a domain few anthropologists venture into. It is titled "The Gatekeepers of Heaven: Anthropological Aspects of Grandiose Architecture."[46] For a theorist who had been interested in the many features of language as a medium of communication, architecture was intriguing to explore because it is a domain in which human beings have expressed ideas, emotions, and feelings

in media other than either spoken language or writing of the ordinary sort which is just a transcription of speech forms. The members of all societies, complex as well as primitive, externalize the ideas they hold about the physical and metaphorical universes, and about the social relations within their own society, by making and manipulating artifacts . . . which are all expressive of *human ideas,*

---

[45] Ibid., p. 29.
[46] Leach "The Gatekeepers of Heaven." This was delivered as part of the Harvey Distinguished Visiting Lecture Series made possible by a grant from Byron Harvey III to the Department of Anthropology, University of New Mexico.

some of which are perfectly well known at a conscious level of human experience, while others are only dimly perceived and exist only as sets of relations within the artificially constructed world of culture.[47]

Leach specifies the kind of semiotic approach he would deploy to "decode the messages which are . . . embodied in human artifacts and their combinations."[48] There is one significant parallel between spoken languages and the languages of non-verbal cultural communication which he would exploit in this essay, namely "the overriding importance of *context*." He says that the "pompous" words, "the space syntax of sacred buildings," may be stated in simpler language to be concerned with simple questions such as: "Why do architects make a fuss about the entrances to grandiose buildings?" and "Does the iconography which is used to decorate grandiose entrances have any distinguishing characteristics?"[49]

The question that Leach was nudging his audience at the University of New Mexico to consider is this: they were familiar with viewing individual displays in Western museums as "beautiful objects" mainly in the tradition of aesthetic values which is now accepted in Europe and America, but what difference could it make to look at such things in their *original* context?

Leach distinguishes two aspects in his explication of *context*, namely "architectural context" and "religious context." By architectural context he has in mind the syntagmatic and paradigmatic linkages and relations between architectural components as groupings in their original settings as temples and palaces. By religious context he has in mind the cosmological schema of complex religious systems such as those in ancient Egypt, India, and Cambodia in which "human kings merge into superhuman gods" and "the palaces of divine kings have a very similar ground plan to the layout of temples." The result is that "topologically speaking the basic layout of all kinds of temples and palaces the world over is almost completely standardized."[50] The Cambodian temple city of Angkor Thom was a replica of the fabled Hindu cosmology, a small model of the universe, a microcosm of the central continent of Jambudvipa with Meru the cosmic mountain rising at its center. Similarly the ancient temple of Edfu, dating from the third century BC, had the cosmographic function of mimicking and recording the structure of the world: the temple was the god's dwelling and the center of the cult, and its layout presupposes a central core which is the throne room, and it is surrounded by concentric

---

[47] Ibid., p. 243. Leach is not including hieroglyphs in this statement.
[48] Ibid., pp. 243–44.   [49] Ibid., p. 244.   [50] Ibid., p. 248.

box-like spaces and a more elaborate sequence of graded spaces leading to the outer entrance.

Since it is Hindu temples, in particular the famous one at Khajuraho with its extraordinary sculpture, that are the main concern of this essay on "Gatekeepers of Heaven" let us pay more attention to them. In elaborate Hindu temples

the principal shrine at the center is nearly always supplemented by subsidiary shrines, which are encountered on the way in or out at each successive threshold, and there is always a relatively major shrine-like edifice just inside or outside the main entrance. The ground plan is not always rectangular; it may be circular or apse shaped, but the nested arrangement by which the human visitor moves from the secular world outside through a series of screened stages, each with its own shrine-like gateway, seems to be invariable.

One infers from Leach's discussion of the relation between the architectural context and the religious context that, while the religious encompasses the architectural and sculptural, in that it is religious conceptions that are being imaged and represented, at the same time it has to be grasped that they are made manifest by the architectural manipulation and molding of space, form, and shape.

The essay is accompanied by a number of pictorial illustrations, the majority of them taken from Khajuraho and other Hindu sites, and the reader must study them closely in conjunction with the text to appreciate the "puzzles" Leach sets up and how he solves them in *anthropological terms*, not necessarily in art historical or formal architectural terms.

It is widely known that the outside surface of the temple buildings at Khajuraho are studded with a multitude of juxtaposed sculptured figures of many different kinds. Let us begin with a pair of them. Leach presents two scantily dressed figures still in situ: one is that of a temple prostitute, "the attribution being due presumably to the scorpion on her leg, which certainly suggests that she has very witch like qualities of some sort."[51] She is a very close cousin to another figure, who appears frequently, and is "described as an apsara, a celestial being, presumably because the properly clothed male figure at her side is in a devotional stance and has four arms, and is therefore a deity."[52] Such juxtapositions exist by the score: scholarly theorizing gyrates around what kind of inference to make – should we infer that these temples were designed for cults concerned with ascetic devotion or with tantric eroticism? Leach does not seek an answer in these terms, but notes that the two ladies standing

---

[51] Ibid., p. 246.   [52] Ibid., p. 246.

lose something if each is considered by herself, and that "such sculptures as groups (may) signify more than each figure taken by itself." And from there he moves on to make an unexpected interpretive suggestion regarding the fact that erotic and ascetic scenes of groups of men and women, deities and humans, deities and animals are found in profusion at Khajuraho, and that they are so located that they can only be recognized if you look rather hard. "They do not have the prominence which the picture books suggest. In context, they look quite different. What is really characteristic of such imagery is *the jumble*: ladies adorning themselves, deities and princes at their devotions, naked women, couples in sexual embrace, a dancer taking a thorn from her foot, a serpent goddess (*nagini*) with cobras providing her halo, *a confusion of the natural and the supernatural*" (emphasis added).[53]

Again, Leach observes that "the *immediate* impact of the sculptured imagery from the observer's point of view is a jumble. And that is the very essence of what I am saying: *the jumble is the message* . . . You should not imagine that this is a peculiarity of Indian architectural style. The same is true of the greatest masterpieces of European medieval church architecture . . . the art historian is of course taught just the opposite." Photographs may pick out a central figure in an ensemble or array, "but *that is not what the designers intended.*"[54]

Leach's seemingly shocking thesis is based on the architectural setting of the sculptured representations and their visual impact on any observer as a jumble and confusion. This inference partly derives from his espousal of semiotic and communication theory (including the concept of redundancy) that suggests that the figures in question as presented must be seen as related to one another as members of a set or array, that at a distance they seem fused. The inference also partly – and perhaps more weightily – derives from considering the cosmology of temples and churches translated into architectural spatial distributions of forms that require that central points, and thresholds, and boundaries surrounding them, be aesthetically imaged in certain appropriate manners, to convey certain experiences to worshipers (and visitors) as they proceed from outside to inside, and from periphery to center.

The two architectural puzzles that Leach sets up and attempts to answer are why jumbles of figures are presented at *certain* places or points in the temple complex, and why gateways are frequently the most elaborate feature of the entire complex.

---

[53] Ibid., pp. 250–51. [54] Ibid., p. 20.

What is engaging about the answers is that Leach resorts to the by now familiar conceptions of mediations and mediators, thresholds and liminal spaces, openings and orifices, boundaries and barriers to penetratingly illuminate aspects of their semiotic and symbolic significance in the shaping and presentation of religious conceptions and the embodying of religious experience.

Shrines and temples, however they may be constructed, are "in reality" physical objects within the confines of the world – they are *gateways* to heaven (or to hell). And equally, of course, the gateways into temples are gateways into gateways, thresholds of thresholds. Artists, architects, poets, mythographers the world over have this common problem: How do we best symbolize this notion of the threshold between the "here and the now" and "the other"?

The true representation of the Other, the Absolute Other, Deity *as such*, is logically impossible, for representation must be in terms of things of this world, and deity, by definition, is not made of the stuff of this world. Consequently all attempts to represent deity in material form may be considered sacrilegious. This is the case in Islam and in iconoclastic forms of Christianity, and also in early Buddhism.[55]

Empty spaces of a mosque; or in the opposite direction, solid objects of abstract shapes with relics in their "womb" around which the pious ambulate (e.g. Buddhist *dagoba* or *stupa*); combinations of abstract geometrical shapes cum naturalist forms like the Hindu lingam-yoni, the Christian crucifix, both of which are depersonalized but have phallic origins – all these devices and vehicles cope with the representation of the absolute centermost and highest.

But the practical iconographic problem is not really how to represent absolute deity in material form . . . the question is rather how to represent the *mediators*, the mystical entities which are betwixt and between, neither altogether divine nor altogether human, but God and man at the same time, the gatekeepers of heaven, the guardians of the threshold. I have already given the answer – the jumble is the message. The betwixt and between is represented by the union and transportation of opposites as in the Christian calvary, where saint and sinner merge with god/man.[56]

In many Hindu and Buddhist transpositions, the relevant imagery, or the relevant shrine, will be found *outside* the shrine or throne room of a higher being. One illustration of this is provided by a group of figures from the Kandariya Mahadeva Temple in Khajuraho (Figure 6 in the original

[55] Ibid., p. 251.   [56] Ibid., p. 253.

text). The scenes presented are enormously complicated, "but two unobvious points about the design emerge only from the context. First, it is located on the inner wall of the ambulatory immediately surrounding the innermost shrine of this particular complex, and the space is so small that the devotee will almost rub up against the figures. Second, it would ordinarily be invisible except by the light of a flickering oil lamp. The visible imagery you see here (in the picture in the text) was never intended; it is the product of modern technology in form of a photoflash![57]

A second illustration is provided by another figure taken from Mukhalingeshvara Temple, Gamjam (ca. 800 AD), of Vishnu in his avatar form of Narasingha, half-lion/half-man, destroying the demon king (Hiranyakasipu). You do not encounter such images in the main shrine of a temple, but only in subsidiary shrines somewhere between the outside and the central core.

(. . . Narasingha eventually destroyed the demon king at dusk (which is neither day nor night), at a threshold (which is neither inside nor outside), by laying his victim on his lap (which is neither on the ground nor in the air), by tearing out his entrails with his claws (which is neither by disease nor by wounding with a weapon).[58]

We can now turn to the issue of why a fuss is made over gateways. "The *usual* characteristic of sacred precincts is that the outermost boundary is distinguished from the secular world of normality either by a zone of tabooed territory or by a wall, or both. Where there is a wall there must be a gate. And this gateway is always relatively elaborate. Quite often it is the *most* elaborate feature of the entire architectural complex. Now this is surely rather odd."[59]

The essence of the matter is that gateways get exaggerated architectural and aesthetic treatment because they are felt to be sacred. They are felt to be sacred because they are, in a quite fundamental sense, intrinsically ambiguous. They are neither on the inside nor on the outside. In crossing boundaries we break down the classifications by which order is established; at the boundary, male becomes female, clean becomes dirty, material becomes immaterial, nature becomes culture, animality becomes humanity, humanity becomes divinity.[60]

At this point, Leach introduces a supporting thought: the homology between the human body and a building. "Most buildings have windows for eyes, a front door for mouth, a back door for anus."[61] Leach remarks that in the drab industrial town of Rochdale in which he grew up, where most of the inhabitants lived in soot-encrusted barracks-like terraced

---

[57] Ibid., p. 251.   [58] Ibid., p. 253.   [59] Ibid., p. 249.   [60] Ibid., p. 256.   [61] Ibid., p. 256.

houses, "at least once a week the front door of each dwelling was scrubbed and scrubbed to a shining whiteness."[62] The human body of course has a more complex set of orifice openings into the external world (e.g. the genitals, mouth, nose, and ears) but the body model is greatly simplified before it is "transformed" into material and architectural imagery. In the religious art of a variety of cultures the world over, the following equations hold good: the top half of the body is treated as homologous to the bottom half; the orifices of the mouth and the nose become the orifices of anus and penis; thus nose = penis. Leach illustrates this with a picture of a spectacular mask from the Sepik River in New Guinea collected by Gregory Bateson. The face is expressly designed to be both man-like and pig-like; the nose is explicitly phallic, and is tipped with the form of a sago weevil, a totemic creature credited with the powers of spontaneous generation. In Hinduism, there is the famous deity with a long nose, Ganesha, son of the god Shiva, guardian of thresholds, not only spatially in that he stands at the front entrance but also in that he is virtually addressed at the beginning of an enterprise.

From here Leach turns his attention to how Hindu sculpture iconographically images the conception of deity

as a kind of latent potency (symbolized as male) and active potency (symbolized as female) . . . while the totality of deity is often represented iconographically by a male, many-armed figure with a female consort at his side, the combination of latent and active potency can also be shown by contrasting the violent activity of a male dancer with the passive stance of a yogi in meditation. Such a combination is the equivalent of the hermaphrodite figure of a male deity, which is likewise very common.[63]

"Still another way of associating the passive latent potency of god with mundane reality is to give deity an animal associate," a vehicle on which he is shown as sitting or standing. "The animal in question then becomes a symbol of the deity even when it is by itself 'in the world'. Thus the passive Shiva with his active consort Durga are often seen together riding a bull, Nandi. But Nandi by himself is the gatekeeper of a Shiva temple, and then stands outside in the world. Similarly, the elephant-headed 'son of Shiva' rides a rat; the rat, like Ganesha the guardian of thresholds, can find a way through all obstacles."[64]

From this discussion, Leach draws these acute inferences which I for one have not seen stated in this original form before: "Roughly

---

[62] Ibid., p. 256.   [63] Ibid., p. 257.   [64] Ibid., pp. 257–58.

speaking, where deity in Hindu iconography is given an explicitly anthropomorphic form and the deities are separate, they belong to the sphere of heaven. When deities are given explicitly animal forms and are separate, they belong to the sphere of earth. But when the male/female/man/animal forms are confused, we are in the intermediate zone; we are then dealing with trickster characters" corresponding to Hermes of Greek mythology, and Ganesha in Hinduism. (That Ganesha's trunk is phallic is an explicit element in the iconography of some sculptures, and it should be appreciated that the figure of Ganesha "as a whole is the equivalent of an androgynous representation of Shiva."[65])

This explication of Hindu iconography, and the fusion and conflation of imagery in mediating and ambiguous "trickster" figures, lead Leach to make another plausible formulation, which adds to what others have called "condensation" and multivalence in object symbols.

Verbal accounts of mythology, since they have to be understood as logical sequences, make clear-cut discriminations, whereas *sculptured forms* simply pile the metaphorical allusions one on top of the other. Lévi-Strauss has established the point that in order to understand verbal expressions of myth we must take sets of myths and lay them one on top of another; contrariwise, in order to understand sculptured forms of myth we must to some extent take the metaphors to pieces, much as I have been doing.

Throughout this essay, as in many of his other writings, while methodologically and interpretively insisting that his structural studies must be linked to and grounded in their context (in this instance, embracing religious, cosmological, iconographic, and architectural conventions), Leach also holds that parallel studies done in different cultural traditions may, and frequently do, yield general similarities. He thus concludes with a risk-taking dazzling "proof" concerning the characterization and representation of St. Peter as a mediator, a gatekeeper of heaven in Christian mythology, frequently shown carrying a set of keys. The reader of the New Testament today is left with the impression that Peter is an ordinary human being (however, although in the gospels he all too humanly denies his association with Christ in quick succession, in Acts, arrested by Herod and put in jail, he walks out of his chains and through the prison walls by supernatural means). In terms of his own structuralist generalization, Leach submits that "St. Peter *ought* to be much more of an ambiguous demigod than he is in fact reported to be." With a pictorial illustration of "the Death of Simon Magus" by Benozzo Gozzoli, and

[65] Ibid., p. 259.

by recourse to *early* Christian mythology, Leach advances the thesis that Simon Peter was "only one half of a dual figure, the other half of which was Simon Magus." "Both in biblical story and Christian legend, the actual performances of these two Simons are almost identical, but where Peter was an *ascetic saint* who works *miracles* in the name of *Christ*, the Magus is a *lecherous sorcerer* who performs *evil magic* in the name of *Satan*. Together they form a Janus-faced trickster."[66] In later Christian tradition Simon Magus appears as the persistent opponent of Simon Peter.

This essay thus, while proposing to art historians a new way of interpreting some features of grandiose architecture, also concludes with a proposal to biblical scholars that the mythology of Christianity as evidenced in biblical and other texts and in some Christian art suggests a way of seeing Simon Peter as a mediator combining dual features. This characterization tends to be erased in later interpretations of the New Testament, and not recognized by contemporary Christians.

Readers of the essay on the Sistine Chapel panels, and of the essays included in the *Structural Implications of Biblical Myth*, which I have already summarized, will have to make assessments of the following kinds. To what extent does the structural (or structuralist) procedure systematically applied yield worthwhile results? Does Leach systematically apply it in all those essays in questions? Is he in certain cases himself guilty of what he called Frazerian errors?

I have already indicated the grounds for admiring two essays – "The Legitimacy of Solomon" and "Melchisedech and the Emperor." But in respect of other essays on biblical myth, readers may find Leach's analogies, "reductions," and equations problematic, and therefore difficult to accept at face value, especially as deployed in the essay "Why Did Moses Have a Sister?" The juxtaposition and making up of a composite picture of Mary, the Virgin, the mother of Jesus, and Mary, the sister of Martha and Lazarus, and Mary Magdalene, and bringing into the discussion Miriam (Mary), the sister of Moses, while appearing bold and revelatory to those willing to engage with "structuralist logic," might be unpalatable to those holding to a strictly literal reading of the Bible.

But even such critics may be willing to make another scrutiny of Leach's formulations after they peruse Jaroslav Pelikan's *Mary Through the Centuries: Her Place in the History of Culture*.[67] This eminent authoritative

---

[66] Ibid., pp. 261–62

[67] Jaroslav Pelikan, *Mary Through the Centuries: Her Place in the History of Culture*, New Haven: Yale University Press, 1996.

scholar and historian of Christian theology sets out to show in a rough chronological order what Mary, the Virgin Bride and Mother of the Church, has meant in the provinces of life and realms of reality in which she has been a prominent force at various periods in history.

Pelikan explores the facets of Marian devotion through a series of images drawn from music, art, and literature. He shows how "an array of theological techniques links her, and the Christian tradition along with her, to the older biblical heritage. Prophecy reveals her bond with Eve. Typology (which identifies Old Testament figures as 'types' of the New) connects her with Miriam, the sister of Moses and Aaron. Through allegory, she becomes Wisdom and the Bride of the Song of Songs. Genealogy endows her with David's lineage."[68] Pelikan develops many themes, but the above associations of Mary with other biblical figures that he establishes may lend plausibility to the analogies and equations postulated by Leach.

There has been little commentary by scholars of art history regarding Leach's forays into their field. Robin Cormack, an art historian, was one of the persons responsible for Leach being invited to the Courtauld Institute in London to make his first public presentation of "Michelangelo's Genesis." So I requested a friend of mine, Norbert Peabody, to ask Cormack what impact it had on the art historians. Cormack's reply was that the lecture was poorly received by them and had been largely ignored ever since. Raymond Firth, who attended the lecture at the Courtauld Institute, has conveyed to me his sense that members of the British audience who heard the lecture had expressed "a general disbelief in his interpretation,"[69] or at best were divided, some regarding it as stimulating and others as unacceptable.

There was some correspondence in the months following the first publication of "Michelangelo's Genesis" in *The Times Literary Supplement* (March 1978), and more commentary after its republication in 1983 in the volume of essays which Leach co-edited with D. Alan Aycock entitled *The Structural Interpretations of Biblical Myth.*

[68] This quotation is taken from Jo Ann Kay McNamara's review of J. Pelikan's book *Mary Through the Centuries* in *New York Times Book Review*, October 27, 1996, pp. 34–35.
[69] Raymond Firth, personal communication dated October 7, 1996.

CHAPTER 13

Individuals, social persons, and masquerade

Two loyal students of Leach in an otherwise laudatory summation of his work[1] found this chink in his armor. Leach seemed unwilling to acknowledge "that both actors themselves, and their conceptions of their own interests, are to some extent culturally constituted. Leach's actor is the maximizing individual of Western utilitarian theory."[2] One of the few well-worn anthropological topics never addressed in Leach's writing is "the concept of the person." They speculate that Leach's unwillingness to do so "had much to do with his antipathy both to the 'social person' (so prominent in the work of Radcliffe-Brown and Fortes), who struck him as a bloodless character implausibly bound by jural rules, and to the unconscious structure postulated by Lévi-Straussian structuralism from which individual agency is expunged."[3]

Although there is something in what they say, I do not agree with the opinion of Fuller and Parry that Leach's "reluctance to 'deconstruct' notions of the 'individual' and notions of 'interest' seems to us the single most serious flaw in his work."[4] This conceptual space he addressed in his own way, without having to buy into the top–down normative conformism of actors implied in the perspectives of the earlier Durkheim, Mauss, Radcliffe-Brown, and Talcott Parsons.

I do not agree with that evaluation by Fuller and Parry because, although they are right in seeing that Leach had an antipathy for the concept of person, they do not quite see that he had *two frameworks* concerned with the relation between "ideas" people hold and their "actual behavior," in which the agency of the strategizing actor and his or her interested actions were sought to be fitted into the horizon of cultural "ideal" models and actors' structured "ideas" and "categories" of thought.

---

[1] Chris Fuller and Jonathan Parry, "Petulant Inconsistency? The Intellectual Achievement of Edmund Leach," *Anthropology Today*, vol. 5, no. 3, June 1989, pp. 11–14.
[2] Ibid., p. 13.   [3] Ibid., p. 13.   [4] Ibid., p. 13.

In *Pul Eliya*, as we saw earlier, Leach trenchantly repudiated that perspective ultimately deriving from the earlier writings of Durkheim, which Radcliffe-Brown and Fortes espoused and elaborated. This perspective conceived society, with its corporate institutions and its mores, as social facts impinging with force upon the actors, who conform to their moral pressure. The schema of social structure constituted of statuses, roles, jural norms, conformity, and deviance produced static equilibrian models.

Leach acknowledged that while he rejected Malinowski's view of the individual as acting to satisfy first and foremost his biological needs, and Malinowski's functionalism which sought to show how everything fitted with everything else as a total seamless, non-conflictual complex, he nevertheless saw individuals not as social automatons but as blood and flesh beings acting to pursue their "power" interests as in *Political Systems of Highland Burma* or their property and "economic" interests as in *Pul Eliya*, and all the social honors that flow from such acquisitions. Malinowskian individuals in action, revised and adapted in pursuit of social ends by Firth, is the legacy into which Leach had been socialized and which was in accord with his own intuitions about individuals whose experiences and motives were not exhausted by social structure conceived as an edifice whose building blocks were statuses and roles, and its cement moral rules and jural norms.

Although Leach's formulations referred to actors pursuing their "private" personal interests, a wording that dangerously suggests that they might be a-social and not culturally influenced, such an interpretation is untenable as we saw in our previous explications of Kachin actors creatively manipulating and filling in the possibilities contained in model category terms such as *gumsa* and *gumlao* (and *shan*), and later of *Pul Eliya* villagers voicing foundational charters, but individually strategizing and pursuing their goals while more or less unaware of the "statistical patterns" or "orderings" formed as outcomes of their collective acts. These "statistical patterns" were, Leach suggested, "social structure" in a new sense, different from Radcliffe-Brown's. Furthermore, how these empirical patterns of conduct related to "ideal models" of kinship, or the tripartite topographical and *pavula* ideal schemes, which the *Pul Eliya* folk voiced, was raised by Leach. The answer on that occasion was that such ideal models, while not generating the actual behavior, did in an "indirect way" relate to them as orientating ideas.

Leach was quite aware that in *Political Systems of Highland Burma* (1954) and in *Pul Eliya* (1961) he had experimented and grappled with two theoretical frameworks which were in tension as well as complementary. In the 1954 work he had espoused a "rationalist" viewpoint by which he meant a focus on the structure of ideas about their society that members hold and articulate; the relation of actual behavior to these ideas was problematic, creative, interpretive, and manipulative. In the 1961 exercise he had espoused an "empiricist" framework, and had taken as his basic task the detailed recording of directly observed, face-to-face behaviors of members of a local community interacting with one another. This ground-up "statistical order" generating individual acts as behavioral patterns did have a structure and patterning (like Durkheim's "suicide rates"), and he surmised that they must have a further relation to the structure of ideas (ideal models) actors hold. What that dialectical relation might be is not adequately clarified in *Pul Eliya* – but I suggest that this "empiricist approach" might have referred quite validly to a Malinowskian formulation: that the empirical orders of acts in *Pul Eliya* (somewhat akin to the Malinowskian "social structure") were given a mytho-historical validation by being referred to an order of ideas shaped as foundational mythic charters (in the Malinowskian sense), and enacted in ritual as symbolic communicative performance.

I shall have more to say about Leach's play, with the "rationalist–empiricist" distinction, when I relate his perspective to that of Lévi-Strauss. Here let me mention that in one context later in time (1976) he said that "the two anthropological viewpoints which I have here summarized as 'empiricist' and 'rationalist' are to be regarded as complementary rather than right or wrong" and that "my own work includes specimen monographs of both types. Leach (1954) is rationalist in style; Leach (1961) is empiricist."[5]

RITUAL ACTION AND PRESENTATION OF SELF

Now I want to suggest that there was a whole domain of thought and action in which Leach was immersed and about which he theorized, and which bypassed any need to formally incorporate the viewpoints of those dealing with the concept of "social person" (and the associated conceptual baggage of "status and role"). This was the domain of ritual as "symbolic communicative performance," which also involved

---

[5] Edmund Leach, *Culture and Communication: The Logic by which Symbols are Connected: An Introduction to the Use of Structuralist Analysis in Social Anthropology*, Cambridge and New York: Cambridge University Press, 1976, p. 6.

the "presentation of self" on various social occasions. This perspective made it possible to bypass the concept of social person and its entailments in the orthodox structural-functionalist mode, while tackling some issues cognate with it.

There are two perspectives evident in the interpretation of ritual action that are complementary, and they deal with the relation between special or marked behavior in ritual occasions and behavior in everyday life.

Into one mode fall those expositions of occasions marked as special time and as transitions between time periods, which call for special presentations of self and for special behavior such as formality, masquerade, and role reversal, and sometimes the alternations between them. This special interest was already set out in an early condensed jewel of an essay called "Time and False Noses"[6] in which Leach attempts to solve the puzzle of why people all over the world mark out their calendars by means of holidays and holy days, feasts and fasts, festivities and rites of passage. These occasions are marked by comparable behaviors, whose varieties are "rather limited yet curiously contradictory. People dress up in uniform, or in funny clothes; they eat special food, or they fast; they behave in solemn restrained manner, or they indulge in licence." "Time is a 'discontinuity of repeated contrasts', a succession of alternations and full stops," and in ritual conduct "*formality* and *masquerade* enact sacred time, but taken together they form a pair of contrasted opposites"; *role reversal* connotes "a complete transfer from secular to sacred, and is sacred time played in reverse, death is converted into birth."[7] At this time of writing Leach was adapting the tripartite schema of Hubert and Mauss consisting of entry from profane time to sacred time, the sacred act itself, and exit/re-entry into profane time, and of Van Gennep consisting of separation from everyday profane time, liminal phase of sacred action, re-aggregation into everyday social life, and elaborating and embellishing both schema with his own playful brilliance.

In both *Political Systems* and *Pul Eliya* Leach changes tack and comes up with a very interesting and theoretically more adequate formulation of how ritual action is related to everyday acts. In *Political Systems* he rejected the Durkheim-influenced division of "social actions into major classes – namely religious rites which are *sacred* and technical acts which are *profane*," on the ground that "there is no class of profane or purely

---

[6] Edmund Leach, "Time and False Noses" first appeared in *Explorations* and was reprinted in Leach, *Rethinking Anthropology*, 1961, pp. 132–36.

[7] Leach, "Time and False Noses," pp. 135–36.

technical acts, because such actions have varying degrees of ritual frills and decorations attached to them."[8] In *Pul Eliya* he likewise rejects the

strict Durkheimian proposition that "things sacred" and "things profane" are quite separate categories, applicable to sets of events which are distinct both in time and place, as not tenable. The category distinction, to be useful, must apply to aspects of all behaviour rather than to separate items of total behaviour.[9] "Rituals", *through which the members of a society manifest to themselves the model schema of the social structure within which they live, occur all the time, in ordinary everyday affairs, just as much in situations which are explicitly ceremonial.*

No doubt it is true that, on the occasion of a wedding or a funeral or a coronation or a degree-taking ceremony or of any similar formal function, the structural relationships between the participants are explicitly and consciously dramatized, and therefore easy to observe, *but, as mere play-acting and pretense, the same kind of structural patterning should be observable in everyday affairs.*[10]

In *Pul Eliya* Leach returned to this theme of how everyday action and explicit ceremonial are related in the context of his struggling to give a coherent account of how the "statistical order" of acts – the normal – relates to the "ideal models" (normative) that people voice in their speech acts and their rituals and myths.

It was the same issue of relation between these two orders that Leach took up in the earlier *Political Systems*, but coming at it from the other "rationalist" and "idealist" direction of how the ideal model thought categories of *gumsa* and *gumlao* related to empirical acts and facts on the ground. In this work, Leach defined formal "ritual" as serving "to express the individual's status as a social person in which he finds himself for the time being"; and similarly, he proposed that myths (especially genealogical myths of origins and lineage pedigree) assert an abstract model of ideal society. And just as actors in everyday politics manipulate and interpret the myths in their variant versions to suit their own positions, claims, and interests, so are their contextual enactments of everyday practices creatively and ambiguously aligned with ritual status claims.

It did not escape Leach that what he had expounded regarding the relation between "sacred" and "profane," and between formal ceremonial/ritual and everyday acts (with ritualized frills), had some

---

[8] Leach, *Political Systems*, pp. 11–13.

[9] Leach alludes here, as examples, to "customary procedures" that contained "aesthetic frills" incorporated in actions pragmatically oriented to technical ends. It is the aesthetic frills surrounding routines of agriculture or cooking which have "meanings as symbols of social states." Leach, *Pul Eliya*, p. 13.

[10] Leach, *Pul Eliya*, p. 295.

affinity with Erving Goffman's book which carried the title *The Presentation of Self in Everyday Life*, in which Goffman developed the thesis that "It is probably no mere historical accident that the word person, in its first meaning is a mask. It is rather a recognition of the fact that everyone is always and everywhere more or less consciously playing a role . . . It is in these roles that we know each other; it is in these roles we know ourselves."[11]

In a remarkably innovative essay, "Masquerade: The Presentation of the Self in Holi-Day Life,"[12] a recognized contribution to visual anthropology written late in his life in 1986, Leach not only quotes this passage from Goffman, but says what he finds especially noteworthy is that Goffman "puts special emphasis on the ambiguity of the boundary between the Sacred and the non-Sacred. Goffman used a variety of metaphors to make his point: 'front stage' versus 'back stage' was perhaps the most effective. In apparently relaxed 'back stage' behavior we are acting out carefully masked roles just as we do when we fill formal costume roles up front." In this late essay Leach extends Goffman's thesis that we engage in role-playing masquerade in everyday life as well as in formal public situations, but also that such play-acting "also involves off-stage ancestors . . . who have to be invented and equipped with the appropriate set of masks in order to justify the multiple roles of the living self."[13]

This essay is both trick and treat for various reasons. Carrying to new heights Leach's comparative and transformational perspective on "us" and "them," it suggests how needing our own family history we may rely on dubious allegedly objective material evidence such as "wills" and photos to fabricate a "true" past which is "mythic" and tendentious. It then presents a set of photographs, some of them depicting "natives" from the era of British colonialism and others from Leach's own family archive pertaining to his Lancashire ancestors, and subjects them to an acute ethnographic reading of the subjects who are photographically "presented" and the "concealed (ambiguous) information" they contain, "not so much about the individual 'selves' of the person depicted as about the total society of which they and the photographer formed a part."[14]

---

[11] Erving Goffman, *The Presentation of Self in Everyday Life*, Edinburgh: University of Edinburgh Press, 1956.

[12] Edmund Leach, "Masquerade: The Presentation of the Self in Holi-Day Life," *Cambridge Anthropology*, vol. 13, no. 3, 1989–90, pp. 47–69. Later published in *Visual Anthropology Review*, vol. 6, no. 2, 1990, pp. 2–13. References are to this latter version.

[13] Leach, "Masquerade," p. 5. [14] Ibid., p. 5.

Leach with humor and an eye for detail discusses the coding of hierarchy in the photos in multiple dimensions – asymmetrical relations between colonial administrators and natives, between men and women, adults and children, and so on – in terms of clothing, headgear, hair styles, seating and standing arrangements, including delicious information on dressing small boys as girls, later in sailor suits, in mid- and late nineteenth-century family portraiture; and a fashion-plate painting of Leach family members of that period in the manner of a French court painter. There is much else, such as pygmies brought to London as exhibits – there is a picture of pygmies at the Houses of Parliament wearing top hats and the same pygmies in a backstreet London slum in very sparse native attire. This anthropological *tour de force* on presentation of selves ranges on the one hand from showing how to decipher representations of actors' social personalities, and their positioning with regard to one another, "in an exaggerated, heavily coded form," to the opposite pole of the continuum in which the images of the subjects *vis-à-vis* one another contain ambiguities such that viewers may read the messages differently.

Thus as if to refute Fuller and Parry, we have in this example Leach, the incurable experimenter with perspectives and inventive adapter of other people's ideas to his own purposes, giving us his exposition of how social persons present their selves to one another. But note that, unlike Goffman who might have held that all the world's a stage, and that we are always "social persons," Leach held that beyond the "social person" there existed the "individual self," richly intimated by great novelists such as Proust, Joyce, and Dostoyevsky, and in any case no mere puppet of jural rules but a dynamic being of experiences and motives that cannot be subsumed by the normative and official forms.

Leach was skeptical of those anthropological theorists who developed phenomenologically oriented accounts of cultures producing qualitatively different social persons as total entities. His rejection of extreme cultural relativism probably prompted his dismissal of Clifford Geertz's thesis of a distinctively Balinese construct of person as "complete rubbish."[15] As we proceed we shall have more to say about Leach's comparitivist perspective and its implications for what is general to, and what is different among, human beings as members of societies.

As Leach eloquently put it, "It seems to me that each of us leads as it were a double existence, one in the life which we reveal to the world in

[15] Edmund Leach, "A Poetics of Power" (review of Clifford Geertz, *Negara*, *New Republic*, vol. 184, April 1981, pp. 30–33).

which we are, and the other to ourselves in our inward thoughts – the two overlap of course but for all that have a separate unity."[16] Or to mimic him, he might say "there is a transformational relation between private existence and public existence, not a direct extension of one into the other."

Be that as it may, I have brought us to the point where I can reasonably make the following submission. Leach, both in *Political Systems* and in *Pul Eliya* (and also in *Rethinking Anthropology*), prepared to bypass that kind of "structuralism" (or "structural-functionalism") stemming from Radcliffe-Brown which approached social action top–down from jural rules, social system and its principles and jural rules to social person. In contrast he highlighted the perspective of individual actors, who while oriented in their talk to an order of thought categories as ideal models, acted in social contexts as strategizing individuals pursuing their interests within the flexibilities embedded in the models. The nature of the relation between the ideal order and the statistical order of aggregated acts was therefore a critical issue that awaited probing, and he offered a range of related answers. I submit that it was Leach's studies in "communication" and "information" theory, and his exposition of "symbolic communicative performance" and the "logic by which symbols are connected" in ritual, in myth, in formal and everyday social acts which additionally filled that seeming gap which Fuller and Parry indicated. The essay on "Masquerade" which we earlier discussed is but one example of his view of social role-playing by social persons, and he demonstrates how these presentations and displays of self are to be decoded in terms of communication theory. As those familiar with his writings know, Leach wrote numerous essays in this mode on a large range of topics, and his *Culture and Communication*, written for a series intended for undergraduate teaching, presents a number of potted summaries and applications of his symbolic communicative theory to an astonishing range of phenomena, including ritual (rites of passage, magic and sorcery, sacrifice), mapping of social space and social time, rank order and hierarchy, mytho-logic, and cosmology.

It would be incorrect and unrealistic to think that Leach dispensed with the language of status and roles. In his analysis of biblical narratives which was discussed in chapter 11 – "The Legitimacy of Solomon" is a good example – he singled out the principal actors and mapped their statuses and their role-playing according to the changes in their

---

[16] Leach, "Masquerade," p. 5.

position in the unfolding of the narratives. In this composition he was concerned to unveil the paradoxical structural contradictions embedded in the text and how they were attributable to existential issues deeply entrenched in Jewish culture and society. Thus he situated statuses and roles in dramatistic terms in a matrix of mutually implicated plot movements. In the essay "Melchisedech and the Emperor," also discussed earlier in chapter 12, Leach again dynamically related the statuses of priest, prophet, and king to the cosmologies and politics of hierarchical orthodoxy and millenarian subversion.

GIFTS AND DEBTS AS NEGOTIATED TRANSACTIONS

In *Social Anthropology* (1982), Leach set out to convey his own view of anthropology from "an egocentric and historical point of view" to lay readers unconnected with professional anthropology.[17] He tried to elucidate in chapter 5, entitled "Debt, Relationship, Power," what is meant by the statement that the "task of the social anthropologist in the field is not simply to observe the details of customary behaviour but to note how the behaviour serves to 'express relationships'".[18]

It may surprise Parry and Fuller (as it did me) that Leach begins that chapter in an "orthodox" manner about the "concept of person," but true to form he then progressively gives his elucidation some twists which tell us why he did not dwell on that orthodoxy, or avoided it, in order to probe deeper into the dynamics of human relationships and interpersonal interactions, and the dialectic between rigid ideal categories and flexible actions and "substitutions" by individuals indexed by class, entrepreneurial choices, and social context.

> In terms of anthropological theory, this chapter, taken as a whole, may be considered an elaboration of Radcliffe-Brown's formula that the core of social anthropology is the study of society considered as "a structure of person to person relationships". I suspect however that parts of my treatment of this theme would have been very uncongenial to Radcliffe-Brown himself . . .
>
> In the language of social anthropology *person* is sharply distinguished from *individual*. The individual is a living biological animal who is born, develops to maturity, grows old and dies; the person is the set of offices and roles which attach to the individual at any particular stage in his life career.
>
> Parts of an individual's day-to-day behaviour are quite idiosyncratic; in general, these fall outside the scope of social anthropology. But very often the major part of an individual's activities stem from the duties and reciprocal obligations

---

[17] Leach, *Social Anthropology*, p. 1.   [18] Ibid., p. 149.

which fall to him by virtue of his roles as a social person. The *network of person-to-person relationships* formula thus refers to sets of rights and duties which find expression in more or less predictable patterns of behaviour. When ethnographers refer to *customs*, the behaviours in question are always of this semi-obligatory predictable kind.[19]

All person-to-person relationships entail reciprocity. There are instances of reciprocal complementary behaviors between two individuals who consider themselves of equal status, such as friends, neighbors who shake hands, engage in reciprocal hospitality, exchange Christmas cards, and so on. "But the majority of person-to-person exchanges are not of this like-for-like kind. Correspondingly most of the persons in a close network of relationships are of unequal rather than equal status. The inequality of the exchange is congruent with the inequality of the status."[20]

These orthodox beginnings lead Leach firstly to indicate a common mistake made by kinship theorists that "a single category word such as *father* can never denote an isolated individual". These "social person labels" are usually brought into association with an array of dyadic counterparts with whom there are context-linked relationships.

Thus it should be obvious (but apparently is not!) that a single kinship category word such as *father* can never denote an isolated individual. It is only one half of several, separable, dyadic relationships, notably: *father/foetus, father/infant child, father/son, father/daughter.* In relational terms the behaviours involved in these four cases may be very different even within a single social context.[21]

In sum, many anthropologists assume that "the word 'father' (or its equivalent in other languages) has a single meaning in itself, whereas in fact it has many different meanings depending upon what other term forms the other half of the dyadic relationship."[22]

Next Leach brings to the elucidation the famous essay of Marcel Mauss on the "gift" and transforms and inverts that discussion into the consideration of "debt":

So far I have given the impression that, if we use the notion of *gift* in the widest possible sense, then gift exchanges constitute the visible expression of what social anthropologists clumsily describe as networks of person-to-person relationships. But that account of my overall argument needs to be qualified in one very major respect.

[19] Ibid., p. 149.   [20] Ibid., p. 150.   [21] Ibid., p. 150.   [22] Ibid., pp. 151–52.

The structure of the relational network is only accessible to the outside observer to the extent that it is visibly manifested in gift-giving performance, but, for the insiders, the actors who actually operate the system, this same structure is felt to consist of rights and obligations. It is not so much a network of gift-giving as a network of indebtedness.

This has very important implications for our interpretation of the coded significance of gift-exchange behaviour. From the actor's point of view, the great majority of gift-giving transactions are partial repayments of debt. I would emphasize the word *partial*. In any context, if a debt is ever fully paid off then the relationship between debtor and creditor ceases to exist.[23]

Thus the assertion is made that "all *enduring* relationships have this quality; when the relationship is activated the parties concerned engage in gift exchange, but at all other times, while the relationship is quiescent, it exists only as a feeling of indebtedness – that is of rights and obligations between the parties."[24]

The underlying general principle is that persisting relationships only exist as feelings of indebtedness. From time to time every such persisting debt relationship needs to be made manifest in an actual gift transaction, but the relationship is in the feeling of indebtedness not in the gift.[25]

To understand the origins or seeds of this "subtext" to Mauss on the spirit of the gift as the axis of exchange theory, and as a subversion of a benign notion of a non-contextualized (non-deconstructed) totalized "person" invested with "rights and duties," we have to go back in time to the beginning, namely the innovative discussion in chapter 5 of *Political Systems of Highland Burma* (1954) of the Kachin *gumsa* categories of *hka* ("debt"), *hpaga* ("trade," "ritual wealth object"), and the normative formulations and actual practices surrounding debt relationships.[26] "Almost any kind of legal obligation that exists between two Kachins is likely to be described as a debt (*hka*). If one pursues the matter further and tries to discover what this 'debt' really implies, one's informant will probably convert it into a list of so many *hpaga*."[27]

The term *hpaga* is used in the double sense of "trade" and "ritual wealth object". Trade transactions are recorded by notches on a tally stick of bamboo which is then split in half, each partner retaining one half as a record; the partners settle up, each debt or notch (*hka*) settled separately on its merits. *Hpaga* as ritual wealth objects include buffalo,

[23] Ibid., p. 152.   [24] Ibid., p. 153.   [25] Ibid., p. 154.
[26] Leach, *Political Systems*, pp. 144–54.   [27] Ibid., p. 144.

gongs of several types, silver bullion, slaves, *n'ba* (several types of shaped cloth which serve as male skirts, blankets and shawls), iron cooking pots, swords (usually a dummy blunt-edged one), silver pipes, opium, bead necklaces, Chinese embroidered coats, etc. These ritual wealth objects only change hands on certain occasions: "The principal occasions are: (a) marriages, (b) funerals, (c) in payment of ritual services by priests or agents, (d) on the occasion of a transfer of residence or the building of a new house, (e) as judicial compensation in settlement of dispute or crime."[28] Covering both contexts of trade transactions and ritual wealth objects, *hpaga* may be "translated as the 'items which are specified in a statement of claim'; . . . for the Kachin legal claims and commercial claims are alike *hka* (debts)."[29]

Now we come to Leach's documentation of the practices relating to the transactions on occasions when ritual wealth objects are transferred. From a formal point of view the payments due on any particular occasion are defined by an agreed local tradition. For each kind of settlement the tradition specifies a number of *hpaga* and gives a title to each *hpaga*. The *hpaga* has the double meaning and mediatory significance of referring simultaneously to the context of the offense and to the settlement of the quarrel as such.

The more significant the occasion – for example, the settlement of a chief's blood feud – the longer the list of titled *hpaga*.

But although the theoretical form of each *hpaga* is meticulously detailed, greater stress is laid on the number and title of the *hpaga* than on its outward form. The real payment is always a matter for agreement between the parties and here *the principle of substitutions (sang ai)* is all important.

What is of especial importance here is the flexibility of the system. By manipulating the principle of substitution to its limits a poor man owning only a few pigs and chickens, and a rich man owning many buffalo can both appear to conform to the same formal code of gift giving. Although they do not in fact contribute goods of the same economic value, they do, by a fiction, contribute the same *hpaga*.

This is important for our understanding of class differences. In theory, gift obligations are scaled according to class . . . In practice the payment depends on the economic standing of the defaultor not on his class status by birth . . . the validation of class status depends more than anything else on an ability to fulfil correctly the gift-giving obligations that are proper to a member of that class. An aristocrat will be accepted as an aristocrat so long as he carries out an aristocrat's obligations. And it is precisely here that *the individual is faced with a choice.*

[28] Ibid., p. 147.   [29] Ibid., p. 146.

Tradition sets the standard of what is proper. But the principle of substitution makes it possible for any man to avoid fulfilling the letter of his obligations if he so chooses; yet if a man fails to pay what is proper he loses face and risks a general loss of status. Paradoxically therefore it is often true, especially of the more enterprising individuals, that they pay as much as they can afford rather than as little as they can haggle for.[30] [emphasis added]

Thus the possibility afforded for "structural rules which have all the appearance of rigidity to be interpreted very freely, thus opening the way for social mobility in a system which purports to be a caste-like hierarchy."[31]

In marriage in theory the same list of *hpaga* is payable. In practice the scale of brideprice payments as measured by the number of cattle tends to be determined by the class status of the bridegroom rather than that of the bride.

The importance of this fact is considerable . . . a crucial element in the structure of *gumsa* society is that when an individual marries out of his or her own social class it is normally the man who marries up and the woman who marries down. If bride price in such cases were fixed according to the status of the bride, the system would break down, for the men of junior status would seldom be able to raise the necessary quantity of cattle and *hpaga*. Nevertheless, despite what happens in practice, Kachin formal theory is that bride price is adjusted to the standing of the *bride*. It is a theory which permits a powerful chief to pick and choose among potential suitors for his daughters and to use their marriage as direct instruments of political alliance.[32]

In principle any outstanding debt, no matter what its origin, is potentially a source of feud. For a Kachin, feud and debt are the same thing – *hka*. It is especially debts between strangers that must be settled quickly otherwise the owner of the debt has a legitimate excuse for resorting to violence; in contrast, debts between relatives, especially affinal relatives, are not urgent matters. Indeed as between *mayu* and *dama* some debts are always left outstanding almost as a matter of principle; *the debt is a kind of credit account which ensures the continuity of the relationship.* There is thus a kind of paradox that the existence of a debt may signify not only a state of hostility but also a state of dependence and friendship.[33]

---

[30] Ibid., pp. 148–49.   [31] Ibid., p. 152.   [32] Ibid., p. 151.   [33] Ibid., p. 153.

CHAPTER 14

Leach and Lévi-Strauss: similarities and differences

Leach himself recognized retrospectively in print in 1982 that there had been some kind of watershed and change of direction in his subject matter and theoretical concerns. This second phase of his writings roughly stretched from the early 1960s to the 1980s.

In the early days my interests, like those of my contemporaries and immediate seniors in the profession, lay mainly in kinship and social organization. These classical fields of anthropological inquiry may not seem very close to the area to which I now devote most of my professional attention which may be described very roughly, as the interface between art and religious ideology. Moreover, in so far as I have a utilizable "theory" which is applicable to the study of art and mythology and religious rituals, it is a theory which developed from the fact that at the time when I conducted my first anthropological field work (among the Yami of Botel Tobago in 1936), I had the competences of an engineer, but not an anthropologist.[1]

We note that in this retrospective look, Leach acknowledges a shift of interest in the substantive phenomena he studied, while affirming a continuity in his approach attributable to his early training as an engineer.

This, as we know from his later experiment with and immersion in "structuralist" analysis, which Leach associated with Saussere, Jakobson, and Lévi-Strauss, is not a complete account of the shift. In fact, in the same book some pages later, Leach sketches another shift that in fact parallels and overlaps with the above.

I myself was first indoctrinated into anthropology by Malinowski and Firth. That is to say I was, at the outset, a "pure" empirical functionalist. Much later I was greatly influenced by the very unempirical structuralism of Lévi-Strauss. This came about because Lévi-Strauss' first magnum opus, *The Elementary Structures of Kinship*, the first edition of which was published in 1949, makes great use of

---

[1] Leach, *Social Anthropology*, p. 8.

the ethnography of the Kachin of North Burma, a people among whom I had lived during much of the period 1939–45.[2]

THE BATTLEGROUND OF KINSHIP

So we know that Leach had already encountered Lévi-Strauss's theories of kinship (especially lineage systems) and marriage (alliance and affinity) by the early 1950s when he was writing *Political Systems of Highland Burma* (which was quite different in perspective from his doctoral thesis). This first encounter was both fruitful and disturbing for Leach, and, as described in detail in chapter 5, it contained the seeds of a complex and ambivalent relationship between the two masters who no doubt appreciated each other's kindred intellects, and yet were distant and unable to form a personal relation of amity and warmth.

The encounters and estrangements, the agreements and disagreements, between the two men, and perhaps the differences between an Anglo-Saxon academic and a French academician regarding what is permissible and expected in scholarly exchange, are difficult to document and interpret. There are some stereotypical stories that one hears whose veracity is unclear: that, for instance, in Britain academic exchanges are frequently polemical, and the thrust and parry of debate are admired and enjoyed. Furthermore, it is alleged that in Britain eminent professors do not necessarily aspire to "found" schools of thought to which "disciples" owe exclusive allegiance under the jealous scrutiny of their masters (Leach for one is an exemplary case of someone who did not want such a following).[3] It is said that in France, leading professors and their disciples form tight circles, loyalty is expected, and cross-cutting links with rival or competitive groups are discouraged, to put it mildly. No doubt some of the basis for the tendency to form exclusive circles of gurus and followers had to do with the competition for research resources and positions and the patronage system that it encourages. Of course, Britain was not innocent of such academic politics.

Leach at one point explains the beginnings of his fateful involvement with Lévi-Strauss in the writing of his book on the Kachins. He says that

[2] Ibid., p. 44.

[3] In Britain, Evans-Pritchard, Firth, and Fortes were known as benign heads of departments who did not insist on conformity; Max Gluckman, however, was apparently more paternal and demanding toward his disciples at Manchester. "Gluckman built a school...The general approach they developed...was an analysis of conflict and of conflict resolution...He built up his team and it was a team with a mascot: The Manchester United Football team." Hilda Kuper, "Function, History, Biography," in George W. Stocking, Jr. (ed.), *Functionalism Historicized: Essays on British Social Anthropology*, Madison: University of Wisconsin Press, 1984, p. 209.

he knew "that a great deal of the ethnography on which Lévi-Strauss had relied was quite inaccurate, but I also knew from first-hand experience that a number of his novel insights concerning this society were very penetrating."[4]

"My first book...besides arguing against the then conventional view that the boundaries of society and the boundaries of culture can be treated as coincident, is also organized as a kind of dialogue between the empiricism of Malinowski and the rationalism of Lévi-Strauss and *these two contrasted strands of my thinking* should be apparent to the reader in all my later writings"(emphasis added).[5] What Leach means by the two strands of thought in dialog within himself is an important issue, which I shall consider after first disposing of the Kachin dispute.

I have in chapter 5, which reviews the 1951 essay on matrilateral cross-cousin marriage and the 1954 *Political Systems of Highland Burma*, discussed the empirical and theoretical grounds on which Leach disagreed with Lévi-Strauss regarding the ethnographical details concerning Kachin wife-giver–wife-taker relations and the direction of the passage of women and the passage of goods as marriage payments. Leach was particularly piqued at Lévi-Strauss's unwillingness to admit his mistakes of fact and his ploy of introducing an exculpating change of wording and trying to paper over his mistake by introducing a hopefully blanket term of "anisogomy" in the French reissue of *Les structures élémentaires* in 1967 and in its English translation published in 1969.

There was also from the beginning a major difference in their understanding of kinship: whether or not it is a system that has intrinsic autonomy in "primitive societies" and whose internal relations and processes explain its dynamics, or whether kinship principles have necessarily to be considered in dynamic relation to economic and political activities in order to understand their patterning and roles in contexts of action. Readers may recognize that Leach reiterated the same question and voiced similar objections in *Pul Eliya* to Fortes's alleged cordoning of kinship systems.

Lévi-Strauss has (at a later time) asserted his invariant view that in primitive societies the rules of kinship and marriage "have an operational value equal to that of economic phenomena in our own society." Hence ethnology should abandon the analysis of the economic infrastucture for that of kinship relations, and only this approach leads to an account of

---

[4] Leach, *Social Anthropology*, p. 44.   [5] Ibid., p. 44.

the "profound structure" of primitive societies. Primitive societies would no longer be the preserve of historical materialism, and the autonomy of social anthropology would be justified by irreducible specificity of the subject, i.e. economic and other activities will be conducted within the fixed framework of kinship relations.[6]

This encompassing view of kinship (which would accord with Fortes's perspective, though Fortes and Lévi-Strauss diverged on the issue of the centrality of affinity and marriage alliance in structuring lineage-based societies) did, as we have explained earlier, inform Lévi-Strauss's model of Kachin society. Lévi-Strauss had argued that in Kachin type matrilateral cross-cousin type marriages, the top strata will progressively accumulate wives and goods and that therefore this kind of asymmetry built from *within the system* of circulating connubium with its speculative possibilities will lead to the periodic breakdown of the chains of generalized exchange. Leach demonstrated not only that Lévi-Strauss got the directions of passage of goods and women wrong, but that such a marriage alliance system fitted with the land tenure and ranking system, and that a hierarchical feudal type system of the *gumsa* type need not necessarily break down. The marriage and kinship domains were not autonomous and had to be integrated to the land tenure and economic system and the political hierarchy to make full sense.

There are other matters concerning the field of kinship study in general on which Leach faulted Lévi-Strauss.[7] Leach disagreed with those theorists, such as Lounsbury, Goodenough, and Scheffler, and with Lévi-Strauss who approved of their formal analysis, who treated kinship vocabulary as a closed set forming an algebraic matrix which refers exclusively to genealogical connections. For one thing, most kinship words have non-kinship meanings as well. Secondly, these theorists attempted to explain the occurrence of a limited number of genealogically based classificatory terminological systems in human societies as being a precipitate of a universal human psychology; this line of thought was quite incompatible with the position of most British functionalist anthropologists who "argue that the different major types of kin terms are a response to different patterns of social organization, rather than to any universal

---

[6] Claude Lévi-Strauss in an interview in *Témoignage Chrétien*, quoted in E. Terray, *Marxism and "Primitive" Societies: Two Studies*, trans. M. Kleppes, New York: Monthly Review Press, 1972, p. 139.

[7] See especially, Edmund Leach, *Lévi-Strauss*, London: Fontana, 1970, chapter 6; and Leach, *Social Anthropology*, where chapters 5 and 6 contain passing comments (for example, pp. 153–56, p. 188).

attribute of the human mind."[8] "Functionalists attach great importance to the study of kinship behaviour"; although the system of verbal categories and the system of behavioral attitudes are interconnected, the two frames cannot be conflated; the analysis of kinship terminologies cannot become an end in itself; "The real subject matter of social anthropology always remains the actual social behaviour of human beings." In any case the logical analysis of kinship term systems "cannot be used to determine whether any particular body of documentary material (and ethnographic reporting) is or is not 'reliable,'" and "facts on the ground" reported by field anthropologists cannot be treated as a tiresome irrelevance in the way some armchair theorists treat them.

There are other problems that arise in relation to Lévi-Strauss's ambitious attempts to formulate universal principles of kinship that rely on ignoring negative instances and on formal deductions that are not tested against all available evidence. Lévi-Strauss has confused "the notion of *descent*, a legal principle governing the transmission of rights from generation to generation, with the notion of *filiation*, the kinship link between parent and child. It is the same kind of confusion which led him to suppose that the incest taboo is simply the converse of exogamy."[9] Lévi-Strauss follows Edward Tylor in taking the rules of exogamy as the converse of the incest taboo, a rudimentary error because incest taboos have to do with sexual relations and exogamy with marriage rules, "and while every teenager knows the difference many anthropologists get them confused."[10] Finally, as has been mentioned before, Lévi-Strauss's ambitious tome, *Elementary Structures of Kinship*, propounds a general theory on the assumption that unilined descent systems are universal, an assumption which is false, and renders certain of his propositions based on it equally suspect.

It is because of an accumulation of such empirical errors, as well as basic differences regarding what the phenomenon of kinship is about, that Leach dismissed Lévi-Strauss's *general* theory of kinship and marriage as faulty and misguided. In making these judgments he was unambiguously aligned with that kind of fieldwork committed to studying the nexus between rules and practices, norms and social action, so

---

[8] Leach, *Lévi-Strauss*, p. 102.

[9] Ibid., p. 108.

[10] R. Fox, *Kinship and Marriage: An Anthropological Perspective*, Harmondsworth: Penguin, 1967, p. 54 (Leach, *Lévi-Strauss*, p. 111). As Leach puts it, "The fact is that in all human societies of which we have detailed knowledge the conventions governing sex relations are quite different from the conventions governing marriage so there is no case for saying that in the beginning the latter must have been derived from the other."

characteristic of most British social anthropologists, whatever their internal differences.

Leach thought that Lévi-Strauss's rationalist and realist predilections were perhaps connected to his somewhat cavalier attitude to and use of empirical data. As an admirer of "Malinowski style intensive fieldwork employing the vernacular, which is now the standard research technique employed by nearly all Anglo-American social anthropologists" and as a tireless advocate of intensive fieldwork and close attention to empirical details, he was contemptuous and dismissive of Lévi-Strauss's own lack of fieldwork and his reliance on problematic documentary sources. "A careful study of *Tristes Tropiques* reveals that, in the whole course of his Brazilian travels, Lévi-Strauss can never have stayed in one place for more than a few weeks at a time and that he was never able to converse easily with any of his native informants in their native language."[11] And the elicitation of information by means of intensive fieldwork is "an entirely different procedure from the careful but uncomprehending description of manners and customs, based on the use of special informants and interpreters, which was the original source for most of the ethnographic observations on which Lévi-Strauss, like his Frazerian predecessors, has chosen to rely."[12]

Leach also warned of another danger that lies in wait for the anthropologist whose sojourn in the field is brief. An experienced anthropologist visiting a new society and working with the aid of competent interpreters

may be able, after a stay of only a few days, to develop in his own mind a fairly comprehensive "model" of how the social system works, but it is also true that if he stays for six months and learns to speak the local language, very little of that original "model" will remain . . . In all his writings Lévi-Strauss assumes that the simple first stage "model" generated by the observer's first impressions corresponds quite closely to a genuine (and very important) ethnographic reality – the "conscious model" which is present in the minds of the anthropologist's informants.[13]

Leach's reference to the demoralizing experience that very little of this initial model, more likely an amalgam of the observer's prejudiced presuppositions, remains in the face of wider and deeper field experience, no doubt gains its force from his own long Kachin experience, and his subsequent intensive documentation in Pul Eliya, in both of which the relation between thought categories and ideal statements and actual

---

[11] Leach, *Lévi-Strauss*, p. 11.   [12] Ibid., pp. 11–12.   [13] Ibid., p. 11.

conduct and practices becomes a major issue for elucidation, something that little troubled or intrigued Lévi-Strauss.

"On this account many would argue that Lévi-Strauss, like Frazer, is insufficiently critical of his source material. He always seems to be able to find just what he is looking for."[14] In his most critical moments, Leach would charge some of Lévi-Strauss's far-ranging comparative forays and allusions in the corpus entitled *Mythologiques* as bearing a resemblance to Frazer's own Liberal and uncritical citations.

ATTRACTION AND AFFINITIES

These critical broadsides represent only one part of the ambivalent attitudes that Leach had toward Lévi-Strauss's writings on kinship. But there are many Lévi-Straussian contributions that Leach was fascinated by, and deeply admired, such as his formulations about "savage" thought,[15] his techniques of decoding myth, and his demonstration of "transformational" analysis.

In fact Leach's little Fontana volume entitled *Lévi-Strauss* (1970), written at a time when already some differences had crystallized between them, is a challenging and fascinating piece of writing to deconstruct. It was translated into six languages and ran to three editions. The opening chapter contains a furious volley against Lévi-Strauss's shallow fieldwork and experience, and his reliance on dubious documents; the penultimate chapter is, as we have seen, a devastating attack on that armchair anthropologist's theory of elementary structures of kinship; but in between we have virtually a celebration (with some skeptical asides) of Lévi-Strauss's structural and transformational analysis of the thought patterns of myth. Some excesses are noted and unprovable generalizations are deflated, but the final judgment is that the journey with Lévi-Strauss into South America is "well worth while."[16] It would seem that Leach on the whole did appreciate Lévi-Strauss's complicated explorations of the thought logic of South American mythology, and was much impressed with his demonstration of homologous and

---

[14] Ibid., p. 12.

[15] "The *Savage Mind* taken as a whole is an entrancing book. The exploration of the way we (the Primitives and the Civilized alike) use different kinds of languages for purposes of classification, and of the way that the categories which relate to social (cultural) space are interwoven with the categories which relate to natural space is packed with immensely stimulating ideas." Leach, *Lévi-Strauss*, pp. 95–96.

[16] Ibid., p. 96.

transformational relations on *many registers* and dimensions. In respect of this mythology, Lévi-Strauss was able to show that:

Sets of relationships among human beings in terms of relative status, friendship and hostility, sexual availability, mutual dependence, may be represented in myth, either in direct or transposed form, as:

1. relationships between different kinds (species) of men, animals, birds, reptiles, insects, supernatural beings;
2. relationships between categories of food – e.g. there being a recurrent analogy between copulation and birth on the one hand, and eating and excretion on the other;
3. relations between categories of sound and silence produced either naturally as animal cries or artificially by means of musical instruments;
4. relations between categories of smell and taste – pleasant/unpleasant, sweet/sour etc.
5. relations between animals and plants, particularly as sources of clothing and of foodstuffs;
6. relations between categories of landscape, seasonal change, time alterations, celestial bodies . . .

or combinations of any of these frames of reference. The main purpose of his South American analysis is not merely to show that such symbolization occurs, for Freud and his followers have already claimed to demonstrate this, but to show that the transformations follow strictly logical rules. Lévi-Strauss displays quite extraordinary ingenuity in the way he exhibits this hidden logic but the argument is extremely complicated and very difficult to evaluate.[17]

Leach was particularly taken with Lévi-Strauss's postulation of the culinary triangle (raw/cooked/rotten *in its primary form* and in its developed form), the relations between different modes of processing food (roasting, boiling, smoking) on the one hand and the relations between social occasions on the other; he acknowledged that Lévi-Strauss had "marshalled a great deal of evidence to show that the process of food preparation and the categories of food with which they are associated are everywhere elaborately structured and that there are universal principles underlying these structures."[18]

It is evident that Lévi-Strauss's ingenious decoding attempts also stimulated Leach, who already had semiotic leanings, to experiment with similar analyses. Leach was ever ready to engage with new thought experiments and with innovative perspectives that opened new vistas

[17] Ibid., pp. 66–67.   [18] Ibid., p. 30.

of understanding. Thus it is transparent in chapter 4 of *Lévi-Strauss* ("The Structure of Myth"), where Leach sets out to instruct the reader about Lévi-Strauss's approach to myth, that he cannot resist the temptation to make an authorial substitution and to play at "Leach imitating Lévi-Strauss."[19] He gives his own analysis in the Lévi-Straussian mode of interconnected Greek myths (e.g. "Kadmos, Europe, and the Dragon"; "Minos and the Minotaur"; "Theseus, Ariadne and the Minotaur"; and others such as the Oedipus cycle), and suggests the plausibility of Lévi-Strauss's central thesis that the function of mythology is to exhibit publicly, though in disguise, unconscious, existential paradoxes; and that myths deal with irresolvable contradictions that we hide from consciousness because their implications run directly counter to the fundamentals of human morality. Leach's own illustrations reveal that there is a matrix formed by the oppositions between the relative positions of human beings and deities and animals, that "the polarity Nature: Culture:Gods:Men . . . affirms that the relationship between gods and men is one of ambiguous and unstable alliance – exemplified by marriage, followed by feud, followed by marriage accompanied by poisoned marriage gifts."[20] From what I have said before, it is easy to see that such myth messages are congenial to Leach's own independently generated ideas on ambiguous and ambivalent liminal entities and on the nearness of sinning and creativeness. One message Leach draws from the whole set of Greek stories he analyzes is that "If society is to go on, daughters must be disloyal to their parents and sons must destroy (replace) their fathers."[21] No doubt this message was in accord with his own personal declaration that at some stage a pupil will have to repudiate his own teacher if he is to be creative himself.

One can point to many other affinities between Leach's sense of metaphorical and metonymical logic and many Lévi-Straussian analogies, such as between eating and sexual intercourse; between honey and menstrual blood; and vomit being not only the correlative and inverse term of coitus and defecation, but also the correlative and inverse term to auditory communication.

Leach was much more cautious than Lévi-Strauss, and modestly agnostic, when it came to the issue of universal trends in the structural patterning of thought categories and other cultural phenomena. He certainly avoided grand pronouncements about the fundamental properties of the human mind, the collective unconscious of the human mind,

---

[19] Ibid., p. 70.   [20] Ibid., p. 74.   [21] Ibid., p. 83.

and underlying relations of an algebraic kind objectively embedded in human thought.

However, a great deal of his own actual analysis of verbal categories, of myths, of representations in art form, and so on did depend on his reliance on binary categories, their contrasts and intersections, and the affective load carried by the overlaps as well as interstices between them. He made liberal use of the Euler diagram to discuss taboo. In certain of his essays he also relied on the tripartite schema of Van Gennep (separation, liminal phase, aggregation) as a general structural pattern applicable to the phenomena at hand (though he would simultaneously insist on understanding the context in which the schema was employed).

Some readers may feel that Leach, the "idealist" and "empiricist," who held that "Ideas are more important than things," that "creative imagination is deeply entangled with the formulation of verbal concepts," and that material objects, things made by man, are "representations of ideas,"[22] did not sufficiently clarify the extent of the generality of binary thought as a human propensity.

Let us consider the following passages by Leach to see where he leads us.

There are some things which seem to be true of all extinct languages so it seems likely that they were true also of all extant human languages. For example, the structure of verbal concepts is binary – I/Other, We/They, Tame/Wild, Good/Bad, Living/Dead . . . and so on. Moreover, at least in an approximate sense, the logic of verbal category formation is "transitive" – things that are opposite to the same thing are equal to one another. We also know that the binary structure of human languages is imposed on the world of experience. The world that is presented to our minds through the interacting operation of sensory signals and verbal categorizations is not how things really are . . . a crucial aspect of this distortion is that, at the level of ideas, categories are clear cut and distinct, but, at the level of fact, the "things" out there that are represented by the verbal categories are fuzzy at the edges. The boundary that separates the inside from the outside is neither one nor the other; it is both inside and outside, an area of confusion loaded with taboo. This applies to the orifices of the human body and also thresholds of houses, and the entrances of cities, and some of the most interesting work on social anthropology in recent years has been concerned with demonstrating the existence of transformational structures in which it is shown that the layout of buildings and of settlements maps both the anatomic organization of the human body and the social anatomy of the body politic.[23]

---

[22] See, for example, Edmund Leach, "A View from the Bridge," *BAR Supplementary Series*, no. 19, 1977, pp. 166–68.

[23] Ibid., pp. 161–62.

Contemporary social anthropology, as exhibited in the work of a great variety of authors including among others, Victor Turner, Mary Douglas, Lévi-Strauss, and myself, owes a great deal to an insight which was developed near the beginning of the century by Robert Hertz and Arnold Van Gennep. Ruthlessly cut down to its bare essentials this insight is that when we encounter a pattern of cultural behaviour which "manifests" a category opposition of the general type which I have indicated above, then the boundary which serves as a marker to distinguish the left hand member of the binary pair, from the right hand member, the "betwixt and between" element is both *ambiguous* and *sacred*, and the whole of religious cult organization is concerned with precisely such border zone cultural phenomena.[24]

It would seem from the foregoing passages (and many other instances) that whatever the philosophical differences between Leach the idealist and Lévi-Strauss the realist, they (as well as certain others such as Douglas and Turner) tended to converge toward a general agreement on this matter: that human thought generally tends toward binary distinctions, and that classifications that are predicated on this binary form, when imposed on the dynamic reality out there, give rise to certain problems of fit, which become the source of affectively laden reactions which are elaborated in cultic form.

However, it is in certain further elaborations and applications of this theoretical bent that we witness the distinctive ways in which Leach's perspective on the work of social anthropology differed from that of Lévi-Strauss.

TRANSFORMATIONAL TRANSCRIPTIONS

We have seen how Leach conveyed in many places his affinity with aspects of Lévi-Straussian structuralism, and that he also attributed this preference to his "mathematical bent" and to the transformational analysis that it enabled. Structuralism was attractive to him because it made possible "cross-cultural transcriptions." He had in *Political Systems of Highland Burma* demonstrated the poverty of treating cultures as well as societies as bounded entities. Transformational analysis, as he saw it, enabled the perception of "schema" or structural designs and arrangements, as transformations of one another. And it is these transformational relations between schema that he identified with the project of cross-cultural comparison. Leach associated these exercises with the analogous operations of mathematical manipulation.

[24] Ibid., p. 170.

The structuralist method, so understood, was applicable just as well to the mythology of Christians and Jews as to the mythologies of the "primitives." The demonstration of this proposition was crucial to Leach's commitment to the possibility of cross-cultural comparison and understanding. Especially in the later phase of his anthropological writing, he lavishly demonstrated that the myths of "primitive peoples," of Hinduism and Buddhism, of classical Greece, of the Bible (Old Testament) were amenable to transformational structural analysis.

While by no means ignoring or not appreciating differences – both cultural and social – in terms of substantive particulars or aesthetic conventions or moral concerns and emphases, Leach saw structural transformational analysis as capable at a higher abstract level of revealing patterns of thought that were general to human beings. Extending beyond the domain of mythology, Leach asserted that the decoding of systems of social representation – such as linguistic usages, manners, styles of dress, food, housing – among different strata of a society, and between societies, was a primary task of the social scientist. The exercise of "decoding" Leach associated with his interests in communication engineering and information processing as well with the possibilities of mathematical manipulation.

The words "transformational transcriptions" were a key expression especially in the later writings of Leach. His illustrations varied from simple or elementary ones to complex correlations between two or more dimensions or domains. Two elementary examples were these: (1) the circle, the ellipse, the parabola, the hyperbola are mathematical abstractions. They can be derived from the geometry of conic sections, and are variations or transformations of one another. (2) In the widely used traffic signal, the ordering of the colours green–yellow–red is the same ordering of the instructions GO–CAUTION–STOP; "the colour system and the signal system have the same 'structure', the one is a transformation of the other."[25]

A more complex situation that could be seen in transformational terms was Leach's characterization of the ideal categories of *gumsa* and *gumlao* which were transformations of each other, whose applications by Kachin actors to the flow of events on the ground took cognizance of, and were dynamically related to, issues of succession to office by ultimogeniture, fission of communities and founding of new ones by eldest sons, economic differentiation, marriage strategies, and so on.

[25] Leach, *Lévi-Strauss*, p. 17.

Leach recognized Lévi-Strauss's small treatise on Australian totemism, in which he postulated a transformational relation between animal-level categories and the social classification and groupings of human beings, as a "major contribution," based on the very widespread phenomenon of the "socialization of animal categories."[26]

To return to Leach's own writings, it was in his notable and remarkable essays focused on biblical materials, early Christian doctrines and art, which have been described in chapters 11 and 12, that he demonstrates to great effect his own brand of virtuosity. These essays contain transformational analyses of thought structures and symbolic complexes together with their dialectical linkage within the larger social contexts and existential concerns of the people who generated and deployed them.

Leach wedded his structuralist transformational analysis to another set of operations that ultimately derived from his work on classificatory categories. Structuralist analysis reveals and exposes symmetries as well as asymmetries, ambiguities as well as liminalities in the relations between postulated categories which humans imposed on the world. The in-between liminal spaces were capable of multiple valuations by actors according to context, as sites of negative error-laden-deviation or of positive creative generation, or alternations between both poles. Leach was fond of pointing out that Cain, the first murderer, was also a sacrificial priest, and Cain's son Enoch returned from the wilderness to build the city, and that these processes were integral to the creation of culture. By temperament and by virtue of his enjoyment of iconoclastic breaching of boundaries, Leach was always fascinated by the in-between spaces and persons – that which was marked as taboo, verbal abuse, the sacred, and persons designated as mediators, gatekeepers, threshold guardians, tricksters, and perhaps most of all, those instances of jumbling and mixing up of gods, humans, and animals. That heavenly gatekeepers invariably turn out to be double-faced tricksters was one of his maxims that were hard to forget.

In one of the seminars he gave at The Johns Hopkins University in the spring of 1976, Leach wrote the following verse on the blackboard:

Ne had the Apple taken been
Ne had never the Our Lady
Been Heavenly Queen

---

[26] Claude Lévi-Strauss, *Totemism*, trans. Rodney Needhan, London: Merlin Press, 1964.

Blessed be the time that apple taken was
Therefore we mour singen *Deo* Gratias (XVth Century Carol)

And below this verse he drew a diagram of two triangles, the points of the inner triangle in particular being the locations of the in-between ambiguous and generative figures (see figure 14.1).

The double triangles mark both the symmetries and the ambiguities. The language of the Bible is not geometrical but it does express polarities. The diagram suggests that the creator is like a sinner, one who breaks rules. Cain and the two Marys suggest this valuation. The serpent is a "biological" trickster – sexual and phallic in nature and ambiguous as regards male or female identity. Some medieval representations of the serpent invest it with Eve's face.

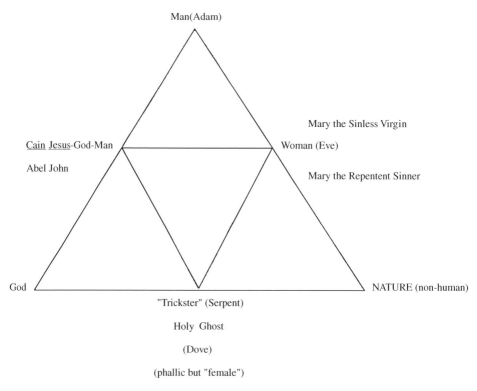

Figure 14.1. Symmetries and ambiguities.

PHILOSOPHICAL DIVERGENCES

While Leach was fascinated by Lévi-Strauss's analysis of thought patterns and mythic thematic oppositions and attempted mediations, and he himself produced similar exercises, he sensed a marked philosophical divide between Lévi-Strauss's "realism" and "rationalism" and his own "idealism" and "empiricism."

Lévi-Strauss saw the universe of human thought as objectively ordered by underlying relations of a mathematical (or algebraic) kind irrespective of human observations. This realism and universalism, combined with a commitment to Cartesian rationalism and a faith in his own reasoning, engendered the view that ethnographic facts and observations may be poor representations of the underlying structural logic which can be imaged in terms of models that objectively inhere in the phenomena studied. He usually assumed that the human brain operated by making binary distinctions, and that related couples of these could be manipulated as in matrix algebra. It is "Lévi-Strauss' bold proposition that the algebra of the brain can be represented as a rectangular matrix of at least two (but perhaps several) dimensions which can be 'read' up and down or side to side like the words of a cross-word puzzle." These operations applied to sound as well as other cultural categories.[27]

In one of the aforementioned seminars at The Johns Hopkins University, Leach identified himself as an Aristotelian, not a Platonist.

There has been an oscillation in Western Philosophy between Plato and Aristotle, between rationalism and realism on the one side, and empiricism and nominalism on the other.

One tradition of Platonism views reality as constituted of essences (or ideas). These essences are really relationships. For example $\Pi = $ circumference$/$diameter, and Π is a relationship, given the context of a circle. This is a specification for all circles which exist, have existed, and might exist. This essence of circularity exists irrespective of humans, and their capacity to think it.

Pure mathematics has created a Platonic universe of essences, which exist in a mathematical sense (but not merely in material terms). What is their status in a non-human universe? Lévi-Strauss and his followers, and a certain brand of Marxists would like to believe that the universe of human relationships exists in this mathematical sense (irrespective of human observations). Ethnographic facts are, or may be, bad representations of the mathematical relationships, but reality can be construed in terms of them as models.

Leach said that he is on the other side of the fence. He is an Aristotelian. He is interested in the facts he can observe, and he looks for organizational principles

---

[27] Leach, *Lévi-Strauss*, p. 52.

that relate them. Anthropology is about a world inhabited by man; human history is made by man. In this respect, Leach is a Vicoist. The limitations of anthropology are human limitations, and anthropology is a product of human mental activity.[28]

Leach saw Lévi-Strauss as a Platonist and a realist. The following passages convey his perception of the Lévi-Straussian project. The search for "fundamental properties" is a recurrent theme in all Lévi-Strauss's writings; what is fundamental and universal must be the essence of our true nature.[29]

Lévi-Strauss is not an idealist in the style of Bishop Berkeley; he is not arguing that Nature has no existence other than in its apprehension by human minds. Lévi-Strauss' Nature is a genuine reality "out there"; it is governed by natural laws which are accessible, at least in part, to human scientific investigation but our capacity to apprehend the nature of Nature is severely restricted by the nature of the apparatus through which we do the apprehending. Lévi-Strauss' thesis is that by noticing *how* we apprehend nature, by observing the qualities of the classifications which we use and the way we manipulate the resulting categories, we shall be able to infer *crucial facts about the mechanism of thinking.*
　　... since human brains are themselves natural objects and since they are substantially the same throughout the species *Homo sapiens*, we must suppose that when cultural products are generated as described above "the process must impart to them certain universal (natural) characteristics of the brain itself." Thus in investigating the elementary structures of cultural phenomena, we are also making discoveries about the nature of Man – facts which are true of you and me as well as of the naked savages of Central Brazil.[30] [emphasis added]

Lévi Strauss is not much concerned with the collective consciousness of any particular social system; his quest rather is to discover the collective *unconscious* of "the human mind" (*l'esprit humain*), and this should apply not merely to speakers of one language, but to speakers of all languages. A famous pronouncement by Lévi-Strauss states: "We are not, therefore, claiming to show how men think the myths, but rather how the myths think themselves out in men and without men's knowledge."[31]

Leach agreed that human thought can frequently be ordered in terms of binary categories, analogical patterns, transformational relations.

---

[28] See Stanley Tambiah, "Personal Accounts: Edmund Leach Situates Himself," *Cambridge Anthropology. Special Issue: Sir Edward Leach*, vol. 13, no. 3, 1989–90, pp. 33–34.
[29] Leach, *Lévi-Strauss*, p. 18.
[30] Ibid., pp. 25–26.
[31] Ibid., p. 51. Leach cites as his source Lévi-Strauss, *Le cru et la cuit*.

These are imputations of the human thinker who imposes these distinctions and categories on the phenomena out there; these thought categories no doubt attempt to grasp, and may reflect characteristics of those phenomena, but there is no one-to-one correspondence between them. The issue of the nature of this correspondence, and its implications, is a major one for anthropology. Leach was skeptical of, and rejected, Lévi-Strauss's realist assertions that the models he postulated *inhered* in the phenomena he studied (a case in point is the status of the models of kinship he elicited in *Elementary Structures of Kinship*).

As his own "structuralist-functionalist" analyses deepened and matured, and his sense of the complementary relationship between his "idealist" tack in *Political Systems of Highland Burma* and his "empiricist" tack in *Pul Eliya* became clear, Leach saw by the mid-1970s how to phrase the philosophical difference between his version of "structuralist-functionalist" analyses and Lévi-Strauss's "structuralism."

In contrast to Lévi-Strauss's rationalism and realism, Leach declared himself an "idealist" (perhaps "nominalist" is a suitable alternative) and "empiricist." His "idealism," we have already noted, consisted in his view that human actors cognitively structure their world (including their interpersonal relations) in terms of "ideal" verbal categories, which are patterned. But note that there is a problem of fit and connection at two levels which becomes the major concern of his kind of anthropology. There is, on the one hand, no one-to-one relation of correspondence between the thought categories and the world out there. (This, for instance, generates the familiar problems of liminal and ambiguous spaces, and overlaps, within systems of classification and hierarchies.) There is, on the other hand, no one-to-one relation between the thought patterns and *actual human conduct* in contexts of social action. The deviations, paradoxes, mediations, and strategic stretching and manipulating of concepts in the contexts of the contingencies and pragmatic circumstances and intentional calculations of action are a major concern that Leach tried to deal with in multiple ways in all his ethnographic writings and his analyses of myth and art.

This commitment to a pragmatic empiricism was what Leach, with unwavering steadfastness, referred to as his Malinowskian legacy and as stemming from his training as an engineer, who always has to test how a model plan works in its implementation in a site. There is always an interesting relation between the mathematics of a model and what happens in the application to practical tasks – a dialectical relation complicated by uncertainties, contingencies, and external influences.

Leach on one occasion contrasted his perspective with that of Lévi-Strauss in the following way. While Lévi-Strauss attempted to reduce cultural and social phenomena to "the laws of the mind," Leach was interested in "ideas" and "facts" that human beings in interaction construct, and he attempts to see the organizational principles that relate to these human figurations. Anthropology is about a world inhabited by human beings, and their history is made by them. He would not oppose anthropology as a discipline to history. This is one of the perspectives that Vico emphasized and in this sense Leach said he was a Vicoist. It was in the context of enunciating this position that Leach stated that the majority of anthropologists shared his "own view that the suggestion that anthropology is solely or even primarily concerned with unconscious mentalist phenomena is totally unacceptable."[32]

In most of his writings, Leach emphasized dealing with the *social context* of thought phenomena as a methodological and interpretive control. In contrast to Lévi-Strauss's reductionist bent of tracing thought to mental processes embedded in the human brain, Leach's thrust, in line with the British structural-functionalist penchant, was more concerned to dialectically relate thought patterns to their social/political/economic and religious contexts to probe their existential logic as well as their contradictions and their ambiguities. Leach felt that Lévi-Strauss progressively departed from this theoretical and methodological perspective, which he had so impressively illustrated in his early Asdiwal essay.[33] We realize how Leach was positioned at the confluence of two anthropological perspectives, British structural-functionalism (itself differentiated and stereotypically summarized as the tension between Radcliffe-Brownian structure and Malinowskian function), and the French structuralism of Lévi-Strauss. His uniqueness and originality lay in combining selectively what he took and transformed from both perspectives, and endeavoring to perform a style of analysis and interpretation that today some would call "practice theory," others as the uniting of "system with event," or of "history and anthropology."

In 1976, at The Johns Hopkins, I heard Leach offer a speculation from his idealist position, which was skeptical of Lévi-Strauss's realist assertion of models inhering in the phenomena studied. He suggested that one should be open to the possibility that thought aids and categories, such as circles, triangles, binary categories, and digital coding that were

---

[32] See Leach, *Social Anthropology*, pp. 34–35.
[33] Lévi-Strauss, "La geste d'Asdiwal."

in vogue at that time, might not be the elements in the construction of computer systems of the future. Such musings were in line with Leach's rejection of Lévi-Strauss's mentalistic thesis that anthropology is primarily concerned with the unconscious cognitive processes inscribed in the mind. As Leach put it in one of his characteristic phrasings, the structuralist's structure is "not in the meat." The processes of the brain have to be understood ultimately in terms of physico-chemical and neurological processes of bio-genetic models.

CHAPTER 15

"A Runaway World?"

"Without contraries is no progression."
William Blake

Leach was invited by the British Broadcasting Corporation (BBC) to deliver the prestigious Reith Lectures in 1967.[1] He was the first anthropologist ever to have been asked (and so far he has had no anthropologist successor). He had been elected Provost of King's College the previous year (another first) and this added to his visibility and reputation as a prominent intellectual. "The central topic was to be the need for change in our moral and social presuppositions in face of the galloping acceleration of the population explosion and the technological revolution, topics which have provided a favourite diet for all the mass communication media for years past. My subject matter was familiar enough though my evolutionist-humanist approach seems to have caused astonishment and at times resentment."[2]

Leach gave six lectures. He was conscious that he was addressing the public at large and had to be direct in style of communication. He appreciated that he should demonstrate how anthropology, usually associated with the study of exotic peoples, places, and customs, had something relevant and vital to say about contemporary global issues, and as usual, he was being himself in being provocative and some might think "prophetic" in his criticism of a passive *status quo* that ought to think ahead.

Leach signaled that his lectures, meant to be all of a piece, were informed by a perspective called "evolutionary humanism as a total attitude to the human situation."[3] And E.M. Forster's famous "only connect" became a motto to convey the multiple interconnections that he hoped to spell out.

---

[1] Edmund Leach, *A Runaway World?* The BBC Reith Lectures, 1967, New York: Oxford University Press, 1968.
[2] Ibid., p. vii.   [3] Ibid., p. 98.

Leach opened the first lecture, "Men and Nature," with the words, "Men have become like gods" in the sense in which scientific knowledge and technology have reached a stage where humans can creatively act like gods to change the world, but the notions of scientific objectivity and detachment concordant with the view that nature out there is orderly and subject to laws make of scientists passive searchers of truth and spectators, evading their responsibility to take active charge of humanity's future at a point in time when science can dramatically change the environment.[4]

The second lecture, "Men and Machines," examined the anxieties humans have toward the very machines which their own technical wizardry has created.

Leach began by saying that all of us are haunted by three ideas that somehow ought to fit together but won't. The first is the idea of nature, the world "out there" that existed before human intervention, but this nature now actually includes the whole animal kingdom, and we humans too are animals. The second is the opposite idea of civilization as opposed to nature, culture and technology being considered as products of human learning and human creativity applied to nature. The third that ought to bridge the two and doesn't in our present thinking is the idea of conscious self, the I, who is part of both nature and culture. This third idea is linked to our suppositions that we act intentionally, we have free will, and we make choices.

This same puzzle was met earlier in the form of "the predicament of scientific detachment" – the scientists' view that nature *must* be orderly

---

[4] Leach remarks that the passive perspective that scientific notions of laws of nature are discovered "objectively" by detached scientists is detrimental to their active participation in the world to shape its future. This attribution contrasts with the different emphasis underscored by Habermas and Foucault. Habermas has argued that the production of scientific knowledge is linked to "interests" and that scientific knowledge has become an important "force of production" intervening in the world on the grounds of its "legitimacy" claims as objective knowledge. In a similar way, Foucault has probed the relation between "knowledge and power," and how that knowledge categorizes and labels the world, disciplines and punishes those defined as deviants, non-conformists, and unnatural. See, for example, Jürgen Habermas, *Towards a Rational Society*, trans. Jeremy J. Shapiro, London: Heinemann, 1971; Michel Foucault, *The Birth of the Clinic: An Archaeology of Medical Perception*, trans. A.M. Sheridan Smith, New York: Pantheon Books, 1973; and *Discipline and Punish: The Birth of the Prison*, trans. A.M. Sheridan, New York: Vintage Books, 1979. Leach is urging them to accept their ethical responsibilities and not hide behind the curtain of objectivity.

Leach, MacIntyre, and Medawar, British intellectuals, take a different tack from Habermas and Foucault, and diagnose the actual situation in Britain in which working scientists are slotted into their niches in their research organizations, and are excluded from making decisions about the development and directions of their sciences. Such decisions are alleged to be the province of superior civil servants, who are trained in the liberal arts and not the sciences, and are ill-equipped to deal with policy issues in an informed and imaginative way.

goes counter to the possibility that the phenomena they are studying might be changing because of their interactional and intentional interventions and thereby defeat their search for causality purely in terms of mechanical rules or probabilty. Scientific investigation might then turn futile to those scientists wedded to detached objectivity.

The same predicament informs the attitude to the machines we make: machines are all right as long as they behave in a predictable way, but what if somewhere along the line they make choices and think and act like us? Why do we feel humiliated and threatened by the idea that we are like machines? If we could find our way to thinking that consciousness is not something that sets us apart from machines (and nature) but something which "connects us all together" then a reconcilable perspective becomes possible.

Leach at this point adumbrates a point of view which illustrates what he meant by "evolutionary humanism." His first move is to point out that evolution is an open-ended theory of change, that it is unpredictable, and that it is neither a simple mechanical process nor a simple randomized change. What then gives direction to change? When environmental conditions are stable physical specialization and accuracy of reproduction are functional, but when the environment changes, it is the more versatile and not overly specialized beings – such as weeds, humans, and rats – that are at a great adaptive advantage. What this versatility implies is that in a situation of random choice, some choices are encouraged by the environment and some are not, and in the outcome the species "learns from experience." Cannot this be equated or aligned with what we mean by "conscious intention" and "free will," which we attribute solely to humans, stripped of their metaphysical connotations?

Recent studies in ethology demonstrate that the classical distinction between animal behavior governed by inborn instinct and human behavior governed by reason and learning must be abandoned. Animals too can learn, and in some cases pass on what they learn to the next generation; and animal habits, like human "customs," can be modified quite rapidly. In this sense animals can make choices, and, pushed further, the usual distinction between evolution as what happens to particular animal species on the one hand and history as events taking place in human societies on the other largely disappears.

It should be mentioned that in attempting to blur the lines between "intentional behavior" and "learning from experience" and "mechanical response," Leach was quite aware of that which, like human speech and language, makes humans different from animals. His push in the service of the interconnectedness between humans, animals, and nature was to argue against the imputed divide between instinct and free will, between animal and human being, and between evolution and history.

It is thus in the service of the same theme of connectedness and participation that Leach now takes up the "relation" between "men and machines."

Leach makes a succinct clarification of what he means by "relation" and "relational structure" (this clarification is a continuation of ideas proffered earlier in *Rethinking Anthropology*). Early in life we are taught to classify things – into kinds of plants, birds, insects – and we are taught to separate one object from another and to label each with a name. It is later that we become interested in how things are related rather than in what they are called. "This is because the comparison of relations is more thought-provoking than the comparison of things." It seems to me that this is a moment at which we can recognize that Leach's insistence and reiteration that his previous training in engineering attuned him to look for the design features of entities and how a thing "works as a whole" by seeing "what connects with what" must be taken seriously. The sets of relations which determine the outward appearance of a whale and the shape of the fuselage of a large aircraft are analogous for the reason "that the relations between a whale and the water through which it swims is very similar to the relations between an aircraft and the air through which it flies . . . In other words, the model – the 'network system of relations' has a much greater explanatory power than the thing itself."[5] Modern science is in this sense concerned with relations and not with objects. And the notion of "relational structures" can be linked to that of "transformation." For example, in transmitting messages "the communication path – my head, my voice, the microphone, the radio transmitter, your receiver, your loud-speaker, your ears, your brain" – shows no break in the sequence. There is a transformation in the forms of the pattern in each stage but not a change in structure.[6]

All this as a preamble brings Leach to the issue of the relation between "men and machines." In his language, Leach said, "machine" means "structured system which works."

From this relational viewpoint, any two machines which work in the same way or do the same kind of job are the same kind of machine even if they are made of quite different substances and operate in quite different environments. And

[5] Ibid., p. 25.   [6] Ibid., p. 27.

we can usefully compare one machine with the other just as we can usefully compare the shape of an aircraft with the shape of a whale . . . Up to a point the human brain is the same kind of machine as a man-made computer.[7]

Leach thus argues that rather than viewing machines as separate from us humans – who think that we are special persons on account of being endowed with consciousness, intentionality, and free will – we might gain some insight into the connectedness between humans and machines (and nature) if we see that there is "no sharp break between what is human and what is mechanical." If one defines machine in general terms as "a structured system which works," that is, as a "relational structure," then *up to a point*[8] the human brain is the same kind of machine as a man-made computer. The relational systems of computer systems and relational systems of brain mechanisms are analogous. This recognition of connectedness between man and machine, that machines are "simply an extension of man" and wholly dependant on the human maker, enables us to relieve our sense of human isolation, loneliness, and separateness, to nurture our participation in an interconnected whole, and to foster our sense of contributing to an open-ended adaptive evolution.

In the third lecture, "Ourselves and Others," Leach deployed his classificatory theory – how humans impose discrete categories on the world and therefore view the liminal in-between spaces and entities as ambiguous and problematic – to suggest why we ourselves, and not only nature and technology, "seem out of control."

Why do we have enemies, and why should we seek to kill our fellow men? The general pattern (except in rare situations) among animal species is that aggression is directed outwards to other species and not inwards, but humans frequently kill one another. "My own guess is that our propensity to murder is a backhanded consequence of our dependence on verbal communication; we use words in such a way that we come to think that men who behave in different ways are members of different species."[9] Because of the way our language is organized we are educated to make categories of contrast and contestation: I and we versus other and them, Englishmen versus Frenchmen, and so on. In daily life, we differentiate closely paired dependent relations such as

---

[7] Ibid., pp. 27–28.

[8] Leach cautioned that one should note his qualification "up to a point," and quotes Medawar as commenting that even if it is inadequate to say that the human brain is a kind of computer it is certainly valid to say that a man-made computer is a kind of brain (p. 28, footnote).

[9] Ibid., pp. 32–33.

parent/child, employer/employee, master/pupil. The extreme of this spectrum is reached when the *other* seems to be very remote and therefore is considered benign. Lying in between the remote heavenly *other* and the close predictable *other* there is a third category which arouses a different kind of emotion: being close at hand it is unreliable, it is out of one's control and becomes a source of fear. The first British colonists' extermination in the eighteenth century of the original Tasmanians, Hitler's slaughter of the Jews, South African apartheid, the labeling as abnormal and consequent shutting up of criminals, lunatics, and the senile, are all part of this fear-inducing predicament. Ultimately the punitive actions are attempts to maintain the values of the existing order against threats which arise from its own internal contradictions. "Cure is the imposition of discipline by force."[10] (This aphorism it seems to me resonates with Foucault's assertions in *Discipline and Punish*.)

Much in the same vein Leach took up next the issue of tensions between generations, normal for any society, but a particular concern in Britain (and elsewhere in the West) in the 1960s in the form of adolescent and youth "rebellion." Leach turned the tables on the older generation who, having failed to create a world fit for young people to live in, show a "rabid hostility" to the young people themselves. "What we have to consider is not 'why are the young so disorderly?' but 'why the old imagine that the young are so disorderly.'" It is because the old allow themselves to feel separated from the young that the young create anxiety.

The anarchist temper of a tiny minority among Britain's pop generation is a healthy attack on English class values. The signals which trigger class prejudice in Britain on the basis of accent, style of dress, commensal habits are once again a case of man imposed separations. The young rebels do not want to inherit a social system in which power is the exclusive preserve of those who happen to have influential parents or of those who are docile and obedient by conforming to parental expectations.

It was almost a natural transition from here for Leach to attribute youthful disorder to "a breakdown of family life." So much "soppy propaganda" has been made about the virtues of "the family" in the English sense that it is imagined to be a universal institution. Contemporary ideas in Britain have been greatly affected by the use of the phrase "The Holy Family" in religious contexts. But the static stereotype of a nuclear family as a universal does not stand up in a comparative context which shows that human beings at one time or other have invented

---

[10] Ibid., p. 36.

different styles and sorts of domestic living. In Britain itself the older bonds of kinship, neighborhood, common occupation and locality have been eroded mainly by the result of economic developments of the past fifty years which have stimulated geographical, occupational, and social mobility. Today the domestic household is isolated; looking inwards upon itself, it intensifies the emotional stress between spouses and between parents and children. "Far from being the basis of good society, the family with its narrow privacy and tawdry secrets, is the source of all our discontents." "Privacy is the source of fear and violence."[11]

"Men and Morality" was the fourth lecture. A theme in previous talks was how fear of the future is tied in with non-participation. Leach considers here "how far this difficulty is simply a problem of morality."

Leach's approach unfolds in a predictable manner in terms of his approach to classification. We impose on the world which is in flow a grid of arbitrary/conventional categories, and the liminal events or phenomena that fall in between the categories are problematic and viewed with fear and/or suppression. Moral rules which distinguish good from bad behavior are actually specified by culture, and "the content of moral prohibitions varies wildly not only as between one society and another but even within the same society as between one social class and another or between one historical period or another."[12] A belief that our more deeply felt moral constraints are shared by all humanity is simply a delusion.

Leach next attempts to answer the question as to why we feel moral rules are important if in fact moral rules vary drastically from place to place and from time to time, and "they cannot have any long-term

[11] A notable reaction in the press to Leach's "dogmatic assertion" (informed by libraries of ethnographic evidence) that "all moral values are arbitrary" was Mr. Philip Toynbee's "equally dogmatic assertion that 'moral fundamentals remain remarkably unchanged'" (Leach, *A Runaway World?*, p. 95). I remember one piece of correspondence in *The Observer* ending with Leach's exasperated exclamation, "Holy Family! Holy Mackerel!"

In any case, viewing the matter from the vantage point of the early 1990s in the United States where an epidemic of charges relating to child abuse, both physical and sexual, battered wives, husbands raping wives (and as I was writing in late January 1994, the murder of their parents by the Menendez brothers for alleged systematic sexual and physical abuse, and the cutting off of Mr. Bobbitt's penis by his wife who allegedly had enough of his raping and his battering) had erupted, Leach may not have been off the mark if he had actually meant "sexual scandals."

As I review this statement in August 1999, I think it is relevant to reflect on two high school tragedies in recent months: the case of two teenagers who killed twelve students and a teacher as well as themselves in Columbine High School at Littleton, Colorado in April, and the copy-cat shooting by a 15-year-old boy of six classmates at a high school in Conyers, Georgia. Easy access to guns, parental ignorance of their children's daily activities, and uncontained rage against some peers at school are said to be ingredients of these excesses.

[12] Leach, *A Runaway World?*, p. 47.

adaptive advantage either for the human species as a whole, or for any incipient sub-species."[13]

His discussion takes off from the structure and functioning of the human brain for receiving and processing sensory signals. In order that the brain may interpret a signal that is fed into it through eyes or ears, it must first of all discriminate. In many instances the receptor mechanisms of the brain are binary and digital, and therefore the received signals are received in either/or terms in order that the interpretation process can start working. But such acts of discrimination call for *repression*, that is, we refuse to or learn to recognize all "in between" shapes and noises, which we interpret as "wrong." When we say that "a particular behaviour is 'wrong' in a moral sense it is because it struck us in the first place as an 'in between' kind of behaviour,"[14] which we either put into a special box labeled "bad things" or else repress it from our consciousness altogether.

There is a way in which these processes are actively used in our perception of phenomena and seeing "patterns" in them: just as when we read a written message we ignore or repress random marks on the paper and recognize sequences of letters and words as forming a patterned message, in the same way our moral categories and codes help us to see a meaningful ordering in other people's behavior which may actually be quite chaotic. There are certain limits within which we tolerate unorthodox behavior and recognize it as patterned, but when deviation becomes too great we type it as immoral and wrong.

When these socially and culturally conditioned cognitive processes are transposed in scale to historical processes certain interesting repressions and valuations are revealed. The London of Charles Dickens's time had troupes of elegantly dressed courtesans parading up and down Regent Street and the Haymarket, but Dickens's allegedly "realistic" novels, in sketching his characters as accepting the prudish conventions of Victorian orthodoxy in their secular lives, display a notable gap in social perception and commentary. Another case of "self-imposed ignorance" relates in our own time to figures such as Stalin and Hitler who were looked upon as great reformers and saints by millions of their fellow countrypeople even in the midst of the Holocaust. "In the thirties, the Russian and German peoples 'refused to know' what was going on under their noses."[15]

"Thus until we know the code, the 'facts as they really are' don't carry any message at all. But once we do know the code we can fit what we

---

[13] Ibid., p. 49.   [14] Ibid., p. 51.   [15] Ibid., p. 54.

see, or hear, or smell, to our expectations. The signals which get us into an emotional muddle are always the border line cases in which the messages are inconsistent."[16] An example from Britain concerns marriage between first cousins which is allowed by law, is quite common, yet suggestive of immorality to those who consider such close marriage to be like incest.

"When social conditions are changing fast, this area of uncertainty gets larger. The old start to denounce the young for their immorality because the code is changing, and they can no longer interpret the signals."[17]

Leach's thinking in this vein, highlighting the discordance between modern social changes and the persistence of conservative moral pressures among the orthodox, and the tendency to resort to the veil of social invisibility, reaches a high point of relevance and immediacy when he lights on urgent and controversial issues such as experimentation on human subjects, the ethics of prolonging the life of persons who are judged to be extremely "abnormal," "senile," or in "chronic pain," and I may add, the ethics of various kinds of genetic engineerings and manipulation that confuse traditional notions of conception and parenthood. Scientists and doctors are expected to explore the unknown, make discoveries, and create innovations – but at the same time we hold that they should not experiment or make guinea pigs out of members of *my* family. Experiments conducted on human subjects, obviously necessary to advance knowledge, are "blacked out" since they contravene orthodox canons of morality.[18]

In the fifth lecture, "Men and Learning," Leach was standing on his own turf of schooling and higher education. Commenting on how the contemporary schools and universities in Britain measure up to imparting genuinely creative and relevant knowledge to youth who face the challenges of a fast-changing world propelled by technological revolution, Leach unbuttons more than ever before and launches a fierce critique in which he too is included as a defaulter.

---

[16] Ibid., p. 55.   [17] Ibid., p. 57.

[18] Such issues have generated heightened feelings and irresolvable conundrums in the USA in recent years. Dr. Kevorkian, who has assisted a number of chronically or terminally ill people to die, was taken to court and released on condition he give up this line of "humanitarian" work. The alleged "scandal" of some medical researchers from Harvard and MIT having experimented in the 1950s with radiation effects on retarded children has made newspaper headlines and news broadcasts. Similar news of experiments on servicemen during wartime has periodically erupted. Litigation and court decisions would no doubt further stir the waters. During the past few years contentions including violent encounters have occurred between those who are anti-abortion and those who support the rights of women to choose abortion. In the UK recently the issue of postmenopausal women giving birth has raised new issues.

Ideally education consists not in the memorizing and storing of facts but the acquisition of the skills by which we can handle them. While everywhere outside the centers of Western capitalism "the normal emphasis of education is on group identity rather than individual identity," the overt values of English formal schooling emphasize individual self-reliance and vicious competitiveness.

The educational institutions, both in the private and public sector, on the one hand cram heads with textbook facts while on the other segregate and classify students into various levels as they pass exams. At its worst the educational system has developed into a ruthless machine for the elimination of the unworthy, and for "picking out the clever conformist." In brief, the British competitive system of selection fails to pick out the kind of people who can cope most effectively with problems of social and technological change, and secondly, the emphasis placed on individual achievement is entirely misplaced.

As in the natural world, so with human beings, it is the versatile "species" that can survive in all sorts of conditions, and not that which has adapted in a very specialized way to a very narrowly defined environment, that has the best prospect of survival in a rapidly changing world. In imparting education it is "the open-ended nonmeasurable kind of ability"[19] that we should look for and foster. Newton, Darwin, Marx, Freud, Picasso were not the products of "academic machines."[20]

Leach next fires salvos at the generational set-up by which in societies like our own, undergoing rapid development, it is the old who impart knowledge to the young. This may be all right in stable conservative societies (as among the earlier Australian aborigines), but in our context, "it is the young adults, not the old ones, who possess the kind of knowledge which young people need to share before they can participate fully in what is going on." "In our runaway world, no one much over the age of forty-five is really fit to teach anybody anything. And that includes me. I am fifty-seven."[21]

The student body in an allegedly "anarchist rebellious mood" have a point when they question the sensitivity to their needs of university committees and university departments all too often managed by old men out of touch with what is now going on. Even worse still,

much of British industry is directed (or misdirected) by elderly gentlemen well over seventy . . . Since those who held offices of power will never willingly give

---

[19] Ibid., p. 69.   [20] Ibid., p. 70.   [21] Ibid., pp. 73–74.

them up . . . the young must somehow or other enforce quite arbitrary rules of early retirement. In those parts of our system which are concerned with research and technological development, either in education, or in industry, or in politics, no one should be allowed to hold any kind of responsible administrative office once he has passed the age of fifty-five.[22]

A footnote in the published lectures says that Leach was advocating that the elderly "should surrender their offices of *power* and not that they should abandon their ordinary occupations." He himself was part of the group of the old not qualified to plan a new world for the rising generation. "Only those who hold the past in complete contempt are ever likely to see visions of the New Jerusalem."[23]

Western societies face this awesome prospect: if powers of preservation of life available to modern medicine are exercised in uninhibited fashion while, "at the same time, we try to tackle the population explosion by reducing the birthrate, then the outcome will be a very decrepit conservative society in which all the political and economic advantages will be with the very old. Most people will dodder on until they are nearly a hundred and half the population will be well past retiring age."[24]

While Leach confessed that he had no solutions to such issues including that of population explosion, he asked whether some kind of ethical re-evaluation of the ethnocentric Christian ethic which stresses the fostering of human life regardless of circumstances was called for, perhaps even a new religious attitude that balances creation and preservation of life with its death and destruction.

In the concluding sixth lecture, "Only Connect . . . ," Leach recapitulated his theme of the total and dynamic interconnectedness of things. It is not the pieces that matter but the evolving system as a whole. And human beings do not stand *outside* the system exercising limitless powers of analytical detached rationality. Leach underscored human flexibility – which makes humans different from mechanical machines – and by virtue of that the possibility of "the total framework of knowable truth to keep on evolving and expanding and changing shape along with the development and refinement of the categories which we use to describe it."[25] Our linguistic behavior demonstrates our capacity to generate and invent new sound patterns of meaning which nevertheless the listener can understand. We are artists with words, we create brand new sentences,[26]

---

[22] Ibid., pp. 75–76.   [23] Ibid., p. 76.   [24] Ibid., p. 59.   [25] Ibid., p. 79.
[26] Leach was, I suppose, voicing Noam Chomsky's ideas on linguistic competence and performance, and the human capacity to generate utterances.

and this is an example of our god-like powers to create and not be afraid of changing situations.

What is alarming about our present situation however is our reluctance to alter our expectations and to change our perspectives. "The monstrous arsenal of modern armaments is manipulated by politicians who talk as if the concept of national sovereignty had remained completely unchanged ever since the eighteenth century."[27]

Large numbers of exceptionally able young people resolutely decline to pursue an orthodox scientific career because they are appalled at the way that science is being used: "Hiroshima, Vietnam, Dr. Kahn's calculations of mega-death," and the willingness to kill off zoological species and spoil the environment on the basis of "the bland unquestioned assumption that national interests always override human interests and that what is man-made and artificial always has priority over what is wild and natural." Actions of this sort can only occur when the decision-maker is totally disorientated about the relations which link ourselves to other people and humankind to nature. But it is humans who are blameworthy, not science. "Science in itself is neutral; it is neither cohesive nor disruptive."[28] The future certainly lies with the people of science and it is altogether essential that they should be people of imagination and good will.

Leach in this final oration was exhorting people not to opt out of taking decisions regarding the problems posed by a world in a runaway condition. He reminded his listeners that

Human beings are superior to other animals because they have a wider choice in the way they can slot experience into expectation, and because they have developed a greater variety of systems of communication. It is our capacity to communicate rather than our capacity to interbreed which has saved the species from disintegration into a number of specialized subtypes. If we are to maintain our human cohesion and dominance it is essential that we allow these two advantages to go on evolving.[29]

We should inhibit the tendency for individuals and groups to separate out as specialized non-communicating systems and we must stimulate the young to elaborate and enlarge their expectations in imaginative ways. We must get out of the habit, which arises from the way our schools are organized, of thinking that reason and imagination are two different kinds of "thing," that the truth of mathematics relates to one kind of fact and the truth of poetry to something quite different.

[27] Ibid., p. 82.   [28] Ibid., p. 84.   [29] Ibid., p. 86.

Leach's bid for human flexibility, to break out of the straitjacket of old classificatory categories and boundaries, to recognize the interconnectedness of things in the world – humans, animals, nature, machines – and to act in tolerance and not so as to dominate and also separate (nationalism, the lamentable delusion that only the separate can be free, is our contemporary disaster), leads him ineluctably to advocating a posture of continuing creativity, which sounds much like Mao Zedong call for permanent revolution. (It may be relevant to note that Mao's cultural revolution was launched around this time.) Leach says that his exhortations

imply that every manifestation of national consciousness is an evil; that respect for tradition is an evil; that every vested interest is at all times open to challenge. They imply a political philosophy of continuous revolution, a persistent disrespect for all forms of bureaucracy . . . You can go on believing that the world ought to be an orderly place even though the quite obvious absence of order fills you with terror, or you can revel in the anarchy and thereby recover your faith in the future instead of hankering after a long dead past.[30]

It is clear that in sounding the call for futuristic thinking Leach was telling the British not to dwell in their past and hanker after their lost colonies and their past imperial glories. Also, at the same time, he embraced the mood of the youth of the mid-1960s, disenchanted as they were with the *status quo* and wanting to change it. Some might think – and did think – that he went too far. One of his capacities – signs of which we have detected earlier – was to push his insights and arguments to their polemical limits, thereby leaving unrecognized surrounding areas of fallibility. Leach was adept at having it both ways: the insider who was simultaneously the tolerable scourge of the establishment, sometimes even playing to the gallery. And no doubt, he full well knew that, whatever his present advocacy, he would have to adopt on the following day a pragmatic attitude to balancing the costs and benefits of institutional continuity and institutional change when exercising the administrative powers of the provostship of King's.

But on this occasion his brief as the Reith lecturer was to shake listeners out of their smug defensiveness and non-action in the face of Britain's looming problems. And his doctrine of evolutionary humanism was a call for creative human responses toward a universe that was indeterminate and open-ended in the way it would evolve.

[30] Ibid., p. 81.

At this point it might be relevant to report what brand of "humanism" Leach professed. The *Humanist News* of January–February 1972 reported the substance of Leach's address entitled "A Personal View."[31] Leach distinguished his "humanism" from that kind of "rationalism" associated with Descartes. Cartesian rationalism (and dualism) was mistaken in equating social science with natural science, and also in not realizing the limits of the doctrine of free will and rational choice theory. These approaches do not adequately deal with and take into account the existential dilemma that other humans must comprehend and respond to us in communication, that actors do not have control of their actions which may produce unexpected unintended consequences. They also do not adequately deal with the fact that "man is an ethical being" and that "human interpersonal relations are governed by moral judgments rather than by logical calculation."

As a "humanist," Leach felt that established religion, by holding that moral codes were ordained by God, simply evades the "responsibility" of individuals for their choices and moreover "cultivates intolerance" toward all who conduct their affairs differently from oneself. A humanist is a person who is willing on every issue to concede that fellow human beings are entitled to hold different opinions from him- or herself. "Tolerance and a personal responsibility are for me the essence of the matter." Much of his advocacy in the Reith Lectures was made in the spirit of and was consistent with this moral philosophical position that in *part* resonates with the existentialist philosophy of Sartre.

DISCUSSION ON THE BBC BY MEDAWAR, MACINTYRE, AND LEACH

Most definitely the most serious and informed discussion of the Reith Lectures was a BBC Third Programme review entitled "A Runaway World Pursued" in which Sir Peter Medawar, Alasdair MacIntyre, and Edmund Leach participated. It was transmitted on New Year's Day 1968 and lasted some forty-five minutes (8.50 p.m. to 9.35 p.m.).[32]

Medawar, the distinguished establishment scientist, MacIntyre, a younger prominent philosopher with a comical sense, and Leach, the

---

[31] I am grateful to Professor Raymond Firth for providing me with the report in *Humanist News*, January–February 1972. The quotations are taken from this report.

[32] In this section based on the broadcast script "A Runaway World Pursued", Edmund Leach, Reith Lecturer for 1967, discusses his lectures with Sir Peter Medawar and Professor Alasdair MacIntyre. Third Programme, BBC, Leach Archive, King's College, Cambridge.

forceful polemical anthropologist, were a good differentiated match to generate an interesting dialog.

The dialog itself, whether planned that way or not, manifested a three-phase pattern. Medawar and MacIntyre as the questioners launched the initial critical thrusts that put Leach on the defensive; next in the long constructive argumentative middle part the three engaged in disputation, Medawar and MacIntyre supporting each other against Leach, MacIntyre differing from Medawar and siding with Leach, Medawar in turn defensively backing away from MacIntyre and veering toward Leach. Finally, in conclusion, all three came together to affirm the importance of some of the prominent themes discussed in the lectures. I must also remark that the dialog sometimes waffled, jumped from one point to another, and recursively returned to an earlier point, but there were some main issues that gave it focus and relevance.

Medawar opened with a query as to what Leach considered the purpose of the Reith Lectures to be, what he had meant to convey, and the style of reasoning behind it, queries he said were prompted by Leach's "asseverative" style of delivery. Leach, agreeing that this comment was fair, said that he had in mind the prospect that the audience for each of his lectures was going to be different, and therefore, rather than following the usual academic style of presentation which progressively attempts an "increasing intensity of analytical nicety," he addressed the general issue of "how we can arrive at a moral consensus throughout society" (in Britain) whose technology was changing fast but which was riven by radical differences of expectations between the older and younger generations, in large part attributable to the educational system which results in class-based strata "ranged in hostile groups." Leach then admitted that "in a changing society it's impossible for everybody to have an agreed moral consensus," but that we could try to introduce the "value of tolerance of difference."

Leach had given an opening to his commentators: is it possible or realistic or desirable to seek moral consensus in a complex society with internal differences and dynamics? MacIntyre was quick to highlight the anomalous nature of the Reith Lectures as "an essentially unfamiliar genre": they are, and have to be, modern sermons, addressed as traditional sermons were, to a broad public in a way that presupposed the very kind of consensus that Leach was saying didn't exist any more. Medawar reinforced this incompatibility in Leach's objective by pointing out that Leach had said in his lectures that "because moral rules vary from time to time and from place to place there is no long-term adaptive advantage for the human species as a whole, or for any incipient sub-species, in adopting any one set of moral rules," and yet he had ended his lectures with a moral exhortation in favor of altruism.

Leach backtracked to clarify the issue of moral consensus and dissensus. Resorting to a kind of language game and speech act approach – which MacIntyre would readily comprehend – Leach observed that participants in social systems – rich and poor, young and old – at any particular time use "a certain set of verbal categories to explain situations to ourselves" and this gives the impression that they agree about how things are. But in fact different segments of society are using these same words quite differently and are strongly committed to such usages. (For example, as regards his own lectures, listeners reacted to some verbal categories he had used – such as "family" – as "trigger words" and reacted "violently" in terms of their expectations about what these words meant.) MacIntyre had earlier made a paradoxical remark that should later have been reassuring to Leach: "If the reaction to your lectures hadn't been confused, turbulent, disagreeing, indeed a lot of your argument would have been wrong."

Leach had indeed taken a moralist position to an undeniable state of affairs: under conditions of technological change, and the natural condition for a moral system in place to be conservative, and the strong tendency for revolutionary codes to revert to a conservative state, "we need a political philosophy of continuous revolution." Anyway on the analog of open-ended evolution that goes forward by "the survival of possible variation" one has to stem what are considered objectionable changes and act in favor of humanitarian values in terms of the ongoing society.

MacIntyre agreed that a morality is conservative in two ways – conservative of the existing social order and in its relation to itself – and in this situation people happily allow quite incompatible and contradictory traditional prescriptions to continue. But the "we" that Leach thought he was addressing was not a unity but very differentiated;[33] "the public at large" is in fact powerless, and among the people who are hostile to Leach's suggestions are those who take short-term decisions, avoid long-term issues, and for them it is important that "the issues should remain

---

[33] Leach disarmingly admitted that he had used the expression "we" as a kind of trick to draw a mass audience into relationship with him, but that his main point throughout was that "we are fragmented into a whole series of mutually hostile and non-communicating segments." In fact he remarked, "I tended to identify myself as a rebel member of the older generation, so that when I was talking about 'we' I was talking about the old who are unnecessarily frightened of the young."

unclear." In this situation, MacIntyre proposed that one should not force on people any positive prescriptions, "but in the first instance simply the necessity of a clear, rational public choice."

But this seemingly forceful call for a public debate on rational choice soon had to face the question of the capacities and roles of scientist, politician, and bureaucrat-civil servant in making decisions, a major issue raised by Leach himself in the lectures which now the three commentators tried to probe further. Leach charged that scientists evade and opt out of making tough decisions instead of taking "a personal view of how things ought to be and then try to bring it about." MacIntyre countered (with a comic sense that was evident throughout the sessions) with the more devastating charge that it is not that they opt out of the tough decisions, but that "they're rarely allowed to come anywhere near them," that in the scientific institutions where they work they are segregated into neat components in which they work on set small finite tasks, and that many of the decisions that Leach was talking about are not taken at all, and are allowed to go by default. They are not settled by the politicians, the bewildered amateurs, "the semi-literate sub-numerate people who rule us." In this context, moral exhortations won't do, because it is a question of "changing social institutions," which is "a matter of politics."

This gave an opening to Leach to reiterate his query about the direction and impact of scientific research. He quite understood how ordinary scientific investigation proceeds (Kuhn's notion of "normal science"[34] was not referred to by Leach), but science can potentially explore in all sorts of directions, and as our knowledge increases research can be devoted to more diverse possible fields and widen its perspectives. But the problem is that there is a huge gulf between the laboratory and the point at which its productions really impact on society; and therefore one needs to know who decides to spend money on directions of scientific development, and makes it possible for the little experiment in the laboratory to hit the public in a big way.

To this query, Medawar, who had authoritative knowledge of scientific institutions, gave the unexpected answer that "there really isn't a machinery by which scientists can express their opinions effectively on the rightness or wrongness of pursuing a particular line of research. Nor...that they need be especially qualified to do it." There is only in

---

[34] Thomas S. Kuhn had published *The Structure of Scientific Revolutions*, Chicago: University of Chicago Press, in 1962.

a looser sense an arena of public debate, exemplified by letters to news-papers, editorial comments, pieces by journalists, that makes it possible for the public to express its misgivings, propose possible solutions, even foolish ones.

This gave an opening to MacIntyre to signal the relevance of another theme in the Reith Lectures: the kind of public educational system in place, in many ways a hangover from the past, which limits in an extreme way public debate on issues, because it leaves out of it most of the people who are going to bear the consequences of decisions taken by those who guide our affairs. On this matter MacIntyre and Leach vigorously came out together in their onslaught on the educational system, with MacIntyre, alluding to what Leach had said, reiterating that it produces the rigid conservative attitude, "built into a system which is competi-tive, selective, and which builds into people norms of competitiveness and selectiveness," which vitiates "such of the high intelligence that gets through the mesh which the whole thing's designed to promote." The target and exemplar of this state of affairs, rejoined Leach, were the elite parts of the Civil Service who control so much of the decision making. Despite the alleged restructuring of admission to the Civil Service, the persons actually recruited are strikingly like the people who are there already, the recruiters inevitably choosing successors suitably like them-selves. In fact the elite civil servants – "these Oxford greats men – nothing against them! . . . nevertheless don't understand what scientists are" and are vaguely contemptuous of them.

Medawar, attempting to mitigate the admittedly grave faults in the Civil Service by referring to the commissional committee under Lord Fulton's chairmanship designed to review and remedy its shortcomings, was treated to MacIntyre's repartee that the statement " 'We are having a commissional committee' . . . strikes cold death in my heart"; in any case although you no longer need to be a Wykehamist to get into the upper reaches of the Civil Service, other schools including grammar schools have been taught to produce substitute Wykehamists. The Reith Lectures ought to make the public aware of this alleged reform in the recruitment of younger generations from the hitherto excluded strata of society, which amounts to the slogan "If you can't in fact beat them let them join *you*."

The next theme discussed, somewhat long and discursive and not or-derly enough to lead to informative clarification, concerned the grounds and processes of creativity and "imagination" and how they relate to "reason" and "mathematical logic." This question arose from Leach's advocacy in the fifth lecture that the current educational system, rather than training people to assimilate and classify facts,[35] should rather be concerned with training students to use their imaginations creatively, for it is from this source that adaptive solutions to technological change can come. Leach had asked whether, granted that one's experience is total and interconnected, there is a kind of upper level at which imagination enters as opposed to the routinized methods of experimentation of "objective science" interacting with the external world. He had invoked Godel (Medawar quipped that referring to Godel always makes a good impression) to raise the issue of different levels of logical analysis, and stated that even to talk about a strictly mathematical system of logic you have to use "a metalanguage which is not itself logical at that point of time," and as you make it consistent there is another higher level that poses the same problem, and so on. When an innovation in scientific theorizing is made, as distinct from a pure piece of experimentation, is this a creative act, and is something new being created? Is altering the frame of reference an act of imagination?

Medawar remarked that the modern view would be that scientific discovery entails an alternation between an imaginative process of thinking up a hypothesis and the critical process of testing it, and that the generative act in a laboratory is an act of imagination. Then, however, he went on to assert that "reason and imagination... are totally different processes, different operations of the mind" and their confusion could be absolutely disastrous.

This assertion triggered MacIntyre's response that "the terms 'reason' and 'imagination' are extremely obfuscating," and if one is going to distinguish between the creation of a hypothesis and its testing, as Medawar had just done, "then it is very important to see that although the imagination is used in the creation of a hypothesis it is a rationally controlled... and rationally informed one."[36] Medawar, seemingly at bay, countered that of course the creative process is rationally informed, but it is "logically unscripted" and you cannot "trace the overt processes of thought" which led to a particular view of the nature of the world.

---

[35] Asked by a skeptical Medawar whether this is the state of affairs today, Leach replied that in response to his lecture on education "by the next post I had no less than six letters from various secondary school masters from all over the country saying – Thank God you've said this – this school is just like that!"

[36] MacIntyre a little later put his position this way: the formal mathematical side of science is part of the creative process, and "training the imagination" involves "training the formal mathematical and logical imagination too."

Leach's concluding remark on the creative process, which evoked the approval of Medawar, was that his "operational" view was that one has to go beyond the notion that scientific reasoning is strictly like logic and mathematics, and that the language employed (words, numbers, symbols) is a system on its own but as the experiment progresses in interaction with the "stuff out there", it in fact takes on new meaning, and acquires new contents, and thereby the frame of truth itself alters as you put more body into your understanding. This operational view contradicts the Cartesian view of a natural world waiting to be discovered, labeled, and classified. It accepts that as we pursue the exploration there is more and more to know, that we are exploring the edge of an unlimited world, that we shall never reach the source of human knowledge. The truth itself changes as you reach into it.

The final point for discussion was Leach's provocative view of the generational gap between the older and younger generations in societies such as our own undergoing rapid development. This issue was reopened by Leach when he remarked that in his experience of Cambridge, the undergraduates connect up with the young dons, with whom they share a larger part of their language, rather than with the senior dons, known as absolutely superb scholars, but who have lost touch with the younger generation. MacIntyre said that this situation of hostility between the generations was one he would pick out as an exciting issue in the lectures. The hostility between the generations, as Leach had said, goes both ways, and he referred to the cues offered by both sides in the educational interaction that form and generalize stereotypes such that "university teachers, school-masters, civil servants become identified with the utterances of judges, bishops and the like."

When Medawar asked what was new about this ("This is *Coningsby* isn't it?"), Leach replied that in an "ideal" stable society, the expectations of the young and old are non-conflictual because the young man is going to move into his father's shoes, and do the job in the same way. If you go a generation back in Britain the society was segmented and "the layer cake" was very sharply class-based, and there was "very little communication between the upper middle class, upper class, the ruling class, the people who talked like you and me around this table really – and the working class . . . a carry over from Disraeli's two nations . . . What is surprising . . . or, interesting about the present time [is that] the cake doesn't cut this way. When the crunch comes, the young of the 'upper class', 'upper middle class' will side with the young of the working class against their elders on both sides in many situations." MacIntyre completed this by saying that these signify "differences of principle and scale because the kind of social identity people have [now] is so different."

MacIntyre had sensed the problem that the Reith Lectures were the only example of the sermon as was traditionally known, addressed to the public at large, and because people were now unused to this genre, "they're likely to react in many strange ways," and produce "relatively random reactions."

Leach, in a postscript to the published Reith Lectures, remarked that they had a *succès de scandale*. There had been commentators of three kinds: firstly, the professional experts in broadcasting technique who, interested not so much in what was said as in the manner of saying it, had approved of his style and delivery; secondly, the journalists and journalist academics (each a Reith lecturer *manqué*) who were consistently hostile (one anonymous intellectual took up four pages of the *Encounter* to denounce the lectures as an "intellectual disaster"); and thirdly members of the general public – he had received from them more than five hundred individual letters – who were for the most part positive and cordial and had "simply listened to what I had to say."[37]

However, Leach also observed in the BBC discussion that many of his critics responded in a rather "trigger-reaction" manner, and that a "substantial number" of people who wrote to him had "either not heard what I've said or read what I've said . . . they've merely picked up a phrase from *The Daily Express* or *Daily Mirror*" or somewhere else and gone to town on that. Certain key words and phrases he had used had "really bounced people off."

The greatest hostility among Leach's critics was triggered by his attack on the conventionally held holiness of family life. Leach in a footnote and the postscript to the book expressed astonishment at this reaction, for what he really had in mind when he spoke of "tawdry secrets" was "the competitive pressures which force us to live beyond our means," notably the stranglehold of hire purchase indebtedness. He did however concede that "at times I trailed my coat just to get a reaction."

Although the lectures evoked comments, both in protest and appreciation, and the ensuing correspondence kept Leach busy for some time, it is equally true that only a limited number of copies of the book were

[37] Ibid., pp. 94–95.

printed, and the book itself is little studied or read in academic circles today. As observed some years later,[38] the book fully deserves a renewed interest at least for the scope and undiminished relevance of the issues, the urgent need for educational reform to suit modern technological changes, the limits of the analogy between human brain and computer technology, the concern for conservation of the environment, the implications of genetic engineering, the basis of intergenerational tensions and conflicts, the role of social stereotyping in producing the curse of racism, and privacy and isolation of individuals and nuclear families as a major source of fear and violence. My recounting of the BBC programme discussion demonstrates that a scientist and a philosopher, both eminent and engaged, deemed the issues he discussed to be of vital concern to Britain.

A BOUQUET FROM AN ESTABLISHMENT FRIEND

A fitting conclusion to my discussion of Leach's *A Runaway World?* is a reference to his Reith Lectures, together with a brief portrait of him, by Noel Annan (1916–2000) in his *Our Age: Portrait of a Generation*,[39] which has been described as "a vast and entertaining survey of the intellectual aristocracy of Noel's generation."[40] Annan, a historian, who among other writings produced a biography of Leslie Stephen which is a vital introduction to the Bloomsbury Group, was Leach's predecessor as Provost of King's College, then went on to become the head of University College, London, and thereafter the first full-time Vice-Chancellor of the University of London. In the course of a busy life as scholar and administrator, he was garlanded with an array of highly prestigious positions in public life: chairman of the trustees of the National Gallery, trustee of the British Museum, and a member of the board of the Royal Opera House.[41]

Chapter 10 of Annan's *Our Age*, entitled "Reaping the Whirlwind," gives a pithy account of the social and political scene of the 1950s and

---

[38] For discussions of the continuing relevance of the Reith Lectures, see Anna Grimshaw, "A Runaway World? Anthropology as a Public Debate," pp. 75–79, and Marilyn Strathern, "Stopping the World: Elmdon and the Reith Lectures," pp. 70–74, both in *Cambridge Anthropology*, vol. 13, no. 3, 1989–90.

[39] Noel Annan, *Our Age: Portrait of a Generation*, London: Weidenfeld & Nicolson, 1990.

[40] Jonathan Mirsky, "On Noel Annan (1916–2000)," *The New York Review of Books*, April 13, 2000, p. 8.

[41] Annan also authored the important Annan Report of 1977 proposing reforms in public broadcasting.

1960s in Britain when "the wall of silence" and taboos about sexual matters faced by the young of every social class in the years between the wars came tumbling down. Here are some of Annan's diagnostic signifiers: medical technology such as the "pill gave women a greater freedom to make love than the condom, the coil or the cap"; if the young "fell prey to anxiety there were tranquillizers, if they were depressed there were purple hearts"; the media struck a new note erasing the distinctions "between high and low culture"; "television and the Italian cinema spread ideas that suddenly appeared realizable as affluence spread and the consumer boom grew"; "teenage culture was transformed as Carnaby Street and King's Road opened their doors in provincial cities."

Annan continues: "Philip Larkin's well known verse that 'sexual intercourse began in 1963 . . . between the end of the Chatterley ban, and the Beatles first LP' was meticulously accurate"; "the Profumo affair like the Chatterley trial, showed how the gap had widened between public opinion and the conventions of the Establishment," and his punishment showed how the Establishment had turned "both apoplectic and vindictive." "Before our eyes we saw the culture of the young transformed," when "American missionaries" in the shape of "hippies preaching Flower Power" invaded Britain; a prominent member of the editorial board of a newspaper, which advised its readers "if you can't turn your parents on, turn on them," was punished as were Keith Richards and Mick Jagger of the Rolling Stones for a first offense of possessing cannabis.

Characterizing Leach as "the most original anthropologist of *Our Age*," and as the "most exuberant of theorists," yet also "Quirky, unpredictable, a believer that truth emerges from contradiction, a roughneck in argument . . . the most charismatic teacher in the subject," Annan gives this commentary based on his reading of the timing and thrust of Leach's BBC performance which was attuned to the context he had sketched:

My successor as provost of King's seized an opportunity to praise the unorthodox. Edmund Leach created a minor sensation with his Reith Lectures of 1967. We are participants in history, he said, and scientists who pride themselves on preserving detachment betray their calling. We should welcome a spot of anarchy and twit the scientists who have set up a pecking order in which the most exact and abstract enquiries – mathematics and physics – are mostly highly praised, and engineering and sociology are treated as scum. "One of our fundamental troubles – particularly we British – take it for granted that there is something intrinsically virtuous and natural about law and order." In fact we are getting more not less conformist every day. Crime is decreasing: the statistics show that more crimes are detected and more crimes are manufactured by Parliament. At a time when most people thought the young were in their heyday, Leach thought they were having a pretty rough time at the hands of judges and moralizing journalists. He considered that they, not their elders, showed the better judgement in rebelling against the Vietnam War, the bomb and hypocrisies of our society such as the class system and the family "with its narrow privacy and tawdry secrets". Far from being the basis of good society the family "is the source of all our discontents". It is in the family that we see the evils of competitiveness – trying to live at a certain economic level – and the competitiveness is intensified in grammar schools, examinations and universities. We should cooperate, we should structure education to discover unorthodox geniuses: instead our schoolmasters cram us with facts instead of teaching us "how to enjoy the pleasures of civilization". The dons who are innovators are rarely over forty: why not compulsory early retirement for the rest? (Leach was not heard to applaud Conservative university policy in the eighties.)[42]

After quoting Leach's provocative denunciation of every manifestation of national consciousness, and advocacy of a political philosophy of continuous revolution, and a permanent disrespect for all forms of bureaucracy, Annan remarks:

Leach achieved his purpose. *Encounter* denounced the lectures as an intellectual disaster, the earnest threw up their hands in horror and the sensible smiled sadly at such characteristic progressive sentiments. The lectures caricatured the liberalism of his generation; but caricatures resemble their originals and the reason Leach gave when he asked his contemporaries to act like gods, confidently and with a show of purpose, was revealing. It was not that the Homeric gods were more likely to achieve their private ambition than mere men who have to bow to fate. But gods have much more fun. That was the authentic voice of our generation.[43]

POSTSCRIPT

After I had completed this biography, I came across Anthony Giddens's *Runaway World*,[44] which "started life as the BBC Reith Lectures for the year 1999." Giddens, himself a celebreated sociologist, presently Director of the London School of Economics and Politics, and before that Professor of Sociology at Cambridge University and a Fellow of

---

[42] Annan, *Our Age*, pp. 140–41.
[43] Ibid., p. 41.
[44] Anthony Giddens, *Runaway World. How Globalization is Reshaping our Lives*, New York: Routledge 2000. Originally published in Great Britain by Profile Books, London 1991.

King's College, made the complimentary remark that the *Runaway World* was the title of the Reith Lectures given by the celebreated anthropologist, Edmund Leach, some quarter of a century ago. However, he put a question mark after his title. I don't think one is needed any more, because "the phrase captures feelings many of us have, living at a time of rapid change."[45] Leach had been prescient.

[45] Ibid., preface, p. 13.

CHAPTER 16

British anthropology and colonialism: challenge and response

THE EXPANSIVE PHASE OF BRITISH STRUCTURAL FUNCTIONALISM

In theory Malinowski's species of functionalist anthropology called for detached first-hand participation and documentation. This in turn called for fieldwork and fieldwork required financial support. Malinowski advocated and supported the notion that trained anthropologists would act as a cohort of trained specialists and that their functional analyses would have practical use in the colonies.[1] Strategically positioning anthropology in this way provided the discipline with important institutional recognition and funding support.[2] Such support also subsidised "the publication of monographs and symposia which followed from fieldwork" and also buttressed an orientation within the discipline away from "the historical tradition toward the strengthening of social scientifically oriented academic research."[3]

I have already, in chapter 3 "Apprenticeship and the Second World War," referred to Jack Goody's account of how, with timely Rockefeller support, a vigorous graduate program was established after the First World War under the leadership of Malinowski at the London School of Economics.[4] The Rockefeller Memorial initially provided the bulk of the grants for research and fellowships; in 1931 it formalized a Fellowship Programme at the International African Institute which enabled a famous group of Africanists, British, European, and African, to become professional anthropologists who would dominate African anthropology (and also make prominent contributions to Australian, Melanesian, and Chinese studies).

---

[1] George W. Stocking, *The Ethnographer's Magic and Other Essays in the History of Anthropology*, Madison: University of Wisconsin Press, 1992, p. 416.
[2] A. Kuper, *Anthropology and Anthropologists, The Modern British School*, London and Boston: Routledge & Kegan Paul, 1983, p. 101.
[3] Stocking, *The Ethnographer's Magic*, pp. 208, 211.
[4] Goody, *The Expansive Moment*.

There are two features to this expansive moment in anthropology. On the one hand it was felt, with much sense of expectation and liberation, that this recognition of the necessity for live fieldwork studies and institutional support for it spelled the demise of the earlier "museum era in Anglo-American anthropology" and the reconstruction of vanishing societies, and the birth of a vigorous new discipline and field of study. On the other hand the all too readily accepted pragmatic and instrumental justification and legitimation of the usefulness of this knowledge, for enlightened practical use by administrators and officers working for imperial regimes, would become the basis for explosive blanket condemnation decades later in the 1970s as part of the post-colonial critique that the anthropologists of this era collaborated in the maintenance of colonialism.

In this regard it is relevant that Cambridge's then famous anthropologists, Rivers and Haddon, though their anthropology was orientated to diffusionism and not functionalism, held the firm view that anthropological training should be primarily for serving the practical needs of colonial administration. Haddon was still influential into the 1930s. Gregory Bateson applied for the Cambridge chair in anticipation of T.C. Hodson's retirement in 1936, and "although he acknowledged a debt to Ruth Benedict's ideas about the 'cultural standardization of personality'", his application, phrased in the language of Radcliffe-Brown, "made a strong case for social anthropology as a 'technical science,' privileging professional research in vanishing cultures over the practical needs of colonial administration." Haddon's firm response was that "the professor of anthropology had an obligation to students who would 'not take up anthropology as a career,' most of them 'Colonial Cadets' who required it primarily 'to enable them to deal sympathetically and efficiently with the natives with whom they will be in contact.' " Haddon feared that Bateson would "soar away from mundane anthropology." In the event, from nine applicants, who included Raymond Firth, Daryll Forde, Reo Fortune, Arthur Hocart, Audrey Richards, and Jack Driberg, John Hutton, who had administrative experience in India and was no high flyer as an anthropologist, was chosen. And he had dutifully, when involved during the First World War in preparing for the Duke of Devonshire's Committee a report on Post War Training for the Colonial Service, "urged the appointment of 'both white and coloured' officers born in the colonies as a great step in the direction of self-government."[5]

---

[5] George W. Stocking, *After Tylor: British Social Anthropology 1888–1951*, Madison: University of Wisconsin Press, 1995, pp. 430–31.

THE CRITIQUE OF ANTHROPOLOGY IN THE LATE
COLONIAL ERA

Because of the powerful general impact of Edward Said's *Orientalism* (1978) on intellectuals and academics, there is a tendency among many of them to view his indictment as the first critique of anthropology's alleged complicity with colonialism. In fact, mounting rumblings of a critical scrutiny of anthropology's connection to colonialism were already audible in previous decades (in the late 1950s and especially in the 1960s). This famous brief statement, unaccompanied by a substantive discussion, was issued by Lévi-Strauss in 1966:

> Anthropology ... is the outcome of a historical process which has made the larger part of mankind subservient to the other, and during which millions of innocent human beings have had their resources plundered and their institutions and beliefs destroyed, whilst they themselves were ruthlessly killed, thrown into bondage, and contaminated by diseases they were unable to resist. Anthropology is daughter to this era of violence: Its capacity to assess more objectively the facts pertaining to the human condition reflects, on the epistemological level, a state of affairs in which one part of mankind treated the other as an object.[6]

There were similar assertions made at this time: a notable instance was *Reinventing Anthropology* edited by Dell Hymes (1972) in which authors raised issues about the political content of fieldwork, the assumptions and practices of ethnographic research and writing, the need to justify fieldwork and to think toward a reflexive and critical anthropology.[7]

Among these questionings from within anthropology and cognate disciplines, I want to single out Talal Asad's edited volume *Anthropology and the Colonial Encounter* (1973), which also preceded by some five years Said's *Orientalism*, for the following reasons. Because Asad was an Oxford-trained anthropologist who mounted an attack from "within" (he was not, however, of British origins), his critique in particular seemed to provide the proximate stimulus that prompted the convening of a seminar at the London School of Economics (LSE) by Peter Loizos. It was at this seminar that some famous anthropologists, either trained at the

---

[6] Claude Lévi-Strauss, "Anthropology: Its Achievements and Its Future," *Current Anthropology*, vol. 7, no. 2, 1966, pp. 124–27. Also see his *The Scope of Anthropology*, trans S. Ortner Paul and R.A. Paul, London: 1967, pp. 51–52.

[7] Dell Hymes (ed.), *Reinventing Anthropology*, New York: Pantheon Books, 1972. See for instance, Hymes, "The Use of Anthropology" and Bob Scholter, "Towards a Reflexive and Critical Anthropology." Also, exchanges in journals such as *Current Anthropology*, *Economy and Society*, *Critique of Anthropology*, and *The Journal of Peasant Studies*.

LSE or teaching there at the time, were invited to respond to the blanket charges that British anthropologists, particularly those working in the colonies in the period between 1930 and 1960, had deeply compromised themselves.[8] The main submissions made by Asad in his introduction were as follows.

"The plausibility of the anthropological enterprise which seemed so self-evident to all its practitioners a mere decade ago, is no longer quite so self-evident."[9] However on the organizational level, British anthropology, exemplified by the Association of Social Anthropologists, flourishes as never before.

On the one hand, the attainment of political independence by colonial, especially African, countries in the late 1950s and 1960s had accelerated socio-economic and planned "developments" accompanied by a shift of power from "tribal" leaders to nationalistic bourgeoisie, and some of the latter's leaders denounced the colonial connections of anthropology. And in response to nationalist expectations some scholars such as J. Vansina began to recover indigenous history,[10] an endeavor which also challenged the functionalist dogma that only written records could provide a reliable basis for reconstructing history.

On the other hand, "ironically, the same forces that were contributing to the ideological dissolution of classical functional anthropology had also contributed to a strengthening of its organizational base."[11] The membership of the Association of Social Anthropologists had increased to 150, and "once this base was in effective operation, social anthropology as institutionalised practice would dispense with the doctrinal specificity it had previously insisted on. Professional distinctiveness could now be maintained through an established network of vested interests . . . rather than by any particular doctrines or methods. Anthropology was now truly a 'profession.'"[12] And furthermore, a boom in anthropological studies occurred in Britain during the Second World War when "economic, political and especially military necessities

---

[8] It is also relevant that Kathleen Gough, a left-wing Cambridge-trained anthropologist, had already published an essay entitled "Anthropology: Child of Imperialism" in the *Monthly Review*, vol. 19, no. 11, 1968, and Rodney Needham from Oxford had written the piece "The Future of Social Anthropology: Disintegration or Metamorphosis?" in *Anniversary Contributions to Anthropology: Twelve Essays*, Leiden: E.J. Brill, 1970.

[9] Talal Asad, "Introduction," in Talal Asad (ed.), *Anthropology and the Colonial Encounter*, London: Ithaca Press, 1973, p. 10.

[10] C.J. Vansina, *Oral Tradition: A Study in Historical Methodology*, trans. H.M. Wright, Chicago: Aldine, 1965.

[11] Asad, "Introduction," p. 14.   [12] Ibid, p. 14.

aroused a new and lively public interest in the African and Asiatic dependencies of Britain and her allies. The plans for post-war economic and social development in these areas generated under pressure of war-time experiences included big schemes of research in the natural and social sciences."[13]

Asad moves from such considerations to these charges:

> It is not a matter of dispute that social anthropology emerged as a distinctive discipline at the beginning of the colonial era, that it became a flourishing academic profession towards its close, or that throughout this period its efforts were devoted to a description and analysis – carried out by Europeans, for a European audience – of non-European societies dominated by European power. And yet there is a strange reluctance on the part of most professional anthropologists to consider seriously the power structure within which their discipline has taken shape.[14]

Echoing Lévi-Strauss's brief 1966 statement on anthropology's relation to colonialism, Asad holds that whatever inspiration the discipline derived from Enlightenment ideas and ideals, it

> is also rooted in an unequal power encounter between the West and Third World which goes back to the emergence of bourgeois Europe, an encounter in which colonialism is merely one historical moment. It is this encounter that gives the West access to cultural and historical information about the societies it has progressively dominated, and thus not only generates a certain kind of universal understanding, but also re-enforces the inequalities in capacity between the European and the non-European worlds (and derivatively, between the Europeanized elites and the "traditional" masses in the Third World).[15]

Asad concludes his Foucauldian indictment with this partial confessional reprieve and hope of resolving contradiction:

> I believe it is a mistake to view social anthropology in the colonial era as primarily an aid to colonial administration, or as the simple reflection of colonial ideology. I say this not because I subscribe to the anthropological establishment's comfortable view of itself, but because bourgeois consciousness, of which social anthropology is merely one fragment, has always contained within itself

---

[13] Ibid., citing Meyer Fortes (ed.), *Social Structure*, Oxford: Clarendon Press, 1949, p. xiii.

[14] Asad, "Introduction," p. 15. With some vehemence Asad turns on Victor Turner for trivializing the relationship between anthropology and colonialism. He quotes passages from Turner's Introduction to Volume III, *Colonialism in Africa 1870–1960*, Cambridge, 1971.

[15] Asad, "Introduction," p. 16.

profound contradictions and ambiguities – and therefore the potentialities for transcending itself.[16]

PERSONAL ACCOUNTS OF FIELD RESEARCH IN BRITISH
COLONIES: MEETING AND MUTING THE CHARGES OF
RADICAL CRITICS

The critical commentary on the anthropological work of British anthropologists working in the period 1930 to 1960, an example of which was Asad's vigorous attack, prompted Peter Loizos to convene a seminar at the London School of Economics. The anthropologists invited were eminently suited to respond on the basis of their field experiences and their own ethnographic and theoretical writings. They were Raymond Firth, Malinowski's heir at the LSE, and Britain's most senior living anthropologist; Audrey Richards and Edmund Leach, both of whom were members of Malinowski's famed seminar; P. Lloyd, who had received his Ph.D. from the LSE; I.M. Lewis, trained at Oxford, who was teaching at the LSE; and Sally Chilver, who was at this time also teaching at LSE and had previous high-level administrative experience with the Colonial Social Science Research Council.[17]

Loizos, in an opening introduction, summarized the main charges mounted by critics, explained the circumstances that led to organizing the seminar, and stated the issues the contributors were requested to address.[18] The charges were:

that functionalist analysis emerged and survived less for any intellectual virtues it might have had than because it was peculiarly well suited to the tasks of imperium; that the anthropologists concerned were, if not the architects of the colonial system then at least its maintenance engineers; and that whatever their motives or their own definitions of the situation, their research in its effects served interests of colonial rulers, rather than those of their subject or science.

Usually these charges are made in a rather general way, with relatively little attempt to differentiate different periods, theoretical persuasions or, and this is crucial surely, different colonial situations. Sometimes, when more *specific*

---

[16] Ibid., p. 18.

[17] The statements made by these participants were published in R.M. Berndt (ed.), "Anthropological Research in British Colonies: Some Personal Accounts," special issue of *Anthropological Forum*, vol. 4, no. 2, 1977. M.G. Smith also participated, but his discussion on corruption in a Hausa emirate was not written up for "diplomatic reasons."

[18] Peter Loizos, "Personal Evidence: Comments on an Acrimonious Argument," in ibid., pp. 137–44.

analyses are undertaken, they are very wide of the mark. Until now there has been relatively little said in reply by the anthropologists thus criticized, and such a reticence may be one reason why students can often produce in headline form the charges, while knowing little of the work or the period in question. Students can be excused this omission perhaps, since were they to master the context of pre-war, or early post-war Anthropology, they would find little time to read more recent work. Meanwhile, however, the stereotypes take on a life of their own. To clear my own head on some of the issues, and to give London Anthropology students and others a chance to ask their own questions, I invited a number of anthropologists who had worked in British colonies to address the following issues at a seminar: how far had they gone into the field critical of the dominant theoretical ideas of their teachers? What constraints had they experienced as a result of the colonial situation, whether in choice of topic, area, informants, the conduct of research, or the publication of results? What use if any had the colonial governments made of their work, and how had their work affected the people they studied?[19]

Since this book is a biography of Leach, it will take us too far afield to report the substance of all the essays. But before dealing with Leach's own response to the charges, I shall highlight some of the responses by all participants that directly problematize, mute, and even question the veracity of the totalizing blanket charges of the critics. Most of the respondents ignored the first question posed regarding their initial theoretical orientations, and focused on their field situations and their relation to the colonial administration. The responses of Audrey Richards and Sally Chilver informatively shed light on the actual linkages between the Colonial Office and professional anthropologists.

A primary feature is that the colonial field situations reported were quite varied (even if they did not cover all situations): Somalia was a "cinderella" of empire where the British administrators were concerned after previous fierce clashes with the Somalis to avoid hurting their feelings; a very different state of affairs prevailed in Sarawak, subject to the antiquated Victorian heritage of the Brooke dynasty and the reluctance of Britain to take over its protection; Nigeria was on the eve of independence with its internal regional and institutional complexity; Leach was mobile in the Kachin Hills in the midst of the war between the British and Japanese, and so on. Not only were the sites different, but the times (between 1930 and 1960) at which the fieldwork was done were different, implying dynamic and changing political and

---

[19] Loizos, "Personal Evidence," p. 137.

economic processes. (One could multiply these variations further – by including urban locations, mining areas, and colonies with a dominant segment of white settlers, etc., which were not represented in the seminar presentation.)

Loizos levels the following judgment against some of the critics, and he includes Asad among them, who "are at pains to condemn colonial government root and branch."

They fail to distinguish between those who saw it as a more or less satisfactory system to be indefinitely sustained, and those who sought to lighten its burden on the colonized while entering many and varied criticisms of it, and often through many acts of support and advice assisting emerging indigenous leaders to independence. They fail, also, to distinguish very much between regimes: one wonders whether they regard all colonial regimes as intrinsically more repressive and exploitive than all independent ones?[20]

And Loizos offers this trenchant comment on why the blanket charges of some radical American critics against British anthropologists may be grounded in their distinctive US politics and interests, a matter on which they exhibit little critical reflexivity:

Many of the harshest criticisms of British anthropologists come from fairly young North American scholars. In a number of cases they have been radicalized by aspects of the Vietnam War, and the knowledge that in Project Camelot and in "counter-insurgency" programmes many American social scientists have played a part in which their scholarship was fairly directly subordinated to immediate and explicit political ends. To come to grips with such issues involves a protracted examination of the United States's historical role in Latin America, the Caribbean, and South Asia, and the long history of her rise as a world power. It is a mistake for American scholars to assume that the relationship of British anthropologists to British Government during the late colonial period was essentially similar to that of some American social scientists to Washington in the 1950s and 1960s. Yet it seems to be precisely such an assumption which fires some of the bitterest criticism. The nature of the actual relationship can be established only by hard work, not by assertion, and the evidence so far suggests it was very different from that of some of the American intellectual Cold Warriors.[21]

[20] Ibid., p. 139. Loizos criticizes the brand of Marxism espoused by Asad thus in footnote 5: "Some authors find it convenient to adopt a version of marxism which insists that the motives and perceptions of individuals are close to irrelevant, as Asad does in both his 1973 essays, and in later publications. Marxism does not *require* this position, however, a position which seriously undercuts Asad's 'scientific' aspirations." Loizos also faults the Marxist critics for the shallowness of their historical research.

[21] Ibid., pp. 141–42.

THE IMPACT OF THE WAR ON LEACH'S WORK
IN THE KACHIN HILLS

Edmund Leach's essay entitled "In Formative Travail with Leviathan" was written for the LSE seminar in response to Loizos's invitation. He began by stating that his "experience as a fieldworking anthropologist was spread over the period 1936 to 1956" and he listed the sites of his fieldwork as follows:

At the beginning I was entirely amateur; at the end I was a professional. Both the geographical and the political contexts of my fieldwork were varied. Botel Tobago, at that time a Japanese colonial possession; Iraqi Kurdistan, Iraq then being independent having recently ceased to be a British mandated territory; North Burma under Governor's rule and subsequently under military administration; British Borneo during the brief post-war period when it was administered from the British Colonial Office, having previously suffered Japanese occupation prior to which it consisted of the bizarre territories of a White Rajah and a British chartered company; Ceylon at a period when Ceylon was already independent but much of the structure of government was still indistinguishable from that of the preceding British regime. Prior to these varied anthropological experiences, I had lived in various parts of China between 1933 and 1936 as a member of the British commercial community.

In the particular context of time and place, the visiting European was in all of these situations in a privileged position. The nature of this privileged status varied very considerably from place to place. Almost any broad generalization on this theme would need to be heavily qualified to meet the particular circumstances of particular contexts.

I therefore propose to confine my recollections in this paper to two particular themes. First, to my contacts with the London School of Economics' social anthropologists between 1937 and 1939; and secondly, to the circumstances of my fieldwork in Burma between 1939 and 1945.[22]

Leach's accounts in this essay as well as in other places about his attendance at Malinowski's seminar at the LSE and the people he met there have already been incorporated in chapter 3. Aside from Malinowski, his other teachers were Raymond Firth and Meyer Fortes, who had recently returned from fieldwork in West Africa. Leach had drawn attention to the fact that, aside from the professional anthropologists, several participants in Malinowski's seminar were colonial administrators home on study leave.

---

[22] Edmund Leach, "In Formative Travail with Leviathan," in Berndt (ed.), "Anthropological Research," p. 190.

Leach remarks that Malinowski was at this time of his career "concerned with the application of his functionalist method to what were described as situations of culture contact."[23] And he makes this significant remark about the political orientations of the papers published at this period by the functionalist social anthropologists who had undertaken fieldwork in British colonial or dominion territories:

The authors had not attempted to grind any particular axes with regard to the equity of the administration of "pre-literate" peoples by imperialist European powers, but it was argued quite explicitly that European administrators working in non-European territories could hardly fail to do a "better" job if they had some understanding of the culture of the people they were supposed to be looking after. I appreciate that the notion of "better" administration is, in such circumstances, ambiguous. Better for whom? The anthropologists themselves would quite certainly have answered "better for the people who are being administered". The point was repeatedly made that many of the most startling injustices which were to be found in the records of colonial administration had arisen simply through the ignorance rather than the malice of the administrators concerned.[24]

The implication is that the authors were not active critics of the colonial regime as such, but that they explicitly held the view, which must have legitimated in their own eyes their own work, that the colonial administrators who had imbibed anthropological knowledge of the local societies could thereby serve as more enlightened rulers.

We now come to Leach's recalling of the circumstances of his fieldwork in Burma. He prefaces this discussion by referring to the events and considerations that led to the British annexation of the coastal strips of southern Burma in 1824–26, and then to the imperialist competition between the British and French in Southeast Asia right through the nineteenth century, which by an ironic serendipitous twist generated ethnographic knowledge.

Both parties took it for granted that before long China would fall apart and become incorporated into the European imperialist hegemony. Quite apart from these imperialist ambitions, this was the great age of railway building, and the British in particular had a mad scheme for driving a railway from Rangoon to Peking! The engineers concerned completely misconceived the nature of the

---

[23] Leach does not dwell on this preoccupation of Malinowski in the latter part of Malinowski's career. B. Malinowski's views on culture contact and change are to be found in *The Dynamics of Cultural Change: An Inquiry into Race Relations in Africa*, edited by Phyllis Kaberry, New Haven: Yale University Press, 1961. First published in 1945.

[24] Leach, "In Formative Travail," pp. 55–56.

terrain difficulties which would face any attempt to build a railway line from Burma into Yunnan, but the engineers in question had a powerful influence on the politicians, and a great deal of the ethnographic information concerning the Shan states and Yunnan and Northern Burma which was accumulated by Europeans between 1840 and 1910 was a kind of by-product of these railway-building projects.[25]

Leach next adverts to a bifurcation in the pattern of British rule over Burma – consisting of two different policies of control exercised over the central lowland core of Burma and over the frontier tribal peoples – which most definitely must have had consequences for his own fieldwork many decades later, but which he had not previously discussed in any of his writings including *Political Systems of Highland Burma*.

The British had in turn annexed a large portion of southern Burma in 1852, and what was left of the original kingdom of Burma in 1885. The military resistance of the central Burmese to British "pacification" turned out to be more persistent than had been anticipated, as evidenced by periodic local rebellions right through the period of occupation down to 1940.

But the British had also initiated and implemented policies that they saw as part of a prolonged and gradual movement toward eventual self-government and independence for Burma. There was an important asymmetry in this programme. It

affected only the Burmese population living in the main valley of the Irrawaddy. It came to involve the Shans of the Eastern frontier only erratically and it did not influence the tribal peoples in the North and West at all. During the period prior to the arrival of the British, these tribal populations had never been fully under the control of the Central Burmese Government, and there was no rational reason why the British should have attempted to administer these areas at all. But the British of those days were obsessed with the idea of *Pax Britannica* and it was taken for granted that law and order must be imposed by force in all territories over which British dominion was claimed.

At a very early stage after the final 1885 annexation, the authorities in Delhi decided that the frontier regions of Burma should be administered quite separately from the central core. And this was how things continued to the end. By 1940, the central heart of Burma had experienced a whole string of constitutional reforms and had moved a very long way toward what was envisaged as ultimate dominion status, in which Burma would have an independent

[25] Ibid., p. 93.

parliamentary constitution similar to that of Australia or New Zealand. The administration of the frontier areas, however, had remained entirely "colonial". Law and order was enforced by an extremely inefficient and corrupt military organization known as the Burma Military Police which consisted, in the main, of Indian troops, while a colonial-style administration was maintained by district officers belonging to a special service, the Burma Frontier Service. The Burmese ministers in the Rangoon government exercised no authority at all in these frontier areas, and even elsewhere there was a curious ambiguity about the status of the European administrators. Most of the senior officers of the Burmese administrative service were members of the Indian Civil Service who had been seconded to Burma and they owed a dual loyalty, taking some of their orders directly from the British Governor General and some from the ministers in Rangoon.

In the late 1930s the position of Europeans who were members neither of the armed forces nor of the administrative services was still extremely privileged as compared with any sector of the local population, but things were on the move. Even if there had been no war with Japan, some type of genuine independence would almost certainly have been achieved by the main Burmese population long before 1945. But what would have happened in the frontier areas is a moot point.

That is the context in which, in the summer of 1939, I was committed to embark upon at least twelve months of social anthropological fieldwork.[26]

Although I have in chapter 3 described, using other sources, Leach's entry into Upper Burma in 1939, and his war experiences and fractured fieldwork, in the essay I am considering here he introduces new information that touches on his wartime involvement with the Kachins whom he had gone out to study. When war broke out in September 1939, Leach volunteered to join the Burma army. Being told he would be called up for training in due course, he made his way to the Kachin Hills and made his first contacts with Hpalang, the village selected for him by Noel Stevenson because it was within the zone of his "Kachin regeneration scheme."[27] Between mid-November and early February Leach underwent a course of military training, and was then joined by Celia Buckmaster who arrived from England to marry him. They returned to Hpalang and Leach conducted fieldwork there until the autumn of 1940 when he was called up for military duty.

The direct involvement of the hills people in the British war effort against Japan also incidentally reminds us of the Americans' deliberate

[26] Ibid., pp. 57–58.
[27] Leach was critical of this scheme and made acid comments about it. Fortunately during the period of his fieldwork in Hpalang, Stevenson was absent, having gone to England on leave.

and more harmful use of the Hmong in their military actions against the Vietcong in Vietnam. Leach informs us as follows:

The Burma army of that time had British officers and local troops. Almost all the troops were recruited from the frontier tribesmen, notably Karens, Chins, and Kachins. Perhaps not very surprisingly, attempts to recruit Burmese and Shans proved largely abortive. At the outbreak of the war this Burma army had consisted of three battalions, and in 1940 the decision was made to expand the force to 10 battalions. This called for an extensive recruiting campaign in the frontier areas, and because of my linguistic knowledge I found myself before long specially earmarked as a recruiting officer for the Kachin Hills. In this role, I visited many parts of the Kachin Hills area which otherwise I would have been very unlikely to see at all. At this point Noel Stevenson once again became a significant factor in my life.

Once the Japanese war started it was perfectly obvious to most of the British civilian administrators, as well as to the civilians in the Burma army, that the British would get pushed out of Burma. It became a military crime to express these views. Nevertheless some action began to be taken. Stevenson was largely responsible for persuading the Governor that it would be feasible to leave behind a network of spies and guerillas until such time as the British armed forces could return. Almost all aspects of this scheme were intrinsically crazy, but nevertheless it resulted in the creation of a special force known as the Kachin Levies. By January 1942 I had been seconded from my Burma Rifles Regiment to a mysterious "X List", and soon found myself embroiled with various shady characters known by letters of the alphabet and numbers. I was never actually a member of the outfit which is referred to in various war diaries either as SO(E) or Force 136, nor was I later involved in either of the Wingate operations, or with "V Force", but peripherally my war was muddled up with all these things as well as others.[28]

It is noteworthy that in writing *Political Systems of Highland Burma* Leach did not consider it relevant to discuss in detail how his extensive recruiting of "frontier tribesmen", and his later involvement with the Kachin Levies, which was "a network of guerillas and spies," actually enabled him to collect information and to gain panoramic insights about the distribution and interrelations between the hills communities. It was this knowledge that considerably widened his vision from a preoccupation with a micro-study of a single village in "functionalist" terms to a macro-perspective of dialectal and dialectical variations among communities oscillating between *gumsa* and *gumlao* structural forms. In the mid-1950s the conventions of writing an innovative interpretive monograph did not require, as they do in the present time among adherents

[28] Ibid., p. 59.

of post-modern dogma, that the author devote substantial space to discussing the manner in which information was elicited, the nature of and the "dialogical" interactions imbued with unequal power relations between anthropologists and subjects that led to "negotiated" understandings of the ethnography reported. Neither British structural functionalism nor Lévi-Straussian "structuralism" – the frameworks that Leach debated and transformed – took the aforementioned issues to be the center of their ethnographic writing.

Leach had the following to say about his war experiences, especially his ambivalent feelings toward and changing fortunes with the British military authorities, and in answer to the query regarding whether his anthropological representation of Kachin society was affected by these interactions:

Between March 1942, when British resistance to the Japanese in Burma was already crumbling, and June 1945 when Japanese resistance to the British in Burma was already crumbling, many strange things happened to me. I was in and out of Burma on many occasions and visited many parts of the Kachin Hills as well as other parts of Western Burma and Assam. In retrospect, I find it very difficult to say just how relevant was my interest in Anthropology to these activities, or how relevant were these activities to my subsequent development as an anthropologist. If I had not had my anthropological background I would not have got seconded into the peculiar cloak-and-dagger activities which were part of my destiny. But what the reader of this series wants to know, presumably, is whether my anthropological findings concerning the Kachins of North Burma would have been different if my research had been conducted in a different sociological climate.

I do not see how I or anyone else could possibly answer such a question. Depending on initial prejudice, all kinds of particular events may be seen as significant. Those who believe that the pre-1950 British social anthropologists were all lackeys of colonial imperialism could draw attention to the fact that by June 1945 I was holding a key position in the military civil affairs service of Burma, with rank approximately equivalent to that of a senior District Commissioner. As counter to that, I might point out that only two years earlier I had narrowly missed being court-martialled; at which time I had been accused by my Corps Commander of being a crypto-communist, and reduced in rank from acting-Major to substantive 2nd Lieutenant![29]

Quite obviously the vicissitudes and frustrations of almost six years of wartime experience severely qualified the kinds of anthropological activity which I could conduct, and they qualified even more severely the kinds of record which I could rescue from the debris. Yet it seems to me that if I had been engaged in

[29] Ibid., pp. 59–60.

Anthropology in a Burma in which neither colonial administrators nor army commanders played their part my anthropological assessment of Kachin society would hardly have been changed. This does not mean that it is a correct assessment, but only that it is my own.[30]

Leach's answer is a surprisingly strong "bracketing" and closing off of that wartime ordeal as irrelevant to his professional anthropological perception and profiling of Kachin society. (Throughout his career, on many occasions, he would express an extreme distaste for what the war had put him through.) However, he concludes his essay with two assertions which amount to a rejection of the Asad-type critique of the anthropology practiced in the colonial period: that anthropology as a discipline aspires to be an objective generalizing science, and it was not part of anthropologists' professional brief to pass judgment on the performance of the colonial regime in whose shadow they conducted fieldwork.

It seems to me now, as it seemed to me then, that the principal task of academic anthropologists in the field is to pursue research which may lead to advances in sociological generalization and that the anthropologist, as such, is not professionally concerned with whether administration is efficient or inefficient, just or unjust. On the other hand I also still believe, as I believed then, that administrators working in the backwoods areas of modern states, whether they be labelled as colonialists, nationalists, communists, or anything else, are likely to be better administrators if they know something about the sociology of the people they are supposed to be administering.

This by no means precludes the possibility that, in my private opinion, the world would be a better place if no such administration existed at all.[31]

To avoid misunderstanding, it should be understood that Leach's stricture that academic anthropologists desist from passing judgment on the colonial regime applies to anthropologists during the time they are in the field. In fact this norm of conduct was laid down by Malinowski himself as explained by Audrey Richards, who writes of her East African fieldwork:

I tried very hard to follow the precept then taught by Malinowski as to the complete neutrality that was desirable for a fieldworker. I made it my business not to criticize European or African officials or to express strong views on policy. This is a rule which I still think important for any research worker while he or she is actually conducting investigations, whether in a colonial territory in the

---

[30] Ibid., p. 60.   [31] Ibid., pp. 60–61.

old days or in Great Britain at the present time. I maintained this position many years later when acting as Director of the East Asian Institute of Social Research in Uganda. It was impossible to be completely neutral in a country which was alive with political and religious disputes, but I felt that we should not make public pronouncements on local issues in the press or at public meetings and that we should never on any account pass information as to crimes or legal disputes which we had observed in the field.[32]

Leach himself did not shy away after he left Burma from commenting from time to time on administrative mistakes, misunderstandings, and misconceived policies, *vis-à-vis* the people who were colonized. For example, in *Political Systems*, there is a devastating account of the "stupidity" of the British administrative policy, even up to 1946, of attempting to treat "Shan and Kachin as separate racial elements" which led to the deterrence of Kachins from settling in Shan territory. In 1889 "in the interests of peace and security" the administration burnt forty-six villages (639 houses), destroyed over 500,000 pounds of paddy, killed seventeen (probably more) Kachins, and sixty-three buffalos.[33] Leach, Firth, Richards, and all the other anthropologists who contributed to the special time of *Anthropological Forum* (1977) were in agreement that whatever his or her personal political preference – left-wing, Liberal/moderate, or right-wing – the professional brief of the anthropologist in the field does not extend to becoming involved in political criticism or activism on behalf of the rulers or the ruled. (This is probably the pragmatic advice still being given in most universities training prospective fieldworkers, although there are today some anthropologists who advocate political activism.) That anthropologists after leaving the field may write critically of government policies, development schemes, and local politics seems to be acceptable practice, although those who wish to return to the same site may pull their punches.

As a prelude to what is to follow in the next section, I would draw attention to the fact that what I have recounted so far are Leach's views expressed in a 1977 publication. But within a few years, in the 1980s, Leach embarked on a more radical critique of the discipline as hitherto practiced, which included a partial admission of deficiency in his own writings on the Kachin.

---

[32] Audrey Richards, "The Colonial Office and the Organization of Social Research," in Berndt (ed.), "Anthropological Research," p. 33.
[33] Leach, *Political Systems*, p. 244.

THE ETHNOGRAPHIC CONTRIBUTIONS
OF COLONIAL ADMINISTRATORS

Leach makes this passing, albeit significant comment on the ethnographic contributions of colonial administrators:

In the various administrative services of the British overseas empire, whether in India or Burma or the Sudan or in the colonies and protectorates, Anthropology was viewed as a hobby rather than as a serious professional pursuit. But it was not officially frowned upon. Many of the major ethnographic monographs were written by colonial administrators in their spare time and, in some cases at least, publication was sponsored by the governmental authorities concerned.[34]

It is relevant that I develop this theme further because Leach's own discussion of the highland Burma (and northeast India) social and political systems owes much to the information provided in reports and sketches by British colonial administrators, as he has himself stated elsewhere, and as indeed does Lévi-Strauss's characterization (without the benefit of direct field experience as in the case of Leach) of "generalized exchange" in the same region.

In South and Southeast Asia in general[35] many civil servants and administrators who crafted census reports, district gazetteers, special reports, and memoirs were also amateur ethnographers, archaeologists, historians, and linguists; additionally there were technical specialists professionally trained as doctors, engineers, surveyors, cartographers, geologists and mining experts, agronomists, crop specialists, military officers, etc., who were also sources of a great deal of knowledge about the living conditions, practices, and systems of local knowledge of the colonized peoples. One outcome in the mid-twentieth century onwards is the reliance of major synthesizing anthropological works of our time on a "critical" but liberal use of these sources. Three examples are Louis Dumont's *Homo Hierarchicus*, Lévi-Strauss's *Elementary Structures of Kinship*, and Leach's own *Political Systems of Highland Burma*.

We are already familiar with Leach's wartime disaster of losing his Hpalang field notes and photographs as a result of enemy action, and then in 1941 his having written from memory a functionalist economic study of Hpalang community before again losing it. Then in 1942 when he reached India he once again sketched out notes of Hpalang which he retained.

[34] Leach, "In Formative Travail," p. 56.
[35] As in other colonial territories in Africa and elsewhere, but we are not concerned with them here. For example, British colonies in West and East Africa yield similar information.

But, as Leach has informed us,[36] during the time of his war service from 1940 to 1945, although he was in the company of Kachins, he never had the opportunity to carry out detailed anthropological study. However, his recruiting military duties gave him the rare and unplanned opportunity to travel widely in the Kachin Hills Area, the northern Shan states and the North Triangle Area. These and other travels gave him a unique opportunity to assess "the totality of Kachin culture." Such notes as he could take during his military tours of 1942–43 he preserved.

What I would suggest is that this wide-ranging travel, which gave him a synchronic view of the region, was supplemented by another panoramic processual view of the region when, in 1946 after being demobilised from the army, he "was permitted by the University of London to prepare a thesis based largely on historical materials relating to the Kachin Hill Area." He remarks that

While preparing this thesis I made a very thorough study of government records and other publications relating to the area, mainly from sources preserved in the India Office library. There are one or two documents which I have never managed to trace, but in general, excluding ephemeral publications issued by the missions, I think I have at one time or another probably read nearly everything that has been published in English, French or German about the Kachin Hills Area during the past 130 years.[37]

In an appendix to this chapter I document a number of historical and ethnographic and other informational materials written mainly by colonial administrators and military officers, and a few missionaries. Lévi-Strauss wholly relied, sometimes uncritically, on these accounts for discussion of north Burma kinship and marriage. Leach's bibliography in *Political Systems* contains the same titles (except for a very few items), plus a number of others absent in Lévi-Strauss's listing, such as Parliamentary Papers, Gazetteers, Reports of Expeditions and Missions, etc. I give in the appendix a list of sources used by Lévi-Strauss, and a list of additional references found in Leach's biography. Against each author's name and published text I have identified his professional status as most helpfully and generously identified for me by F.K. Lehman, who has an author-itative knowledge of these writings. It is noteworthy that many of these texts were published locally in Calcutta and Rangoon, and the rest in

---

[36] See chapter 3. My main source here is Appendix VII, "A Note on the Qualifications of the Author," *Political Systems*, pp. 311–12.
[37] Leach, *Political Systems*, p. 312.

Metropolitan London. I have make a few comments on these authors, while referring the reader to the appendix.

The majority of these authors published their writings in the early 1900s and onwards, their positions and work occurring after the conquest of Upper Burma in 1895. The missionary authors turn out to be few: O. Hanson, who wrote two texts on Kachin language and customs, was a Baptist missionary of Swedish extraction, and C. Gilhodes, who wrote on Kachin religion and marriage and on the condition of their women, was a French Roman Catholic missionary. (It seems likely that a certain W.C. Smith who wrote a book on the Ao Naga of Assam was also a missionary.)

It is interesting that J.P. Mills, who wrote three books on the Nagas, and J.H. Hutton, who wrote two books on them, were members of the elite Indian Civil Service (ICS) seconded to work for the Frontier Service. They are said to have been rivals. Hutton also later served as Commissioner of the 1931 Census, and succeeded Haddon to the Chair of Anthropology at Cambridge University. There were a few others who were also seconded from the ICS such as J.H. Green, who contributed to the 1931 Census, and W. Grigson, who wrote about the Gonds of Bastar.

The largest number of authors were civilian administrators directly recruited to serve in Burma, some of the more famous bearing the rank of Deputy Commissioner. For example, N.E. Parry, who wrote a well-known text on the Lakhers, was a Deputy Commissioner serving in the Lushai Hills; W.R. Head, who wrote the pamphlet on the Haka Chin (whom Lévi-Strauss had confused with the Kachin), was a Deputy Commissioner in the northern Chin Hills; A. Playfair, who wrote another valuable text on the Garos, and P.R.T. Gurdon, who wrote on the Khasis, were similarly administrators.

An early author, with a somewhat different background, associated with the production of the multiple volumes of the Gazetteer of Upper Burma and the Shan States (1900–1) was J.G. Scott, who was of merchant origins, and was given an official appointment as the first administrator of the Shan states after the British conquest of Upper Burma in 1885.

Among the administrators may also be included a minority of military officers who were seconded for work as administrators in the Frontier Service. Examples are H.R. Hertz, who wrote on Kachin (or Jinghpaw) language and customs, and T.C. Hodson (who came from a line of officers who served in India), who dealt with the Naga tribes of Manipur.

A wholly different source of information came from persons who went on expeditions, explorations, and diplomatic missions before the conquest of Upper Burma, on the one hand representing the interests of a wealthy class of merchants operating in Calcutta and Rangoon who had direct access to the Colonial Office in London to represent their mercantile causes, and on the other hand serving the interests of the British government which was interested in information of military significance, and in making a direct railway link between Burma and Yunnan bypassing the French lines of communication. This combination of military, mining and trading, missionary and imperial interests came together in the impossibly utopian railway scheme that Leach referred to as indirectly generating valuable ethnographic information. Captain S.F. Hannay, whose journal of a route traveled in 1835–36 from Ava to the amber mines in the southeastern frontier of Assam as related by Captain Pemberton, is a case in point. Hannay produced his informative three works on the Shans of Burma before the mid-nineteenth century. D. Richardson was a medical doctor who, with the support of Christian missions, went on intelligence-gathering expeditions to the border regions, around the same time. So did E.B. Sladen who explored the possibility of a trade route to China via Bhamo. Instances pertaining to the latter decades of the nineteenth century were General Walker, who compiled notes on the "Kachin Tribes of the Northeast Frontier of Upper Burma," and J. Anderson, who wrote about an expedition to western Yunnan via Bhamo.

We may conclude from this discussion that the much admired and acclaimed original perspective on the Kachin Hills that Leach's *Political Systems* offered is the felicitous outcome of his integrating and assessing his initial study of Hpalang community in 1940, and subsequently his wartime experiences from 1940 to 1945, with his critical reading of the "colonial" literature on the region dating from about the late 1830s onward to the mid-1940s.

Another remark is in order. The idea that the professional anthropologists who worked in the British colonies from the 1930s to the 1950s may have faced various kinds of difficulties with the district officers and other colonial authorities has to be muted by the consideration that some administrators of this time, including their predecessors, were themselves the authors of valuable ethnographic information used by the professional anthropologists. Moreover, some of these same administrators also went to the major British and other European universities on study leave to write theses for higher academic degrees. A few attained academic positions in these universities.[38] This kind

---

[38] Some examples are J.H. Hutton (Cambridge), the great A.M. Hocart and G.I. Jones (Cambridge).

of blurring in some instances of the distinctions between colonial administrators and professional anthropologists, archaeologists and linguists, does not however negate the marked differences of perspective and role definition that applied in other cases.

In conclusion, I should draw attention to the strong "post-colonialist" critique mounted by certain scholars in respect of India of the very categories of knowledge and representation of Indian society crafted by colonial administrators and missionaries, and used by many scholars of India, including Louis Dumont. The main allegation is that the documents and reports crafted by them were intellectual creations produced in the service of configuring, dominating, dividing, and ruling the colonies. This argument, which directly or indirectly conjoins ideas from Marx, the Frankfurt School of Critical Sociology (e.g. Adorno, Horkheimer, and Habermas), and from a different direction, ideas propagated by Foucault, especially his twinning of "knowledge and power," has adherents and expounders in modern anthropology. An original exemplar of this genre is Bernard Cohn of the University of Chicago, and his followers-successors such as Nicholas Dirks.[39] A powerful advocacy originating separately is the series of studies (for example, five volumes published between 1982 and 1987) penned by a galaxy of scholars, mostly Indian, of the "Subaltern Studies Collective," led by Ranajit Guha. They, too, have adapted and transformed Marxian and Foucauldian theories and Antonio Gramsci's notion of the subaltern[40] in their historical and anthropological studies of India.

There has been no extensive parallel critique of the colonial literature on Burma written in Leach's time. Leach himself did criticize that literature's categorization of peoples of Upper Burma into discrete tribes, and he initiated a major revision of that classificatory reification.[41] In chapter 17 I shall review one of his last broadsides which indirectly suggests his engagement with such new currents of thought.

---

[39] See for example Bernard Cohn, *Colonialism and Its Forms of Knowledge: The British in India,* Princeton: Princeton University Press, 1996; also Cohn, *Anthropologist Among the Historians and Other Essays,* Princeton: Princeton University Press, 1988. Nicholas Dirks, "Castes of Mind," *Representations,* no. 37, Winter 1992, pp. 56–78; also Dirks, "The Invention of Caste: Civil Society in Colonial India," *Social Analysis,* vol. 25, Autumn 1989, pp. 42–52.

[40] It is not necessary to review some of the major studies here. Ranajit Guha's "The Prose of Counter-Insurgency" is thought to be "a classic statement of the principle of their work." ("Editor's Note" in *Selected Subaltern Studies,* Ranajit Guha and Gayatri Chakravorty Spivak (eds.), New York: Oxford University Press, 1988.)

[41] Benedict Anderson added a new chapter to his 1991 revised edition of *Imagined Communities,* London and New York: Verso, 1991, where he refers to "Census, Map, Museum" (chapter 10) as the three institutions that profoundly shaped the way in which the colonial state imagined its dominion. But curiously he makes no reference to Bernard Cohn who led the way in such formulation. Neither Burma nor Leach figures in Anderson's coverage of Southeast Asia.

Appendix: The sources authored by colonial administrators (and missionaries) used by Lévi-Strauss and Edmund Leach

LÉVI-STRAUSS'S DOCUMENTARY SOURCES

Lévi-Strauss was heavily dependent on sources authored by British administrators in his characterization of "generalized exchange" in northern Burma and northeast India in Part II, chapters 15–18 of his grand classic *The Elementary Structures of Kinship* (1969). He had no direct field experience of life in this region. Since the original French version, *Les structures élémentaires de la parenté*, was published in 1949, and Leach refers to it in *Political Systems*, I document a number of Lévi-Strauss's sources first before I deal with Leach's sources.[1]

W.J.S. Carrapiett. *The Kachin Tribes of Burma*. Rangoon. 1929. An administrator in the Kachin Hills, British of Armenian origins.

C. Gilhodes. *The Kachins: Religion and Customs*. Calcutta. 1922. A French Roman Catholic missionary.
"Marriage et condition de la femme chez les Katchin, Birmanie" *Anthropos*. Vol. VIII.

W. Grigson. *The Maria Gonds of Bastar*. Oxford. 1938. A member of the Indian Civil Service, who served as an administrator.

P.R.T. Gurdon. *The Khasis*. London. 1914. An administrator.

O. Hanson. *A Grammar of the Kachin Language*. Rangoon. 1896. A Baptist missionary of Swedish extraction.
The Kachins: Their Customs and Traditions. Rangoon. 1913.

W.R. Head. *Handbook of the Haka Chin Customs*. Rangoon. 1917. Deputy Commissioner, Northern Chin Hills.

H.F. Hertz. *A Practical Handbook of the Kachin or Chingpaw Language etc. with an Appendix on Kachin Customs, Laws and Religion*. Rangoon. 1915. A military officer seconded to work as an administrator in the Frontier Service.

T.C. Hodson. *The Naga Tribes of Manipur*. London. 1923. Military officer seconded to work in the Frontier Service.

---

[1] Lévi-Strauss also mentions other European sources such as J.P. Wehrli, and a few sources by Indian writers, but his information is not integral to the point I am making here.

J.H. Hutton. *The Sema Nagas.* London. 1921. A member of the ICS who served in the Frontier Service and was Commissioner of the 1931 Census.
The Angami Nagas. London. 1921.
J.P. Mills. *The Lhota Nagas.* London. 1922. A member of the ICS who served in the Frontier Service.
The Ao Nagas. London. 1926.
The Rengma Nagas. London. 1937.
A. Playfair. *The Garos.* London. 1909. An administrator.
J. Shakespear. *The Lushei Kuki Clans.* London. 1912. A military colonel who served in the Frontier Service.

Finally, I must mention H.N.C. Stevenson's essay "Feasting and Meat Division among the Zahau Chins of Burma," *Journal of the Royal Anthropological Institute*, vol. 67, 1937, pp. 15–32. Stevenson, who had served as Assistant Superintendent, Sinlum, and was the administrator in charge of the "Kachin Regeneration Scheme," was the one who invited Edmund Leach to begin his fieldwork in Hpalang located in the regions of the scheme, and who, as mentioned earlier, was the author of *The Economics of the Central Chin Tribes*, Bombay, 1943, which Leach used in his own work.

LEACH'S DOCUMENTARY SOURCES, ADDITIONAL TO THE TITLES ALREADY LISTED BY LEVI-STRAUSS

J. Anderson. *A Report on the Expedition to Western Yunnan via Bhamo.* Calcutta. 1871. Associated with opening communication between Burma and Yunnan.
J.T.O. Barnard. "The Frontier of Burma," *Journal of the Royal Central Asia Society*, vol. 15, 1930.
H. Burney. "On the Population of the Burman Empire," *Journal of the Statistical Society.* London. 1941. Participated in diplomatic missions from the government of India to the Kingdom of Burma.
E.A. Gait. *A History of Assam.* Calcutta. 1906.
J.H. Green. "A Note on the Indigenous Races of Burma." *Census* 1931, XI, Report. 1933. Probably ICS, seconded to Frontier Service at the request of J.H. Hutton.
"The Tribes of Upper Burma North of 24 Latitude and their Classification." Typescript, Haddon Library, Cambridge. 1933.
S.F. Hannay. "Abstract of the Journal of a Route travelled by Captain S.F. Hannay in 1835–36 from the Capital of Ava, to the Amber Mines of the Hukawng Valley on the South Eastern Frontier of Assam," by Captain R. Boileau Pemberton. *Transactions of the Asiatic Society of Bengal*, vol. 6, April 1837. A military officer who had connections with trading interests.
Sketch of the Singhphos or Kakhyens of Burma. Calcutta. 1847.
The Shan or Tai Nation. Calcutta. 1848.
Continuation of Notes on the Shans, Part II (Shans of Assam). Calcutta. 1848.

H.F. Hertz. *A Practical Handbook of the Kachin or Chingpaw Language.* Calcutta. 1943. A military officer seconded to the Frontier Service.

W.A. Hertz. *Burma Gazetteer.* Myitkyina District. Vol. A. Rangoon. 1948. An administrator.

A. Mackenzie. *History of the Relations of the Government with the Hills Tribes of North Eastern: Frontier of Bengal.* Calcutta. 1884. An administrator.

N.E. Parry. *The Lakhers.* London. 1932. Deputy Commissioner, Lushai Hills.

D. Richardson. "Copy of papers relating to the route of Captain W.C. McCleod from Moulmein to the Frontiers of China to the route of Dr. Richardson on his fourth mission to the Shan Provinces of Burma (1837), or extracts from the same," *Parliamentary Papers 1868–69,* XLVI. A medical doctor who was a member of an intelligence-gathering expedition to the border regions, probably funded by missionary sources.

J.G. Scott and J.P. Hardiman. *Gazetteer of Upper Burma and the Shan States.* Part 1, 2 vols.; Part 2, 3 vols. Rangoon. 1900–1. Scott was of merchant origins and received an official appointment as first administrator of the Shan states after the British conquest of 1885. Hardiman was an administrator who assisted Scott.

L.W. Shakespear. *History of Upper Burma, Upper Assam and North Eastern Frontier.* London. 1914. An administrator.

E.B. Sladen. "Official Narrative of the Expedition to Explore the Trade Route to China via Bhamo," *Parliamentary Papers 1867–68.* Like Richardson, not an official but went on expedition with government assent.

W.C. Smith. *The Ao Naga Tribe of Assam.* London. 1925. Probably a missionary.

J.J. Walker. "Expeditions among the Kachin Tribes of the Northeast Frontier of Upper Burma compiled by General J.J. Walker from the reports of Lieut. Elliot, Assistant Commissioner," *Proceedings of the Royal Geographical Society,* vol. 14, 1892. A military officer involved with expeditions gathering intelligence information.

CHAPTER 17

Retrospective assessment and rethinking anthropology

On March 4, 1980, Leach gave a lecture at the University of Washington, Seattle, entitled "Political Systems of Highland Burma: A Retrospective Assessment." Professor C.F. Keyes, who had invited him and probably suggested the theme, has kindly provided me with some rough hand-written, telegraphic notes he had taken at the lecture.[1]

A telling comment in the lecture was how in retrospect, some twenty-six years after *Political Systems of Highland Burma* was published, Leach makes a revision of that text. This looking back was no doubt influenced by certain new trends being aired in anthropology especially as regards the taking into account of historical processes in ethnographic writing. Leach remarked that in *Political Systems* he had tried to come to grips with the condition that no entities identifiable as distinct tribes existed on the ground, and that the social organization of the region was a continuum with no clear boundaries or frontiers. Moreover, the literature on the Kachin ranging in date from 1780 to 1940 (the first Europeans arrived in 1825) had in fact indicated that there had been continuities as well as discontinuities. There was evidence that alien powers such as Chinese, Burmese, and later the British had made war-like intrusions into the Kachin region, and that Kachins had increasingly become dependent on articles and goods of foreign manufacture. There were internal political changes generated in response to these external influences. Moreover Kachin and Shan had lived in a state of interdigitation for at least five centuries.

Leach openly admitted to his audience that his book had been, there-fore, in some respects "reductionist" in that it had postulated categories such as Burmese, *shan*, Kachin, *gumlao* and *gumsa*, while leaving out of consideration the play of historical forces on their usage. The Kachin

---

[1] On the following day Leach gave a second lecture whose contents, dealing with the anthropo-logical study of small-scale societies and the methodology of structuralism, are not relevant to the present discussion.

category, for example, was originally used by Burmese to refer to people living on the China–Burma border; and the British used to refer to all of them as Jinghpaw speakers. Now, in post-independence times, Kachin is a term that present-day Kachins have adopted to label themselves.

Having made this retrospective observation, Leach then proceeded in his lecture to explain how he had attempted in *Political Systems* to give some sort of order to events in a fluid field situation in dialog with the theoretical trends of the 1950s. He had represented the community of Hpalang, the site of his first fieldwork in 1939–40, as a microcosm of the region, and that sketch contained many of the insights he would develop regarding Kachin social and political dynamics. Myths varied from individual teller to teller, and each teller manipulated them to enhance his individual status. There was no true version of a myth – its claims varied with the teller and also the group to which he belonged. But individual tellings and interpretations of key concepts were variations on a theme and, in this sense, they exhibited a common structure. Although the actors might suppose that their linguistic labels were separated by significant boundaries, what distinguishes one type of Kachin from another is the interpretation of key concepts, which at a deeper level manifested a structure.

Leach remarked that *Political Systems* was written in reaction to the regnant theory of unilineal descent systems as enunciated by Evans-Pritchard regarding the Nuer and by Fortes concerning the Tallensi. He was pushed into supporting alliance theory because it fitted his data better, and not because he was a defender of Lévi-Strauss. In fact in the region as a whole non-unilineal kinship systems outnumber unilineal-alliance systems.

There are other submissions of value in the book. He had documented the range of polysemic meanings relating to the Kachin house and long house, which linked with others in the settlement, which in turn was a microcosm of the larger society. This flexible range of uses was helpful to Kachin social discourse, and allegedly precise and bounded anthropo-logical concepts such as household, lineage, and clan were out of place in representing Jinghpaw language usages. He also drew attention to the Kachin notion of *kha* as debt and how ongoing debt linked persons in relationships. Settling a debt in full was a hostile act. This discussion of debt contributed to the general theory of exchange.

The writing of *Political Systems* was completed in 1952, and it was more concerned with politics than economics. In writing it Leach had taken into account Lévi-Strauss's *Elementary Structures* (the French version was first published in 1949). He was also influenced by Pareto[2] whose homeostatic model he found more illuminating than Marx. He had attempted to validate, based on historical evidence covering a long stretch of time, his thesis of an oscillation between *gumsa* and *gumlao* models.

One could infer from such retrospective comments that Leach, at the time he wrote *Political Systems* in the early 1950s, was proposing a way of dealing with long-term historical process in a more dynamic way than the more static equilibrium models employed by the structural-functional anthropologists of his time. In this context, it is relevant to note that his dispute with Lévi-Strauss in the 1950s also entailed the charge that Lévi-Strauss's "internalist" analysis of the dynamics of Kachin kinship as an autonomous phenomenon had failed to recognize that Kachin society had undergone radical changes in the previous 140 years in response to "external" pressures and forces which had not originated from within, though of course these external intrusions affected internal relations.

A few years after the Seattle lecture Leach returned to the issue of historical writing, but this time taking up another theme than that stated above. The provocative ruminations expressed in the 1984 essay "Glimpses of the Unmentionable in the History of British Social Anthropology"[3] contain some brief remarks concerning the value of historical writing in terms of the actors' perceptions and verbalizations rather than in terms of the categories and schema of the (Western) observer. He drew attention to the writings of Marshall Sahlins and Valerio Valeri on Hawaii[4] in this mode and expressed his excitement about them. He mused that he had, in a pioneering and groping way, tried to portray Kachin thought and action in terms of how Kachins formulated for themselves, via myth, ritual, and speech acts, the way they saw their historical process unfolding. We now see more clearly how to read historical ethnography from the point of view of the observed rather than that of the observer.[5]

In tandem with this observation Leach introduced a related but quite different, and what may be termed today "postmodern," concern

---

[2] See footnote 14 in chapter 5 regarding Leach's use of Pareto.

[3] Published in *Annual Review of Anthropology*, vol. 13, 1984, pp. 1–23. I shall deal with this essay in chapter 19.

[4] Marshall Sahlins, *Islands of History*, Chicago: University of Chicago Press, 1985; Valerio Valeri, *Kingship and Sacrifice: Ritual and Society in Ancient Hawaii*, Chicago: University of Chicago Press, 1985.

[5] It is with regard to this aspect of Leach's submissions in *Political Systems* that Parry and Fuller correctly remarked that Leach's "attempt to grapple with the problems of history and a culturally specific 'historicity' was years ahead of its time." (Fuller and Parry, "Petulant Inconsistency?", p. 13.)

regarding the impact of the ethnographer's presence on those studied and the degree of validity of the authorial claim to objective reporting. He voiced a realization, much more sharply than he had ever done before, but not in terms of a sustained demonstration, "that in no circumstances has the 'European' observer – anthropologist, missionary, ship's captain, traveller – ever been able to give an objective account of the manners and customs of primitive society. The very fact that the observer was there at all completely altered the nature of what was observed. The 'Death of Cook business' is an extreme example, but the case is general." This is an unqualified radical opinion in the form expressed here. Let us see whether and how he fills out this radical view in subsequent writings.

A POLEMICAL PARTING SHOT

A lecture bearing the title "Tribal Ethnography: Past, Present, Future," polemical and probably disconcerting to his audience consisting primarily of fellow British anthropologists, was delivered by Leach at the twenty-seventh annual conference of the Association of Social Anthropologists of Britain and the Commonwealth (ASA), held at the University of East Anglia, during Easter 1987.[6] It was one of his last appearances on stage; he was scarred by illness, and he delivered a parting shot, so to speak, the accuracy and fairness of which I shall try to evaluate after describing it.

Leach begins with the statement that he is concerned with "the problems of objectivity in fieldwork," and fires two salvos. The first is that he has reached the "radical conclusion that all ethnography is fiction," in the sense that "any ethnographic monograph has much more in common with an historical novel than with a treatise in natural science."[7] Throughout the essay he will refer to (what he means by) "fiction" in multiple ways. The second salvo is that the "still widespread belief that the pre-literate societies of classical ethnography were static and outside history is wholly unjustified."[8] He also glosses this issue in many ways in the essay. He asserts that it is a recent development that the words "tribe" and "tribal" are now seldom used by British social anthropologists; the word tribe appeared in the writings of Radcliffe-Brown

---

[6] This lecture was published first in *Cambridge Anthropology*, vol. 11, no. 2, 1987, pp. 1–14. It is from this text that I shall quote. The same text was published posthumously in Elizabeth Tonkin, Maryon McDonald, and Malcolm Chapman (eds.), *History and Ethnicity*, ASA Volume, London: Routledge, 1989, pp. 34–47.

[7] Leach, "Tribal Ethnography," p. 1.   [8] Ibid., p. 1.

regarding the "Australian Tribes" (1931), of Fortes on the Tallensi as a "Trans-Volta Tribe," and of Gluckman about East and South African tribes (1960s). Even Roger Keesing's 1981 textbook[9] is about "The Tribal World." The recent substitution of the term "traditional society" for "tribe" also carries the suggestion of "stasis" and it is "the target of [his] attack."[10]

"Tribal ethnography" concentrated on communities "in which the level of literacy among the older members of the adult population is very low and in which there is a very marked gap between the technological resources of the ethnographers themselves and those whom they are studying."[11] And in the past tribal ethnographers have been primarily interested in the contrast between European culture and non-European culture. Leach makes the following charge against the earlier tribal ethnographers (which he extends to recent ethnographers as well). By the time the ethnographer came on the scene the empirical contrast between European and non-European cultures had usually become blurred, yet "in order to bring things into sharper focus palpably European elements in the ethnographer's notes were omitted from the published record or else treated as an alien contamination grafted onto whatever was there before."[12] Leach makes the associated charge that further distortion is perpetrated by the omission in the evidence of "nearly all references to the cultural background of the ethnographer him(her)self"; "yet there are many situations in which the ethnographer's personal 'cargo' must have had drastic repercussions."[13]

These charges are further developed under the compass of the major issue of "the relationship between history and ethnography . . . which itself has a history which deserves attention."[14] Leach mentions that ethnography became more closely linked with "fictitious history" after Columbus's discovery of the Americas, and the speculations on how the American Indians first got there, and how the differences between "the savage" and "the civilized" came about (a question that also concerned the ancient Greeks in a more rudimentary way). But more proximately and consequentially two kinds of "pseudo-historical theories of social development" dominated the stage during most of the eighteenth century and again during the latter half of the nineteenth century. They were evolutionism and diffusionism. The supposition by the former that customs of primeval man had evolved over time like the species

---

[9] Roger M. Keesing, *Cultural Anthropology: A Contemporary Perspective*, New York: Holt, Rinehart, & Winston, 1981.
[10] Ibid., p. 1.   [11] Ibid., p. 1.   [12] Ibid., p. 2.   [13] Ibid., p. 2.   [14] Ibid., p. 2.

in a Darwinian tree fitted very well with the age of European colonial expansion since the non-white local inhabitants of the colonial territories could be rated as inferior by nature. And diffusionism, fashionable among anthropologists from about 1890 onwards (and still favored by some archaeologists), focused on past movements of peoples and of cultural traits and their points of origin. "Both doctrines assumed that mankind was made of numbers of 'races,' like 'species' of birds and animals, who were of different genetic origin, spoke different languages, had different manners and customs, and therefore did not mix. If they mixed, this was an aberration brought about by the impact of colonialism and the diffusion of individual 'traits.' "[15]

W.H.R. Rivers, an ardent diffusionist, died in 1924, and Malinowski launched his functionalism at the London School of Economics. Although the reconstruction of prehistory was no longer on the agenda, the understanding of how tribal society worked before the coming of the Europeans was a prime objective in the mapping of the alleged pre-colonial "traditional" society. The perspective and methodology of this project that occupied the majority of British functionalists/ structural-functionalists, past and present (including himself, presumably in his writings of the fifties?), is the target of Leach's trenchant attack.

The enterprise of these ethnographers assumed "that it was possible to know about what had been the case in the past by observing a different state of affairs in the present. Despite the obvious flaw in such a premise the specious guarantee of stability provided by colonial rule at first gave this new, sociological, style of enquiry an appearance of scientific objectivity."

The central pitfall was "the belief that ethnographic records, made by direct observation during the present century, can with suitable editing, be treated as referring to a 'traditional culture' which was free of European influence and had existed from time immemorial."[16] "The details of what the ethnographer reports as survivals from the 'traditional past' may have been derived from many sources but the story is always phrased as if it were an objective description of known facts, rather than the author's personal interpretation of ambiguous history."[17] One example of assumed evidence of long-term cultural stability is when a datable historical document appears to match up with modern ethnographic records. Another example of tendentious interpretation is to think that

---

[15] Ibid., p. 3.   [16] Ibid., p. 4.   [17] Ibid., p. 4.

European traders, Christian missionaries, and colonial administrators are the prime destructive cause of detribalization, while the impact of "Indian and Chinese traders, or Buddhist and Islamic missionaries or the ethnographer him(her)self [is] not accorded this privileged status."[18]

Leach proceeds to illustrate these tendencies "from the classics of British social anthropology but they are also typical of much more recent work."[19] The following are some examples.

The first is Raymond Firth, Leach's teacher and close friend, garlanded as "by a wide margin the greatest living ethnographer,"[20] but guilty in his numerous writings of the assumptions, firstly, that "traditional" Tikopia society had objective reality and, secondly, that it was more or less impervious to historical change.

Firth reports that in 1928 about half the population of Tikopia were baptized Christians but in his earlier Tikopia monographs he pays little attention to this fact. Even in *Social Change in Tikopia* (1959), which is explicitly intended to point up the key difference between Tikopia society in 1929 and Tikopia society in 1952 (when 100% of the population was nominally Christian), Firth continues as if he believed that if it hadn't been for the missionaries and the administration no changes would have occurred at all.[21]

Leach offers other examples of Firth's alleged commitment to the continuity of Tikopia as a "traditional society." His 1985 dictionary of Tikopia language put "loan words" which he does not consider to be authentic Polynesian in an appendix. Leach suggests that Firth assumes that the (secular) *fono* (public assemblies) he observed in 1952 and 1966 would have been ethnographically identical to *fono* held in 1928/29 if they had been held at that time.

Leach offers as the alternative interpretation that the *fono* which Firth witnessed during his later visits were "an innovative response to colonialism and perhaps even to ideas Firth, with his wide knowledge of comparative Polynesian ethnography had himself introduced into the thinking of high ranking individuals!"[22]

This speculation is used as a preface to making the assertion that even the most experienced "ethnographers might be 'contaminating' their own evidence by being there at all," that indeed "it is impossible for any ethnographer ever to record 'uncontaminated' evidence." "Traditional culture" is not simply there for inspection, "the observer is *always* a key part of the *changing* scene that he/she observes, and this is especially the

[18] Ibid., p. 4.   [19] Ibid., p. 4.   [20] Ibid., p. 4.   [21] Ibid., p. 5.   [22] Ibid., p. 6.

case when the number of persons involved is very small and the economic resources of the observees technically impoverished."[23] Moreover, since most professional field research is a cooperative effort between observer and observee, each learning from the other, it is possible that many of the "objective" observations of earlier ethnographers could be rated as a reflexive feedback of what the observer had unintentionally suggested in the first place.

An example of this can be found in Leach's own records. "The Christian missionaries (Catholic and Baptist) and also the earliest British administrators, who worked among the Kachins of North Burma at the end of the nineteenth century all reported that the Kachin name for the Supreme Being is 'Karai Kasang'." The French Catholic missionary, Father Gilhodes, devoted a whole chapter of his monograph (*The Kachins: Religions and Customs*)[24] to this subject "largely because he had been given special instructions by the German-Catholic Pater Schmidt to look out for evidence of an original autochthonous belief in a High God. But no cult or mythology of Karai Kasang was recorded by any of the early ethnographers, and Gilhodes notes that Karai Kasang is quite unlike any analogous term in neighbouring languages."[25] Therefore, Leach finds it plausible to suggest that "the name Karai Kasang is a corruption of some version of Christian/Chretien." But he would not on that account treat it as a "loan word." Modern Kachin Christians are distinguished from non-Christians by the fact that they worship Karai Kasang.

Leach next sets his sights on Evans-Pritchard's account of the Nuer, especially Nuer religion.[26] In contrast to Firth the committed atheist, who may have belittled the possibility that the presence of Christians on Tikopia could have influenced his own observation, Evans-Pritchard was "an ardent Roman Catholic convert" whose main texts "hardly make reference to the dense population of Roman Catholic missionaries to whom the author elsewhere expresses his debt."[27] The same is true of Godfrey Lienhardt's account of the Dinka,[28] immediate neighbors of the Nuer. Leach alleges that the "various 'traditional' Nuer and Dinka

---

[23] Ibid., pp. 6–7.
[24] C. Gilhodes, *The Kachins: Religion and Customs*, Calcutta: Catholic Orphan Press, 1922.
[25] Leach, "Tribal Ethnography," p. 7.
[26] E.E. Evans-Pritchard, *The Nuer: A Description of the Modes of Livelihood and Political Institutions of a Nilotic People*, Oxford: Clarendon Press, 1940.
[27] Leach, "Tribal Ethnography," p. 8.
[28] Godfrey Lienhardt, *Divinity and Experience: The Religion of the Dinka*, Oxford: Clarendon Press, 1961.

religions which these authors describe appear to have a number of strikingly Jesuitical characteristics."[29]

Leach includes among his critique of ethnographic classics Ian Hogbin's study of the Solomon Islands (1939) whose contents were organized in terms of a functionalist tripartite scheme of The Past, The Present, and The Future.[30] Hogbin stated that his aim was to examine how the aboriginal culture has been modified and changed by Western contact. What he actually observed in the field was "The Present, which is all about exploitation by Traders, Plantation Owners, Administrators and Missionaries";[31] his Past, a reconstruction, is an invention, and yet it is this Past that "he writes about in the present tense"[32] and it provides him with his images of social reality. The contents of traditional custom may have been chosen to fit in with the ethnographer's prejudices.

Leach takes some of the sting from his critique by granting that the task "we were set" (i.e. students of Malinowski, and he seems to include himself) was to describe the institutions of the local "traditional tribal society," and "to this end the ethnographer was entitled to ignore all 'obviously recent' European influences."[33]

How then did this perspective affect Leach's own ethnographic work? He addresses this query to his study of the Kachin. At the time of writing the *Political Systems of Highland Burma* (1954), he admits: "I still accepted the conventional view that my task was to discuss an indigenous social system of which I myself was not a part. Thus the missionaries and the colonial administrators and the British military recruiting officers were not really part of my story. I see now that this was a mistake."[34] (One may add to this Leach's remarks in the 1980 Seattle lecture about 140 years of foreign intrusions in the Kachin region and their impact on the internal dynamics of local social organization.) Leach, however, submitted that "Only in one respect do I claim any superiority over most of my anthropological contemporaries. When I came to study the Kachin it quicky became obvious that although the existing ethnographic literature was full of reference to 'tribes' there were in fact no tribes and no tribal boundaries."[35] A central theme in *Political Systems of Highland Burma* was "that an individual might start life as a Kachin and fetch up as a Shan, or vice versa. In the concluding pages, I expressed considerable

---

[29] Leach, "Tribal Ethnography," p. 8.
[30] H. Ian Hogbin, *Experiments in Civilisation: The Effects of European Culture on a Native Community in the Solomon Islands*, London: G. Routledge & Sons, 1939.
[31] Leach, "Tribal Ethnography," p. 7.
[32] Ibid., p. 7.   [33] Ibid., p. 9.   [34] Ibid., p. 10.   [35] Ibid., p. 10.

scepticism concerning the ethnographic validity of the various mono-graphs by J.H. Hutton, J.P. Mills and others about the tribal peoples of Assam."[36]

Leach changes tack and comments on how "traditional society" is presented in the areas of visual anthropology and material culture. He had already in the essay "Masquerade" made some acute observations on the social and political implications of staged photographs.[37] He re-marks here that "wider familiarity with nineteenth century photographic archives has shown how impossible it is to draw a sharp demarcation line between the 'detribalized' present and the 'tribal' past." Yet Evans-Pritchard's "Nuer are nearly all naked," though Francis Muding Deng,[38] son of a former Dinka paramount chief, informs that the first motor car arrived in Dinka-land before Evans-Pritchard began his Nuer researches, and that a full-scale brick-built Romanesque cathedral was built at the Catholic missionary headquarters at Wau. All the individuals in Deng's photographs are fully clothed. "Firth's early photographs of Tikopia never reveal a European artifact,"[39] and the photograph of Malinowski in his "ethnographer's tent," probably taken by the trader Billy Hancock, shows no item of European origin except his typewriter.

The manner in which many museum exhibitions have been mounted in the past with rare ethnographic objects displayed in isolation with the minimum of contextual explanation had been a subject of Leach's criticism for some time. In this essay Leach comments on three spe-cial exhibitions mounted in 1986 by the Museum of Mankind (which is a Department of Ethnography of the British Museum) – one in which objects were presented as if they were entirely "uncontaminated" by European influence; a second mounted with the collaboration of the artist Eduardo Paolozzi displayed photographs from the colonial era in which Europeans and "natives" are prominently copresent,[40] and the material objects from the "tribal" world show strong evidence of European influence; the third exhibition was of Kalahari funerary screens that date from the eighteenth and nineteenth centuries when the Kalahari were flourishing middlemen in the slave trade: "The

[36] Ibid., p. 9.
[37] See chapter 13 where I deal with Leach's essay "Masquerade," in which he interprets the coding of hierarchy in photoghraphs.
[38] Francis M. Deng, *The Dinka of the Sudan*, New York: Holt, Rinehart & Winston, 1972.
[39] Leach, "Tribal Ethnography," p. 8.
[40] Leach remarks that "white colonial administrators in their preposterous white solar topees were certainly quite as interesting as ethnographic images as the Nigerian chiefs with their ebony walking sticks and European style suitings." Ibid., p. 10.

imagery of the screen is a wonderful combination of African and European elements."[41] Historical information about the Kalahari from the sixteenth century onwards is well documented in the log books of European sea captains. In fact at no time during the past 450 years has there existed a "traditional" Kalahari society outside history.

These submissions bring out the methodological and substantive limitations of the era that encompassed Malinowski and Radcliffe-Brown and their associates. The alleged organic unity of the culture being studied could only be shown, even approximately, only if the depth of their data was very shallow. Diachronic historical studies cannot be accommodated to synchronic functionalist studies unless reformulated as structural transformations after the manner of Michel Foucault,[42] but the functionalist acceptance of Durkheim's thesis of organic unity of society led to the ignoring of historical change, and to imagining that the original pre-colonial tribal society existed "inside a carapace of colonial and post-colonial bureaucracy and western technology."[43]

Nineteenth-century ethnographers in particular felt a commitment to social stability, and they equated the variety of "cultures" with a variety of "races," which in turn were viewed as virtually equivalent to zoological species with hard edges that could not mix. "In the circumstances of colonialism European culture bumped into non-European culture without merging. Even in the late 1930s respected anthropologists still wrote about 'the study of culture contact' as if 'cultures' were separate unit entities."

We know much better than formerly "just how culturally destructive was the third World's experience of the colonial expansion of Europe," but "precisely because of this destruction, the polarization of traditional/post-traditional, tribal/detribalized, has often seemed sharper than before."[44] The agents of colonial expansion felt that because they had accomplished a greater technical and political mastery over the environment, these other "primitive" societies had stood still, "awaiting 'detribalization' and incorporation into the cheap labour market required by colonial capitalism."[45]

While colonial governments usually encouraged the various agents of "detribalization," many anthropologists have usually (but not always)

---

[41] Ibid., p. 10.
[42] But even if some of the later generation of anthropologists, asserts Leach, have substituted the algebra of structural transformation for the missing sequences of recorded history, the past becomes a fiction invented by the ethnographer.
[43] Ibid., pp. 10–11.   [44] Ibid., p. 10.   [45] Ibid., p. 11.

adopted a conservationist approach, and just like rare species of mammals are preserved in a zoo, so specimens of antique "cultures" have been sought to be preserved "on native reservations under the supervision of white skinned jailors."[46] "This is all familiar country but it is easy to forget that something like 95% of what passes for the ethnography of 'traditional' American Indian cultures derives from research carried out on native reservations."[47]

In this critique devoted mainly (but not exclusively) to the tendentious perspectives of classical British ethnographers deriving from Malinowski's brand of functionalism, Leach also on two occasions launches his condemnation of Lévi-Strauss's famous opposition between "cold" static primitive societies, which tend to run on and on like clockwork, and to remain indefinitely in their initial state, and "hot" modern hierarchical societies, which work like steam engines, and constantly evolve through self-generated internal contradictions. Leach's refrain that "primitive" societies however defined are, like "modern" societies, caught up in history is as much directed at Lévi-Strauss as at Malinowski and his disciples.

In the concluding paragraphs Leach returns to the theme of the effect of the ethnographer's presence on the subjects he interacts with and studies: "There can be no future for tribal ethnography of a purportedly 'objective' kind. Ethnographers must admit the reflexivity of their activities; they must become autobiographical. But with this changed orientation they should be able to contribute to the better understanding of historical ethnography."[48]

Historical Anthropology is not just a matter of recognizing that the way "we," the ethnographers, see them, the people about whom we write our books, changes over time; there is also the question of how they see us. We need to look again at the "mythology" and "traditions" of "tribal peoples" to see what it can tell us about their *changing* evaluations of the others (i.e. the foreigners especially the Europeans).[49]

RETHINKING ETHNOGRAPHIC WRITING

How accurate was Leach in his criticism of the anthropologists he names? How do his remarks apply to his own past work? How much clarity is there to his assertions? Finally, how do his reflections relate to his past formulations, and to what extent are they congruent with or possibly

---

[46] Ibid., p. 11.   [47] Ibid., p. 11.   [48] Ibid., p. 12.   [49] Ibid., p. 13.

influenced by certain texts that appeared in the late 1970s and 1980s authored by such writers as Michel Foucault, Bakhtin, Edward Said, Johannes Fabian, James Clifford, and others, but none of whom he cares to cite? One knows, however, that he was an avid reader and that he kept up with the flow of literature in a variety of fields.

What did Leach mean when he said that "all ethnography is fiction," and that an ethnographic monograph has more in common with a historical novel than a scientific work grounded in claims of objectivity? The words "historical novel" bring to mind Sir Walter Scott's "historical novels." It is not to that genre that he can be referring. Nor is it possible that Leach is equating the ethnographic text with the "novel" as fiction. He in fact had much admiration for the great novelists. On several occasions I heard him say that their texts, works of imagination and literary skill, cast greater light on the complex dilemmas and behavior of human beings than the ethnographic writings of anthropologists which purport to represent the occurrences of real life. At another point, Leach introduces another complication by saying that, "All the traditional societies of the ethnographic map are products of the ethnographic imagination. In this respect a monograph in social anthropology is no different from a monograph in history." In terms of present-day alignment of anthropological and historical writing, this analogy can be considered as appropriate, although the historian's dialog is with written archival sources.

I think Leach would have conveyed more clarity if he had restated his remarks thus: that all ethnography is "constructed" (rather than "fiction"), and that ethnographers develop their information and reflexive interpretation of the forms of life they are studying through interaction with and negotiated understandings with their subjects/informants.[50] That these interactions are imbued with asymmetrical power relations between the ethnographers (predominantly white and Western) and the colonized "natives," and that if the ethnographers addressing their own professional audience feel free to represent their subjects and their changes over time, they make little or no effort to record and track the subjects' own changing perception of the foreigner ethnographers as encoded in their myths, rituals, and folk tales. A connected submission is that the very presence of foreign ethnographers in the local community – bearing their own "cargo" of superior status (and, I imagine, their paraphernalia of equipment, gifts, and connections to officials) – alters the

---

[50] Mariza Peirano has reminded me that Leach's earlier coinage of the term "as if" model could be invoked to clarify his position.

situation they are studying, and this dynamic intervention is usually missing in the older ethnography as an integral part of the anthropologists' reflexivity.

The most telling of Leach's indictments is that "primitive societies, however defined, are like 'modern' societies caught up in history." They have never existed outside history. This point of view can hardly be perceived in the writings of earlier anthropologists, and it has ramifications even for those anthropologists who have focused on "historical ethnography" (and on the relation between history and anthropology). Notably relevant is the remark that anthropologists working in the present find the need to project a "traditional" past on flimsy evidence or simply by projecting backwards from the present as a prelude to an alleged new phase of discussing a changing present. This is another manifestation of fictional historical ethnography. And in this essay, as on other occasions, Leach shows he had a keen eye for the implications of staged photographs and museum exhibits which are guilty of erasing or ignoring evidence of colonial influences and objects in order to present an alleged authentic traditional culture. I may add in support of Leach that this preservationist ethic is manifested by many who wield the camera, and it may scarcely reflect the circumstances and sentiments of those photographed; and the ethic of rescuing a disappearing past guides the manner of documenting current rituals and ceremonies. But in fact, cultural traditions have always been changing; "old ceremonies" have continually incorporated newly arriving prestigious objects and currently relevant themes, and their being alive is related to this changing dynamic. Furthermore, it is an exaggeration to hold that it is only with European colonial contact that changes have occurred in the old order.

Looked at from one perspective, I would suggest that these ideas are a further development of those Leach had offered in the mid- and late 1960s, and which I have recounted in chapter 10. He had by that time rejected typological contrasts, based in evolutionary thought, between "primitive" and "modern," "cold" and "hot" societies; and between "primitive" ignorance and "rational" thought of civilized beings. He espoused a universalist as opposed to a relativist stance in holding that in certain important ways primitives are like us moderns, their experiences illuminate ours. And he proposed a comparative method which mapped cross-cultural schema, and their transcription via transformational analysis. Now he goes a step further in indicating the anthropologist's cotemporality with his othered subjects, and their mutual effects upon one another through interaction and copresence.

From another perspective, Leach's remarks made in 1987 remind me of Johannes Fabian's powerful text *Time and the Other: How Anthropology Makes Its Object*, published in 1983.[51] Fabian's main argument is that anthropology has practiced a "denial of coevalness" with the "Other" it has studied and represented. Various "distancing devices," existential, rhetorical, and political, have been employed in this denial of coevalness, thereby persistently and systematically placing "the referent(s) of anthropology in a Time other than the present of the producer of anthropological discourses."[52] He dubs this denial of coevalness the "allochronism" of anthropology.

Fabian asserts that "We [the anthropologists] need to cover up for a fundamental contradiction: on the one hand we dogmatically insist that anthropology exists on ethnographic research involving personal, prolonged interaction with the Other. And then we pronounce upon the knowledge gained from such research a discourse which construes the Other in terms of distance, spatial and temporal" in order "to keep the Other outside the Time of Anthropology."[53]

Fabian foregrounds a conception of "Time" as central to his submission: Time is a "form through which we define the content of relations between Self and Other", it is integral to the dialectical constitution of the Other in its temporal, political, and historical conditions.[54] Moreover, we anthropologists have not "paid much attention to intersubjective Time, which does not measure but constitutes those practices of communication we customarily call fieldwork."[55] If co-equalness, sharing of present time, is a condition of communication, then anthropological knowledge which claims its sources in ethnography is integrally involved in this kind of communication. Fabian thus calls for a recognition of "the radical contemporaneity of mankind" in the praxis and politics of anthropological research.[56]

There is much here that is congruent with Leach's assertions. In my view it is likely that Leach had read Fabian, though he does not cite him, nor had he reviewed him. In one respect Fabian goes beyond Leach in attributing culpability to virtually all genres of anthropological writing – such as the structural-functionalism of British anthropology, American cultural anthropology, especially those like Ruth Benedict,

---

[51] Johannes Fabian, *Time and the Other: How Anthropology Makes Its Object*, New York: Columbia University Press, 1983, acknowledges among others the influence and/or concordance between his submissions and those of Foucault, and of Said (whose *Orientalism* [1978] appeared after Fabian had completed his essays).

[52] Fabian, *Time and the Other*, p. 31.

[53] Ibid., p. xi.   [54] Ibid., p. x.   [55] Ibid., p. xii.   [56] Ibid., p. x.

Margaret Mead, Clyde Kluckhohn (and others) who produced studies of "culture at a distance" during the Second World War which combined "cultural relativism" and patterns of "national character" with a justification of American warfare against the Nazis and the Japanese;[57] and French structuralism, especially that of Lévi-Strauss, and his distinction between hot and cold societies (which Leach had preceded Fabian in criticizing).

Leach puts his finger on a presupposition stemming from an earlier phase of Malinowski's ahistorical functionalism, which also set the agenda for many of his disciples including Leach himself, that it was their task to recover the traditional cultural and social forms of "tribal society," and in this process to ignore the influences of colonial contact. This prescription relates especially to Malinowski's writings on "traditional" life in the Trobriand Islands. As discussed earlier Leach's first study of Hpalang in north Burma aspired to be a "functionalist" community study of this kind.

However, Malinowski did engage in another kind of advocacy especially from 1929 and 1930 onwards when, in his capacity as director of the Fellowship Programme of the International African Institute, he argued with intensifying vehemence against the highest colonial administrators of East Africa (for example P.E. Mitchell, provincial commissioner in Tanganyika and later governor of Kenya) that field studies had their usefulness as "practical anthropology" providing the colonial administrators with an accurate and sympathetic understanding of tribal life, but not as a handmaid-tool of imperial objectives. He also advocated that the theoretically oriented anthropologist, in also becoming an agent of "practical" knowledge, should "become more concerned in the anthropology of the changing African, and in the anthropology of the contact of white and coloured, of European culture and primitive tribal life . . ."[58] Although Malinowski had in an earlier phase of this debate argued for anthropology's practical relevance as a scientific and neutral objective inquiry into the life forms of tribal life, he progressively argued in a

---

[57] Examples of such studies are: Ruth Benedict, *The Chrysanthemum and the Sword: Patterns of Japanese Culture*, Boston: Haughton Mifflin, 1946, and Margaret Mead and Rhoda Métraux (eds.), *The Study of Culture at a Distance*, Chicago: The University of Chicago Press, 1953.

[58] Bronislaw Malinowski, "Practical Anthropology," *Africa*, vol. 2, 1929, pp. 22–38. For an informative discussion of Malinowski's engagement in debate with Mitchell on the role of anthropology in relation to British colonial objectives, see Wendy James, "The Anthropologist as Reluctant Imperialist," in Talal Asad (ed.), *Anthropology and the Colonial Encounter*, London: Ithaca Press, 1973, pp. 42–69.

hardening view against Mitchell's colonialist view, that anthropology directly serve as a practical tool of imperialism, that social scientists had to become politically involved in their work on behalf of native interests. His most powerful statements in this vein, a "sign of increasing disaffection with the apolitical, amoral natural science approach of those strongly influenced by Radcliffe-Brown, and of a deepening radical commitment,"[59] are to be found in his posthumously published collection of essays under the title *The Dynamics of Culture Change* (1945).[60] In the first chapter he trenchantly asserted:

There is a moral obligation to every calling. The duty of the anthropologist is to be fair and true interpreter of the Native . . . In reality, the historian of the future will have to register that Europeans in the past sometimes exterminated whole island peoples; that they expropriated most of the patrimony of savage races; that they introduced slavery in a specially cruel, and pernicious form . . . The Native still needs help. The anthropologist who is unable to perceive this, unable to register the tragic errors committed . . . remains an antiquarian covered with academic dust and in a fool's paradise . . . Research in order to be of use must be inspired by courage and purpose . . . Shall we therefore, mix politics with science? In one way, decidedly "yes" . . .[61]

Wendy James remarks that "the increasingly political stand taken by Malinowski is an indication of his sympathy for the growing nationalist movements of Africa." Jomo Kenyatta's presence at Malinowski's seminars in London in the thirties, and Malinowski's own visits to Africa, where he called on several of his own students engaged in field-work, must have opened his eyes to the explosive situation in what had been peaceful anthropological territory. Malinowski wrote the introduction to Kenyatta's *Facing Mount Kenya* (1938), a record of his own Kikuyu as a people who suffered conquest, subjugation and loss of land, and an intimation of their growing nationalist challenge to colonial rule. It has to be understood that Malinowski can hardly be viewed as espousing a radical revolutionary stance: he was afraid of the dangers of extreme nationalism and its spread, but he was sympathetic to the African peoples' sufferings, and his sense of the "scientist's duty" included the improvement of their social and economic conditions by means of knowledge-based liberal reforms.

[59] James, "The Anthropologist as Reluctant Imperialist," p. 66.
[60] Bronislaw Malinowski, *The Dynamics of Culture Change: An Inquiry into Race Relations in Africa*, edited by Phyllis Kaberry, New Haven: Yale University Press, 1961. First Published in 1945. The references here are to the 1961 edition with a new introduction by P. Kaberry.
[61] Ibid., pp. 3–4. James, "The Anthropologist as Reluctant Imperialist," p. 66.

In this context it is worth remembering that among the anthropologists trained by Malinowski and advised to conduct investigations of the colonial contact situation and its "practical" implication was Audrey Richards, whose *Land, Labour and Diet in Northern Rhodesia* (1939) focused on the hard realities of survival and subsistence in rural areas drained of manpower by the developing mining and industrial towns. Another associate of Malinowski, I. Schapera, was the author of multiple studies in South Africa on issues of contact and historical changes. A notable example is his *Migrant Labour and Tribal Life: A Study of Conditions in Bechuanaland Protectorate* (1947).[62]

Returning to Leach's polemical essay "Tribal Ethnography: Past, Present, and Future," it is curious that his memory of Malinowski's theoretical influence on his disciples is confined to his conception of integrative functionalism, which he had elaborated in relation to Melanesia, and except for a passing reference, Leach ignores his advocacy of the study of dynamics of colonial contact and culture change with regard to Africa. As Audrey Richards has remarked, "Many of Malinowski's pupils worked among the larger African tribes of the greatest political importance and where European contact had been at its maximum."[63] And some of them addressed the issues he publicized.

Although unlike his copious writings on Melanesia, Malinowski did not himself produce ethnography of any significance concerning Africa, he did hold that Africa was the site of societies in flux and change, that the rapidity of their change was informed by the play of unexpected forces and factors such as African nationalism and autonomous African churches, and that "the whole range of European influences, interests, good intentions, and predatory drives must become an essential part of African culture change." Moreover, he significantly discarded for this kind of study an approach that would treat "the complex situation of change as one 'well integrated whole', [for it] ignores the whole dynamism of the process," and he also saw the contact situation as highly one sided, in which the higher dominant culture acts "upon a simpler more passive one."[64] The Europeans wield the instruments of physical power and aggression, control the economic enterprises, and economically exploit the natives of West Africa and Uganda, and do not admit Africans to relations of social, political, or even religious equality.

---

[62] London and New York: Oxford University Press, 1947.
[63] Andrey I. Richards, "Practical Anthropology in the Lifetime of the International African Institute," *Africa*, vol. 14, 1944, pp. 289–301.
[64] Malinowski, *The Dynamics of Culture Change*, pp. 9, 15, 57.

I am introducing this information about Malinowski's advocacy of studies of the dynamics of unequal colonial contact in Africa, not only to problematize the blanket charge of anthropology's conscious or unconscious complicity in the Western imperial project, but also to mute that part of Leach's own undifferentiated indictment of those anthropologists of the period of the 1930s to 1950s who are alleged to have sought to construct a pre-colonial "traditional" tribal society as a bounded whole, impervious to change before colonial contact, and/or, when studying the societies during the colonial period, to ignore or bracket the impact of colonial administrators, missionaries, and commercial entrepreneurs on their subject peoples. Leach's neglect or amnesia regarding Malinowski's programatic advocacy of his version of "practical anthropology" joined with the study of the dynamics of the colonial encounter may be, I surmise, linked to his negative attitude toward "applied anthropology" in the service of alleged economic and social development of subject native populations.

Leach may well have been on target when criticizing the ahistorical perspectives adopted by Radcliffe-Brown on Australian tribes, by Fortes on the Tallensi, Evans-Pritchard on the Nuer, and also himself for not dealing adequately with Kachins' exposure to 140 years of external contacts. But he might have been more generous about Firth's alleged avoidance of these issues, especially when the same 1977 issue of *Anthropological Forum*, in which Leach discussed the colonial and wartime context of his Kachin work, carried a lengthy and retrospective report by Firth on his multiple, varied research projects undertaken during his long career. In this essay entitled "Whose Frame of Reference? One Anthropologist's Experience,"[65] Firth not only makes a spirited and nuanced response, the response of a Liberal, a humanist, and a veteran fieldworker, to Asad's queries, but also in an almost prescient way he anticipates and answers to some degree the charges leveled by Leach, in his 1987/89 parting shot, which is that Leach launched this critique a full decade after Firth's 1977 essay, of which Leach must have been aware since they both participated in the same LSE seminar. Especially relevant here is Firth's brief recounting of his three field trips to Tikopia, and the nature of his engagement with the Christian missions, and the changes he encountered over time. It should be considered as providing some counter-evidence to Leach's remarks on gaps in Firth's ethnography.

[65] Raymond Firth, "Whose Frame of Reference? One Anthropologist's Experience," in R.M. Berndt (ed.), "Anthropological Research in the British Colonies: Some Personal Accounts," special issue of *Anthropological Forum*, vol. 14, no. 2, 1977, pp. 145–67.

A question that must necessarily be raised is to what extent Leach's remarks of this nature – that all ethnography is "fictional," that there is no future for ethnography of a purported "objective" kind, that ethnographers must reflexively consider how their very presence changes the situation they are studying, that a "historical ethnography" reporting how we see them, the subjects of our study, should also ideally deal with how they see us over time – apply to his two principal ethnographic texts, *Political Systems of Highland Burma* (1954) and *Pul Eliya* (1961). How do these observations and prescriptions apply to his idealist-empiricist position that he argued for earlier in relation to *Political Systems*, further reinforced some years later with a "materialist bent" in *Pul Eliya*, which text claimed that the proof of its inferences was embedded in its thick documentation of empirical facts?[66]

Leach did not in his 1987/89 critique of "Tribal Ethnography" refer to *Pul Eliya*.[67] His fieldwork in Sri Lanka was of short duration, intensely focused on a local community on which he gathered a wealth of information, and although he had contact with the local district office (where records were located), his research did not extend to include a deep study of island-wide politics, though he was well aware of both colonial and post-independence developments.

His main ethnographic reflections and memories were throughout his life focused on Burma, especially north Burma, the site of his stimulating as well as harrowing wartime experiences, and also the site of his dissenting controversy with Lévi-Strauss, and therefore one wonders how his parting shot directed at the stalwarts of British anthropology relates to his own *Political Systems* and associated essays on Burma.

On the question of how he had dealt with processes of change and continuity in the Kachin Hills in 1954, and how he might have dealt with them in light of subsequent discussions on "historical ethnography" expressed in the seventies and eighties, Leach offered complex answers. As my documentation in foregoing chapters shows, on the one hand he proposed that he had innovatively struggled to take into account the records and reports dealing with Kachin political processes over a period of some 140 years, and that he had situated them in

---

[66] I have myself in chapter 7 appreciatively described Leach in relation to *Pul Eliya* as "a master ethnographer meticulously engaged with micro-details."

[67] My speculation is that if asked about *Pul Eliya* he might retrospectively at this date have admitted its authorial defects, but he would still have stuck to the validity of his critique of unilineal descent group theory, and been proud of his historical analysis of land tenure records of the Old Field from 1890 to 1954 and of his knowledge of dry zone hydraulic works.

a theoretical framework of oscillating equilibrium between *gumsa* and *gumlao* as polar ideal type categories. Again, he remarked that he had experimentally tried to characterize the Kachins' own sense of historical process in terms of their categories, instead of from the point of view of an external Western observer's view of history. He saw that this prescient approach had been more fully realized in some recent writings. And he reminded that his rejection of Lévi-Strauss's "internalist" analysis of kinship that was insulated from the impact of the structures and forces of political economy was evidence of his processual approach.

On the other hand, in his reassessment of *Political Systems* over three decades later, he also recognized that the literature on the Kachins, even from before the arrival of the British, showed the exposure of the Kachin and Shan (and other) peoples to waves of external contact that surely had generated internal changes, and that seen in this light his own text had failed to convey the dynamics of such interaction, in terms of both continuities and discontinuities. In fact *Political Systems* did in its concluding discussions contain programatic declarations that societies are "continuously adaptive subsystems within an unbounded matrix," and that historical processes are "open-ended" and "cannot be represented in causal deterministic evolutionary terms." But these insights were not systematically developed.

Leach, the polemicist, continuously open to, and experimenting with, new ideas and insights, and in doing so, conceding some of his past inconsistencies and insufficiencies, would have accomplished a final feat if he had actually written a text documenting the dynamic historical experiences and changes in the highlands of Burma, and what in his previous writings on the Kachin Hills he would revise, reformulate, even repudiate. He had begun to illustrate what he now meant by the idea that primitive societies, however defined, are like modern societies and that the anthropologists and their subjects were co-temporal, but a longer demonstration would have engaged both his admirers and his critics, and embellished his already considerable contributions.

It has to be recognized that by the mid-1980s he was hobbled by illness and in decline, and could not have had the time or energy to marshal the evidence and to compose a substantial text on these issues. However, since he had blamed Evans-Pritchard, Lienhardt, and Firth for scarcely taking into account the impact of Christian missionaries on the native peoples they described in their monographs, Leach might have earlier in 1954, or more likely later, given a demonstration of how he would tackle this issue with regard to the Kachins themselves. In *Political Systems* there are eight scattered and brief references in the text or in footnotes of the following kind:

> In 1940, about one-fifth of the Hpalang community [his main field site] were nominally Christians, more or less equally divided between Roman Catholics and American Baptists. Sectarian affiliations served admirably as a banner for factionalism, but missionary activity had not had as much effect upon the structural organization of the community as might perhaps have been expected. The cleavages between the Catholics and the Baptists and the Pagans were certainly marked, but exactly the same groups of people have been involved in fratricidal bickering before the coming of Christianity.[68]

Leach's attention throughout is focused on the religious rituals and festivals of the majority "pagans." The two major communal festivals – one at sowing time and the other toward the end of August before the rice came to ear – were the occasions on which according to orthodox *gumsa* practice the rival claims to the chieftainship were asserted and emphasized.[69] The cult of the *nats*, a hierarchy of ancestral spirits, is described as the central framework of ritual action: the annual sacrifices on behalf of the community sponsored by the chief and conducted by the "priests" and ritual butchers; the consultations by mediums through trance with *nats* and recently deceased ancestors; the divination procedures to seek answers to marriage partners, lost property, and so on; and the recitals of the saga tellers.[70]

Despite the supremacy of the pagan religion as briefly mentioned above, it seems that the Catholic versus Baptist affiliations had a play in factional politics in Hpalang community, which in 1940 divided into two main factions of long standing, each subdivided into five and four villages, and these in turn into named lineages. Leach describes a controversial betrothal between a couple, both Catholic but belonging to the opposed factions; the fractional bifurcation became further charged because of "internal rivalries within Summut village between the headman's lineage who were Baptists and the Jangman village [from which one betrothed member came] who were Catholics."[71] Leach dissects

---

[68] Leach, *Political Systems*, p. 72.

[69] Ibid., p. 72.

[70] Ibid., pp. 189–95. On p. 173, Leach says that the *nats* are spirits, "non-natural men" in Lang's famous phrase, who "extend the human class hierarchy to a higher level and are continuous with it."

[71] Ibid., pp. 77–78. It may be noted that marriage was conducted according to their respective Christian ritual by Baptists and Catholics.

another dispute that bears on severance of an affinal *mayu–dama* relationship, which has a bearing on rank and title to land, between the previously mentioned Summut village primarily peopled by Baptist Christians and a number of leading Dashi members (of Gauri village) who had recently become Catholics.[72] The Summut–Dashi rank claims further ramify with the issue of speech dialect affiliations which also tie in with claims of ancestry.[73] Elsewhere in the book he refers to "the 19th-century feud" between the Gauri chiefs of the Mahtang area and their neighbors of the Sinlum–Lawdan group of villages, and indicates that the latter, mainly Baptists, were now in the 1950s ascendent over their Catholic rivals.[74]

There are some other observations about the Kachin Hills in general which speak of the duration and impact of the missions which arrived even before the British administration. "The Catholics had a permanent station at Bhamo from 1874; the American Baptists from 1875. Most of the Kachin leaders of today (1954) are nominally Christians. This does not necessarily mean much more than they have attended a Christian school."[75] However, "the Christian god Karai Kasang seems to have been well assimilated to Kachin ideas; he is Karai Wa and treated as a kind of superior sky nat."[76] Leach is skeptical of the claim of the missions that the Kachins had the notion of a superior high god from the beginning, and he suspects that Karai Kasang was simply a confused pronunciation of Christian. (In his 1987 essay, as we have already seen, he charges the French missionary Father Gilhodes with fulfilling the instructions of Father Schmidt to search for a high god at the summit of the Kachin pantheon.)

I have brought together the scattered references to the impact of the Christian missions to pose some questions about Leach's treatment of this issue at the beginning of his professional career in the 1950s. Like Firth before him among the Tikopia, and many other structural-functionalists of that time, the "pagan" part of the religion was viewed as anthropologically more enduring, relevant, and interesting than the shallower impact of the Christian missions. Leach was perhaps at that time not interested in the issue of colonial and Christian "contact," and the coevalness of Kachins, Shans, and Westerners – a problematical matter for anthropologists at a later time. In *Political Systems* he did not

---

[72] Ibid., p. 83.   [73] Ibid., p. 94.   [74] Ibid., p. 273.
[75] Ibid., p. 245. In a later reference on p. 259, Leach observes neutrally that "most of the Kachins now in authority were educated in mission schools."
[76] Ibid., pp. 245–46.

tackle the issue of syncretic integration of, or incompatibilities between, pagan and Christian beliefs and ritual components, and their articulation with dialectical and territorial affiliations.

In the eighties Leach was, as I have suggested, probably reading the newer "poststructuralist," "post-colonial," and "postmodern," "subaltern" and "historical-ethnographic" genres of literature, and I suppose that if he had the time and energy he would have responded to these highly self-conscious and trenchant writings selectively in his own characteristic receptive as well as debunking manner, stretching the frontiers of his own interpretive understanding, and unsettling received orthodoxies and new claims.

In concluding this commentary, let me therefore refer to some of the texts that have addressed the large topic of the problems and character of anthropological (and comparative civilizational) studies in colonial, post-colonial, and late modern times. I have already dealt with one of them by Fabian.

Not the first chronologically, but the longest, sustained critique indicting all knowledge constructed in the context and service of imperial conquest and domination, especially in respect of Egypt (and the Middle East), was Edward Said's *Orientalism* published in 1978.[77] Some of the main allegations were that the Orient was a field created, ordered, and bounded by primarily Western scholars. There was a tendency to portray Islam as unchanging and mired in stasis, and to ignore and downplay internal differences, contestations, and variation within the Islamic societies and civilizations. Orientalism as an imperial intellectual project – in which anthropology participated – sought to essentialize and homogenize the Other in order to be better able to grasp, absorb, and subordinate it. The scholarly and non-scholarly writings of the orientalist genre were meant for Western readers and institutions and not for the majority of Arabs for whom the literature was inaccessible. Indeed, the prevailing attitude of scholars was one of disapproval of and hostility toward Islam and the Arabs, even among those who had devoted much energy and time to their studies. By comparison such a negative bias was not found among many scholars engaged in classical Greek, or Buddhist, or sinological studies.

---

[77] Edward W. Said, *Orientalism*, New York: Random House, 1978. See also Edward W. Said, "Representing the Colonized: Anthropology's Interlocutors," *Critical Inquiry*, vol. 15, no. 2, Winter 1989, pp. 205–25, in which Said reviews anthropological writings specifically, including those that support his main indictment of Orientalism (for example, Asad, Fabian, and Gérard Leclerc).

A theme, which has a prior and parallel expression in Foucault's writings,[78] is Said's treatment of the relation between knowledge, power, and authority to define, intervene, and dominate the world. Said's own take as literary critic is phrased in terms of the implications of "representation." Said's thesis is that "knowledge of the Orient because generated out of strength, in a sense *creates* the Orient, the Oriental, and his world."

> Representation, or more particularly the act of representing (and hence reducing) others almost always involves violence of some sort to the subject of the representation . . . This is one of the irresolvable problems of anthropology, which is constituted essentially as the discourse of representation of an Other epistemologically defined as radically inferior (whether labelled primitive, or backward, or simply Other); the whole science or discourse of anthropology depends on the silence of the other.[79]

The view of anthropological representation as violence committed on the "other" in a context of unequal power relations, which also silences the voices of the "other," and the unrealistic "myth" of the lone ethnographer who in fact was complicit with imperialist domination, became common themes in the writings of many anthropologists, some of whom appear in the pages of the timely overview and survey in *Anthropology as Cultural Critique* (1986)[80] and rhetorically even more forcefully in James Clifford and George Marcus's *Writing Culture: The Poetics and Politics of Ethnography* (1986),[81] and Clifford, *The Predicament of Culture: Twentieth-Century Ethnography, Literature, and Art* (1988).[82]

Among Clifford's "postmodern" deconstructive submissions I would foreground his questioning of the grounds on which, and the strategies by which, ethnographers claim their "authority" to give objective accounts.[83] The assumption that "primitive" cultures can be described

---

[78] Michel Foucault's powerful writings influenced Said, Asad, Fabian, and other critics I have mentioned. Among Foucault's numerous texts I might select these as examples: *Madness and Civilization: A History of Insanity in the Age of Reason*, trans. R. Husard, London: Tavistock Publications, 1971; *The Birth of the Clinic: An Archaeology of Medical Perception*, trans. A.M. Sheriden Smith, New York: Pantheon Books, 1973; *Discipline and Punish: The Birth of the Prison*, trans. A. Sheriden, New York: Vintage Books, 1979. (The dates of their original publications in French were 1961, 1963, and 1975 respectively.)

[79] Said, *Orientalism*, p. 40.

[80] George E. Marcus and Michael M.J. Fischer. *Anthropology as Cultural Critique: An Experimental Moment in the Human Sciences*, Chicago: The University of Chicago Press, 1986.

[81] James Clifford and George E. Marcus, *Writing Culture: The Poetics and Politics of Ethnography*, Berkeley: University of California Press, 1986.

[82] James Clifford, *The Predicament of Culture: Twentieth-Century Ethnography, Literature, and Art*, Cambridge, MA: Harvard University Press, 1988.

[83] I refer here to Clifford, *The Predicament of Culture*. Also see James Clifford, "On Ethnographic Authority," *Representations*, vol. 1, Spring 1983.

synchronically and as coherent wholes, combined with the methodological claim that participant observation gives the ethnographer first-hand experience and scientific knowledge, downplayed the textual nature of ethnographies. Ethnographies are authored *texts*, not direct reflections of experience; and there cannot be a definitive "reading" of a culture.

There are at least two passages from experience to text. An ethnographer records experience in fieldnotes, and then, going home, converts them and memories into a manuscript. In this process, particular situations are liable to be flattened into generalized patterns, individuals become composite "typical" cases, conversations are distanced into observations, and cultures are reified.

Drawing on Bakhtin's discussion of the dialogical and intersubjective exchanges of utterances, and of genres, heteroglossia, and polyphony in differentiated communities, Clifford develops the argument that ethnographic reports are actually the outcomes of constructive negotiations and shared understandings between ethnographer and his or her subjects (interlocutors). A "culture" as a construction is an open-ended creative dialog of subcultures, of insiders and outsiders, and of diverse factions; and "a 'language' is the interplay and struggle of regional dialects, professional jargons, generic commonplaces, the speech of different age groups, individuals, and so forth."[84]

This kind of "postmodern" commentary on the practices of anthropologists has evoked certain criticisms from different quarters. Said has criticized postmodernism's relative detachment from urgent historical and political concerns that have informed the work of certain kinds of post-colonial writers and artists. As antidote one may turn to the writings of the "subaltern commune" on India that focus on peasant resistance and alternative narratives to the official narratives of the colonial regime and of the post-independence nation-state. Aside from looking away from issues of historic injustice and unequal power relations, the postmodern writings in question have been criticized for being narcissistic and navel-contemplating, concentrating more on the preoccupations of the introspective anthropologist rather than the people being studied, and on the desk-occupying anthropologists composing their text rather than the cross-checking ardors of the fieldworkers collecting information through a variety of techniques and interpersonal dialogs. If Foucault is right that discourse, including experimental ethnography, is integrally related to power relations and empowerment, and to

[84] Clifford, *The Predicament of Culture*, p. 46.

acquiring, as Bourdieu would say, cultural and symbolic capital, then ironically the postmodernists themselves may not be adequately reflexive as to how their advocacy may be related to their political and academic goals. Perhaps this commentary should terminate here at the threshold of considering the ideological, intellectual, social, and political conditions constituting postmodernism and its spatial and temporal manifestations in architecture, aesthetics (literature, music, painting), the media (film, video, information technology, etc.), and economics (late multinational capitalism, globalism). These themes have been famously tackled from a neo-Marxist perspective by Fredric Jameson,[85] David Harvey,[86] and others. Harvey for example summarizes his submission as follows: "There has been a sea-change in cultural as well as in political-economic practices since around 1972 . . . there is some kind of necessary relation between the rise of postmodern cultural forms, the emergence of more flexible modes of capital accumulations and a new round of 'time–space' compression in the organization of capitalism."[87] Jameson places postmodernism in "late capitalism," an age when culture sees an "immense dilation of its sphere (the sphere of commodities)", an age of "simulacra" and "virtual reality" and historical shallowness. Its characteristic phenomena are commodity fetishism and shopping fever, glitz architecture and depthless art, computer culture and cyberpunk, MTV, and global gentrification.

[85] Fredric Jameson, *Postmodernism, or, The Cultural Logic of Late Capitalism*, Durham, NC: Duke University Press, 1991.
[86] David Harvey, *The Condition of Postmodernity: An Enquiry into the Origins of Cultural Change*, Oxford and Cambridge, MA: Basil Blackwell, 1989. Both Jameson and Harvey interpret from a neo-Marxist perspective.
[87] Harvey, *The Condition of Postmodernity*, p. vii.

CHAPTER 18

The work of sustaining institutions: Provost of King's College (1966–1979)

Edmund Leach was elected a Fellow of King's College in 1960 and Provost in 1966. "Though still relatively new to the College, his election as Provost in 1966 came as no surprise. It fitted the mood of the times, a mood for change."[1] It seems that the liberals, and the left wing forming the Junior Caucus, saw him as eligible and congenial.

We may recall that Mao's Cultural Revolution had begun in 1966 (and raged for a decade) in China. By the late sixties student activism and radical politics including demonstrations against nuclear weapons were in ferment both in Europe and in the United States. May 1968 saw the militant student uprising in Paris; soon afterwards in the United States the repudiation of the Vietnam War and opposition to conscription came to a boil. It is possible that taking cognizance of the Cultural Revolution in China, and seeing signs of impending student militant politics, Leach used the Reith Lectures as a platform to talk of necessary change in Britain and the need for scientists and policymakers to act creatively and responsibly. As we saw in chapter 15 on *A Runaway World?* Leach had upbraided the older generation for having failed to create a world for young people to live in; he linked youthful disorder to a breakdown of family life, and urged a reform in the current educational system, the proper task of which is to impart genuinely creative and relevant knowledge to face the challenges of a world propelled by technological revolution. By the late sixties, many students in Cambridge wanted representation in college councils, and were advocating withdrawal from financial involvements in South Africa.

Let me begin with a reporting of the manner in which the College Council and the College Congregation chaired by Provost Leach tackled

---

[1] Stephen Hugh-Jones, "Edmund Leach 1910–1989," a memoir prepared by direction of the Council of King's College, Cambridge, 1989, p. 31.

the important issues that came up during the first eight years of Leach's tenure.

The year 1969, four years after Leach was installed as Provost, proved to be one of the most critical in the history of King's College. The issue arising concerned the admission of women into the exclusively male colleges of Cambridge,[2] and King's was destined to lead the way.

This issue had been discussed in King's in preceding years. On March 5, 1966 (some seven months before Leach's election as Provost) at a Congregation held in the Combination Room "for the special purpose of considering alterations of Status," the conservative motion that "No woman shall be a member of the College whether on the Foundation or otherwise" was carried by "Ayes 42 and the Provost" (Noel Annan). The number of votes against and the number of abstentions were not recorded in the minutes.[3]

It is very surprising that some three years later, on May 27, 1969, at an "Ordinary Congregation" the motion "That the governing Body of King's College agree in principle to the admission of women to the College, the principle to be put into effect when a satisfactory method of admission of women has been worked out" was carried with "Ayes 48 and the Provost, Noes 5, Abstentions 6." The Minutes make special mention that "Dr. E.M. Forster [the famous novelist and long-lived resident Honorary Fellow] also attended the Meeting."[4]

The Minutes, like all other Minutes phrased in a brief matter-of-fact style, do not convey the high drama and intrigue that led to this historic decision and reversal of former resistance. Leach's own informal jubilant account of how it was engineered will be related shortly. The admission of women into "co-residence" and to college fellowships was smoothly implemented without delay after negotiations with the women's colleges. In due course, Dr. Tess Adkins, the first woman Senior Tutor of King's (and of any other co-residential college in Cambridge) was appointed after the eminent classicist Dr. Geoffrey Lloyd stepped

---

[2] The established exclusively women's colleges in Cambridge University were the older institutions of Newnham and Girton, and the more recently founded New Hall.

[3] I am most grateful to the present Provost, Dr. Patrick Bateson, for generously permitting me to look at the Minutes of the Congregation pertaining to the years relevant to Leach's tenure as Provost. I shall hereafter quote from the Minutes of the Congregation held at various times without further attribution.

[4] E.M. Forster died shortly afterwards, and at an Ordinary Congregation held on July 18, 1970 the following motion was "carried unanimously, the Provost and Fellows upstanding": "The Provost and Fellows desire to place on record their sorrow on the death in his 92nd year of their much beloved friend Edward Morgan Forster, Honorary Fellow and a resident member of the College for the past 24 years."

down from this important position, having served in it from 1969 to 1973.[5]

The year 1970 was a distinctive year in the affairs of King's and was, I imagine, an anxious time for Provost Leach. The repressive acts of the authoritarian regime in South Africa were repugnant to all liberals and radicals, and the radicalized Student Union of King's passed a motion that called upon the college: "(a) to take steps immediately to withdraw permanently all indirect investments wherever it is possible to trace the relevant links to South Africa; (b) to terminate its account in Barclay's Bank, in view of that bank's collaboration with the South African Government, and if possible, to transfer its account to the Co-operative Society."

On February 21, 1970, at an Ordinary Congregation held as usual in the Combination Room, the question of South African investments was discussed. It was proposed by Mr. Wood (a Research Fellow in economics) and Provost Leach that the Provost be authorized "to request the Estates Committee to report to the Governing Body on the issues raised by" the Student Union motion. The motion was carried, with an amendment proposed by Professor Kaldor, the prominent economist of socialist persuasion, "to insert after the word 'Committee' the words 'to reaffirm its original decision in 1961 not to hold shares in companies operating mainly in South Africa.'" Clearly the liberal and left-wing Fellows of King's had for quite some time, before the Student Union motion, been advocating a similar action. In May of 1970 the Congregation acknowledged receipt of the Bursar's report on South African investments, and discussed the Student Union motion relating to the college's bankers.

The denouement to the student agitation about South Africa was that the College Council was persuaded that the college should withdraw its accounts with Barclay's Bank unless the bank severed its business connections with South Africa. As the sanctions against the bank were about to be applied, the bank declared that it would comply.

It seems that it was partly, at least as a response to student agitation, to be allowed to participate in the college's decision making on politically important matters[6] that the same year of 1970 saw the renewal

---

[5] Before that Lloyd had served as assistant tutor from 1964 to 1967. The Annual Congregation of November 1973 thanked Dr. Lloyd for "his vigorous and enlightened services both as Assistant Tutor, and more particularly, as Tutor."

[6] Another instance of student activism resulting in this case is the forced entry into the Garden House Hotel in Cambridge that will be related shortly.

of deliberations on what was to be an innovative leap taken by King's, namely the admission of student representatives on the College Council and other college committees. It took some years of discussions by the College Council about the feasibility of this proposal, and the required changes in the college's statutes and ordinances, to enable its implementation. In July 1974, the Congregation accepted the following recommendation made by the Council: four resident members of the college *in statu pupillari*, at least one of whom shall be an undergraduate and one a graduate student, may attend meetings of the Council on being elected in secret ballot by the resident members.[7]

These four student members thus joined the Council which had until then consisted of the Provost, Vice Provost, and "such number not less than twelve," which included holders of specified college offices and the remainder elected every year by the Annual Congregation. Only three students were elected to serve on the Council for 1974, but this number increased to the permissible four in subsequent years.

Concerning Leach's performance as Provost, Hugh-Jones writes that:

The stage was set for a rethinking of the College and changes there were – the Hall was turned back to front, the servery became a self-servery, the high table was made low, and English not Latin became the Provost's language in Chapel. More significantly it was under his Provostship that King's, after years of discussion and contention, finally decided to admit women as undergraduates and Fellows. Edmund took personal pleasure in the fact that, despite the wrangles, the final vote was approved *nem con* at the congregation on 21 February 1970.[8] At a subsequent congregation, the Provost inaugurated the proceedings with the customary "Gentlemen, we should perhaps begin" whereupon a junior research fellow, Dennis Mollison, jumped to his feet to protest – the Provost appeared to have overlooked that there were now women on the Fellowship. Momentarily nonplussed, then rescued by a bold stroke of anthropological inspiration, the Provost replied "For the purposes of this meeting women shall be deemed to be men."

The admission of women went hand in hand with another change in the social make up of the College, an increasing number of students from state schools, the result of an admissions policy inaugurated by Provost Annan and championed by Edmund and his ex-student and colleague Alan Bilsborough [physical anthropologist]. The students' relations with this Provost were respectful rather

---

[7] The motion stipulated that elected student members to the Council "shall not attend meetings declared by the chairman to be reserved areas of business which include appointments, promotions, and other matters affecting the personal position of members of the Governing Body or staff of the College, the admission of individuals or their academic assessment." This restriction did not disallow students from discussing college policies on other matters.

[8] Hugh-Jones is in error here. His error actually stems from a misremembering, committed by Leach himself. According to the College Minutes, which I have already reported, the vote on admission of women was taken on May 27, 1969.

than close; they admired him but did not know him well. These were also years of student militancy and here, rather to the surprise of many, especially the students themselves, the same man who, in his Reith Lectures, had seemed to advocate greater permissiveness and the ceding of power from the old to the young, now seemed to play a cautious and often rather conservative role.

An enthusiastic supporter of another major change, student representation on the College council and other administrative bodies, he was rather less enthusiastic about the targets and manner of their other demands and protests. Though a rebel himself, when confronted by other rebels his conservatism came to the fore. For Edmund they simply did not go about it all in the right kind of way nor behave in the manner that he thought students ought. With students in mind he expressed his views as follows – "the whole system of things and people which surrounds us coerces us to be conformist; even if you want to be a rebel you will still have to go about things in a conventional way if you are to gain recognition and not to be rated insane."

An active and efficient administrator, he took pleasure in "making things work". He certainly liked power but it was not power over people that he wanted but the power to put his ideas and plans into effect and then watch them run. This mechanic's interest in systems fitted with his anthropologist's interest in people and their institutions. In the machinations of College affairs he was neither autocratic nor devious and he knew how to delegate. With Provost Leach in the chair, College meetings were never dull affairs and at times became quite stormy as his emotions and exasperation let fly. An effective chairman, he expressed his own views forthrightly and expected others to do the same, canvassing round the table for different points of view and commenting silently on the proceedings with his virtuoso range of facial expressions. After meetings he would often issue his jovial invitation "come and have a drink". The drink was usually in the kitchen but it was his convivial nature and love of conversation, not kitchen politics, that took him there. It was in such ad hoc informal gatherings that his great warmth and humanity came to the fore.

As an observer, Edmund was fascinated by ceremony – ritual was a major focus of his anthropology – he was a keen reader of books on etiquette and the "ridiculous" ceremonials of College life provided him with an endless source of amusement. He was intrigued by the activities surrounding the conferral of his Knighthood in 1975 and delighted a student audience with an instant and perceptive analysis of the proceedings. But his hatred of all forms of insincerity, pretence, pomposity and sham made him reluctant and acutely uncomfortable as a participant, a reluctance that applied in particular to some of the trappings of organised religion. The nadir came each year on Founder's day with the laying of lilies and roses on the Chapel altar, a "preposterous ceremony . . . which belongs so obviously to the taste of the Kingsmen of 50 years ago."[9] His style

---

[9] I feel compelled to add a footnote to this, which illustrates Leach's anthropological interest in ritual and his own divided sentiments about himself participating in old rituals. His Lady Day Sermon at King's, later published as "Noah's Second Son" in *Anthropology Today*, vol. 4, no. 4, August 1988, was about race prejudice. But on the margins of the essay Leach reproduced excerpts from

added greatly to a new more informal atmosphere in the College but here, as everywhere in his life, he drew an idiosyncratic line, often hard for others to follow or understand, between a radical iconoclasm and "going too far".

The years of his Provostship coincided with his emergence as a man of public affairs, the holder of numerous appointments, and with a gradual transition from young Turk to an Establishment figure. As Chairman of its [the university's] Needs Committee he played an important role during his period on the General Board. A tough, independent and determined administrator with a good strategic mind, he championed the need for long term planning within the University and helped to push through a number of structural reforms, most notably the grouping of the Arts faculties into Inter-faculty Committees in line with the Sciences.[10]

Edmund retired from the Anthropology Department in 1978 and from the provostship the year after and became an elder statesman, full of wise council and ever ready to back and encourage new projects and initiatives. Apart from a truly splendid farewell feast in the Hall, marked by his memorable speech about himself as a "dying god," he went out of his way to avoid all forms of memorial, festschrift, and the like.[11]

We may now add some events and views to fill out Hugh-Jones's affectionate and tolerant account. I myself would like to refer to an episode. I had been elected a Fellow of King's in 1970 (I went there from Clare Hall), and soon afterwards also was appointed supervisor to the college's undergraduates in social anthropology, and tutor for graduate studies. It was possibly in 1971 that two doctoral students in anthropology by the name of Stephen Hugh-Jones and Peter Silverwood-Cope, both of whom had conducted fieldwork in South America, persuaded me that at the annual party for graduate students I was to host in the Fellows Garden a Rastafarian band should be engaged to provide the music. The Senior Tutor, Geoffrey Lloyd, had supported my request, and a nervous Provost had also been nudged to give his consent. During the open-air party in the afternoon, Edmund Leach ambled in on an unexpected visit, and was greatly relieved to discover that the party was orderly and that the Rastafarians, alleged to be members of a protest cult, were charming music makers. (Afterwards there was a late-night party in a cottage in the woods outside Cambridge which I was unable to attend, so I cannot report on what happened there.)

An Account of the Different Ceremonies Observed in the Senate House of the University of Cambridge by Adam Wall (1798) describing the events, including the order of the procession, observed on March 25, the foundation day (Lady Day) at King's College. The tradition we are told goes back to the seventeenth century.

[10] Hugh-Jones, "Edmund Leach" (Memoir), pp. 31–32.   [11] Ibid., p. 34.

Geoffrey Lloyd, the distinguished classicist and presently Master of Darwin College, was Senior Tutor at King's from 1969 to 1973. Earlier, when both Leach and Lloyd were Fellows (before holding the positions respectively of Provost and Senior Tutor), they had had cordial and fruitful intellectual exchanges, and Lloyd's book, *Polarity and Analogy*,[12] gave evidence of his incorporation of anthropological conceptions in his interpretation of Greek thought. As frequently happens, administrative work can be so demanding of time, energy, and patience that it can take its toll on leisurely exchange of knowledge; furthermore, academic bureaucratic roles can sometimes put serious strains on pre-existing friendships when the participants are strongly committed to their tasks as they conceive them.

In 1992 I requested Lloyd, by now President of Darwin (I had met him on several occasions since my leaving King's in 1973), to convey to me some of his memories and thoughts on his relationship with Leach during his provostship. He sent me this letter, saying, "This is all very impressionistic and for your eyes only, but maybe there will be something that you can use." I reproduce here the bulk of his letter.

I was convener of the Junior Caucus when we elected him and one of his staunchest backers. What he stood for was a real openness of spirit and readiness to rethink educational issues, as well as himself giving great intellectual leadership. But in practice he turned out to be far more the conventional academic administrator than I, for one, had expected. We carried through such policy changes as the inauguration of co-residency very smoothly. That issue had been discussed originally some five or six years before we finally took our decision, and the immediate pressure group that led to our finally making the change consisted in part of graduate students. But Edmund exercised a benign overview of the discussion and was very supportive.

On a number of occasions when relations were difficult between King's and other colleges, between the University and the town, between students and the police (the Garden House affair), Edmund was again very helpful.

But certainly from time to time, as he got into his provostship, the autocratic streak in him came out, and he certainly did not like bringing anything to a vote on the College Council if there was any chance of his being defeated.

Whilst I had been very happy to work with him in my first term of office as Senior Tutor, I had to take stock of my own position when it came to my reappointment, and I certainly thought it wiser to limit my commitments, given the way things were going. So I only accepted reappointment for a shorter term than would be normal. In part, because of what seemed to me to be

---

[12] Geoffrey E.R. Lloyd, *Polarity and Analogy: Two Types of Argumentation in Early Greek Thought*, Cambridge: Cambridge University Press, 1966.

the increasing inflexibility of Edmund as chairman of all the major College committees.

That also affected such little chance as I had to discuss intellectual matters with him. The excitement of my initial meeting with him when he introduced me to the work of Needham, Hertz and others was tremendous. But it became increasingly difficult to sustain our discussions on matters to do with the history of ideas or the methodology of the social sciences when in the thick of College politics. I expect, Tambi, the same has to be said rather of my relationship with you when you came to King's, and there we were in next door offices month in month out, but with hardly an opportunity to talk about Austin.[13]

When I had given up the tutorship things became easier between me and Edmund, but he was still pretty preoccupied with running the College, and the first flush of enthusiasm for the exchange of ideas when we first met was never really repeated. But I still read everything of his that I could lay my hands on and still discussed occasionally what was happening in social anthropology.

He was a truly great social anthropologist, and I count myself extremely fortunate to have known him personally – even if I also have to add that working closely with him in College was sometimes rather bumpy.

Let me describe what "the Garden House affair" that Lloyd was referring to was about. This well-known hotel, picturesquely overlooking the Cam and the summer-time boating parties, was hosting a tourist promotion on behalf of the Greek government, which at that time was controlled by the infamous and repressive Greek "colonels." The radical students at Cambridge staged a demonstration planned by the Communist Party in front of the hotel. A certain number of these demonstrators were from King's, and prominent among the leaders of the protest were two young dons, both economists, one from King's (Bob Rowthorn)[14] and the other from Queens' (a certain Mr. Singh). Some four policemen were posted at the entrance to the hotel, but the demonstrators, about two hundred strong, rushed to the back of the hotel, entered it, and overturned some furniture. The Cambridge police were immediately notified, and they came in force and arrested some six leaders of the demonstration. In due course the Proctors of the relevant colleges met with the police and secured the release of the arrested. Leach was actively supportive of the settlement with the police.

When I was on one of my visits to Cambridge in the mid-1990s to read the Leach papers, I ran into John Dunn, eminent Professor of Politics

---

[13] Lloyd is here referring to J.L. Austin, the Oxford linguistic philosopher.
[14] This account of the incident was given to me, some decades after it happened, by Bob Rowthorn himself during one of my visits to King's in the mid-1990s. The incident took place in either 1969 or 1970.

at Cambridge. He has been a long-time Fellow of King's, including the years when Leach served as Provost. On my request he gave me an informal oral account of his view of Leach's stewardship.

The early years of his provostship, when Edmund was finding his way, were also the time when the college's Student Union was vociferous that the college should terminate its accounts with Barclay's Bank, unless it divested itself of its investments in South Africa. The "junior members" of the college were volatile, even disorderly at this time, and Edmund was nervous, even "panicky," and concerned that nothing should happen to disrupt and destabilize the college.

Dunn reminisced that Edmund was a "large man" who could get very angry. Indeed he was famously involved in staging some shows of temper at Council meetings. But the positive side of this behavior was that Edmund was frank and up front and not devious, and this aspect of his conduct was appreciated in due course.

In retrospect, Edmund's reputation as Provost had been rising after his retirement. Noel Annan, his predecessor, had intellectual merits but was egocentric. Bernard Williams, Edmund's successor, was distant, even indirect, and fastidious, and was not really committed to King's as an institution. Edmund instantiated with great enthusiasm and energy his own commitment to the intellectual life. Until the very end, he vigorously engaged with, and was intrigued by, new ideas, and most importantly he envisaged the intellectual enterprise as the vocation of the college as a collectivity. Although he was not the founder of the college's Research Centre, he was actively involved in giving it purpose and direction.

It was for these achievements that he is being increasingly regarded as one of the most stimulating and notable Provosts of recent times. He had a great sense of what King's should be as an academic institution.

Adam Kuper's "An Interview with Edmund Leach" printed in *Current Anthropology*[15] was certainly unconventional, irreverent, and outspoken. It contains Leach's own account of how the vote on admission of women was successfully obtained. By way of leading up to it, let me report that Kuper reminded Leach that when Kuper was a research student at King's in 1962 "you were part of the opposition," not only within the Department of Archaeology and Anthropology but also at King's concerning the way that the college was then run; moreover, he was in opposition to what British anthropology then stood for. "It was therefore strange

---

[15] *Current Anthropology*, vol. 27, no. 4, August–October 1986, pp. 375–81. All following quotations are taken from this piece, especially pp. 381–82.

for me to see you become, later, in some way a successful Establishment figure."

Leach replied: "Well, it seems strange to me, too. But having won most of my battles I could hardly turn around and become the leader of the Counter-Reformation." Kuper countered that Leach is now perceived by a younger generation as an "archetypal Establishment figure," and that he personally was "astonished to find that in some circles you have come to be seen as a reactionary."

Now I will quote in full Leach's self-congratulatory and artful account of the campaign to admit women:

I don't find it so strange, there can be guile in these matters. Here in King's I am certainly seen as very conservative. It has already been forgotten that women became members of the College for the first time (after 525 years) while I was Provost. It is an interesting story.

To make the proposal plausible, we had to have allies. There was much backstage negotiation with our neighbours, Clare and Churchill. Both these colleges eventually first admitted women at the same time as King's. But they had problems. In Clare the Master was enthusiastic; at Churchill the Master was opposed. The Clare story was that the Old Guard dug up a retired fellow who had not been seen for 20 years. He turned up in a Bath chair and cast his vote against the admission of women. So they were back at square one.

We took things slowly and talked it out for a couple of years or perhaps more. The opposition were clearly in a minority, but we had to win by a two-thirds majority of the whole Governing Body (that is, all the Fellows, about 100 individuals). At the last minute, when I thought all was lost, the leader of the opposition got up and made a highly emotional speech to the effect that this was the most important vote that the College had faced during the last 500 years. He could see that his supporters were in a minority, so he asked them to change sides and let this historic decision go through on a unanimous vote. One splendid old boy refused to take that one and said he must abstain. So King's voted for the admission of women *nem. con.*!

That could only have happened in King's. But there was some anthropology in it, too. If I had not already begun to acquire the reputation of being much more conservative than my erratic predecessor, I doubt if we would have made it at all. I am no fisherman, but it was all rather like landing a salmon.

Hugh-Jones characterized Leach as a "shrewd administrator," active and efficient and taking pleasure in results. By and large this was so, and certain other Fellows when asked did agree, with the caveat that he did get what he wanted when he managed to keep his temper! He was seen as "unconventional" at times. I have been told by a member of the Council that Leach sometimes simply did not turn up at some meetings if the vote on a "disagreeable" item on the agenda might go against his deeply felt judgment. Outbursts of temper and absences may be unconventional but strategic dramatistic devices, and the use of them may have been part of his "guile" as administrator.

It is inevitable that there would be variant versions of the famous vote on the admission of women to King's. As I have reported before, the official College Minutes of the Congregation held in 1969 noted that the motion for the admission of women was carried almost unanimously with five noes and six abstentions. Leach, the famous explicator of variant renderings of the "same" myth according to the narrators' different interests and positionings, himself proudly claimed that the final vote was approved *nem. con.* This was an "inaccuracy" which has been repeated by some of his younger disciples such as Stephen Hugh-Jones and Caroline Humphreys, who became Fellows of the college some years after the event. I imagine if Leach had been confronted with the recorded Minutes, he would have genially admitted that such a momentous event with mythic possibilities might be reported in various ways by participants. The current Provost of King's, Patrick Bateson, who was present at the voting, gave me his version as follows. At the final discussion before voting Leach asked with some provocation "Isn't there ANYONE AGAINST?", and in not exactly spontaneous reply, there were five votes against. Bateson was almost accurate: he had not remembered the six abstentions. In 1996 when I happened to have tea with Tony Tanner, the renowned commentator on American literature, and some other Fellows who had been present at the voting, none of them could remember with certainty whether the vote was unanimous or whether there had been a few dissenters.

Leach voluntarily stepped down as Provost in 1979. I had myself heard that at the time of his election in 1966, he had stated that he did not think he would want to stay in office for more than ten years. This was in line with sentiments expressed in the Reith Lectures about the undesirability of old persons serving as administrative heads. He had only exceeded his original intention by two years. He was succeeded by the philosopher Bernard Williams.

At the Congregation of the college held in the Combination Room on Saturday, March 3, 1979, the vote of thanks proposed by the new Provost, and seconded by Professor Braithwaite, the venerable philosopher, was worded as follows: "that the thanks of the College be given to Sir Edmund Leach for the dedication which he has given to the College in the twelve years for which he has been Provost, for the imagination with which he has addressed its problems, and the understanding he has shown towards the members."

Leach did not aspire to be a High Table wit or a Combination Room sparkling raconteur. However, when he was comfortably relaxed he did recount funny episodes, and this one was related to Susan Drucker-Brown, who was granted an "interview" with him in April 1984.[16] Leach had stepped down as Provost some five years earlier and was Emeritus.

> I [Drucker-Brown] cycled up to King's wondering uncomfortably if I would be waiting long since I thought I was early by 5 minutes, but I could see his tall figure from a distance. He was wearing a white cloth tennis hat and didn't see me though I waved to him. He had said to meet on the "cobbles" but, as I got off my bike he said "You can leave your bike around at Webbs [Webb Court], there's some kind of gas works going on here," and I could see that the entrance to King's was more than usually cluttered. We walked down King's parade and I said I was unused to the vocabulary of "cobbles" and "Webbs" for parts of King's College. He laughed and said that the cobbles had been a point of great dispute when he first arrived at King's. The front of the college was paved with cobbles but they were very nasty ones ... large and rough and people were forever falling on them. Michael Jaffee [a Fellow who became Director of the Fitzwilliam Museum] presented a nice plan for repaving the front of King's with flags of slate. At which point a Fellow got up and made an impassioned speech ... it must have gone on for twenty minutes, about the infamy of replacing the sacred cobbles. If the college could not find the money he said, he and others would go down to the beach at Hunstanton and with their own hands they would bring back cobbles to repave the front of King's ...

Aside from his acts of generosity toward research students through the Esperanza Trust (of which more shortly), and from his own private funds, Leach made some gifts to King's. He transferred to the college his quite substantial house and garden at Storey's Way, and had willed half the proceeds of the sale of his valuable library for making long-overdue improvements to the library of the college.

I have earlier indicated how Edmund and Celia Leach lived a modest style of life, allowing themselves only occasional luxuries and pleasure trips. Leach had been personally distressed by the hardships suffered especially by the poor and the working class during the Depression. He found it hard to reconcile his wealth with his socialist preferences. As an undergraduate he had written to a friend with regard to his forebears: "by a process of exploitation that would not be even dreamed of by the most ambitious of present day industrialists, they proceeded

---

[16] I have referred to this interview in chapter 4. See footnote 3.

to amass very considerable fortunes at the expense of the unfortunate population of Lancashire."[17] This same unease, reflected in his modest lifestyle, accompanied him throughout his life. It also resulted in his quite extraordinary generosity. "He gave money to innumerable people and institutions without hesitation and without a backward thought if he felt so inclined."[18]

FELLOW AND PRESIDENT OF THE ROYAL ANTHROPOLOGICAL INSTITUTE

The Institute is very close to my heart. (Leach)

The following notice of Leach's passing away composed by Adrian C. Mayer appeared in *Anthropology Today*:

Professor Sir Edmund Leach, born in 1910, died in Cambridge on 6 January 1989. An Obituary will be published shortly in A.T.: but Fellows and Members of the Royal Anthropological Institute owe a special debt to Edmund which should be separately expressed.

From the time when he was first elected to the Council in 1946, Edmund was one of the most active supporters of the Institute, seeing the help he gave it as being part of his more general advocacy of anthropology in the world at large. During the late 1950s and 1960s, he took a leading part in moves to enlarge the Fellowship and reorganize the Institute's publications. But his greatest challenge came in 1971, when his Presidency coincided with the Institute's loss of its premises in Bedford Square and with a low point in its finances. It was characteristic of his commitment that he agreed to serve an extended four-year term, by the end of which the Institute's affairs had started to turn, under the long-term objectives set out by the Development Committee he had formed in 1972. Thereafter, Edmund continued as an active Vice-President, attending most Council meetings – at which his contributions were, as might be expected, imaginative and controversial as well as helpful.

It will be a cause of great satisfaction to his colleagues to know that he lived to see the Institute attain most of its objectives for which he had worked, often through the generous support of the Esperanza Trust, of which he was the donor and principal trustee. Without its help, the purchase of the Institute's premises would have been jeopardized, the development of A.T. put at risk, and many of its academic initiatives weakened. That the Institute has been able to respond

---

[17] Rosemary Firth, "A Cambridge Undergraduate: Some Early Letters from Edmund Leach," *Cambridge Anthropology. Special Issue: Sir Edmund Leach*, vol. 13, no. 3, 1989–90, p. 13.

[18] Hugh-Jones, "Edmund Leach" (Memoir).

to a changing world has to an important degree been due to Edmund's initiative and practical support.[19]

The RAI published (as its Occasional Paper no. 42) "a near-complete bibliography of his publications over the fifty years of his career, as a tribute to its former President and as a working tool for scholars ... The first item in the bibliography is a letter to *The Times* published in 1935 about reforms in China; the last (apart from posthumous publications) is an anonymous leaflet on the Great Windows of King's College Chapel, Cambridge, co-authored with the Dean of King's."[20] Among other things, the preface to the bibliography written by the then President of the RAI, Eric Sunderland, says: "he established and generously endowed the Esperanza Trust for Anthropological Research, and he continued to be intimately involved in its affairs, which included assisting in the purchase of the Institute's current premises, its launching and sustaining of *Anthropology Today*, and myriad other matters of concern to anthropology generally, under the umbrella of the RAI."[21]

At several points it has been mentioned how funds from the Esperanza Trust that Leach had set up were used to support research: the trust was named after the sugar factory, La Esperanza, on the estates of Hermanos Leach in the Argentinian province of Jujuy, and was funded from money Leach had inherited from its sale. A statement by the RAI says "According to the Founder's wish, the Trust gives unobtrusive support to the Institute's work in many ways as well as funding the Leach/RAI Fellowships."[22] As Mayer and Sunderland have already intimated Leach made other benefactions to the institute: a small collection of antique Chinese ceramics was given to it to auction; and he left half the proceeds of the sale of his valuable library to it. Leach effectively used his financial and administrative skills to help the institute regain its vitality. He also no less importantly vigorously urged and led the launch of, as a

---

[19] *Anthropology Today*, vol. 5, no. 1, February 1989, p. 1. The obituary written by Chris Fuller and Jonathan Parry, "Petulant Inconsistency? The Intellectual Achievement of Edmund Leach" was published in *Anthropology Today*, vol. 5, no. 3, June 1989, pp. 11–14.

[20] Publication notice of the RAI Distribution Centre, Letchworth. *The Great Windows of King's College Chapel, Cambridge*. Anonymous leaflet, coauthored by Edmund Leach and Rev. John Drury, published by King's College Chapel, 1988.

[21] Royal Anthropological Institute of Great Britain and Ireland, *Edmund Leach: A Bibliography*, Occasional Paper no. 42, 1990, p. 1.

[22] Edmund Leach served as Chair of the Esperanza Fund until his death. Audrey Richards was one of the trustees (among others), and after her retirement Jean la Fontaine replaced her. After Leach's death, La Fontaine became Chair.

supplement to the *Journal*, another publication, *Anthropology Today*, which would deal with contemporary issues and new intellectual and artistic pursuits that would appeal to a wider reading public than the professionals. He saw the relevance of giving more visibility to ongoing studies on race relations, refugee studies, studies of feminist issues, and ongoing efforts in visual anthropology, including the burst of ethnographic and other documentary films.

His own concern with the state of racial prejudice and race relations in Britain is reflected in "Noah's Second Son," a Lady Day Sermon at King's College, Cambridge, published in *Anthropology Today*.[23] The second son is of course Ham, whose descendants were condemned to be "servants of servants unto his brethren," also by extension "black" skinned. Leach condemns the notion that people can be sorted into exclusive "racial categories." Although he does refer critically to "apartheid" in South Africa, and other perhaps softer versions of it in India (the caste system), and in Israel where "racist prejudice" prevails, his main message is "let us worry about our own society" in Britain. Discussion of this issue is timely because "If 'race' is now a matter of public debate it is because things are changing rather than because they are standing still." The important changes taking place in Britain are linked with greater opportunities in education: "the many defects of our present system of attitudes are not immutable. If we fully understand that fact we must not be complacent but we need not despair."[24]

[23] *Anthropology Today*, vol. 4, no. 4, August 1988, pp. 2–5.   [24] Ibid., p. 5.

CHAPTER 19

Retirement, retrospection, and final illness

The creator is like a sinner, one who breaks rules.

Leach

Although he had relinquished his positions as Professor of Anthropology in 1978 and, a year later, as Provost of King's College, Leach continued to be active and productive until the beginning of August 1988 when he became very ill and never recovered.

Celia and Edmund went to live outside Cambridge in the village of Barrington. "The Birk" consisted of a simple cottage, and a functional study and compact library. Its marvelous feature was the large garden and orchard, and beyond them an acre of woods kept as a natural reserve. The entire property was about six acres in extent, and it was this ecological haven for birds and small animals, and the chance to keep it intact in the face of expanding urban "development," that had prompted the Leaches to acquire the property as their sanctuary for their retirement. There they lived a simple life, with modest furniture and no television, but surrounded by a collection of paintings, books, and newspapers, and, not to be left out, the dog, whom they both cared for as a companion. The evening meal was important, and the occasion for good food and good wine.

Celia had always been tall, beautiful, gracious, warm, and lively; while Edmund was absorbed in his intellectual work, Celia too had been creatively involved with her painting and her writing of novels. They relied on each other for many things. As Hugh-Jones puts it, "In Celia, a talented painter and writer, he found his complement and in her he found and admired the things that were missing or remained unexpressed in himself."[1] In his writings on several occasions Leach had conveyed his admiration for artists – painters, composers, and novelists – as having the

[1] Hugh-Jones, "Edmund Leach" (memoir).

capacity and sensibility and intuition to communicate human emotive truths, which anthropologists rarely match in their mode of ethnographic writing. Celia once told me that while he was certainly interested in her paintings and would comment on them, she did not think Edmund had read her novels. She in turn usually did not read Edmund's writings, except when occasionally he handed over some piece to her with a "have a look at this" request. But of course, given their common interests in art, architecture, visual representation, music, and nature's creatures, there was much conversational exchange.

In retirement, Leach remained quite busy until the end of 1988 not only attending seminars and meetings both in Cambridge and London, but also lecturing abroad especially in the United States. For example, in the fall of 1979 he, accompanied by Celia, spent a term at Cornell University as a Senior Fellow of the Andrew Dixon White Society for the Humanities, and visited a number of universities to give lectures (including Harvard). He contributed the position paper entitled "Past/Present: Continuity or Discontinuity" to the Second Annual Symposium on Historical Linguistics and Philology held at the University of Michigan, April 1982[2] and he contributed to the Harvey Lecture Series at the University of New Mexico (1983)[3] and the Patten Foundation Lectures at Indiana University (1984–85).[4] Earlier in 1983 Leach served as the President of XV Pacific Science Congress held at Dunedin, New Zealand, and delivered the address "Ocean of Opportunity."[5] In the same year, he participated as the discussant for a symposium entitled "Text, Play, Story," organized by The American Ethnological Society (February 11–14, 1983) in Baton Rouge, Louisiana. The symposium was planned to coincide with the Mardi Gras in New Orleans.[6]

A conference entitled "Symbolism Through Time" supported by the Wenner-Gren Foundation Anthropological Research was held in the

---

[2] This was published in the *Journal of Historical Linguistics and Philology*, vol. 1, no. 1, 1983, pp. 70–87.

[3] The lecture entitled "The Gatekeepers of Heaven: Anthropological Aspects of Grandiose Architecture" was published in the *Journal of Anthropological Research*, vol. 39, no. 3, Fall 1983, pp. 243–64.

[4] The titles of the two Patten lectures were "Semiotics, Ethnology, and the Limits of Human Understanding" and "Michelangelo's Genesis: A Structuralist Interpretation of the Central Panels of the Sistine Chapel" which was later published in *Semiotica*, vol. 56, nos. 1/2, December 1985, pp. 1–30.

[5] A revised version of this address was published in *Pacific Viewpoint*, vol. 24, no. 2, 1983, pp. 99–111.

[6] The proceedings were published as *Text, Play, Story: The Construction and Reconstruction of Self and Society*, Stuart Plattner (Proceedings Editor), and Edward B. Bruner (Editor and Symposium Organizer), Washington, D.C.: The American Ethnological Society, 1984. Edmund Leach's comments as discussant appear under the title "Conclusion: Further Thoughts on the Realm of Folly," pp. 356–64.

city of Fez, Morocco on January 13–20, 1986. Edmund Leach contributed a paper entitled "Aryan Invasions over Four Millennia," which was published in a volume edited by Emiko Ohnuki-Tierney, *Culture Through Time: Anthropological Approaches.*[7] The volume was posthumously dedicated by the editor "to Edmund Leach, a towering intellect and a modest man."

In this essay, in characteristically trenchant and debunking style Leach charges that the well-entrenched claim of the arrival of Indo-Aryan-speaking people and the spread of Indo-Aryan languages in India is a mythical fantasy for which there is not a shred of archaeological evidence. A whole array of famous philologists, ranging from William Jones and Max Muller to Dumezil, and archaeologists, such as Smart Piggott, Mortimer Wheeler and the Allchins, have no hard evidence for associating the alleged spread of Indo-Aryan languages with a massive invasion of Aryan people from the northwest in the second millennium BC.

This fantasy is a product of the theory of "unilineal segmentary history of language development" espoused by philologists. The mythology of Aryan invaders in the past fits in with the racist framework and dogma of British colonial imperialism whose elite administrators saw themselves as bringing "pure" civilization to a morally corrupt and decrepit India. Leach concludes disarmingly that of course no one is going to believe that the Aryan invasions never happened at all. (As an aside I may remark that Leach would have been ironically surprised, if he had followed Indian politics in his last years, that the advocates of resurgent Hindu nationalism in the 1980s and 1990s, especially organizations such as the Rashtriya Swayamsevak Sangh (RSS), the Vishwa Hindu Parishad (VHP), and the Bharatiya Janata Party (BJP), have declared that the Aryan invasion is an invented myth and that the Sanskrit language was produced indigenously and locally. The defining feature of India, they assert, is its Hindu culture, a doctrine that sees Muslims and Islam as foreign alien invaders. This counter-mythology has its own political purpose, and played a part in enabling the BJP to capture political power in the late 1990s.)[8]

Leach made his last visit to the United States to present "Masquerade: The Presentation of the Self in Holi-day Life" at the tenth anniversary

---

[7] Stanford: Stanford University Press, 1990. Leach's essay appears on pp. 227–45.

[8] See Christophe Jaffrelot, *The Hindu Nationalist Movement in India*, New York: Columbia University Press, 1996.

celebration of the Department of Anthropology at The Johns Hopkins University, and at Harvard University in April 1986.

A cursory look at the list of his publications after retirement between the years 1978 and 1988 as given in the Royal Anthropological Institute *Bibliography*[9] shows the enormous number of pieces he wrote especially in the form of book reviews, an activity he assiduously engaged in, and enjoyed, throughout his career. He was a voracious reader with a phenomenal memory.

In the last years of his life, Leach was engaged in an activity, even a pastime, which he obviously enjoyed. The man who cared not for a commemorative *festschrift* from his past students, his colleagues, and friends, who was embarrassed by praise and preferred argument, attempted to set the record straight about his social and family background, his career, his experiences as well as his prejudices, in a mode of writing and speaking that combined humor and irreverence, frankness and a near-breaking of academic etiquette. Informative, and in places unconventional, the essay "Glimpses of the Unmentionable in the History of British Social Anthropology" was written for the *Annual Review of Anthropology* (1984).[10] The "traditional" invitation by the *Review* to eminent professors *emeriti* and *emeritae* magisterially to reminisce about their careers was turned into an engrossing polemical and experimental exercise in the sociology of knowledge. (This text has been cited many times in this book, but its most innovative and controversial thesis concerning the link between the theorizing of some eminent anthropologists and their social class and nationality has yet to be discussed, in the following section.) In addition, Leach gave the long interview to Adam Kuper that was published in *Current Anthropology* (1986) under the title "An Interview with Edmund Leach."[11] All these biographical memories and reminiscences, reflexive commentary and tendentious confessions, are stories of the past by a narrator who knew only too well the mythic properties and ambiguities and contextual uses of "history." He also felt toward the end that "if contemporary ethnography is to have any 'bite' at all it must be at least partly autobiographical,"[12] a sentiment that accords with some postmodern trends.

[9] Royal Anthropological Institute, *Edmund Leach: A Bibliography*.
[10] Edmund Leach, "Glimpses of the Unmentionable in the History of British Social Anthropology," *Annual Review of Anthropology*, vol. 13, 1984, pp. 1–23.
[11] *Current Anthropology*, vol. 27, no. 4, August–October 1986, pp. 375–81.
[12] Leach in a letter to Tambiah dated May 13, 1986. This comment was made with regard to my own book *Sri Lanka: Ethnic Fratricide and the Dismantling of Democracy*, Chicago: University of Chicago Press, 1985.

THE IMPACT OF SOCIAL CLASS AND NATIONALITY
ON BRITISH ANTHROPOLOGY

In "Glimpses of the Unmentionable" (1984), writing as a retired senior practitioner on the theme of "anthropology in my time", Leach devoted a good part of the essay to the unusual theme of how "differences in social class played a crucial role in what happened in British anthropology during the first 40 years of this century."[13] He attempted to relate the anthropological writings of the major figures of his time in Britain to their biographical facts relating to national identity, social class origins, and the circumstances operating in the politics of British academia, especially Oxbridge and London. His frankness included the express recognition of his own upper-middle-class status and biases, and of the class and racial prejudices prevailing in Cambridge that hindered the acceptance of anthropology as a full-fledged discipline.

Coming from someone who had a firm commitment to empirical fieldwork, and who always upheld the value of studying "other" societies as a way of throwing light on our own, it may at first sight seem unexpected to be told that "the assumption that ethnographic 'facts' recorded by anthropological observers in the field have some kind of objective reality" was mistaken. The reverse was the case: "the data which derive from fieldwork are subjective not objective . . . every anthropological observer, no matter how well he/she has been trained, will see something that no other such observer can recognise, namely a kind of harmonious projection of the observer's own personality, and when these monographs are 'written-up' in monograph or any other form, the observer's personality will again distort any purported objectivity."[14] He further asserted that anthropological texts are interesting in themselves and not because they tell us about the external world. They can be real in two quite different ways. In the first case "text is text, just as the Bible is a text, interesting in itself because it is structured in discoverable ways, full of hidden meanings both intended and unintended."[15] But the text cannot be assumed to be corresponding to any kind of "reality."

"In the second case we can read a text with the set purpose of discovering *projections* of the author's personality, of finding a record of how he or she reacted to what was going on."[16] Some pages earlier, adumbrating the assertion that "the sociology of the environment of social anthropologists has a bearing on the history of social anthropology," he suggested

---

[13] Leach, "Glimpses of the Unmentionable," p. 2.
[14] Ibid., p. 22.   [15] Ibid., p. 22.   [16] Ibid., p. 22.

that, "Whatever they did or said as anthropologists was simply a '*structural/metaphoric transformation*' of what they did or said in quite nonanthropological contexts. There is a *continuity* in such matters and the particular style of an individual scholar's anthropology is meshed in with other aspects of his/her personality. Such *continuities are difficult* to demonstrate directly, but they sometimes show up in *unpredictable consistencies of behaviour*" (emphasis added).[17] He concluded this large interpretive proposition with this caution: "Unless we pay much closer attention than has been customary to the personal background of the authors of anthropological works, we shall miss out on most of what these texts are capable of telling us about the history of anthropology."[18]

What are we to make of this advocacy made by Leach at the end of his career? Deliberate inconsistency or a change of tack? There might be some overtones in this statement deriving from contemporary postmodern questioning of authorial claims to representational objectivity. Be that as it may, I think what he has done in pursuing this new line of inquiry is to "bracket" the issue of how ethnographic reports relate to "the reality out there" being studied. (His previous ethnographic writings had wrestled with that issue.) He now affirms his own structuralist perspective on pattern recognition in anthropological monographs as texts, and dialectically links that to the sociology of small local worlds – that is, how the biographical features of anthropologists and their perception of the social contexts in which they lived and worked had significant continuities with what they wrote.

This latter connection is what Leach called the unrecognized "nonsense" of the history of anthropology as opposed to its recognized official "sense," the "hidden" part he wanted to place on the agenda. The inveterate experimenter with perspectives was indulging in one final game. We note that Leach employs a host of words to label the nexus he explores, such as "projections," "structural/metaphoric transformations," "continuities," which are not exactly parallel or homologous, and do not in any case specify a clear procedure of interpretation. Nevertheless, it is my hypothesis that there is a subtext, or perhaps a not so "hidden" aspect to Leach's exercise, which is that he was using the small arena of British anthropology, at a certain period of time, also to situate himself, and by contrast to convey to the reader what might be the connections between his own life and times, his works and his achievements in academia and public life, and to what extent his own social

---

[17] Ibid., p. 3.   [18] Ibid., p. 22.

class origins and Englishness played a vital but usually "unmentioned" role.

Leach faults certain histories of the discipline such as Langham (1981) and Adam Kuper (1983)[19] for providing "only the barest minimum of information about the geographical, ethnic, family, and class background of the individual concerned. Nor is the reader given any feel of the major intellectual innovations of the period as they were generated by such contemporary titans as Bertrand Russell and Sigmund Freud."[20]

In the years 1900–36, British social anthropology revolved around events that took place within the triangle Oxford–Cambridge–London:

on such a minuscule stage the relation of actors to their social surrounding deserves close attention . . . very few of the leading characters [such as Malinowski, Firth, Fortes, Nadel] were born in the British Isles and fewer still belonged to that exclusive "upper and upper-middle" social class whose members were then alone in feeling themselves fully at home in the vacuous conservatism of Oxford and Cambridge Universities.[21]

Leach refers to two aristocracies in Britain in the period in question. One is the "titled aristocracy" listed in *Burke's Peerage* and *Burke's Landed Gentry*. The other is what Noel Annan has called "the intellectual aristocracy," the members of a small group of closely intermarried families who came to dominate the affairs of Oxford and Cambridge, especially the latter, from about the middle of the nineteenth century. They were the Darwins, the Huxleys, the Chadwicks, the Wedgwoods, mostly "upper middle class" in origin whose original affluence derived from the Industrial Revolution of the late eighteenth century. They tended to be evangelical in religious attitude.

The two kinds were not wholly distinct, but "the interests of the intellectual aristocrats who ruled the universities and the titled aristocrats who ruled the Empire were almost identical."[22] Leach said that he himself was not "an aristocrat of either variety."[23]

Now, the conventional story is that between 1898 and 1925 academic anthropology was triumphantly established in Cambridge, especially by Haddon and Rivers, but the real fact is that during this period "they

---

[19] Ian Langham, *The Building of British Social Anthropology: W.H.R. Rivers and His Cambridge Disciples in the Development of Kinship Studies, 1898–1931*, Studies in the History of Modern Science, vol. VIII, Dordrecht and Boston: D. Reidel, 1981; Adam Kuper, *Anthropology and Anthropologists: The Modern British School*, rev. edn London and Boston: Routledge & Kegan Paul, 1983.
[20] Leach, "Glimpses of the Unmentionable," pp. 2–3.
[21] Ibid., p. 3.   [22] Ibid., p. 4.
[23] Ibid., p. 7. Leach's family's wealth, as we have seen earlier, originated from the Lancashire mills of the nineteenth century, and he also belonged to the upper-middle-class stratum.

failed to establish anything at all."[24] No doubt Haddon was a Fellow of Christ's College and Rivers was elected to a fellowship tardily at St. John's College only in 1902. Although Rivers came to be highly respected in his college, he was not influential in university politics. The main reason for the marginality of these two men was their social class: they were not "gentlemen." Being not of gentry status, they carried little weight in university politics, and thereby failed to establish anthropology as a recognized mainline discipline. "Cambridge anthropology survived between 1900 and 1925 only because Haddon's marginal post was attached to the Museum of Archaeology and Ethnology."[25]

Leach sees the same fate as befalling Tylor in Oxford: he was not a "gentleman," and anthropology in Oxford was a non-subject. Leach states that what he says is not intended to belittle Rivers's considerable intellectual contributions to both anthropology and psychology:

My point is simply that any history of British developments in these fields needs to take into account not only the overwhelming dominance and academic prestige of Oxford and Cambridge but also the conservatism and social arrogance of those who were effectively in control of these two great institutions during the early part of this century. Haddon and Rivers were fighting to gain recognition in a most hostile environment and they were losing the battle.[26]

By contrast with Oxford and Cambridge, London presented a different situation. The London School of Economics was, in the 1920s and 1930s, considered an upstart "very low status institution." It was a platform for Fabian ideas. Edward Westermarck began to teach a rich combination of theoretical sociology and fieldwork-based social anthropology as early as 1904.

After that all the significant developments in social anthropology which occurred in Britain during the first quarter of this century were focused around the LSE. And, by feedback, the greater the successes of LSE anthropology [or for that matter, University College, London anthropology sponsored by Elliot Smith and W.J. Perry] the less likely it became that the conservative Establishment in Oxford and Cambridge would touch the subject with the end of a barge pole.[27]

After 1920 things began to change but only very slowly. From 1924 on almost all the Oxford and Cambridge graduates who, for one reason or another, found themselves interested in "social anthropology", migrated to London to sit at the feet of Bronislaw Malinowski. They included Edward Evans-Pritchard,

---

[24] Ibid., p. 4.   [25] Ibid., p. 6.   [26] Ibid., p. 6.   [27] Ibid., p. 6.

Camilla Wedgwood, Audrey Richards, Monica Hunter (later Wilson), and Gregory Bateson.[28]

Wedgwood, Richards, and Bateson belonged to the "intellectual aristocracy" and two of them were women, who could not come into their own at Cambridge. At this period Cambridge had an official policy of complete sexual segregation – there were two women's colleges, and women received separate degrees even though they took the same courses as men. It was to this Cambridge that Leach went as an undergraduate from 1929 to 1932, and his reaction to it, and more widely to the general political turmoil of that time, the General Strike of 1926, the onset of the Depression, and the ominous rise of Hitler's Nazism, has been dealt with in chapter 3.

Let us now make the leap to the 1950s and 60s, and review Leach's commentary on the social and national identities and situations of the prominent British social anthropologists of that time. I shall leave aside Evans-Pritchard for the moment.

With varying degrees of enthusiasm and varying degrees of success Malinowski, Firth, Schapera, Fortes, Nadel, and the other foreigners who were mainly responsible for the high prestige that was attributed to "British" social anthropology in the 1950s and 1960s . . . eventually assimilated themselves into the lifestyle and cultural conventions of Oxbridge academics, but they remained "outsiders" with a highly ambivalent attitude toward the values of their adopted academic milieu. This ambivalence is both reflected in and a reflection of their approach to the study of anthropology.[29]

> Meyer Fortes serves as an example. His basic social identity was that of the son of an impoverished South African Jew of Russian descent. Except for a period during the second World War when he returned to West Africa, Fortes was associated with the faculty of either Oxford or Cambridge from late 1939 until his retirement, and for the last thirty-one years of his life he lived in Cambridge as a Professorial Fellow (later Honorary Fellow) of King's College. When he arrived from Oxford in 1951, King's College was still a bastion of British upper-class values of the most archaic kind.

Although those values stood in glaring contrast to those to which Fortes was acculturated in his South African homeland, he gave the impression that he "venerated" King's and Cambridge. But it was the veneration of an outsider:

In relation to the College, he was, as he had been during his fieldwork in West Africa, an acute "participant observer". But fieldworking anthropologists do not

---

[28] Ibid., p. 8.   [29] Ibid., p. 11.

ordinarily seek to intervene in the affairs in which they participate; and so it was with Fortes in King's. He was much liked and respected by his colleagues, but he never played an active executive role in College affairs. Indeed, to a quite disconcerting extent, he never seemed to understand how the system really worked.[30]

Let us also leave Firth aside (he receives a special commentary[31]) and focus on Leach's point that the British-born anthropologists

were trying to get away from a homeland that they found archaic whereas "the 'foreigners' were looking for a new idealized homeland that would offer a kind of stable respectability which their own original homeland lacked. Schapera, Hunter, Fortes, and Gluckman were all from South Africa. Is it too fanciful to suggest that the prominence that several of these authors were later to give to the notion of homeostatic social equilibrium and to the belief that social structures persist even when there are drastic changes in cultural appearances derived from their personal need for a stable homeland?"[32]

Though "Glimpses of the Unmentionable" has an interesting sympathetic sketch of Firth's brief adaptation to Britain and his theoretical

---

[30] Ibid., p. 12.

[31] Ibid., pp. 12–13 where Leach gives this sketch: Firth was a New Zealander, and the country of his youth was not unstable and had "the merits of quiet provincialism," and its "values were egalitarian, do-it-yourself, rational . . . When Firth first came to England at the age of 23 he was clearly fascinated by the aesthetic resources of the metropolis and of Europe generally, but the irrational snobberies of the English upper-middle class must have seemed both alien and bizarre. Yet for the New Zealanders of that time Great Britain was still 'home'; a homeland of tradition." At the age of 82 (when Leach's essay "Glimpses of the Unmentionable" was published in 1984), Firth was the unchallenged "senior elder" among British social anthropologists.(Raymond Firth is still alive in year 2000.) Over the years his influence upon how the subject has developed has been immense, but it owes nothing whatever to any "Oxbridge" connection. Firth never involved himself in British national politics, but his general stance has been consistently that of a moderate conservative. As in his anthropology, he displays a formal interest in the way society changes over time but tends nevertheless to view such changes as superficial. Certainly he has never shown any enthusiasm for change for its own sake.

In academic argument he has been consistently skeptical about all forms of reductionist generalization. He has never allowed himself to use ethnographic detail simply to exemplify a proposition which he has arrived at by a priori reasoning; the argument grows out of the evidence which is presented in massive detail. The enthusiasm for "theory" isolated from empirical evidence which is often displayed by Oxbridge academics and by their Parisian counterparts arouses Firth's undisguised contempt. Here at least he shows himself a true follower of Malinowski. This is all of a piece with his private passion for Romanesque art and architecture, a style in which extreme intricacy of decorative detail is fitted to structures of almost brutal solidity and which stands in sharp contrast to the mathematical elegance of the gothic architecture of later centuries.

On the other hand, despite Firth's avoidance of the abstract rhetoric of national politics, he has been a lifelong do-it-yourself politician of quite another kind. He has consistently displayed a deep commitment to the preservation and development of the academic discipline of social anthropology, and his achievements in that area have been very remarkable. From the 1940s to the 1960s he had a wide variety of personal but quite informal ties with senior civil servants in key positions. He used these contacts with outstanding skill.

[32] Ibid., p. 12.

bent, and brief sketches of others such as Evans-Pritchard, Nadel, and Radcliffe-Brown,[33] the main point I want to highlight here is Leach's comparison of the backgrounds of "outsiders" and of "foreigners" like Fortes in particular (and certain others such as Gluckman and Schapera), and the concordance between the logic of their conservative adaptation to British academic institutions and their espousal of formal structural anthropology, with his own background as a British upper-middle-class "insider" whose reaction to his home society was more critical, and in parallel, whose anthropological theorizing was of a different, more dynamic kind. He was opposed particularly to the Radcliffe-Brown and Fortes type of highly abstract and jural concept of social structure in stable equilibrium, and countered their structural-functional typologies with his own versions, first of the dialectic between idealism (ideal categories of thought) and empiricism (actors' manipulative social uses of them to further their interests) in *Political Systems of Highland Burma* and *Pul Eliya*, and later of the dialectic between structuralism (patterned system of ideas in myth and ritual) and functionalism (the use by actors of their ambiguities, contradictions and possibilities to solve existential dilemmas) as in the analysis of biblical narratives.

Ultimately it seems as if Leach, by using a contrastive device, is trying to sum up his overall career in Cambridge as anthropologist and academic administrator. Earlier in the century, Rivers and Haddon, though academically respectable, had failed to establish firmly in Cambridge the discipline of anthropology, because of their being shut out of university politics because of their lower social class, non-gentleman status. Later in time, Fortes had been in double jeopardy – as foreigner and out of place in the Cambridge social hierarchy – and he had passively adjusted to it. He had not been active in running the university, and a sign of this in Leach's eyes was his inability at the beginning of Leach's own career at Cambridge to secure the promised fellowship at a college, and his less than prominent success in securing timely fellowships for other anthropologists.

Leach had begun his tenure at Cambridge in a somewhat ambiguous situation. By social class and by virtue of a renowned public school and

---

33 Leach, who disliked Radcliffe-Brown, slighted his pretensions to being "by lineage and upbringing an English country gentleman" with an assumed hyphenated name, and referred to his early education as having its start at the Royal Commercial Travellers School at Pinner in Middlesex. Leach in contrast recognized Evans-Pritchard as "a very English Englishman despite his Welsh name," educated at the ultra-prestigious Winchester and later at Oxford. He was a "true scholar." Although Evans-Pritchard was associated with Radcliffe-Brown earlier on, Leach considered that he had deviated later to follow different theoretical ideas.

a Cambridge undergraduate education he was an insider, eligible to find his way into the Establishment; but the discipline of anthropology had a somewhat depressed status, and he would have to prove its academic worthiness, which in time he did. His election to Provost of King's was a sign of his scholarly eligibility. His argument was that precisely *because* he was an insider, he could, up to a point, be emancipated from undue veneration for a Cambridge institution which dates from 1442; he could join others in reforming it from the inside – to admit women, to recruit less-privileged students from non-public schools, while conserving its meritorious past, and so on. And he had seen to it that King's would be a haven for anthropologists who were yet to become academic Brahmins.

These aspects of the presentation in "Glimpses of the Unmentionable" are ambivalently revealing. Leach in his public pronouncements and in his private life was fiercely anti-racist; he similarly deplored colonialism and exploitation of the poor, espoused humanist, socialist values, and supported the Labour Party. He abhorred conspicuous consumption and gave generously to those in need. He was an Establishment figure who appreciated the unconventionality of the intellectual aristocracy: he admired Gregory Bateson who had an impressive academic pedigree (his grandfather William Henry Bateson had been Master of St. John's College, Cambridge) as his image of an "Englishman's Englishman," and Gregory had renounced Cambridge.

However, Leach also knew that social class prejudices and inclusions/exclusions were an entrenched part of British social life. And he was also honest enough to recognize that social class mattered not only in general, but also to himself, for he was socialized into some of its preferences and prejudices. His unconventionality in "Glimpses of the Unmentionable" was facing up to implications of both dimensions for the history of anthropology in Britain and for the trajectory of his own career. As he put it on another occasion: "I cannot really imagine a social system in which there was no social class hierarchy; but social classes which are soft at the edges are to be preferred to those of race in which the edges are very hard."[34] He had done what he could to enable social mobility, to widen the doors of opportunity, and to make Cambridge life more egalitarian.

I find it difficult to give a commentary on Leach's provocative statements on the sensitive issues of class and country of origin. One of the

---

[34] Leach, "Noah's Second Son," p. 5.

dictionary glosses of a gentleman is that he is "a man of good birth or high social standing," which seems to be the sense in which Leach is using the word. Firth has remarked to me that Rivers seems to him a respectable name. A disciple, close friend, and admirer of Fortes, Susan Drucker-Brown has vigorously objected in a personal communication to me (dated March 17, 1997) that Leach was inaccurate in stating that Fortes's " 'primary social identity' was that of an impoverished South African Jew of Russian descent."[35] And Leach himself, who had a difficult time obtaining a college fellowship, narrated in his favor that as an insider he had with ease "climbed the wall between Clare and King's."

Leach's "Glimpses of the Unmentionable," touching on sensitive issues of class and nationality within British academia, was received, as might be expected, with mixed emotions by his peers. However, I have also personally heard remarks in admiration of his innovative venture into a tabooed but nevertheless important issue in British academic and social life. He no doubt wanted to provoke and expected the reactions he received, but must have felt it as therapeutic that the controversial hidden issues he had raised should be debated in the open.

That Leach was in all probability correct that constraining anti-Semitic and anti-feminist prejudices were prevalent among some of the ruling conservative dons of the Cambridge Establishment of the 1940s is attested by an oral account given to George W. Stocking, the noted historian of anthropology in both Britain and the United States, by no less a person than Evans-Pritchard, a sparkling raconteur of somewhat embellished narratives. Anthropology at Cambridge gave promise of a more theory- and research-oriented future in 1945 when Hutton was able to get Evans-Pritchard released from military service to accept what turned out to be a one-year appointment as Reader in Anthropology. To quote

[35] Susan Drucker-Brown says that Fortes's father was a Russian Jew, and that Meyer was born in South Africa. Meyer arrived in London, aged 21, in 1927, and lived in Bloomsbury, London, for about ten years and taught at the LSE before the war; he also had worked at Emmanuel Miller's child guidance clinic. He moved to Oxford with his wife Sonia and child Natalie at the end of 1939. Susan says that he was "far more identified with London than with Oxford, certainly until E-P moved there." He became a British citizen only after he took the chair at Cambridge. The "Oxbridge" demeanor of Meyer was probably a late construction. Godfrey Lienhardt had told Susan (for what it is worth) that Meyer's accent was not British until he came to Cambridge. Susan says it was "unfair of Edmund to play down the radical element in Meyer's life and work," which he actually did appreciate and admire. She also points out that Meyer was, like Leach, a life-long member of the Society of Humanists, and that he was non-observant, and it was only after Sonia's death that he attended the synagogue on Yom Kippur. For an informative portrait of Meyer Fortes (1906–83) see Jack Goody's 1991 memoir in the *Proceedings of the British Academy*, vol. 80, pp. 275–287, entitled "1991 Lectures and Memoirs."

from Stocking, who relates Evans-Pritchard's account of a critical and diagnostic event:

Four years later, it was Evans-Pritchard, as one of the external electors for Hutton's successor, who played a key role in winning Cambridge for social anthropology. He and the other Oxford elector, T.K. Penniman, along with the Vice-Chancellor (who by tradition was expected to vote with the external electors), favored the candidacy of Meyer Fortes against Fürer-Haimendorf, who was Hutton's choice. Fortes, however, was opposed by three of the four internal electors, for what Evans-Pritchard recalled as anti-Semitic reasons, with the fourth, the psychologist F.C. Barlett, remaining undecided. At one point Evans-Pritchard was asked to leave the room, and was told upon his return that the board was unanimous in proposing him. When he refused, they thought of Audrey Richards, but she had been previously discouraged from applying because the Disney Professor of Archaeology was a woman, and having two women in the same field was felt to be impossible. With Bartlett's support, Fortes was finally elected by one vote, and a generation after Hodson's choice had saved Cambridge from diffusionist extremists, it was finally won for social anthropology.[36]

ILLNESS

Already in the early 1970s when I was still in Cambridge, Leach was bothered by some skin eruptions on his head. They gradually worsened and developed into a skin cancer. The disease must have had its beginnings during his wartime travels in Upper Burma. Celia once remarked that the horrendous, exposed, wearing seven-week march from Upper Burma to Kunming in China might have taken its toll.

Though bothersome, the skin cancer did not slow down Leach during his active years, but by 1984 he had undergone surgical treatment: a plate-like disc was visible on his head "under which his hair, still not all gray, [grew] over his brow in a rather boyish thatch."[37] He wore a white cloth hat on the street, and had begun to use a hearing aid. A battered academic soldier, he still had unfinished business at hand as we saw earlier. Other medical interventions followed. "Though inwardly shaken and worried, outwardly he brushed aside the humiliation of disfigurement and pain of treatment with wit and cheerfulness, even reappearing after one particularly gruelling operation to announce with a proud grin 'look I've been remodelled.' "[38]

---

[36] George W. Stocking, *After Tylor: British Social Anthropology, 1888–1951*, Madison: University of Wisconsin Press, 1995, p. 431. The Hodson referred to is T.C. Hodson who was appointed to the readership in 1926, and retired in 1936, being succeeded by J.H. Hutton.
[37] Susan Drucker-Brown interview with Tambiah, 1984.
[38] Hugh-Jones, "Edmund Leach" (memoir), p. 38.

By early 1986 his debilitating skin cancer had reached a danger-ous and painful level. But that did not keep him from traveling to the United States in order to attend the celebration of the tenth an-niversary of the Department of Anthropology at The Johns Hopkins University which, at the invitation of Sidney Mintz in 1976, he had to help launch. Leach sent me copies of two of his letters to Sid Mintz, after I had, with Mintz's connivance, persuaded Leach to visit Harvard after Baltimore.

Here are excerpts from the letter of February 17, 1986.

I gather that Tambi and you have been involved in a plot. Having firmly said that I *must* return home direct from Baltimore and declined an invitation to New York accordingly, I find that one way or another my schedule seems to be taking me to Boston.

I am not in good shape medically. I have skin cancer on my face which has been treated at intervals both by radiation and skin grafting over a number of years. It looks as if I shall have to go into hospital for another graft next month. My medical adviser assured me this morning this *ought* not to prejudice my trip to the States, – apart from having a bandage round my head. But the surgeon might take a different view. This makes things difficult. I shall be seeing the surgeon and the radiation expert together on February 28th. I will then report immediately on where I stand.

I have been working on my theme ["The Presentation of the Self in Holi-Day Life"] for some time and I have a pretty clear idea about what I want to say but the effectiveness will depend on getting the right slides. There may be some snags in this regard. As I suggested six months back it would be an advantage if there were two slide projectors displaying images side by side so as to make direct visual comparison. But if that is difficult it is not essential.

On March 1, 1986 Leach wrote again:

My head is a mess but the skin graft surgeon proposes to leave it alone lest worse befall. It looks ugly and is sometimes painful but the alternative is a fairly major operation which would keep me in hospital for a month and might not work anyway. I see the radiation man again at the end of this month but, provided there has been no major deterioration (which is not expected), he is not likely to propose further treatment for the time being.

This leaves me free to come to the States. Please process my travel arrange-ments accordingly.

I have not yet completed my lecture. It is turning out different from what I had originally planned though the title is O.K. There will be a lot of pictures (normal 35mm slides) but I have difficulty about getting hold of some of them and that raises problems. I think I originally told you I would need two projectors, side by side. That will be unnecessary but I would like to have a projector where I operate the thing myself from the rostrum pressing buttons to go forwards and backwards.

Greetings to everyone. Many apologies for being so hesitant.

In April 1986, having given his lecture at Baltimore, Leach arrived in Cambridge, Massachusetts. His head was heavily bandaged, and he was obviously very tired, and visibly ill. (I had not realized that he had been subject to taxing radiation treatment.) His public lecture given on April 19 was as usual well attended: with great strength of will he gave "Masquerade: The Presentation of the Self in Holi-Day Life" and showed the numerous slides that went with it. Fortunately he had sent me an advance copy, and it became possible to publish the text of this innovative and experimental effort in visual anthropology posthumously in *Cambridge Anthropology*.[39]

Tired and ill as he was, he nevertheless spent most of the following afternoon meeting and informally conversing with the graduate students I had assembled to meet him. He talked with students individually. After food and drinks, we sat around him, and for quite some time he answered questions raised by the students concerning his writings and his experiences. Students later spontaneously remarked to me how accessible and genuinely interested in their progress he was.[40]

Leach left Cambridge, Massachusetts, for England on April 22. I later received this gracious letter from him dated 13 May 1986:

This is weeks overdue but perhaps there are extenuating circumstances. As must have been all too obvious my private Chernobyl disaster was causing me a lot of pain and nausea throughout the time that I was in Cambridge (Mass.) and as things since then have got worse rather than better it has been difficult to get down to writing letters.

The medical team who are looking after me here in Cambridge (Eng.) are probably the best in the country and they seem to be cautiously confident that they will get things under control before long but meanwhile it is all very depressing!

I am immensely grateful for the warmth of your hospitality; not just from you and Mary Wynne but from everyone whom I met, both old acquaintances and new. I enjoyed myself even as I was a wet blanket to others!

I admire the moral courage that lies behind your book on the Sri Lankan Tamil disaster.[41] It confirms my feeling that if contemporary ethnography is to

---

[39] *Cambridge Anthropology. Special Issue: Sir Edmund Leach*, vol. 13, no. 3, 1989–90, pp. 47–69.

[40] Professor Arthur Kleinman told me recently that in 1976 Leach had visited the University of Washington in Seattle, and he had been greatly impressed with the manner in which Leach, at the reception after his lecture, engaged with the students and talked with them individually.

[41] Leach was referring to my book *Sri Lanka: Ethnic Fratricide and the Dismantling of Democracy*.

have any "bite" at all it must be at least partially autobiographical. I hope it gets properly reviewed by someone who understands what is at issue.

Greetings to you all; and thanks again. Special messages of greeting not only from Celia but also from Susan Drucker-Brown whom I ran into on the street yesterday.

I did not see him again until August 1988 when I visited him at Barrington on a late morning. Stephen Gudeman, his former student, a personal friend, and a trustee of the Esperanza Fund was also there. Leach's health had taken a very serious turn, and it was clear that the end was near. It was not only the skin cancer any more. He had developed an inoperable tumor on the brain, and this was a cruel and dispiriting blow to him:

Edmund, who had set a supreme importance on communication, was now unable to read and write and had to struggle hard to express himself at all. Yet even here his bravery shone through – to do as he did and take delight in the fact that, in struggling to speak, he made the same classic metaphoric and metonymic displacements of which his hero Jakobson had written required considerable guts. He was indeed a very courageous man.[42]

When Gudeman and I saw him, Leach was not in a mood or in a state to communicate. He was diminished both physically and mentally and we could only sit and watch in misery as he sat in a wheelchair with a rug draped over his legs. Celia later told me that he had been much frustrated by his slowing down; I can't remember the exact words, but they were to the effect that "his computer broke down just as Edmund was winding down." (He had held on to an old model computer for many years and had repeatedly fixed it.)

I had planned to visit Edmund again in mid-January 1989, one last time. But news reached me in the States from Celia, via Stephen Hugh-Jones, that he was fast sinking and would not last until my intended visit. So I immediately left for Cambridge on December 30, 1988. Stephen and Christine Hugh-Jones had visited Edmund on the previous evening, and had told him that I was on my way. He had asked: "Tomorrow?", one of the very few words he had spoken, when Stephen and Christine took their leave:

When we knew he had only a short time to live my wife and I went to say goodbye to him. Holding his hand, Christine said to him "Edmund, you have

---

[42] Hugh-Jones, "Edmund Leach" (memoir), pp. 38–39. Stephen is here referring to Roman Jakobson's famous essay "Two Aspects of Language and Two Types of Aphasic Disturbance" in R. Jakobson and M. Halle, *Fundamentals of Language*, The Hague: Mouton, 1956.

been very important to us both." He looked at us with those ever mobile and very expressive eyes of his and said just one word. "Why?" We came away with tears in our eyes, laughing with delight at the subtlety of a simple question, so typical of him and which condensed so much of himself.[43]

For about a week Edmund had been cared for at a hospice called Arthur Rank House on Mill Road, Cambridge. It was a long vigil for his family. On New Year's Day January 1, 1989, I went to see Edmund in the company of Celia and Alexander who had come from Australia to see his father. Edmund was unable to talk. He gave me three or four sidelong glances in recognition, and he nodded his head to Celia when I said Mary Wynne (my wife) sent him her love. We sat around him, and Alexander peeled a mandarin orange and fed Edmund a few sections, and in a spontaneous act of commensality, we also ate a section each. A silent last communion in which by chance I had been included. (Louisa Brown, their daughter, was at that moment driving up to Cambridge from London.)

When I next visited Edmund on the afternoon of January 3, a doctor and attending nurses informed me that he was under sedation – he had been given morphine to ease the pain – and that he should be able to sleep comfortably. I was alone in his room, and I sat and watched him for quite some time. The large head and face that I knew were shrunken and held under a taut skin. He would no more open his eyes or wake up from his induced sleep. Then I looked at his hands. They were the same as they always had been, large muscular hands with long, big fingers: the engineer's hands that tinkered with machines and did many odd jobs around the house and garden, the right hand that wrote so many letters and comments in a bold, angular script, the hands that worked long hours on the computer. I felt those hands; they were warm, and they seemed to retain their vitality even in death.

Then Celia and Louisa arrived, and we simply sat and watched him. I returned to the States the next day.

Edmund Leach passed away two days later. He had not wanted a memorial service for the same reason he had not wanted a *festschrift* to commemorate his retirement in 1978. But there was a funeral service at King's College Chapel at which the college's famed angelic choir sang for him:

Edmund died on Twelfth Night, Friday the 6th of January in his 79th year. His funeral in the Chapel he loved was a dignified and grand affair, just the kind of

---

[43] Hugh-Jones, "Edmund Leach" (memoir), p. 38.

occasion that he, in life, would have loved to observe, the very stuff of ceremony. His shrewd anthropologist's eye would not have missed the fact that his death coincided both with the winter solstice and with the death of Emperor Hirohito, an Asian god-king.[44]

The high points of the service, besides the singing of the choir, were "the Address," given by Stephen Hugh-Jones, and the reading by John Rylands of John Donne's poem:

> Death, be not proud, though some have called thee
> Mighty and dreadful, for thou art not so;
> For those whom thou think'st thou dost overthrow
> Die not, poor Death, not yet canst thou kill me.
> . . .
> One short sleep past we wake eternally,
> And Death shall be no more. Death, thou shalt die.

A friend of mine who had attended the service wrote to me: "The funeral was sad but consoling, and Stephen's speech was beautifully delivered as was the John Donne sonnet, which was recited in a magnificent baritone voice by an aged don who walked with a cane but apparently had been an actor in his youth."[45]

At the end of the service, there was a solemn and moving procession from the chapel, round the front court to the gateway, in this order (which Leach would have anticipated): coffin, family, Provost, Vice-Provost, participants in the service, and Fellows in significant order. An observer noted that above the buildings the setting sun and rising full moon coincided. I would add that if there had been a sudden shower of rain, and if an arching rainbow had appeared over King's Chapel, the ending would have been perfect.

After the cremation, tea was served in the College Hall to all the guests.

---

[44] Ibid., p. 39 (memoir).
[45] Susan Drucker-Brown to the author in a letter dated January 19, 1989.

Bibliography

Abrahams, Ray. "Edmund Leach: Some Early Memories," *Cambridge Anthropology. Special Issue: Sir Edmund Leach*, vol. 13, no. 3, 1989–90, pp. 19–30.

Anderson, Benedict. *Imagined Communities*, rev. edn (London and New York: Verso), 1991.

Annan, Noel. *Our Age: Portrait of a Generation* (London: Weidenfeld & Nicolson), 1990.

Asad, Talal (ed.). *Anthropology and the Colonial Encounter* (London: Ithaca Press), 1973.

"Introduction," in *Anthropology and the Colonial Encounter* (London: Ithaca Press), 1973.

Austen, Leo W. "Procreation among the Trobriand Islanders," *Oceania*, vol. 5, 1934, pp. 102–13.

Bateson, Gregory. *Naven* (Cambridge: Cambridge University Press), 1936.

Benedict, Paul K. "Thai, Kadai and Indonesian: A New Alignment in Southeastern Asia," *American Anthropologist*, vol. 44, 1942, pp. 578–601.

Austro-Thai Language and Culture, with a Glossary of Roots (New Haven: HRAF Press), 1975.

Benedict, Ruth. *The Chrysanthemum and the Sword: Patterns of Japanese Culture* (Boston: Houghton Mifflin), 1946.

Berndt, R.M. (ed.). "Anthropological Research in British Colonies: Some Personal Accounts," special issue of *Anthropological Forum*, vol. 4, no. 2, 1977.

Bloch, Marc. *Feudal Society*, trans. L.A. Manyon (Chicago: The University of Chicago Press), 1963.

Bourdieu, Pierre. *Esquisse d'une théorie de la pratique, précédé de trois études d'ethnologie kabyle* (Geneva: Librarie Droz), 1972.

Outline of a Theory of Practice, trans. R. Nice (Cambridge: Cambridge University Press), 1977.

Brohier, R.L. *Ancient Irrigation Works in Ceylon* (Colombo: Government Publications Bureau), 1934.

Calverton, F.C. and S.D. Schmalhausen. *Sex in Civilization* (London: G. Allen & Unwin), 1929.

Cambridge Anthropology. Special Issue: Sir Edmund Leach, vol. 13, no. 3, 1989–90.

Chamberlain, James R. "A Critical Framework for the Study of Thao Houng or Cheuang," paper presented at the First International Conference on the Literary, Historical, and Cultural Aspects of the Thao Hung Thao Chueang, Bangkok, January 18–19, 1996.

Clifford, James. "On Ethnographic Authority," *Representations*, vol. 1, Spring 1983.

The Predicament of Culture: Twentieth-Century Ethnography, Literature, and Art (Cambridge, MA: Harvard University Press), 1988.

Clifford, James and George Marcus. *Writing Culture: The Poetics and Politics of Ethnography* (Berkeley: University of California Press), 1986.

Codrington, H.W. *Ancient Land Tenure and Revenue in Ceylon* (Colombo: Ceylon Government Press), 1938.

Cohn, Bernard S. "Review of *Pul Eliya: A Village in Ceylon*," *Journal of the American Oriental Society*, vol. 82, no. 1, 1962.

Anthropologist Among the Historians and Other Essays (Princeton: Princeton University Press), 1988.

Colonialism and Its Forms of Knowledge: The British in India (Princeton, Princeton University Press), 1996.

Cohn, Norman. *The Pursuit of the Millennium* (London: Secker & Warburg), 1957.

"Medieval Millenarism: Its Bearing on the Comparative Study of Millenarian Movements," in S.L. Thrupp (ed.), *Millennial Dreams in Action* (The Hague: Mouton), 1962.

Colonial Social Science Research Council. *First Annual Report 1944/45*.

Deng, Francis M. *The Dinka of the Sudan* (New York: Holt, Rinehart & Winston), 1972.

Dirks, Nicholas B. "The Invention of Caste: Civil Society in Colonial India," *Social Analysis*, vol. 25, Autumn 1989, pp. 42–52.

"Castes of Mind," *Representations*, no. 37, Winter 1992, pp. 56–78.

Dixon, R.M.W. "Virgin Birth Correspondence," *Man* (n.s.), vol. 3, no. 4, 1968, pp. 652–54.

Douglas, Mary. *Purity and Danger: An Analysis of Concepts of Pollution and Taboo* (London: Routledge & Kegan Paul), 1966.

Implicit Meanings: Essays in Anthropology (London and Boston: Routledge & Kegan Paul), 1975.

Drucker-Brown, Susan. Transcript of interview with Edmund Leach.

Dyen, Isidore. "Comment," in Appendix to Edmund Leach, "Frontiers of 'Burma,'" *Comparative Studies in Society and History*, vol. 3, no. 1, 1960, pp. 69–71.

Edney, Matthew H. *Mapping an Empire: The Geographical Construction of British India, 1765–1843* (Chicago: The University of Chicago Press), 1997.

Embree, Ainslie I. *Imagining India: Essays on Indian History* (Delhi and New York: Oxford University Press), 1989.

Epigraphia Zeylanica (Colombo: Printed at the Dept. of Govt. Printing, Sri Lanka [Ceylon] for the Archeological Dept.), 1933.

Evans-Pritchard, E.E. *The Nuer: A Description of the Modes of Livelihood and Political Institutions of a Nilotic People* (Oxford: Clarendon Press), 1940.

Fabian, Johannes. *Time and the Other: How Anthropology Makes Its Object* (New York: Columbia University Press), 1983.

Farmer, B.H. *Pioneer Peasant Colonisation in Ceylon: A Study in Asian Agrarian Problems* (London and New York: Oxford University Press), 1957.

Firth, Raymond. "Marriage and the Classificatory System of Relationship," *Journal of the Royal Anthropological Institute*, vol. 60, 1930, pp. 235–68.

We, the Tikopia: A Sociological Study of Kinship in Primitive Polynesia (New York: American Book Co.), 1936.

Malay Fishermen: Their Peasant Economy (London: K. Paul, Trench, Trubner & Co.), 1946.

Elements of Social Organization (London: Watts), 1951. The Josiah Mason Lectures, 1947; also published New York: Philosophical Library, 1951.

(ed.) *Man and Culture: An Evaluation of the World of Bronislaw Malinowski* (London: Routledge & Kegan Paul), 1957.

"Whose Frame of Reference? One Anthropologist's Experience," in R.M. Berndt (ed.), "Anthropological Research in the British Colonies: Some Personal Accounts," special issue of *Anthropological Forum*, vol. 4, no. 2, 1977, pp. 145–67.

Firth, Rosemary. "A Cambridge Undergraduate: Some Early Letters from Edmund Leach," *Cambridge Anthropology. Special Issue: Sir Edmund Leach*, vol. 13, no. 3, 1989–90, pp. 9–18.

"Biographical Sketch of Sir Edmund Ronald Leach (1910–1989)," in C.S. Nicholas (ed.), *The Dictionary of National Biography* (Oxford: Oxford University Press), 1986–1990.

Fortes, Meyer. *The Dynamics of Clanship Among the Tallensi: Being the First Part of an Analysis of the Social Structure of a Trans-Volta Tribe* (London and New York: Oxford University Press for the International African Institute), 1945.

Social Structure: Studies Presented to A.R. Radcliffe-Brown (Oxford: Clarendon Press, 1949.

"The Structure of Unilineal Descent Groups," *American Anthropologist*, vol. 55, 1953, pp. 17–41.

Kinship and the Social Order: The Legacy of Lewis Henry Morgan (Chicago: Aldine), 1969.

Fortune, Reo F. *Sorcerers of Dobu: The Social Anthropology of the Dobu Islanders of the Western Pacific*, rev. edn (London: Routledge & Kegan Paul), 1963.

Foucault, Michel. *Madness and Civilization: A History of Insanity in the Age of Reason*, trans. R. Howard (London: Tavistock Publications), 1971.

The Birth of the Clinic: An Archaeology of Medical Perception, trans. A.M. Sheridan Smith (New York: Pantheon Books), 1973.

Discipline and Punish: The Birth of the Prison, trans. A. Sheridan (New York: Vintage Books), 1979.

Fox, R. *Kinship and Marriage: An Anthropological Perspective* (Harmondsworth: Penguin), 1967. Also published by Cambridge University Press, 1983.

Freud, Sigmund. *Totem and Taboo: Resemblances between the Psychic Lives of Savages and Neurotics* (New York: Moffat, Yard & Co.), 1918.

Fuller, Chris and Jonathan Parry. "Petulant Inconsistency? The Intellectual Achievement of Edmund Leach," *Anthropology Today*, vol. 5, no. 3, June 1989, pp. 11–14.

Geertz, Clifford. "Religion as a Cultural System," in Michael Banton (ed.), *Anthropological Approaches to the Study of Religion*, Association for Social Anthropology Monograph 3 (London: Tavistock Publications), 1966, pp. 1–46.

The Interpretation of Cultures: Selected Essays (New York: Basic Books), 1973.

Geiger, Wilhelm (trans.). *Cūlavamsa* (2 vols., Colombo: Ceylon Government Information Department), 1953.

(ed.) *The Mahāvamsa* (London: Luzac for the Pali Text Society), 1958.

Gellner, Ernest. "Time and Theory in Social Anthropology," *Mind* (n.s.), vol. 67, no. 266, April 1958.

Gilhodes, C. *The Kachins: Religion and Customs* (Calcutta: Catholic Orphan Press), 1922.

Girling, F.K. *The Acholi of Uganda*, Colonial Research Studies no. 30 (London: HMSO), 1960.

Goody, John R. "A Comparative Approach to Incest and Adultery," *British Journal of Sociology*, vol. 7, no. 4, 1956, pp. 286–305.

The Developmental Cycle in Domestic Groups, Cambridge Papers in Social Anthropology no. 1 (Cambridge: University Press for the Dept. of Archaeology and Anthropology), 1958.

"1991 Lectures and Memoirs," *Proceedings of the British Academy*, vol. 80, 1991, pp. 275–87.

The Expansive Moment: The Rise of Social Anthropology in Britain and Africa 1918–1970 (Cambridge and New York: Cambridge University Press), 1995.

Gough, Kathleen E. "Female Initiation Rites on the Malabar Coast," *Journal of the Royal Anthropological Institute*, vol. 85, 1955, pp. 45–80.

"Anthropology: Child of Imperialism," *Monthly Review*, vol. 19, no. 11, 1968.

Grimshaw, Anna. "A Runaway World? Anthropology as a Public Debate," *Cambridge Anthropology*, vol. 13, no. 3, 1989–90, pp. 75–79.

Guha, Ranajit. "The Prose of Counter-Insurgency," in Ranajit Guha and Gayatri Chakravorty Spivak (eds.), *Selected Subaltern Studies* (New York: Oxford University Press), 1988.

Gunawardana, R.A.L.H. "Irrigation and Hydraulic Society in Early Medieval Ceylon," *Past and Present*, vol. 53, November 1971, pp. 3–27.

Robe and Plough: Monasticism and Economic Interest in Early Medieval Sri Lanka (Tucson: University of Arizona Press for the Association for Asian Studies), 1979.

Habermas, Jürgen. *Towards a Rational Society*, trans. Jeremy J. Shapiro (London: Heinemann), 1971.

Habib, Irfan. *The Agrarian System of Mughal India, 1556–1707* (Bombay and New York: Asia Publishing House for the Dept. of History, Aligarh Muslim University), 1963.

Hall, D.G.E. *A History of South-East Asia* (Londan: Macmillan, and New York: St. Martin's Press), 1955.

Harvey, David. *The Condition of Postmodernity: An Enquiry into the Origins of Cultural Change* (Oxford and Cambridge, MA: Basil Blackwell), 1989.

Head, W.R. *Handbook of the Haka Chin Customs* ([S.I.]: Ministry of Chin Affairs, Government of the Union of Burma), 1955.

Hill, Christopher. *The World Turned Upside Down: Radical Ideas during the English Revolution* (London: Temple Smith), 1972.

Hocart, A.M. *The Temple of the Tooth in Kandy*, Memoirs of the Archaeological Survey of Ceylon, vol. IV (London: Luzac & Co. for the Government of Ceylon), 1931.

Hogbin, H. Ian. *Experiments in Civilization: The Effects of European Culture on a Native Community in the Solomon Islands* (London: G. Routledge & Sons), 1939.

Hugh-Jones, Stephen. "Edmund Leach 1910–1989," a memoir prepared by direction of the Council of King's College, Cambridge, 1989.

"Edmund Leach 1910–1989," *Cambridge Anthropology. Special Issue: Sir Edmund Leach*, vol. 13, no. 3, 1989–90.

Hymes, Dell (ed.). *Reinventing Anthropology* (New York: Pantheon Books), 1972.

Ievers, R.W. *Notes on Tanks Lying Below the Kalawewa Yoda-Ela*, Sessional Paper 29 of 1886 (Colombo: Government Press), 1887.

Manual of the North-Central Province, Ceylon (Colombo: Ceylon Government Press), 1899.

Jaffrelot, Christophe. *The Hindu Nationalist Movement in India* (New York: Columbia University Press), 1996.

Jakobson, Roman and Morris Halle. "Two Aspects of Language and Two Types of Aphasic Disturbance," in *Fundamentals of Language* (The Hague: Mouton), 1956.

James, Wendy. "The Anthropologist as Reluctant Imperialist," in Talal Asad (ed.), *Anthropology and the Colonial Encounter*, London: Ithaca Press, 1973, pp. 42–69.

Jameson, Fredric. *Postmodernism, or, The Cultural Logic of Late Capitalism* (Durham, NC: Duke University Press), 1991.

Jones, Ernest. "Mother-Right and the Sexual Ignorance of Savages," *International Journal of Psycho-Analysis*, vol. 6, 1924, pp. 109–30.

Kaberry, Phyllis. "Virgin Birth," *Man* (n.s.), vol. 3, no. 2, 1968, pp. 310–13.

Keesing, Roger M. *Cultural Anthropology: A Contemporary Perspective* (New York: Holt, Rinehart & Winston), 1981.

Keyes, C.F. *The Golden Peninsula: Culture and Adaptation in Mainland Southeast Asia* (New York: Macmillan), 1977.

Kirsch, A. Thomas. *Feasting and Social Oscillation: A Working Paper on Religion and Society in Upland Southeast Asia*, Cornell University Southeast Asia Program Data Paper no. 92 (Ithaca: Cornell University Department of Asian Studies), 1973.

Knox, Robert. *An Historical Relation of the Island of Ceylon in the East Indies* (Glasgow: James MacLehose & Sons), 1911; original edition 1689.

Korn, Francis and Rodney Needham. *Lévi-Strauss on the Elementary Structures of Kinship: A Concordance to Pagination* (London: William Cloves & Sons), 1969.

Krader, Lawrence (ed.). *The Ethnological Notebooks of Karl Marx* (Assen: Van Gorcum), 1972.

Kuhn, Thomas S. *The Structure of Scientific Revolutions* (Chicago: The University of Chicago Press), 1962.

Kuper, Adam. *Anthropology and Anthropologists: The Modern British School*, rev. edn (London and Boston: Routledge & Kegan Paul), 1983.

"An Interview with Edmund Leach," *Current Anthropology*, vol. 27, no. 4, August–October 1986, pp. 375–81.

"In Uncle Henry's Footsteps," *The Guardian*, Tuesday, January 10, 1989.

Kuper, Hilda. "Function, History, Biography," in George W. Stocking, Jr. (ed.), *Functionalism Historicized: Essays on British Social Anthropology* (Madison: University of Wisconsin Press), 1984.

La Raw, Maran. "Towards a Basis for Understanding the Minorities of Burma: the Kachin Example," in P. Kunstadter (ed.), *Southeast Asian Tribes, Minorities and Nations* (Princeton: Princeton University Press), 1967.

Langham, Ian. *The Building of British Social Anthropology: W.H.R. Rivers and His Cambridge Disciples in the Development of Kinship Studies, 1898–1931*, Studies in the History of Modern Science, vol. VIII (Dordrecht and Boston: D. Reidel), 1981.

Latour, Bruno. *Science in Action: How to Follow Scientists and Engineers through Society* (Cambridge, MA: Harvard University Press), 1987.

Leach, Edmund. *Social and Economic Organisation of Rowanduz Kurds*, London School of Economics Monographs on Social Anthropology no. 3. London. 1940.

"Jinghphaw Kinship Terminology: An Experiment in Ethnographic Algebra," *Journal of the Royal Anthropological Institute*, vol. 75, 1945, pp. 59–72.

Social Science Research in Sarawak, Colonial Research Studies no. 1 (London: HMSO for Great Britain Colonial Office), 1950.

"The Structural Implications of Matrilateral Cross-Cousin Marriage," *Journal of the Royal Anthropological Institute*, vol. 81, 1951, pp. 23–55.

"Cronus and Chronos," *Explorations*, no. 1, 1953, pp. 15–23.

"Aesthetics," in E.E. Evans-Pritchard, Raymond Firth, Edmund Leach et al., *The Institutions of Primitive Society: A Series of Broadcast Talks* (Oxford: Blackwell), 1954. Reprinted as "Art in Cultural Context," in Peter B. Hammond (ed.), *Cultural and Social Anthropology: Selected Readings*, New York: MacMillan, 1964, pp. 344–50.

Political Systems of Highland Burma: A Study of Kachin Social Structure (London: G. Bell & Sons for The London School of Economics and Political Science), 1954. Reprinted with introductory note by the author in 1964.

"Land Tenure in a Sinhalese Village, North Central Province, Ceylon," Summary in *Man*, vol. 55, article 178, 1955, pp. 166–67.

"Polyandry, Inheritance and the Definition of Marriage, with Particular Reference to Sinhalese Customary Law," *Man*, vol. 55, article 199, 1955, pp. 182–86. Reprinted in *Rethinking Anthropology*, 1961.

"Aspects of Bridewealth and Marriage Stability among the Kachin and Lakher," *Man*, vol. 57, 1957, pp. 50–55. Reprinted in *Rethinking Anthropology*, 1961, pp. 114–23.

"Structural Continuity in a Sinhalese Village (Ceylon Northern Dry Zone)," Proceedings of the Ninth Pacific Science Congress of the Pacific Science Association, held at Chulalongkorn University, Bangkok, Thailand (Bangkok: Pacific Science Congress), 1957.

"Concerning Trobriand Clans and the Kinship Category 'Tabu'," in Jack Goody (ed.), *The Developmental Cycle in Domestic Groups*, Cambridge Papers in Social Anthropology no. 1 (Cambridge: University Press for the Dept. of Archaeology and Anthropology), 1958.

"Magical Hair," Curl Bequest Essay, 1957, *Journal of the Royal Anthropological Institute*, 1958, vol. 88, Part 2, pp. 147–64.

"Hydraulic Society in Ceylon," *Past and Present*, no. 15, April 1959, pp. 2–26.

(ed.) *Aspects of Caste in South India, Ceylon and North-West Pakistan*, Cambridge Papers in Social Anthropology no. 2 (Cambridge: Cambridge University Press), 1960.

"The Frontiers of 'Burma,'" *Comparative Studies in History and Society*, vol. 3, no. 1, 1960, pp. 49–68.

"Golden Bough or Gilded Twig?" *Daedalus (Journal of the American Academy of Arts and Sciences)*, vol. 90, no. 2, Spring 1961, pp. 371–87.

"Lévi-Strauss in the Garden of Eden: An Examination of Some Recent Developments in the Analysis of Myth," *Transactions of the New York Academy of Sciences*, series 2, vol. 23. no. 4, 1961, pp. 386–96.

Pul Eliya, a Village in Ceylon: A Study of Land Tenure and Kinship (Cambridge: Cambridge University Press), 1961.

Rethinking Anthropology, London School of Economics Monographs on Social Anthropology no. 22 (London: University of London/Athlone Press), 1961.

"Time and False Noses," in *Rethinking Anthropology*, London School of Economics Monographs on Social Anthropology no. 22 (London: University of London/Athlone Press), 1961, pp. 132–36.

"Genesis as Myth," *Discovery*, vol. 23, no. 5, May 1962.

"Pulleyar and the Lord Buddha: An Aspect of Religious Syncretism in Ceylon," *Psychoanalysis and the Psychoanalytic Review*, vol. 49, no. 2, Summer 1962, pp. 81–102.

"Review of Lévi-Strauss' *Le totémism aujourd'hui* and *La pensée sauvage*," *Man*, vol. 63, art. 50, 1963, pp. 76–77.

"Telstar et les aborigènes ou 'La pensée sauvage,'" *Annales: Economies, Sociétées, Civilisations*, vol. 19, no. 6, November–December 1964; reprinted in English as "Telstar and the Aborigines," 1970.

"Review of Claude Lévi-Strauss's *Mythologiques: Le cru et le cuit*," *American Anthropologist*, vol. 67, no. 3, 1965, pp. 776–80.

"The Legitimacy of Solomon: Some Structural Aspects of Old Testament History," *European Journal of Sociology*, vol. 7, no. 1, 1966, pp. 58–101. Reprinted in *Genesis as Myth and Other Essays*, 1969, pp. 25–83.

"Virgin Birth," The Henry Myers Lecture, *Proceedings of the Anthropological Institute of Great Britain and Ireland*, 1966, pp. 39–49.

A Runaway World? The BBC Reith Lectures, 1967 (New York: Oxford University Press), 1968.

"A Runaway World Pursued," Broadcast Script – Edmund Leach, 1967 Reith Lecturer, discusses his lectures with Sir Peter Medawar and Professor Alasdair MacIntyre. Third Programme, BBC, Leach Archive, King's College Library, Cambridge.

(ed.) *The Structural Study of Myth and Totemism* (London: Tavistock Publications), 1967.

Correspondence in *Man* (n.s.), vol. 3, no. 1, 1968.

"Virgin Birth Correspondence," *Man* (n.s.), vol. 3, no. 1, 1968.

"Virgin Birth Correspondence," *Man* (n.s.), vol. 3, no. 4, 1968.

Genesis as Myth and Other Essays (London: Cape), 1969.

" 'Kachin' and 'Haka Chin': A Rejoinder to Lévi-Strauss," *Man* (n.s.), vol. 4, no. 2, 1969, pp. 277–85.

"A Critique of Yalman's Interpretation of Sinhalese Girl's Puberty Ceremonial," in Jean Pouillion and Pierre Maranda (eds.), *Echanges et communications: Mélanges offerts à Claude Lévi-Strauss à l'occasion de son 60ème anniversaire*, The Hague: Mouton, 1970, vol. II, pp. 818–28.

Lévi-Strauss (London: Fontana), 1970.

"Telstar and the Aborigines," in Dorothy Emmet and Alasdair MacIntyre (eds.), *Sociological Theory and Philosophical Analysis* (New York: Macmillan), 1970, pp. 183–203; English version of "Telstar et les aborigènes," 1964.

"A Personal View," *Humanist News*, January–February 1972.

Culture and Communication: The Logic by which Symbols are Connected: An Introduction to the Use of Structuralist Analysis in Social Anthropology (Cambridge and New York: Cambridge University Press), 1976.

"Social Anthropology: A Natural Science of Society?" Radcliffe-Brown Lecture, 1976, published in *Proceedings of the British Academy*, vol. 62, 1976, pp. 157–80.

Custom, Law and Terrorist Violence (Edinburgh: University Press), 1977.

"In Formative Travail with Leviathan," in R.M. Berndt (ed.), "Anthropological Research in British Colonies: Some Personal Accounts," special issue of *Anthropological Forum*, vol. 4, no. 2, 1977, pp. 190–97.

"A View from the Bridge," *BAR Supplementary Series*, no. 19, 1977, pp. 161–76.

"Michelangelo's Genesis: Structural Comments on the Paintings of the Sistine Chapel Ceiling," *The Times Literary Supplement*, March 18, 1978.

"Literacy Be Damned," opening address, National Communications Conference, June 13–15, 1979.

"A Poetics of Power" (review of Clifford Geertz, *Negara*), *New Republic*, vol. 184, April 1981, pp. 30–33.

Social Anthropology (Glasgow: Fontana Paperbacks), 1982.

"Against Genres: Are Parables Lights Set in Candlesticks or Put Under a Bushel?" in E. Leach and D.A. Aycock, *Structuralist Interpretations of Biblical Myth* (Cambridge and New York: Cambridge University Press), 1983, pp. 89–112.

"The Gatekeepers of Heaven: Anthropological Aspects of Grandiose Architecture," *Journal of Anthropological Research*, vol. 39, no. 3, Fall, 1983, pp. 243–64.

"Imaginary Kachins," *Man* (n.s.), vol. 18, no. 1, 1983, pp. 191–99.

"Melchisedech and the Emperor: Icons of Subversion and Orthodoxy," in E. Leach and D.A. Aycock, *Structuralist Interpretations of Biblical Myth* (Cambridge and New York: Cambridge University Press), 1983, pp. 67–88.

"Ocean of Opportunity," *Pacific Viewpoint* vol. 24, no. 2, 1983, pp. 99–111.

"Past/Present: Continuity or Discontinuity," *Journal of Historical Linguistics and Philology*, vol. 1, no. 1, 1983, pp. 70–87.

"Why Did Moses Have a Sister?" in Edmund Leach and D. Alan Aycock, *Structuralist Interpretations of Biblical Myth* (Cambridge: Cambridge University Press), 1983, pp. 33–66.

"Conclusion: Further Thoughts on the Realm of Folly," in S. Plattner (ed.), *Text, Play, and Story: The Construction and Reconstruction of Self and Society* (Washington, D.C.: The American Ethnological Society), 1984, pp. 356–64.

"Glimpses of the Unmentionable in the History of British Social Anthropology," *Annual Review of Anthropology*, vol. 13, 1984, pp. 1–23.

"Michelangelo's Genesis: A Structuralist Interpretation of the Central Panels of the Sistine Chapel," *Semiotica*, vol. 56, nos. 1/2, December 1985, pp. 1–30.

"Tribal Ethnography: Past, Present, Future," lecture given at the 27th Annual Conference of the Association of Social Anthropologists of Britain and the Commonwealth (ASA), published in *Cambridge Anthropology*, vol. 11, no. 2, 1987, pp. 1–14, and posthumously published in E. Tonkin, M. McDonald, and M. Chapman (eds.), *History and Ethnicity*, ASA Volume (London: Routledge), 1989, pp. 34–47.

"Noah's Second Son," *Anthropology Today* vol. 4, no. 4, August 1988, pp. 2–5.

"Aryan Invasions over Four Millennia," in Emiko Ohnuki-Tierney (ed.), *Culture Through Time: Anthropological Approaches* (Stanford: Stanford University Press), 1990, pp. 227–45.

"Masquerade: The Presentation of the Self in Holi-Day Life," *Cambridge Anthropology*. Special Issue: Sir Edmund Leach, vol. 13, no. 3, 1989–90, pp. 47–69; also published in *Visual Anthropology Review*, vol. 6, no. 2, 1990, pp. 2–13.

Edmund Leach Papers, Modern Archive Centre, King's College Library, Cambridge.

Leach, Edmund and John Drury. *The Great Windows of King's College Chapel, Cambridge* (Cambridge: King's College Press), 1988. Anonymous leaflet.

Lehman, F.K. *The Structure of Chin Society: A Tribal People of Burma Adapted to a Non-Western Civilization*, Illinois Studies in Anthropology No. 3 (Urbana: University of Illinois Press), 1963.

Lévi-Strauss, Claude. *Les structures élémentaires de la parenté*, Paris: Presses Universités de France, 1949. Second edition 1967, Paris and The Hague: Marton.

"The Structural Study of Myth," *Journal of American Folklore*, vol. 68, no. 270, 1955, pp. 428–44.

"La geste d'Asdiwal," *Annuaire de l'E.P.H.E. (Sciences Religieuses)*, 1958–59.

"La structure et la forme: réflexions sur un ouvrage de Vladimir Propp," *Cahiers de l'Institut de Science Economique Appliquée*, series M, no. 7, 1960.

La pensée sauvage (Paris: Plon), 1962.

Anthropologie Structurale (Paris: Plon), 1963; reprinted in English as *Structural Anthropology* trans. Claire Jacobsen and Brooke Grundfest Schoepf (New York: Basic Books, 1963).

Le totémism aujourd'hui (Paris: Presses Universitaires de France), 1962.

Mythologiques, vol. I: Le cru et le cuit (Paris: Plon), 1964.

Totemism, trans. Rodney Needham (London: Merlin Press), 1964.

"Anthropology: Its Achievements and Its Future," *Current Anthropology*, vol. 7, no. 2, 1966, pp. 124–27.

Mythologiques, vol. II: Du miel aux cendres (Paris: Plon), 1966; English version: *From Honey to Ashes*, 1973.

The Scope of Anthropology, trans. S. Ortner Paul and R.A. Paul (London: Cape), 1967.

The Elementary Structures of Kinship, trans. J.H. Bell, J.R. van Sturmer, and R. Needham, and edited by R. Needham, Boston, MA: Beacon Press; London: Eyre & Spottiswoode, 1969. First published as *Les structures élémentaires de la parenté* (1949).

Interview *in Temoignage Chrétien*, quoted in E. Terray, *Marxism and "Primitive" Societies: Two Studies*, trans. M. Klepper (New York: Monthly Review Press), 1972.

From Honey to Ashes, trans. J. and D. Weightman (New York: Harper & Row), 1973.

Léy-Ward, Annick and Sophie and Pierre Clément. "Some Observations on the Map of the Ethnic Groups Speaking Thai Languages," *Journal of the Siam Society*, vol. 76, 1988, pp. 29–41.

Lienhardt, Godfrey. *Divinity and Experience: The Religion of the Dinka* (Oxford: Clarendon Press), 1961.

Lingat, R. "Evolution of the Conception of Law in Burma and Siam," *Journal of the Siam Society*, vol. 38, 1950.

Les sources du droit dans le système traditionnel de l'Inde (Paisard The Hague: Mouton), 1967.

Lloyd, Geoffrey E.R. *Polarity and Analogy: Two Types of Argumentation in Early Greek Thought* (Cambridge: Cambridge University Press), 1966.

McLennan, John F. *Primitive Marriage* (London: Quaritch), 1865.

McMahon, Sir A. Henry. "International Boundaries," *Journal of the Royal Society of Arts*, vol. 84, 1935.

McNamara, Jo Ann Kay. "Review of Pelikan, J., *Mary Through the Centuries: Her Place in the History of Culture*," *New York Times Book Review*, October 27, 1996.

Maine, Henry. *Ancient Law* (London: J. Murray), 1861.

Village Communities in the East and West (London: J. Murray), 1871.

The Early History of Institutions (London: J. Murray), 1875.

Malamat, Abraham. "Comments on E. Leach: The Legitimacy of Solomon – Some Structural Aspects of Old Testament History," *Archives Européennes de Sociologie*, vol. 8, 1967.

Malinowski, Bronislaw. *Argonauts of the Western Pacific: An Account of Native Enterprise and Adventure in the Archipelagos of Melanesian New Guinea* (London: G. Routledge & Sons), 1922.

"The Problem of Meaning in Primitive Languages," in C.K. Ogden and I.A. Richards (eds.), *The Meaning of Meaning: A Study of the Influence of Language upon Thought and of the Science of Symbolism* (London: K. Paul, Trench, Trubner & Co. for the International Library of Psychology, Philosophy and Scientific Method), 1923, pp. 296–336.

"Psycho-Analysis and Anthropology," *Psyche*, vol. 4, 1924, pp. 293–332.

Sex and Repression in Savage Society (London: K. Paul, Trench, Trubner & Co. for the International Library of Psychology, Philosophy and Scientific Method), 1927.

"Practical Anthropology," *Africa*, vol. 2, 1929, pp. 22–38.

The Sexual Life of the Savages in North-Western Melanesia: An Ethnographic Account of Courtship, Marriage, and Family Life among the Natives of the Trobriand Islands, British New Guinea (London: G. Routledge & Sons), 1929.

"Parenthood: The Basis of Social Structure," in V.F. Calverton and S.D. Schmalhausen (eds.), *The New Generation: The Intimate Problems of Modern Parents and Children* (London: n.p.), 1930, pp. 113–68.

Coral Gardens and Their Magic: A Study of the Methods of Tilling the Soil and of Agricultural Rites in the Trobriand Islands (2 vols., London: G. Allen & Unwin), 1935.

The Dynamics of Culture Change: An Inquiry into Race Relations in Africa, edited by Phyllis Kaberry (New Haven: Yale University Press), 1961. First published 1945.

Marcus, George E. and Michael M.J. Fischer. *Anthropology as Cultural Critique: An Experimental Moment in the Human Sciences* (Chicago: The University of Chicago Press), 1986.

Maspero, H. "Les langues tibéto-birmanes," in A. Meillet and M. Cohen (eds.), *Les langues du monde* (Paris: Centre National de la Recherche Scientifique), 1952, pp. 529–70.

Maybury-Lewis, David. "Review of *Mythologiques: Du miel aux cendres*," *American Anthropologist*, vol. 71, 1969, pp. 114–20.

Mayer, Adrian C. "Obituary," *Anthropology Today*, vol. 5, no. 1, February 1989.

Mead, Margaret and Rhoda Métraux (eds.). *The Study of Culture at a Distance* (Chicago: The University of Chicago Press), 1953.

Mendelson, E. Michael. *Sangha and State in Burma: A Study of Monastic Sectarianism and Leadership*, edited by John P. Ferguson (Ithaca: Cornell University Press), 1975.

Mirsky, Jonathan. "On Noel Annan (1916–2000)," *The New York Review of Books*, April 13, 2000.

Murdock, G.P. "Genetic Classification of the Austronesian Languages: A Key to Oceanic Culture History," *Ethnology*, vol. 3, no. 2, 1964, pp. 117–26.

Murphey, Rhoads. "The Ruin of Ancient Ceylon," *Journal of Asian Studies*, vol. 16, no. 2, 1957, pp. 181–200.

Nash, Manning. *The Golden Road to Modernity: Village Life in Contemporary Burma* (New York: Wiley), 1965.

Needham, Rodney. "The Future of Social Anthropology: Disintegration or Metamorphosis?" *Anniversary Contributions to Anthropology: Twelve Essays* (Leiden: E.J. Brill), 1970.

Neusner, J. "The Talmud as Anthropology," Annual Samuel Friedland Lecture, The Jewish Theological Seminary of America, 1979.

Nicholas, C.W. "A Short Account of the History of Irrigation Works up to the 11th Century," *Journal of the Ceylon Branch of the Royal Society* (n.s.) vol. 7, 1960.

Obeyesekere, Gananath. *Land Tenure in Village Ceylon: A Sociological and Historical Study* (Cambridge: Cambridge University Press), 1967.

"Obituaries: Professor Sir Edmund Leach, Critical Rethinker of Social Anthropology," *The Times*, Saturday 7 [month missing], 1989.

Ogden, C.K. and I.A. Richards (eds.). *The Meaning of Meaning: A Study of the Influence of Language upon Thought and of the Science of Symbolism* (London: K. Paul, Trench, Trubner & Co. for the International Library of Psychology, Philosophy and Scientific Method), 1923.

Oliver, Douglas. "Pul Eliya, a Village in Ceylon: A Study in Land Tenure and Kinship," *American Anthropologist*, vol. 64, 1962, pp. 621–22.

Paranavitana, S. *Inscriptions of Ceylon* (Colombo: Archaeological Survey of Ceylon, 1970).

Pareto, Vilfredo. *Traité de sociologie générale*, edited by Pierre Boven (Lausanne and Paris: Payot & Cie), 1917–19. English translation as *The Mind and Society*, edited by Arthur Livingston, New York: Dover Publications, 1963.

Parker, H. *Report on the Proposed Deduru Oya Project*, Sessional Paper 3 of 1889 (Colombo: Government Press), 1889.

Parsons, Talcott. *Structure of Social Action: A Study in Social Theory with Special Reference to a Group of Recent European Writers* (New York: McGraw-Hill), 1937.

Pelikan, Jaroslav. *Mary Through the Centuries: Her Place in the History of Culture* (New Haven: Yale University Press), 1996.

Pelliot, P. *Mémoires sur les coutumes du Cambodge de Tcheou Ta-Kouan, Oeuvres posthumes de Paul Pelliot* no. 3 (Paris: Librairie d'Amerique et d'Orient, A. Maisonneuve), 1951.

Phear, John B. *The Aryan Village in India and Ceylon* (London: Macmillan), 1880.

Pieris, Ralph. *Sinhalese Social Organization: The Kandyan Period* (Colombo: Ceylon University Press Board), 1956.

Pinkerton, John. *A General Collection of the Best and Most Interesting Voyages and Travels in All Parts of the World* (17 vols., London: Longman, Hurst, Rees, & Orme), 1808–14.

Powell, H.A. "An Analysis of Present Day Social Structure in the Trobriand Islands," Ph.D. Thesis, University of London, 1956.

"Virgin Birth Correspondence," *Man* (n.s), vol. 3, no. 4, 1968, pp. 651–56.

Propp, Vladimir. "Morphology of the Folk Tale," *International Journal of American Linguistics*, pt. 3, vol. 24, no. 4, 1958.

Ratanaporn Sethakul. "The Tai 'Chiang' in the Upper-Mekong River Basin: Their Origins and Historical Significance," paper presented at conference entitled "The Tai Peoples before the Coming of Civilization" at Thammasat University, Bangkok, May 27–28, 1999.

Richards, Audrey I. *Land, Labour and Diet in Northern Rhodesia: An Economic Study of the Bemba Tribe* (London and New York: Oxford University Press for the International Institute of African Languages and Cultures), 1939.

"Practical Anthropology in the Lifetime of the International African Institute," *Africa*, vol. 14, 1944, pp. 289–301.

"The Colonial Office and the Organization of Social Research," in R.M. Berndt (ed.), "Anthropological Research in British Colonies: Some Personal Accounts," special issue of *Anthropological Forum*, vol. 4, no. 2, 1977, pp. 168–89.

Robinson, Marguerite S. *Political Structure in a Changing Sinhalese Village* (Cambridge and New York: Cambridge University Press), 1975.

Roth, Walter E. *Superstition, Magic and Medicine*, North Queensland Ethnographic Bulletin no. 5 (Brisbane: G.A. Vaughan), 1903.

Royal Anthropological Institute of Great Britain and Ireland. *Edmund Leach: A Bibliography*, Occasional Paper no. 42, 1990.

Russell, Bertrand. *Marriage and Morals* (New York: H. Liveright), 1929.

Sahlins, Marshall. *Islands of History* (Chicago: The University of Chicago Press), 1985.

Said, Edward W. *Orientalism* (New York: Random House), 1978.

"Representing the Colonized: Anthropology's Interlocutors," *Critical Inquiry* vol. 15, no. 2, Winter 1989, pp. 205–25.

Schapera, Isaac. *Migrant Labour and Tribal Life: A Study of Conditions in the Bechuanaland Protectorate* (London and New York: Oxford University Press), 1947.

Schneider, David M. "Virgin Birth Correspondence," *Man* (n.s), vol. 3, no. 1, 1968, pp. 126–29.

Scott, J. George and J.P. Hardiman. *Gazetteer of Upper Burma and the Shan States, 1900–01*, vol. II, part 2 (Rangoon: Government Printing), 1900.

Seneviratne, H.L. *Rituals of the Kandyan State* (Cambridge: Cambridge University Press), 1978.

The Work of Kings: The New Buddhism in Sri Lanka (Chicago. The University of Chicago Press), 1999.

Sinding-Larsen, S. "A Re-Reading of the Sistine Ceiling," in *Acta ad Archaeologiam et Artum Historiam Pertinentia*, vol. 4, 1969.

Smith, Adam. *The Wealth of Nations: An Inquiry into the Nature and Causes of the Wealth of Nations* (Dublin: Whitestone), 1776.

Spiro, Melford E. "Religion: Problems of Definition and Explanation," in Michael Banton (ed.), *Anthropological Approaches to the Study of Religion*, Association of Social Anthropologists Monograph 3 (London: Tavistock Publications), 1966.

"Virgin Birth, Parthogenesis, and Physiological Paternity: An Essay in Cultural Interpretation," *Man* (n.s.), vol. 3, no. 2, 1968, pp. 242–61.

Kinship and Marriage in Burma: A Cultural and Psychodynamic Analysis (Berkeley: University of California Press), 1977.

Steinberg, Les. "The Line of Fate of Michelangelo's Painting," *Critical Inquiry*, vol. 6, no. 3, 1980.

Stevenson, H.N.C. *The Economics of the Central Chin Tribes* (Bombay: Times of India Press), 1943.

Stocking, George W., Jr. (ed.). *Malinowski, Rivers, Benedict, and Others: Essays on Culture and Personality*, History of Anthropology vol. IV (Madison: University of Wisconsin Press), 1986.

The Ethnographer's Magic and Other Essays in the History of Anthropology (Madison: University of Wisconsin Press), 1992.

After Tylor: British Social Anthropology, 1888–1951 (Madison: University of Wisconsin Press), 1995.

Strathern, Marilyn. "Stopping the World: Elmdon and the Reith Lectures," *Cambridge Anthropology*, vol. 13, no. 3, 1989–90, pp. 70–74.

Suravira, A.V. (ed.). *Pujavaliya* (Colombo: n.p.), 1961.

Talmon, Shemaryahu. "Letter to E. Leach, Sept. 4th, 1966," Modern Archive Centre, King's College Library, Cambridge.

Tambiah, Stanley J. "The Structure of Kinship and Its Relationship to Land Possession and Residence in Pata Dumbara, Central Ceylon," *The Journal of the Royal Anthropological Institute*, vol. 88, pt. 1, 1958, pp. 21–44.

"Kinship Fact and Fiction in Relation to the Kandyan Sinhalese," *The Journal of the Royal Anthropological Institute*, vol. 95, part 2, 1965, pp. 131–73.

"Polyandry in Ceylon – with Special Reference to the Laggala Region," in C. von Fürer-Haimendorf (ed.), *Caste and Kin in Nepal, India and Ceylon: Anthropological Studies in Hindu–Buddhist Contact Zones* (Bombay and New York: Asia Publishing House), 1966.

World Conqueror and World Renouncer: A Study in Buddhism and Polity in Thailand against a Historical Background, Cambridge Studies in Social Anthropology (Cambridge and New York: Cambridge University Press), 1976.

"The Galactic Polity in Southeast Asia," in Stanley J. Tambiah (ed.), *Culture, Thought and Social Action: An Anthropological Perspective* (Cambridge, MA: Harvard University Press), 1985, pp. 252–76.

Sri Lanka: Ethnic Fratricide and the Dismantling of Democracy (Chicago: The University of Chicago Press), 1986.

"Buddhist Conceptions of Universal King and Their Manifestations in South and Southeast Asia," Kuala Lumpur, University of Malaya, 1987.

"King Mahāsammata: The First King in the Buddhist Story of Creation, and His Persisting Relevance," *Journal of the Anthropological Society of Oxford*, vol. 20, no. 2, 1989, pp. 101–22.

"Personal Accounts: Edmund Leach Situates Himself," *Cambridge Anthropology. Special Issue: Sir Edmund Leach*, vol. 13, no. 3, 1989–90.

Buddhism Betrayed? Religion, Politics, and Violence in Sri Lanka (Chicago: The University of Chicago Press), 1992.

Taylor, L.F. "General Structure of Languages Spoken in Burma," *Journal of the Burma Research Society*, vol. 39, 1956.

Tennent, James E. *Ceylon* (2 vols., London: Longman, Green, Longman & Roberts), 1860.

Thongchai Winichakul. *Siam Mapped: A History of the Geo-body of a Nation* (Honolulu: University of Hawaii Press), 1994.

Tooker, Deborah. "Modular Modern: The Compartmentalization of Group Identity in Northern Thailand," unpublished essay.

Turner, Terence. "Le dénicheur d'oiseaux en contexte," *Anthropologie et Société*, vol. 4, no. 3, 1980, pp. 85–116.

Valeri, Valerio. *Kingship and Sacrifice: Ritual and Society in Ancient Hawaii*, trans. P. Wissing (Chicago. The University of Chicago Press), 1985.

Vansina, C.J. *Oral Tradition: A Study in Historical Methodology*, trans. H.M. Wright (Chicago: Aldine), 1965.

Wall, Adam. *An Account of the Different Ceremonies Observed in the Senate House of the University of Cambridge* (Cambridge: John Burges), 1798.

Wilbert, Johannes. *Folk Literature of South American Indians: General Index*, UCLA Latin American Studies vol. 80 (Los Angeles: University of California Press), 1992.

Wittfogel, Karl. *Oriental Despotism: A Comparative Study of Total Power* (New Haven: Yale University Press), 1957.

Wolters, O.W. *History, Culture, and Region in Southeast Asian Perspectives* (Singapore: Institute of Southeast Asian Studies), 1982.

Yalman, Nur. "On the Purity of Women in the Castes of Ceylon and Malabar," *Journal of the Royal Anthropological Institute*, vol. 93, part 1, 1963, pp. 25–58.

Under the Bo Tree: Studies in Caste, Kinship, and Marriage in the Interior of Ceylon (Berkeley: University of California Press), 1967.

Index